Advanced Oracle Tuning and Administration

TO,
AMANDA
BEST WISHES

Noorali

About the Authors

Eyal Aronoff is Vice President of Products at Quest Software. Eyal is the inventor of AdHawk and SQLab database monitoring, administration, and application tuning tools. He is a certified DBA and a frequent presenter at New York Oracle User Group and the International Oracle User Week.

Kevin Loney is a certified Oracle DBA and the author of two of the first three books published by Oracle Press: *Oracle DBA Handbook* and (with George Koch) *Oracle: The Complete Reference*. He is the lead DBA for a large pharmaceutical company and has written over a dozen technical articles for *Oracle* magazine.

Noorali Sonawalla is the president and founder of Sunrise Systems, a New Jersey consultancy. He is an expert in Oracle database tuning and replication and is the author of numerous articles on those subjects.

ORACLE®   *Oracle Press*™

Advanced Oracle Tuning and Administration

Eyal Aronoff
Kevin Loney
Noorali Sonawalla

Osborne **McGraw-Hill**

Berkeley New York St. Louis
San Francisco Auckland Bogotá Hamburg London Madrid
Mexico City Milan Montreal New Delhi Panama City
Paris São Paulo Singapore Sydney Tokyo Toronto

Osborne **McGraw-Hill**
2600 Tenth Street
Berkeley, California 94710
U.S.A.

For information on translations or book distributors outside the U.S.A., or to
arrange bulk purchase discounts for sales promotions, premiums, or fundraisers,
please contact Osborne/**McGraw-Hill** at the above address.

Advanced Oracle Tuning and Administration

1234567890 DOC 9987

ISBN 0-07-882241-6

Publisher
Brandon A. Nordin

Editor in Chief
Scott Rogers

Project Editor
Claire Splan

Associate Project Editor
Heidi Poulin

Technical Editor
Rachel Carmichael

Copy Editor
Gary Morris

Proofreader
Pat Mannion

Indexer
Valerie Robbins

Computer Designer
Marcela Hancik

Illustrator
Richard Whitaker

Series Design
Jani Beckwith

Quality Control Specialist
Joe Scuderi

Cover Photo
Jeff Smith, Image Bank

Contents At A Glance

PART 1
Managing Database Size, Performance, and Emergencies

1   Managing Database Size, Performance, and Emergencies   3

PART 2
Administration of a Growing Database

2   Planning for Your Database Growth   19
3   Memory and CPU Tuning Issues   33
4   Hardware Tuning Issues   51
5   Managing the Space Inside Your Database   79
6   Database Shutdown/Startup Kit   119

PART 3
Tuning a Growing Database

7   Managing for Performance   135
8   Monitoring   149
9   Environment Tuning   177
10 EXPLAINing SQL Statement Tuning   193
11 The Top Ten SQL Tuning Tips   261

PART 4
Advanced Tuning Options

12 Parallel Options   321
13 When All Else Fails: New and Improved Tuning Options   . .   357

PART 5
The Oracle DBA Certification Exam

14 Oracle7 DBA Certification Exam Candidate
    Bulletin of Information   417
15 Oracle7 DBA Practice Questions   445
16 Analysis of the Practice Questions   481
17 The Oracle7 Database Administrator Practice Test   545

    Index   577

Contents

ACKNOWLEDGMENTS, XXI
INTRODUCTION, XXV

PART 1
Managing Database Size, Performance, and Emergencies

1   Managing Database Size, Performance, and Emergencies 3
    The Spiral Cycle of Application Deployment   4
        Phase One: Initial Deployment of the Application   4
        Phase Two: Hardware Upgrades and
            Tuning Efforts   5
        Phase Three: Redeployment   7
        Phase Four: Another Redeployment   8
        Phase Five: Major Redeployment   9
    Planning for the Spiral Cycle of
        Application Deployment   10

Lowering the Crisis Level   11
Managing Resource Requirements   13
Managing the Hardware Issues   14
Preparing for the Future   15

PART 2
Administration of a Growing Database

2 Planning for Your Database Growth **19**
Growth Profiles   20
    Business Reference Tables   20
    Application Reference Tables   22
    Business Transaction Tables   25
    Temporary/Interface Tables   27
Using Growth Profiles in Planning   30

3 Memory and CPU Tuning Issues **33**
Types of Applications   34
    How Oracle Addresses OLTP Data Access Needs   34
    How Oracle Addresses Batch Data Access Needs   37
How to Calculate the Hit Ratio   39
Factors That Impact the Hit Ratio   41
    Dictionary Tables Activity   41
    Temporary Segment Activity   42
    Rollback Segment Activity   43
    Index Activity   43
    Table Scans   44
    OLTP and Batch Application Types   45
Memory and CPU Tuning Issues   46
Selecting a Target Hit Ratio for
   Your Application   47
Memory and CPU Requirements   48

4 Hardware Tuning Issues **51**
Estimating Disk Capacity Requirements   52
    Space Inside the Database   52
    External Space Used by Oracle   54
    Application Administration Space   56
    Redundancy/Emergency Storage Space   57
Identifying I/O Bottlenecks   57
Traditional Hardware Approaches   60
    Separation of Files   61
    Data Striping   62

How to Use RAID Technologies   64
    How RAID Works   65
    When to Use Striping   69
    When to Use Mirroring   70
    When to Use Parity-Based Systems   70
    Choosing a RAID Configuration   72
Raw Devices and File Systems   73
    Management Considerations of Raw Devices   75
Supporting Changing Capacity Requirements   76

5   Managing the Space Inside Your Database **79**
Types of Tables   80
Managing Extents   81
    How Oracle Allocates Extents   81
    Sizing Extents for Performance   86
Managing Tables   91
    Highwatermarks   92
    Inside the Blocks   94
    Clusters   97
Managing Indexes   98
Managing Temporary Segments   99
Managing Rollback Segments   102
Managing Free Space   107
Storage Parameters Reference   113
    initial   113
    next   114
    pctincrease   114
    minextents   114
    maxextents   114
    tablespace   114
    pctfree   115
    pctused   115
    size   115
    freelists and freelist groups   115
    initrans and maxtrans   116
    optimal   116

6   Database Shutdown/Startup Kit **119**
Items in the Shutdown/Startup Kit   120
    Delete or Archive Old Trace Files and Logs   120
    Rename the Alert Log   122
    Generate a *create controlfile* Command   123
    Pin Packages   124
    Create an Owner-to-Object Location Map   126

Recompute Statistics   128
Shrink Rollback Segments That Have Extended
    Past optimal   129
Implementing the Shutdown/Startup Kit   131

PART 3
Tuning a Growing Database

7   Managing for Performance **135**
Where to Start   136
    Ensure a Consistent Production Environment   136
    Categorizing Application Transactions and Queries   139
    Focus on Offensive SQL   140
    Tune Specific Long-Running Processes
        and Batch Jobs   141
    Tune the Access to Individual Tables   142
Using the Optimizers   142
    The Rule-Based Optimizer   143
    The Cost-Based Optimizer   143
    A Hybrid Approach   143
    Selecting the Optimizer   144
    Implementing the Cost-Based Optimizer   144
    Additional Optimizer Goals   146
Where to Go Next   146

8   Monitoring **149**
Types of Monitoring   150
Oracle Performance Statistics Issues   152
    Value Ranges   152
    Precision   153
    Performance of the Statistics Views   153
    Naming   154
Gathering the Statistics   154
Interpreting the Statistics   156
    Query Processing   156
    Transaction Management   162
    Memory and CPU Usage   163
    Database Management   166
    User Statistics   169
Enterprise Manager   171
Developing a Monitoring Plan   174

9 Environment Tuning **177**

Key init.ora Parameters   178
      DB_BLOCK_SIZE   178
      DB_BLOCK_BUFFERS   178
      SHARED_POOL_SIZE   179
      LOG_BUFFER   179
      DB_WRITERS   180
      DB_FILE_MULTIBLOCK_READ_COUNT   180
      SORT_AREA_SIZE and SORT_AREA_RETAINED_SIZE   181
      SORT_DIRECT_WRITES   181
      ROLLBACK_SEGMENTS   182
Memory Tuning   182
      Contention for Overall Memory   183
      Setting up Shared Memory   184
      Setting up Semaphores   185
      Managing Memory Trade-Offs   186
I/O Tuning   186
      Implement the Optimal Flexible Architecture   187
      Distribute I/O   188
CPU Tuning   190
Tuning your Application   191

10 EXPLAINing SQL Statement Tuning **193**

How to Generate the Explain Plan for a Query   194
      Automatically Generating Explain Plans in Oracle7.3   198
      Interpreting the Order of Operations   199
Operations   199
      Conventions Used in Execution Path Illustrations   202
      AND-EQUAL   203
      CONCATENATION   204
      CONNECT BY   206
      COUNT   209
      COUNT STOPKEY   211
      FILTER   212
      FOR UPDATE   213
      HASH JOIN   215
      INDEX RANGE SCAN   216
      INDEX UNIQUE SCAN   218
      INTERSECTION   219
      MERGE JOIN   222
      MINUS   223
      NESTED LOOPS   225

OUTER JOIN   228
PROJECTION   229
REMOTE   230
SEQUENCE   232
SORT AGGREGATE   233
SORT GROUP BY   234
SORT JOIN   235
SORT ORDER BY   237
SORT UNIQUE   238
TABLE ACCESS BY ROWID   238
TABLE ACCESS CLUSTER   240
TABLE ACCESS FULL   241
TABLE ACCESS HASH   242
UNION   243
VIEW   244
Interpreting the Explain Plan Output   246
      New Features in Oracle7.3   249
Applying Query Tuning to Process Tuning   250
Using Hints   250
ALL_ROWS   251
AND-EQUAL   252
CACHE   252
CHOOSE   253
CLUSTER   253
FIRST_ROWS   253
FULL   254
HASH   254
HASH_AJ   255
INDEX   255
INDEX_ASC   255
INDEX_DESC   255
MERGE_AJ   256
NO_MERGE   256
NOCACHE   256
NOPARALLEL   256
ORDERED   256
PARALLEL   257
ROWID   257
RULE   257
STAR   257
USE_CONCAT   258
USE_HASH   258

USE_MERGE   258
USE_NL   258

11 The Top Ten SQL Tuning Tips **261**
The Objective of the SQL Tuning Tips   262
The Ten Tips   262
    1. Avoid Unplanned Full Table Scans   263
    2. Use Only Selective Indexes   265
    3. Manage Multi-Table Joins
       (NESTED LOOPS and MERGE JOINs)   269
    4. Manage SQL Statements Containing Views   282
    5. Tune Subqueries   287
    6. Use Composite Keys/Star Queries   294
    7. Properly Index CONNECT BY Operations   301
    8. Limit Remote Table Accesses   305
    9. Manage Very Large Table Accesses   308
    10. Revisit the Tuning Process   317

PART 4
Advanced Tuning Options

12 Parallel Options **321**
The Impact of the Parallel Options   322
What Are the Options?   322
How Parallel Query Works   323
    Conventional Query Processing   323
    Parallel Query Processing for a Table Scan   324
    Parallel Query Processing for a Table Scan with
      One Sort   325
How to Manage and Tune the Parallel Query Option   327
    How Query Server Processes Are Assigned   328
    How to Manage the Query Server Pool   329
    Init.ora Parameters Affecting the
      Degree of Parallelism   330
    Defining the Degree of Parallelism at
      the Table Level   331
    Using Query Hints to Force Parallelism   332
    How to Monitor the Parallel Query Option   333
    Understanding Explain Plan Outputs   336
    Tuning Parallelized Operations   345
    How Oracle Determines the Degree of Parallelism   346
    The Art of Selecting a Degree of Parallelism   347

Disadvantages of Enabling Parallel Query at
   the Instance Level   348
Additional Parallel Options   349
   Parallel create table   349
   Parallel create index   350
   Parallel Data Loading   351
   Parallel Recovery   353
   Oracle Parallel Server   353
Choosing Among the Parallel Options   354

13   When All Else Fails: New and Improved Tuning Options . .   357

Optimizer Changes   358
   Histograms   358
   Hash Joins   365
   Star Queries   369
Performance-Related Changes   369
   unrecoverable Actions   370
   Direct Path Export   371
   Dedicated Temporary Tablespaces   372
   Sort Direct Writes   373
Object Administration Changes   374
   maxextents unlimited   374
   Deallocation of Unused Space from
     Tables and Indexes   375
   Fast Index Recreate   378
   Bitmap Indexes   379
   User-Specified Hash Clusters   381
   Partitioned Views   382
   Stored Triggers   385
Database Administration Changes   386
   Resizeable Datafiles   386
   Dynamically Changeable init.ora Parameters   389
   Tablespace Coalesce   391
   Read-Only Tablespaces   393
   Shrinking Rollback Segments   394
   Standby Databases   394
   Media Recovery Status   395
   Replication   396
   General Replication Issues   396
   Asynchronous and Synchronous Replication   397
   Snapshots   398
   Advanced Replication   401
   Object Groups   404

Updateable Snapshots   404
Row-Level and Procedural Replication   405
Additional Changes in Oracle7.3   405
Comparing Replicated Tables   406
Replication Challenges   408
Multi-Threaded Server   409
Delayed-Logging Block Cleanout   410
Scalable Buffer Cache   411
New Database Administration Utilities   411
TRACE   411
DB_VERIFY   412

PART 5
The Oracle DBA Certification Exam

**14 Oracle7 DBA Certification Exam Candidate
Bulletin of Information** **417**
Contacting the Oracle7 Database Administrator Examination
Program Staff   419
The Oracle7 Database Administrator Examination   419
A Word about The Chauncey Group International   419
Oracle DBA Job Analysis   420
About the Examination   420
Test Development   421
Test Dates   421
Fees   421
Test Preparation   421
Test-Taking Strategies   422
Test Content   423
Registration—Scheduling Your Computer-Based Assessment
(U.S. and Canada)   425
Note: Americans with Disabilities Act   425
Changing or Canceling Your
Oracle7 DBA Appointment   426
Refunds   426
Inclement Weather   426
Retake Policy   426
Identification Requirements   427
On the Day of the Examination   427
Test Center Regulations   429
Additional Security Measures   429
Grounds for Dismissal   429

Name Registry   430
Reporting Test Results and Passing Scores   430
Final Scores   430
Score Reliability   431
Determination of Passing Scores   431
FAQs   432
List of Computer-Based Testing Centers   432
Registration—International   435
Oracle Education   439

15   Oracle7 DBA Practice Questions **445**
Question Format   446
Recording Your Answers   447
What to Do If You're Stumped   447
What's a Passing Grade?   447
Time Limits   447
The Questions   447
Answer Form for the Practice Questions   478

16   Analysis of the Practice Questions **481**
Answer Key to the Practice Questions   482
General Analysis of the Practice Questions   482
References   484
    General Reference   485
    Backup and Recovery   486
    Resource Management   486
    Maintenance and Operations   487
    Security   487
    Tuning and Troubleshooting   488
    Data Administration   489
    Architecture and Options   489
Question Analysis   490

17   The Oracle7 Database Administrator Practice Test **545**
How to Use the Practice Test Material   547
Marking the Answer Sheet   548
Test Taking Strategies   548
Test Content   549
    I. Oracle Architecture and Options (11-13%)   549
    II. Security (13-15%)   549
    III. Data Administration (11-13%)   549
    IV. Backup and Recovery (16-18%)   550
    V. Software Maintenance and Operation (13-15%)   550
    VI. Resource Management (13-15%)   550

      VII. Tuning and Troubleshooting (13-15%)   550
Overview and Directions   551
Practice Database Description   561
      Section 1-SGA Summary   562
      Section 2-Initialization Parameters (init.ora)   562
      Section 3-Tablespace Information   563
      Section 4-Rollback Segment Information   563
      Section 5-User Information   564
      Section 6-List of Roles   564
      Section 7-Granted Roles   565
      Section 8-Tablespace Quotas   565
      Section 9-Table Information   566
Answer Sheet/Score Interpretation Guide
   Oracle7 DBA Practice Examination   567
      Score Interpretation for the
         Oracle DBA Sample Exercise   568

Index **577**

Acknowledgments

For a while now, I have been collecting information about Oracle performance and administration. Oracle has evolved over time and so has my understanding of it. To date, I keep getting surprised by aspects and behavior of the product that I did not anticipate. My Oracle monitoring products, AdHawk Monitor, AdHawk Spacer, and most noticeably SQLab, forced me to spend nights and days trying to figure out "what does it all mean." This book is the result of a relentless pursuit to understand what is under the covers. We tried whenever possible to explain why things happen the way they happen and why to take each action.

I wish to thank a number of people who gave me support throughout my career and through the process of writing this book.

Thanks to Dorith Kleinstein and Yigal Amit for introducing me to Oracle back in 1985. To Marcus Halside of John Bryce for putting me to work on benchmarks of Oracle V6, opening the door for my first understanding of Oracle internals. To Clara Castano, Alfred Ferrito, and Carol Delbene of Johnson & Johnson, who gave me my first experience with a very large scale production environment. Special thanks to my co-author and friend, Noorali Sonawalla, who kept stimulating me and challenging me to solve "interesting" problems and to publish articles about them. Without this experience and the material it generated, I could not have come up with this book. Thanks to my clients and colleagues at the New York and New Jersey Oracle User Groups who many times were the guinea pigs for my new talks (and products).

Thanks to Rachel Carmichael and Marlene Theriault for introducing me to Kevin Loney in ECO95. Special thanks to Kevin Loney who orchestrated the creation of this book. His relentless pursuit for accuracy and simplicity made this book what it is.

To David Kreines and the people of ETS (The Chauncey Group) for their cooperation in the DBA certification exam. To Scott Rogers and the people of Osborne McGraw-Hill who made it simple for us to come up with the book and were willing to accommodate our unusual needs.

Last but not least, to my wife Yael and my new daughter Leya for being there and supporting me.

Eyal Aronoff

Putting together a book like this, even with two co-authors, is no small feat—and one does not realize that until one is drawn well into the process! It is a humbling realization of the extent of support and effort needed from everyone involved.

First and foremost, thanks to my family for their patience and for putting up with my long hours and hibernation. Their silent contribution to this book was critical to its success.

Special thanks to my co-author and friend, Eyal Aronoff, with whom I have enjoyed many long hours of thought-provoking interactions. His thirst for understanding how Oracle works and his insight into many issues gave depth to this book.

Special thanks to my co-author Kevin Loney for his meticulous and unflinching dedication to this work. I got associated with Kevin only recently, and in a short span of time, I have developed great admiration and respect for his talent and ability to put things "simply."

Thanks to my brother, Nuruddin Sonawalla, for the research and for his significant contributions to Chapters 12 and 13. He kept those chapters moving, even during my few weeks of absence. Thanks also to Vinod Banginwar for helping with the research and to Rachel Carmichael for the technical edits and for keeping us honest. Thanks to Joel Kenan for the valuable feedback and input.

On the work front, I would like to take this opportunity to thank all my clients, associates, and friends, with whom I have had the privilege to work over the years (you know who you are). I have learned from each and every one of you. Thank you for the opportunity.

Over at Oracle Press, thanks to Scott Rogers for his patience and understanding and to Daniela Dell'Orco, Claire Splan, Gary Morris, and Jani Beckwith for their help. Thanks to everyone at New Jersey, New York and other Oracle user groups for putting up with my talks over the years.

Noorali Sonawalla

Thanks first to my family for their patience and support.

Thanks to Riley and his family for helping me keep things in focus. Amazingly, he turned 3. We are measured not by what we achieve, but by what we overcome.

I have been blessed by the altruism of many. Thanks go to the people who helped for no good reason other than to help: to Jay Warshell of Astra Merck and to Rachel Carmichael. Jay was particularly helpful with Chapters 4, 8, and 9. Rachel played a key role in the creation of this book, as she was the person who introduced me to Eyal Aronoff and who later performed technical and developmental reviews for the book. She has also contributed or inspired (maybe "insisted on" is a more proper term) material, most notably for Chapters 4 and 6. Both Rachel and Jay were willing to work based on my schedule (like DBWR, I write in bursts). Thanks to Carl Dudley for his work on hash clusters, as presented at IOUW94.

Thanks to those who have supported and inspired me over the years; the list keeps growing. On the work front, thanks to Clint Gilliam and Rob Cohen for their support and leadership. To my draft editors and team members: Andy Nelson, John Abrams, Mike Janesch, Jim Viscusi, Steve Rodi, Mike McDonnell, Ray Tulchinsky, Tod Kehrli, Joe Waldron, Frank Frederick, Sharada Bhat, Narayanan Krishnan, and Diane Masciantonio—thanks for the support and assistance. Special thanks to Andy Arnold for his edits and insights. Thanks as always to the long-term supporters such as Marie, Rob, Chris, Decky, and Bill for their support.

Thanks to Eyal Aronoff, Noorali Sonawalla, and Nuruddin Sonawalla for their in-depth research and superb contributions to this effort. Their dedication and diligence helped see this book to the completion of its goal—the creation of a highly useful, thoroughly researched, and user-focused book. This book would not have been possible without them, and I am grateful to have had the opportunity to work with them.

Over at Oracle Press, thanks goes to Scott Rogers, Daniela Dell'Orco, Gary Morris, Claire Splan, and Jani Beckwith. Thanks to the team at The Chauncey Group for their assistance. Julie Gibbs of Oracle has been my editor and friend for many years now, and I am grateful for her efforts.

Lastly, thanks go to my readers and users over the years, who by their questions help direct the answers that this book provides. The scripts shown in this book are provided on the CD; also, check out the Oracle Press section of the Osborne Web page (**http://www.osborne.com**) for information on new releases and updates. You can also use the Osborne Web page to send messages to the publisher regarding this book or books you'd like to see. If you keep asking questions, we'll keep working out the answers.

Kevin Loney

Introduction

Whether you are a database administrator or application developer, you need to be able to tune and manage your database as it grows. In this book, you will find database tuning and administration techniques that are designed to help you maintain your application's performance throughout its entire lifecycle. If you are an experienced DBA, the section of this book that is devoted to the Oracle7 DBA Certification Exam should help you to direct your self-study and training efforts. Regardless of your role or experience level, you can use the advanced techniques and insight provided in this book to tune your database environment and your applications. You could also use the question provided to develop a set of interview questions for use during interviews of DBA candidates.

The book is divided into five sections according to topic. Part 1 of this book introduces the spiral model of application deployment, and describes its influence on database size and query performance—along with the related rise in crisis level as perceived by the application administrators.

In Part 2, the management of space both outside and inside the database is described in detail. You'll see the impact of RAID sets, raw devices, and memory availability on your application—and you will very likely never look at extents or hit ratios the same again. Each technology and internal Oracle characteristic is discussed in depth, enabling you to make the right choices for your database and its growth rate. At the end of Part 2, a database shutdown/startup kit is provided to help improve the performance and ease of management for your databases.

In Part 3, you'll see a step-by-step guide to tuning your application environment and its SQL. The relevant internal Oracle statistics are described in detail, followed by information on monitoring and interpreting them. Once the environment is sound, you can focus on tuning the most offensive SQL—and the later chapters of this section provide an intensive explanation of every operation you've ever seen in an Oracle7 explain plan, along with how to tune the statement that uses the operation.

Part 4 describes the implementation of the most recent and significant changes available for Oracle administration and tuning. The parallel options are described here, as are new features such as histograms, fast index recreates, dedicated temporary tablespaces, and Advanced Replication.

If you are ready to take the Oracle7 DBA Certification Exam, then Part 5 will provide the information you need to help determine your level of preparedness for the exam. In addition to the official candidate bulletin of information and practice test for the exam, this section includes a large number of questions designed to help you determine which areas of study you should focus on in order to become a more fully-rounded DBA. By completing the practice test and working through the practice questions, you should be able to determine which areas you need to study and practice prior to taking the exam.

If you are an application developer, the material on interpreting the explain plan operations and SQL tuning tips in Part 3 may be of immediate interest. If you are an experienced DBA, you may start with Part 4 to quickly skim the latest features available. However, you should be sure to read through the space management material in Part 2 for insight into the management of the data you are querying.

The objective of this book is to guide you through the steps involved in managing a database as its database size increases. For each component of an Oracle installation—disks, memory, CPU, database options—the details regarding its proper implementation and monitoring are provided, along with the criteria used to select the proper options. With the proper components implemented correctly, you will be able to maintain high system performance while managing a growing database.

PART 1

Managing Database Size, Performance, and Emergencies

CHAPTER 1

Managing Database Size, Performance, and Emergencies

Almost all databases have one thing in common: change. Change takes many forms: tables may grow in size, instances may grow in number, and applications may become more distributed. Unless you are prepared to manage the changes that occur, each change can cause you to enter "crisis mode" until the performance and management problems caused by the change are resolved.

In this book, you'll find the techniques used to manage a changing database throughout its full life cycle. You'll see how to design a database that anticipates change, how to manage its growth, how to monitor it, and how to tune it.

Real-world examples are used throughout, to make it as easy as possible to apply the information to your environment.

The Spiral Cycle of Application Deployment

In this chapter, you'll see the application development life cycle, from the vantage point of the database administrator (DBA). From the user perspective, the application development life cycle is a series of production releases, maintenance releases, and occasional performance problems. From the DBA perspective, the application development life cycle is a continuing spiral of application deployments involving three factors: the database size, the response time, and the crisis level. The tips and techniques in this book, when applied, will allow you to minimize the crisis level at each phase of the application's life cycle. In this section, you'll see how the crisis level, database size, and response time change immediately following the deployment phases of an application.

Phase One: Initial Deployment of the Application

Throughout this chapter, the term *crisis level* refers to the urgency used when resolving problems. The crisis level can be quantified by measuring how much time you spend administering the system after hours. If you are constantly monitoring, modifying, and tuning the system during nights and weekends, the crisis level is high. If you are spending no effort on the administration of the system, the crisis level is very low.

As shown by the "Crisis Level" line in Figure 1-1, the crisis level is high at the initial deployment of an application. As users begin to work with the application, the crisis level drops. As users become more experienced in using the system, the perceived urgency of their problems and the number of errors made decrease.

As the users enter data into the system, the *database size* increases, as shown by the "Database Size" line in Figure 1-1. The database size refers not to the allocated space for the database, but rather to the total number of records in the database. As users begin to use the application for their work processes, the number of rows in tables increases steadily.

The database size directly impacts the *response time*, as shown by the "Response Time" line in Figure 1-1. The response time is a measure of the time needed to fulfill the most commonly executed queries within the system. As more and more records are added to the system by the users, the response time grows.

At some point following the initial deployment of the application, the response time grows to an unacceptable level. Queries begin to take too long to execute,

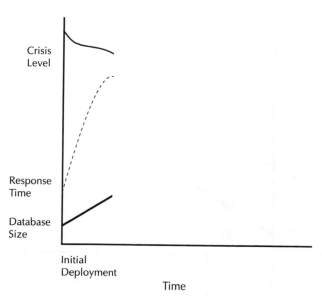

FIGURE 1-1.   *Phase One: Initial deployment*

and the hardware on which the application has been deployed can no longer support the application's processing needs. At that point, you enter the second phase of application deployment: upgrading the system and tuning the application.

Phase Two: Hardware Upgrades and Tuning Efforts

The goal of upgrading the hardware is to improve the system performance. The improvement in system performance helps to reduce the crisis level involved in supporting the application. Chapters 2, 3, and 4 describe the alternatives available during hardware upgrades. Alternatives include acquiring additional CPUs for the current server, moving to a faster server, using advanced I/O systems, and adding memory to the server. Each of these alternatives has a cost—and a benefit, in the improved performance of the application.

As shown in Figure 1-2, upgrading the hardware should have an impact on the response time. If you are able to use Oracle's Parallel Query Option, you can involve multiple CPUs in the resolution of many database activities. For details on how to implement and exploit Oracle's parallel query architecture, see Chapter 12.

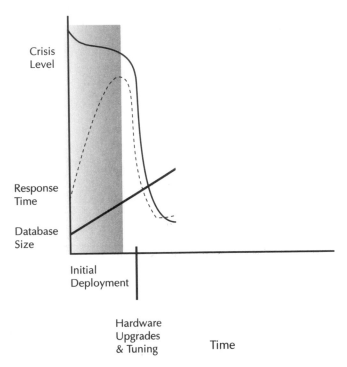

Crisis
Level

Response
Time

Database
Size

Initial
Deployment

Hardware
Upgrades
& Tuning

Time

FIGURE 1-2. *Phase Two: Hardware upgrades and tuning efforts*

Upgrading the hardware should have no impact on the database size. You may choose to increase the allocated size of the databases (for example, by adding space to the temporary tablespace areas), but that does not alter the rate at which rows are inserted into the database. The database size continues to rise at a fairly steady rate.

In addition to upgrading the hardware, you may also tune the Oracle environment to take advantage of the operating environment changes. Environment tuning may include increasing the space available to the memory and sort areas within the database. The tuning process, which begins with environment tuning and ends with tuning specific "offensive" SQL statements, is described in Part 3 of this book. The tips in Chapter 11 are provided with a changing, growing database in mind.

Once the response time problems have been addressed, the crisis level decreases rapidly. The system performs acceptably well, and the database grows at a constant rate. Meanwhile, the users have been working with the system and have developed the requirements for the next phase of the application deployment: modifications to the original application. In most cases, the application modifications consist of additions to the application's base set of tables and increased integration with other applications.

Phase Three: Redeployment

As the database size grows, the response time gradually increases. As shown in Figure 1-3, the crisis level decreases or remains constant until a second part of the application is deployed. When a new part of the application is deployed in production, the crisis level increases. Often, it is not possible to fully simulate production usage and data volumes in a system test environment. Because you may not be able to adequately model production usage, you may not be able to correctly forecast the performance of the revised production application. The response time grows suddenly worse, usually as a result of a very small set of queries. The focus on "offensive" SQL in an otherwise acceptable environment is a key part of the tuning methodology described in Chapter 7.

As a new set of tables is added to the application during the redeployment phase, the database size increases; the number of users likely increases as well. The crisis level stays high during the redeployment phase until the most offensive

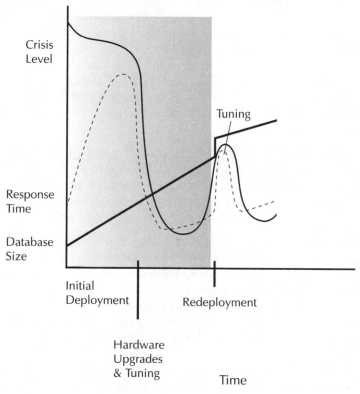

FIGURE 1-3.   *Phase Three: Redeployment*

queries have been tuned and performance has returned to an acceptable level. Because the database has grown in size, the backup strategy may no longer be appropriate; your backups may now take longer than the allotted time. Because the backups take longer to complete, the recovery process may take longer as well. The modifications to the backup process further increase the crisis level.

Because the database size continues to increase, it is likely that the response time will continue to increase over the life of the application. The best response time following redeployment is usually worse than the best response time following the prior hardware upgrade and tuning phase.

Phase Four: Another Redeployment

Following the initial redeployment, further modifications will be made to the application, usually at regular intervals. By this point in the application's life cycle, a full set of version numbers has been assigned to each deployed version of the application. Smaller redeployments get combined into larger ones as the testing and rollout processes involved in deploying the application grow more and more complex.

As shown in Figure 1-4, the response time grows with each redeployment. Each of the three variables discussed in this chapter has quickly established a pattern within the application development cycle:

■ *Database size grows over time.* The size of the database increases with each redeployment, as users and functionality are added to it. In systems that periodically delete older data from the database, the rate of growth may gradually level off.

■ *Response time is cyclic.* Left alone, response time will gradually worsen because of the increasing database size. When the hardware is upgraded, response will usually improve. At each redeployment, response time will get worse, as changes to the database structure and size affect existing queries, while new queries are added to the production environment.

■ *Crisis level is cyclic, closely mirroring response time.* Figure 1-4 reflects the production database support experience for many applications: there are significant efforts over very short periods of time, followed by extended periods during which the crisis level is low. The crisis level increases as the response time increases, and decreases when the response time decreases. The crisis level also increases each time the backup procedures have to change to accommodate the increased database size.

These three trends hold true even during an extreme change to the application. One more application phase will be considered in the next section to illustrate this point: a major redeployment.

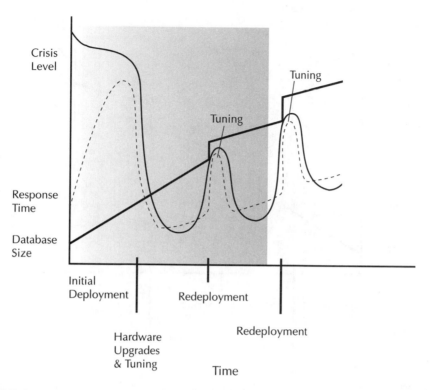

FIGURE 1-4.   *Phase Four: Another redeployment*

Phase Five: Major Redeployment

During a major redeployment of the application, the application may be rewritten or greatly expanded. As a result, the database size may dramatically increase. For example, an application that was previously used to track internal customers may be expanded to do the same for external customers, or a financial system may be expanded by adding new modules. During preparations for the major redeployment, the new database size is estimated and the disk space allocation is planned. Figure 1-5 shows the effects of the major redeployment.

As shown in Figure 1-5, the sudden increase in database size during a major redeployment can have a dramatic effect on the response time of the system. The crisis level rapidly increases; dealing with a major redeployment is like dealing with an entirely new system. All of the past work—the hardware upgrades and the tuning efforts following each smaller redeployment—may be completely overwhelmed by the processing requirements of the new system.

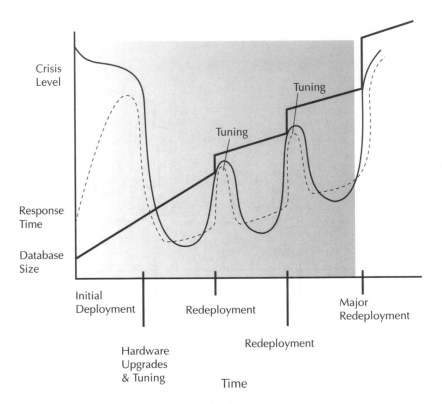

FIGURE 1-5. *Phase Five: Major redeployment*

The good news is that you know how the cycle will proceed in the new system. The database size will increase at a fairly steady rate, with incremental increases during subsequent redeployments. The response time will grow steadily worse over time, and will be particularly bad immediately following each redeployment. During each redeployment, the crisis level will increase as you try to tune the system to minimize the performance impact of the system changes on transaction performance and backup performance.

Planning for the Spiral Cycle of Application Deployment

The cycle of application growth shown in Figure 1-5—steady database size increase, with cyclic increases in the response time and the crisis level—is called the *spiral cycle of application deployment.* If you do not properly plan to support it, the spiral cycle will eventually make your system unmanageable.

Throughout this book, you will find details on how to manage the spiral cycle. There are three critical areas of management effort:

1. *Plan for database size growth.* You must create your applications with an understanding of their future growth patterns, requiring you to cooperate closely with both the user community and the application developers.

2. *Tune effectively.* You must be able to identify and resolve the tuning problems caused during redeployments and system growth.

3. *Stay current.* You must be familiar with the latest Oracle and hardware technology so you can take the best advantage of it during your tuning and system management efforts.

Planning for database size growth is covered throughout Part 2 of this book. Part 3 covers monitoring and tuning for databases, including an exhaustive look at the operations shown via the **explain plan** command. In Part 4, you'll see details on implementing the latest options within Oracle, such as the Parallel Query Option and the data warehousing-related options. In Part 5, you'll find information related to the Oracle7 DBA Certification Exam, designed to help you determine which areas of database administration you need to concentrate on during your self-study. A thorough understanding of all of these areas will allow you to confidently manage the spiral cycle of application deployment for your applications.

Since the bulk of this book is dedicated to technical solutions to the problems caused by the spiral cycle, the rest of this chapter will focus on nontechnical solutions. In the next sections, you will see management tips for building an environment that can support a major redeployment. Once the environment is in place to support the major redeployment, you can begin to use the technical tuning advice provided in this book to resolve the response time problems. The goal of the management advice is to make sure you have the chance to use the tuning advice before the crisis level rules out any alternatives. Before you can respond to a crisis, you have to have enough time—and the proper tools—to respond to it.

Lowering the Crisis Level

Crisis level increases come from several sources, including requirements, expectations, and human resources. The first major source of crisis level increase, for many systems, is that the *requirements change or expand dramatically over time.* As a result, the core system of the initial production deployment is used in ways never imagined during the original system analysis and design. For example, consider a system that started as a small database application—until the corporation using the application was bought by a larger corporation. As a result of the corporate change, the application's requirements may be expanded to include requirements from the new parent corporation.

Often, the changes to requirements are implemented by adding new functionality to the existing system without reanalyzing the impact on the original design. Thus, as shown in Figure 1-5, you cannot correctly forecast the response time impact of even a minor redeployment. Since the system was not completely replanned, the performance of the system cannot be completely replanned, and response time problems result.

The second major source of crisis level increases is *high expectations from users.* As users become more computer literate, their expectations of the application developers increase. For example, users may expect modifications to a multiuser, highly integrated application to be performed as rapidly as if the application being modified was a single-user PC-based system that had no integration points with other applications. Because servers are less expensive than before, users may also expect that the life cycle costs for the application should decrease dramatically as well. If users expect more modifications, made faster and for less cost, then the crisis level will remain high throughout the entire application life cycle.

The third major source of crisis level increases are *personnel availability.* In order to develop systems faster, you need to have developers who understand the business requirements and the users' needs. To use the latest technology, you need developers who are adequately trained on the latest technology, with relevant experience. To support the growing database size and periodic response-time problems, you need a DBA staff that is experienced in managing databases of varying size and growth rates, and who are properly equipped to resolve tuning problems. You therefore need a staff that is highly capable and highly flexible, coupled with a corporate organization dedicated to training and making use of the most current technology.

Of the three causes described here—changing requirements, unrealistic expectations, and personnel availability—the two most difficult causes to deal with are the requirements and expectations problems. The way in which a change in requirements is integrated into an application is dependent on the systems development methodology for your databases; unless full reanalysis of the system is a part of that methodology, it will be very difficult to extend the analysis phase of a modification project to include reanalysis of the whole system. Similarly, problems with unrealistic expectations are cultural in nature, and require effective communications for their resolution. Just as the developers need to understand the business requirements of the application, the users need to understand the technical implications of their requirements. Ideally, the business users and system developers operate as a single team, sharing the responsibility and success for the system.

The most opportune time for revising expectations comes when a new technology or architecture is introduced. For example, when your users decide they want to use a decision support system architecture, you need to help them understand the implications of that architecture and the costs—in terms of time, training, and practice—that go along with it. The objective of this communication is not to stop the new architecture from being implemented, but rather to properly set the users' expectations. The more tightly integrated the development team and business users are, the more likely the projected costs are to be accepted.

Another way of managing expectations is to make the system response time estimates part of the system design documentation; if the system design changes, change the response time estimates. By doing so, you can then use the design documentation as a communications vehicle for response-time implications, and make the users aware early in the process of the implications of their design decisions. If possible, perform stress tests that help improve the accuracy of your performance estimates, and evaluate the impact on your backup strategies.

Managing Resource Requirements

The role of the DBA and application developer changes as rapidly as the application architectures and database versions change. The basic DBA duties change little, but other facets—such as development support and production support—can change greatly depending on how the environment is created and used. For example, when using the Parallel Query Option (see Chapter 12), the process of creating tables changes little (or not at all depending on your implementation). However, the monitoring of the pool of query server processes available for use by the Parallel Query Option is not part of the standard database monitoring process. As a result, the monitoring portion of the DBA role must expand to adequately support the implementation of the new technology.

The development support portion of the DBA role also changes rapidly. Consider the changes that occur when you change from rule-based to cost-based optimization. Suddenly, the frequency of actions by the DBA (how often is each table analyzed?), the methods used by the DBA (does the DBA use **estimate statistics** or **compute statistics**?), and the database version in use (are histograms available?) have a direct impact on the developers. As a result, the DBA must be integrated into the development teams. If not, the response-time peaks during deployments (see Figure 1-5) will grow higher and higher—and there may not be a simple tuning resolution available.

Production control responsibilities of the DBA include all of the development support responsibilities, plus:

■ Configuration management of key database files (such as object creation scripts and database configuration files)

■ Impact analysis of changes to the production environment

■ Proactive monitoring of database space allocation and usage

■ Creation and implementation of standard procedures for security and database backups

■ Creation and implementation of procedures in the event a disaster recovery is necessary

There are two steps that help lower the crisis-level effects of the resource requirements issue: train your database administrators adequately, and fully integrate them with the developers and users they support. You will need a way to monitor the training requirements of your database administrators; to help evaluate training needs, a set of DBA training questions (with answers) is provided in Part 5 of this book.

Managing the Hardware Issues

In order to properly plan and implement your database application in your physical operating environment, you need to integrate your operating system and network support team with your development team. As noted in Chapters 3 and 4, there are a number of hardware implementation alternatives available to you. However, the time required to acquire the necessary hardware may prohibit you from using it during application development. It is important that the application team be able to understand the implications of the hardware choices they make, just as the business users would be aware of the technical choices they make.

Integrating the hardware maintenance and development teams can be difficult, because DBAs usually have little control over the organizational alignment of the operating system and network management team. However, it is an important step. If there is no integration between the operating system management, network management, and development teams, how will the development team answer the following questions?

■ Should the application use file systems or raw devices?

■ How much of a transaction load can the network handle?

■ Should the application use a transaction monitor?

■ Should the application replicate data? If so, during what times?

■ Can the operating system and network environment handle the projected growth of the application?

If there is no integration between the operating system management, network management, and development teams, there is no guarantee that the development team will guess correctly about any of the above questions. As a result, the application's response time will be unpredictable, and its ability to be managed throughout the spiral cycle of application deployment is questionable.

The DBAs will be integrated with the operating system and network management teams via their participation in the development teams, but you should also try to integrate the DBAs directly with the hardware maintenance teams. DBAs will frequently need to make judgments regarding which technology should be used for an application—judgments often based on the available hardware. If you do not know the plans for the hardware systems, you cannot make plans for the applications that use them. Chapters 3 and 4 provide discussions of hardware-related issues, but they assume that the DBA knows the current hardware environment and the plans for it. In a client-server development environment, the DBA also needs to make sure the client device support team is included in the technical architecture discussions with the development team.

Preparing for the Future

To prepare for the future of your database, you must prepare for its growth. As described in the earlier sections, some of the preparation involves organization changes (integrating teams), and some involves cultural changes (focusing on training, and setting user expectations). The following sections of this book provide the technical details necessary to prepare for change, but they will have the greatest effect only if you have first resolved the organizational and cultural issues that affect the crisis level. The following sections describe:

1. Planning for growth, both inside and outside your database.

2. Tuning your database environment.

3. Tuning SQL statements, accompanied by an in-depth look at the data access and manipulation operations.

4. Implementing new technology, such as the parallel options and the features of Oracle7.3.

5. Evaluating the study needs of your personnel via the practice questions provided. Information on the Oracle7 DBA Certification Exam is also provided.

If your application is going to be used tomorrow, its database size will grow tomorrow. Its response time may be affected—and the DBA's crisis level may increase. To allow your database to grow without adversely affecting the response time (and crisis level), you must first plan for growth. Chapter 2 provides a framework for planning your management of the database growth.

PART 2

Administration of a Growing Database

CHAPTER 2

Planning for Your Database Growth

As described in Chapter 1, the spiral cycle of application deployment depicts an ever-growing database. With each successive redeployment of an application component, the size of the database increases. In this section of this book, you will see how to manage the space used by a growing database—both inside and outside the database.

This section consists of five chapters. In Chapter 3, you will see how memory and CPU resources are used by the database, and how to select the optimal memory and CPU configuration for your databases. In Chapter 4, you will see how the different I/O technologies such as raw devices and RAID technologies can be applied to your databases. Chapters 5 and 6 provide information on the effective management of the internal database structures.

To effectively use the chapters in this section, you should know the characteristic growth patterns of the major types of database objects used by applications. In this chapter, you will see the major database object types described, and their growth patterns illustrated. If you understand the growth patterns of your application's database objects, and how the objects fit into established growth profiles, you will be able to apply the tuning advice provided throughout this section and this book.

Growth Profiles

A *growth profile* describes the growth of a database object, based on three characteristics:

- The space used by the data
- The volatility of the data
- The growth rate of the data

In the following sections, you will see illustrations of the growth profiles for four categories of database tables used by applications. The categories are business reference tables, application reference tables, business transaction tables, and temporary/interface tables. Each of the sections contains examples of the tables within the category, along with brief discussions of common tuning issues for the category. Full discussions of the relevant tuning issues are provided in later chapters.

Business Reference Tables

The most common tables in most applications are categorized as *business reference tables.* Business reference tables store the reference data for your business. For example, the MTL_SYSTEM_ITEMS table of Oracle Financials stores product structure rows that are specific to your customization of Oracle Financials. The size of business reference tables usually corresponds to the size of the business. Large businesses will usually have large business reference tables.

Although business reference tables grow, their growth rate is small compared to that of the rest of the application's tables. Their records tend to change little over time; the growth within them is usually due to insertions of records that reflect a change in the business.

The growth profile for business reference tables is shown in Figure 2-1. The timeline from Chapter 1's application deployment cycle is used to show the change

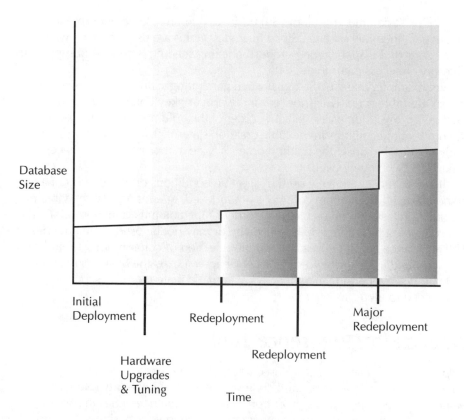

FIGURE 2-1. *Growth profile for business reference tables*

in the size of the business reference tables over time. As shown in Figure 2-1, this is a slow process, with incremental increases coinciding with each deployment of the application. The growth rate of business reference tables tends to follow that of the company.

Common Tuning Issues for Business Reference Tables

The tuning issues for business reference tables depend on the size and the growth rate of the tables. If the business reference tables are small and will stay small, you should consider fully-indexed tables and cached tables, as described in the "Application Reference Tables" section below in this chapter. If they are large, you should consider the tuning issues for large tables, as described in the "Business Transaction Tables" section below in this chapter and in Chapter 11.

The most common problem with business reference table performance is an inadequate indexing scheme. Since reference tables are used in many ways by many parts of the application, a robust indexing scheme is needed to support the diversity of access paths to the data.

For example, many CASE tools, when generating scripts for tables, will generate the **create table** script with indexes on the primary key columns and sometimes on the foreign key columns as well. The order of the columns in the indexes is usually the order of the columns in the table creation statement. There are two common tuning issues that arise: the column order may be inappropriate, and necessary indexes may be overlooked.

If a column is frequently used by limiting conditions during queries of a table, it should be indexed. If the column is not indexed, queries against the table may result in a full scan of the table. If the order of the columns is inappropriate, the index may not have the proper selectivity, or may not be used during queries. The avoidance of full table scans and the selection of column order for indexes are described in the first two sections of Chapter 11. As the business reference table grows, the performance penalty of an inadequate indexing scheme is guaranteed to increase.

Application Reference Tables

Application reference tables are used to provide reference data to the application, such as a list of valid code values as a data integrity reference. Application reference tables differ from business reference tables in several ways. First, they store data that may not be unique to your business. Second, they are small by nature. Third, they are nonvolatile, and grow very slowly. For example, a laboratory results application may have a code table called TEMPERATURE_CODES to provide a list of valid types of temperature readings (Fahrenheit, Celsius, or Kelvin). It is unlikely that the TEMPERATURE_CODES table will dramatically increase in size. It is also unlikely that the existing records in the table will be frequently modified. The table is nonvolatile and does not grow rapidly.

The growth profile for application reference tables is shown in Figure 2-2. The timeline from Chapter 1's application deployment cycle is used to show the change in the size of the application reference tables over time. As shown in Figure 2-2, the application reference tables increase in size during each deployment of the application, as new reference tables are added. Between deployments, they are static in size.

Common Tuning Issues for Application Reference Tables

Application reference tables are frequently very small. They are ideal candidates for being referenced as fully indexed tables or cached tables. In a fully indexed

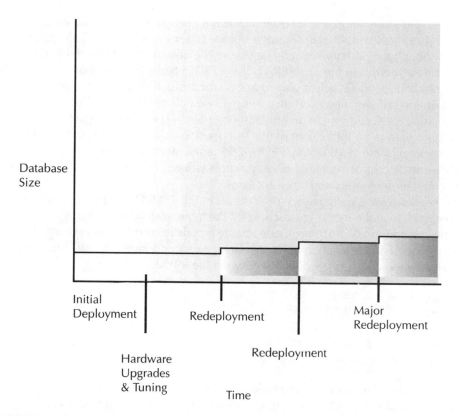

Database Size

Initial Deployment

Hardware Upgrades & Tuning

Redeployment

Redeployment

Major Redeployment

Time

FIGURE 2-2. *Growth profile for application reference tables*

table, all of the columns are indexed in concatenated indexes. For example, the valid temperature codes can be stored in a table named TEMPERATURE_CODES. The **create table** command for the TEMPERATURE_CODES table is shown in the following listing.

```
create table TEMPERATURE_CODES
(Temp_Code    VARCHAR2(1) primary key,
 Description VARCHAR2(25));
```

As shown in the preceding listing, the TEMPERATURE_CODES table has two columns: a Temp_Code column (for the code values, such as 'C'), and a Description column (for the code descriptions, such as 'Celsius'). The primary key of the table is the Temp_Code column. Since a primary key is created on the Temp_Code column, Oracle creates a unique index on the Temp_Code column.

Although the primary key index enforces the uniqueness of the Temp_Code column for records in the TEMPERATURE_CODES table, the index on Temp_Code may not be the most efficient way to access the table. If you need to query the Description column along with the Temp_Code column (for example, while populating a selection list in an application), then you will need to perform either a full table scan or an index scan of the Temp_Code column's index, followed by a table access of the TEMPERATURE_CODES table. Since the table is so small, an index-only access or a table scan-only access will require less processing time than a combination of index and table accesses.

To improve the performance of accesses to the TEMPERATURE_CODES table, you can change the indexing structure for the table. Instead of creating a single-column index on Temp_Code, create a concatenated index on both the Temp_Code and Description columns. Create a second index on the concatenation of Description and Temp_Code, as shown in the following listing.

```
create index I_TEMP_CODE$CODE_DESC
on TEMPERATURE_CODES (Temp_Code, Description);

create index I_TEMP_CODE$DESC_CODE
on TEMPERATURE_CODES (Description, Temp_Code);
```

When the two indexes in the preceding listing are created, the TEMPERATURE_CODES table is fully indexed. Any access to the table can be performed solely via an indexed access, with no need to query the table directly. As a result, the performance of queries that involve index-based accesses to TEMPERATURE_CODES table will improve.

If the table is to be accessed via full table scans, its data will not be held long in memory; when another user queries the table, the table will have to be read from disk again. To preserve the table in memory for as long as possible, mark it as a *cached table* via the **alter table** command, as shown in the following listing.

```
alter table TEMPERATURE_CODES cache;
```

Tables marked as cached tables that are read via full table scans will be kept within the database's SGA as long as if they had been accessed via indexed accesses. Fully-indexed tables and cached tables are described in Chapters 3 and 11.

Business Transaction Tables

Business transaction tables store the majority of the transactions within the application. For example, the table that stores the line items in an ordering system is a business transaction table. Business transaction tables tend to be extremely volatile; they are usually among the most volatile tables in the entire application. They have a very high growth rate; in fact, the growth rate of the business transaction tables is the leading contributor to the growth rate of the application's overall database size.

The growth profile for business transaction tables is shown in Figure 2-3. The timeline from Chapter 1's application deployment cycle is used to show the change in the size of the business transaction tables over time. As shown in Figure 2-3, the business transaction tables increase in size constantly, with incremental increases immediately following each deployment of the application. The growth rate of the business transaction tables tends to increase as the number of users of the application increases.

Common Tuning Issues for Business Transaction Tables

Since business transaction tables grow so rapidly, the space management and tuning options used for them change over time. For example, the best type of joins performed within queries using business transaction tables may change rapidly as the tables increase in size. Chapter 11 provides tips for the management of joins and the order in which joins are processed. As the business transaction tables grow larger than the available memory area, you need to evaluate your tuning strategy again (see Chapter 11). The growth rate of the business transaction tables drives the growth rate of the database size.

The indexes associated with business transaction tables grow as well. If a row is deleted from a business transaction table, the space previously used by the row's index entries will not be reused by Oracle. If a business transaction table has many deletes and inserts, but does not grow in size, then its indexes may grow in size. The table's indexes grow in size because more and more space within the index becomes unusable as the number of deletions increases—a condition called *index stagnation* (see Chapter 5 for a full description of the causes and remedies of this problem). Thus, a business transaction table that contains chronologically based data, such as the last 24 months worth of sales orders, will stay a constant size while its indexes increase in size. To remedy the situation, you will need to rebuild the indexes (see "Fast Index Rebuilds" in Chapter 13).

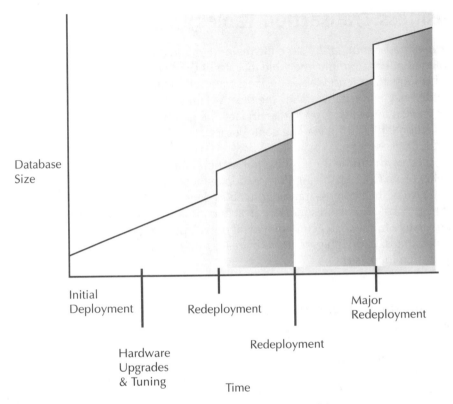

Database Size

Initial Deployment

Hardware Upgrades & Tuning

Redeployment

Redeployment

Major Redeployment

Time

FIGURE 2-3. *Growth profile for business transaction tables*

If the growth rate of the business transaction tables is largely due to growth in one or two tables, you may elect to move those tables to their own tablespaces. Doing so gives you more options regarding the tuning of the I/O involving those tables. Chapter 4 addresses the I/O options available to you for tuning very active business transaction tables.

In order to improve the performance of queries against the business transaction tables, you may create tables that store aggregated values from the business transaction tables. For example, you may store frequently requested summary values from the transaction tables into aggregation tables. As a result, the total database size increases again—without any user transactions being performed. Aggregation tables are typically created during tuning efforts, and may cause the database size attributed to the business transaction tables to increase even more rapidly than shown in Figure 2-3.

To improve the performance of the creation of aggregate tables, you can take advantage of Oracle's Parallel Query Option (PQO), available as of Oracle7.1. As described in Chapter 12, PQO allows the CPU burden of a transaction to be distributed across multiple CPUs within a single server. PQO is ideal for the creation of aggregate tables, since the table scanning and sorting operations involved in generating aggregate tables can all be parallelized. To further improve performance, the **create table as select** and **create index** commands can take advantage of the **unrecoverable** clause (as of Oracle7.2) to eliminate the writing of entries to the online redo log files during the object creation. Full details for the implementation of PQO are provided in Chapter 12.

Temporary/Interface Tables

Temporary/interface tables are used temporarily during data processing. They are not used for long-term storage of data but rather to assist in the data migration process. They are not directly accessed by the users of the application.

For example, the GL_INTERFACE table of Oracle Financials is a temporary/interface table. Like writes to most temporary/interface tables, writes to GL_INTERFACE occur in short bursts; afterwards, the data is queried out of the table and the table's records are deleted. Temporary/interface tables have very high volatility; they do not contain the same records for a long period of time. Their growth is sporadic; depending on the schedule for data loading, there may be no representative growth rate unless you look at the growth rate over a very large time period. The size of interface tables can vary widely, and can be volatile.

The growth profile for temporary/interface tables is shown in Figure 2-4. The timeline from Chapter 1's application deployment cycle is used to show the change in the size of the temporary/interface tables over time. As shown in Figure 2-4, the temporary/interface tables increase in size intermittently, with subsequent deletion of rows. Because of their nonstandard growth rate, the size needed by temporary/interface tables is difficult to predict and is a frequent cause of problems during data migration.

Common Tuning Issues for Temporary/Interface Tables

Temporary/interface tables are prone to the index stagnation problem described earlier, and to a second problem called the *highwatermark problem*. When data is written to a table, Oracle records the number of the highest block to which data was written. That block number—the highwatermark —is kept with the table header block information.

The high-water mark is used in two different situations. First, when you perform a SQL*Loader Direct Path load, the highwatermark is used to determine where the data should start to be loaded. The formatted blocks of data generated by SQL*Loader Direct Path are inserted above the highwatermark of the table.

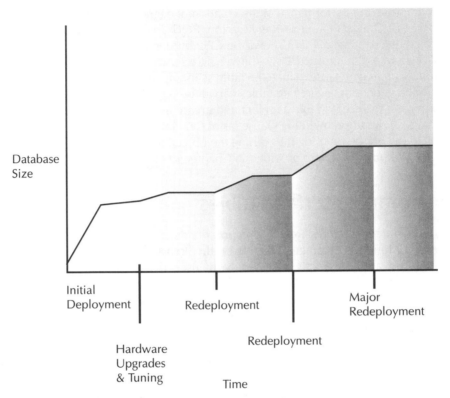

FIGURE 2-4. *Growth profile for temporary/interface tables*

Second, when you perform a full table scan of the table, Oracle will scan up to the highwatermark of the table, regardless of the number of records in the table.

Let's consider the SQL*Loader Direct Path problem first. If you perform a Direct Path load into the table, then delete all the records from the table, and then perform a second Direct Path load into the table, you will need to have enough space to store the loaded data *twice*. As shown in Figure 2-5, the space used by the first data load is unused by the second, because of the highwatermark value generated by the first data load. The second data load starts at the highwatermark.

As shown in Figure 2-5, the loaded data requires twice the amount of space it should, because of the unused space within the table. To reset the highwatermark, you could have **truncate**d the table to delete the records from the first data load. Other than **truncate**, the only way to reset the highwatermark is to recreate the table.

Table

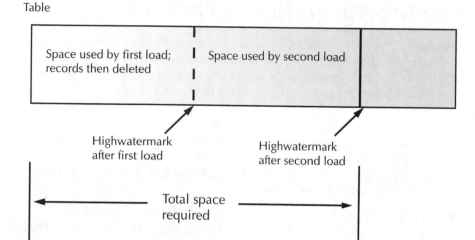

FIGURE 2-5.   *Highwatermark problem for Direct Path Loads*

The second problem caused by the highwatermark is the performance of full table scans. If you delete the records from the second data load in Figure 2-5, the table will have no records in it. How long will it take to execute the following query, assuming GL_INTERFACE is the table for the Direct Path load examples?

```
select count(*) from GL_INTERFACE;
```

The query in the preceding listing requires a full table scan of GL_INTERFACE. During the full table scan, Oracle will read up to the highwatermark—*even if all the blocks are empty*. The query will return a count of 0, but only after it has scanned all of the blocks previously used by the first and second data loads. If the table had been **truncate**d, the highwatermark would have been reset. If the highwatermark had been reset, the full table scan of the GL_INTERFACE table would have completed almost immediately.

As of Oracle7.3, you can deallocate space from tables, clusters, and indexes. When you deallocate space from a segment, as described in Chapter 13, you can only deallocate space that exists beyond the highwatermark of the table. Thus, if you have temporary/interface tables whose true highwatermark is constantly changing, but whose recorded highwatermark never decreases, you should periodically arrange to clear all the records from the table with the **truncate** command. For details on determining the highwatermark of your tables, see Chapter 5.

Using Growth Profiles in Planning

To prepare for growth within your database, you should first categorize your tables based on the definitions in the preceding sections of this chapter. The tables (and their indexes) that are categorized as either business transaction tables or business reference tables need to be monitored for growth. You can monitor growth in several ways:

- *Monitor the space allocated to the segment.* The DBA_SEGMENTS data dictionary view shows the number of bytes and database blocks allocated to each segment. You can query DBA_SEGMENTS for the space allocated to both the table and its indexes.

- *Analyze the table.* After you analyze a table, you can query the DBA_TABLES, DBA_INDEXES, and DBA_IND_COLUMNS data dictionary views to see how many rows are in the table and the impact on the table's indexes.

- *Select the count of records in the table (***select count***(*)* **from** *table_name;).* This method does not allow you to see the index space usage changes.

You can store the database sizing data in a separate table and track the change in the table size over time. By tracking the rate of change to the size of your fastest growing business transaction table, you can very closely approximate the growth rate for the entire database. Be sure to consider the growth rate of the indexes when calculating that of your database, and add in the space intermittently required by the temporary/interface tables.

Indexes that contain updateable columns should be watched very closely. The more the values in the index can be updated, the more likely the index is to experience index stagnation (described earlier in this chapter, and in detail in Chapter 5). As index stagnation grows, the number of empty and unusable blocks within an index grows. Thus, the growth rate of indexes with updateable columns may be significantly higher than predicted unless you periodically rebuild the indexes.

In Oracle7.3, the process of rebuilding indexes is simpler than in previous versions. The **alter index** *index_name* **rebuild** command rebuilds the *index_name* index, using the current index as the data source for the new index. Because the current index is used as the data source, the index creation process is faster than if the table were used as the index's data source. You can also use the **rebuild** option of the **alter index** command to specify storage parameters and tablespace designations for the index. As described in Chapter 13, the **rebuild** option for indexes requires that you have enough storage space available to store both the old and the new versions of the index simultaneously.

Once you have determined the growth rate of your database, you can evaluate the options available to you for managing the response time of the database. These options, including hardware tuning, memory tuning, space tuning, and SQL tuning, are described in Parts 2, 3, and 4 of this book. As illustrated in Chapter 1, the addition of hardware (such as CPUs, memory, and disks) will not solve the core performance problems, but it may decrease the crisis level enough so you have the time to address the core performance problems properly.

If system performance is not an immediate problem, you still need to be able to forecast your system needs—and potential problems. In Chapters 3 and 4, you will see how to anticipate the memory, CPU, and hardware tuning issues your database will encounter as it grows in size and user base. As the data is being used in more of the enterprise's critical processes, the value of the data increases—and so does the penalty for losing the data. The ability to quickly and reliably back up and recover the data helps reduce the crisis level associated with data availability issues. In Chapter 4, you will see the hardware solutions available, when to use them, and how to configure them so that your growing application could take advantage of them.

CHAPTER 3

Memory and CPU Tuning Issues

Most tuning efforts involving memory management in Oracle focus on the *hit ratio*—a measure of how often data is read from memory instead of from disk. Unfortunately, most general discussions of target values for the hit ratio fail to consider the impact of factors such as application type and Oracle's I/O mechanisms. In this chapter, you will see how different types of data accesses artificially increase or decrease the overall hit ratio, and how to set appropriate target values of the hit ratio for your applications. You'll also see that Oracle's I/O processing is CPU-bound, and how to use this information to set appropriate minimum hit ratio levels.

Since I/O processing and CPU processing are related in Oracle, memory and CPU tuning issues must be considered together. In the first part of this chapter, you'll see the techniques Oracle uses to address application data access needs. You'll see the impact of temporary segment activity and rollback segment activity on the hit ratio, as well as the impact of index scans. Given the actions Oracle takes when resolving data access requests, you will then be able to determine what your database's minimum and target hit ratio values will be.

Types of Applications

From the perspective of memory management, there are two types of Oracle database applications:

- *OLTP (On-Line Transaction Processing) applications*, in which many users activate small transactions. The performance of an OLTP application is measured by the response time of random queries executed by online users.

- *Batch applications*, in which a small number of users execute large transactions. The response time of batch applications is measured by the overall time to complete the transactions.

The distinction between OLTP and batch applications during tuning efforts is addressed in detail in Chapter 7; the focus in this chapter is merely to establish that there are two separate types of applications. Most production applications incorporate a mix of batch and OLTP characteristics. For example, a financial tracking system may have many online transactions against its ledger (OLTP), but may also receive periodic data loads from outside sources (batch). The challenge is to service the needs of both types of transactions with the available memory, disk, and CPU resources.

Since applications tend to use both OLTP and batch transactions, you need to know how each type of transaction is processed and what features are available to improve the performance of the transactions. In the next sections, you will see how Oracle addresses the data access needs of OLTP and batch transactions. The goal is to build a database that will perform well for the online users and can be optimized for frequently-used batch transactions.

How Oracle Addresses OLTP Data Access Needs

OLTP applications have a large number of users executing random queries against the database. The challenge within OLTP applications is to reduce the response time for accessing a small amount of data. However, the data access pattern is random; you cannot predict the next data the users will request.

Within OLTP applications, a *random hot-spot* pattern usually evolves. A *hot spot* is an area on a disk that is frequently accessed. If an area on disk is accessed once, there is a good chance that the same area will be accessed again. Even though many users are accessing the data, the same sections of the database—and the disks—are used repeatedly. The particular physical location is random, but the area is accessed repeatedly.

For example, consider a financial ledger application. Users who enter new ledger data into the ledger tables are entering data to the free blocks at the end of the ledger table; those transactions will reuse the same blocks, regardless of the user entering the data. The index blocks associated with those records will also be reused frequently. During data entry, the new ledger entries will be validated based on the referential integrity constraints defined by the application and the database. Since the users all use the same ledger table, they will all use the same tables via referential integrity checks. As a result, the tables accessed via referential integrity checks will become hot spots for short "lookup" queries.

To enhance the performance of OLTP applications, you can use three of Oracle's features. First, the *data block buffer cache* of the SGA stores blocks of data that have been read from the datafiles. Since the data is already in memory, another user accessing the same data can read the data without incurring an additional physical I/O against the datafile. Second, the *shared SQL area* of the SGA stores the parsed version of the SQL commands run against the database. Users who execute very similar queries can therefore have their queries processed more quickly by the database. Third, *indexes* allow for quick access to data. Most access to tables in OLTP applications occurs via an index; if the columns of an index are used as limiting conditions in the queries, the index provides a quick way for Oracle to find the row required by the query.

Within the data block buffer cache, Oracle manages the available space via a Least Recently Used (LRU) algorithm. If Oracle tries to read a new block into the data block buffer cache and discovers that there is no more free space within it, old blocks must be written out of it to make room for the new block. To determine which blocks must be removed, Oracle checks the LRU list. The blocks that have been least recently used are removed from the data block buffer cache and (if they have been changed) are written to disk, making room for the new blocks. If the most-used data can remain in the data block buffer cache for many users to access, your users will see improved performance because the most-used data is being read from memory instead of from disk.

The efficiency of the data block buffer cache is expressed via the hit ratio for the database. In general, a 90 percent hit ratio assumes that each block read into the data block buffer cache will be read nine times before it must be written back to disk (if it has been changed; otherwise, it is simply removed from the cache). As noted at the beginning of this chapter, there are a number of factors within an application that can skew the hit ratio measurement. See the "How to Calculate the

Hit Ratio" and "Factors That Impact the Hit Ratio" sections later in this chapter for details on hit ratio calculations.

Data blocks that are read into the data block buffer cache via full table scans are placed at the bottom of the LRU list, and are the first blocks to be discarded from the cache when more space is needed. OLTP applications that have many small application reference tables may have queries that force full table scans of the small tables (since a full scan of a small table may be faster than an index scan followed by a table lookup). The small tables, since they were read via full table scans, are likely to be quickly removed from the data block buffer cache. To keep the small tables actively in the data block buffer cache, you can create a fully-indexed table or, as of Oracle7.1, you can mark the table as a cache table.

To fully index a table, create an index that contains all of the columns of the table. The index blocks read during queries of the table will stay in the data block buffer cache longer than if the same data had been read via a full table scan. Fully indexing a table is appropriate if the table is small and nonvolatile. If the table's data changes frequently, the cost of maintaining the index will outweigh the performance benefits of fully indexing the table.

To mark a table as a cache table, specify the **cache** clause in either the **create table** or **alter table** command. If a table is marked as a cache table, that table's blocks will be considered as the most recently used blocks in the data block buffer cache—even if they were read via a full table scan. Thus, you can avoid having your small tables' blocks frequently removed from the data block buffer cache. In the following example, the ACCOUNT_CODES table is marked as a cache table. The first time its blocks are read into the data block buffer cache, they will be marked as the most recently used blocks in the cache.

```
alter table ACCOUNT_CODES cache;
```

If a table is not a cache table, you can embed the CACHE hint as part of your queries to force the table to be cached (see "Using Hints" in Chapter 10). To deactivate the cache status of a table, use the **nocache** clause of the **alter table** command.

The combination of index accesses, the data block buffer cache, and the shared SQL area dramatically improves the performance of OLTP applications by minimizing the number of times the database has to perform I/O for random hot-spot reads. Unfortunately, most applications also have batch features, either in the form of data loads or long-running reports. You need to determine the prevalence of batch transactions within your OLTP application in order to properly plan for the impact of batch data access on your data block buffer cache effectiveness.

How Oracle Addresses Batch Data Access Needs

Batch applications have a characteristic disk access pattern for each user. Usually, a batch job works on its own data in the same pattern each time it is run. Since the performance of a batch transaction is measured by its throughput, Oracle implemented solutions to improve the throughput of batch transactions.

Most batch data access solutions involve tuning full table scans. Oracle implemented four techniques to optimize full table scans:

- *Multiblock reads.* Multiple blocks are read from the table in a single "read" request.

- *Buffer aging.* Blocks read via full table scans are quickly removed from the data block buffer cache.

- *One consistent get per block.* Instead of checking the timestamp of each record, Oracle checks the timestamp of each block during a full table scan.

- *No special reads for migrated rows.* Chained rows are read based on their current physical location, not their original location.

As a result of these four techniques, full table scans can perform well while minimizing the impact on possible concurrent OLTP actions. In the following sections, you will see detailed descriptions of each technique and its impact on batch data access performance.

Multiblock Reads

Multiple blocks are read into the data block buffer cache during a single read request. The number of blocks to read is determined by a number of factors—some that you can set, and some that are operating system-dependent. The two factors that you can set are the database block size and the multiblock read count factor.

The database block size is set via the DB_BLOCK_SIZE parameter in the database's init.ora file when the database is created. You cannot easily change the database block size of an existing database. To do so, you need to perform a full database Export, completely rebuild the database with a new database block size specified, and then Import the data back into the database. The default database block size is 2KB; you should use at least a 4KB database block size for your databases, since the increase in database block size improves performance for both OLTP and batch applications. Batch applications typically realize up to 40 percent performance improvement when the database block size is increased from 2KB to 4KB, and performance is further improved by using a database block size of 8KB or greater.

The multiblock read count factor is set via the DB_FILE_MULTIBLOCK_READ_ COUNT parameter in the database's init.ora file. The DB_FILE_MULTIBLOCK_ READ_COUNT parameter can be changed after a database has been created; as of Oracle7.3, it can be changed while the database is running (see Chapter 13). DB_FILE_MULTIBLOCK_READ_COUNT tells Oracle how many blocks to read during a single read request. The usage and effectiveness of the multiblock read differs among operating systems. In many operating systems, the time it takes to read eight blocks is only slightly longer than the time it takes to read one block. As a result, the overall cost of reading the blocks decreases.

The amount of data read during a single read request is the product of the database block size and the multiblock read count factor. If the database block size is 4KB, and the multiblock read count factor is 8, then eight database blocks (32KB worth of data) will be read into the buffer during a database read. The operating system limits the amount of data that can be read during a single read request. In the HP-UX operating system, for example, 64K can be read during a single read request. Therefore, if the database block size is 4KB, then no more than sixteen database blocks can be read during a single read. You should set the DB_BLOCK_SIZE and DB_FILE_MULTIBLOCK_READ_COUNT parameters to take greatest advantage of the operating system's ability to read multiple blocks in a single read.

Buffer Aging
When one user is reading data via a full table scan, it is unlikely that any other user will need to read the scanned blocks. Therefore, a portion of the data block buffer cache is reserved for use by blocks read via full table scans. The size of the reserved portion is equal to that of the data read during a single read (see the preceding "Multiblock Reads" section). As described in the "How Oracle Addresses OLTP Data Access Needs" earlier in this chapter, the blocks read via full table scans are marked as least recently used and are quickly removed from the data block buffer cache (the process is referred to as *buffer aging*). If buffer aging did not occur, then a single user performing a full table scan could completely overwrite the data block buffer cache.

The only problem with buffer aging is that it assumes that index accesses and their subsequent table accesses are highly shareable among users. Although this is often the case, index accesses against extremely large tables may cause the index blocks read to overwrite the entire data block buffer cache. If you are frequently querying very large tables, see the "Manage Very Large Table Accesses" section of Chapter 11.

One Consistent Get per Block
When reading data, Oracle checks the data's SCN (System Change Number) to make sure you will receive data that is both timely and consistent. If the SCN is

greater than the SCN recorded when the transaction began, the data has changed since the transaction started. SCNs are used to ensure a consistent view of data and to determine which data need recovery during recovery operations following media failures.

If the data has changed since the transaction started, Oracle checks the rollback segments for the original data for the blocks you are requesting. The data read from the rollback segment will be consistent with the rest of the data required for your transaction, or the query will fail. Block accesses involving SCN checks are called *consistent gets.*

When a row's SCN is changed, the SCN for the block in which the row is stored is changed too. During a full table scan, it is enough to check the SCN for the entire block and to ignore the SCNs for the rows in the block. If the block was not changed since the transaction started, the scan of rows inside the block is executed with no additional consistent gets. Thus, the overhead of checking the SCN for each row is avoided; depending on the number of rows in each block, this technique, automatically used by Oracle, can save as much as 50 percent in processing time.

No Special Reads for Migrated/Chained Rows

Migrated and *chained rows* are rows that are no longer stored in their original blocks, usually because the row "grew" when its column values were updated to longer values. The migrated or chained rows will be referenced twice within the table—in their original locations and in their current locations. When performing a table scan, Oracle does not handle the chained rows as part of the original block. Rather, it reads the rows in the physical order in which they occur in the table. Since the entire table is being read, the query process will eventually read all of the rows in the table and it can skip the references to migrated or chained rows. The exception to this rule are chained rows that are larger than the database block size; these are called *spanned rows.* When reading spanned rows, Oracle does "jump" back and forth during the scan to assemble the row fragments.

The combination of these four techniques—multiblock reads, buffer aging, one consistent get per block, and no special reads for chained rows—improves the performance of full table scan operations and minimizes their Impact on the data block buffer cache efficiency.

How to Calculate the Hit Ratio

The data block buffer cache efficiency, as measured by the hit ratio, records the percentage of times the data block requested by a query is already in memory. The more frequently the data is found in memory, the higher the hit ratio will be.

You can calculate the hit ratio by determining the number of logical reads and physical reads that occur during a time interval. The interval chosen is important; the database records the cumulative logical reads and physical reads since the database was started. If you select the cumulative hit ratio from the database, the hit ratio will reflect not only the application's logical reads but also the logical reads performed when the database was first opened. Since the data block buffer cache is empty when the database is first opened, the cumulative hit ratio for a database will generally be lower than the hit ratio during a specific period of online usage. The utlbstat.sql and utlestat.sql scripts found in the /RDBMS/ADMIN subdirectory under the Oracle software home directory can be used to determine the number of logical and physical reads during a given interval.

Logical and physical read statistics can be queried via the V$SYSSTAT dynamic performance view. Logical reads are the sum of 'consistent gets' and 'db block gets'. The 'db block gets' statistic value is incremented when a block is read for update and when segment header blocks are accessed. Physical reads are recorded in the line for the 'physical reads' statistic. The query in the following listing will display the cumulative hit ratio for a database.

```
select
    SUM(DECODE(Name, 'consistent gets',Value,0)) Consistent,
    SUM(DECODE(Name, 'db block gets',Value,0)) Dbblockgets,
    SUM(DECODE(Name, 'physical reads',Value,0)) Physrds,
    ROUND((((SUM(DECODE(Name, 'consistent gets', Value, 0))+
        SUM(DECODE(Name, 'db block gets', Value, 0)) -
        SUM(DECODE(Name, 'physical reads', Value, 0)) )/
        (SUM(DECODE(Name, 'consistent gets',Value,0))+
        SUM(DECODE(Name, 'db block gets', Value, 0))))
        *100,2) Hitratio
from V$SYSSTAT;
```

The query in the preceding listing displays the cumulative consistent gets, database block gets, and physical reads from the V$SYSSTAT view. The consistent gets and database block gets, added together, are the logical reads from the database. Subtracting the physical reads from the logical reads and dividing the difference by the logical reads gives you the hit ratio. Sample output from the preceding query is shown in the following listing.

```
CONSISTENT DBBLOCKGETS   PHYSRDS    HITRATIO
---------- ----------- ---------- ----------
  81538694     4008468   8793798       89.72
```

NOTE
A logical read that causes a physical read to occur increments the statistic values for both logical reads and physical reads. To avoid counting the same read twice in the hit ratio calculation, the physical reads are subtracted from the logical reads; the difference is divided by the logical reads.

The query output shows that 81 million consistent gets have been performed, along with 4 million database block gets. To service the 85 million logical reads, over 8 million physical reads were performed, generating a cumulative hit ratio of 89.72.

Given the hit ratio, you may be tempted to offer advice on tuning the application. However, you need to know more about the application in order to judge whether the hit ratio is acceptable or unacceptable. In the next section, you will see how the different types of segments used impact the hit ratio—for better or worse.

Factors That Impact the Hit Ratio

In principle, the hit ratio can reveal the degree to which reports and batch transactions interfere with the work of online users in an OLTP environment. A high hit ratio might suggest that interference is low, while a low hit ratio may suggest that interference is high. Unfortunately, the reality is not so simple.

To understand the factors that impact the hit ratio, you must consider the different segments involved in processing the data in the data block buffer cache. As described in the following sections, you must consider the impact of dictionary tables, temporary segments, rollback segments, index scans, and table scans.

Dictionary Tables Activity

When a SQL statement first arrives at the Oracle kernel, the database parses the SQL statement. The data dictionary objects involved in the query are resolved, and the SQL execution path is generated. If the SQL statement refers to an object (such as a table or view) that is not already in the SGA, Oracle executes a SQL statement to query the data dictionary for information about the object. The query of the dictionary table is called a *recursive query*.

A recursive query is similar to a regular query, except that the database's dictionary tables are queried instead of user tables. The database dictionary tables are owned by SYS, and most of the database dictionary table names end with a "$". The data dictionary tables contain all of the data needed to manage the database—such as the object names, types, and privileges.

Like regular queries, the blocks read from the data dictionary tables are read into the data buffers in the SGA. Since each of the data dictionary tables is small, the caching of these tables is expected to be good, and the hit ratio against these tables will be high. For example, you would expect that if all users are using the same application, they will be using the same database objects; and since those objects are represented as rows in the data dictionary tables, the same rows of the data dictionary tables will be queried repeatedly. As a result, the queries of the data dictionary tables will artificially increase the hit ratio of OLTP applications. Since the data blocks of the data dictionary tables take up space in the SGA, they effectively reduce the space available to your tables' blocks while increasing the overall hit ratio. If the data dictionary information required by the query is already in the data dictionary cache of the SGA, then no recursive call is necessary.

Temporary Segment Activity

When a user executes a query that requires a sort, Oracle tries to sort all of the rows inside the *sort area* in memory. The size of the sort area is determined by the setting of the SORT_AREA_SIZE parameter in your database's init.ora file. If Oracle requires more sort area than is available in memory, a temporary segment is allocated to store data associated with the sort. The allocation and release of a temporary segment involves more than ten recursive SQL statements. As of Oracle7.3, you can minimize the cost of temporary segment allocation; see the "Dedicated Temporary Tablespaces" section of Chapter 13 for details.

Once the temporary segment is allocated, Oracle tries to keep the cost of the sort to a minimum by writing data to and from the temporary segment in an unformatted fashion. Since the temporary segment activity is performed on unformatted data, Oracle does not use the consistent get mechanism to read the data—and no logical reads are recorded! Oracle does perform physical reads and writes to move the data to and from the temporary segment. As a result, it is possible to have a *negative* hit ratio.

For example, if there is 1 logical read and 100 physical reads for the temporary segment, the hit ratio will be (1-100)/1 = -99 = -9900 percent! Since accesses to temporary segments add physical reads without increasing the logical reads, temporary segment activity artificially decreases the hit ratio for both OLTP and batch applications. Temporary segment accesses should be avoided during OLTP applications; be sure the SORT_AREA_SIZE parameter is set high enough to avoid the need for temporary segments.

Rollback Segment Activity

Rollback segment activity is divided into two distinct activities: *rollback activity* and *rollback segment header activity*. Rollback segment header activity controls the writing of changed data blocks to the rollback segment. The rollback segment header is a data block, and it is frequently modified; therefore, the rollback segment header block will remain in the data block buffer cache for long periods of time. Accesses to the rollback segment header block will thus increase the hit ratio for your application, even though it is not related to your data blocks. The impact of the rollback segment header activity on your hit ratio will be greatest for OLTP systems that feature many small transactions. The "consistent changes" and "data blocks consistent reads—undo records applied" statistics (see Chapter 8) can be used to determine the frequency with which users access data from rollback segments.

Rollback activity is recorded in the blocks of the rollback segment. The rollback activity recorded in the rollback segments has little significant impact on the hit ratio. Queries that require access to both the data segments and rollback segments typically perform slower than if the data segments by themselves had been accessed.

Index Activity

Typical access to data involves an access to the index to get the RowID and a TABLE ACCESS BY ROWID operation to get the data block (see Chapter 10 for a description of data access operations). Since the index and the table operate separately, consistent gets are used to read both inside the index and from the table.

Every time a nonunique index or a partial key (only the leading part of an index) is used in the query, an INDEX RANGE SCAN operation is executed (see Chapter 10). The number of logical reads in an INDEX RANGE SCAN can be calculated as the sum of the height of the index (typically 3) and twice the number of rows in the scanned range (see Figure 3-1). The INDEX RANGE SCAN operation creates a large number of logical reads on a relatively small number of blocks. For example, a query on 10,000 rows out of a 500,000-row test table resulted in an 86 percent hit ratio *even though none of the blocks was cached prior to the query execution*! The hit ratio will artificially increase due to index range scan activity if all the data is not found in the index. If all the data is found in the index, there will be no artificial impact on the hit ratio.

Figure 3-1 shows the logical reads needed to resolve a query of the COMPANY table via an indexed access. When the query is executed, a logical read of the "root" node of the index (Read #1) directs the query to use the proper index "leaf"

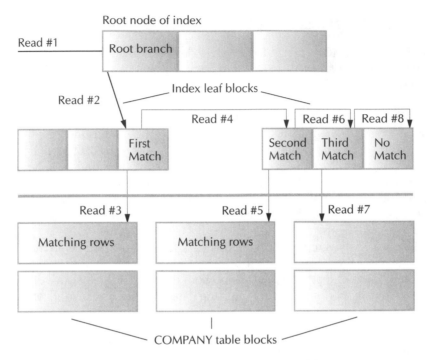

FIGURE 3-1.   *Logical Reads for Indexed Accesses to Tables*

nodes. A logical read is then performed against the first "leaf" node (Read #2), followed by a subsequent table access to the COMPANY table (Read #3). The next value from the leaf node is obtained (Read #4), followed by another table access (Read #5). The cycle of repeated logical reads against the index and table continues until the scan of the index encounters an entry that does not match the search criteria. The total number of logical reads required for the query is two times the number of records returned (one read for the index leaf, plus one read to the table) plus two (for Read #1 and Read #8, the first and last reads). If the index has 3 levels, then an additional read will be required before reaching the index leaf nodes.

Table Scans

As previously described, the blocks read via table scans are not kept long in the data block buffer cache. As a result, table scans will lower the overall hit ratio for both OLTP applications and batch applications. Also, there is only one consistent get per block for a full table scan, while an index scan may have several consistent gets per row (see Figure 3-1)!

To improve the performance of table scan and sorting operations, you can use Oracle's parallel options. The parallel options distribute the processing requirements of a query among multiple processes. As a result, the query may be able to use more system resources concurrently and complete faster. See Chapter 12 for a full description of the parallel options available.

OLTP and Batch Application Types

As described in the preceding sections, the hit ratio is not as simple as it seems. Since there is no way to calculate the hit ratio of accesses to your tables separate from the rest of the database, you must consider the impact of the different database segments when evaluating your hit ratio.

For OLTP applications, the impact of the different segment types is shown in Table 3-1.

As shown in Table 3-1, the two factors that lower the hit ratio—temporary segment accesses and table scans—are not commonly found in OLTP applications. On the other hand, the factors that increase the hit ratio—particularly data dictionary accesses and index scans—are frequently found in OLTP applications. Therefore, the hit ratio for OLTP applications will be artificially inflated just by the nature of the application.

For batch applications, the impact of the different segment types is shown in Table 3-2.

As shown in Table 3-2, the two factors that lower the hit ratio—temporary segment accesses and table scans—are commonly found in batch applications. The factors that increase the hit ratio—particularly data dictionary accesses and index scans—are infrequently found in batch applications. Data dictionary accesses are low because fewer tables are accessed by batch applications than

Type of Activity	Overall Impact on Hit Ratio	Frequency of Occurrence
Data dictionary segments	High increase	High
Rollback segments	Low increase	Low
Index scans	Medium increase	High
Temporary segments	High decrease	Low
Table scans	Medium decrease	Low

TABLE 3-1. *Impact on Hit Ratio for OLTP Applications*

Type of Activity	Overall Impact on Hit Ratio	Frequency of Occurrence
Data dictionary segments	High increase	Low
Rollback segments	Low increase	Variable
Index scans	Medium increase	Medium
Temporary segments	High decrease	Medium
Table scans	Medium decrease	High

TABLE 3-2. *Impact on Hit Ratio for Batch Applications*

by OLTP applications. If the batch transaction is running a report, the rollback segment activity would be zero; if the batch transaction is performing data modifications, then the rollback segment activity may be high, but with little overall impact on the hit ratio. From the information provided in Table 3-2, the hit ratio for batch applications will be artificially decreased just by the nature of the application.

Before setting a target hit ratio for your application, you need to consider the relationship between I/O and CPU within Oracle, as described in the following section.

Memory and CPU Tuning Issues

When a data access request is able to be successfully completed by accessing only the data already in memory, that request is called a *hit*. If the data is not in memory, the access request is called a *miss*, and a physical I/O read has to be performed. A hit in the SGA returns the data immediately to the application, while a miss requires the intervention of the buffer manager.

The buffer manager coordinates the space usage in the data block buffer cache. If the data block buffer cache is full, and a miss occurs (new data is read from disk), the buffer manager has to evaluate the blocks already in memory, remove blocks from memory and queue them to be written to disk (if the data in the blocks has changed), and place the new blocks in the data block buffer cache. Because of the processing requirements of the buffer manager, it takes eight times more CPU to execute a physical read than it takes to access cached data directly. As a result, Oracle I/O operations are CPU-intensive—I/O operations require CPU resources to constantly manage the contents of the SGA.

You can use the CPU cost of Oracle I/O operations to estimate a break-even point between the CPU usage for physical reads and reads from memory. From our tests, the break-even point is an 89 percent hit ratio. The break-even point indicates that if the hit ratio is 89 percent for 100 logical reads, the CPU required to perform the first 89 reads is equal to that required to perform the 11 physical reads. Since physical I/O operations are CPU-bound, reducing the number of I/O operations reduces the CPU requirements of your application. One of the best ways to reduce physical I/O is by minimizing the use of full table scans, particularly in the optimization of OLTP applications (see Chapter 11 for SQL tuning advice). See Chapter 4 for information on tuning issues related to I/O.

Selecting a Target Hit Ratio for Your Application

For all applications, your hit ratio should exceed 89 percent in order to minimize the impact of the CPU costs for I/O operations. Even if your application is largely batch-oriented, you should strive to achieve a hit ratio of greater than 89 percent.

The target hit ratio for an application depends on the mix of OLTP and batch users within the database. If you have an OLTP application, featuring many users executing small transactions, then your target hit ratio should be 98 percent or above. As described earlier in this chapter, the nature of OLTP applications and the database objects involved artificially inflates the hit ratio; you need to increase your target hit ratio as well.

Often, an application will mix OLTP users with batch users. You can use the V$SESS_IO dynamic performance view to display the hit ratio for each current user in the database. To measure the hit ratio of batch processes, you could display the results of the following query as the process is starting and just before it completes.

```
column HitRatio format 999.99
select Username,
       Consistent_Gets,
       Block_Gets,
       Physical_Reads,
       100*(Consistent_Gets+Block_Gets-Physical_Reads)/
           (Consistent_Gets+Block_Gets) HitRatio
  from V$SESSION, V$SESS_IO
 where V$SESSION.SID = V$SESS_IO.SID
   and (Consistent_Gets+Block_Gets)>0
   and Username is not null;
```

Sample output from the query is shown in the following listing. The hit ratio for each user session is displayed, along with the logical and physical reads statistics (provided the user has performed at least one logical read). The **Username is not null** clause eliminates the Oracle background processes from the output.

USERNAME	CONSISTENT_GETS	BLOCK_GETS	PHYSICAL_READS	HITRATIO
SYSTEM	298	9	25	91.86
GLORIA	112	4	23	80.17
MARY	190	6	48	75.51
PEACH	145	10	22	85.81
BETTY	2065	128	381	82.63
STACI	47825	40424	4312	95.11
KELLI	532	10	46	91.51
FLORA	112350	25	4711	95.81
POLLY	23891	1061	337	98.65

If you have 20 or more users, and batch users cause less than 50 percent of the logical reads within your database, you should aim for a hit ratio of between 94 and 97 percent. If you have fewer than 20 users, the sharing of data among users depends heavily on the application, so you should aim for a hit ratio in the 89 to 94 percent range.

If your OLTP application is truly random, with very little sharing of data, you will not be able to use the SGA effectively. The SGA's caches allow for blocks read by one user to be read by a second user without needing to perform a physical I/O. If the OLTP application has a random hot-spot data access pattern, you should be able to read each block an average of nine times or more before it is removed from memory, achieving your target hit ratio.

Memory and CPU Requirements

Memory requirements are qualified by both your application's needs and the hardware vendor you are using. There are three areas of memory used by a database application: the application's memory area, the user's PGA (used for session context and sort-related information), and the SGA. The emphasis throughout this chapter is on tuning the SGA, since it is the largest of the three areas and bears the greatest impact on performance. The two most important SGA memory structures are the buffer cache and the shared SQL area. Of the shared memory areas required by Oracle, these two parts of the SGA are the largest.

To ensure good performance, a large enough SGA should be allocated. You should set an extremely high hit ratio (98 percent or better) for OLTP applications while settling for a lower hit ratio (89 percent) for batch applications. Although batch data access operations could settle for an even lower hit ratio, that lower hit ratio does not usually translate to a smaller SGA.

As the database grows, the buffer cache should grow accordingly. You should periodically review the size of your SGA and the size of the database and increase it accordingly. On average, the size of the data block buffer cache should be about

1 to 2 percent of your database size. If your database is so large that you cannot allocate the necessary memory for the SGA, you should concentrate on optimizing the database I/O as explained in detail in Chapter 4.

The shared SQL area also consumes a large amount of memory. In applications that make use of stored procedures or the Multi-Threaded Server (MTS), the shared SQL area may be larger than the data block buffer cache. The shared SQL area is used as a memory area for "competing" shared structures, including the library cache (which caches information about database objects such as stored procedures and views) and the cursor cache that caches SQL statements. In an MTS configuration, the shared SQL area is used to store session-specific information such as the context area and the sort area.

The demand on the shared SQL area is directly dependent on the breadth of your application. OLTP applications require more shared memory than batch-oriented applications, because there are more users executing more distinct transactions. Aggravating the memory requirements for shared SQL area is the implementation of stored procedures, packages triggers, and even views in the shared memory. You can use the DBA_OBJECT_SIZE view to show how much memory is actually taken by each object (see Chapter 6). The shared SQL area can grow quickly; for example, an Oracle Financials version 10 implementation could use a 200 MB shared SQL area.

From the CPU perspective, Oracle's architecture allows it to use as much of the CPU resources as you have available. If you have more than one CPU on a server, Oracle can use multiple CPUs during the resolution of a single transaction. Advanced features such as the Parallel Query option (covered in depth in Chapter 12) give you more flexibility regarding the use of the available CPU resources. When these resources are exhausted, it could be a result of either real workload or nonoptimal SQL (since poorly written SQL increases the number of physical I/O operations, and Oracle I/O operations are CPU-intensive).

Before performing extensive SQL tuning, it is prudent to upgrade the CPU and increase the available memory so that environmental factors can be excluded as the cause of poor performance. Once your CPU and memory resources are adequate for your application, you can concentrate on tuning the SQL that most affects the hit ratio of your application users. If the hit ratio is in your target range, you will be making the best use of the memory and CPU resources available. For information on how to tune SQL statements, see Section III of this book.

CHAPTER 4

Hardware Tuning Issues

Every system's performance is ultimately bounded by the speed of its slowest component. Since disk I/O speed is usually much slower than CPU speed, improving the performance of a database system often involves improving the performance of disk accesses. However, before you choose a hardware solution, there are a number of tuning and administration aspects to consider.

In this chapter, you will see a guide to estimating your required disk capacity, followed by descriptions of traditional and advanced solutions to resolving disk access performance problems. Solutions described include RAID implementations and raw devices. You will see the implementation and tuning issues associated with the advanced techniques, as well as their impact on administrative activities such as backup and recovery.

Estimating Disk Capacity Requirements

The disk capacity required by a database is the total of the disk space required by four separate categories of database-related space:

■ Space inside the database

■ External space used by Oracle

■ Application administration space

■ Redundancy/emergency storage space

In the following sections you will see information regarding the estimation of the space requirements for each type of space used by an application.

Space Inside the Database

Before a database is implemented, you need to determine how much data is going to be loaded into the tables. If the data comes from an outside source, you can use the size of the input files as a gross estimate of the required database space. If the data comes from transactions, you will need to estimate the average row size and the total number of rows in order to estimate the space required to store the rows. You can use the space calculations provided in the Oracle documentation to generate exact space requirements; however, exact space calculations are not necessary at this point in the space planning process. At this stage, you are only trying to generate an estimate of the space required rather than the actual space allocations used during object creations.

Once you have estimated the space required by the tables, you need to consider the space that is used as overhead within each database block that stores the tables' data. Inside each database block, Oracle leaves space for the expansion of the rows stored in the block. This space is defined by the **pctfree** storage parameter for the table. However, the **pctfree** setting usually only accounts for a portion of the database block overhead space. In normal transaction processing applications, rows are added and deleted continuously from the database blocks. The adding and deleting of rows causes the data in the blocks to become increasingly sparse over time; the amount of free space within the blocks will grow. If your database block size is ten times the average row length, you should expect that the free space within your database blocks will eventually reach 25 to 30 percent. If your database block size is small, and your row size is large, the free space percentage within the blocks will be even greater—possibly as high as 40 percent.

Now that you have estimated the space requirements for the table and its free space, add an additional 10 to 15 percent to the estimate. The additional space is required because of the way in which Oracle allocates space for segments. Each time more space is required by a segment, Oracle allocates a new extent for the segment (the extent's size is determined by the **next** and **pctincrease** storage parameters for the segment). Initially, the new extent is mostly empty. The space cost of the new extent may be significant; often, the second extent of a table is sized to be 25 to 50 percent of the size of the initial extent of the table. To avoid the significant cost of new (and largely empty) extents, make the initial extent large enough to handle new records. The additional space for the initial extents is particularly important for business reference tables (see Chapter 2). Adding in the free space overhead for the table and the free space buffer against extent allocation can increase the table's space requirements by 50 percent.

Once the tables' storage requirements are known, you can estimate the index space requirements. In general, the total size of the indexes is comparable with the total size of the tables. Systems that have high ad hoc query and end-user reporting activity will use indexes that are about 50 percent greater in size than the size of the tables.

The sizing of temporary segments and rollback segments presents more of a problem. In principle, you should allocate a rollback segment whose size is comparable to the largest transaction in the database for each rollback segment. However, in most applications, read consistency and concurrency requirements dictate the need for multiple rollback segments that are used by multiple small transactions. You need to have enough rollback segment space available to handle all of the concurrent transactions, plus an additional rollback segment specifically sized to handle the largest transactions.

The temporary tablespace requirements depend on the types of sorting operations performed within your application. If you are using the **compute statistics** option of the **analyze** command, you may need to support a temporary segment that is four times as large as the table being analyzed. The temporary segments and rollback segments may account for as much as 25 to 30 percent of the total database size.

Lastly, add in the space required by the SYSTEM tablespace. The SYSTEM tablespace stores the data dictionary information. In a production environment that uses stored objects (such as procedures, packages, functions, and triggers), your SYSTEM tablespace will likely exceed 100MB in size. The SYSTEM tablespace space requirements of stored objects arise from several tables stored in the SYSTEM tablespace; among them are SOURCE$, which stores the source code for packages, functions, and procedures; TRIGGER$, which stores the source code for triggers; and IDL_UB1$ and IDL_UB2$, which store compiled p-code for procedural objects.

If you use Oracle's Advanced Replication option (formerly called Symmetric Replication), its large number of stored objects will likely cause your SYSTEM tablespace to exceed 200MB in size; your TOOLS tablespace may require even more space than that. The replication catalog tables (REPCAT$) and the deferred queue table for replication are stored in the TOOLS tablespace, as are all of the error tables for replication. Each record queued for replication to another site is written to a table in the TOOLS tablespace; if a record received via replication fails during insert in the local database, the error records are written to tables in the TOOLS tablespace. You need to properly size the TOOLS tablespace if you will be using the Advanced Replication option. If you use the same instance for both production and development, the space requirements in the SYSTEM tablespace can increase dramatically, again because of the space used by stored objects.

External Space Used by Oracle

In addition to the space used within the database, disk capacity requirements estimates should include the space that the database needs external to the datafiles. The online redo log files and the archived redo log files are external to the datafiles, but are a critical part of the database; they record the transactions that occur within the database. The control files, although small in size, are also critical files for the database.

Since the log files record the transactions within a database, the space requirements of the log files depend on the transaction activity within the database. When an online redo log file fills, a *log switch* occurs. On a volatile production system, you should have enough online redo log files so that a log switch will occur no more often than every 20 to 30 minutes. To view how often log switches occur in your system, you can query V$LOG_HISTORY, which records the time of each log switch in the database for the most recent 100 log switches. The following query will show the time of each log switch during the past day (provided fewer than 100 log switches occurred in that time frame).

```
select TO_CHAR(TO_DATE(Time, 'MM/DD/YY HH24:MI:SS'),
               'HH24:MI:SS')
  from V$LOG_HISTORY
 where TO_DATE(Time,'MM/DD/YY HH24:MI:SS') > SysDate-1
 order by TO_DATE(Time, 'MM/DD/YY HH24:MI:SS')  desc;
```

In the query, you need to use the TO_DATE function on the Time column because Time is stored as a character field. Sample output of the V$LOG_HISTORY query is shown in the following listing.

```
TIME
-------------------
16:26:02
16:23:01
16:19:58
15:52:11
15:50:17
15:48:51
15:46:14
15:43:15
15:41:11
15:39:41
14:56:51
14:50:52
14:29:27
14:07:51
13:50:18
13:30:53
13:28:52
13:27:03
12:57:51
12:56:03

20 rows selected.
```

The sample output from the V$LOG_HISTORY query shows a typical usage pattern; there are times of high activity (shown by the seven log switches that occur from 15:39:41 to 15:52:11) followed by lower levels of activity (no log switches occur between 15:52:11 and 16:19:58). Each entry in V$LOG_HISTORY represents a single log switch. Thus, for the system shown in the sample query output, the online redo log files are too small. During periods of high activity, log switches are occurring every two minutes—instead of every 20 minutes. Based on the log switch timing information, the sample database's online redo log files are one-tenth of the size they should be.

V$LOG_HISTORY will only show the last 100 log switches. Therefore, you can query V$LOG_HISTORY to determine the cumulative time for the last 100 log switches by selecting the minimum Time value. The difference between the current system time and the minimum time value will be the cumulative time required for the last 100 log switches in days, as selected by the query in the following listing.

```
select SysDate - MIN(TO_DATE(Time,'MM/DD/YY HH24:MI:SS'))
        Days_for_last_100_switches
  from V$LOG_HISTORY;
```

The time for the last 100 log switches, as reported by the preceding query, will be displayed in terms of days.

You should have at least two redundant groups of log files. You can either use the operating system to mirror the online redo log files or you can establish redundant sets of online redo log files within Oracle (in which Oracle performs the mirroring). You may want to keep as much as two to four hours of work in your online redo log files. Depending on the size of these files and the transaction volume in the database, you may need six to ten online redo log files.

The optimal space required for the archived redo log disk area should be large enough to contain all the accumulated logs since the last backup. Having that many archived redo log files available will make ordinary media recovery very fast. Single tablespace recovery of a day's work could take only a few minutes if all archived redo log files are still on disk. However, for very large and volatile databases, it is not practical to have all the archived redo log files from the last backup stored on disk. Nevertheless, it is a good practice to allocate at least enough space for a day or two of archived redo log files. For example, in an Oracle Financials system with 200 online users and 10 to 15 batch jobs daily, you may use an online redo log file configuration with two sets of six online redo log files 50MB each for a total of 600MB (two sets of files*six files*50MB per file = 600MB). The archived redo log disk area containing a day and a half of archived redo log files could consume 4GB of space.

You also need to consider the space required by the Oracle software used by the database. A typical Oracle installation will require about 200MB of disk space. The instance, when opened, creates a file for the SGA's memory map. The size of the SGA file depends on the size of the SGA and the operating system used.

Application Administration Space

As the application grows and the database grows, more and more reports are printed and each report grows in size. Interim files generated by the batch process or input files that come via the network also keep growing in volume. You need to budget space for the files used to move data into and out of the database. The space required for the interim files and the spool files will increase over time, and you need to factor it into the disk capacity requirements for the application.

Redundancy/Emergency Storage Space

When your data size grows to over 10GB, your total database size (including free space, index space, rollback segments, temporary space, and external file space) will likely approach 30 to 40GB. For a database of that size, it may take longer than a long weekend to recreate and reload all the data for the database. To minimize the impact of a disk failure, and therefore eliminate the need for recovery time, you should consider using an advanced hardware architecture, such as disk mirroring or a RAID implementation (as described later in this chapter). Disk mirroring techniques will impact your storage requirements; for example, 1-to-1 mirroring of all your disks will double your storage space requirements.

When a failure happens or when a major Oracle upgrade is necessary, the time it takes to recover can be directly related to the amount of disk space available. For example, if you can copy many of your archived log files from tape to disk, database recovery could speed up significantly. If an application glitch corrupts a table, the ability to store Export dump files on disk could provide for a means of at least partial recovery. For example, if you need to recover business reference tables without impacting your application transaction tables, you may need to use an Export dump file that is no longer available on disk. To perform the recovery quickly, you will need to copy the Export dump file from tape onto disk—and to make that copy, you will need adequate space to hold the Export dump file.

Figure 4-1 shows the total disk space requirements in proportion to the initial input data. As the database grows in size, the different space areas of the database—data, indexes, rollback segments, temporary segments, free space, and application administration space—also grow. Each type of space is shown in a separate area of the figure; the sum of all areas shows the total space needed by the database at any time. After a major redeployment (see Chapter 1), you may need to use a disk mirroring strategy in order to support your database recovery requirements. The space required for redundancy and emergency storage may dramatically increase your space requirements; as shown in Figure 4-1, the space costs of redundant storage are incurred after the recovery time requirements force you to use a different database backup strategy.

Identifying I/O Bottlenecks

Most I/O-bounded systems are bounded by *read* I/O (as opposed to *write* I/O). If your database block buffer hit ratio (see Chapter 3) is not in the high 90s and you

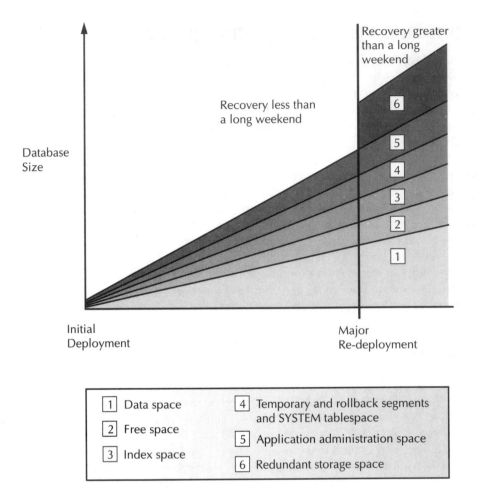

FIGURE 4-1. *Impact of database growth on disk capacity requirements*

have a database with hundreds or thousands of objects, many type of transactions, and many online users, you should first try to increase the size of your database block buffer cache. If response time is still very slow (especially for the most important processes) after you have increased the size of your database block buffer cache to the point where the buffer hit ratio is in the high 90s, then you should try to tune the SQL statements in your applications (see Section III). However, some applications have such intensive I/O needs that I/O becomes an issue to them. How can you identify I/O bottlenecks?

First, query the V$FILESTAT dynamic performance table. To check the file I/O distribution during a specific time interval, you can use the utlbstat.sql and utlestat.sql files provided by Oracle—the output will show the read and write I/O distribution across the datafiles. If the V$FILESTAT view shows that the file I/O is not concentrated on one or two files, you should check the operating system monitoring utilities. If your I/O rate to individual disk drives, as shown by the operating system monitor, approaches the operating environment's maximum during the period of high activity, you will need to use one of the advanced I/O architecture options described in the following sections of this chapter.

In the following listing, the V$FILESTAT view is joined to the V$DATAFILE view; the result will show the total I/O by datafile. The I/O is expressed in terms of database blocks read and written.

```
select DF.Name File_Name,
       FS.Phyblkrd Blocks_Read,
       FS.Phyblkwrt Blocks_Written,
       FS.Phyblkrd+FS.Phyblkwrt Total_IOs
  from V$FILESTAT FS, V$DATAFILE DF
 where DF.File#=FS.File#
 order by FS.Phyblkrd+FS.Phyblkwrt desc;
```

FILE_NAME	BLOCKS_READ	BLOCKS_WRITTEN	TOTAL_IOS
/db10/oracle/DEV/sys01.dbf	1095747	6580	1102327
/db13/oracle/DEV/appdata01.dbf	278310	11845	290155
/db10/oracle/DEV/sys02.dbf	256668	3681	260349
/db10/oracle/DEV/appindex01.dbf	155168	1928	157096
/db10/oracle/DEV/temp01.dbf	3524	17745	21269
/db02/oracle/DEV/users01.dbf	12756	0	12756
/db10/oracle/DEV/rbs01.dbf	630	11219	11849
/db01/oracle/DEV/rbs02.dbf	9134	0	9134
/db13/oracle/DEV/users02.dbf	98	1545	1643
/db05/oracle/DEV/tools01.dbf	600	92	700
/db05/oracle/DEV/tools02.dbf	0	0	0

```
11 rows selected.
```

In the preceding listing, the datafiles are listed in descending order of total I/O activity. The "read" and "write" I/Os are shown as well, since the type of I/O operations performed influences the solution for resolving an I/O bottleneck. In the preceding example, the datafiles for the SYSTEM tablespace account for most of the I/O activity, followed by the data tablespace for the application (the "appdata01" datafile). The application is read-intensive, with many more reads than writes.

When writing to the database, Oracle uses a technique involving "lazy writes." The lazy writes technique involves leaving modified blocks of data in the SGA for some time before they finally get written to the datafiles. The writing of modified blocks to the datafiles is performed by the DBWR background process. DBWR "wakes up" periodically to perform the writes; it can also be triggered when modified blocks are removed from the SGA's data block buffer cache.

When DBWR writes data to the datafiles, it locks some portions of the SGA's data block buffer cache for the duration of the write and writes the modified blocks to the datafiles. If there are not enough DBWR processes available in a database with many write operations, you will see what is known as the *hiccup syndrome*. The symptoms of the hiccup syndrome are very short intermittent periods of very high write activity to the database (see Chapter 8 for database monitoring guidelines). During the "hiccups," there will be a very high write rate (200 to 300 writes per second), followed by a period of no writes at all. Graphically, the write rate will not be constant, but will instead be a series of intermittent bursts of large write activity—the hiccups. When a hiccup happens, the write rate increases and the user activity diminishes to zero because the SGA's data block buffer cache is locked by the DBWR process.

If you are experiencing the hiccup syndrome, you need to increase the number of DBWR processes available to your database. The number of available DBWR processes is controlled by the DB_WRITERS parameter in your database's init.ora file. The number of DBWR processes should be proportional to the number of transactions and users that update the database simultaneously. In general, you should have one DBWR process for every 50 online (query and update) users, and one DBWR process for every two batch jobs that update the database.

For example, if you have 100 online users, and four batch jobs running concurrently, you should modify your database's init.ora file to include the line

```
DB_WRITERS = 4
```

If you still experience the hiccup syndrome after increasing the number of DBWR processes, you can add more DBWR processes until the problem is resolved.

The lazy write technique used by Oracle also impacts the choice of RAID technologies to use, as described in the "Choosing a RAID Configuration" section later in this chapter.

Traditional Hardware Approaches

If you have identified an I/O bottleneck in your database, you can choose from a number of tuning approaches. The basic approaches, described in the following section, involve separating files and striping data. Following the description of the basic approaches, you will see how to implement the advanced RAID options and raw devices.

Separation of Files

To avoid contention between database files, there are several basic rules used when designing the physical layout of your database. If you are experiencing I/O contention, you should first make sure that I/O contention has not been designed into your system by violating one of these rules. The following rules refer to separation of files across drives; files should be placed on different I/O channels as well, to avoid the possibility of the I/O card becoming an I/O bottleneck.

- *Separate tables and indexes.* The datafiles used for tables and their indexes should be stored on separate disks to avoid contention during queries. A query that involves an index access to a table followed by an access of the same table will encounter I/O contention if the index and table are stored on the same device.

- *Separate rollback segments and tables and indexes.* Rollback segments are used during data manipulation transactions—as are the tables and indexes that store the data being manipulated.

- *Separate rollback segments and online redo log files.* As transaction-related data is being written to the rollback segments, a record of the transaction is being written to the online redo log files. Since rollback segment entries and online redo log file entries are being written concurrently, you should store them on separate devices.

- *Separate online redo log files and archived redo log files.* If you are running your database in ARCHIVELOG mode, the online redo log files will be archived. During periods of high activity, there may be I/O contention between the online and archived redo log files unless you keep them on separate disks.

- *Separate temporary tablespaces from tables and indexes.* Temporary segments are used during large queries and sorting operations (see Chapter 11). Since the table and index segments will also be read during large queries, they should be stored apart from temporary segments.

- *Separate the SYSTEM tablespace from the rest of the database.* Accesses to the data dictionary tables, as well as to the stored objects (procedures, packages, functions and triggers), cause the SYSTEM tablespace to be read. Store the SYSTEM tablespace apart from the rest of the database.

If you have followed these rules and you still are experiencing I/O contention, you should consider one of the advanced I/O methods described in the next sections of this chapter. RAID technology and raw devices are implemented at the operating system level. Another option, *data striping*, is available within the database as well. Most operating systems that have some form of logical volume management offer data striping options as well.

Data Striping

If you have multiple disks available for your data tablespaces, you can distribute the data across multiple disks via a technique called *data striping*. In data striping, the data in a table is spread across multiple disks by placing the table's extents on multiple disks.

For example, you could create a tablespace comprising two datafiles, as shown in the following listing. In the example, the datafiles in the tablespace are stored on two separate disks.

```
create tablespace DATA_1
datafile '/db01/oracle/DEV/data_1a.dbf' size 100M,
        '/db02/oracle/DEV/data_1b.dbf' size 100M;
```

The DATA_1 tablespace's datafiles are equally sized, and are stored on separate disks. Because the datafiles are stored on separate disks, you can distribute the I/O against the tablespace across the two disks. For example, you can create a table in the DATA_1 tablespace that has two extents, each of which will be stored in a separate datafile. You can use the **datafile** parameter of the **alter table allocate extent** command to specify a datafile, but you can also force the table to use multiple files when you create the table. In the following example, a table is created in the DATA_1 tablespace with two extents (via the **minextents 2** clause). The table's extents are sized (via their **initial** and **next** clauses) to consume most of the available space in the datafiles. Because the two extents cannot both fit into the first datafile, the first extent will be stored in the first datafile and the second in the second datafile.

```
create table TEST
(Column1   VARCHAR2(20))
tablespace DATA_1
storage (initial 98M next 98M pctincrease 0 minextents 2);
```

In the preceding example, the extent sizes are slightly smaller than allocated datafile space to allow for Oracle's overhead space within the datafile. When the table is created, two 98MB extents will be created for the TEST table.

The TEST table will now have two extents. Each extent will be in a separate datafile, since they both cannot fit in the first datafile, and extents cannot span datafiles. Since the datafiles are stored on separate disks, the table's data will be striped across the disks, potentially reducing I/O contention. At the start, the table will be empty. As data is written to the table, the first extent will begin to fill with data. When the first extent has no more free space left, data will be written to the second extent. Thus, although the table is striped across multiple disks, the table's data is not striped across the disks until *after* the first extent has filled with data.

In the following example, the TEST table created previously is dropped and recreated in the DATA_1 tablespace. The TEST table is created with one extent, which will be stored in the first datafile of the tablespace. The **alter table allocate extent** command is then executed to create a second extent of the table explicitly stored in the second datafile in the tablespace.

```
drop table TEST;

create table TEST
(Column1    VARCHAR2(20))
tablespace DATA_1
storage (initial 40M next 40M pctincrease 0 minextents 1);

alter table TEST allocate extent
(datafile '/db02/oracle/DEV/data_1b.dbf');
```

In the preceding example, the storage parameters for the TEST table were changed—the **initial** extent is 40MB in size, the **next** extent is 40MB in size, and the **minextents** value is 1. When the table is created, a single 40MB extent will be created in the DATA_1 tablespace. The first extent will allocate 40MB of space in the first datafile in DATA_1, which is 100MB in size; 60MB of the datafile will be free. When the second 40MB extent is created for the TEST table (via the **alter table allocate extent** command), the extent would normally be stored in the free space available in the first datafile (since the free space is large enough to hold the extent). Since the second datafile is specified in the **alter table** command, the second extent will be stored in the second datafile.

Data striping allows you to distribute the I/O costs of accesses to datafiles. Data striping helps most when the data for the table is already available and the table is nonvolatile. If the table is used to store transactional data, you will get little benefit from the striping until the first extent has filled. To get immediate striping of all your data, you should use one of the operating system methods described in the following sections.

How to Use RAID Technologies

RAID technologies are becoming an integral part of database solutions. In this section you will see how to take advantage of RAID technology and how to select the proper configuration for your applications.

The term "RAID" stands for Redundant Array of Inexpensive (or Independent) Disks. In RAID environments, a collection of disks is configured to operate collectively under the control of special hardware or software. The collection of disks provides advantages in several areas:

- *Media reliability and availability.* In RAID environments, data is stored on multiple disks; therefore, the loss of a single disk does not affect the availability of the data.

- *Serviceability.* Since data is stored redundantly, you can service one of the disks involved in a RAID environment without interrupting the application that uses the disks. This "hot swap" capability is manufacturer-dependent; some RAID controllers do not support the ability to remove one of the drives during operation. If the hot swap capability is not supported, the system must be shut down before the disk can be serviced.

- *Configurability.* As described in the following sections, you can configure the RAID environment to suit your application.

- *Performance.* Since more disks are involved in I/O requests against RAID environments, you can distribute the I/O load of a transaction across multiple disks in a very consistent and simple manner. Although the RAID controller adds overhead to the I/O operations, in a properly designed RAID set, the performance gain from the distribution of I/O access to the data should far exceed the overhead cost of the RAID controller. Additionally, a caching controller further minimizes the RAID controller's overhead, as described in the "Cache Issues" section later in this chapter.

RAID implementations use many techniques to provide data redundancy, error checking, data distribution, and data buffering. Although RAID implementation is controlled at the operating system level, you need to be aware of the implementation used on your disks in order to best manage your database's I/O burden. In general, RAID implementations are most commonly used when you have databases that are large or critical, or have high availability requirements or very short recovery times available.

NOTE
In some operating systems, the RAID sets are not controlled by the operating system; a number of manufacturers now implement RAID controllers at the drive level, so the operating system may not know it is communicating with a RAID set.

In the next sections, you'll see a brief overview of RAID technologies, followed by implementation advice.

How RAID Works

There are multiple RAID levels, as shown in Table 4-1. The descriptions in Table 4-1 refer to a *RAID set*. A RAID set is the set of disks that work together in a RAID environment. For example, if there are four disks working together in a RAID environment, the four disks together make up the RAID set.

Level	Description
RAID-0	Block striping, with no parity checks
RAID-1	1-to-1 disk mirroring
RAID-0+1	A combination of striping and mirroring
RAID-2	No longer used; was replaced by RAID-3
RAID-3	Byte striping with dedicated parity (parity allows recovery from failure of one disk of the RAID set)
RAID-4	Block striping with dedicated parity (parity allows recovery from failure of one disk of the RAID set)
RAID-5	Block striping with distributed parity (parity allows recovery from failure of one disk of the RAID set)
RAID-6	Block striping with two sets of distributed parity (parity allows recovery from failure of two disks of the RAID set)
RAID-7	Higher-performance version of RAID-5
RAID-S	Higher-performance version of RAID-5

TABLE 4-1.   *RAID Levels*

As shown in Table 4-1, there are numerous RAID levels available. The RAID levels make use of a combination of *mirroring* and *parity* to achieve the data availability and performance objectives.

NOTE
The RAID levels available to you are dependent on the hardware and operating system in use.

In mirroring, two disks are kept in sync; whenever data is written to one disk, it is also written to the second disk. A user who requests data from a datafile may read the data from either disk. As a result, the performance of transactions against the mirrored set of disks may improve, because the I/O load against the disks may be balanced (particularly for reads). However, there is a cost to mirroring—you double the disk space you need and the number of writes performed.

Figure 4-2 shows how parity helps to reduce the number of disks required to ensure availability. In a parity-based system, data from a single file is distributed across multiple disks. For example, four-disk RAID-3 environments place the first byte of a file on Disk 1, the second on Disk 2, the third on Disk 3, and a parity check byte on Disk 4. If Disk 1 becomes unavailable, the data that had been on Disk 1 can be recreated by the operating system, since the data from Disks 2 and 3 and the parity check from Disk 4 is still available. As shown in Figure 4-2, a mirrored set of four disks allows you to store two disks' worth of data on four disks;

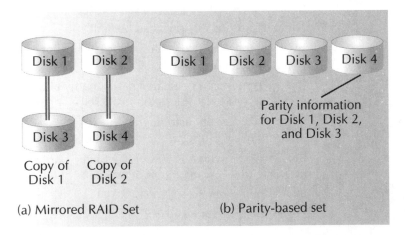

FIGURE 4-2. *Mirrored and Parity-Based Sets*

a parity-based set of disks allows you to store three disks worth of data on four disks, a 50 percent improvement in space availability.

In a RAID environment, one or more array controllers control the disks involved in the RAID set. As shown in Figure 4-3, the data is distributed across multiple disks. The manner in which data is striped across the disks and parity is handled identifies the RAID level in use.

NOTE

In a RAID environment, the size of the data segment is the same for each drive (see Figure 4-3). For RAID-3, each data segment is one byte in length; for RAID-5, each data segment is one block in length.

In a RAID environment, the disks are independent. That is, data is read from or written to each disk independently. In RAID-0, data is spread across a set of disks in the form of user-defined segments. Reading and writing use multiple disks concurrently via available I/O channels, increasing the I/O throughput available. Since a single disk has physical limits to its data transfer rate, getting multiple disks to transfer data cooperatively improves the overall throughput rate of an I/O request. In a RAID-0 environment, striping is performed at the operating system level, improving the concurrency and scalability of data access for a multiuser system.

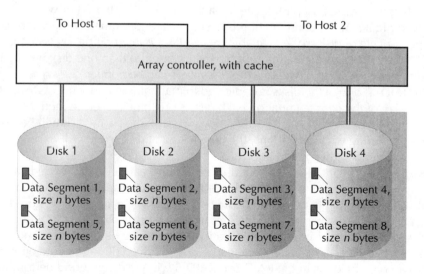

FIGURE 4-3. *RAID configuration, with array controller*

In RAID-1, a copy of a disk's data is stored on a second disk via mirroring (see the "Mirrored Set" portion of Figure 4-2). The effective disk capacity is one-half of the available disks, since half of the disks are used as the mirror set. There is no data striping used in RAID-1. If one of the disks fails, the other can continue to operate. I/O requests against the disks can be directed to either disk; the operating system controls the distribution of the I/O load to each disk in the mirror set, and reconciles changes against the disks.

In RAID-0+1, data is duplicated on mirrored disks and is also striped across groups of mirrored disks. RAID-0+1 allows you to gain the advantages of both RAID-0 and RAID-1; the system will have increased concurrency of data across disks, increased throughput, and data protection via full redundancy. As with RAID-0, the full redundancy of data requires that half of the disks be dedicated to mirroring.

In RAID-3, the data is striped across multiple disks. As described in Table 4-1, the size of the data segment on each disk is only one byte in length (shown in Figure 4-3). One of the disks in each RAID set is dedicated to maintaining the parity information for the other disks, which is used to reconstruct missing data in the event of a disk failure. RAID-3 will yield good performance for large sequential data reads (>32KB in size); for small reads (<32KB), the performance will be comparable to conventional non-RAID disks. If the transactions are small, you may obtain better performance from balancing the load across a larger number of small-capacity disks via RAID-0 or RAID-5. RAID-3 is not effective for multi-use systems with high transaction rates.

For write operations, the load on the RAID-3 parity disk could be very high, since the parity disk must participate in each write I/O. Each read or write command in a RAID-3 configuration is executed at approximately the same speed. The percentage of disk space available in a RAID-3 configuration exceeds that of a RAID-1 RAID-0+1 configuration, but the failure of more than one disk will cause the system to become unavailable (until backups can be applied).

In RAID-4, one of the disks is dedicated to maintaining parity (as in RAID-3), but the size of the data segment on each disk is one block (user-defined RAID stripe) instead of one byte. In a RAID-4 environment, the parity disk will be used frequently during write operations, the percentage of disk space will exceed that of a comparable RAID-0 configuration.

RAID-5 is similar to RAID-4, but uses distributed parity instead of dedicated parity. The parity information is interleaved with the corresponding data blocks on the RAID set. The parity block for the first set of data segments may be stored on Disk 4, while the parity block for the second may be stored on Disk 3, with a data block written to Disk 4 instead. The location of the parity block rotates among the disks in the RAID set. As a result, the parity disk involved during a write operation rotates among the disks in the RAID set. RAID-5 will yield very good performance for applications that have many more reads than writes. In RAID-5 environments, writes typically take twice as long as reads. RAID-6, RAID-7, and RAID-5 are some of the more recently introduced variations of RAID-5 by various vendors.

When to Use Striping

Hardware-based striping of data via RAID technology is advantageous to many applications and is easier to manage than the data striping described earlier in this chapter. For applications with many online users performing small transactions, RAID provides a high level of concurrency across the disks, reducing disk I/O bottlenecks.

A single sequential process (such as a large batch transaction) usually does not benefit from striping unless it can consume more I/O than a single disk can provide. If multiple disks are available, the large sequential process may be able to use the disks to generate a higher rate of data throughput. When using the Parallel Query option, you will obtain better throughput for your queries only if the data is stored across multiple disks; see Chapter 12 for information on the implementation and management of the Parallel Query option.

Since all disks in a RAID set can participate in large I/Os, you must have many spindles in order to effectively use striping. A larger number of smaller drives (more spindles) is preferable to a smaller number of larger drives in an array.

When configuring striped disks, you should count a RAID set as one logical spindle and spread tables and indexes across different logical spindles. If tables and indexes are on the same logical spindles, you will still see significant improvements for many small, random I/Os, but large I/Os going across multiple disks will result in the same spindles conflicting for table and index I/O. Earlier in this chapter, the rules for datafile separation stated that you should separate the files used by tables and indexes. To separate tables and indexes in a RAID environment, you must store them on separate sets of RAID disks.

The stripe size or the block size to use depends on the size of a single, physical I/O request in the system—often the operating system block size. For example, in the HP/UX Unix operating system, the default block size is 8KB. A physical I/O *must be satisfied* from one disk in block striping (not byte striping). If the same I/O is spread on more than one disk, all disks need to return parts of the data before the request is complete—resulting in more overhead per read. Therefore, the stripe size must be much greater than the I/O block size to minimize the impact of the read overhead. Stripe sizes of 64KB to 128KB are commonly used in database configurations. If the stripe size is too large relative to the amount of data requested by the read, the controller will be waiting to retrieve more data than the application needs.

When to Use Mirroring

Mirroring is the best way to provide redundancy. If one disk fails, the second continues to work with no reconstruction penalty. In a parity-based system, there is a reconstruction penalty when a disk fails—the operating system or controllers must reconstruct the contents of the lost disk from the available ones. Although there is no data lost, and the system remains available, there is a performance penalty in parity-based systems due to the additional reconstruction processing requirements. The system can dynamically recover—with no loss of availability—from the loss of any disk in a RAID set (even the parity disk in a dedicated parity RAID configuration). There is no such reconstruction penalty in mirrored systems.

In a mirrored environment, overall I/O to the operating system is doubled—you are writing everything twice. However, the benefits of mirroring are great. The operating system distributes I/O requests among the disks dynamically, and you have a complete copy of all of your data. You can use your mirrored disks to dramatically improve the performance of your backups as well. To do so, "break" the mirrored set and use the mirror set (the copy of the data disks) during the backups, while the data disks are accessed by users. When the backups are complete, reestablish the mirror and the disks will be resynchronized. In order to maintain a mirror of the production environment while backing up data from the original mirrored set, you may create a second mirror of the same master disk—doubling the disk space required for the mirrors, but guaranteeing that your data is always mirrored.

You should use mirroring if you can spare half of your disks, and have well-distributed data. Since a mirrored system that does not use striping will not receive the benefits of automatic striping that the parity-based solutions provide, you must stripe the data and balance the I/O load yourself. With mirroring (RAID-1), you could also use operating system striping (RAID-0+1), so that you would not need to stripe manually.

When to Use Parity-Based Systems

Parity-based systems provide an alternative to mirroring. The number of disks available for data storage is greater in a parity-based system than in a mirrored system, and the data is automatically striped across the RAID set. However, there are potential costs during intensive write operations. During a write operation, the parity disk is involved in every I/O; therefore, the benefits of striping may be lost in the cost of the I/O burden on the parity disk. You should use a distributed parity system such as RAID-5 to distribute the I/O burden on the parity disk across the disks.

In a parity-based environment, you can only recover (without system downtime) from the loss of a limited number of disks. In RAID-3 and RAID-5, for example, you can only recover from the loss of a single disk in each RAID set. If you lose more than one disk in a RAID set, the operating system will not have enough information to dynamically reconstruct the missing data. In RAID-6, which uses two sets of distributed parity blocks, you can recover from the loss of two disks in a RAID set.

If you lose a disk in a parity-based system, the remaining disks in the RAID set will *all* be used during each I/O request. During reconstruction, data must be read from all disks and written to the data and the parity disks. In a distributed parity configuration, there is increased read and write activity to all disks. By comparison, mirrored systems do not have the same reconstruction performance penalty.

Cache Issues

In general, using parity-based systems allows you to provide data protection at a low cost in terms of disk overhead. Whereas mirror-based systems dedicate half of the available disks to data redundancy, parity-based systems dedicate only one disk per RAID set to data protection. If you have the same number of disks available for each, you will have more available disk space in a parity-based system than in a mirror-based system.

During a write operation to a parity-based system, you actually perform multiple writes, since the parity information has to be continuously updated. This may cause performance problems, which occur in dedicated parity systems such as RAID-3 (due to the single parity disk I/O bottleneck), and in distributed parity systems like RAID-5 (due to block striping; all other data in the parity block must be reread during writes).

To avoid potential performance problems in parity-based systems, make sure the disk controllers use a large cache. In general, the larger the cache is, the better the performance will be for both reads and writes against the RAID set, although the degree of the performance gain is dependent on operating system specifics such as how data is accessed and where it is physically located on the disk. However, there is a potential data integrity issue associated with the controller's caching method.

The cache used during writes to the disk (called the *write cache*) can be either synchronous (in which the controller does not respond with a "done" signal until the data makes it to the disk) or asynchronous (in which the controller responds with a "done" signal after the data has been written to the cache and before the writing of the data to the disk is complete). If the write cache is asynchronous, there is a risk of losing data if the disk fails prior to the completion of the data writing process. With asynchronous caches, there is an exposure window between the writing of the data to the cache and the writing of the data to the disk.

There are several alternatives available to help you avoid the potential data loss problem. You could use a fully protected caching scheme in which the disk subsystem guarantees either that the cache is nonvolatile or, more commonly, that there is a backup power supply for the disk subsystem and hardware redundancy. In the case of a power failure, the subsystem can ensure that all unwritten cache information is physically written somewhere on the disks in the short time span between the detection of the power failure and the system shutdown. If this operational guarantee is not available for your operating environment, you should make sure that asynchronous caching is not used for the RAID sets used by Oracle.

Choosing a RAID Configuration

The advantages of RAID configurations—data redundancy, automatic striping, and distribution of I/O for improved performance—can help you deal with the problems created by growing databases. In the previous sections, you've seen the characteristics of the available RAID configurations described, along with potential benefits and costs of each.

Most applications will benefit from intelligent, application-aware striping. Since the proper RAID configuration will change based on the application's needs, there is no single configuration that will be appropriate for every application. However, there are some general guidelines that can be applied:

- Data warehousing applications, which feature large batch writes and many small queries, are well-suited for parity-based systems like RAID-5. Small writes perform poorly in RAID-5 configurations, since the entire block and its associated parity block have to be read and written for even a small write. For example, you would have to read and write an entire 512-byte block and its parity block for a small 8-byte write operation. Read operations perform well in RAID-5 configurations because the entire block is read into the disk's cache each time data from the block is requested, minimizing the time required for subsequent data requests from the same block. Reads perform twice as fast as writes in RAID-5 environments. If there are not enough read requests from the application to keep all the disks in the RAID set busy, you will not achieve the full performance potential from your RAID-5 implementation.

- If the time available to data loading is very short, or your application is write-intensive, you should consider RAID-0+1. Since you will not pay the performance penalty of maintaining the parity information during the write operations, a mirrored-based system should perform well in a write-intensive environment.

- If the costs of disks for a mirrored system exceed your budget, you will need to either selectively mirror only certain disks or use a parity-based system. Use a parity-based system with distributed parity (such as RAID-5) to distribute the costs of the I/O to the parity blocks. You can mix RAID methods on the same server, so you could have a mix of RAID-1 and RAID-5 disks.

The lazy write technique used by Oracle, as described in the "Identifying I/O Bottlenecks" section earlier in this chapter, impacts the decision of what RAID configuration you should use. As previously described, RAID-5 calculates the parity every time a block is written. If the DBWR process "hiccups" and writes 20 blocks at one time, DBWR will have to wait for the completion of 20 block writes (of the new data), 20 block reads (of the original parity), and then 20 block writes (of the new parity). Altogether, the transaction requires 60 block I/Os, instead of the 20 block I/Os that would have been required in a non-RAID environment. A mirrored environment would require the 20 blocks to be written twice, for a total of 40 block I/Os. If you are using a parity-based system, you need to ensure that you have enough DBWR processes so there are very few "hiccups." In systems with high transaction activity, online redo log files can be located on their own non-RAID devices or on RAID-1 devices in order to minimize the penalty for frequent small writes. If you locate the online redo log files on non-RAID disks, you should use Oracle to mirror the files; if you place them on RAID-1 devices, they will be mirrored by the operating system.

Regardless of the implementation you choose, you should be aware of the way in which the hardware is configured. You should use as large a cache as possible, with either a synchronous cache or a protected asynchronous cache. You also need to know how the disks and controllers are configured. If the same disk controllers are used across all of the RAID sets, you may create an I/O bottleneck at the array controller level—and not only will it be difficult to diagnose, it may cause you a significant performance problem! When implementing RAID environments, you need to work with your operating system administration personnel to make sure you understand how the RAID system has been configured.

Raw Devices and File Systems

When formatting a new disk drive for a Unix system, you first need to partition the disk drive into logical devices. When partitioning the disk drive, you have the option to create a file system on each device (in which case it looks like a normal disk with a standard directory structure) or leave it in a raw format, with no Unix file system on it (in which case it is called a *raw device*).

If a file system is created on the disk drive, the file system will use some of the space on the disk drive to store the "block map" for the disk and the file pointers (called *inodes*). After the file system is mounted by the operating system, files and directories can be created on the disk. Every file and directory will have an inode allocated to it to keep information about file locations.

On a raw device, inodes do not exist. You cannot create directories or list the files that are stored on a raw device. Once the size of a raw device is set, you cannot change the size of the raw device from the operating system without reformatting the disk, although logical volume management tools allow you to extend raw devices. Despite their administrative drawbacks, raw devices are sometimes used to improve I/O performance. The more I/O-intensive your application is, the more it can benefit from using raw devices.

NOTE
Most operating systems that support raw devices allow you to have both file systems and raw devices on the same server.

If one or two of your data files are very actively used, you can move them to raw devices while leaving the rest of your database in file systems. You can query V$FILESTAT and V$DATAFILE to show the distribution of I/O across the files, as shown in the following listing. The query in the following listing is identical to the datafile I/O query shown earlier in this chapter, with the addition of a **where** clause to eliminate datafiles that have no read I/Os.

```
select DF.Name File_Name,
       FS.Phyblkrd Blocks_Read,
       FS.Phyblkwrt Blocks_Written,
       FS.Phyblkrd+FS.Phyblkwrt Total_IOs
  from V$FILESTAT FS, V$DATAFILE DF
 where DF.File#=FS.File#
   and FS.Phyblkrd >0
 order by FS.Phyblkrd+FS.Phyblkwrt desc;
```

FILE_NAME	BLOCKS_READ	BLOCKS_WRITTEN	TOTAL_IOS
/db10/oracle/DEV/sys01.dbf	1095747	6580	1102327
/db13/oracle/DEV/appdata01.dbf	278310	11845	290155
/db10/oracle/DEV/sys02.dbf	256668	3681	260349
/db10/oracle/DEV/appindex01.dbf	155168	1928	157096
/db10/oracle/DEV/temp01.dbf	3524	17745	21269

```
/db02/oracle/DEV/users01.dbf          12756          0      12756
/db10/oracle/DEV/rbs01.dbf              630      11219      11849
/db01/oracle/DEV/rbs02.dbf             9134          0       9134
/db13/oracle/DEV/users02.dbf             98       1545       1643
/db05/oracle/DEV/tools01.dbf            608         92        700

10 rows selected.
```

The query in the preceding listing shows the read and write I/O against the datafiles for all datafiles that have nonzero I/O. The datafiles are listed in descending order of I/O activity, with the most active files listed first. The most active datafiles are those that would benefit most by being moved to raw devices. If the database objects have been properly separated (see "Identifying I/O Bottlenecks" earlier in this chapter), and there are still a few datafiles that account for the majority of the database's I/O burden, those datafiles are candidates for being moved to raw devices.

Many file systems lock access to a file when a user is reading the file—the memory file descriptor that contains the inode and other information about the file is locked for a very short time. When that lock occurs, the operating system will not allow multiple simultaneous readers of the same file. Therefore, if you use disk management systems to stripe a database file across multiple disk drives, only one user process at a time will be able to gain access to a file. Since raw devices do not impose any such restrictions on concurrency, raw devices will yield improved parallelism of disk access.

The applications that gain most from using raw devices are those that have multiple batch jobs or ad hoc queries running simultaneously. You will particularly see benefit using raw devices if the batch jobs adversely impact the response time experienced by online users. Applications that take advantage of the Parallel Query option (see Chapter 12) are able to use raw devices to perform concurrent I/O accesses to the same file. If the majority of your database activity is from online users executing small transactions, you will likely see little or no performance benefit from using raw devices.

Management Considerations of Raw Devices

Although they can improve the performance of your I/O operations, raw devices may make the administration of your database more difficult. The potential problems include:

■ *Backups.* The only standard Unix command that can be used to backup a raw device is the *dd* command—*tar* and *cpio* cannot be used for raw devices. If the raw device is larger than the tape being used for the backup, *dd* will not prompt for the next tape automatically. Also, you will not be able to recover a single file from the backup of a raw device—you have to recover the entire raw device unless you know where (in blocks) the file starts. Also, *dd* does not allow you to verify that the writes to the tape drive are accurate. It is strongly recommended that you use a third-party backup utility to manage the backups of your raw devices.

■ *Sizing.* You may not be able to change the size of your existing raw devices, so you need to communicate with your Unix system administrators regarding the sizing and administration of raw devices. As previously noted, some logical volume management tools allow you to extend existing raw devices.

■ *Space allocation.* When creating a database file on a raw device, size the file to be smaller than the raw device space by at least two database blocks. Allocating the space in this manner will ensure you do not overwrite the header block of the raw device.

■ *Performance.* Raw devices can improve the performance of read/write-intensive applications, but will not improve the response time of online transaction-based applications. As a result, you should set up a test environment to evaluate whether the performance benefit that may be gained offsets the management costs.

If your application can take advantage of raw devices to improve the database performance, you need to manage the impacts of raw devices on your system administration. The impact on your backup options is particularly significant. If you modify your backup plans to use *dd*, you need to validate your backup plans—and revalidate them every time the raw device structures change. If you cannot guarantee the recoverability of your data via *dd* or a third-party backup utility, you should not use raw devices. If you reuse tapes from old backups, your system administration personnel should establish a schedule for removing old tapes from the tape backup cycle, since there is no way to verify the accuracy of a *dd*-based backup.

Supporting Changing Capacity Requirements

As shown earlier in Figure 4-1, a steadily increasing database size will eventually cause your backup and recovery operations to take longer than the longest available time window. As a result, you may be forced to consider the use of mirroring strategies in order to meet your recovery time requirements. Managing the datafiles and the space that is "outside" the database allows you to focus your administration and tuning efforts on the database internals.

Mirrored systems are expensive in terms of disk space; the mirrored data requires twice as much space as it used to. As the database continues to grow in size, the cost of mirroring grows rapidly. You may therefore consider going to a parity-based system in order to achieve the benefits of data redundancy while minimizing the disk overhead required. The disk overhead costs for a parity-based system will continue to grow as the database size grows, but will not be as great a cost as a mirrored system.

The side benefit of parity-based systems—particularly those with distributed parity—is the automatic striping of your data. The I/O burden of a query can thus be distributed among all available disks, enabling you to avoid potential I/O bottlenecks. The data will be striped from the start, rather than having to wait for extents to fill before data striping efforts have an impact. You can also use raw devices to further enhance your I/O performance, but at a cost of increased management difficulties. In a mirrored system, you could also use striping if you implemented RAID-0+1 instead of RAID-0.

If you do not use the operating system to perform striping, you can force the database to stripe the data internally. However, data striping within the database often does not have an immediate impact for business transaction tables; it will have a greater immediate impact for business reference tables and other tables whose data is already available. Striping data within the database requires accurate estimates of the sizes of the available extents. If extents are properly sized, there is no performance penalty for having multiple extents in a database object. The proper sizing of extents and the impact of database growth and transaction activity on database objects are described in Chapter 5.

CHAPTER 5

Managing the Space Inside Your Database

In Chapters 3 and 4, the focus was on the management of the physical storage for your data. In this chapter, you will see the internals of the data storage and their impact on the database as it grows.

The first part of this chapter uses the application table types described in Chapter 2 to categorize the tables within an application. You'll see the impact of the table type on its space usage and management, along with the impact of techniques such as row packing and extent sizing. Following that section, you'll see space implementation advice for each distinct type of segment (such as indexes and temporary segments), along with specific advice regarding the proper storage parameters to use. If the techniques in this chapter are followed, you should not encounter any major space management problems within your database, nor should the space utilization lead to performance problems. If the space utilization is not increasing the crisis level, you can focus on the root causes of any performance problems that arise within your database, and quickly respond to any response time increases.

Types of Tables

As described in Chapter 2, there are four types of tables, each with a different growth profile. They are:

- *Business reference tables,* which store the reference data for your business

- *Application reference tables,* which store reference data for the particular application

- *Business transaction tables,* which store the majority of the transactions for the application

- *Temporary/interface tables,* used during data processing steps

The different types of tables have different growth profiles (see Chapter 2). However, all of their growth profiles have one feature in common: between deployments, the growth of the tables is fairly linear. In the following sections, you will see how the linear growth rate of the tables can be used to properly estimate and distribute their space requirements.

NOTE
If the user base of an application rises suddenly, the database size may grow in a nonlinear manner for a short period. Over a larger period of time, however, the overall growth rate of the database size should approximate a straight line between each deployment stage.

In Oracle, objects store their data in *segments.* Each table, index, rollback segment, cluster, and temporary segment has an associated segment. Segments consist of *extents.* Each segment has at least one extent. An extent is a set of contiguous blocks; it cannot span the datafiles within a tablespace. Figure 5-1 shows the relationship between segments and extents.

For a segment to grow, it must allocate a new extent. Initially, the new extent will be mostly empty; as rows are added to the segment, the extent will gradually fill with data. When the extent cannot hold the amount of data inserted, a new extent will be allocated to the segment.

Since allocation of extents is the mechanism by which segments grow, you need to understand the performance implications of extents in order to manage the

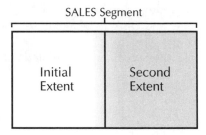

FIGURE 5-1.   *Segments and extents*

impact of database size on database response time. In the following section, you will see that extents, if properly sized, have no measurable impact on performance. Minimizing the number of extents may make managing the segments simpler, but extents—despite their reputation—are not inherently evil. As you will see in the following sections, there are even benefits to having multiple extents.

Managing Extents

Depending on the type of segment in use, extents serve different purposes. Within rollback segments, for example, extents contain temporary copies of blocks that are changed during transactions. In versions of Oracle prior to Oracle7.3, the maximum number of extents that any segment can obtain is limited based on the database block size. For a 4KB block size on many Unix platforms, the maximum number of extents per segment is 249 unless you use the **maxextents unlimited** clause available in Oracle7.3 (see Chapter 13).

Because the maximum number of extents within a segment is limited (although in Oracle7.3, the limit increases to over two billion), the allocation of extents can cause problems. Since an extent is mostly empty when it is first allocated, the allocation of an extent may require a great deal of space—although the space allocation may be triggered by a very small transaction! As a result, you need to manage the space parameters used by Oracle to calculate the size of each extent.

How Oracle Allocates Extents

Each segment has, as part of its definition, a set of parameters that tell the database how to allocate extents for the segment. The segment's space allocation parameters are set via the **storage** clause of the command used to create or alter the segment (such as **create table** or **alter index**). You can query DBA_TABLES to see the storage parameters for a table, and DBA_INDEXES to see the storage parameters for an index.

In the following example, the SALES table is created with an initial extent size (see Figure 5-1) of 8MB.

```
create table SALES
(Company_ID  NUMBER,
Period_ID    NUMBER,
Sales_Total  NUMBER,
constraint SALES_PK primary key (Company_ID, Period_ID))
storage (initial 8M next 4M pctincrease 0
         minextents 1 maxextents 200)
tablespace APP_DATA;
```

The **storage** clause of the **create table** script shown in the preceding listing follows a number of rules for extent sizing that will be explained in this chapter.

When the SALES segment is created, Oracle will attempt to create an extent that is 8MB in size for the segment. The size of the first extent is determined by the value of the **initial** parameter. The extent will be allocated in whole blocks. Thus, if you specify an extent size that would force the database to split a database block, the size of the extent will be rounded up to the nearest block.

As of Oracle7, the database rounds or alters the extent allocations dynamically. For example, if you specify an initial extent of just two blocks, the database will round the extent size up to five blocks (for a 2KB database block size; the rounding factor may change with the block size). In the SALES segment example, 8MB was specified for the initial extent. Given a database block size of 4KB, the initial extent will consist of 2048 database blocks. If there is a section of available free space 2050 database blocks in size, the database may choose to expand the initial SALES extent to use all of that free space.

The goals of dynamic rounding of extents sizes are to maximize the reuse of extents that have been dropped and to avoid fragmenting your database with small, unusable extents. If all of your extents are created with the same storage parameters, or if they follow the same sizing rules—for example, that you always allocate extents in multiples of five database blocks—then you increase the likelihood that a segment's extents can be easily reused after the segment is dropped.

When the segment allocates a second extent, Oracle uses the **next** parameter of the **storage** clause to generate the size of the second extent. As with the initial extent, the size of the second extent may be dynamically modified by Oracle based on its rounding criteria and the available storage space.

To size subsequent extents, Oracle uses three values: the **next** parameter, the **pctincrease** parameter, and the number of the extent. For the third extent of the segment, Oracle uses the formula (**next***(1+(**pctincrease**/100))). For example, the SALES table had a **next** value of 4MB and a **pctincrease** value of 0. Therefore, the size of the third extent will be (4MB*(1+(0/100))) = 4MB. If the **pctincrease** value had been 50, the third extent would be 50 percent greater than the second extent (6MB), and the fourth extent would be 50 percent greater than the third extent (9MB).

If you have a non-zero value for **pctincrease**, the growth of your space allocation will be nonlinear. As shown in Figure 5-2, a non-zero **pctincrease** forces the total space allocated by the database to increase geometrically. However, the database size—the space *used* by the data—grows linearly, as shown in Figure 5-2. Thus, if **pctincrease** is set to a non-zero value, each new extent unnecessarily allocates a greater amount of unused space—until there is no more space left in the tablespace.

NOTE
Since growth rates, viewed over long enough time periods, are linear between deployments, you should use a **pctincrease** value of 0 for your segments, with properly set **initial** and **next** values.

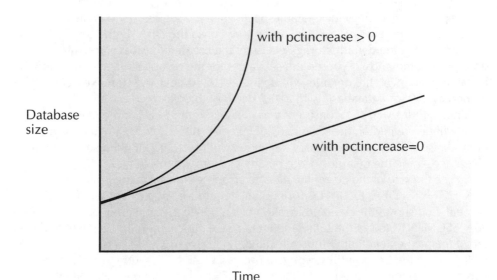

FIGURE 5-2.   *Impact of pctincrease on database size*

If the segment is empty when it is first created, Oracle will create the number of extents specified by the **minextents** parameter value. The maximum number of extents is set via the **maxextents** parameter value. Once a segment reaches the maximum number of extents possible for its database block size (pre-Oracle7.3), you cannot extend the segment. Therefore, you should set the **maxextents** parameter value to a number that is lower than the maximum number of extents allowable for that database block size. For example, if the maximum number of extents allowable for the database block size is 249, set the **maxextents** value to 200; if your **maxextents** setting is reached, you can alter the **next** parameter value to change the size of future extents, thereby preventing the segment from reaching the maximum allowable number of extents. If the SALES segment attempts to allocate 201 extents, the extent allocation will fail, and you will know that your storage estimates were incorrect.

NOTE
Set **maxextents** to a value that is lower than the maximum number of allowable extents for your database block size.

You can use the **minextents** parameter to stripe data across multiple devices, distributing the I/O operations against the table across multiple disks. See Chapter 4 for information on data striping.

If you don't set values for storage parameters, segments will inherit the default storage parameter settings for the tablespace when the segments are created. Default storage parameters, which can be viewed via the DBA_TABLESPACES view, are set via the **default storage** clause of the **create tablespace** and **alter tablespace** commands. If you do not set values for the default storage parameters at the tablespace level, the defaults will be **initial** 10240 **next** 10240 **maxextents** 121 **pctincrease** 50 for a database with a 4KB database block size.

Since a PRIMARY KEY constraint was created on the SALES table, a unique index will be created on the (Company_ID, Period_ID) columns. Since no **using index** clause was used, the primary key index will be created in the user's default tablespace, using the default storage parameters for the tablespace.

To see the size of the currently allocated extents for a segment, you can query DBA_EXTENTS. DBA_EXTENTS displays one record for each extent within the segment, and shows the size and location of each extent. You can query DBA_SEGMENTS to see the total amount of space allocated to the segment and the size of the next extent that will be allocated.

If you use the Export utility, you can use its COMPRESS option to reduce the segment to a single extent. For example, if SALES had extended to two extents (8MB and 4MB), you could use Export to compress those two extents to a single 12MB extent. After exporting the SALES table, you could **truncate** it and then use the Import utility to recreate and load it.

When the SALES table is recreated via Import, the **initial** size will have been changed based on the total amount of space previously allocated to the segment (as reported in the Bytes column of DBA_SEGMENTS). The **initial** value will now be 12MB. The **next** value will have been left unchanged.

Although reducing SALES to a single extent may make it simpler to manage, it may also cause management problems. For example, what if the tablespace in which SALES previously existed consists of two datafiles, each 10MB in length? Since an extent cannot span datafiles, the SALES segment's new 12MB initial extent cannot be created—*so the table creation during Import will fail.* If the segment is successfully created in a larger datafile, the initial extent size will reflect the total previous space allocation—not the total space used by rows.

Each extent is a contiguous set of database blocks. However, not all blocks are used by rows. You can determine the number of blocks used by rows via two methods, both of which involve full table scans of the table. First, you can query the RowID pseudo-column values of the rows in the table. The first 8 characters of the RowID are the block ID; characters 15 through 18 are the file ID. The combination of the block ID and the file ID uniquely identifies each block within the tablespace. Therefore, the following query, which concatenates the block ID and file ID of each row, reports the number of distinct blocks used by rows in the table—the number of used blocks.

```
select COUNT(DISTINCT(SUBSTR(RowID,1,8)||
                      SUBSTR(RowID,15,4)))
   from SALES;
```

A second method for calculating the number of blocks used by the rows in a segment requires using the **analyze** command. Analyze the table, and then query the Blocks column from the DBA_TABLES view, as shown in the following listing. Due to the overhead associated with the **analyze** command, this method of calculating the number of used blocks may be slower than the RowID-based method shown in the previous listing.

```
analyze table SALES compute statistics;

select Blocks
   from DBA_TABLES
 where Table_Name = 'SALES';
```

NOTE
If you are *only* interested in the number of blocks, you can use the **analyze table estimate statistics for 1 rows** command. The number of blocks is taken directly from the segment header, so the entire table does not have to be scanned to determine the value of this statistic.

Before using the COMPRESS option of Export, you should make sure that the total allocated bytes, if compressed to a single extent, can fit into the available space within your tablespace; and that the allocated size of the segment accurately reflects the used space within the segment.

As a result of recreating and repopulating the segment, you should receive performance benefits, which are often incorrectly attributed to the compression of the extents. The benefits from the segment recreation are:

■ *Improved data density.* The data is reinserted into the segment, usually resulting in more rows stored per block.

■ *No migrated rows.* Since the data has not been updated, no rows should have been migrated from their original blocks. If a row is larger than the database block size, you will have spanned rows.

■ *Index defragmentation.* Index stagnation, described in the "Indexes" section later in this chapter, can cause significant performance problems. By truncating or dropping the table, you are also truncating or dropping the indexes on the table. When you recreate the index (after the rows have been reinserted), the index will be as small and efficient as possible.

■ *The highwatermark is reset.* Each time a full table scan is performed, Oracle scans all the blocks below the highwatermark of the table. When the table is **truncate**d or recreated, the highwatermark is reset, reducing the number of blocks scanned during full table scans.

The combination of the four factors listed above has a significant impact on the performance of all queries that use the table. No matter what type of query is executed against the table, it should perform better than queries against the previous SALES table. The performance improvement depends on the volatility of the SALES table prior to its Export. If the data in SALES was frequently updated or deleted, the performance improvement generated by recreating the table can be significant.

Although it's tempting to attribute the performance improvement to the compression of the extents into a single extent, you would have generated the exact same performance improvements if you had used COMPRESS=N during the Export and created the SALES table with its original storage parameters. In the next section, you will see how to size extents so they will not have negative impacts on your performance.

Sizing Extents for Performance

Extents are often blamed for performance problems; however, their impact on performance is minimal and can be completely avoided. In fact, careful use of extents can improve your response time by distributing your I/O operations across multiple devices. To understand the impact of extents on performance, you need to consider the two different methods of reading data from a table: by RowID and by full table scan.

Oracle's preferred method of reading records for OLTP applications is by the row's RowID value. For example, an index range scan may generate a list of RowIDs that match a query's limiting condition. The query in the following listing would perform a range scan on the SALES table's primary key index (Company_ID, Period_ID).

```
select *
  from SALES
 where Company_ID > 100;
```

Since all columns are selected from the SALES table, the index alone cannot satisfy the query. Once the index has been scanned for the RowID values for rows that meet the limiting condition on the Company_ID column, the SALES table will be accessed via a TABLE ACCESS BY ROWID operation.

The RowID pseudo-column has three components. The RowID components are, in order: a block number (of the block within the file), a sequence number (of the row within the block), and a file number (of the file within the database). For example, the RowID 00001234.0000.0009 corresponds to the first row (sequence number 0000) in block 00001234 of file 09 (note that the numbers are in hexadecimal). Once Oracle has the RowID for a row, it knows exactly which block of which file the row is located in, and it knows exactly where within the block the row resides.

What the RowID *does not* contain—information regarding the extent in which the row resides—is just as significant as what it does contain. Accesses to the table that use a RowID-based method, such as indexed-based accesses, are blind to the extent allocation within the segment. Extents only impact full table scans.

NOTE
The following comparison of the extent size with respect to I/O size for saving I/O is significant only when the I/O size (64KB) and the extent size are of the same order of magnitude. It becomes insignificant if I/O size is much less than extent size.

During a full table scan, Oracle uses its multiblock read capability (see Chapter 3) to scan multiple blocks at a time. The number of blocks read at a time is determined by the database's DB_FILE_MULTIBLOCK_READ_COUNT setting in the init.ora file and by the limitations of the operating system's read buffers. For example, if you are limited to a 64KB buffer for the operating system, and the database block size is 4KB, you can read no more than 16 database blocks during a single read.

Consider the original SALES table again. With its original storage parameters, SALES has an 8MB initial extent and a 4MB second extent. For this example, assume that the highwatermark of SALES is located at the end of the second extent. In the first extent, there are 2048 database blocks, 4KB each in size. During a full table scan, those blocks will be read 16 at a time, for a total of 128 reads (2048/16 = 128). In the second extent, there are 1024 database blocks. During a full table scan, those blocks will be read 16 at a time, for a total of 64 reads (1024/16=64). Thus, scanning the entire table will require 192 reads (128 for the first extent, plus 64 for the second extent).

What if the two extents were combined, each having the same highwatermark? The combined extent would be 12MB in size, consisting of 3072 database blocks. During a full table scan, those blocks will be read 16 at a time, for a total of 192 reads. *Despite the fact that the extents have been compressed into a single extent, the exact same number of reads is required because of the way the extents were sized.* As you will see in the next section, the location of the extents may influence the efficiency of the reads, but the number of reads is the same in both the single-extent and two-extent examples.

What if SALES had 192 extents, each one 16 blocks in length? A full table scan would read 16 blocks at a time, for a total of 192 reads. *Thus, whether the SALES table had 1, 2, or 192 extents, the exact same number of reads was required to perform the full table scan.* The size of the extents is critical—the size of each extent must be a multiple of the number of blocks read during each multiblock read (set via the DB_FILE_MULTIBLOCK_READ_COUNT init.ora parameter value).

In the 192-extent example, the extent size matched the setting of the DB_FILE_MULTIBLOCK_READ_COUNT value (16). If each extent had been 20 blocks (instead of 16 blocks), how many reads would be required?

The SALES table contains 3072 blocks of data (12MB total). If each extent is 20 blocks each, you'll need 154 extents to store the 3072 blocks of data. When reading the first extent during a full table scan, Oracle will read the first 16 blocks of the extent (as dictated by the DB_FILE_MULTIBLOCK_READ_COUNT). Because there are four blocks left in the extent Oracle will issue a second read for that extent. Reads cannot span extents, so only four blocks are read by the second read. Therefore, the 20-block extent requires two reads. Since each extent is 20 blocks in length, each extent will require two reads. Because there are 154 extents, a full table scan of SALES will now require 308 reads—a 60 percent increase over the 192 reads previously required!

As shown in Table 5-1, the number of extents in a table does not affect the performance of full table scans of the table as long as the size of the extents is a multiple of the size of each read that is performed.

Size of extents	Number of extents	Number of reads required by a full table scan
12MB	1	192
8MB, 4MB	2	192
64KB	192	192
80KB	154	308

TABLE 5-1. *Impact of extent sizes on full table scans*

The examples listed in Table 5-1 show two important facts about extents relative to performance:

1. If the extents are properly sized, the number of extents has no impact on the number of reads required by table scans.

2. If the extents are not properly sized, the number and size of the extents can greatly increase the amount of work performed by the database during a full table scan.

Proper sizing of extents is a key factor in managing the performance of full table scans. To eliminate the potential impact of multiple extents on performance, you need to make sure that the size of each extent is a multiple of the number of blocks read during each multiblock read. In many systems, 64KB or 128KB is read during each read (in the SALES example, 64KB was used). Therefore, size your extents so that each is an even multiple of 64KB or 128KB. As shown in Table 5-1, choosing an extent size that is not an even multiple of this value (such as 80KB) can increase the amount of work performed during a full table scan. If the extents are properly sized, there is no impact on the required number of reads.

Although increasing the number of extents does not necessarily increase the number of reads required, the complexity of managing the impact of extents increases as the number of extents increases. Consider, for example, the size of the extents; although you may calculate them to minimize the number of unnecessary reads, Oracle may dynamically change the extent size based on its rounding functions. The only way to reduce the effect of dynamic space allocation rounding is to reduce the number of extents.

Database objects frequently read via large scans—either full table scans or large index range scans—should be stored in a small number of extents. The additional extents, if properly sized, will not negatively impact performance.

Keeping the number of extents small makes it more likely that the next data to be read is physically near the data currently being read.

Location of Extents

If having multiple properly sized extents does not necessarily hurt your performance at the database level, what impact does it have at the operating system level?

In prior versions of Oracle, you could create contiguous datafiles when a tablespace was created—the files would be located in a contiguous set of blocks on the operating system device. However, as of Oracle Version 6, there has been no way to guarantee (from within the database) that the datafiles you create are located on contiguous areas of disk. Thus, two consecutive blocks within the same extent may be physically located on different sections of the same disk.

If the blocks of a datafile were all contiguous on a disk, then each time you completed one read, the disk hardware would be properly positioned to execute the next read. But since there is no guarantee that the data you are reading from a single extent is contiguous on the disk, there is no guarantee that the disk hardware is properly positioned for the next read regardless of the number of extents in the table. Any potential benefit from disk hardware positioning is therefore eliminated unless you can guarantee that the file is located on a contiguous area on a disk. If you create a new file system on a new disk, and create a datafile as the first file in that file system, you increase the likelihood that the file's blocks are physically contiguous.

If a database object is not read by large scans, the number of extents has no impact on the performance of queries against it. In OLTP applications, the typical access to database files is via random "hot-spot" reads (see Chapter 3); the efficiency of the reads may be improved if the hot spots are near each other, but the number of extents in which the hot spots are stored makes little difference to the performance of the data accesses. When designing your database to take advantage of the physical location of data, you need to be aware of the I/O management techniques in use on the server. The advanced I/O management techniques available, such as RAID technologies (see Chapter 4), use striping methods to split a file across multiple disks—so data that appears to be on the same device is actually stored on separate disks. Because RAID systems distribute data from the same file across multiple disks, you cannot be certain of the physical location of a data hot spot, nor that two hot spots are stored on the same disk.

The Benefits of Multiple Extents

Having a single extent may make an object simple to manage—provided the object fits into a single datafile. However, forcing each object in your database to have just one extent will yield little in the way of performance improvements, and may actually hurt your performance.

If you have only one extent in the SALES table, you cannot stripe the SALES data within the database (see Chapter 4). The SALES table would be stored in a single datafile and, by extension, on a single disk. All queries against SALES will use the same disk, and you will be unable to distribute the I/O operations across multiple disks unless you use some form of operating system-level striping.

If you have only one extent for SALES, you will not be able to effectively use the Parallel Query option (PQO) for queries against the table. In the PQO (see Chapter 12), multiple processes concurrently perform the work of a query. If the data queried by the multiple processes is all located on the same disk, using the PQO for queries of the data may create an I/O bottleneck on the disk!

Lastly, having a single extent for an object prevents you from using the available extents to determine the growth rate for an object. For example, if you create a large initial extent for a small business transaction table, you will have to periodically check the number of rows in the table in order to determine its growth rate. If the extents were more reasonably sized, you would be able to determine its growth pattern by checking its extent allocations. Also, a single large extent wastes space within the object. Although you can reclaim allocated space as of Oracle7.3 (see Chapter 13), there is usually little benefit to preallocating large volumes of unused space.

If the size of each extent is a multiple of the data volume read during a single multiblock read from the database, there is no performance penalty for using multiple extents—and if you are using database striping or PQO methods, there is potential performance *benefit*. You can use the **maxextents unlimited** clause of Oracle7.3 (see Chapter 13) to allow your objects to have over two billion extents—but such a high number would likely be difficult to manage. Although multiple extents do not have to hurt your performance, they can make your database more difficult to administer. For database tables that will grow—primarily the business transaction tables—monitor their extent allocation and determine their growth rate. If the business transaction tables extend no more often than once every few months, the management effort required for them will remain low.

Managing Tables

When managing a set of tables, you need to manage several space-related issues, including the allocation and sizing of extents, as described in the previous section. If the table is volatile—particularly if it is a temporary/interface table—you need to manage its highwatermark. You also need to manage the space usage within the blocks, and, if used, within clusters. In the following sections, you'll see how to manage highwatermarks and data blocks.

Highwatermarks

When a table is created—and after it has been truncated—its *highwatermark* is set to the beginning of the table. The highwatermark records the number of the highest block in which records have been stored within the table (the highwatermark increases in five-block increments). Each time the table is read via a full table scan, Oracle reads up to the highwatermark of the table—even if there are no records in the table. As described in Chapter 2, an incorrect highwatermark can have significant impact on operations that use the highwatermark—particularly SQL*Loader Direct Path loads and full table scans.

For example, if you insert 100,000 blocks worth of data into a table and then use the **delete** command to delete the records, there will be no rows in the table—but the highwatermark will be set at 100,000. The next time you perform a full table scan of the table, Oracle will scan through 100,000 empty blocks. If you have ever performed a **select count(*)** from a table immediately after a full **delete** of the table, you may have seen the performance penalty associated with the previous setting of the highwatermark.

Moreover, the deletion may have unintended effects on the storage of data within the table. Each table maintains a *free list*—a list of free blocks within the table. Blocks are added to the free list in order of their arrival—so the newly freed blocks will be placed at the bottom of the free list. When records are inserted into the table now, the first records will be inserted at a point in the datafile beyond the blocks that previously held data.

If you use SQL*Loader Direct Path, Oracle inserts formatted blocks of data into the table, starting at its current highwatermark. If the highwatermark does not accurately reflect the data in the table, your data loads may require a great deal of space—while leaving space beneath the highwatermark untouched. If there are empty blocks available below the highwatermark, SQL*Loader Direct Path will not be able to use them during data loads—thus increasing the space required by the table being loaded.

There are two methods you can use to determine the highwatermark of the table. The first method uses the **analyze** command, and the second uses the DBMS_SPACE package introduced with Oracle7.3.

The **analyze** command updates the statistics in DBA_TABLES for the analyzed table. In the following listing, the SALES table is analyzed, using the **compute statistics** option of the **analyze** command.

```
analyze table SALES compute statistics;
```

The number of blocks allocated to the SALES table can be queried via DBA_SEGMENTS:

```
select Blocks
   from DBA_SEGMENTS
 where Owner = 'APPOWNER'
   and Segment_Name = 'SALES';
```

The number of blocks above the highwatermark can be selected from DBA_TABLES:

```
select Empty_Blocks
   from DBA_TABLES
 where Owner = 'APPOWNER'
   and Table_Name = 'SALES';
```

The highwatermark (HWM) for the table can be calculated via the formula shown in the following listing. In the formula, you subtract the number of empty blocks from the number of allocated blocks to determine the number of used blocks. An additional block is subtracted in order to account for the block used as the table header block.

```
HWM = DBA_SEGMENTS.Blocks - DBA_TABLES.Empty_Blocks - 1
```

The second method for determining the highwatermark is available as of Oracle7.3. You can use the new DBMS_SPACE package to see the space allocation in the table, as shown in the following listing. The first three parameters passed to DBMS_SPACE.UNUSED_SPACE procedure shown below are the schema that owns the object, the object's name, and the object type (table, index, or cluster). Four variables are defined to hold the output of the DBMS_SPACE.UNUSED_SPACE procedure.

```
declare
        OP1 number;
        OP2 number;
        OP3 number;
        OP4 number;
        OP5 number;
        OP6 number;
        OP7 number;
 begin
dbms_space.unused_space('APPOWNER','SALES','TABLE',
                        OP1,OP2,OP3,OP4,OP5,OP6,OP7);
    dbms_output.put_line('OBJECT_NAME       = SALES');
    dbms_output.put_line('--------------------------');
    dbms_output.put_line('TOTAL_BLOCKS      = '||OP1);
    dbms_output.put_line('TOTAL_BYTES       = '||OP2);
```

```
    dbms_output.put_line('UNUSED_BLOCKS    = '||OP3);
    dbms_output.put_line('UNUSED_BYTES     = '||OP4);
end;
/
```

The output of the preceding script for a 2MB SALES table is shown in the following listing.

```
OBJECT_NAME     = SALES
---------------------------
TOTAL_BLOCKS    = 500
TOTAL_BYTES     = 2048000
UNUSED_BLOCKS   = 200
UNUSED_BYTES    = 819200
```

The DBMS_SPACE package's output combines the data that could have been queried via DBA_SEGMENTS and DBA_TABLES. In the preceding example, there are 500 allocated blocks (including blocks both above and below the highwatermark). There are 200 unused (empty) blocks above the highwatermark. Thus, the highwatermark for the SALES table would be 299 (500-200-1).

To reset the highwatermark for a table, you must either drop and recreate the table, or you must **truncate** it. Since both methods remove data from the table, you may need to save a copy of the data prior to resetting the highwatermark.

Inside the Blocks

In order to optimize the transactions that use the rows of a table, you need to optimize two features related to the rows' physical storage: the number of rows per block and the order of rows within the block.

The more rows there are per block, the fewer blocks you will need to read during range scans and table scans. As described in the "Extents" section earlier in this chapter, Oracle can read multiple blocks during a single "multiblock" read from a table during a full table scan. A small increase in the number of blocks read may have only a small impact on the number of multiblock reads required; a large increase in the number of blocks read may have a large impact on the number of multiblock reads required. For example, if your multiblock reads read 16 blocks at a time, then increasing the number of blocks to be read by 10 adds only one read to the query processing; adding 160 new blocks adds 10 reads to the query processing.

The more densely packed the rows are within your tables' blocks, the fewer blocks you will need to read. Each database block has a header/trailer area, an area used by the rows' data, and free space. To improve the row density within your blocks, you need to consider all three of these areas during your space management efforts.

The size of the header area for a database block varies little among blocks of different sizes. Therefore, you can increase the amount of available (nonheader) space within a block by using a larger block size. For example, if the header area occupies 204 bytes in a 2KB block, only 90 percent of the block is usable for data and free space; in a 4KB block, 95 percent of the block would be usable for data and free space. As you increase the database block size, you also increase the percentage of usable space within each block.

The free space and row space within a database block must be managed in concert. The free space within a block is used to hold new rows as they are added, and updated values as rows are updated. The **pctfree** parameter tells Oracle how much space in each block should be reserved as free space within the block. For example, if you have specified **pctfree 10** for a table, no new records will be written to the block if fewer than 10 percent of the block is free.

The free space must be large enough to handle the updates to the rows' columns, particularly if values are updated from null values to long text strings. The more volatile your data, the more free space you'll need in the block—and the larger your **pctfree** should be. If the free space available within the block is too small to handle the expansion of a row, the row may be "migrated" to another block to handle its space requirements.

Once the **pctfree** limit has been crossed, no new rows may be inserted into the block until the percentage of the block used (not free) passes the **pctused** setting for the table. The **pctused** setting is at 40 percent by default. Tables that are very volatile, especially those that experience a high volume of **insert**s and **delete**s, will eventually reach the point where most of the blocks are just 40 percent populated if they use the default value. As a result of the low **pctused** setting, the blocks are very sparsely populated by the rows, and the work performed by scanning operations increases accordingly.

If the data is very volatile, you will need to schedule periodic maintenance in order to improve the density of rows within blocks; otherwise, your scans of the table will read more blocks than necessary. If your application is **delete**-intensive, you should set a high value for **pctused**; if your application is **update**-intensive, you should set a value for **pctfree** that reflects the average growth of rows in the table.

Generally, it's better to have a small **pctfree** and some migrated rows than a high **pctfree** and only a few rows per block. The **pctfree** parameter setting impacts all the blocks in the table; migrated rows only impact a few rows and only when performing access via an index. To find out if you have migrated (chained) rows problem in the table, select the Chained_Rows column from DBA_TABLES. To fix the migrated (chained) rows problem, use the **analyze table** command with the **list chained rows** clause; the RowIDs of the chained rows is written into a table named CHAINED_ROWS (created via the utlchain.sql script in $ORACLE_HOME/rdbms/admin). Deleting and reinserting the chained rows into the table resolves the chained rows problem with no need to reorganize the entire table. If after fixing this problem you still have chained rows, they are probably "spanned" rows that are larger than a database block. In general, the larger the database block size, the fewer problems there are with migrated rows. Row chaining decreases as database block size increases because **pctfree 10** for an 8KB block is 800 bytes and for a 2KB block is 200 bytes; if one in every four rows grows over 200 bytes in length due to updates, there will be many chained rows for the 2KB block table and none for the 8KB block table.

You can use the Export and Import utilities to save and reload the data for your tables. If you do, be sure to recreate or **truncate** the table between the Export and the Import steps in order to reset the highwatermark for the table. Import executes a series of **insert** commands, which causes the rows to be packed densely within the blocks. If the rows are unlikely to be updated after being reloaded, you can set a lower value for **pctfree** prior to the Import to reduce the amount of free space within each block.

Within the block, the order of rows—*row proximity*—is important. The larger the table, the greater the impact row proximity will have on your performance. For example, if you frequently query records from the COMPANY table based on range scans of Company_ID values, you should order the rows within the blocks by their Company_ID value. If the rows are ordered, all of the records you need will be stored together—reducing the number of blocks you need to read. Row proximity is another form of row density; instead of managing the number of rows per block, you manage the number of related rows per block.

Row proximity can have a great impact on the performance of queries from very large tables (see the "Manage Very Large Table Accesses" section of Chapter 11). Ideally, you could reorder rows for a table by creating a second table, via the **create table as select** command. However, this and the **insert as select** command do not allow you to specify an **order by** clause.

To circumvent this limitation, create a view on the base table. The view should group by *all* of the columns of the table plus the RowNum pseudo-column. The view shown in the following listing selects and groups by all of the columns in the COMPANY table.

```
create or replace view COMPANY_VIEW as
select Company_ID,
       Name,
       Address,
       City,
       State,
       Zip,
       Parent_Company_ID,
       Active_Flag
  from COMPANY
```

```
group by Company_ID,
        Name,
        Address,
        City,
        State,
        Zip,
        Parent_Company_ID,
        Active_Flag,
        RowNum;
```

The **group by** clause will force the use of a sorting operation within Oracle during queries—and the rows selected from COMPANY_VIEW will be sorted in order of Company_ID. This allows you to then create a table selecting from COMPANY_VIEW; the effect will be that a duplicate copy of COMPANY will be created, with the rows properly sorted.

```
create table COMPANY_ORDERED
    as select * from COMPANY_VIEW;
```

In the preceding example, the data was ordered by the Company_ID value. Often, you may need to order the data by an attribute column instead, such as the Name column. If the data is ordered to support the most-used range queries, and is densely stored within each block, then you can minimize the number of blocks read during each query and thereby improve the performance of your queries. You need to add RowNum to the **group by** clause so that duplicate rows in COMPANY will be copied from COMPANY to COMPANY_ORDERED.

Clusters

Clusters are used for two purposes. If a cluster is used for a single table, the rows of the table will be physically sorted in ascending order of the column designated as the *cluster key*. If a cluster is used to store multiple tables, the records from the tables are stored within the same blocks, potentially reducing the number of blocks read during a join.

Clusters, however, have significant costs from a performance perspective. Transactions on clustered tables are six to eight times slower than the same transactions on unclustered tables, and generate a far greater amount of rollback and redo log information. Therefore, you should not use clusters for your business transaction tables, since the overhead for maintaining the clusters will impact the performance experienced by your online users.

You could consider using clusters for static tables—such as the application reference tables—but the poor performance of clusters during transactions means that the performance of recovery operations for those tables will be poor. To derive the cluster's benefits (sorted data) without its costs (poor transaction performance), leave your tables unclustered and periodically unload all the data, sort it by the shared key, and reload it, as described in the previous section.

Hash Clusters

If your tables are very large and static, and are used primarily by equivalence queries, you may be able to effectively use hash clusters. In a hash cluster, the values of the *hash key* (such as the primary key column of the table) are used to generate the physical location of the row. Hash clusters perform poorly for range queries and require a large amount of space. The ability to specify a user-defined hash formula, available as of Oracle7.2, allows you to take advantage of hash clusters for large tables with sequential (nonintelligent) keys. See the "Manage Very Large Tables Accesses" section of Chapter 11 for details on implementing hash clusters.

Managing Indexes

Indexes on business transaction and temporary/interface tables pose special challenges to DBAs and application administrators. Each record with a value for the indexed column will have an entry in the index. When an indexed value is updated in the table, the old value is deleted from the index, and the new value is inserted into a separate part of the index. The space released by the old value may never be used again.

As indexed values are updated or deleted, the amount of unusable space within the index increases—a condition called *index stagnation*. Because a stagnated index contains a mixture of data and empty areas, scans of an index will be less efficient as the index grows more stagnated. To resolve index stagnation, you need to drop and recreate the index.

As of Oracle7.3, you can use the "fast index rebuild" method to recreate indexes. During a fast index rebuild, the new index uses the old index as its data source, instead of using the table as its data source. During a fast index rebuild, you need to have enough space available to store both the new and old indexes concurrently. See Chapter 13 for information on implementing the fast index rebuild method.

When you create a UNIQUE or PRIMARY KEY constraint, you should use the **using index** clause to specify the **tablespace** and **storage** parameters for the index. If you do not specify **tablespace** and **storage** parameters for an index, it will be created in your default tablespace, using the default storage parameters for the tablespace. As of Oracle7.1, a **using index** clause is also available for the **create snapshot** command; the only index affected by this clause is the one created on the M_ROW$$ column of a simple snapshot (see "Replication" in Chapter 13).

As of Oracle7.2, you can use the **unrecoverable** clause with the **create index** and **create table as select** commands. When you use the **unrecoverable** clause with the **create index** command, no redo log information is written for the object creation; thus, if you recover the database by applying archived redo log files, you will not be able to recover the index. However, there is no data that is uniquely stored in the index! If you cannot recover the index from the archived redo log files, you can recreate it manually by reissuing the **create index** command following the completion of the recovery process. By using the **unrecoverable** option you can speed up index and table creation significantly and reduce the negative impact of those operations on other database transactions that are happening at the same time. The **unrecoverable** option is appropriate for temporary/interface tables that feature frequent data modification and deletion, particularly if you use the parallel options (see Chapter 12).

When creating an index, you should specify a very low value for **pctfree**. Since you cannot update a value inside an index, there is no benefit to maintaining a large amount of free space within the blocks of an index. Since the space used by deleted entries within an index may not be reused, you cannot set a **pctused** value for indexes.

Because of the performance degradation caused by index stagnation, you should schedule periodic recreations of all indexes whose data is volatile. For the temporary/interface tables, you should drop and recreate all of the tables' indexes after each major data manipulation process. For your business transaction tables, the indexes on commonly updated columns should be periodically dropped and recreated. If records are frequently deleted from your business transaction tables, you should periodically drop and recreate all of the indexes on those tables. If your business transaction tables are **insert**-only, there is no need to drop and recreate the indexes unless you need to change the **storage** or **tablespace** parameters.

Managing Temporary Segments

A temporary segment is used whenever sorts cannot be performed in memory. When a process needs a temporary segment, Oracle creates a segment in the user's temporary tablespace (as defined by the **temporary tablespace** clause of the **alter user** and **create user** commands). The temporary segment will be named for the file and block at which it starts; a temporary segment in file 15 starting at block 2001 will be named 15.2001.

Most applications need no more than two types of temporary segments: one for use during queries of business transaction tables, and one for use during very large sorting operations associated with temporary/interface tables. Your temporary tablespace that supports the business transaction table queries must be able to support multiple users with small temporary segment requirements. The temporary tablespace used for the large sorting operations—or for application administration tasks such as analyzing tables—must be able to handle a small number of large temporary segments. Since the space usage characteristics for the two types of temporary segments differ greatly, two separate temporary tablespaces can be created.

The temporary tablespace for multiple users is typically named TEMP. Each temporary segment created in TEMP will use TEMP's default storage parameters for its storage parameters. The default storage parameters for TEMP are set via the **default storage** clause of the **alter tablespace** and **create tablespace** commands. The default parameters for TEMP should be sized to allow multiple small temporary segments to be created, while allowing each of the temporary segments to extend.

For example, if TEMP consisted of a single 100MB datafile, and you anticipated having as many as ten different temporary segments concurrently, you could specify the default storage for the tablespace as:

```
alter tablespace TEMP
default storage (initial 1M next 1M pctincrease 0
        minextents 1 maxextents 249);
```

Given the default storage parameters in the preceding listing, each temporary segment in TEMP will consist of 1MB extents. When sizing temporary segments, there are several important rules to follow:

1. *Use pctincrease 0*. Using a non-zero value for **pctincrease** will cause the temporary segments to grow geometrically (see the "Extents" section earlier in this chapter); if a large extent is not available, the transaction using the temporary segment may fail.

2. *Set initial and next to the same value.* Temporary segments are frequently created and dropped. To increase the reusability of the free extents from dropped temporary segments, you should make all extents the same size.

3. *To set initial, divide the total available space by the number of concurrent users of temporary segments; divide that result by 10 to determine initial.* For the example, there were ten concurrent users of 100MB of temporary segment space, so **initial** and **next** were set to 1MB each. These settings allowed small temporary segments to consume very little space, while larger temporary segments could expand as needed.

To see the temporary segments currently in use, query DBA_SEGMENTS, as shown in the following listing.

```
select *
  from DBA_SEGMENTS
 where Segment_Type = 'TEMPORARY';
```

Since the default **pctincrease** value for TEMP is set to 0, the SMON background process will not automatically coalesce neighboring free extents within TEMP. Therefore, TEMP will, over time, consist of a large number of previously used extents. If you follow the rules given previously in this section, each of the extents will be the same size—and will be reusable by all new or expanding temporary segments. If you change the values for **initial** and **next**, drop and recreate the TEMP tablespace; otherwise, you may not be able to easily reuse the previously used—and now free—extents. If you are using Oracle7.3, you could use the

```
alter tablespace TEMP coalesce;
```

command as an alternative to dropping and recreating the TEMP tablespace following a change to its storage parameters.

As of Oracle7.3, you can create a dedicated temporary tablespace. In this kind of tablespace, a single temporary segment is created; it supports multiple users concurrently. The temporary segment does not get dropped when the users no longer need it; instead, it remains in the temporary tablespace awaiting another user request for temporary segment space. Keeping the temporary segment in place avoids the costs associated with the creation and dropping of temporary segments. You can mark a tablespace as a dedicated temporary tablespace by specifying the **temporary** clause in the **alter tablespace** or **create tablespace** command. See the "Dedicated Temporary Tablespaces" section in Chapter 13 for implementation details.

Temporary tablespaces that are dedicated to supporting very large sorting operations associated with temporary/interface tables need to be carefully managed. In general, you will need to support a few very large temporary segments. For example, in order to use the **compute statistics** option when you **analyze** a table, you generally need to be able to create a temporary segment that is four times as large as the analyzed table. The default storage parameters for the tablespace therefore need to be set to allow the creation of a large temporary segment. If the application is small, you may be able to support the large transactions within the TEMP tablespace. As the database size increases, however, you may need to create a second temporary tablespace that is dedicated to large temporary segment activity.

The temporary tablespace for large temporary segments—for this example, called TEMP_LARGE—should have default storage parameters that follow the sizing rules given earlier. The default **pctincrease** value should be 0, and **initial** and **next** should be equal. When applying the third rule, regarding the size of the extents, you need to take into account that far fewer transactions will be concurrently using TEMP_LARGE than used TEMP.

If you use the parallel **create table as select** or parallel **create index** option, then you need to be very careful with your usage of temporary segments. These parallel options, as described in Chapter 12, create multiple processes that work together to complete the requested task. When creating a table in parallel, each of the processes creates an extent (of size **initial**) for the table and adds more extents as necessary. When the statement completes, the data from the temporary segments are merged into a single table, and the temporary segments are dropped. Thus, for the duration of the table or index creation process, you must have enough temporary segment space to support multiple copies of the object—and the greater the degree of parallelism, the more space you need!

Occasionally, temporary segments will not be properly dropped by Oracle. You can query DBA_SEGMENTS (as shown earlier in this section) to see the current temporary segments, but you cannot drop the segments. To release the space used by the segments, perform a database shutdown, followed by a startup. When the database is restarted, the temporary segments will have been dropped.

Managing Rollback Segments

Transactions against database tables—**insert**s, **update**s, and **delete**s—generate entries in *rollback segments*. The rollback segments store the previous image of a block as it existed before the transaction started. The entries within the rollback segment are used for two purposes:

- To rollback changes, in the event the transaction is not committed
- To present a read-consistent view of data to all users

In order to present a read-consistent view of data to all users, rollback segments provide data to users who are querying data that has been changed but not yet committed. If a user executes a query that uses data that has been changed but not yet committed by a second user, the query will return the data as it existed before the change was made. The query will read the previous version of the data from the rollback segment. If the data required by the query has been overwritten by data from another transaction, the user executing the query will receive an ORA-1555 ("snapshot too old") error message.

The goal of rollback segment management is to reduce contention and prevent "snapshot too old" errors without wasting too much disk space. However, large and small transactions compete for the same rollback segments. Unless you specifically use the **set transaction use rollback segment** command *after every commit*, you have no control over how Oracle balances the rollback segment usage across transactions. Moreover, hundreds of OLTP users may only have a few actual transactions open at any time. You need to balance the number of rollback segments, the number of extents for each rollback segment, and the total space allocated to the rollback segment tablespace.

To support a production application, you will typically need two distinct types of rollback segments. For transactions against application reference tables, business reference tables, and business transaction tables, you will need multiple small rollback segments. For transactions against the temporary/interface tables, you will need a small number of large rollback segments. The number of each type of rollback segment required is most directly related to the number of concurrent transactions within the database. If there are many small transactions performed concurrently within the database, you will need multiple rollback segments, each designed to handle multiple transactions.

A single rollback segment can store the data from multiple transactions. Each transaction generates a rollback segment entry consisting of the "before image" version of the blocks that have changed. To simplify the management of multiple rollback segment entries within a rollback segment, you should size the rollback segment so that each of its extents is large enough to support a typical transaction.

When a transaction's rollback segment entry cannot be stored within a single extent, the entry *wraps* into a second extent within the rollback segment. The extents within a rollback segment are assigned cyclically, so a rollback segment entry can wrap from the last extent of the rollback segment to its first extent— provided there is not an active rollback segment entry already in the first extent. If there is an active rollback segment entry already in the first extent, the rollback segment will extend.

To control the extension of rollback segments, you can set an **optimal** size for the rollback segment. To do so, use the **optimal** parameter of the **storage** clause when executing the **create rollback segment** or **alter rollback segment** commands. Although you can specify a default **optimal** value at the tablespace level (prior to Oracle7.3), rollback segments within that tablespace will not inherit that **optimal** setting from the tablespace; you need to specify **optimal** separately for each rollback segment.

In the following listing, the R1, R2, and R3 rollback segments are created in the RBS tablespace. Each of the rollback segments is created with the exact same storage parameters.

```
create rollback segment R1
tablespace RBS
storage (initial 2M next 2M minextents 2 maxextents 249
        optimal 20M);
```

```
create rollback segment R2
tablespace RBS
storage (initial 2M next 2M minextents 2 maxextents 249
        optimal 20M);

create rollback segment R3
tablespace RBS
storage (initial 2M next 2M minextents 2 maxextents 249
        optimal 20M);
```

When creating rollback segments for your OLTP users, you should follow these rules:

1. Dedicate a tablespace for rollback segments only. This tablespace could contain multiple files stored on different drives to help distribute I/O against the rollback segments across multiple disks.

2. Make all of the rollback segments the same size. Oracle will assign the rollback segments in a round-robin fashion (unless the user specifically requests a rollback segment to be used via the **set transaction use rollback segment** command), so creating rollback segments of differing sizes will not improve your ability to support transactions.

3. Make **initial** and **next** equal. In the event that the rollback segment is dropped, you want to maximize the chances that the dropped extents can be reused by another rollback segment. For rollback segments, you cannot specify a value for **pctincrease**; it will always be 0. The **pctincrease 0** setting guarantees that when the rollback segment shrinks to its **optimal** size, the space released could be used by another rollback segment.

4. Create extents that are large enough to prevent wrapping. Ideally, each transaction would be stored in its own rollback segment. Since that is not likely to be the case, each transaction should be able to be stored in its own extent. Create extents that are large enough to support most of the transactions without wrapping.

5. Set **optimal** high enough to avoid dynamic extensions of the rollback segment. If the rollback segment has to constantly extend beyond its **optimal** setting and then shrink back to its **optimal** setting, it is performing a great deal of unnecessary space management work. If a rollback segment extends frequently, it is not properly sized to handle the transaction load it is supporting.

6. Leave enough free space in the tablespace for a larger-than-usual transaction to be able to extend whatever rollback segment it is using. The **optimal** setting will cause that rollback segment to shrink later. Leaving adequate free space for extensions ensures that many small transactions and few large transactions can coexist in the rollback segments without running into the "snapshot too old" problem. It is common to have more than 70 percent of the rollback segment tablespace free for future rollback segment extents.

When a rollback segment extends beyond its **optimal** setting the first time, the rollback segment will not shrink. The second time the rollback segment extends beyond its **optimal** setting, the rollback segment will shrink—provided the second transaction forced the rollback segment to allocate a new extent. Setting a value for the **optimal** parameter will not prevent all space management issues, but can help limit the space management issues associated with rollback segments.

In the prior example, R1, R2, and R3 were all created with two extents—the minimum number in a rollback segment. As the rollback segments grow, they will eventually reach the **optimal** setting of 20MB each (ten extents). Although the rollback segments will use 60MB when they are all at their **optimal** size, you will need to have more than 60MB available in order to support the occasional extensions of the rollback segments.

To see the **optimal** setting for the rollback segment, along with the number of times the rollback segments have extended, wrapped, and shrunk, you can query V$ROLLSTAT and V$ROLLNAME, as shown in the following example. V$ROLLSTAT records the statistics related to rollback segment use since the last time the database was started.

```
select Name,
       OptSize,
       Shrinks,
       AveShrink,
       Wraps,
       Extends
  from V$ROLLSTAT, V$ROLLNAME
 where V$ROLLSTAT.USN=V$ROLLNAME.USN;
```

NAME	OPTSIZE	SHRINKS	AVESHRINK	WRAPS	EXTENDS
SYSTEM		0	0	0	0
R1	20971520	14	1787611	295	47
R2	20971520	9	1360782	248	23
R3	20971520	10	1703936	295	32

As shown in the previous listing, most problems with rollback segments show up in more than one rollback segment at a time. The values for the Wraps column (the cumulative number of wraps) are non-zero, so the extent sizes are not large enough to support the transactions. The rollback segments keep extending and shrinking (the Extends and Shrinks columns), so the **optimal** size is too low. The average amount of space reclaimed during a shrink (as shown in the AveShrink column) is less than 2MB.

To avoid the space management costs associated with constant extensions and shrinks of the rollback segments, increase the **optimal** parameter by at least the average shrink value—in this case, by 2MB in each rollback segment. The wraps problem is more difficult to resolve. As the V$ROLLSTAT output shows, wraps are occurring for many different transactions; to avoid wraps, you will need to drop and recreate the rollback segments with higher extent sizes.

As of Oracle7.2, you can use the **alter rollback segment** command to shrink rollback segments to a size of your choosing. The rollback segments will still have a minimum of two extents. If you do not specify a size to shrink to, the rollback segment will shrink to its **optimal** size. In the following listing, the R2 rollback segment is shrunk back to its **optimal** size.

```
alter rollback segment R2 shrink;
```

See Chapter 6 for information on automating the rollback segment shrinkage process during a database shutdown/startup cycle.

As the database grows, the size of the transactions against the business transaction tables and reference tables will typically remain constant in size or grow very slowly. However, the size of the transactions against your temporary/ interface tables may grow rapidly. To support the transactions against the temporary/interface tables, you should create a second rollback segment tablespace (such as RBS_BIG) that is specifically designed to support large transactions.

To support large transactions, you need large rollback segments—with large extent sizes and a high setting for **optimal**. When you are not using the large rollback segments, you should disable them. The command shown in the following listing will mark the R_BIG rollback segment as offline.

```
alter rollback segment R_BIG offline;
```

To bring the R_BIG rollback segment back online prior to a large transaction against the temporary/interface tables, you can use the following command:

```
alter rollback segment R_BIG online;
```

To minimize the need for large rollback segments, you can use the following methods:

- Frequently **commit** in large transactions and batch jobs.

- Fetch through, close, and release every cursor of long-running queries as soon as possible. The rollback is not released until there are no users with a cursor open that require data from that "old" image, even though the data itself was committed by its own transaction.

- To reduce the size of a **create table as select** or **insert as select** transaction, use the SQL*Plus **copy** command to force data to be committed periodically throughout the transaction.

- To reduce the size of the rollback segment entries caused by complete refreshes of snapshots, use simple snapshots with fast refreshes instead. See Chapter 13 for descriptions of the available replication options.

- To reduce the size of transactions generated by the Import utility, specify the COMMIT=Y keyword, along with a BUFFER value to force Import to periodically commit while inserting records into a table.

- To reduce the size of rollback segment entries generated by deletions, structure your tables to allow you to use the **truncate** command instead. The **truncate** command cannot be rolled back; it is a DDL command that immediately deletes all records from a table and resets its highwatermark. To execute the **truncate** command, you must have been granted the DROP_ANY_TABLE system privilege.

If you are using **create table as select** or **create index** commands, investigate the use of the **unrecoverable** option. See Chapter 13 for a full description of the **unrecoverable** option.

Managing Free Space

Extents that have not been allocated to segments are called *free extents*. Free extents within Oracle have two different origins:

■ The space allocated to a tablespace that has never been used by any segment

■ The space previously used by segments that have since been dropped or resized

If none of your segments will ever be dropped, you only need to be concerned with the free extents created when a tablespace is created. As with the extents of a segment, free extents cannot span datafiles. Thus, the **create tablespace** command shown in the following listing creates two free extents in the APP_REF tablespace.

```
create tablespace APP_REF
datafile '/db02/oracle/APP/app_ref01.dbf' size 100M,
         '/db03/oracle/APP/app_ref02.dbf' size 50M
default storage (initial 1M next 1M pctincrease 0
          maxextents 249);
```

When the APP_REF tablespace is created, one database block (4KB for this example) will be reserved as a header block within each datafile. The rest of each file will be a single, large free extent. The second file will be a 50MB free extent (less its header block). You can see the physical locations of free extents by querying DBA_FREE_SPACE, as shown in the following listing. DBA_FREE_SPACE lists the File_ID and Block_ID of the starting point of each free extent within a tablespace (identified via the Tablespace_Name column); for each file in the tablespace, the starting Block_ID will be "2". The size of the free extent is listed in both bytes (the Bytes column) and database blocks (the Blocks column).

```
select File_ID,
       Block_ID,
       Bytes,
       Blocks
  from DBA_FREE_SPACE
 where Tablespace_Name = 'APP_REF'
 order by File_ID, Block_ID;


FILE_ID   BLOCK_ID        BYTES      BLOCKS
--------- ---------- ----------- ----------
7         2           104853504      25599
8         2            52424704      12799
```

The output from DBA_FREE_SPACE shows the free extents created when the APP_REF tablespace was created. The free extents within the APP_REF tablespace are shown in Figure 5-3.

First datafile

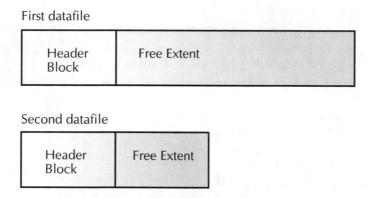

Second datafile

FIGURE 5-3. *Free extents in the APP_REF tablespace*

When a new extent is created in the APP_REF tablespace (either by the creation of a new object or the extension of an existing object), Oracle will evaluate the free extents within the tablespace to find an acceptable storage site for the extent. The evaluation process usually starts at the beginning of the first file in the tablespace, and continues through the end of the last file in the tablespace. If no free extent can support the new extent request, Oracle may dynamically coalesce neighboring free extents within a tablespace to form a larger free extent. Oracle can only do this if the extents are next to each other with no segments between them, and are in the same file. Because the two APP_REF free extents are in different files, they cannot be combined into a single free extent.

If the space within a tablespace has never been used, each of the tablespace's datafiles should contain a single free extent. As segments are created, the space at the beginning of the datafile is used, leaving a large free extent at the rear of the datafiles. Figure 5-4 shows the APP_REF tablespace after four tables have been created.

If the third segment is now dropped, the space used by that segment will be marked as a free extent. The other segments will not move; instead, the space freed by the third segment will remain between the second and fourth segment—a condition referred to as free space fragmentation (this type of free space fragmentation is sometimes referred to as "Swiss cheese" fragmentation). Figure 5-5 shows the result of the dropping of the third segment.

The management of free space created by dropped objects is far more complex than the management of free space created during datafile creations. Ideally, the space freed by the third segment should be completely reused before the large free extent at the end of the datafile is used. To encourage the reuse of dropped extents,

First datafile

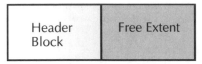

| Header Block | First Segment | Second Segment | Third Segment | Fourth Segment | Free Extent |

Second datafile

| Header Block | Free Extent |

FIGURE 5-4. *Four segments in the APP_REF tablespace*

several techniques are available—some implemented by Oracle automatically, and others enforced through proper extent sizing.

As previously described in the "Extents" section of this chapter, Oracle dynamically rounds the sizes of the extents it creates—usually to multiples of five blocks. Oracle may also dynamically decide to change the requested extent size depending on the available space. For example, if you requested an extent that was 10 database blocks in size, and a 12-block free extent was available, Oracle may allocate the entire 12-block free extent to your segment.

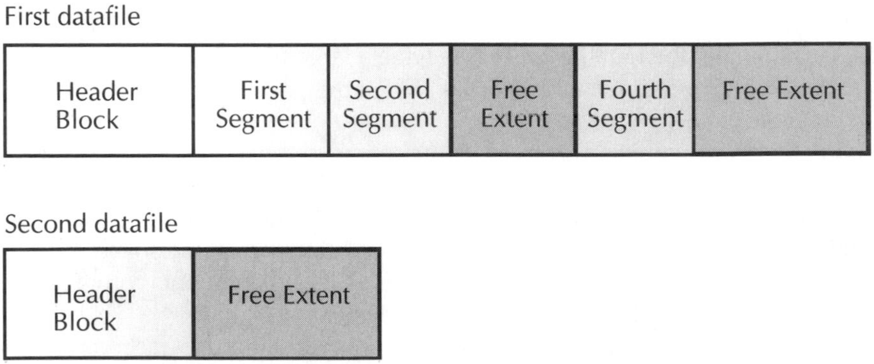

First datafile

| Header Block | First Segment | Second Segment | Free Extent | Fourth Segment | Free Extent |

Second datafile

| Header Block | Free Extent |

FIGURE 5-5. *Free space fragmentation in the APP_REF tablespace*

If you use standard sizes for your segments and extents, you will increase the likelihood that the extents can be reused. As described in the "Sizing Extents for Performance" section earlier in this chapter, each extent should be a multiple of the amount of space read during a multiblock read of the table. There are therefore a limited set of extent values to choose from. If a multiblock read reads 64KB worth of data, the valid extent sizes include 64KB, 128KB, 256KB, 512KB, 1MB, and 2MB. Extent sizes between these values (such as 1MB + 64KB) are also valid extent sizes, but may be more difficult to reuse when dropped.

Consider the third segment that was dropped for Figure 5-5. If the segment consisted of a single extent 8MB in size, the other segments could easily reuse the dropped space if they request space in extents of 1MB, 2MB, or 4MB.

To maximize the likelihood of free extent reuse, create a list of valid extent sizes, each of which is twice as large as the previous valid size. For example, you could use 1MB, 2MB, 4MB, 8MB, 16MB, and 32MB as your extent sizes. If a 16MB extent is dropped, its space could be used by another 16MB extent, or by two 8MB extents, or by four 4MB extents, or by eight 2MB extents, or by some combination of multiple extent sizes. By carefully selecting the list of possible extent values, you greatly increase the likelihood that the dropped space will be reused without additional dynamic space manipulation by Oracle.

If the fourth segment is dropped, the dropped extent will be marked as a free extent. Since the default **pctincrease** for the APP_REF tablespace is set to 0, the dropped extent will *not* be coalesced with the free extent created when the third segment was dropped. Figure 5-6 shows the segments and the free extents within the APP_REF tablespace. The type of free space fragmentation that features neighboring uncombined free extents is sometimes referred to as "honeycomb" fragmentation.

Within the first datafile, there are three extents that are next to each other—but they are not combined into a single large extent. If a new extent allocation request is issued, and the two smaller free extents cannot service the request by themselves, then the large free extent at the end of the datafile will do so—further aggravating the fragmentation situation (see Figure 5-5).

If the default **pctincrease** value for the tablespace had been set to a non-zero value, the SMON background process would have dynamically coalesced all of the neighboring free extents into a single large free extent—making the reuse of dropped extents a much simpler job to manage. However, if you use a non-zero **pctincrease** for your segments, they will grow geometrically (see Figure 5-2).

As of Oracle7.3, you can manually coalesce neighboring free extents into larger extents. The **coalesce** clause of the **alter tablespace** command manually performs the work that SMON performs automatically. SMON does not coalesce free extents in tablespaces whose default **pctincrease** values are non-zero. The

First datafile

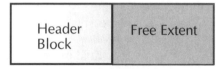

Second datafile

Header Block	Free Extent

FIGURE 5-6. *Honeycomb fragmentation in the APP_REF tablespace*

command shown in the following listing will coalesce the APP_REF tablespace's fragmented free space in the first datafile into a single large extent.

```
alter tablespace APP_REF coalesce;
```

There is a way to get the best of both worlds—to get SMON to coalesce your free extents without forcing your segments to grow at an accelerated pace. To use this method, you must specify a **pctincrease** value for each segment created within the tablespace. You should only use this method for tablespaces that contain tables and indexes—never for tablespaces that may contain rollback segments or temporary tablespaces, including the TEMP, RBS, and SYSTEM tablespaces.

First, specify a default **pctincrease** value of 1 for the tablespace:

```
alter tablespace APP_REF
default storage (pctincrease 1);
```

Next, when you create a segment within the APP_REF tablespace, specify a **pctincrease** of 0 for the segment—since the growth rate of segments is linear (see the "Extents" section earlier in this chapter).

```
create table TEST_TABLE
(x  VARCHAR2(10))
tablespace APP_REF
storage (initial 1M next 1M pctincrease 0);
```

The **pctincrease** setting at the table level will override the default **pctincrease** setting for the tablespace when the table is created. Specify the **pctincrease** value of 0 for each segment as it is created.

Since the default **pctincrease** value for the tablespace is non-zero, the SMON background process will dynamically coalesce any neighboring free extents that are created. Since the **pctincrease** value specified at the table level is 0, the segments will grow in a linear fashion and will be able to maximize the likelihood that the free extents created when a segment is dropped will be reused.

To further minimize the impact of dropped segments, you should segregate objects that are likely to be dropped (or shrunk—see Chapter 13 for information on deallocation of space from tables, indexes, and clusters). Place the objects that are likely to be dropped into a tablespace apart from objects that are unlikely to be dropped. For example, the indexes on application reference tables are very unlikely to require rebuilding; the indexes on volatile temporary/interface tables are likely to require periodic rebuilding. Therefore, you should store the indexes for temporary/interface tables apart from the rest of the application's indexes, to minimize the impact of their dropped extents on your free space management efforts.

If you are using one of Oracle's replication methods (see Chapter 13), you should store the replicated data in a tablespace apart from the rest of your application's data. Since the replicated data may be updated in one or more remote databases, you do not control it and cannot accurately predict its growth rate. To perform system administration activities, you may need to periodically drop and recreate the replica; segregating the replicated objects will minimize their impact on the space management activity within your environment.

Storage Parameters Reference

In the following sections, you will see the tuning and management advice related to each of the storage parameters. The advice given in this section is based on the examples and discussions earlier in this chapter. The storage parameters are listed in the order in which they are normally specified in an object creation.

initial

The extents within a segment must be multiples of the space read during a multiblock read of the database (such as 64KB or 128KB). To further improve the likelihood of space reuse, you should generate a list of valid extent sizes, with each valid size twice as large as the previous—for example, 128KB, 256KB, 512KB, 1MB, 2MB, 4MB, 8MB, 16MB. The setting for the **initial** parameter should be chosen from the list of valid extent sizes. Select values for initial that reflect the segment's planned size, and use consistent extent sizes.

next

To maximize space reuse, the value for the **next** parameter should come from the same list as the possible **initial** extent sizes. Set **next** equal to **initial** for rollback segments and temporary segments.

pctincrease

For objects, the **pctincrease** value should always be set to 0. For tablespaces that contain no temporary segments, rollback segments, or data dictionary objects, you can set the default **pctincrease** value to 1 to force SMON to coalesce the neighboring free extents in the tablespace; if you use this method, you must specify **pctincrease 0** when creating objects within the tablespace.

minextents

For rollback segments, **minextents** must be set to at least 2. For all other objects, set a **minextents** value of 1 unless you want to stripe the data within the database (as described in Chapter 4).

maxextents

Prior to Oracle7.3, the maximum number of extents an extent can have is limited, based on the database block size. Set the **maxextents** parameter to be less than the maximum allowed for your database block size. As of Oracle7.3, you can set **maxextents unlimited** for your objects (see Chapter 13), although this is not an advised setting for temporary segments and rollback segments.

tablespace

In addition to separating tables from indexes, you should separate the objects used to support the temporary/interface tables from the rest of the database objects. The rollback segments and temporary segments used during batch data loads of the temporary/interface tables should be stored apart from the rest of the rollback segments and temporary segments. The indexes for temporary/interface tables, which may require frequent reorganization, should be stored apart from the rest of the indexes in the database, to minimize the impact of dropped extents on your free space management.

pctfree

For tables, **pctfree** should be set to reserve enough space within a block to hold updates to the records in the block. If the table is *not* updateable, set **pctfree** very low (for example, **pctfree 1**) to minimize the amount of space left free within the block. There is no single **pctfree** value that will correctly apply to all of your tables. Instead, use a very low **pctfree** value for the application reference and business reference tables, and evaluate the update frequency within your business transaction and temporary/interface tables to determine a proper **pctfree** setting for them. If you set **pctfree** too low for a table, the rows within the table's blocks may become chained to other blocks, or may have to be migrated when they grow. If you set **pctfree** too high, you will waste space and will store fewer rows per block. For indexes, specify **pctfree 1**.

pctused

For tables experiencing high **delete/insert** activity, set a high value for **pctused**; otherwise, a large portion of each block may be left unused. For all other tables, the default of **pctused 40** is adequate. The **pctused** parameter cannot be specified for indexes, since indexes may not reuse the space freed within the index when an indexed value is deleted.

size

The **size** parameter is only used by clusters. Due to the high performance overhead incurred by transactions against clusters, avoid using clusters for your data storage.

freelists and freelist groups

The **freelists** parameter determines the number of free lists. A *free list* is a list of database blocks that have been allocated for the segment's extents and have free space greater than the **pctfree** setting. In general, the default value of **freelists 1** is adequate; if you have multiple processes performing large **insert** operations concurrently, increase the **freelists** parameter. If you are using the Oracle Parallel Server option, you can use the **freelist groups** parameter to specify the number of groups of free lists available to the instances; the default value is adequate unless you are performing multiple large concurrent **insert**s.

initrans and maxtrans

The **initrans** parameter sets the initial number of "transaction entries" allocated within each data block. If not enough space is available for multiple concurrent transactions, the transaction entries will dynamically allocate space from the available free space in the block. The **maxtrans** parameter sets the maximum number of transactions that can concurrently update a data block. The **initrans** and **maxtrans** parameters do not affect queries, and should not be changed from their default values.

optimal

The **optimal** parameter is used only by rollback segments. You should specify an **optimal** value for each rollback segment. Monitor the rollback segment via V$ROLLSTAT to determine if the rollback segment is being forced to dynamically extend beyond its **optimal** setting. When setting the **optimal** parameter for a rollback segment, you must specify the parameter via the **create rollback segment** or **alter rollback segment** command; the setting will not be inherited from the default storage parameters for the tablespace.

CHAPTER 6

Database Shutdown/ Startup Kit

A database shutdown and startup cycle can be a great opportunity for the DBA, since no other users are using the database while the shutdown and startup are taking place. If a user is logged into the database prior to the shutdown, then his or her account will be disconnected during the shutdown process (if a **shutdown immediate** or **shutdown abort** is used). After the instance is restarted, no users are connected until they explicitly request to connect to the database.

During the time that no users are logged into the database, you can perform a number of database administration functions that enhance the manageability and performance of your database. In this chapter you will see a set of operations that should be performed inside and outside the database during the shutdown/startup cycle. You'll also see details for the implementation of each operation.

Items in the Shutdown/Startup Kit

There are seven items in the basic shutdown/startup kit, as follows:

- While the database is shutdown, delete or archive old trace files/logs.

- While the database is shutdown, rename the alert log.

- Generate a **create controlfile** command for your instance via the **alter database backup controlfile to trace** command.

- Pin your most-used packages in the SGA.

- Create an owner-to-object location map, showing who owns what where in the database.

- Recompute statistics on your most-accessed tables and indexes.

- Shrink rollback segments that have extended past **optimal**.

In the following sections, you'll see full descriptions of each of these steps, along with implementation guidance. The operating system steps are listed first, followed by the internal database steps.

Delete or Archive Old Trace Files and Logs

As you use an Oracle instance, Oracle writes diagnostic information about the instance to many trace files and logs. Each of the background processes creates a trace file, which is stored in the directory identified by the BACKGROUND_DUMP_DEST parameter in the init.ora or config.ora file. Users create trace files; and sometimes the database, when encountering an internal error, creates a trace file. Users' trace files are created in the directory identified by the USER_DUMP_DEST parameter in the init.ora or config.ora file.

Depending on your operating system configuration, the number of trace files stored for your instance may be infinite. In some Unix systems, for example, the trace files for the background processes start with a single digit, followed by an underscore and the process number for the background process—for example, the file could be named 3_12345.trc. The next time you shutdown and startup the instance, a new file will be created for the same background process, but will likely have a different process number—for example, 3_33214.trc. The previous file will not be deleted by the database.

Left unchecked, the background processes' trace files will grow in number. User trace files written to USER_DUMP_DEST will also continue to grow in number. Since trace files are often stored in a subdirectory under the Oracle software home directory, an unchecked population of trace files can consume all of the free space on the device used by the Oracle software.

To avoid having trace files consume all available free space, you need to actively manage them. The method of managing the trace file population depends on the needs of your environment; do you need to be able to view trace files from last month? from last year? Do you need to keep them all online? From a problem diagnosis perspective, trace files are important. However, you should be able to develop a management solution that allows you to compress, back up, and remove trace files from your directories. It is best to perform these actions while the database is down—otherwise, the trace files used by the background processes will still be active during your file management process.

SQL*Net also creates log files. For SQL*Net V1, the file is called orasrv.log; enter the command

```
tcpctl stat
```

to see the location of the trace file. The SQL*Net V1 log file grows in size over time; its rate of size increase is directly related to the debug level chosen for the orasrv process. While SQL*Net V1 is shutdown, you can delete or rename the orasrv.log file; a new log file will be created in its place when SQL*Net V1 is restarted.

For SQL*Net V2, listener.log is the name of the log file. To determine its location, enter the command

```
lsnrctl status
```

The SQL*Net V2 Listener log file grows in size over time. While the SQL*Net V2 Listener is shutdown, you can delete or rename the listener.log file; a new log file will be created in its place when the SQL*Net V2 Listener is restarted. An example of the listener.log rename process is shown in the following listing.

```
> lsnrctl stop
> mv listener.log old_list.log
> lsnrctl start
```

NOTE
Don't shutdown SQL*Net unless the databases on the host have already been shutdown. If you shutdown SQL*Net while users are connected to the databases on the server, then any user connected via SQL*Net will be disconnected from his or her database session.

In the preceding example, the SQL*Net V2 Listener process was shutdown via the **lsnrctl stop** command. The Unix *mv* command was used to rename the listener.log file, and the Listener process was restarted.

Rename the Alert Log

As you use an Oracle instance, Oracle writes diagnostic information changes within the instance to an *alert log*. The alert log is stored in the directory identified by the BACKGROUND_DUMP_DEST parameter in the init.ora or config.ora file. The alert log is usually named after the instance—for an instance named PROD, the alert log may be named alert_prod.log.

The alert log contains information about major database events, including startups, shutdowns, redo log switches, tablespace changes, file changes, internal errors, and tablespace backup status changes. The information in the alert log has two critical characteristics: it is important, and it grows rapidly. If something is important enough to be written to the alert log, then the DBA should be aware of it. For example, what errors or warning messages were encountered the last time the instance was started? How many redo log switches were occurring during a critical performance test? All of this information is written to the alert log, and you should be aware of it.

Unfortunately, the alert log fills quickly. If you let it grow unchecked, the log will eventually grow to an unmanageable—and unreadable—size. New entries to the alert log are appended to the bottom of the file, and the file will grow until there is no more space left on the device on which it is stored. Since BACKGROUND_DUMP_DEST may be located on the same device as your Oracle software home directory, the growth of your alert log may impact the space available for your software directory.

To solve these two problems—uncontrolled space usage and unread data—keep the alert log to a small size by renaming it periodically. The alert log can be renamed at any time, even while the database is open. If Oracle cannot find a properly named alert log file in BACKGROUND_DUMP_DEST to append to, it will create a new file with the proper name in that directory. Although it is not necessary to rename the alert log during a shutdown/startup cycle, the periodic, scheduled nature of a shutdown/startup cycle makes it an ideal time to schedule a rename of the alert log.

For example, after shutting down the instance, you may enter the following command from within the BACKGROUND_DUMP_DEST directory for your PROD instance:

```
> mv alert_prod.log old_alert.log
```

In the preceding example, the alert log for the PROD instance is renamed using the Unix *mv* command. You can now read, mail, or print the old_alert.log file and review it for potential problems or diagnostic information.

Generate a *create controlfile* command

The **create controlfile** command has two uses: to build a controlfile from scratch after your existing controlfiles have been damaged, and to alter database-level parameters such as MAXDATAFILES. The **create controlfile** command must list all of the files associated with the database, and the syntax is very specific. Oracle will create the full syntax for the **create controlfile** command for you if you use a variant of the **alter database** command. The ideal time to run this command is at the end of a physical file backup and during a shutdown/startup cycle, immediately following the startup.

From within SQLDBA, Server Manager, or SQL*Plus, enter the command

```
alter database backup controlfile to trace;
```

When the preceding command is executed, Oracle will create a trace file in your user dump file directory. The user dump file directory is defined by the USER_DUMP_DEST parameter in the instance's init.ora or config.ora file. The file will be named using the standard naming convention for your operating system; it may simply be named after your process ID on the operating system (for example, ora_1234.trc).

The trace file will contain the full syntax for your database's **create controlfile** command. Rename the trace file to a more meaningful name. You may also wish to move the file to make it easy to find.

If you do not immediately move or rename the trace file that is created by the **alter database backup controlfile to trace** command, you may either have difficulty finding the proper trace file or you may inadvertently remove the trace file as part of your cleanup of old trace files. Since the trace file will be written to your USER_DUMP_DEST directory, and will be named according to the naming standard for your trace files, the new trace file's name will not be easily differentiated from existing files. For example, in some Unix systems, the trace filename format is ora_*process*.trc, where *process* is the operating system process ID of the process that created the file. If you don't know the process number of the process that created the trace file, you will need to search through the files (using a command such as the Unix *grep* command) to find the file containing the **create controlfile** command. If you need to search the files manually, use the timestamps on the files to narrow your search—only search the files created around the time your shutdown/startup cycle occurred.

Pin Packages

PL/SQL objects, when used, are stored in the library cache of the shared SQL area within the SGA. If a package has already been loaded into memory by a user, other users will experience improved performance when executing that package. Thus, keeping a package "pinned" in memory decreases the response time to the user during package executions.

To improve the ability to keep large PL/SQL objects pinned in the library cache, you should load them into the SGA as soon as the database is opened. Pinning packages immediately after startup increases the likelihood that a contiguous section of memory will be available to store the package. As of Oracle7.1, the DBMS_SHARED_POOL package can be used to pin PL/SQL objects in the SGA.

To use DBMS_SHARED_POOL, you first need to reference the objects that you want to pin in memory. To load a package in memory, you can reference a dummy procedure defined in the package or you can recompile the package. The core set of packages provided by Oracle does not need to be referenced or recompiled before pinning and will be loaded the first time it is executed. You can pin a cursor by executing its SQL statement.

Once the object has been referenced, you can execute the DBMS_SHARED_POOL.KEEP procedure to pin the object. The KEEP procedure of DBMS_SHARED_POOL, as shown in the following listing, takes as its input parameters the name of the object and the type of object ('P' for packages, 'C' for cursors).

```
alter package APPOWNER.ADD_CLIENT compile;
execute DBMS_SHARED_POOL.KEEP('APPOWNER.ADD_CLIENT');
```

The example shown in the preceding listing illustrates the two-step process involved in pinning packages in memory: the package is first referenced (via the compilation step), and is then marked for keeping.

To allow a pinned object to be removed from the SGA via the normal Least Recently Used algorithm for cache management, use the UNKEEP procedure of the DBMS_SHARED_POOL package. As shown in the following listing, the UNKEEP procedure takes the same parameters as the KEEP procedure took—the object name and the object type.

```
execute DBMS_SHARED_POOL.UNKEEP('APPOWNER.ADD_CLIENT');
```

UNKEEP is usually not needed, but you can use it to manage your memory allocations within the SGA if you do not have a lot of system memory available.

Pinning your most-used packages in memory immediately after startup will improve your chances of acquiring contiguous space for them within the SGA. This is less of an issue in Oracle7.3 than in the earlier versions of Oracle7, but it is a good practice to follow regardless of the version used.

Selecting Packages to Pin

Each database will have two sets of packages to pin: the core set used by each database, and the set of packages specific to a particular application. The core set of packages to pin is listed in Table 6-1. All of the packages shown in Table 6-1 are owned by SYS.

If you are using the Symmetric Replication features of Oracle7, you should pin all of the packages listed in Table 6-1; databases not using Symetric Replication should pin the packages listed in the first column. If you are using Symmetric Replication, then application-specific packages are created for the tables in the replication schema. These packages are named after the table, with the suffixes "$RP" and "$RR". For example, for the COMPANY table, the packages would be named COMPANY$RP (used to queue deferred calls) and COMPANY$RR (the conflict resolution package for incoming transactions). The application-specific packages for Symmetric Replication should be pinned in the SGA for replicated tables with a very high level of update/insert/delete activity.

For Common Applications	Additional Packages for Symmetric Replication
DIUTIL	DBMS_DEFER
STANDARD	DBMS_REPUTIL
DIANA	DBMS_SNAPSHOT
DBMS_SYS_SQL	DBMS_REFRESH
DBMS_SQL	DBMS_DEFER_INTERNAL_SYS
DBMS_UTILITY	REP$WHAT_AM_I
DBMS_DESCRIBE	
DBMS_JOB	
DBMS_STANDARD	
DBMS_OUTPUT	
PIDL	

TABLE 6-1.   *Core Packages to Pin*

You should pin the largest packages first. To determine the proper order, you can use the script shown in the following listing. It uses the DBA_OBJECT_SIZE view to list the order in which the objects will be pinned.

```
select Owner,
       Name,
       Type,
   Source_Size+Code_Size+Parsed_Size+Error_Size   Total_Bytes
  from DBA_OBJECT_SIZE
 where Type = 'PACKAGE BODY'
 order by 4 desc;
```

Create an Owner-to-Object Location Map

During recovery, maintenance, and tuning operations, it is useful to know which users own objects in which tablespaces. You can only get this information from the database while the database is open and available; the ideal time to query for this information is immediately following a database startup.

There are two components to the owner-to-object location map: owners in tablespaces, and tablespaces used by owners. Very similar queries are used to generate this information (as shown in the following listings); the only difference between the two queries is the order in which the information is presented.

The query in the following listing selects from DBA_SEGMENTS to determine which owners have objects in which tablespace. Sample data is shown with the query.

```
break on Tablespace_Name skip 1 on Owner
select Tablespace_Name, Owner, Segment_Name, Segment_Type
  from DBA_SEGMENTS
 order by Tablespace_Name, Owner, Segment_Name;
```

TABLESPACE_NAME	OWNER	SEGMENT_NAME	SEGMENT_TYPE
APP_DATA	APPOWNER	LINE_ITEMS	TABLE
		ORDERS	TABLE
	SHOSHEE	CONTACTS	TABLE
APP_INDEXES	APPOWNER	LINE_ITEMS_PK	INDEX
		ORDERS_PK	INDEX
		ORDERS_TEMP	TABLE

The sample data in the preceding listing shows that in the APP_DATA tablespace, two users own objects, and all of those objects are tables. In APP_INDEXES, APPOWNER is the only owner account—but one of its objects there is a table (named ORDERS_TEMP).

The preceding example shows two ways in which the owner-to-object location map query is useful. First, during recovery operations, you could use the query results to see which objects were located in which tablespace, and could therefore make more educated decisions about your recovery needs and options. If you lost the APP_INDEXES tablespace, for example, you could use the output shown in the preceding example to determine that you could not replace the tablespace's objects just by recreating the indexes that had been in it; you would also need to recover the APPOWNER.ORDERS_TEMP table.

The second use for the owner-to-object location map query is to display irregularities in the locations of your applications' objects. Why is there a table created in the APP_INDEXES tablespace? Scanning the user object locations during each startup helps you to manage the locations of your objects.

While performing Imports of data, it is useful to know if a user owns objects in multiple tablespaces. If a user's tables are confined to a single tablespace, it may be possible to perform a complete Import of that user; otherwise, a table-by-table Import may be necessary. To view the owner-to-object location map by owner, reorder the columns in the query and change the break logic, as shown in the following example.

```
break on Owner skip 1 on Tablespace_Name
select Owner, Tablespace_Name, Segment_Name, Segment_Type
  from DBA_SEGMENTS
 order by Owner, Tablespace_Name, Segment_Name;
```

OWNER	TABLESPACE_NAME	SEGMENT_NAME	SEGMENT_TYPE
APPOWNER	APP_DATA	LINE_ITEMS	TABLE
		ORDERS	TABLE
	APP_INDEXES	LINE_ITEMS_PK	INDEX
		ORDERS_PK	INDEX
		ORDERS_TEMP	TABLE
SHOSHEE	APP_DATA	CONTACTS	TABLE

As shown in the preceding listing, the APPOWNER user only owns objects in the APP_DATA and APP_INDEXES tablespaces. When your listings show the objects owned by many users, it is useful to see the data presented in this format.

Creating an Owner-to-Datafile Location Map

You can also see object locations on a datafile-by-datafile basis. In the preceding examples, the objects' location was shown at a tablespace-by-tablespace level. If a tablespace comprises multiple datafiles, you should also generate an owner-to-datafile location map. Otherwise, if you lose a single datafile from a tablespace, you will not know which objects had extents within that file.

As a segment extends, it acquires space in the datafiles associated with its tablespace. The extents of a segment can be stored in multiple datafiles. The example in the following listing shows the SQL script that generates the owner-to-datafile location map (by joining DBA_EXTENTS to DBA_DATA_FILES), along with sample output for the APP_DATA tablespace.

```
break on Owner on Segment_Name

select DBA_EXTENTS.Owner,
       DBA_EXTENTS.Segment_Name,
       DBA_DATA_FILES.Tablespace_Name,
       DBA_DATA_FILES.File_Name,
       SUM(DBA_EXTENTS.Bytes) Bytes
  from DBA_EXTENTS, DBA_DATA_FILES
 where DBA_EXTENTS.File_ID = DBA_DATA_FILES.File_ID
 group by DBA_EXTENTS.Owner, DBA_EXTENTS.Segment_Name,
   DBA_DATA_FILES.Tablespace_Name, DBA_DATA_FILES.File_Name;
```

```
OWNER      SEGMENT_NAME TABLESPACE FILE_NAME                           BYTES
---------- ------------ ---------- ------------------------------- ---------
APPOWNER   LINE_ITEMS   APP_DATA   /db01/oracle/APP/data01.dbf      13045760
                        APP_DATA   /db02/oracle/APP/data02.dbf       5457920
           ORDERS       APP_DATA   /db01/oracle/APP/data01.dbf       2048000
SHOSHEE    CONTACTS     APP_DATA   /db01/oracle/APP/data01.dbf       2048000
```

The query output in the preceding listing shows that the LINE_ITEMS segment has extents in two datafiles. ORDERS and CONTACTS have extents in only one datafile. All of the segments shown in the previous listing are in the APP_DATA tablespace (from the previous report in this section), but only LINE_ITEMS has extents in the second datafile in that tablespace.

Recompute Statistics

In Oracle7, statistics for tables and indexes are regenerated only on demand. To generate statistics for use by the cost-based optimizer, use the **analyze** command, as shown in the following listing.

```
analyze table ORDERS compute statistics;
```

You can also use the **estimate** keyword to estimate statistics, but the **compute** option gives the most exact results. If you analyze statistics on a table, the table's indexes are analyzed too (although in Oracle7.3 you can specify that the table's indexes are not to be analyzed with the table).

NOTE
The **analyze table... compute statistics** command can create very large temporary segments during its processing.

You can only compute statistics on objects when the database is open. Due to the resource-intensive nature of the **analyze** command, it is best to perform table analysis while no other users are using the database. The time immediately following a database startup may therefore be ideal for analyzing your objects, particularly if no one will be logging into your database for a long enough period of time.

To facilitate analyzing a large number of objects, you can use the ANALYZE_SCHEMA procedure of the DBMS_UTILITY package. The ANALYZE_SCHEMA procedure has two input parameters: the name of the schema that owns the objects to be analyzed, and the method to use during analysis ('COMPUTE' or 'ESTIMATE'). In the following example, the APPOWNER account's objects will be analyzed using the **compute statistics** method.

```
execute DBMS_UTILITY.ANALYZE_SCHEMA('APPOWNER','COMPUTE');
```

When the command in the preceding listing is executed, all of the APPOWNER account's objects will be analyzed using the **compute statistics** method.

Shrink Rollback Segments That Have Extended Past optimal

Each rollback segment in your database should have a setting for its **optimal** storage parameter (see the Optsize column in V$ROLLSTAT). **optimal** indicates the size to which the rollback segment should "shrink" during usage. If the rollback segment extends past its **optimal** size, it will stay overextended; the next transaction that forces it to extend again will, when complete, cause the rollback segment to shrink back to its **optimal** size.

A rollback segment will stay overextended, beyond its **optimal** size, until a second transaction forces it to extend past its current size. For example, if a rollback segment R1 had an **optimal** size of 10M, and it is used to handle a 12M transaction, then R1 will extend to 12M in size. The R1 rollback segment will *not* shrink back to 10M automatically. If a second transaction uses more than 12M in R1, then once the second transaction is complete, R1 will shrink back to its **optimal** 10M size. The following commented listing shows an example of the forced-shrinkage process. In the example, a deletion from a table named TEMP_TABLE is used to reset R1 to its **optimal** size.

```
REM  Force the R1 rollback segment to be used
REM  Ensure the SET TRANSACTION command is used by the
REM    DELETE command.
rollback;
set transaction use rollback segment R1
REM  Delete from the 12M table; DO NOT COMMIT!
delete from TEMP_TABLE;
REM  Rollback the deletion
rollback;
```

In Oracle7.0 and Oracle7.1, the only way to shrink a rollback segment back to its **optimal** size (without dropping and recreating the rollback segment) is to create transactions that force the rollback segments to extend again, as shown in the preceding example. As of Oracle7.2, a new option is available for rollback segment shrinkage. You can use the **shrink** option of the **alter rollback segment** command to shrink rollback segments. If you do not specify a size the rollback segment should shrink to, it will shrink to its **optimal** size. You cannot shrink a rollback segment to less than its **optimal** size.

In the following listing, the R1 rollback segment is altered twice. The first command shrinks R1 to 15M. The second command shrinks the R1 rollback segment to its **optimal** size. The **shrink** option of the **alter rollback segment** command is only available in Oracle7.2 and above.

```
alter rollback segment R1 shrink to 15M;
alter rollback segment R1 shrink;
```

Following a startup, you can quickly reset all of your rollback segments to their **optimal** sizes using the methods described in this section. If you are using Oracle7.0 or Oracle7.1, you will need to create a large transaction in each targeted rollback segment. If you are using Oracle7.2 and above, you can use the **alter rollback segment** command's **shrink** option to automate the resizing process.

Implementing the Shutdown/Startup Kit

Most of the items described in this chapter require customization for your databases—for example, you will need to specify which procedures should be pinned for each instance. In general, the scheduling of the items relative to the shutdown/startup cycle is:

1. Shutdown the instance.

2. Delete or archive old trace files and logs.

3. Rename the alert log.

4. Startup the instance.

5. Generate a **create controlfile** command for your instance via the **alter database backup controlfile to trace** command.

6. Reference your most-used packages.

7. Use DBMS_SHARED_POOL to pin your most-used packages and procedures in the SGA.

8. Create an owner-to-object and owner-to-datafile location map, showing who owns what where in the database.

9. Recompute statistics on your most-accessed tables and indexes.

10. Shrink rollback segments that have extended past **optimal**.

These steps, when performed with each shutdown/startup cycle, will improve the recoverability, performance, and ease of management for your database.

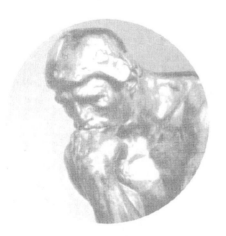

PART 3

Tuning a Growing Database

CHAPTER 7

Managing for Performance

Tuning production applications, whether they are custom or packaged (purchased) applications, can be a difficult balancing act. You need to find a way to improve the performance of the system without making changes that will damage the stability of the system. This chapter describes a tuning methodology that allows you to tune an existing production system while minimizing the chances of adverse effects.

This section of this book comprises five chapters. In this chapter, application profiles and the major tuning steps will be described. The following chapters describe how to monitor the database, how to tune the database environment, and how to analyze and tune SQL statements.

Where to Start

Often, the most difficult part of a task is knowing where to start. In the case of tuning, there are five common steps involved. They are, in order:

1. Ensure a consistent production environment.

2. Categorize the application's transactions and queries.

3. Focus on offensive SQL.

4. Tune specific long-running processes and batch jobs.

5. Tune the access to individual tables.

In the following sections, you will see descriptions of each of these steps, which are covered in detail in subsequent chapters.

Ensure a Consistent Production Environment

When an application is first deployed to production, it performs according to its system requirements—otherwise, it would not meet the business requirements of its users. As described in Chapter 1, nothing is guaranteed to stay the same once an application goes into production. The space used by the data grows, more users are added, and the system may be used for purposes beyond its original scope. Change to the performance of the system is to be expected.

Most users save old files on their personal computers, old mail messages in their e-mail accounts, and old data in the database. As a database administrator, it is almost unheard of for a user to request that you remove data—or tables, or functionality—from an application. Your production environment must therefore be stable enough to withstand the impact of growth in the usage and size of the system.

Ensuring a consistent production environment with respect to performance consists of several factors, described in the following sections. Your goal should be to remove environmental factors as the major cause of any performance problems the system encounters. If the production environment is managed in a consistent fashion, your tuning efforts can be focused on specific SQL problems.

Managing Memory Requirements

The memory areas within the SGA play a critical role in the performance of applications—particularly for multiuser applications. The data block buffer cache is the part of the SGA that allows Oracle to minimize the number of physical reads required to satisfy a query. The size of the cache is determined by the setting of the DB_BLOCK_BUFFERS setting in your init.ora file (you specify the number of blocks in the data block buffer cache). If the data required by a query has already been read into the cache by another user, Oracle can use the cache's data to resolve the query. Chapter 8 describes how to monitor the *hit ratio* for a database. A hit ratio of 0.90 means that each block read into the data block buffer cache is used nine times before it is removed from the SGA.

The Shared Pool in the SGA contains multiple large structures. The *Shared SQL Area* contains the parse tree and execution plan for SQL statements (the more complex the statement, the more space required in the Shared SQL Area). The *Library Cache* within the Shared Pool contains the list of all the data dictionary objects currently used, and the relationships between them. The *Row Cache* within the Shared Pool contains cached data dictionary information. In the Shared SQL Area, identical SQL statements share execution information, just as they share data in the data block buffer cache. The size of the Shared SQL Area is determined by the setting of the SHARED_POOL_SIZE parameter in your instance's init.ora file (you set the number of bytes for the Shared SQL Area). The more procedures and packages you use, the more space you will need in the Shared SQL Area. The default value for the SHARED_POOL_SIZE parameter is 3.5 MB, but this setting is far too low. If you have multiple concurrent users in your database, you should start with a SHARED_POOL_SIZE setting of at least 10 MB. If you are actively using packages and procedures, you will need to increase the SHARED_POOL_SIZE setting further.

If you are using the multi-threaded server configuration, the SGA (the data block buffer cache combined with the Shared Pool) should use about 50 to 75 percent of the entire memory available for the database. In a multi-threaded server configuration, the user processes do not take any memory, especially in Client/Server applications. Therefore, if a machine is dedicated to Oracle applications, and you are using the multi-threaded server configuration, the shared memory on the machine should amount to about 70 percent of the total memory, and most of the shared memory should be allocated to the SGA.

Chapters 8 and 9 describe the monitoring of the SGA objects. Adequate memory allocation is a critical part of establishing a consistent production environment.

Managing Data Location

In addition to managing the memory areas of the database, you also need to manage the physical storage used by the different types of database files. Regarding physical storage, your main goal should be to avoid I/O contention among your database files. By monitoring the I/O associated with the database's disks (see Chapter 8), you can determine which files and disk drives could potentially cause I/O bottlenecks. Chapter 4 describes the use of advanced I/O architectures (such as RAID and LVM) to help distribute the I/O.

Within the datafiles, you should manage your extent usage. As described in Chapter 5, there is no performance penalty for having multiple extents if the extents are properly sized. However, there is a management penalty—the more extents you have, the more difficult it is to know which data is stored in which datafile. Since Oracle reports I/O by datafile, you need to know the exact locations of your tables in order to properly correlate I/O usage to tables.

Another I/O management issue, *data proximity,* is described in Chapter 11. Data proximity—the order in which data is physically stored in the table—becomes an issue when a table grows very large. If a table is frequently queried by range scans of a particular column (such as State or Name), then physically ordering the rows of the table by that column will improve the performance of range scans against the table. As the table grows larger, improving the data proximity can have a great effect on the performance of range scans against it. Managing data proximity helps improve the I/O within the database and limit the environmental causes of performance problems.

Monitoring

Monitoring and tuning of the database environment is covered in Chapters 8 and 9. To ensure a consistent production environment, your monitoring should include:

- *Production monitoring.* A monitoring system should be in place to notify you if a database is suddenly inaccessible.

- *Trend monitoring.* You should store values about specific key factors—such as the percentage of free space in each tablespace—and use the results to see the changes in the factors over time. Once a consistent trend has been established, you will be able to use the data for forecasting as well.

- *Ad hoc monitoring of the database.* You should be able to monitor the database during set time periods. Oracle's utlbstat.sql and utlestat.sql scripts help you to monitor the changes in system statistics during a set period of time. The output of utlestat.sql will help you identify areas requiring tuning attention.

- *Ad hoc monitoring of application SQL.* You should be able to see the current SQL being used by the applications in your database. It is complicated to query this data from the system tables, so you may need to look at advanced Oracle or third-party tools to perform this type of monitoring.

If you have production and trend monitoring in place, you will have advance warning of potential problems within the database. When a problem does arise, you can use your ad hoc monitoring tools to isolate the SQL or table that is causing the trouble. Having created a consistent production environment, you can focus your tuning efforts on the factors most affecting your performance—the most "offensive" SQL used within your application. Before you can judge the SQL, you first need to understand the application it serves. In the next section, you will see the application categorization process.

Categorizing Application Transactions and Queries

Very few systems consider long-term performance implications during their implementations. System usage changes that are five years away are usually not part of the base requirements for the implementation of the first version of an application. (Consider, for example, applications that are released as production applications in 1998 that do not take into account how they will handle date manipulation after the year 2000.) The spiral pattern of application deployment shown in Chapter 1 holds true—the system grows until something *must* be done about its performance.

Custom Versus Packaged Applications
You will find the spiral pattern to hold true for both custom applications and third-party packages. Often, packages encounter performance problems before custom applications, for two primary reasons:

■ *The developers devised the package for general system requirements—not for your requirements.* The developers did not know your specific business rules, nor did they know the pattern of usage or growth within your application. Judged against their development requirements, theirs is a high-quality package, and they are less likely to implement radical changes for one customer.

■ *The developers devised the package to run on databases other than Oracle.* In order to create applications that could run on multiple databases, the developers may not have been able to take advantage of some of Oracle's more advanced features (such as hints).

For those two reasons, you need to pay close attention to the performance of packaged software as the system that uses it grows. Since packaged software most likely does not conform to your naming and account usage conventions, the tuning and administration of packages can be more difficult than that of custom applications.

From a tuning perspective, the approach is the same for both packaged software and custom applications. You will likely spend more pre-implementation time tuning packages than custom applications, and will have less control over the changes made to database objects in subsequent versions. Other than those two issues, there is little difference between the tuning processes for custom or packaged applications.

OLTP (On-Line Transaction Processing) Versus Batch

The most significant distinction you can make when categorizing a system for tuning purposes concerns the system's transaction pattern. The differences in the transaction patterns for OLTP (online transaction processing) applications and batch applications are shown in Table 7-1.

As defined in Table 7-1, OLTP applications support multiple users who perform many small, random queries, and who judge the system's performance by its response time to those queries. In a batch environment, the transactions are larger and fewer in number. The performance of batch transactions is judged by the time it takes for the entire process to complete. Batch transactions also tend to be very consistent in their patterns of data access—for example, batch reports may always join a certain set of tables, whereas OLTP users could dynamically join a variety of tables.

Use the characteristics in Table 7-1 to categorize your applications. You may find that your applications are a hybrid of the two categories. If you have a hybrid application, you will need to consider the tuning aspects of each part separately. As described in the following chapters, the performance requirements of OLTP and batch transactions will lead you down differing execution paths when tuning SQL.

Focus on Offensive SQL

Once the application has been categorized as an OLTP or batch transaction application, you need to focus on tuning the most "offensive" SQL. In general, a small number of SQL statements are responsible for most of the activity that occurs in a database. Rather than trying to learn and understand an application in its entirety (a particularly long task if you are tuning packaged software), focus on the few SQL statements that dominate the database activity.

OLTP	Batch
Many users	Few users
Small transactions	Large transactions
Few SQL calls per transaction	Many SQL calls per transaction
Response time is critical	Total throughput time is critical
Random access to data	Characteristic disk access pattern by user

TABLE 7-1.   *Characteristics of OLTP and Batch Applications*

Unfortunately, it is not simple to determine which SQL statements are using the majority of the system resources. As described in the "Ensure a Consistent Production Environment" section earlier in this chapter, you need to monitor for exception conditions. In the case of performance, you should establish the control limits for system resource usage. When a transaction exceeds that limit, it is marked as being "out of control" and needs to be addressed. Control limits are usually expressed as either a percentage of the total available CPU used or the total time to complete the process.

In most production databases, fewer than ten transactions account for over 80 percent of the resource usage. In some cases, a transaction may appear to be rather small—but it may be executed so many times that it becomes a major resource user within the system. For each of the problem transactions, examine its execution path. The procedure for generating and understanding the execution path (also known as the *explain plan*) is described in Chapter 10. The procedure to follow when tuning SQL is described in Chapter 11.

Tune Specific Long-Running Processes and Batch Jobs

As noted in Table 7-1, a batch transaction may include multiple smaller transactions. Each of these component transactions may perform well on its own; as part of a larger whole, it may cause a performance problem.

For example, consider a pair of queries that select data from different sections of the same large table; the queries are run in succession and use indexed access to the table. The first query reads the data from the large table into the SGA via index scans and table accesses by RowID. The blocks read by the first query stay in the SGA. The second query selects data from a different part of the table—and is unable to use the table blocks already read into the SGA by the first query. The ordering of queries, and the operations they use, can impact their performance when they are paired as part of a larger batch transaction.

A second example of batch transactions that perform poorly involves data changes to tables. If the first transaction updates records in a table without committing the changes, a second transaction that queries the same data must repeatedly check the rollback segment involved in the first transaction. If the data from the first transaction had been committed, the additional query processing would not have been necessary.

Even if two transactions perform well separately, you cannot guarantee they will perform well together until you analyze their actions as a set. Typically, problems with batch performance are first noticed when the overall batch transaction performance grows worse. In many cases, the problem within the batch transaction is isolated to a small number of individual transactions or interactions between transactions.

Tune the Access to Individual Tables

Once the most offensive SQL statements in a consistent production environment have been tuned, you should evaluate the use of individual tables within your database. There are several categories of tables that are cause for greater attention during tuning efforts:

- *Frequently-used tables.* If a table is frequently used by multiple users, then tuning the access to the table should have a positive impact on performance for multiple users. Make sure the most frequently used tables are properly indexed, since they are likely to be frequently joined to other tables or to have limiting conditions on their columns. Frequently-used tables may be moved to different disks to reduce I/O contention. You should also make sure the table's indexes are stored in a different tablespace; by storing the tablespaces' datafiles on different disks, you can reduce I/O contention between a table and its indexes.

- *Extremely large tables.* Tables that are significantly larger than your SGA's data block buffer cache require special attention during tuning efforts. The performance management techniques for queries involving very large tables differ significantly from those used for smaller tables.

- *Extremely volatile tables.* Tables that have a high ratio of insert and delete versus updates (such as GL_INTERFACE in Oracle Financials) or tables that have high volume of updates to indexed columns should be looked at very carefully for reorganization opportunities (see Chapter 5 for information on index and table stagnation).

- *Remote tables.* If queries reference database objects via database links, you need to be particularly careful during your tuning efforts. The selection of driving tables for NESTED LOOPS joins involving remote tables is particularly important.

Chapter 11 provides tuning tips specific to each of these categories.

Using the Optimizers

When using the Oracle optimizers, there are three primary options available. The mode used for optimization is set via the OPTIMIZER_MODE parameter in each instance's init.ora file; it can be overridden via the **alter session set optimizer_goal** command and via the use of hints (see the "Using Hints" section of Chapter 10). Valid values for the optimizer goal are COST, RULE, and CHOOSE. As of Oracle7.2, you can also specify FIRST_ROWS and ALL_ROWS as the optimizer goal, although it is usually preferable to use either RULE or COST.

The Rule-Based Optimizer

Rule-based optimization uses syntactical rules to evaluate the different execution paths that a query could use. Each possible execution path is graded, and the one with the best score is used to perform the query. Unless you have specifically tuned your queries to use rule-based optimization, it is possible that some of them will perform poorly using this option.

The Cost-Based Optimizer

If you have analyzed your tables and indexes, then the *cost-based optimizer* can use statistics gathered about those objects to evaluate the available execution paths. The cost-based optimizer will know how many records are in each table and how selective each index is. In Oracle7.3, the cost-based optimizer can also know about the distribution of data values within a table. All of these statistics will be used when evaluating the potential execution paths, and the execution path with the lowest estimated "cost" will be selected. The statistics are gathered each time you run the **analyze** command for the objects (see the "Implementing the Cost-Based Optimizer" section later in this chapter).

A Hybrid Approach

You may choose to use cost-based optimization for some queries and rule-based optimization for others. This hybrid approach is usually seen in new versions of old applications. For example, the existing queries that were tuned with rule-based optimization may continue to use that option, while new tables added to the application are analyzed, and thus can use cost-based optimization. In general, a hybrid approach in which you don't control which optimizer is used is not advisable. If you want to use both the cost-based and the rule-based optimizers, you should use the cost-based optimizer, and use the RULE hint to override it when necessary.

If your OPTIMIZER_MODE value in init.ora is set to CHOOSE, Oracle will use cost-based optimization if statistics are available on the tables involved in a query. If some of the tables have not been analyzed, the optimizer may choose to perform full-table scans on those tables. Since multiple large full-table scans will likely harm the performance of a query, users of the cost-based optimizer should make sure that all tables involved in a query have been analyzed.

NOTE
CHOOSE is helpful if queries reference either all-analyzed tables or all-nonanalyzed tables. If a query references both analyzed and nonanalyzed tables, and CHOOSE is the optimizer mode, then the optimizer may use a nonoptimal execution path.

Selecting the Optimizer

In general, the hybrid approach is very difficult to manage if more than a few queries are involved. For example, if the optimizer goal is set to COST, you will need to regularly analyze the tables used by queries using the cost-based optimizer. On the other hand, if the optimizer goal is RULE, and the tables within an application grow at different rates, the best execution path may change—and the optimizer will not use it unless you change the syntax of the query.

Change is constant. The rule-based optimizer does not allow you to handle changes to the data without also making changes to the application code that accesses the data. Since the cost-based optimizer allows the execution path to change as the data changes, you should use the cost-based optimizer where appropriate. You can still use rule-based optimization for specific queries via the use of the RULE hint (see the "Using Hints" section of Chapter 10). Using a RULE hint in a query will clearly label it as a query that has been specifically tuned for rule-based optimization.

Oracle's implementation of its cost-based optimizer has rapidly improved with each release of Oracle7. Oracle has continued to add new features to it (see Chapter 13 for information on the data histogram features), and has continued to improve its existing features. As a result, performance when using the cost-based optimizer should be consistently predictable. Although the RULE hint may be available in Oracle8, the role of rule-based optimization will probably diminish over time, and you should begin converting to cost-based optimization if you have not already done so.

Implementing the Cost-Based Optimizer

Effective use of the cost-based optimizer requires that the tables and indexes in your application be analyzed regularly. The frequency with which you analyze the objects depends on the rate of change within the objects. For batch transaction applications, you should re-analyze the objects after each large set of batch transactions. For OLTP applications, you should re-analyze the objects on a time-based schedule (such as via a weekly or nightly process).

Statistics on objects are gathered via the **analyze** command. If you analyze a table, then its associated indexes are automatically analyzed as well. In Oracle7.3, you can specify that only the table be re-analyzed, but this should only be done if the only changes to the table were in nonindexed columns. Also in Oracle7.3, you can analyze only the indexed columns, speeding the analysis process. In general, you should analyze a table's indexes each time you analyze the table. In the following listing, the COMPANY table and all of its indexes are completely scanned and their statistics are gathered by the first **analyze** command. The second command, for Oracle7.3 and above, analyzes just the table and its indexed columns.

```
analyze table COMPANY compute statistics;
analyze table COMPANY compute statistics for table
    for all indexed columns;
```

The statistics on the COMPANY table and its indexes can be viewed via DBA_TABLES, DBA_TAB_COLUMNS, and DBA_INDEXES. For example, the Distinct_Keys column of DBA_INDEXES displays the number of distinct keys in an index; the Num_Rows column of DBA_TABLES displays the number of rows within a table. See the "Use Only Selective Indexes" section of Chapter 11 for further information on the use of the **analyze** command.

To **analyze** all objects in a schema, you can use the ANALYZE_SCHEMA procedure within the DBMS_UTILITY package. As shown in the following listing, it has two parameters: the name of the schema, and the **analyze** option used (**compute** or **estimate**).

```
execute DBMS_UTILITY.ANALYZE_SCHEMA('APPOWNER','COMPUTE');
```

When the command in the preceding listing is executed, all of the objects belonging to the APPOWNER schema will be analyzed, using the **compute statistics** option of the **analyze** command. If you are using rule-based optimization, then the statistics, although not used during the optimization process, will provide useful information to the developers during the query tuning process.

Implications of compute statistics
In the examples in the preceding section, the **compute statistics** option of the **analyze** command was used to gather statistics about objects. Oracle also provides an **estimate statistics** option, which, by default, scans only the first 1064 rows of a table during its analysis. The **estimate statistics** option, therefore, may not be appropriate if your tables will be growing—since values in new records added to the table might not be considered during subsequent analyses of the table. If you

choose to use **estimate statistics**, analyze as much of the table as possible (you can specify a percentage of the rows to analyze)—at least 10 percent. If you do not analyze enough of the table, your statistics will not accurately reflect the data in the table; in the first releases of Oracle7.0, failing to analyze enough rows in the table could cause ORA-0600 errors during queries of the table.

To generate the most accurate statistics, you should use the **compute statistics** option wherever possible. There are, however, management issues associated with the **compute statistics** option of the **analyze** command. Specifically, **compute statistics** can require large amounts of temporary segment space (up to four times the size of the table). You need to make sure that the user performing the analysis has the proper temporary tablespace settings and that the temporary tablespace can handle the space requirements. As the table grows over time, the temporary segment space requirements of **compute statistics** will grow. Although **compute statistics** places an additional management burden on the system, the benefits gained from the use of accurate statistics should outweigh the management burdens.

Additional Optimizer Goals

As new versions of Oracle7 are released, new optimizer goals are made available. For example, as of Oracle7.2, you can set the instance's OPTIMIZER_MODE value to ALL_ROWS. You should be very careful when using these goals, since they apply to all transactions within the instance—including the RBDMS's transactions against the data dictionary tables. If you can get acceptable performance from COST or RULE, use them. Handle exceptions by means of embedded hints.

Where to Go Next

At the start of this chapter, a five-step approach to tuning was provided. As part of ensuring a consistent production environment, you should perform the monitoring and environment tuning described in Chapters 8 and 9. If your database environment is already well-tuned and appropriately monitored, you should read through the operations descriptions in Chapter 10, followed by the detailed tuning tips provided in Chapter 11. Chapters 12 and 13 offer advice on the usage of advanced tuning options, such as hash joins and the Parallel Query Option. Before spending a great deal of time tuning your SQL, first make sure you have guaranteed that your production environment is both consistent and appropriate for your application.

CHAPTER 8

Monitoring

Monitoring your database is the only way to be sure that it is performing consistently. Although monitoring the database environment can reveal a critical flaw in the environment, more commonly it eliminates the environment as a factor in performance problems.

In this chapter, you will see the different types of monitoring available and the focus is on the internal statistics provided by Oracle. You'll see the issues regarding the internal statistics' ranges and precision, followed by instructions for gathering the statistics during specific time intervals. Each of the major statistics provided by Oracle is then described so that you will be able to properly interpret the statistics—and understand the environment changes necessary to resolve any indicated problems.

In Chapter 9, you will see the tuning objectives directly related to the monitored statistics. To evaluate your database against those objectives, you should first gather and interpret the database statistics, as described in this chapter.

Types of Monitoring

Database environment monitoring efforts can be divided into two major classifications. The first involves notification in the event of a database service outage. Events that cause outages include:

- *The failure of an instance.* If a database is shutdown, no one can access it.

- *The failure of SQL*Net.* If the SQL*Net V1 "orasrv" process or the SQL*Net V2 "Listener" process is shutdown or is not working properly, new connections to the database via SQL*Net will be prevented, and restarting SQL*Net to correct the problem will disconnect the current users.

- *The filling of the archived redo log file destination disk.* If the database is in ARCHIVELOG mode and there is no free space in the archived redo log file destination directory, no new database actions will be allowed until space is freed for new archived redo log files.

In addition to database-related causes of a database service outage, you also need to monitor the environment in which the database operates. The environment usually includes a server component and a network component. If possible, you should establish a common monitoring program for all components that affect the database service availability.

A system that can monitor for database availability can usually be expanded to track critical factors about the database over time, and report trends in the changes of specified values. For example, you may use the monitoring tool to track the percentage of free space within a tablespace, and generate trend reports allowing you to estimate when the tablespace will no longer be able to support its space requirements. Thus, monitoring tools can be used to both report on events and predict future events (such as a lack of free space in a tablespace).

The second class of monitoring tools is used to monitor the database in an ad hoc fashion. Although the database may be available for users, there may be an environmental factor that causes performance problems—which may be significant enough that the application using the database is unable to meet its goals for transaction performance. If this is the case, the database service is effectively unavailable. If the database environment is not part of the problem, you will need to check individual SQL statements for performance problems (as described in Chapters 10 and 11).

There are three types of monitors for Oracle databases: client-centric, server-centric, and hybrid (also known as client/agent). Each type of monitor has advantages and disadvantages. The advantages of a *client-centric* monitor are that it is easy to install and operate, and that it inflicts overhead on the monitored system only when the tool is being actively used. However, client-centric monitoring tools have limited capabilities for detecting database service outages; therefore, they are effective as ad hoc monitoring tools but not for service outage monitoring.

Server-centric monitoring tools continuously poll the database for status information (at custom-defined intervals). The constant polling creates steady overhead on the application; however, it enables these products to perform database service outage monitoring and trend monitoring. Because they are server-centric, the user interface for these tools may be more difficult to use than that of the client-centric tools.

A *hybrid* solution uses agents on the server to monitor for service outages but has a client front-end that can connect to the database. With a hybrid solution, you can use the monitoring tool as both a service outage monitor and an ad hoc monitor.

Most monitors get information from the database using three main sources:

- *V$ and X$ views*—structures inside Oracle that record statistics about the database.

- *Oracle SNMP MIB*—SNMP (Simple Network Management Protocol) is a common communications protocol for collecting management information from devices on a network. The information is collected by "agents" in the devices and recorded in the MIB (Management Information Base). SNMP management utilities can collect the MIB information and present it to an administrator or operator on a management console.

- *Oracle's monitoring API*—a set of Oracle programs that can be used to report performance statistics to calling programs.

The most common data source—and the one that can be easily used by every DBA—is the set of dynamic performance tables known as the *V$ views*. These views, whose names start with "V$", are derived from views of the memory structures Oracle uses to run the database. The low-level views of the memory structures are called the "X$" views because their names all start with "X$". The V$ views query the X$ views. The view syntax of the V$ views is defined in the Oracle software and is not part of the data dictionary. On top of the V$ views, the Oracle installation routines generate views called the V_$ views. The V_$ views are based on the V$ views.

For example, V$SESSION can be queried for user session-related information. In fact, V$SESSION is a public synonym for a SYS-owned view named V_$SESSION. V_$SESSION, in turn, is a view of SYS.V$SESSION—which is a view of a X$KSUSE. No user but SYS can select from X$KSUSE, so the public synonym V$SESSION gives non-SYS users a way to see the statistical information available via X$KSUSE.

There are a number of third-party tools available to complement Oracle's ad hoc monitoring tools (such as Server Manager and, as of Oracle7.3, Enterprise Manager). Most ad hoc monitoring tools use the internal V$ statistics views to generate statistics about the database. The utlbstat.sql and utlestat.sql scripts, which are useful for monitoring statistics during predetermined intervals, provide information on the database environment during specific periods of time. All of these ad hoc tools rely on Oracle's internal statistics. In the following section, you will see the limitations of these statistics, followed by descriptions of the major statistics available.

Oracle Performance Statistics Issues

Oracle's V$SESSTAT and V$SYSSTAT views contain a large number of statistics. In the following sections, you will see general information regarding the interpretation of statistics and specific information about the usage of the major statistics.

The internal statistics were added to the Oracle kernel to help debug Oracle and, later, to help tune Oracle's performance on industry-standard benchmarks. The V$ tables were not designed to be a public method to monitor Oracle activity. Because they were not originally designed for public use, there are potential inconsistencies with the interpretation and overall function of the V$ views. Starting with Oracle7.2, Oracle has significantly improved the consistency of the statistics in the V$ views. In the following sections, you will see the key considerations when interpreting the statistics.

Value Ranges

In Oracle versions prior to Oracle7.3, the statistics are stored as 32-bit unsigned counters. This storage method means that statistics values can only range between 0 and 2,147,483,647. Although this may seem to be an unreachable value, it is too small for time, memory, and buffer access statistics. If the counter exceeds the maximum value in its range, it wraps around and starts from 0 again. Furthermore, when selecting from the V$SYSSTAT using SQL*Plus, the numbers are returned as signed 32-bit counters; so numbers greater than 1,073,741,823 will appear as *negative* numbers. When the upper limit of a value is exceeded, or when a statistic is returned as a negative number, all derived calculations will return an erroneous value.

For example, suppose a database is accessing the buffer 2000 times per second. In one day there will be 172,800,00 buffer accesses. After a single week of continuous operation the 'consistent gets' statistic, instead of reading

1,209,600,000, will be a negative number. After two weeks, the 'consistent get' reading will exceed two billion (internally) and will appear to start from 0 again. Thus, after the first week, the hit ratio (see Chapter 3) will show a nonsensical reading! As of Oracle7.3, some of the statistics are now stored as double long integers. Among the statistics that changed are those related to logical reads; this change significantly reduces the value range problem.

Precision

Several of the available statistics are incremented in an inconsistent fashion. For example, there are cases in which a sort is being used and the sort count does not increment; cases in which the number of executions in the SQL cache statistics table and the V$ statistics tables do not match; and times when the number of physical reads in the V$FILESTAT view does not match the 'physical read' count in the V$ statistics tables. Additionally, there is no read consistency mechanism when reading from the V$ statistics tables, so while you are reading, the data in the internal statistics views is changing.

It is difficult to monitor a database without influencing the database via the monitoring program. For example, if you periodically select free space statistics from a database, the queries for that information use the database to return that information—and the internal database statistics reflect the database operations used to resolve the free space query. If you are monitoring statistics that are unrelated to memory and I/O issues, the effect may be negligible. However, if you are using the V$ views for memory or I/O monitoring, all of your queries against the V$ views affect the data in the V$ views. You should therefore expect that the precision of the values selected from the V$ views is indeterminate.

Performance of the Statistics Views

The performance of queries against the V$SYSSTAT view is reasonable. Every access to V$SYSSTAT is equivalent to a full table scan of a table with fewer than 200 rows (145 rows in Oracle7.3.2), with no physical reads. When accessing the V$SESSTAT view, some accesses scan a table that is equivalent to 145 times the maximum number of sessions that can be opened (as defined in the SESSIONS parameter in the init.ora configuration file). For example, suppose your database has 50 concurrent users. You may choose to define the SESSION parameter at 200 to avoid reaching the maximum number of allowable users. Every time you want to see how many logical reads a user has done (from V$SESSTAT), Oracle will execute the equivalent of a 200*145 = 29,000-row table scan. The V$SESSTAT query will execute many logical reads even if only one user is actually connected to the database.

As of Oracle7.2 (and improved in Oracle7.3), the database enables use of a key (similar to an index) when accessing the statistics based on some key criteria. For example, the V$SESSTAT is keyed by columns named SID (Session ID) and Statistic# (the identifying number for the statistic). If you can specify the SID or the Statistic# as a limiting condition for your query of V$SESSTAT, the access time to the statistics will be reasonable. For most practical usage, the addition of the key significantly resolves the performance problems. User SID values can be selected from V$SESSION; Statistic# values can be selected from V$SYSSTAT.

Naming

The statistics are organized into groups; each subgroup usually corresponds to a sub-development group in the Oracle kernel development team or to some function of the database. In many cases, the statistics were added to views with no naming convention in mind. As a result, the name used may not be descriptive (or may even be misleading). For example, in the case of physical reads, the 'physical reads' statistic is counted in blocks in V$SYSSTAT; in the V$FILESTAT view, the 'physical reads' statistic is counted in read requests and the 'physical block reads' statistic in blocks.

Gathering the Statistics

You can query V$SYSSTAT to see the cumulative statistics for the database since the last time the database was started. The cumulative statistics will reflect all of the database activity since it was opened—including the initial population of the SGA.

Often, you may need to measure the statistics during a specific interval. Doing so will allow you to discount the impact of the database startup activities. For example, when the database is first started, the data block buffer cache is empty. The first queries against the database will result in physical reads no matter how well-tuned they are—since the data block buffer cache doesn't contain the query's data yet, the query cannot be resolved via data already in memory. Therefore, the cumulative hit ratio, which measures the percentage of block reads read from memory, will always be depressed because of the physical reads that occur during the first queries following database startup.

To measure the statistics for a specific interval, you can use the utlbstat.sql and utlestat.sql scripts provided by Oracle. The scripts are located in the /rdbms/admin subdirectory under the Oracle software home directory. At the start of the period you wish to monitor, run the utlbstat.sql script from within SQLDBA (or within Server Manager, for Oracle7.1 and above), while connected as INTERNAL. The following listing shows the running of the utlbstat.sql script from within the Server Manager line mode interface.

```
> svrmgrl
SVRMGR> connect internal;
Connected.
SVRMGR> @$ORACLE_HOME/rdbms/admin/utlbstat
```

The utlbstat.sql script creates tables that record the current cumulative statistics for a number of statistics tables, as well as empty tables that will later store the statistics at the end of the monitoring period.

At the end of the monitoring period, run the utlestat.sql script from within SQLDBA or Server Manager, as shown in the following listing.

```
> svrmgrl
SVRMGR> connect internal;
Connected.
SVRMGR> @$ORACLE_HOME/rdbms/admin/utlestat
```

The utlestat.sql script will populate the statistics tables with the cumulative statistics at the end of the monitoring period. It will then generate a report (named report.txt) that shows the differences in the cumulative statistics between the time that utlbstat.sql was run and the time that utlestat.sql was run. You can therefore determine the statistics for the database during any given time interval—provided that the database is not shutdown during the time interval (which would reset the statistics), and that the time period is not too long (see the previous section on "Value Ranges").

Most server-centric and hybrid monitoring tools allow you to monitor the database for changes in cumulative statistics during particular time periods. Most client-centric tuning tools let you see the cumulative statistics but do not let you specify monitoring intervals. Regardless of the monitoring tool you use, you can supplement it with utlbstat.sql and utlestat.sql to refine the statistics monitoring process for use during specific database activity periods.

To see the cumulative statistics at any time, you can directly query V$SYSSTAT, as shown in the following listing.

```
select Name,
       Value
  from V$SYSSTAT
 order by Name;
```

NOTE
The output from this query of V$SYSSTAT will be shown throughout this chapter, using a sample database that includes both batch and OLTP characteristics.

In the following section, you will see how to interpret the systemwide V$SYSSTAT statistics. The interpretation of the file I/O statistics of the V$FILESTAT view is discussed in Chapter 4.

Interpreting the Statistics

In the following sections, the major statistics from V$SYSSTAT are grouped according to the database actions they monitor. The groups are:

Query Processing	Statistics directly associated with retrieving and sorting data for queries
Transaction Management	Statistics related to the processing of data changes
Memory and CPU Usage	Statistics related to the management of memory and CPU resources in the database
Database Management	Statistics related to the database's background processing
User Statistics	Statistics related to user actions

In the following sections, you will see descriptions of the major statistics within the categories listed. Since many of the statistics deal with memory areas, some of them cross categories. In those cases, the statistics are shown in only one category.

Query Processing

The statistics within the Query Processing category describe how Oracle retrieves data. The Query Processing category includes the statistics used to calculate the hit ratio for the database.

'Consistent Gets'

The 'consistent gets' statistic reflects the number of accesses made to the block buffer to retrieve data in a consistent mode. Most accesses to the buffer are done with the consistent get mechanism, which uses the SCN (System Change Number) to make sure the data being read has not changed since the query was started. The 'consistent gets' statistic is incremented in the following ways, according to the operation performed:

■ *For full table scans:* 'consistent gets' increments by 1 per block read.

■ *For table access through the index:* 'consistent gets' increments by Index height (usually 2) + 2 * keys in the range.

The number of consistent gets when reading table data using an index is much higher than when doing a full table scan because there are two gets for every row during the index-based read, while in a table scan there is one consistent get per block.

■ *For access inside the index only:* 'consistent gets' increments by 1 per block read. If the SQL statement accesses only columns that are stored in an index, there will be no access to tables. Accessing data via index-only reads is the shortest path to the data.

'db Block Gets'

The 'db block gets' statistic reflects the number of blocks accessed via single block gets (i.e., *not* through the consistent get mechanism). The 'db block gets' statistic number is incremented when a block is read for update and when segment header blocks are accessed. Segment header blocks are accessed for multiple purposes, including extent allocation, update of the highwatermark (see Chapter 2), and rollback segment mapping.

The sum of 'consistent gets' and 'db block gets' is the total number of logical reads performed by the database. To see the 'consistent gets' and 'db block gets' statistics on a user-by-user basis, query the Consistent_Gets and Block_Gets columns of V$SESS_IO.

'Physical Reads'

The 'physical reads' statistic reflects the cumulative number of blocks read from disk. The statistic's value is incremented once per read block regardless of whether the read request was for a multiblock read or a single block read. Most physical reads load data, index, and rollback blocks from the disk into the buffer cache. However, if the SORT_DIRECT_WRITE init.ora parameter is set to TRUE or AUTO, physical reads from temporary segments place blocks directly into the session's sort area.

Physical reads are initiated by logical reads (except in the case of reads from temporary segments, which do not count as logical reads). The overall hit ratio for the data block buffer cache is derived by subtracting the number of physical reads from the number of logical reads, and dividing the difference by the number of logical reads. See Chapter 3 for information on setting target values for your database's hit ratio.

The following listing shows sample output for the statistics used to calculate the hit ratio. For the values displayed, the logical reads total is 103,024,687. Since there were 12,953,867 physical reads required to satisfy the logical reads, the hit ratio is 87.43—(103024687-12953867)/103024867. This hit ratio value is below the minimum target hit ratio value of 89 percent (see Chapter 3).

```
consistent gets                  97363982
db block gets                     5660705
physical reads                   12953867
```

To see the hit ratio on a session-by-session basis, query V$SESS_IO. V$SESS_IO can be joined to V$SESSION by the SID column, allowing you to select the Username as part of the query. See Chapter 3 for a sample user hit ratio listing.

'Physical Writes'

The 'physical writes' statistic reflects the cumulative number of blocks written to disk. The statistic's value is incremented once per block written regardless of whether the write request was for a multiblock or single block write. Most physical writes are done by the DBWR background processes. The DBWR process writes modified data, index, and rollback blocks from the SGA's buffer cache to disk. Writes to temporary segments are executed by the user and the blocks may be taken directly from the session's sort area.

'Write Requests'

The 'write requests' statistic reflects the cumulative number of write requests. The ratio of 'physical writes' to 'write requests' shows the average number of blocks written in a single write to the database. If your application is batch-oriented and write-intensive, you may be able to reduce write contention by increasing the number of DBWR processes available (by increasing the DB_WRITER init.ora parameter). Doing so helps to reduce contention for free buffers within the data block buffer cache.

'db Block Changes'

The 'db block changes' statistic reflects the cumulative number of modified blocks chained to the "dirty" list. Once the block is in the "dirty" list, additional changes to that block are not counted as block changes. If a block was written to disk and removed from the "dirty" list, the next change will cause the 'db block changes' statistic's value to increment. This statistic cannot be used to show the number of rows updated, nor does it represent the number of blocks updated—at best it is a combination of both.

'Consistent Changes' and 'Data Blocks Consistent Reads– Undo Records Applied'

The name of the 'consistent changes' statistic is misleading. It does not indicate the number of updates (or changes), but rather, the number of times a consistent get had to retrieve an "old" version of a block because of updates that occurred after the cursor had been opened. A report or batch job that causes a high 'consistent changes' value may be a precursor for a 'snapshot too old' situation (see Chapter 7). As of Oracle7.3, a more accurate statistic was added. Named 'data blocks consistent reads—undo records applied', the new statistic gives the actual number of data records applied.

'Table Scans (Short Tables)' and 'Table Scans (Long Tables)'

The 'table scans (short tables)' and 'table scans (long tables)', added together, reflect the cumulative number of full table scans. Until Oracle7.2, a table is classified as "short" or "long" by comparing the table's size with the _SMALL_TABLE_THRESHOLD init.ora parameter (this parameter is no longer used in Oracle7.3). Since Oracle7.2, every cached table (see Chapter 3) is classified as "short" as well as any table under 5 database blocks in size (as defined by the highwatermark for the table).

When a "long" table scan is executed, the blocks fetched from disk are marked as "old" as soon as the application finishes scanning through them. These blocks will be first on the list to age out of the buffer cache. The result is that even if many users scan the same table, there will be only limited caching among the users, and limited reuse of the same blocks within the data block buffer cache of the SGA. When a "short" table scan is executed, the blocks are loaded into the Least Recently Used list (see Chapter 3), which improves their chance of staying in the buffer long enough to be "hit" by multiple scanning users. The highwatermark for a table, which determines its "size," is incremented every time a new block is inserted into the table. However, the highwatermark is *not* decreased even if all of the rows are deleted from the table (see Chapter 2). For large instances with enough memory and a large data block buffer cache, using the **cache** option for small tables should translate into fewer physical reads and better overall performance for short full table scans.

The sample output in the following listing shows that full table scans are used frequently for small tables; however, there have been over 7000 full table scans of "large" tables, possibly contributing to the unacceptable hit ratio shown previously in this chapter.

```
table scans (long tables)              7202
table scans (short tables)           192089
```

'Table Scans (Cache Partitions)' and 'Table Scans (RowID Ranges)'

The 'table scans (cache partitions)' and 'table scans (rowid ranges)' statistics are used with the Parallel Query option. The number of RowID ranges corresponds to the number of simultaneous query server processes that scan the table (see Chapter 12).

'Table Scans Rows Gotten' and 'Table Scan Blocks Gotten'

The 'table scans rows gotten' statistic reflects the cumulative number of rows read for full table scans. The 'table scan blocks gotten' statistic reflects the cumulative number of blocks read for full table scans.

'Table Fetch by RowID'

The 'table fetch by rowid' statistic reflects the cumulative number of rows fetched from tables using a TABLE ACCESS BY ROWID operation. Usually, table fetch with RowID is the result of an index access. The consistent gets inside the index do not cause this statistic's value to increment.

'Table Fetch Continued Row'

The 'table fetch continued row' statistic reflects the cumulative number of continued rows fetched. This statistic's value is incremented when accessing a row that is longer than a block in length and when accessing "migrated" rows. Migrated rows are rows that were relocated from their original location to a new location because of an **update** that increased their size to the point where they could no longer be accommodated inside their original block. Access to migrated rows will cause this statistic's value to increment only if the access is performed by RowID. Full table scans of tables that contain migrated rows do not cause this counter to increment.

The statistics value in the following listing shows that migrated rows have been accessed by RowID over 5000 times since the database was last started.

```
table fetch continued row                    5638
```

'Cluster Key Scans' and 'Cluster Key Scan Block Gets'

A cluster is a grouping of one or more tables. Records in a cluster with the same cluster key will be stored in physical proximity, in one or more cluster blocks. Cluster blocks are **not** equivalent to database blocks. The cluster block size is predefined in the **create cluster** statement. A cluster block may span one or more database blocks; alternatively, a database block may contain several cluster blocks.

The 'cluster scans' statistic reflects the number of requests for record reads for a given cluster key. The 'cluster key scan block gets' statistic reflects the number of database blocks accessed to retrieve a set of clustered records. When the records sharing the same key cannot fit in one cluster block, a *continuation cluster block* is allocated. When a cluster read request for this large set of records is received, multiple blocks are returned to satisfy the read request. If the ratio of blocks read to the number of scan requests is much greater than 1, there are too many continuation cluster blocks. Therefore, the cluster block's size—as defined by the **size** parameter when the cluster is created—is too small.

Oracle uses clusters to store some of the data dictionary tables. Usually, these clusters are sized much too small. As a result, most instances will have a large ratio of 'cluster Key Scan block gets' to 'cluster key scans'. In our benchmark tests, transactions on clustered tables are six to eight times slower than the same transactions on unclustered tables. The amount of rollback and redo log information created by the clustered tables is an order of magnitude greater than that created by transactions on unclustered tables. Because of the poor transaction processing performance, cluster loading and recovery can be very time-consuming. To derive the cluster's benefits (sorted data) without its costs (poor transaction performance), you should leave your tables unclustered and periodically unload all the data, sort it by the shared key, and reload it.

'Sorts (Memory)' and 'Sorts (Disk)'

The "sort" statistics record the sort activity. The 'sorts (memory)' statistic reflects the number of sorts small enough to be performed entirely in sort areas without using temporary segments. The 'sorts (disk)' statistic reflects the number of sorts that were large enough to require the use of temporary segments for sorting. The memory area available for sorting is set via the SORT_AREA_SIZE and SORT_AREA_RETAINED_SIZE init.ora parameters.

Rather than allocating the entire SORT_AREA_SIZE for every cursor that requires an **order by**, **group by**, or even **COUNT(*)**, memory is allocated from the sort area in small increments (8KB in our tests). After the last row is fetched from a cursor, the cursor is immediately invalidated and the sort area used by that cursor is freed for other cursors in the session to use. This improvement in memory management is especially important for SQL*Forms applications where all the cursors inside a form remain open until an **EXIT** or **NEWFRM** command is executed. Since the sort area is released after the last row is fetched from the cursor, one or two sort areas may be sufficient for the entire session. This means that the SORT_AREA_SIZE can be increased to several MB as memory permits—but be careful when setting a high sort area size if you are using the parallel options (see Chapter 12). You should set the SORT_AREA_RETAINED_SIZE to a much smaller number (a few KB), so users that need a lot of memory for only one sort release it after the sort is over.

The statistic values in the following listing show that sorts are performed in memory 99.66 percent of the time for the sample database; temporary segments are rarely used.

```
sorts (disk)              216
sorts (memory)          64048
```

Transaction Management

The statistics within the Transaction Management category describe how Oracle manages transactional data. There is an overlap of some statistics between the Query Processing and Transaction Management categories (since transactions may involve queries, and queries may be affected by data changes).

'Opened Cursors Current'
The 'opened cursors current' statistic reflects the number of the currently active SQL statements. To see the actual SQL statements, query SYS.V_$OPEN_CURSOR.

'Opened Cursors Cumulative'
The 'opened cursors cumulative' statistic reflects the cumulative number of cursors opened since the database was started. You can use this statistic's value to calculate the rate at which cursors are opened within the database.

'User Commits'
The 'user commits' statistic reflects the number of times users issued **commit** calls to the database. Commits may be executed explicitly via the **commit** command, or implicitly via DDL commands.

'User Rollbacks'
The 'user rollbacks' statistic reflects the number of **rollback** calls issued by users. From a performance standpoint, **rollback** is one of the most expensive database operations. A high ratio of **rollback**s to **commit**s may indicate a potential performance problem. However, SQL*Forms uses **commit** and **rollback** when exiting from a form, even if there were no **update**s, in case a lock was pending. A **rollback** with no transaction takes almost no resources.

The statistics in the following listing show that **commit**s account for over 98 percent of the transactions in the sample database.

```
user commits           10593
user rollbacks           197
```

'Redo Log Space Requests'
The 'redo log space requests' statistic reflects the number of times a user process waits for space in the redo log buffer area of the SGA. If the value of this statistic is

non-zero, you should increase the size of the redo log buffer area of the SGA (set via the LOG_BUFFER parameter in the init.ora file). Increasing the size of the online redo log files may also help decrease the number of waits associated with redo log entries.

The following listing, showing output from V$SYSSTAT, indicates that there are frequent waits in the redo log buffer area. The DBA should increase the size of the redo log buffer area.

```
redo log space requests            3169
```

To see how large the redo log buffer area is, you can query V$PARAMETER, as shown in the following listing.

```
select Name,
       Value
  from V$PARAMETER
 where Name = 'log_buffer';

NAME                               VALUE
-----------------------------      ------------------
log_buffer                         38912
```

'Redo Synch Writes'
The 'redo synch writes' statistic reflects the number of user commits, the number of checkpoints, and the number of log switches. The statistic's value is incremented every time a user commits, at every checkpoint and every log switch.

Memory and CPU Usage

The statistics within the Memory and CPU Usage category describe how Oracle manages its memory areas. There is an overlap of some statistics between the Query Processing and Memory and CPU Usage categories (since queries read data into and out of memory).

'Recursive Calls' and 'Recursive CPU Usage'
Recursive SQL statements are SQL statements that are generated by the Oracle kernel rather than by user applications. The 'recursive calls' statistic reflects the sum of the describe, parse, open, fetch, close, and execute calls of all recursive SQL statements. There are several types of recursive SQL statements, as described in the following sections. Some recursive activity—consisting of recursive calls and their associated CPU usage—is unavoidable.

For example, in the sample database there had been 103 million logical reads. To support those logical reads, there had been over 3 million recursive reads, as shown in the following listing.

```
recursive calls                3707963
```

Data Dictionary Cache Load   Whenever the database parses a SQL statement, it scans the text for syntax and semantic correctness. The semantic check requires cross-referencing of the information in the SQL statement and the data dictionary, including the table names, columns-to-table relationships, column names, data types, and security access privileges. To resolve the relationships, Oracle uses the data dictionary cache in the SGA. When the data sought is not in the cache, Oracle executes SQL statements to retrieve the data dictionary information from the SYSTEM tablespace into the dictionary cache. These statements for data dictionary information represent one type of recursive SQL statement. To reduce the number of recursive calls caused by statements of this type, the dictionary cache size should be increased. In Oracle7, the dictionary cache resides inside the shared pool area. To increase the size available to the dictionary cache, increase the size of the shared pool area (via the SHARED_POOL_SIZE init.ora parameter).

Data Dictionary Maintenance   When a DDL statement is received by the database, the statement is translated into a variety of DML statements that maintain the data dictionary tables. One **create table** statement, for example, can generate hundreds of **insert**s, **update**s, and **delete**s to the TAB$, COL$, and other data dictionary tables.

Object Allocation   When a table or an index is first created or requires a new extent for its storage, the database performs space management activities via two tables, UET$ (Used Extents Table) and FET$ (Free Extents Table). The manipulation of these tables is a relatively "expensive" operation, involving the execution of an average of four DML statements for each space allocation.

Because object allocation is costly in terms of the recursive calls it requires, temporary segment usage is costly from a performance standpoint. The allocation and release of each temporary segment requires the execution of about eight to ten DML statements. In Oracle7.3, you can define dedicated temporary tablespaces, thereby reducing the need to perform object allocation when using temporary segments (see Chapter 13).

PL/SQL Compilation   PL/SQL compilation uses recursive calls in much the same way as SQL statements do—for syntax and semantic correctness checks.

Execution of SQL Statements Inside PL/SQL Blocks   Probably the most misleading effect when measuring the number of recursive calls is the fact that when a SQL statement is executed inside a PL/SQL block, it is counted as a recursive statement, even though it is a user who actually caused the SQL statement to execute.

'Session Logical Reads'

The 'session logical reads' statistic is the sum of consistent gets and db block gets. Although its name starts with 'session', this statistic is recorded at the system level via V$SYSSTAT.

As shown earlier in this chapter, there were 103,024,687 logical reads in the database (as calculated by adding the values of the 'consistent gets' and 'db block gets' statistics). However, the 'session logical reads' statistic is not equal to this value! The value is off by 0.7 percent in this example because the V$ views' statistics are not maintained consistently. As described in the prior section on "Precision," the different V$ views are apparently updated at different times.

```
consistent gets            97363982
db block gets               5660705
session logical reads     102325777
```

'CPU Used When Call Started' and 'CPU Used by This Session'

The 'CPU' statistics record CPU usage in hundredths of seconds.

To calculate the amount of CPU used by the current SQL statement, use the equation shown in the following listing.

```
CPU used by current SQL = 'CPU used by this session'
                        - 'CPU used when call started'
```

To determine the CPU utilization for the current session, divide the 'CPU used by this session' statistic's value by the 'session connect time' statistic's value. The value for 'session connect time' will be 0 unless you have set TIMED_STATISTICS to TRUE in your database's init.ora file.

'Session UGA Memory', 'Session UGA Memory Max', 'Session PGA Memory', and 'Session PGA Memory Max'

In the V$SESSTAT table, the memory statistics show the amount of memory allocated to each user inside and outside the global area. In the V$SYSSTAT table, the memory statistics are the cumulative sum of memory allocated to all users since the instance started. The memory statistics are cumulative—they are *not* the total memory currently used by users. The memory statistics are useful only on the session level.

Database Management

The statistics within the Database Management category describe how Oracle manages its processes and internal messaging.

'Background Timeouts'
The 'background timeouts' statistic reflects the number of timeouts issued for Oracle background processes. This statistic's value is incremented every one to three seconds depending on the machine and operating system. On Sun/Solaris (like most other Unix operating systems), a timeout occurs approximately every 1.5 seconds.

'Messages Sent' and 'Messages Received'
The 'messages sent' and 'messages received' statistics reflect the communications between the various Oracle background processes. Generally, a message is sent every time a **commit** is made or a new connection to the database is opened.

'Enqueue Timeouts', 'Enqueue Waits', 'Enqueue Requests', and 'Enqueue Releases'
The enqueue-related statistics reflect the actions of the Oracle locking mechanisms. The locking scheme in Oracle is implemented via an enqueue mechanism. Whenever a lock is requested, an enqueue request is issued. When a **commit** or **rollback** occurs, the enqueue is released. The difference between the 'enqueue requests' statistics value and the 'enqueue releases' statistics value represents the number of locks currently being held and the number of requests that have timed out. If 'enqueue waits' is non-zero, there are not enough enqueues available in the database (as set via the ENQUEUE_RESOURCES init.ora parameter).

The following listing shows the value of the 'enqueue waits' statistic for the sample database. Since the value is non-zero, more enqueue resources should be added to the database.

```
enqueue waits                 51
```

'Free Buffer Requested', 'CR Blocks Created', and 'Current Blocks Converted for CR'
Free buffers in the data block buffer cache are requested for multiple reasons. When data is **insert**ed into the database, a free buffer is requested every time a new block is needed. On **update**s, free buffers are requested to contain the rollback

information. Overall, this is an indicator of how many new blocks are created, but because we cannot distinguish between database blocks, rollback blocks, and other blocks, these statistics are not useful except for a general analysis of buffer cache activity—which is better measured by the 'consistent gets', 'db block gets', and 'physical reads' statistics.

Buffer Waits

In addition to the statistics provided via V$SYSSTAT and V$SESSTAT, you can see statistics related to "wait" events in V$WAITSTAT. In versions of Oracle prior to Oracle7.3, the statistics in V$WAITSTAT were collectively reported under the 'buffer busy waits' statistic in V$SYSSTAT; that statistic is no longer used.

To see the V$WAITSTAT statistics classes and the number of times each type of wait has occurred, execute the query shown in the following listing.

```
select Class,
       Count
  from V$WAITSTAT;
```

V$WAITSTAT shows the number of times a user process had to wait for each of ten different types of buffers. Most of the buffer wait statistics will be zero; however, non-zero values for certain buffer statistics values in V$WAITSTAT indicate potential process conflicts in the database. Table 8-1 shows the common types of buffer waits and the most common diagnosis for each type of block contention.

'Recovery Blocks Read', 'Recovery Array Reads', and 'Recovery Array Read Time'

During a recovery operation, the recovery statistics monitor the rate of recovery. As of Oracle7.3, two new V$ views are available for monitoring the status of file recovery operations (see Chapter 13).

'SQL*Net Roundtrips to/from Client', 'Bytes Received via SQL*Net from Client', and 'Bytes Sent via SQL*Net to Client'

Several SQL*Net-related statistics are available as of Oracle7.2; they are reported via V$SYSSTAT and by using the **set autotrace on** command (see Chapter 10). These new Oracle7.2 statistics show the amount of traffic between a SQL*Net client and the server. The number of "round trips" is the number of times a message was sent and an acknowledgment received. The actual number of bytes sent and received is also shown. On a wide area network (WAN), the number of round trips may be more important than the number of bytes that is sent back and forth due to the inherent network latency. As a rule of thumb, network latency on a WAN could be as high as 1 millisecond per every 250 miles and 3 to 10 milliseconds for every

Buffer wait type	Diagnosis
'data blocks'	Usually occurs when there are too many modified blocks in the buffer cache; reduce contention by adding DBWR processes.
'sort blocks'	Rarely seen except when the Parallel Query option is used; reduce contention by reducing the degree of parallelism (see Chapter 12) or decreasing the SORT_AREA_SIZE init.ora parameter setting.
'segment header'	May occur when many full table scans execute simultaneously with data loading processes; aggravated by the parallel options. Reschedule data loading jobs to reduce contention.
'free list'	May occur if multiple data loading programs run simultaneously. If the loads must run simultaneously, see the "Scalable Buffer Cache" section of Chapter 13.
'undo header'	May occur if there are not enough rollback segments to support the number of concurrent transactions.
'undo block'	Very rarely occurs; may be caused by multiple users updating records in the same data block at a very fast rate; can usually resolve the contention by increasing the **pctfree** of the tables being modified.

TABLE 8-1.   *V$WAITSTAT Buffer Contention Types*

network router encountered. The network latency delay is in addition to the delay caused by the network bandwidth.

> **NOTE**
> In Oracle7.3, the **set autotrace on** command in SQL*Plus shows statistics related to each transaction as the transaction completes. The 'bytes sent via SQL*Net to client', 'bytes received via SQL*Net from client', and 'SQL*Net roundtrips to/from client' statistics are among the statistics automatically displayed for each transaction by **set autotrace on**.

'SQL*Net Roundtrips to/from dblink', 'Bytes Received via SQL*Net from dblink', and 'Bytes Sent via SQL*Net to dblink'

Several SQL*Net and database-related statistics are available as of Oracle7.3. These new Oracle7.3 statistics show the amount of traffic between instances using database links. The number of "round trips" is the number of times a message was sent and an acknowledgment received. The actual number of bytes sent and received is also shown.

If you are using NESTED LOOPS joins involving remote tables, you can use the 'SQL*Net roundtrips to/from dblink' statistic value to determine the impact of the execution path on the network traffic. See the "Limit Remote Table Accesses" section of Chapter 11 for information on tuning queries involving database links.

User Statistics

The statistics within the User Statistics category describe how Oracle manages its processes and internal messaging. Since some of the statistics are cumulative, you may need to know when the database was started. The startup time of the database can be queried from the V$INSTANCE view, as shown in the following listing.

```
select TO_CHAR(TO_DATE(D.Value,'J'),'MM/DD/YYYY')||' '||
       TO_CHAR(TO_DATE(S.Value,'SSSSS'),'HH24:MI:SS')
            Startup_Time
  from V$INSTANCE D, V$INSTANCE S
 where D.Key = 'STARTUP TIME - JULIAN'
   and S.Key = 'STARTUP TIME - SECONDS';
```

'Logons Cumulative'
The 'logons cumulative' statistic reflects the cumulative number of connections to the database (including the connection you used to query V$SYSSTAT for this value). This statistic's value is useful for calculating the connection rate.

'Logons Current'
The 'logons current' statistic reflects the current number of open sessions in the database. The process and session information for current users is available via V$SESSION and V$PROCESS. The V$LICENSE table shows the maximum number of users that were concurrently logged onto the database since it started.

'Parse Time CPU', 'Parse Time Elapsed', and 'Parse Count'
Parsing is the process of matching the SQL statement with the data dictionary, binding all bind variables, and creating the explain plan. Traditionally, parsing required 15 and 25 percent of the database activity. With the introduction of the shared SQL area in Oracle7, parsing overhead should not be that high. The parse-related statistics, however, do not show the improvements. The 'parse count' statistic is incremented for every parse request whether or not the SQL statement is already in the shared SQL area.

'Execute Count'

The 'execute count' statistic is incremented for every execute request and for every time a cursor is opened.

'User Calls'

The 'user calls' statistic reflects the number of calls from applications to the database. Calls can be any of the following: describe, parse, open, fetch, close, or execute. If a SQL statement fetches more than one row at a time, each array read will count as one user call. Therefore, user calls are not an accurate indication of the number of rows retrieved. In the past, the 'user calls' statistic was used to estimate the amount of network traffic. Today, with the new OCI (Oracle Call Interface) calls that group many actions together, 'user calls' no longer translates to a measure of network traffic.

'Session Connect Time' and 'Process Last Non-Idle Time'

The 'session connect time' and 'process last non-idle time' statistics measure time in units of hundredths of a second. The 'session connect time' statistic reflects the time the session connected. The 'session last non-idle time' statistic shows the timestamp of the last user call. The current timestamp can be queried via V$TIMER. The query shown in the following listing returns the time the current user was connected to the system (provided you have set TIMED_STATISTICS to TRUE in your database's init.ora file prior to the last database startup):

NOTE
This information is not available on all platforms.

```
select SID,TO_CHAR(SysDate - (Hsecs-S.Value)/(24*3600*100)
          ,'MM/DD/YYYY HH24:MI:SS')  Connection_Time
  from V$SESSTAT S, V$STATNAME N, V$TIMER
 where N.Name = 'session connect time'
   and N.Statistic# = S.Statistic#
   and S.Value != 0;
```

NOTE
The Hsecs column in V$TIMER returns the current time in hundredths of a second.

The following query will display the time the current user was last active. For the query to return data, you must have set TIMED_STATISTICS to TRUE in your database's init.ora file prior to its last startup.

```
select SID,TO_CHAR(SysDate - (Hsecs-S.Value)/(24*3600*100)
            ,'MM/DD/YYYY HH24:MI:SS')  Last_Non_Idle_Time
from V$SESSTAT S, V$STATNAME N, V$TIMER
where N.Name = 'process last non-idle time'
and N.Statistic# = S.Statistic#
and S.Value != 0;
```

Enterprise Manager

Enterprise Manager (EM), available from Oracle, is a hybrid database monitoring tool. EM has a client front-end that can connect to the database, along with agents that reside on servers. Presently available on the Windows NT operating system, EM can be used for database administration and monitoring.

EM's architecture is a departure from earlier Oracle tools such as SQLDBA and Server Manager. Its architecture includes:

- A centralized command center for multiple, distributed databases

- Distributed, intelligent agents located on servers throughout the network

- Integrated job scheduling across network servers

- A software distribution utility to simplify the process of installing and upgrading Oracle software

- A customizable client front-end tool for database object management

- Integration points for third-party tools

Each of the tools within EM uses the common EM architecture. A repository stores the messages received from intelligent agents via communication daemons, as shown in Figure 8-1. Information related to the tasks performed by the DBA is stored in the DBA's repository (which can be either a local or a remote database). When you connect to EM, you need to specify the connection information for the database in which your repository information is stored. Before attempting to use

Enterprise Manager Console

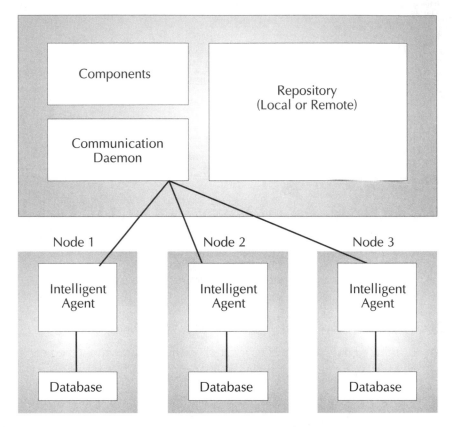

FIGURE 8-1. *Overview of Enterprise Manager Architecture*

EM's database administration commands, you should be sure you have enabled the proper database roles (such as DBA) or privileges (such as ALTER TABLESPACE).

To simplify the database monitoring and administration process, EM provides a core set of administration capabilities as well as a set of add-on products that can be purchased separately and integrated into your EM configuration. In the following sections, you will see descriptions of the components of EM.

Server Manager 2.3   A line-mode interface to Server Manager is used whenever you are using EM in a non-graphical mode. The line mode is used when running EM from batch jobs, such as for performing automated database shutdowns and startups.

Enterprise Manager Console   The EM Console is a collection of tools, including Navigator (to view and administer objects and users on the network), Map (to monitor the system), Job Scheduler (to schedule jobs across the servers), and Event Management (to monitor event status as reported by the agents). You can use the EM Console for most basic administration tasks, such as service outage reporting and user creation.

Database Administration Toolset   In addition to the EM Console capabilities, a number of components provided via EM are specifically created to aid in database administration (similar in function to the screens of Server Manager). The Database Administration Toolset of EM includes a Security Manager component, an Instance Manager, a Schema Manager, and a Storage Manager to simplify the execution of database administration commands. Backup Manager not only executes backup commands, it also provides a backup "wizard" to aid in the generation of backup scripts; Recovery Manager can be used to automate database recovery efforts. Data Manager provides an interface to the Export, Import, and SQL*Loader utilities. You can use Software Manager to distribute software packages to network servers, and a SQL Worksheet is provided to support SQL statements from within the Database Administration Toolset.

Enterprise Manager Performance Pack   In addition to the tools provided as part of EM, you can purchase several tools to facilitate the monitoring and administration of your database. The tools, collectively referred to as the EM Performance Pack, include:

- *Oracle Performance Manager*—for graphical display of database statistics, including the ability to drill down to the user session level.

- *Oracle Lock Manager*—to display the sessions that are waiting for or holding locks within the database.

- *Oracle TopSessions Monitor*—to display the top sessions for any statistic, allowing you to isolate the sessions executing the most resource-intensive SQL commands; the SQL being executed can be displayed along with its execution path.

- *Oracle Tablespace Manager*—to manage database storage space at the tablespace level, including the ability to drill down to the segment and extent level.

- *Oracle Expert*—to provide recommendations for performance improvements, based on an analysis of the database activity and system usage; "what if" scenarios can be used to generate capacity planning information.

- *Oracle Trace*—to monitor system statistics on an event-based rather than a time-based schedule; events to be monitored include contention for I/O services and insufficient size of the data block buffer cache (see the "Buffer Waits" and "Query Processing" sections earlier in this chapter).

Other Integrated Applications   In addition to the applications listed in the previous sections, EM also includes Oracle Replication Manager. Currently in Beta release, Oracle Replication Manager provides a graphical interface to the management of the Advanced Replication Option (see Chapter 13). A Computer-Based Training (CBT) program for EM is also included.

Developing a Monitoring Plan

Regardless of the monitoring tool you use, you should develop a set of statistics that should be monitored regularly. You can use time-based monitoring systems to detect trends in the system resource usage, and event-based monitoring systems to further investigate the cause of performance problems you have detected. All of the tools use the Oracle internal statistics, so it is important to understand their usage in order to best monitor your database. Once those internal statistics are being monitored, you can begin to tune your environment.

If the environment is tuned, it will be a less likely source of performance problems. Most likely, performance problems will be caused by a small number of offensive SQL statements that require more system resources than are available in the environment. In Chapter 9, you will see how to use the internal statistics to tune your environment.

CHAPTER 9

Environment Tuning

A tuned environment is an essential part of an effective database. If the database environment has not been tuned, the environment may negatively impact every transaction that users execute, regardless of the efficiency of the transaction. In this chapter, you will see the basic building blocks of a successful database application environment.

In this chapter, you will see advice on key init.ora parameters that influence the performance of your database environment. Later sections of the chapter cover tuning of the components of the environment—memory, CPU, I/O, and networking—in greater depth. While this chapter provides an overview of environment tuning issues, Chapters 3 and 4 provide detailed discussions of CPU, memory, and I/O tuning options. In this chapter, all of the environmental factors are considered relative to their cumulative effect on the database's operating environment.

Key init.ora Parameters

Most of the important init.ora parameters are explained throughout this book where appropriate. Of the many parameters provided by Oracle, you need to focus on ten of them to establish a sound database environment.

DB_BLOCK_SIZE

The DB_BLOCK_SIZE parameter is set when the database is created; it determines the size of each block within the database. You cannot change the block size of an existing database; the only method available for increasing the block size is to perform a full database Export, recreate the database with a different DB_BLOCK_SIZE value, and Import the database. The full recreation of the database is typically a costly operation in terms of time, effort, and crisis level. Therefore, you should be sure to set the proper database block size when the database is first created.

In most environments, the default value for DB_BLOCK_SIZE is 2048 bytes (2KB). If your operating environment permits, you should increase this value to 4KB, 8KB, or higher. The performance gains obtained by using a larger block size are significant for both OLTP and batch applications. In general, each doubling of the database block size will reduce the time required for I/O-intensive batch operations by around 40 percent. As the database block size increases, your overall memory requirements may increase.

DB_BLOCK_BUFFERS

The DB_BLOCK_BUFFERS parameter sets the size, in database blocks, of the data block buffer cache in the SGA. The larger the data block buffer cache is, the more memory will be available for sharing data already in memory among users—reducing the need for physical reads. You can determine the effectiveness of the data block buffer cache by measuring the hit ratio of the database. See Chapter 3 for a description of the factors that impact the hit ratio, and Chapter 8 for statistics to monitor.

The init.ora file provides three DB_BLOCK_BUFFERS values by default (labeled as 'SMALL', 'MEDIUM', and 'LARGE'). The labels refer to the number of users; a 'MEDIUM' database has six to ten concurrent users. If you have fewer than six, start with the 'SMALL' setting; if more than ten, start with the 'LARGE' setting. Once the database has been in use, monitor the hit ratio to determine if the DB_BLOCK_BUFFERS setting needs to be increased. If you have few users, the

'SMALL' or 'MEDIUM' setting may be appropriate; otherwise, you will need to use settings at or above 'LARGE'. In general, the size of the data block buffer cache should be about 1 to 2 percent of the size of the physical database.

SHARED_POOL_SIZE

The SHARED_POOL_SIZE parameter sets the size, in bytes, of the shared pool in the SGA. As described in Chapter 3, the shared pool stores data for the library cache and (for systems using the Multi-Threaded Server) session-specific data, plus the shared SQL area. If your application is OLTP-oriented, and you use packages and other procedural objects, you'll need a large shared SQL area. In environments using a large number of procedural objects, the size of your shared pool may exceed your data block buffer cache. If you use the Multi-Threaded Server (MTS), you may need to double the size of your shared pool from its pre-MTS size. See Chapter 6 for information on pinning packages in the shared SQL area.

The init.ora file provides three SHARED_POOL_SIZE values by default (labeled as 'SMALL', 'MEDIUM', and 'LARGE'). Do not use anything except the 'LARGE' setting as a default value unless you are not using any procedural objects or the MTS. If you have many users, you should increase the SHARED_POOL_SIZE parameter each time you increase the DB_BLOCK_BUFFERS parameter. The more procedural objects you have, the larger your shared pool should be; in package-intensive applications, it is common for the shared pool to be larger than the data block buffer cache.

LOG_BUFFER

The LOG_BUFFER parameter sets the size, in bytes, of the redo log buffer area in the SGA. The default is set to four times the maximum database block size for the operating system. For an OLTP application in which many users perform transactions, the LOG_BUFFER parameter needs to be increased beyond its default value. If the 'redo log space requests' statistic in V$SYSSTAT (see Chapter 8) is non-zero, you should increase LOG_BUFFER to support the transaction load without forcing transactions to wait for accesses to the redo log buffer.

To determine the size of your various SGA regions, you can query V$SGA, as shown in the following listing. The sample database in the listing has a shared pool that is greater in size (44,958,712 bytes) than the data block buffer cache (30,720,000 bytes). The redo log buffer, however, has been left at 164KB (a common default value for Unix systems). If the application is transaction-intensive, users will likely encounter resource contention problems within the redo log buffer.

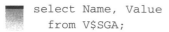

```
select Name, Value
  from V$SGA;

NAME                                                   Value
----------------------------------------------------- -------------
Fixed Size                                                    46384
Variable Size                                              44958712
Database Buffers                                           30720000
Redo Buffers                                                 163840
```

You can also issue the **show sga** command from within SQLDBA or Server Manager to see the SGA regions' sizes, along with the total size of the SGA.

DB_WRITERS

Once the database block size and memory areas are properly established, tune the way in which Oracle writes data from memory. If your operating system permits you to use multiple DBWR processes, set a value greater than '1' for the DB_WRITERS parameter. If you start more than one DBWR process, you may be able to reduce contention for blocks within the data block buffer cache. If there is only one DBWR process available, it becomes a possible bottleneck during I/O operations, even if the data is distributed among multiple devices. See Chapter 4 for further information on managing the I/O demands of Oracle applications.

You can use several factors to help estimate the number of DBWR processes you will need. First, you can determine the number of concurrent logons (see Chapter 8). You can query V$LICENSE for the maximum number of concurrent logons since the database was started. You can also use the file I/O distribution queries from Chapter 4 to verify the need for additional DBWR processes. The number of DBWR processes should be proportional to the number of transactions and users that update the database simultaneously. In general, you should have one DBWR process for every 50 online (query and update) users, and one DBWR process for every two batch jobs that update the database.

DB_FILE_MULTIBLOCK_READ_COUNT

As described in Chapter 4, the DB_FILE_MULTIBLOCK_READ_COUNT parameter helps determine how many blocks are read at a time by the database during full table scans.

NOTE
This parameter only affects the performance of full table scans.

You should set the DB_FILE_MULTIBLOCK_READ_COUNT parameter to a value that takes the greatest advantage of the operating system's buffer during reads. For example, suppose the operating system buffer available for reads is 64KB in size. If your database block size is 2KB, you should set DB_FILE_MULTIBLOCK_READ_COUNT to 32; if the block size is 4KB, set DB_FILE_MULTIBLOCK_READ_COUNT to 16. In some operating systems, the available buffer size is configurable.

SORT_AREA_SIZE and SORT_AREA_RETAINED_SIZE

Once you have established an environment that can read the data into memory effectively, you need to establish the size of the memory areas used for sorting. If the sort area is not large enough, Oracle will create temporary segments to use during sort operations. As described in Chapter 3, temporary segments will artificially decrease your hit ratio; they will also decrease the performance of the query performing the sort. If you can perform the entire sort in memory, you can eliminate the cost of writing data to temporary segments.

The SORT_AREA_SIZE parameter specifies the maximum amount of memory, in bytes, the user has available for sorting. SORT_AREA_RETAINED_SIZE sets the maximum amount of memory, in bytes, that will be used for an in-memory sort. You can determine if your sort-related parameters are set adequately by examining the 'sorts (memory)' and 'sorts (disk)' statistics from V$SYSSTAT (as described in Chapter 8). If sorts requiring temporary segments (as defined by the 'sorts (disk)' statistic) account for more than 5 to 10 percent of the memory-based sorts (as defined by the 'sorts (memory)' statistic), then you may consider increasing the size of SORT_AREA_SIZE and SORT_AREA_RETAINED_SIZE. Ideally, the 'sorts (disk)' value will be zero, and all sorts will be performed in memory.

SORT_DIRECT_WRITES

As of Oracle7.2, Oracle enables writes to temporary segments to bypass the data block buffer cache via a technique called *sort direct writes*. As a result, sorting performance of queries requiring temporary segments significantly improves—the performance improvement is usually around 40 percent. To enable sort direct writes, set the SORT_DIRECT_WRITES parameter to TRUE in your init.ora file; set SORT_WRITE_BUFFERS to 4, and set SORT_WRITE_BUFFER_SIZE to 65536. See Chapter 13 for further information on sort direct writes.

ROLLBACK_SEGMENTS

To properly support the transactions within your database, you need to have enough rollback segments. The more concurrent transactions that occur within your database, the more rollback segments you need. If you have too few rollback segments, the contention for the rollback segments—and for the disks on which the rollback segments are stored—may create an I/O bottleneck during transaction processing.

As described in Chapter 5, you should have a set of rollback segments specifically designed to support the most frequently executed transactions within your application. You should have a separate set of rollback segments that are sized to support large transactions against your temporary/interface tables. To determine if you have enough rollback segments, you can query V$WAITSTAT, as described in the "Buffer Waits" section of Chapter 8. The Class column of V$WAITSTAT lists the different types of wait statistics recorded. If the V$WAITSTAT statistic for "undo header" waits is a high, continually increasing number, then you need to add more rollback segments in order to effectively support the transactions in the database. To distribute the I/O operations against rollback segments, you can distribute the datafiles for the rollback segments' tablespace across multiple disks (see Chapter 4).

Memory Tuning

Ideally, a database performs as few physical reads as possible, using the SGA areas to share previously read data among users. Operating systems use similar strategies, such as file system buffers, to improve the I/O performance of the system.

As described in Chapter 4, Unix systems can use either raw devices or file systems. When file systems are used, the operating system reads data into the Unix buffer cache, which is a part of the kernel's memory; the data is then transferred to the Oracle buffer cache in the SGA, which is a part of process memory within the operating system. Both the process memory and the kernel's memory come from the same limited physical (available) memory and must be managed as a whole. Depending on the disk hardware used, disk arrays may provide additional buffering to decrease I/O times, particularly for read-intensive applications (see Chapter 4).

When managing memory for an Oracle database application, you should first manage the memory within Oracle. See Chapter 3 for a full description of the way in which Oracle uses its memory areas and the impact of different operations on the reported hit ratio. As you create a stable environment for the memory areas within Oracle, you should also reduce the likelihood of contention for overall memory at the operating-system level.

Contention for Overall Memory

To reduce contention for overall memory, you need to manage the occurrences of two operating-system-level virtual memory management techniques: *swapping*, in which an entire process is moved out of memory and onto disk; and *paging*, in which selected sections of a process are read in or written out of memory.

In the following sections, you will see each of these described, along with architecture trade-offs and issues related to semaphores and shared memory setup. In the following sections, Unix will be used as the prototype operating system for the discussion; the general concepts are found in many multiuser operating systems.

Swapping

When Unix needs memory to service the process demands on the system, and the amount of available memory has dropped below a predefined threshold, the operating system will make space available by attempting to move entire processes out of memory to secondary storage allocated on disk, known as *swap space*. The swapping operation places an additional processing overhead for the operating system. Also, the processes that get swapped out must be swapped back into memory before they can continue to be executed. An outgoing process is said to be *swapped out*, while the incoming process is *swapped in*.

Swap space is an area on disk allocated to the operating system to store the memory used by processes that have been swapped out. Traditionally, smaller Unix systems were often configured with swap space up to four times greater than memory size. Larger systems could be configured with an amount of swap space at least equal to physical memory. For Oracle, it is strongly recommended that swap space be configured at least two to four times the amount of physical memory. A shortage of swap space can result in limited memory usage due to the system's inability to reserve swap space for a new process to be loaded into memory. Use the **pstat -s** command on BSD Unix or the **swap -l** command on Unix System V to monitor swap space.

From a memory management perspective, the objective is to minimize or eliminate swap-outs—especially for shared processes like the Oracle background processes. Use the **sar -w** command on Unix System V or the **vmstat -S** command on BSD Unix to check for swapping. If you see excessive swapping, you should reduce your processes' memory usage or add more memory to the system.

Paging

Most operating systems also provide a finer level of memory management, in which only selected pages (individual pieces of memory) of a process are read in or written out of memory. This process is called *paging*, and is usually driven by LRU (Least Recently Used) algorithms, similar to Oracle's SGA memory management method. Although paging presents less of a problem than swapping, it must nevertheless be monitored and controlled to reduce the impact of its resource usage on the overall system performance. Use the **sar -p** command on Unix System V or the **vmstat -S** command on BSD Unix to detect high page-out activity for your system. Memory that has been written out of memory via paging is written into swap space.

Setting up Shared Memory

Shared memory is a kernel-managed memory structure used by multiple processes to share information. On most operating systems, Oracle is implemented as multitask architecture where the various processes access shared resources and data through the SGA. All Oracle processes must attach to the SGA. The size of the SGA is determined at database startup, based on a few key parameters (see the "Key init.ora Parameters" section earlier in this chapter). Oracle must be able to acquire adequate space for the SGA at startup.

The SGA resides in the shared memory area in Unix; therefore, adequate shared memory must be available within the operating system when the database is started. Shared memory is available in segments, and multiple segments can be attached by a process. You may need to adjust the following shared memory parameters on your system. On some operating systems, adjusting shared memory parameters may require relinking the kernel.

SHMMAX	The maximum size, in bytes, of a single shared memory segment
SHMSEG	The maximum number of shared memory segments that can be attached to a single process
SHMALL	The total number of shared memory segments available in the entire system

Each Oracle instance requires its own SGA—and thus its own shared memory area. Oracle recommends trying to accommodate the SGA for a single instance in one shared memory segment. If the SGA is too large, this may have implications for other non-Oracle applications on the system that also use shared memory. The total amount of memory used by your SGA can be queried from V$SGA, as shown in the "Key init.ora Parameters" section earlier in this chapter.

If you get shared memory errors during database startup, check the shared memory parameters, adjust them as necessary, relink the kernel if required, and reboot. You can use the Unix **ipcs -b** command to obtain a list of current shared memory segments in use. Your system administrators can use Oracle's **tstshm** utility, available on some Unix platforms, to evaluate existing shared memory configuration.

Setting up Semaphores

You can use the Unix **ipcs -b** command to obtain a list of current *semaphores* (operating system flags used to control shared resources) in use. Unix processes are usually written to use semaphores to coordinate access to shared resources. If a shared resource is locked, a process will suspend and wait for that resource to become available. Typically, Oracle uses one semaphore per Oracle process. Minimally, there should be more semaphores than the value of the PROCESSES parameter in init.ora. In fact, since semaphores are a systemwide resource, the kernel settings for semaphores must be adequate to handle the needs of all concurrent applications on the system. If you have multiple instances on the same server, you will need enough semaphores to support all of the instances that will be open at any one time.

Semaphores are allocated in sets, with each set having multiple semaphores and the system having multiple sets. There is a system-defined upper limit on the total number of individual semaphores. Oracle claims all the semaphores it will use at instance startup by claiming complete sets of semaphores. Any unused semaphores in the last set are not available to other processes. Some of the important parameters governing semaphore allocation are:

SEMMNI	The maximum number of semaphore sets on the system
SEMMSL	The maximum number of semaphores per set
SEMMNS	The maximum number of semaphores available systemwide

The maximum number of available semaphores on the system is the lesser of SEMMNS and the product (SEMMNI * SEMMSL).

The balance between the number of semaphores and the number of sets must be selected based on the number of Oracle instances and other applications running concurrently on your server. Since semaphores do not use many system resources, it is generally acceptable to set the number of semaphores and semaphore sets values high to avoid potential problems. However, you should not set the number of semaphores so high as to cause the operating system to scan unusually large numbers of semaphores that will not be used. If you attempt to start a database and not enough semaphores are available to support the defined number of processes (based on the PROCESSES setting in init.ora), the database will not start.

Managing Memory Trade-Offs

The purpose of Oracle's memory structure is to provide a good hit ratio for accesses within Oracle. If the SGA area is too large and begins to page excessively to disk because not enough memory is available for other processes, caching can become an overhead instead of an asset. Moreover, the operating system paging overhead is not obvious from within Oracle.

For example, if part of the SGA is paged out, and a read is made against a block that has been written to the swap space, then the operating system has to go to the disk to satisfy a request for the data. The trip to the disk is caused by a *page fault* (the page is not in memory) and recorded as a page-in. As far as Oracle is concerned, once the page is brought into memory, the read request is satisfied within the buffer cache and recorded as a logical read with no physical read. From within Oracle, it appears that there is no memory problem, and the paging activities are not recorded in the hit ratio statistics. Your systems administration personnel need to monitor for paging to make sure the SGA is not so large that paging is occurring.

Unix always reads from disks in units of the operating system block size. The Oracle database block size should be a multiple of the operating system block size. For example, if the operating system block size is 8KB and Oracle block size is 2KB, for every block request from Oracle (single block request), the operating system fetches an 8KB block, stores it in an 8KB area in the operating system buffers, and Oracle then picks up only 2KB from it to put into the SGA! Given the fact that the overall time (seek + latency + read) to read an 8KB block at random is almost the same as it is for a read of a 2KB block, incorrectly sized database block sizes waste the server's I/O cache resources for data that may not be used. The operating system I/O block size is usually different from the sector size on the disk, which is usually 512 bytes.

I/O Tuning

Chapter 4 covers many advanced I/O techniques, such as RAID systems and raw devices. To make the best use of such techniques, you should first establish a file organization plan that is optimal and flexible. If you use Oracle's default installation programs, you will generate a directory structure that allows you to easily manage the Oracle software and the database files. Appropriately, Oracle's file architecture is named the Optimal Flexible Architecture.

Implement the Optimal Flexible Architecture

Optimal Flexible Architecture (OFA) is a set of requirements and rules that define installation guidelines—including uniform directory structures, naming standards, and database file layout guidelines—to simplify administration of the Oracle environment. OFA is not mandatory for setting up an efficient and high-performance database that's easy to administer; rather, it is a set of guidelines that standardizes the database file setup and increases the likelihood that the database file layout will be efficiently designed and easily administered. Many facets of OFA are implemented by default by the Oracle7.3 installation programs; you need to establish your customization of OFA prior to creating your databases or installing Oracle software.

OFA consists of 13 requirements and 11 rules. The requirements may be considered goals and objectives for setting up a flexible, optimal database environment. These requirements include:

- File system organization and naming standards that make the environment scalable and easy to administer

- Distribution of files for balanced and efficient I/O

- Appropriate isolation for multiple versions of multiple Oracle environments (DEVELOPMENT, TEST, PRODUCTION, etc.) on the same server

The 11 OFA rules serve as an example of organizing the directories and file layout for Oracle databases in a Unix environment. They include:

- Directory organization rules

- Directory and file naming conventions

- File organization and layout rules

- Tablespace naming guidelines

- Raw device guidelines

NOTE
The 11 OFA rules are intended to inform, not to dictate the naming conventions. The exact file and directory names chosen are not important as long as the names are simple and standardized and do not cause confusion. Any other approach that satisfies the goals and objectives with simplicity can function as well as OFA.

The most important objective related to database file management is to guarantee that all datafiles are at the same depth of directory structure, using a consistent naming convention. For example, if the instance name is PROD, the directory structure used by the datafiles could be

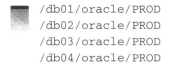

```
/db01/oracle/PROD
/db02/oracle/PROD
/db03/oracle/PROD
/db04/oracle/PROD
```

The directory structure for the TEST instance could be

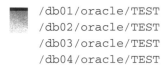

```
/db01/oracle/TEST
/db02/oracle/TEST
/db03/oracle/TEST
/db04/oracle/TEST
```

Within each directory, name the files consistently. If each instance has a separate directory, you do not need to include the name of the instance in any of the filenames. If more space is needed for files than is available under current directory structures (for example, for large numbers of trace files), relocate the files as necessary but maintain the OFA directory structures by using symbolic links to point to the new file locations. Use symbolic links to point to raw partitions to maintain the ease of file management.

When using any type of network file systems (NFS, DFS, or AFS), do not place any Oracle database file on any network file system, since network file systems do not have robust enough concurrency controls. If you place Oracle database files on a network file system, your data integrity could be jeopardized. Executables and message files can be placed on network file systems if the access times are acceptable.

Using a consistent naming standard and directory structure greatly simplifies administration, especially for backup procedures and operating system (shell) scripts. Techniques for balancing I/O, separating segments with different I/O loads, and managing performance are covered extensively outside of the OFA framework. See Chapter 4 for details on identifying and resolving problems related to I/O distribution and performance.

Distribute I/O

As described in Chapter 4, the I/O throughput of devices can be a limiting factor on the performance of your application. You can distribute the I/O both within the database and outside of the database. For example, within the database you can move the most frequently accessed objects into their own tablespaces; separate tables and their related indexes; separate rollback segments from tables; and separate the data dictionary segments from all other objects. Outside of the database, you need to make sure that your file distribution supports the logical distribution within the database.

For example, if you have separated your two most-used tables into their own tablespaces, but placed the datafiles for those tablespaces on the same disk device, then you have not eliminated the potential for I/O contention between the tables—you may as well have placed both tables in the same tablespace. If you put tables and indexes into separate tablespaces, but place the datafiles for those tablespaces on the same RAID set (see Chapter 4), you have not necessarily avoided the potential table/index I/O bottleneck.

Within the database, the tuning of SQL statements, as described in Chapters 10 and 11, is critical to reducing the I/O operations required by the application. Some operating systems allow you to implement additional I/O management techniques, including:

- *List I/O*—allows multiple I/O requests to be combined in a list and treated as a single I/O request, thereby reducing I/O overhead.

- *Asynchronous I/O*—allows a process to proceed with the next operation without having to wait for the I/O to complete after issuing a write.

Multiple DBWR Processes

The use of multiple database writers is possible with List or Asynchronous I/O, depending on the operating system. Using multiple DBWR processes improves I/O performance. Coupled with List I/O or Asynchronous writes, if available on the operating system, multiple DBWR processes can provide dramatic improvements for write-intensive systems.

NOTE
Consult with Oracle Support to determine the optimal configuration for your environment. Many multiuser operating systems support the use of multiple DBWR processes.

You can monitor the distribution of I/O within the database via the V$FILESTAT view (see Chapter 4). At the operating-system level, you can monitor how long I/O requests have to wait before being serviced. Long queues of requests are caused by having either too many I/O requests for the disk or requests that take too long to service. In Unix System V, use the **sar -d** command to monitor disk request queues; in BSD Unix, use the **iostat** command. The queues should be near zero. Monitor the disk I/O queue length in conjunction with the disk activity rate to determine if you need to further distribute your I/O operations.

If too many requests are being issued for the disk, there may be multiple busy files on the same disk; if the files are datafiles, you can use V$FILESTAT to determine which database files are being used by the accesses. Since disk I/O rates can be a limiting factor for your query performance, the goal is to involve multiple disks in processing the same I/O.

Striping, another option for I/O distribution, can be performed both within the database and at the operating system level. See Chapter 4 for a discussion of issues related to striping, including the selection criteria to use when selecting among RAID options for striping at the operating-system level. If the data is properly distributed, you can use the Parallel Query option (see Chapter 12) to involve multiple processes in the resolution of a single transaction. If the data is not distributed, the Parallel Query option may cause I/O bottlenecks to occur within your system as multiple processes try to access the same device.

CPU Tuning

If the I/O operations for your database are minimized and distributed, and adequate memory is allocated, your application will be CPU-bound. CPU can be consumed during user activities, system activities, and I/O activities (see Chapter 3). Any CPU time that is not consumed is considered idle time. To check for CPU contention, use the **sar** command for Unix System V, or the **vmstat** and **iostat** commands for BSD Unix; the **top** command is also useful for displaying the top CPU consumers. The goal of CPU tuning is to maximize the CPU devoted to users while minimizing the CPU impact of I/O waits and overhead.

New CPU options with greatly improved performance are announced or introduced frequently. As a result, designing your application to be CPU-bound (by fully distributing its I/O requests and using enough memory) allows you to handle an expansion to the application by expanding the CPU capacity of the server on which the database resides. For example, if your application is CPU-intensive, but only 75 percent of the CPU is used by the application, then doubling the number of application users does not require a redistribution of I/O; it requires adding more CPUs to the server. The tuning issue related to the increased number of users thus becomes a server management issue, not an application maintenance issue.

Oracle exploits Symmetric Multi-Processing (SMP) architectures (featuring multiple CPUs on a single server) extremely well due to its multitasking architecture. For example, the parallel options (see Chapter 12) allow multiple CPUs to participate in a variety of database operations, including full table scans, sorts, index creations, recovery, and data loading. If using the parallel options results in disk sorts being converted to memory sorts, dramatic performance gains will be realized.

Most operating systems do a good job of scheduling CPU usage in an SMP environment. Nevertheless, whenever a process is switched from one CPU to another, there is migration overhead associated with the process switch. The systems management personnel can use processor affinity/binding, if supported on your system, to carefully manage process affinity.

Tuning your Application

The application does not exist apart from its environment, but rather, through its use of disk I/O, memory resources, and CPU, directly influences its operating environment. You must therefore consider tuning your application to be a critical step in tuning your environment.

Beyond the init.ora parameters discussed at the start of this chapter, tuning a database application consists of tuning the application's architecture and tuning the SQL it uses. Typically, a very small number of SQL statements are responsible for most of the resource consumption by an application. You need to identify the most offensive parts of the application, and use the tuning advice in the next several chapters to tune them. In Chapter 10, you will see descriptions of the operations Oracle uses to access and manipulate data. In Chapter 11, you'll see resolutions to the major tuning issues related to SQL statements. In Part 4 of this book, you'll see implementation advice for new tuning options such as the parallel options.

Once you have tuned your application, you need to revisit your environment tuning process to make sure the changes in the application do not cause problems within the environment. For example, greatly expanding the memory requirements of your application may cause paging and swapping, as described earlier in this chapter. In general, the better tuned the application is, the easier it will be to tune the environment that supports the application. You can then focus on the limited set of tuning problems caused by the most resource-intensive SQL in your application.

CHAPTER 10

EXPLAINing SQL Statement Tuning

To tune your queries, you must first determine the steps the optimizer is following when resolving the queries. You can use Oracle's **explain plan** command to display the path the optimizer will use for any given query. In this chapter you will see how to use the **explain plan** command, a full description of the operations listed in the **explain plan** results, and a method for modifying the execution path Oracle chooses for the query.

Even if you are already familiar with the **explain plan** command, you should review the "Operations" and "Using Hints" sections of this chapter prior to reading Chapter 11.

How to Generate the Explain Plan for a Query

You can determine the path that Oracle will choose for a query's execution (known as the *execution path* or the *explain plan*) without running the query. To determine the execution path, you must use the **explain plan** command in Oracle. This command will evaluate the steps in the execution path for a query, and will place one row for each step into a table named PLAN_TABLE. The records in PLAN_TABLE will describe the operations used at each step of the query execution, and the relationships between the execution path steps. If you are using the cost-based optimizer in Oracle7.3, the **explain plan** will show the relative "cost" of each step in the execution path.

To use **explain plan**, you first need to create a PLAN_TABLE table in the schema that you will be using (usually, the schema that owns the tables used by the query). Oracle provides a script to create the PLAN_TABLE; named utlxplan.sql, it is usually stored in the /RDBMS/ADMIN subdirectory under the Oracle software home directory. Run the utlxplan.sql script from within SQL*Plus, as shown in the following example of a Unix user creating PLAN_TABLE.

```
> sqlplus hobbes/tiger
SQL> @$ORACLE_HOME/rdbms/admin/utlxplan

Table created.
```

In the example, the user named Hobbes ran the utlxplan.sql script to create PLAN_TABLE in the Hobbes schema. Although you can rename PLAN_TABLE, it is simpler to use the default name. If the utlxplan.sql script fails, you lack one of the following:

- the CREATE TABLE privilege
- adequate free space within your default tablespace
- any more space within your space quota for your default tablespace

NOTE
The utlxplan.sql script may change between Oracle versions and sometimes between minor releases. You should drop PLAN_TABLE and run this script every time you upgrade your Oracle version to guarantee you will see all available execution path information.

The **create table** command for PLAN_TABLE comes from the utlxplan.sql script for Oracle7.3.2, and is provided to show the PLAN_TABLE column structures.

```
rem
rem
Rem Copyright (c) 1988 by Oracle Corporation
Rem NAME
Rem UTLXPLAN.SQL
Rem FUNCTION
Rem This is the format for the table that is used by the
Rem EXPLAIN PLAN statement.  The explain statement requires
Rem the presence of this table in order to store the
Rem descriptions of the row sources.

create table PLAN_TABLE (
statement_id     varchar2(30),
timestamp        date,
remarks          varchar2(80),
operation        varchar2(30),
options          varchar2(30),
object_node      varchar2(128),
object_owner     varchar2(30),
object_name      varchar2(30),
object_instance numeric,
object_type      varchar2(30),
optimizer        varchar2(255),
search_columns   numeric,
id               numeric,
parent_id        numeric,
position         numeric,
cost             numeric,
cardinality      numeric,
bytes            numeric,
other_tag        varchar2(255),
other            long);
```

Four of the columns (Cost, Cardinality, Bytes, and Other_Tag) are not available unless you are using Oracle7.3. If you have upgraded a pre-Oracle7.3 instance containing a PLAN_TABLE table to Oracle7.3, you need to drop PLAN_TABLE and recreate it by running the Oracle7.3 version of utlxplan.sql.

Once PLAN_TABLE has been created in your schema, you can begin to determine the execution paths of selected queries. The columns in PLAN_TABLE are described in Table 10-1.

Column	Description
Statement_ID	The Statement_ID you set in the **explain plan** command; it "names" the query for future reference.
Timestamp	A timestamp recording when the **explain plan** command was issued.
Remarks	A remark column; you can add remarks to existing records in PLAN_TABLE via the **update** command.
Operation	The SQL operation performed in the step.
Options	The option used for the operation, such as UNIQUE SCAN or RANGE SCAN for the INDEX operation.
Object_Node	The database link used to refer to an object, or, in the Parallel Query Option, the query server process used by the operation.
Object_Owner	The owner of the object being referenced by the operation.
Object_Name	The name of the object being referenced by the operation.
Object_Instance	The ordinal position of the object, as it exists in the SQL being explained.
Object_Type	An attribute of the object, such as UNIQUE for indexes.
Optimizer	The optimizer mode used (such as FIRST_ROWS or RULE).
Search_Columns	Not currently used.
ID	A number assigned to each step in the explain plan; with Parent_ID, establishes the hierarchy of steps in the execution path.
Parent_ID	The ID of the step that is the "parent" of the current step in the hierarchy of the execution path.
Position	The order of processing for steps that have the same Parent_ID. In the first row generated for an explain plan, this column contains the optimizer's estimation of the statement's "cost" (if cost-based optimization is used; otherwise, no cost is calculated).

TABLE 10-1. *Column Descriptions for PLAN_TABLE*

Column	Description
Cost	Relative cost for the step, if cost-based optimization is used; only available in Oracle7.3.
Cardinality	Only available in Oracle7.3; the expected number of rows returned from the operation.
Bytes	Only available in Oracle7.3; the "width" of each returned row.
Other_Tag	Only available in Oracle7.3; if the value is SERIAL_FROM_REMOTE, the SQL in the Other column will be executed on the remote node. The other values for Other_Tag describe the operation's usage within the Parallel Query option (see Chapter 12 for a full description of parallel-related Other_Tag values).
Other	For distributed queries, Other contains the text of the SQL that is executed on the remote node.

TABLE 10-1.   *Column Descriptions for PLAN_TABLE (continued)*

To determine the execution path of a query, prefix the query with the following SQL:

```
explain plan
set Statement_ID = 'TEST'
for
```

To make the tuning process simpler, always use the same Statement_ID value, and delete the records for each execution path before using the **explain plan** command a second time.

An example of execution of the **explain plan** command is shown in the following listing. The query shown in the listing will not be run during the command; only its execution path steps will be generated, and they will be inserted as records in PLAN_TABLE.

```
explain plan
set Statement_ID = 'TEST'
for
select Name, City, State
  from COMPANY
 where City = 'Roanoke'
   and State = 'VA';

Statement processed.
```

The records have now been inserted into PLAN_TABLE. You can query the PLAN_TABLE using the following query. The results of this query will show the operations performed at each step, and the parent-child relationships between the execution path steps.

```
select
  LPAD(' ',2*Level)||Operation||' '||Options
                ||' '||Object_Name   Q_Plan
from PLAN_TABLE
where Statement_ID = 'TEST'
connect by prior ID = Parent_ID and Statement_ID = 'TEST'
start with ID=1;
```

The query shown in the preceding listing uses the CONNECT BY operator to evaluate the hierarchy of steps in the query's execution path. The query in the listing assumes the Statement_ID field has been set to 'TEST'. The execution path steps will be displayed in the column given the "Q_Plan" alias.

If the COMPANY table in the prior example had two single-column, nonunique indexes on its City and State columns, then the Q_Plan value—the execution path—would be the same as the one shown in the following listing.

```
Q_PLAN
--------------------------------------------------------
TABLE ACCESS COMPANY BY ROWID
  AND-EQUAL
    INDEX RANGE SCAN COMPANY$CITY
    INDEX RANGE SCAN COMPANY$STATE
```

Automatically Generating Explain Plans in Oracle7.3

If you are using Oracle7.3, you can have the explain plan automatically generated for every transaction you execute within SQL*Plus. The **set autotrace on** command will cause each query, *after* being executed, to display both its execution path and high-level trace information about the processing involved in resolving the query.

In order to use the **set autotrace on** command, you must have first created the PLAN_TABLE table within your account. When using the **set autotrace on** command, you do not set a Statement_ID, and you do not have to manage the records within the PLAN_TABLE. To disable the autotrace feature, use the **set autotrace off** command.

If you use the **set autotrace on** command, you will not see the explain plan for your queries until after they complete. The **explain plan** command shows the execution paths without running the queries first. Therefore, if the performance of a query is unknown, use the **explain plan** command before running it. If you are fairly certain that the performance of a query is acceptable, use **set autotrace on** to verify its execution path.

Interpreting the Order of Operations

The execution path shown in the preceding listing uses indenting to show the parent-child relationships between three operations: TABLE ACCESS BY ROWID, AND-EQUAL, and INDEX RANGE SCAN. *The plan is executed from inside out and from top to bottom.* Thus, the two INDEX RANGE SCAN operations must provide data to the AND-EQUAL operation. The AND-EQUAL operation is the only operation that provides information to the TABLE ACCESS BY ROWID operation. You'll see descriptions and examples of each operation (AND-EQUAL, etc.) in the "Operations" section of this chapter.

Of the two INDEX RANGE SCAN operations in the preceding example, which occurs first? Since the range scans on City and State both have the same "parent" step in the execution path (the AND-EQUAL step), you need to look at the PLAN_TABLE.Position column to determine which occurs first. If you use the query shown previously to select records from PLAN_TABLE, you should read the execution path from the inside out, and from top to bottom. Applying this order to the execution path shown in the preceding listing, the index range scan on City provides the first input to the AND-EQUAL operation.

You should now delete the execution path records from PLAN_TABLE prior to using the **explain plan** command again with the same Statement_ID value:

```
delete from PLAN_TABLE;
```

In the following section, you will see each available operation fully described. The operation descriptions include example queries and execution paths, along with written and pictorial interpretations of the generated plans. Once you understand the implications of the operations, it is easier to understand the potential performance problems for a query.

Operations

To interpret an explain plan and correctly evaluate your SQL tuning options, you need to first understand the differences between the available database operations. In the following sections, you'll see each of the database access operations identified by the name given to it via the **explain plan** command, along with its characteristics. For each type of operation, an example is provided.

The operations are listed in alphabetical order. In some cases, the example for an operation will use operations described later in the chapter (such as MERGE JOIN, which always uses a SORT JOIN operation, or MINUS, which always uses a PROJECTION).

The operations are all classified as *row operations* or *set operations*. The differences between row and set operations are shown in the following list.

Row Operations	Set Operations
Executed on one row at a time.	Executed on a result set of rows.
Will be executed at the FETCH stage, if there is no set operation involved.	Executed at the EXECUTE stage when the cursor is opened.
The user can see the first result before the last row is fetched.	The user cannot see the first result until all rows are fetched and processed.
Example: A full table scan.	*Example:* A full table scan with a GROUP BY clause.

In the following sections, each operation will be described as either a row operation or a set operation. For each operation, you'll see a sample query that illustrates the operation's use, along with the explain plan for the query and written and pictorial interpretations of the explain plan.

The operations covered in the following sections are listed in Table 10-2.

In the examples in this chapter, you'll see references to three tables, shown in Figure 10-1. The COMPANY table in Figure 10-1 has four indexes on it: a primary key index on its Company_ID column, a nonunique index on its City column, a nonunique index on its State column, and a nonunique index on its Parent_Company_ID column. Parent_Company_ID is a foreign key back to the COMPANY.Company_ID column.

The COMPETITOR table is used to track data about products that compete directly with your company. Its only index is a two-part primary key on the Company_ID and Product_ID columns. The COMPETITOR.Company_ID column is a foreign key back to the COMPANY.Company_ID column.

The SALES table reports sales totals by company and time period. The only index on the SALES table is a two-part primary key (Company_ID and Period_ID). The SALES.Company_ID column is a foreign key back to the COMPANY.Company_ID column.

NOTE
In the following examples, you'll see the COMPANY table many times. Be sure you are familiar with its index structure before reading the examples. The columns' datatypes are provided strictly for reference.

Operation

AND-EQUAL

CONCATENATION

CONNECT BY

COUNT

COUNT STOPKEY

FILTER

FOR UPDATE

HASH JOIN

INDEX RANGE SCAN

INDEX UNIQUE SCAN

INTERSECTION

MERGE JOIN

MINUS

NESTED LOOPS

OUTER JOIN

PROJECTION

REMOTE

SEQUENCE

SORT AGGREGATE

SORT GROUP BY

SORT JOIN

SORT ORDER BY

SORT UNIQUE

TABLE ACCESS BY ROWID

TABLE ACCESS CLUSTER

TABLE ACCESS FULL

TABLE ACCESS HASH

UNION

VIEW

TABLE 10-2. *SQL Operations*

```
COMPANY
    Company_ID      NUMBER      -primary key COMPANY_PK
    Name            VARCHAR2
    Address         VARCHAR2
    City            VARCHAR2    -nonunique index COMPANY$CITY
    State           VARCHAR2    -nonunique index COMPANY$STATE
    Zip             VARCHAR2
    Parent_Company_ID NUMBER -nonunique index COMPANY$PARENT
    Active_Flag        CHAR
```

```
COMPETITOR
    Company_ID      NUMBER      -first column of primary key
                                    COMPETITOR_PK
                                -foreign key to COMPANY_PK

    Product_ID      NUMBER      -second column of primary key
                                    COMPETITOR_PK
```

```
SALES
    Company_ID      NUMBER      -first column of primary key SALES_PK
                                -foreign key to COMPANY_PK

    Period_ID       NUMBER      -second column of primary key SALES_PK
    Sales_Total     NUMBER
```

FIGURE 10-1. *Tables used in Chapter 10 examples*

Conventions Used in Execution Path Illustrations

In the Interpretations section under each operation listed below, you will find an illustration of the way the operation is used as part of a query. Read the illustrations from left to right—they show a time sequence of the operations within the execution path. Each operation will be shown in a separate box, and arrows will be

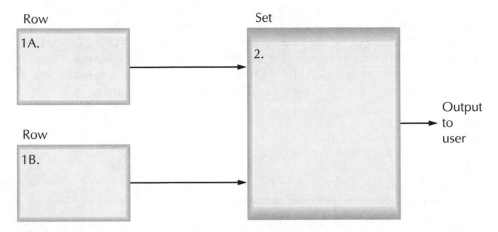

FIGURE 10-2. *Sample execution path illustration*

used to indicate the flow of data. Row operations will have "Row" written over their boxes, and set operations will have "Set" written over theirs.

Operations that occur at the same time are shown in the same vertical column, and will have the same identifying number, with a letter suffix. Thus, in Figure 10-2, two concurrent row operations, labeled "1A" and "1B", provide data to a set operation labeled "2". The output of operation "2" is the data that is provided to the user.

AND-EQUAL

Operation type: Row

Description
AND-EQUAL merges sorted lists of values returned by indexes. It returns the list of values that are common to both lists (such as RowIDs that are found in two separate indexes). AND-EQUAL is used for merges of nonunique indexes and range scans of unique indexes.

Example

```
select Name, City, State
  from COMPANY
 where City = 'Roanoke'
   and State = 'VA';
```

The query shown in the preceding listing selects from the COMPANY table based on two criteria in its WHERE clause. The criteria can use the COMPANY$CITY index on the City column and the COMPANY$STATE index on the State column to obtain RowIDs for the rows to be returned. Since the Name column is required by the query, the COMPANY table will have to be accessed; the other column values are already available via the index searches.

The Plan

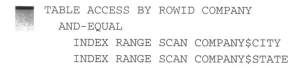

```
TABLE ACCESS BY ROWID COMPANY
   AND-EQUAL
      INDEX RANGE SCAN COMPANY$CITY
      INDEX RANGE SCAN COMPANY$STATE
```

Interpreting the Plan

The plan shows that the two nonunique indexes—on the City column and on the State column—are scanned for values matching the WHERE clause criteria. The RowIDs from each index scan are placed in sorted lists. The AND-EQUAL operation merges the two lists and generates a single list of RowIDs that were in both lists. If a RowID exists only on one of the indexes, it will not be returned by the AND-EQUAL operation. Since the WHERE clause contains an AND clause, the AND-EQUAL operation is used to prevent RowIDs from being returned from the indexes unless the RowIDs are found in both indexes.

The RowIDs are then used to access the rows in the COMPANY table that satisfy the WHERE clause criteria, and the query is complete. Figure 10-3 shows this execution path.

CONCATENATION

Operation type: Row

Description

CONCATENATION does a UNION ALL (a UNION without elimination of duplicate values) of result sets.

Example

```
select Name, City, State
  from COMPANY
 where State = 'TX'
   and City in ('Houston', 'Austin', 'Dallas');
```

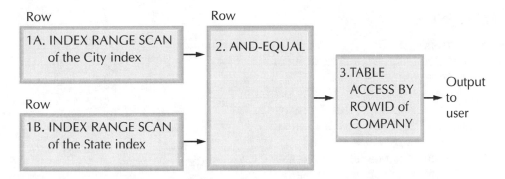

FIGURE 10-3. *AND-EQUAL example execution path*

The query shown in the preceding listing selects from the COMPANY table based on two criteria in its WHERE clause. The criteria can use the COMPANY$CITY index and the COMPANY$STATE index to obtain RowIDs for the rows to be returned. Since the Name column is required by the query, the COMPANY table will have to be accessed; the other column values are already available via the index searches.

The query of the City column uses an IN clause, which is functionally equivalent to an OR clause. The query could be rewritten as

```
select Name, City, State
  from COMPANY
 where State = 'TX'
   and (City = 'Houston'
        or City = 'Austin'
        or City = 'Dallas');
```

Taking this expansion one step further, the State portion of the query can be placed into each section of the OR clause. The revised query would now read

```
select Name, City, State
  from COMPANY
 where (State = 'TX' and City = 'Houston')
    or (State = 'TX' and City = 'Austin')
    or (State = 'TX' and City = 'Dallas');
```

Viewing the query in the last preceding format helps to understand the plan that is generated, as shown in the following section.

The Plan

```
CONCATENATION
  TABLE ACCESS BY ROWID COMPANY
    AND-EQUAL
       INDEX RANGE SCAN COMPANY$CITY
       INDEX RANGE SCAN COMPANY$STATE
  TABLE ACCESS BY ROWID COMPANY
    AND-EQUAL
       INDEX RANGE SCAN COMPANY$CITY
       INDEX RANGE SCAN COMPANY$STATE
  TABLE ACCESS BY ROWID COMPANY
    AND-EQUAL
       INDEX RANGE SCAN COMPANY$CITY
       INDEX RANGE SCAN COMPANY$STATE
```

Interpreting the Plan

The plan shows that the query is executed as if the IN clause is rewritten as an OR clause, and the other criteria are placed within the OR clauses. Within each OR clause, an AND-EQUAL operation is performed to merge the lists of RowIDs returned from the index scans. The RowIDs returned by the AND-EQUAL operations are then used to select the requested columns from the COMPANY table via a TABLE ACCESS BY ROWID operation. The resulting records from each part of the query are then concatenated to carry out the OR clause. Figure 10-4 shows the execution path.

NOTE
If the query is very complex, the optimizer may decide not to use the CONCATENATION operation; instead, partial index range scans will be performed. If you want to force the use of the CONCATENATION operation, you may need to use the last query format shown in the preceding example.

CONNECT BY

Operation type: Row

Description

CONNECT BY does a recursive join of a table to itself, in a hierarchical fashion.

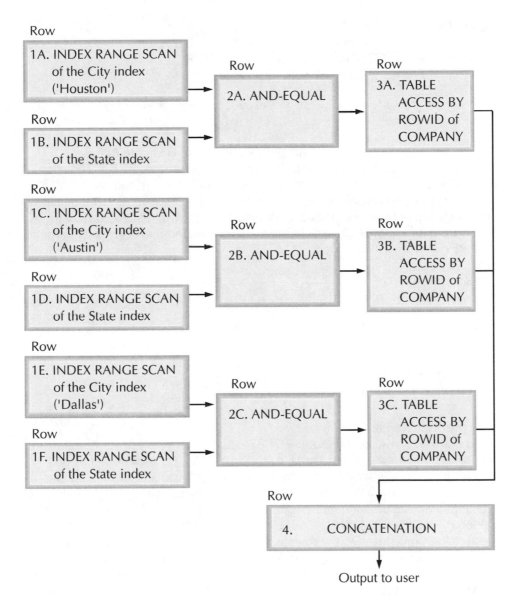

FIGURE 10-4. *CONCATENATION example execution path*

Example

```
select Company_ID, Name
  from COMPANY
 where State = 'VA'
connect by Parent_Company_ID = prior Company_ID
 start with Company_ID = 1;
```

The query shown in the preceding listing selects companies from the COMPANY table in a hierarchical fashion; that is, it returns the rows based on each company's parent company. If there are multiple levels of company parentage, those levels can be displayed in the report. See Chapter 11 for details on implementing and tuning CONNECT BY. The query shown in the preceding listing selects from the COMPANY table based on parentage and one other criterion in its WHERE clause (the State value).

The Plan

```
FILTER
  CONNECT BY
     INDEX UNIQUE SCAN COMPANY_PK
     TABLE ACCESS BY ROWID COMPANY
     TABLE ACCESS BY ROWID COMPANY
        INDEX RANGE SCAN COMPANY$PARENT
```

Interpreting the Plan

If you don't regularly use the CONNECT BY operation in your queries, the explain plan (which includes separate TABLE ACCESS BY ROWID operations) may be confusing. The plan shows that first the COMPANY_PK index is used to find the root node (Company_ID = 1), then the index on the Parent_Company_ID column is used to provide values for queries against the Company_ID column in an iterative fashion (hence the two separate TABLE ACCESS BY ROWID operations). After the hierarchy of Company_IDs is complete, the FILTER operation—the WHERE clause related to the State value—is applied. The query does not use the index on the State column, although it is available and the column is used in the WHERE clause. For advice on tuning SQL statements that use the CONNECT BY operator, see Chapter 11. Figure 10-5 shows the execution path.

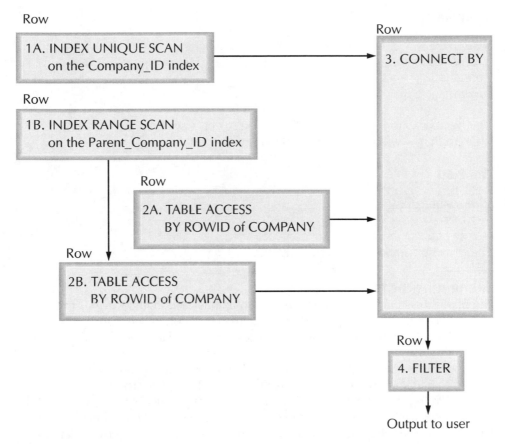

FIGURE 10-5. *CONNECT BY example execution path*

COUNT

Operation type: Row

Description

COUNT is executed when the RowNum pseudo-column is used without specifying a maximum value for RowNum. COUNT receives rows from its child operations and increments the RowNum counter. If a limiting counter is used on the RowNum pseudo-column, then the COUNT STOPKEY operation is used instead of COUNT.

Example

```
select Name, City, State, RowNum
  from COMPANY
 where City > 'Roanoke'
 order by Zip;
```

The query shown in the preceding listing selects rows from the COMPANY table. Each row will have the original row number returned.

The Plan

```
SORT ORDER BY
   COUNT
      TABLE ACCESS BY ROWID COMPANY
         INDEX RANGE SCAN COMPANY$CITY
```

Interpreting the Plan

The plan shows that the index on the City column is used to find RowIDs in the COMPANY table that satisfy the WHERE clause condition (where City > 'Roanoke'). The RowIDs from the City index scan are used to query the COMPANY table for the Name and State column values. For each row returned, the counter is incremented. Because of the use of the index, the rows that are returned will be the "lowest" city names that are greater than the value 'Roanoke'. The rows will be returned from the COMPANY$CITY index in ascending order of the City column's value. The RowNum pseudo-column will then be calculated and put into the row. The SORT ORDER BY operation will order the rows by Zip, as requested in the ORDER BY clause. Figure 10-6 shows the execution path for the query.

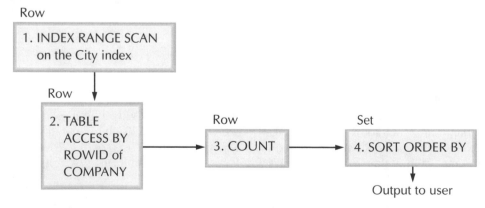

FIGURE 10-6. *COUNT example execution path*

NOTE
The RowNum values are assigned *before* the ordering takes place.

COUNT STOPKEY

Operation type: Row

Description
COUNT STOPKEY is executed when the RowNum pseudo-column is used with a limiting counter. COUNT STOPKEY receives rows from the previous operation and increments a counter; if the counter reaches a given threshold, a "No More Rows" condition is generated.

Example

```
select Name, City, State
   from COMPANY
 where City > 'Roanoke'
   and RowNum <= 100;
```

The query shown in the preceding listing selects from the COMPANY table based on two criteria in its WHERE clause. The first criterion can use the COMPANY$CITY index to obtain RowIDs for the rows to return. The second criterion limits the number of returned records to 100. Since the Name and State columns are required by the query, the COMPANY table will have to be accessed; the City values are already available via the index searches.

The Plan

```
COUNT STOPKEY
   TABLE ACCESS BY ROWID COMPANY
      INDEX RANGE SCAN COMPANY$CITY
```

Interpreting the Plan
The plan shows that the index on the City column is used to find RowIDs in the COMPANY table that satisfy the City value condition. The RowIDs from the index scan are used to query the COMPANY table for the Name and State values. For each row returned, the counter is incremented so that only 100 rows are returned. Because of the use of the index, the rows that are returned will be the 100 "lowest" City names that are greater than the value 'Roanoke', and the records will be sorted by City. Figure 10-7 shows the execution path.

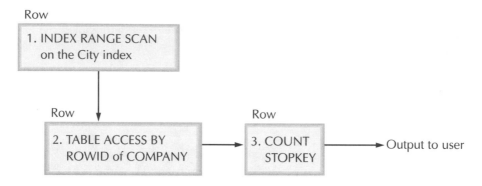

FIGURE 10-7. *COUNT STOPKEY example execution path*

FILTER

Operation type: Row

Description
FILTER performs a WHERE clause condition when no index can be used to assist in the evaluation. Unfortunately, the FILTER operation is sometimes implicit. Any FILTER condition that is applied when performing a table access (such as during a TABLE ACCESS BY ROWID) does not show up in the plan. When FILTER shows up in an explain plan, it is usually the result of a missing index or the disabling of an existing index.

Example
The FILTER operation was in a prior example in this chapter—the CONNECT BY operation's example. In the query shown in the following listing, the WHERE criterion on the State column is not applied until after the CONNECT BY hierarchy has completed; the resulting rows are filtered to determine which meet the specified State criteria.

```
select Company_ID, Name
  from COMPANY
 where State = 'VA'
connect by Parent_Company_ID = prior Company_ID
 start with Company_ID = 1;
```

The Plan

```
FILTER
  CONNECT BY
    INDEX UNIQUE SCAN COMPANY_PK
    TABLE ACCESS BY ROWID COMPANY
    TABLE ACCESS BY ROWID COMPANY
      INDEX RANGE SCAN COMPANY$PARENT
```

Interpreting the Plan

Since the example is designed to focus on the FILTER operation, you can ignore most of the CONNECT BY processing in the plan for this example. The important part (from the FILTER operation perspective) is the line

```
where State = 'VA'
```

The limiting condition on State will not be applied until all of the rows are returned by the CONNECT BY operation. The FILTER operation applies the limiting condition to the rows. The index on the State column is not used in this example, because a CONNECT BY operation is used to generate the result set before the limiting condition is applied.

If you are familiar with the CONNECT BY operation processing, you can see how the plan illustrates the execution path for the query. The plan shows that first the COMPANY_PK index is being used to find the root node (Company_ID = 1); then the index on the Parent_Company_ID column is used to provide values for queries against the Company_ID column in an iterative fashion (requiring two separate TABLE ACCESS BY ROWID operations). After the hierarchy of Company_IDs is complete, the FILTER operation—the WHERE clause related to the State value—is applied. The query does not use the index on the State column, although it is available and the column is used in the WHERE clause. Figure 10-8 shows the execution path.

FOR UPDATE

Operation type: Set

Description

FOR UPDATE places a row-level lock on all the rows that can be retrieved from the **select** statement.

Using FOR UPDATE allows you to use the **where current of** clause in **insert, update,** and **delete** commands. A **commit** will invalidate the cursor, so you will need to reissue the **select for update** after every **commit**.

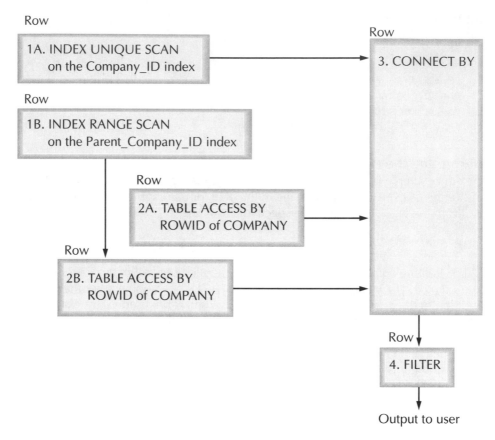

FIGURE 10-8. *FILTER example execution path*

Example

```
select Name, City, State
  from COMPANY
 where City > 'Roanoke'
   and Active_Flag = 'Y'
   for update of Name;
```

The Plan

```
FOR UPDATE
  TABLE ACCESS BY ROWID COMPANY
    INDEX RANGE SCAN COMPANY$CITY
```

Interpreting the Plan

The plan shows that the index on the City column is used to find RowIDs in the COMPANY table that satisfy the limiting condition on the City value (City > 'Roanoke'). The RowIDs from the index scan are used to query the COMPANY table for the Name and State values. The "Active_Flag='Y'" criterion is implicitly applied during the TABLE ACCESS BY ROWID operation (see the FILTER operation section). The FOR UPDATE operation is then applied to give the user row-level locks on each row returned from the query. Figure 10-9 shows the execution path.

HASH JOIN

Operation type: Hybrid of row and set operations

Description

HASH JOIN joins tables by creating an in-memory bitmap of one of the tables and then using a hashing function to locate the join rows in the second table. Hash joins are available as of Oracle7.3, and are described in detail in Chapter 13.

Example

In the following query, the COMPANY and SALES tables are joined based on their common Company_ID column.

```
select COMPANY.Name
  from COMPANY, SALES
 where COMPANY.Company_ID = SALES.Company_ID
   and SALES.Period_ID =3
   and SALES.Sales_Total>1000;
```

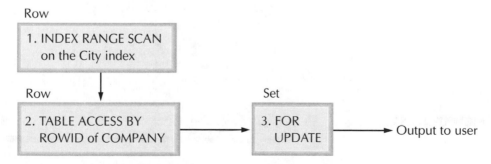

FIGURE 10-9. *FOR UPDATE example execution path*

The Plan

```
HASH JOIN
   TABLE ACCESS FULL SALES
   TABLE ACCESS FULL COMPANY
```

Interpreting the Plan

The plan shows that the SALES table is used as the first table in the hash join. SALES will be read into memory. Oracle will use a hashing function to compare the values in COMPANY to the records that have been read into memory.

If one of the tables is significantly smaller than the other in the join, and the smaller table fits into the available memory area, then the optimizer will generally use a hash join instead of a traditional NESTED LOOPS join. Even if an index is available for the join, a hash join may be preferable to a NESTED LOOPS join. See Chapter 13 for a detailed description of hash joins and the system parameters that affect them.

Figure 10-10 shows the execution path.

INDEX RANGE SCAN

Operation type: Row

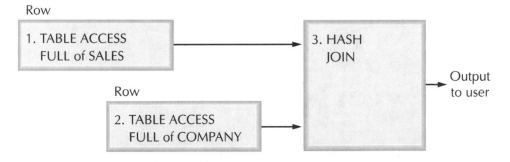

FIGURE 10-10. *HASH JOIN example execution path*

Description

INDEX RANGE SCAN selects a range of values from an index; the index can be either unique or nonunique. Range scans are used when one of the following conditions is met:

- a range operator (such as < or >) is used

- the BETWEEN clause is used

- a search string with a wildcard is used (such as 'A%')

- only part of a concatenated index is used (such as by using only the leading column of a two-column index)

The access to the range of values within the index starts with an index search for the first row that is included in the range. After the first row has been located, there is a "horizontal" scan of the index blocks until the last row inside the range is found.

NOTE
The efficiency of an INDEX RANGE SCAN is directly related to two factors: the number of keys in the selected range (the more values, the longer the search), and the condition of the index (the more fragmented, the longer the search).

Example

```
select Name, City, State
  from COMPANY
 where City > 'Roanoke';
```

The Plan

```
TABLE ACCESS BY ROWID COMPANY
   INDEX RANGE SCAN COMPANY$CITY
```

Interpreting the Plan

The plan shows that the index on the City column is used to find RowIDs in the COMPANY table that satisfy the limiting condition on the City value. Since a range of values is specified (City > 'Roanoke'), an INDEX RANGE SCAN is performed. The first value that falls within the range is found in the index; the rest of the index is then searched for the remaining values. For each matching value, the RowID is recorded. The RowIDs from the INDEX RANGE SCAN are used to query the COMPANY table for the Name and State values. Figure 10-11 shows the execution path.

INDEX UNIQUE SCAN

Operation type: Row

Description
INDEX UNIQUE SCAN, which selects a unique value from a unique index, is the most efficient method of selecting a row from known field values.

Each unique index access is built from a separate access into the index's B*tree structure, drilling down from the index root to the leaf blocks. On average, three blocks are read to fulfill the unique index access (see Chapter 5).

Example

```
select Name, City, State
  from COMPANY
 where Company_ID = 12345;
```

The Plan

```
TABLE ACCESS BY ROWID COMPANY
   INDEX UNIQUE SCAN COMPANY_PK
```

Interpreting the Plan
The query uses the Company_ID column as the sole criteria in its WHERE clause. Since Company_ID is the primary key of the COMPANY table, it has a unique index associated with it. The unique index for the Company_ID primary key is named COMPANY_PK.

During the query, the COMPANY_PK index is scanned for one Company_ID value ('12345'). When the Company_ID value is found, the RowID associated

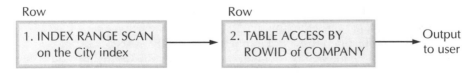

FIGURE 10-11. *INDEX RANGE SCAN example execution path*

with that COMPANY_ID is used to query the COMPANY table. Figure 10-12 shows the execution path.

INTERSECTION

Operation type: Set

Description
INTERSECTION is used to merge sets of records returned by multiple queries; in this sense, it is analogous to the index record merge performed by AND-EQUAL. INTERSECTION is used when the INTERSECT clause is used in a query.

Example
Most INTERSECT queries should be rewritten to use joins instead, to improve their ability to use row instead of set operations. The following example could be rewritten to use a join, but for purposes of illustration is shown using an INTERSECT clause.

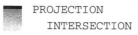

```
select Company_ID
   from COMPANY
 where State = 'AZ' and Parent_Company_ID is null
INTERSECT
select Company_ID
   from COMPETITOR;
```

The query in the previous listing will select all Company_IDs from the COMPANY table whose state value is "AZ", whose Parent_Company_ID value is null, and whose Company_ID value also is present in the COMPETITOR table.

The Plan

```
PROJECTION
   INTERSECTION
```

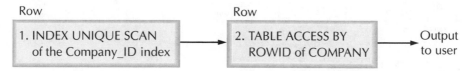

FIGURE 10-12. *INDEX UNIQUE SCAN example execution path*

```
SORT UNIQUE
   TABLE ACCESS BY ROWID COMPANY
      INDEX RANGE SCAN COMPANY$STATE
SORT UNIQUE
   TABLE ACCESS FULL COMPETITOR
```

Interpreting the Plan

The plan shows the INTERSECTION operation, along with two operations described later in this chapter: SORT UNIQUE and PROJECTION.

The plan shows that each of the queries is executed separately, and the results of the two queries are returned to the INTERSECTION operation. In the first (top) query, the index on the State column is used, and the RowID values returned from that index scan are used to select records from the COMPANY table. During the TABLE ACCESS BY ROWID on the COMPANY table, the "Parent_Company_ID is null" criteria is applied (via an implicit FILTER operation).

The second (bottom) query does not have any WHERE clause criteria, so a TABLE ACCESS FULL (full table scan) of the COMPETITOR table is performed. The results of each query are then sorted separately via the SORT UNIQUE operations—only unique Company_ID values will be passed on to the INTERSECTION operation.

The INTERSECTION operation takes the sorted rows from the two queries and returns to the user the rows that are common to both queries via the PROJECTION operation (which makes the two result sets appear as one). Figure 10-13 shows the execution path.

An Advanced INTERSECTION Example

A second example of INTERSECTION involves the CONNECT BY operation. Let's assume that you want to add a row into the COMPANY table, with a Company_ID =10 and Parent_Company_ID =5. How can you be sure that there will be no loops in the hierarchical structure of the data in the COMPANY table? The query in the following listing checks for the intersection of two searches—one up the tree, and one down the tree. If the intersection of these two queries returns a row, there is a loop in the hierarchy of the Company_ID values.

```
select Company_ID, Name
  from COMPANY
 where State = 'VA'
connect by Parent_Company_ID
        = prior Company_ID /*down the tree*/
 start with Company_ID = 10
INTERSECT
select Company_ID, Name
```

```
  from COMPANY
 where State = 'VA'
connect by Company_ID
        = prior Parent_Company_ID /*up the tree*/
 start with Company_ID = 5;
```

If the query in the preceding listing does not return any rows, there will be no loop in the Company_ID hierarchy if you insert a row with a Company_ID value of 10 and a Parent_Company_ID value of 5. The first part of the query starts down the hierarchy of Company_IDs, starting with a Company_ID value of 10. The second query starts up the hierarchy of Company_IDs, starting with a Company_ID of 5. If both queries return the same record, the INTERSECTION operation will return a record—and a loop exists in the Company_ID hierarchy for that combination of Company_ID and Parent_ID values.

The following listing shows the execution path for the preceding query. Although the execution path is complex, it can be interpreted fairly easily. The

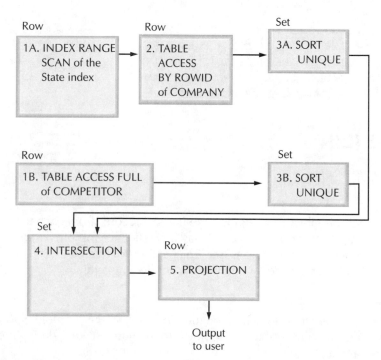

FIGURE 10-13. *INTERSECTION example execution path*

SORT UNIQUE, INTERSECTION, and PROJECTION operations are caused by the use of the INTERSECT operator in the query. The separate CONNECT BY operations generate the rows that are FILTERed (the State = 'VA' limiting condition) and are used as input to the INTERSECTION operation. Note that different indexes are used within the CONNECT BY operation, depending on the syntax of the CONNECT BY condition in the query. See Chapter 11 for information on tuning queries that use the CONNECT BY operation.

```
PROJECTION
   INTERSECTION
      SORT UNIQUE
         FILTER
            CONNECT BY
               INDEX UNIQUE SCAN COMPANY_PK
               TABLE ACCESS BY ROWID COMPANY
               TABLE ACCESS BY ROWID COMPANY
                  INDEX RANGE SCAN COMPANY$PARENT
      SORT UNIQUE
         FILTER
            CONNECT BY
               INDEX UNIQUE SCAN COMPANY_PK
               TABLE ACCESS BY ROWID COMPANY
               TABLE ACCESS BY ROWID COMPANY
                  INDEX UNIQUE SCAN COMPANY_PK
```

MERGE JOIN

Operation type: Set

Description
MERGE JOIN joins tables by merging sorted lists of records from each table. It is effective for large batch operations, but may be ineffective for joins used by transaction-processing applications (see Chapter 11). MERGE JOIN is used whenever Oracle cannot use an index while conducting a join.

Example
All of the tables used in this chapter are fully indexed, so the example below deliberately disables the indexes by adding 0 to the numeric keys during the join, in order to force a merge join to occur.

```
select COMPANY.Name
  from COMPANY, SALES
```

```
where COMPANY.Company_ID+0 = SALES.Company_ID+0
   and SALES.Period_ID =3
   and SALES.Sales_Total>1000;
```

The Plan

```
MERGE JOIN
   SORT JOIN
      TABLE ACCESS FULL SALES
   SORT JOIN
      TABLE ACCESS FULL COMPANY
```

Interpreting the Plan

There are two potential indexes that could be used by a query joining COMPANY to SALES. First, there is an index on COMPANY.Company_ID—but that index cannot be used because of the "+0" value added to it (disabling indexes is described in detail in Chapter 11, "Top ten SQL Tuning Tips"). Second, there is an index whose first column is SALES.Company_ID—but that index cannot be used, for the same reason.

As shown in the plan, Oracle will perform a full table scan (TABLE ACCESS FULL) on each table, sort the results (using the SORT JOIN operations), and merge the result sets. The use of merge joins indicates that indexes are either unavailable or disabled by the query's syntax. Figure 10-14 shows the execution path.

MINUS

Operation type: Set

Description

MINUS returns the set of rows from one query that is not present in the set of rows returned by a second query. The MINUS operation is used whenever you use the MINUS clause in a query.

Example

```
select Company_ID
   from COMPANY
MINUS
select Company_ID
   from COMPETITOR;
```

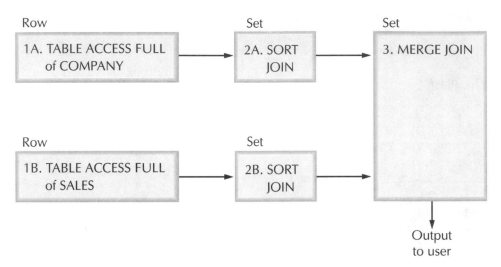

FIGURE 10-14. *MERGE JOIN example execution path*

NOTE
This example forces the use of full table scans; rewriting the query to use the NOT EXISTS clause could enable it to take advantage of indexes. See the section on subqueries in Chapter 11.

The Plan

```
PROJECTION
  MINUS
    SORT UNIQUE
      TABLE ACCESS FULL COMPANY
    SORT UNIQUE
      TABLE ACCESS FULL COMPETITOR
```

Interpreting the Plan

Since there are no WHERE conditions, no indexes will be used by the query. Each part of the larger query will be executed separately. Both tables will be fully scanned. When the scans are complete, the SORT UNIQUE operations will sort the results of each query and remove any duplicate rows within each set. The MINUS operation then returns to the user the rows that are returned from the first query but are not returned from the second query via the PROJECTION operation (which makes the two result sets appear as one). Figure 10-15 shows the execution path.

NESTED LOOPS

Operation type: Row

Description
NESTED LOOPS joins table access operations when at least one of the joined columns is indexed. The importance of the join order during NESTED LOOPS joins is discussed in Chapter 11.

Example
The query from the MERGE JOIN section will be used again as an example; this time, the indexes will not be disabled.

```
select COMPANY.Name
  from COMPANY, SALES
 where COMPANY.Company_ID = SALES.Company_ID
   and SALES.Period_ID =3
   and SALES.Sales_Total>1000;
```

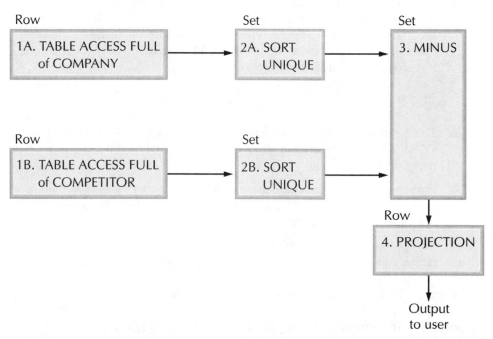

FIGURE 10-15. *MINUS example execution path*

The Plan

```
NESTED LOOPS
  TABLE ACCESS FULL SALES
  TABLE ACCESS BY ROWID COMPANY
    INDEX UNIQUE SCAN COMPANY_PK
```

Interpreting the Plan

The plan shows that the SALES table is used as the *driving table* for the query.

During NESTED LOOPS joins, one table is always used to drive the query; this example shows how the driving table is used. Chapter 11 provides tuning guidance on the selection of a driving table for a NESTED LOOPS operation.

For each Company_ID value in the SALES table, the Company_ID index on the COMPANY table will be checked to see if a matching value exists. If a match exists, that record is returned to the user via the NESTED LOOPS operation.

There are several important things to note about this query:

- Although all of the SALES table's primary key columns were specified in the query, the SALES_PK index was not used. The SALES_PK index was not used because there was not a limiting condition on the leading column (the Company_ID column) of the SALES_PK index. The only condition on SALES.Company_ID is a join condition.

- The optimizer could have selected either table as the driving table. If COMPANY was the driving table, it would have had a full table scan performed on it.

- In rule-based optimization, if there is an equal chance of using an index regardless of the choice of the driving table, the driving table will be the one that is listed last in the FROM clause.

- In cost-based optimization, the optimizer will consider the size of the tables and the selectivity of the indexes while selecting a driving table.

Figure 10-16 shows the execution path.

Interpreting the Order of Operations within NESTED LOOPS

NESTED LOOPS operations pose a special challenge when reading the output from PLAN_TABLE. Given the execution path shown in the following listing, it appears that the first step in the execution path is the scan of the COMPANY_PK index, since that is the innermost step of the execution path.

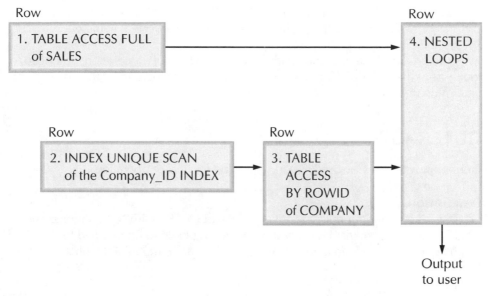

FIGURE 10-16.   *NESTED LOOPS example execution path*

```
NESTED LOOPS
  TABLE ACCESS FULL SALES
  TABLE ACCESS BY ROWID COMPANY
    INDEX UNIQUE SCAN COMPANY_PK
```

Despite its placement as the innermost step, the scan of the COMPANY_PK index is *not* the first step in the execution path. A NESTED LOOPS join needs to be driven by a row source (such as a full table scan or an index scan)—so to determine the first step within a NESTED LOOPS join, you need to determine which operations directly provide data to the NESTED LOOPS operation. In this example, two operations provide data directly to the NESTED LOOPS operation—the full table scan of SALES, and the RowID access of COMPANY.

Of the two operations that provide data to the NESTED LOOPS operation, the full table scan of SALES is listed first. Therefore, within the NESTED LOOPS operation, the order of operations is as follows.

1. The full table scan of SALES.

2. For each record in SALES, access COMPANY by Company_ID. Since an index (COMPANY_PK) is available on COMPANY.Company_ID, use that index via a unique scan.

3. For each RowID returned from the COMPANY_PK index, access the COMPANY table (to get the Name value, as requested by the query).

When reading the execution path for a NESTED LOOPS operation, you need to look first at the order of the operations that directly provide data to it, and determine their order.

OUTER JOIN

Operation type: May be used as part of either a row or set operation.

Description
OUTER is an option for both NESTED LOOPS and MERGE JOIN operations. The OUTER JOIN option enables rows from the driving table to be returned to the calling query although no matching rows were found in the joined table.

Example
The query from the NESTED LOOPS section will be used again as an example; this time, an OUTER JOIN is used.

```
select COMPANY.Name
  from COMPANY, SALES
 where COMPANY.Company_ID = SALES.Company_ID (+)
   and SALES.Period_ID = 3
   and SALES.Sales_Total >1000;
```

The Plan

```
NESTED LOOPS OUTER
   TABLE ACCESS FULL COMPANY
   TABLE ACCESS BY ROWID SALES
     INDEX RANGE SCAN SALES_PK
```

Interpreting the Plan
The plan shows that COMPANY is used as the driving table for the query. For each Company_ID value in COMPANY, the primary key index on the SALES table will be checked to see if a matching value exists. Even if a match does not exist, that record is returned to the user via the NESTED LOOPS OUTER operation. Figure 10-17 shows the execution path.

PROJECTION

Operation type: Row

Description
PROJECTION is used by the INTERSECTION, MINUS, and UNION operations to return a single set of records from the results of multiple queries.

Example
The following listing shows the MINUS operation's example from earlier in this chapter.

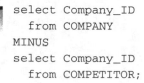

```
select Company_ID
   from COMPANY
MINUS
select Company_ID
   from COMPETITOR;
```

The Plan

```
PROJECTION
   MINUS
```

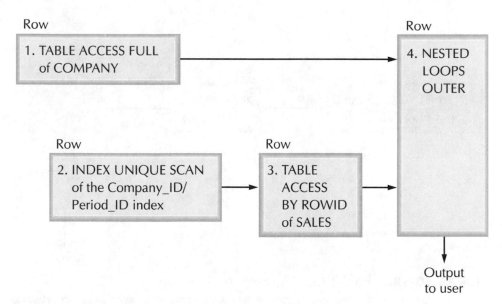

FIGURE 10-17. *OUTER JOIN example execution path*

```
SORT UNIQUE
   TABLE ACCESS FULL COMPANY
SORT UNIQUE
   TABLE ACCESS FULL COMPETITOR
```

Interpreting the Plan

The plan shows that after the MINUS operation is performed (see the "MINUS" section earlier in this chapter), the PROJECTION operation resolves the output into a single set of data for output to the user. PROJECTION is always used in conjunction with the MINUS, INTERSECTION, and UNION operations. Figure 10-18 shows the execution path.

REMOTE

Operation type: Can be either row or set

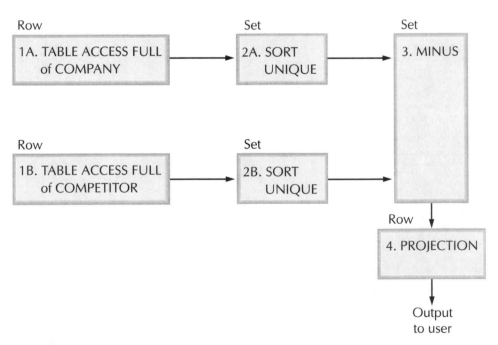

FIGURE 10-18. *PROJECTION example execution path*

Description
REMOTE sends a SQL statement to be executed at a remote node via a database link. The syntax of the SQL statement sent to the remote node is shown in the Other column of PLAN_TABLE.

Example
Since REMOTE requires a remote database access, a database link will be created for this example. The database link connects to the Hobbes account in the database that is identified via the 'test' service name in the local tnsnames.ora file.

```
create database link REMOTE1
connect to hobbes identified by tiger
 using 'test';
```

In the example query, a local COMPANY table is joined to a remote SALES table via a NESTED LOOPS join.

```
select COMPANY.Name
  from COMPANY, SALES@REMOTE1
 where COMPANY.Company_ID = SALES.Company_ID
   and SALES.Period_ID = 3
   and SALES.Sales_Total > 1000;
```

The Plan

```
NESTED LOOPS
  REMOTE
  TABLE ACCESS BY ROWID COMPANY
    INDEX UNIQUE SCAN COMPANY_PK
```

For the step with the REMOTE operation, you can query PLAN_TABLE for the syntax of the query sent to the remote node:

```
select Other
  from PLAN_TABLE
 where Operation = 'REMOTE';
```

The value of the Other column for this example is

```
SELECT "COMPANY_ID","PERIOD_ID","SALES_TOTAL"
  FROM "SALES" SALES
 WHERE "SALES_TOTAL">1000 AND "PERIOD_ID"=3
```

Interpreting the Plan

The plan shows that the remote SALES table is used as the driving table for the NESTED LOOPS join (see the NESTED LOOPS operation for a brief discussion of driving tables). The text in the PLAN_TABLE.Other column shows the query that is executed in the remote database. For each Company_ID value returned by the query of the remote SALES table, the COMPANY_PK index will be checked to see if a matching Company_ID value exists in the COMPANY table. If a match exists, that row is returned to the user via the NESTED LOOPS operation. Figure 10-19 shows the execution path for the example query.

> **NOTE**
> See Chapter 11 for tuning guidance regarding the selection of driving tables in NESTED LOOPS joins that involve remote tables.

SEQUENCE

Operation type: Row

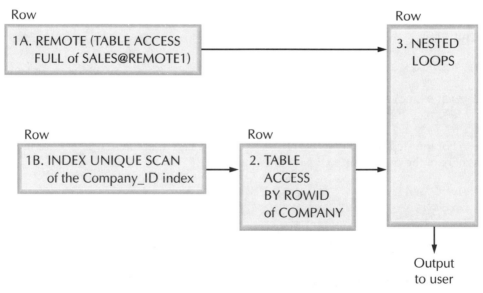

FIGURE 10-19. *REMOTE example execution path*

Description
SEQUENCE is used when accessing a database sequence via the NextVal and CurrVal pseudo-columns.

Example
Since the SEQUENCE operation requires a sequence to exist, a sequence named COMPANY_ID_SEQ will be created for this example:

```
create sequence COMPANY_ID_SEQ
 start with 1 increment by 1;
```

In the example query, the next value is selected from the sequence by selecting the sequence's NextVal pseudo-column from DUAL.

```
select COMPANY_ID_SEQ.NextVal
  from DUAL;
```

The Plan

```
SEQUENCE COMPANY_ID_SEQ
  TABLE ACCESS FULL DUAL
```

Interpreting the Plan
The plan shows that the DUAL table (comprising one row and owned by SYS) is scanned. The COMPANY_ID_SEQ sequence is used to generate the value of the NextVal pseudo-column for the returned row, using the SEQUENCE operation. Figure 10-20 shows the execution path for the query.

SORT AGGREGATE

Operation type: Set

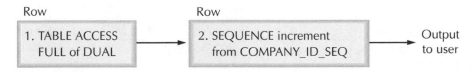

FIGURE 10-20. *SEQUENCE example execution path*

Description
SORT AGGREGATE is used to sort and aggregate result sets whenever a grouping function appears in a SQL statement without a GROUP BY clause. Grouping functions include MAX, MIN, COUNT, SUM, and AVG.

Example

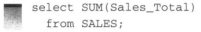

```
select SUM(Sales_Total)
  from SALES;
```

The Plan

```
SORT AGGREGATE
  TABLE ACCESS FULL SALES
```

Interpreting the Plan
The plan shows that after the SALES table is scanned (via the TABLE ACCESS FULL operation), the records are passed to the SORT AGGREGATE operation. SORT AGGREGATE sums the Sales_Total values and returns the output to the user. Figure 10-21 shows the execution path for the query.

SORT GROUP BY

Operation type: Set

Description
SORT GROUP BY performs grouping functions on sets of records.

Example

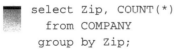

```
select Zip, COUNT(*)
  from COMPANY
 group by Zip;
```

FIGURE 10-21. *SORT AGGREGATE example execution path*

The query shown in the preceding listing selects the number of rows in each Zip, as listed in the COMPANY table. One record will be returned for each distinct value in the Zip column.

The Plan

```
SORT GROUP BY
    TABLE ACCESS FULL COMPANY
```

Interpreting the Plan

The plan shows that the COMPANY table will be scanned. After the table has been read, the SORT operation will sort and group the records according to the value of their Zip columns. Each group will then be counted, and the result will be returned to the user. Figure 10-22 shows this execution path.

SORT JOIN

Operation type: Set

Description

SORT JOIN sorts a set of records that is to be used in a MERGE JOIN operation.

Example

The example from the MERGE JOIN section earlier in this chapter will be used again. All of the tables used in this example are fully indexed, so the example below deliberately disables the indexes by adding 0 to the numeric keys during the join, in order to force a merge join to occur.

```
select COMPANY.Name
    from COMPANY, SALES
```

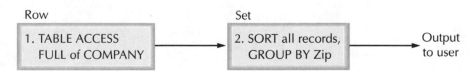

FIGURE 10-22. *SORT GROUP BY example execution path*

```
where COMPANY.Company_ID+0 = SALES.Company_ID+0
  and SALES.Period_ID =3
  and SALES.Sales_Total>1000;
```

The Plan

```
MERGE JOIN
  SORT JOIN
    TABLE ACCESS FULL SALES
  SORT JOIN
    TABLE ACCESS FULL COMPANY
```

Interpreting the Plan

The plan shows that the COMPANY and SALES tables will be accessed via TABLE ACCESS FULL operations. Before the records from those tables are passed to the MERGE JOIN operation, they will first be processed by SORT JOIN operations that sort the records. The SORT JOIN output is used as input to the MERGE JOIN operation. Figure 10-23 shows the execution path.

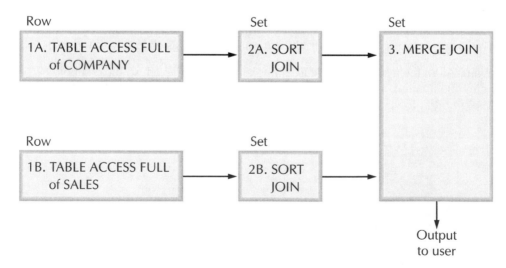

FIGURE 10-23. *SORT JOIN example execution path*

SORT ORDER BY

Operation type: Set

Description
SORT ORDER BY is used to sort result sets without elimination of duplicate records.

Example

```
select Name
  from COMPANY
 order by Name;
```

The Plan

```
SORT ORDER BY
   TABLE ACCESS FULL COMPANY
```

Interpreting the Plan
The plan shows that after the query is resolved (by the TABLE ACCESS FULL operation), the records are passed to the SORT ORDER BY operation for ordering. The SORT ORDER BY operation orders the records by their Name values and sends the output to the user. Figure 10-24 shows the execution path for the example query.

>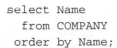
>
> **NOTE**
> If the example had used the Company_ID column instead of the Name column, the optimizer would have used the COMPANY_PK index to perform the ordering.

FIGURE 10-24. *SORT ORDER BY example execution path*

SORT UNIQUE

Operation type: Set

Description
SORT UNIQUE is used to sort result sets and eliminate duplicate records prior to processing by the MINUS, INTERSECTION and UNION operations.

Example
A MINUS operation will be used in this example, although the SORT UNIQUE operation is also shown in the "INTERSECTION" and "UNION" sections of this chapter.

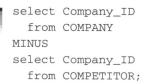

```
select Company_ID
  from COMPANY
MINUS
select Company_ID
  from COMPETITOR;
```

The Plan

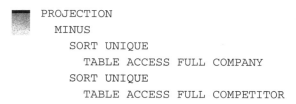

```
PROJECTION
  MINUS
    SORT UNIQUE
      TABLE ACCESS FULL COMPANY
    SORT UNIQUE
      TABLE ACCESS FULL COMPETITOR
```

Interpreting the Plan
The plan shows that after each of the queries is separately resolved (by the TABLE ACCESS FULL operations), the records are passed to the SORT UNIQUE operation prior to being input into the MINUS operation. The SORT UNIQUE operation sorts the records and eliminates any duplicates, and then sends the records to the MINUS operation. Figure 10-25 shows the execution path.

TABLE ACCESS BY ROWID

Operation type: Row

Description
TABLE ACCESS BY ROWID returns a single row from a table, based on the RowID provided to the operation. This is the fastest way to return data from a table.

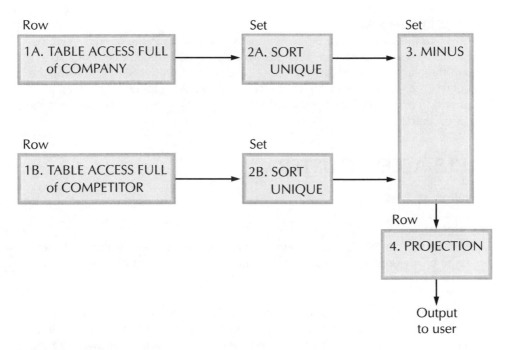

FIGURE 10-25. *SORT UNIQUE example execution path*

NOTE
TABLE ACCESS BY ROWID may also represent an implicit FILTER operation.

Example

```
select Name
  from COMPANY
 where Company_ID = 12345
   and Active_Flag = 'Y';
```

The Plan

```
TABLE ACCESS BY ROWID COMPANY
  INDEX UNIQUE SCAN COMPANY_PK
```

Interpreting the Plan

As shown in the plan, the use of the Company_ID column in the query's WHERE clause allowed the COMPANY_PK index to be used. That index does not also contain the Name column, so Oracle must access the COMPANY table, using the RowID returned by the index, to get the Name value. An implicit FILTER is then performed to return only the rows with Active_Flag = 'Y'. Figure 10-26 shows the execution path.

TABLE ACCESS CLUSTER

Operation type: Row

Description

TABLE ACCESS CLUSTER returns rows from a table that is stored within a cluster, when the cluster key is used. Chapter 5 contains a discussion of clusters.

Example

The query from the NESTED LOOPS section will be used here again as an example. For the purposes of this example, assume that COMPANY is stored in a cluster, named COMPANY_CLUSTER, and the cluster key is the Company_ID column. The name of the cluster key index (on Company_ID) is COMPANY_CLUSTER_NDX.

```
select COMPANY.Name
  from COMPANY, SALES
 where COMPANY.Company_ID = SALES.Company_ID
   and SALES.Period_ID = 3
   and SALES.Sales_Total>1000;
```

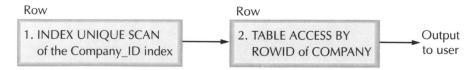

FIGURE 10-26. *TABLE ACCESS BY ROWID example execution path*

The Plan

```
NESTED LOOPS
   TABLE ACCESS FULL SALES
   TABLE ACCESS CLUSTER COMPANY
      INDEX UNIQUE SCAN COMPANY_CLUSTER_NDX
```

Interpreting the Plan

The plan shows that SALES is used as the driving table for the query. For each Company_ID value in the SALES table, there will be an access to the COMPANY table using the cluster index on the Company_ID column. Figure 10-27 shows the execution path.

TABLE ACCESS FULL

Operation type: Row

Description

TABLE ACCESS FULL returns rows from a table when the RowID is not available for the row search. Oracle scans each block in the given table until all rows are read.

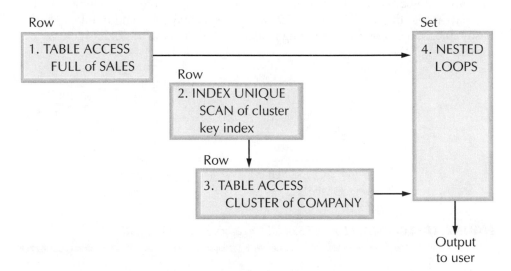

FIGURE 10-27. *TABLE ACCESS CLUSTER example execution path*

Example

```
select *
  from COMPANY;
```

The Plan

```
TABLE ACCESS FULL COMPANY
```

Interpreting the Plan

Since no restraining conditions are placed on the query, all records and all
columns will be returned. Oracle will sequentially read through all of the table's
blocks and will return them to the user as output. Figure 10-28 shows the
execution path.

TABLE ACCESS HASH

Operation type: Row

Description

TABLE ACCESS HASH is analogous to TABLE ACCESS BY ROWID; instead of
accessing rows by ROWID, the optimizer calculates the location of the row inside
the table using a hash formula on the key columns of the table and then uses that
value to access the rows. In Oracle7.2, you can specify your own formula for the
hash table. See Chapter 11 for tuning guidance related to the use of hash clusters
for very large tables.

FIGURE 10-28. *TABLE ACCESS FULL example execution path*

Example
Assume that COMPANY is stored in a hash cluster:

```
select Name
  from COMPANY
 where Company_ID = 12345
   and Active_Flag = 'Y';
```

The Plan

```
TABLE ACCESS HASH COMPANY
```

Interpreting the Plan
Since the Company_ID is the primary key for the COMPANY table, the hash
formula uses the Company_ID value to determine the RowID of the sought row.
Since the RowID will be determined by the hash formula, there is no need for an
index access to retrieve the specified row. Figure 10-29 shows the execution path.

UNION

Operation type: Set

Description
UNION returns a single set of rows from the results of two or more queries. To
perform this operation, Oracle first retrieves all the rows from both SELECT
statements, sorts them, and then performs the Union merge. Using the UNION ALL
clause prevents duplicate rows from being eliminated during the UNION
operation. The description in this section covers both UNION and UNION ALL.

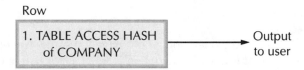

FIGURE 10-29. *TABLE ACCESS HASH example execution path*

Example

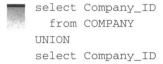

```
select Company_ID
  from COMPANY
UNION
select Company_ID
  from COMPETITOR;
```

The query in the preceding listing will return a single set of Company_ID values—all Company_ID values in either COMPANY or COMPETITOR. Duplicate COMPANY_ID values will be eliminated.

The Plan

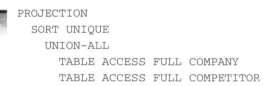

```
PROJECTION
  SORT UNIQUE
    UNION-ALL
      TABLE ACCESS FULL COMPANY
      TABLE ACCESS FULL COMPETITOR
```

Interpreting the Plan

The plan contains a surprise—a UNION actually does a UNION ALL! UNION returns unique records that are found in two separate queries. UNION ALL returns all records, including duplicates, that are found in two separate queries. A UNION is, within the optimizer, the combination of a UNION ALL (which makes one concatenated result set out of the two queries' output) and a SORT UNIQUE (which then eliminates the duplicates).

Since no WHERE clauses are used in either query, Oracle will perform a full table scan on each table. The UNION-ALL operation merges the two result sets into a single result set. SORT UNIQUE then eliminates the duplicate values and sends the records to the PROJECTION operation for output to the user. Figure 10-30 shows the execution path.

> **NOTE**
> A UNION ALL operation would have the same execution path, except that it would not contain a SORT UNIQUE operation.

VIEW

Operation type: Set

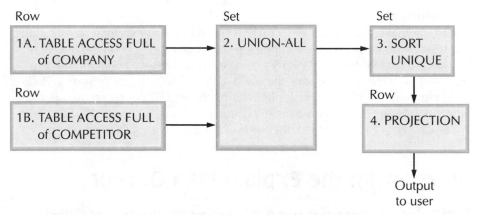

FIGURE 10-30.   *UNION example execution path*

Description
VIEW resolves any query nested deeper than the VIEW operation into a temporary area. The use of VIEW may be caused by correlated queries or by the inability of Oracle to pull a view's query into the rest of a larger query, forcing it to resolve the view separately.

Example
The example is in two parts: a view is created and then queried. The plan that follows applies only to the query of the view, not to the view creation itself.

```
create view COMPANY_COUNT as
select Zip, COUNT(*) Company_Count
  from COMPANY
 group by Zip;

select Zip, Company_Count
  from COMPANY_COUNT
 where Company_Count BETWEEN 10 and 20;
```

The Plan

```
VIEW COMPANY_COUNT
  FILTER
    SORT GROUP BY
      TABLE ACCESS FULL COMPANY
```

Interpreting the Plan

Because there is a set operation (GROUP BY) within the view syntax, the optimizer must resolve the view before executing the conditions specified in the query. All the rows are fetched from COMPANY using a full table scan, and then they are sorted and counted by Zip during the SORT GROUP BY operation. The WHERE clause condition in the query is applied during the FILTER operation on the result of the view. Figure 10-31 shows the execution path.

See Chapter 11 for a detailed discussion of the use of views during tuning efforts.

Interpreting the Explain Plan Output

The output of the **explain plan** command, as shown at the beginning of this chapter, is a set of records in PLAN_TABLE that illustrate the relationships between the data access operations in the execution path. All of the available operations are described and illustrated in the preceding "Operations" section. Even the most complex queries can be understood if their execution paths are generated, since every step in the path will be an operation. With the explain plan output showing the parent-child relationships between steps, you can construct a visual image of the query, and can understand where potential performance problems may arise.

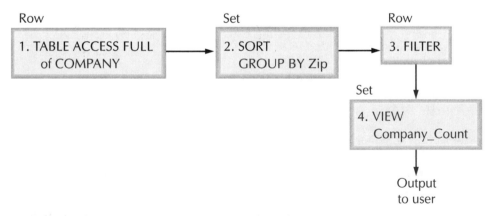

FIGURE 10-31. *VIEW example execution path*

Consider the following explain plan. An Order column is shown as well, to illustrate the order in which operations are performed.

```
ORDER Q_PLAN
----- ------------------------------------------------------
   10 PROJECTION
    9  SORT UNIQUE
    8   UNION-ALL
    5    MERGE JOIN
    2     SORT JOIN
    1      TABLE ACCESS FULL COMPANY
    4     SORT JOIN
    3      TABLE ACCESS FULL SALES
    7    TABLE ACCESS BY ROWID COMPETITOR
    6     INDEX UNIQUE SCAN COMPETITOR_PK
```

See Figure 10-32 for the graphical representation of the execution path. In the following discussion, the references to step numbers refer to the Order column shown in the preceding listing. To minimize confusion, the step numbering scheme used in prior illustrations in this chapter is not used here.

Without even seeing the query, we can make some judgments about its performance. First, the final operation performed for this query is a UNION—the combination of PROJECTION, SORT UNIQUE, and UNION-ALL shows that (see "UNION" earlier in this chapter). UNION (steps 8, 9, and 10) is a set operation, so it will not return any rows to the user until the UNION completes. Second, one of the operations that directly feeds the UNION is another set operation, MERGE JOIN (step 5). The UNION cannot begin until the MERGE JOIN completes. The second operation that feeds into the UNION is a row operation, TABLE ACCESS BY ROWID of the COMPETITOR table (step 7).

Consider the execution path again, this time simplifying it to just the major operations (collapsing the UNION steps into a single step):

```
Q_PLAN
------------------------------------------------------
UNION
  MERGE JOIN
    SORT JOIN
      TABLE ACCESS FULL COMPANY
    SORT JOIN
      TABLE ACCESS FULL SALES
  TABLE ACCESS BY ROWID COMPETITOR
    INDEX UNIQUE SCAN COMPETITOR_PK
```

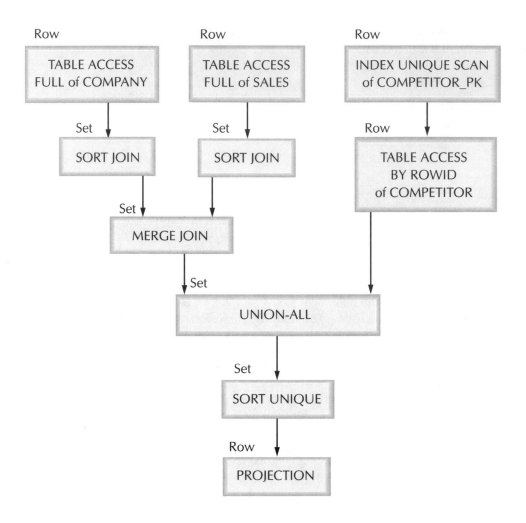

FIGURE 10-32. *Explain plan example execution path*

Looking at the steps in the previous listing strictly from an operation-type viewpoint, the execution path is:

```
Q_PLAN
------------------------------------------------------------
SET
  SET
    SET
        ROW
    SET
        ROW
  ROW
    ROW
```

The three set operations are nested—the outermost one (the UNION), the last to complete, cannot begin until the inner ones (the MERGE JOINs and the SORT JOINs) complete. This query may not perform well in an online environment—it cannot take advantage of the row operations' ability to return rows quickly. If the MERGE JOIN had been replaced by a NESTED LOOPS operation (which is a row operation), there would only be a single set operation (the UNION) remaining in the query.

Can the query be tuned? Since we haven't seen the query, and don't know its use, it is too soon to say—but you can now understand its processing, and the implications of its processing, at a glance. See Chapter 11 for a detailed discussion of join options.

New Features in Oracle7.3

Each query that involves an analyzed table will report a "Cost" during its explain plan analysis. The "Cost" value only applies to the query being analyzed—it can be used to compare queries that return the same data, but cannot be used to compare the performance of unlike queries. The Cost value reflects the relative cost for the throughput required by the query, and does not consider the time required to return the first row of the return set.

The cost for the query is stored in the Position column for the first step of the query (the step for which the Parent_ID value is null, and ID=0). The PLAN_TABLE.Position column contains the optimizer's estimation of the statement's "cost" (if cost-based optimization is used; otherwise, no cost is calculated).

In Oracle7.3, Oracle provides the Cost associated with each step of a query. Thus, you can now tell how much each step in the query contributes to the query's throughput. The cost for each step is stored in the Cost column of PLAN_TABLE. With the step cost data, you can more easily identify the most costly steps in the execution path.

Applying Query Tuning to Process Tuning

Which operation should you use when accessing your data? It depends. Different types of processes have different ways of measuring performance: online applications rate performance based on the time it takes to return the first row of the query, while batch applications rate performance based on the time it takes for the entire query to complete. Process tuning typically involves batch processes, so the goal should be to achieve the best throughput in your process's queries.

By default, Oracle optimizes queries to achieve best throughput—ideal for batch processes. Using best throughput as a goal may cause Oracle to use set instead of row operations, while row operations would be favored if your goal was the performance of returning the first row. In addition, set processing may involve full table scans, which do not cache well in the SGA. Set processing may create disk I/O bottlenecks.

For example, when joining two tables, the primary choices are NESTED LOOPS and MERGE JOIN operations. NESTED LOOPS is a row operation, while MERGE JOIN is a set operation. Based on the available statistics, Oracle may decide that a MERGE JOIN operation will complete faster than a NESTED LOOPS operation for a given query. For batch processing, it would be faster to use the MERGE JOIN operation in that case. However, if the same query is to be used as part of an online application, it should be modified to use the NESTED LOOPS operation.

In the next section, "Using Hints," you'll see how to influence the choices that the optimizer makes when evaluating the data access operations available during the execution of a query.

Using Hints

You can use *hints* to alter the execution path chosen by the cost-based optimizer. Hints are embedded within SQL statements, and only modify the execution path for the statements in which they appear. The start of a hint is indicated by the following string,

/ * +

following a **SELECT**, **DELETE**, or **UPDATE**. A hint's text is terminated by

* /

The syntax for hints is almost identical to that of comments within SQL—the only difference is the addition of the "+" sign to indicate the start of the hint. The "+" cannot be preceded by a space.

NOTE
If a hint is specified incorrectly, the optimizer will ignore it and will *not* report an error.

In the following sections, you'll see descriptions of the available hints, and examples of their usage. Many of the hints shown in the following sections are referenced in Chapter 11. The operations referenced by the hints are described in the "Operations" sections earlier in this chapter.

NOTE
Many of the hints allow you to list specific table names. If you use table aliases in your query, refer to the tables by their aliases within the hints.

ALL_ROWS

The ALL_ROWS hint tells Oracle to optimize the query for the best throughput—that is, to minimize the time it takes for all rows to be returned by the query. This is the default action of the Oracle optimizer, and is appropriate for batch operations. An example is shown in the following listing.

```
select /*+ ALL_ROWS */
       COMPANY.Name
  from COMPANY, SALES
 where COMPANY.Company_ID = SALES.Company_ID
   and SALES.Period_ID =3
   and SALES.Sales_Total>1000;
```

The example shown in the previous example would normally use a NESTED LOOPS operation during the query's execution (see the "NESTED LOOPS" section earlier in this chapter). ALL_ROWS will force the optimizer to consider using a MERGE JOIN instead.

NOTE
If you specify ALL_ROWS, you must have previously analyzed the tables used by the query. If you have not done this, the optimizer estimates missing statistics and uses them while choosing an execution path.

AND-EQUAL

The AND-EQUAL hint tells the optimizer to perform an AND-EQUAL operation on the indexes listed within the hint. An example of this hint is shown in the following listing.

```
select /*+ AND-EQUAL COMPANY$CITY, COMPANY$STATE */
       Name, City, State
  from COMPANY
 where City = 'Roanoke'
   and State = 'VA';
```

CACHE

The CACHE hint, when used for a table in a query, tells Oracle to treat the table as a cached table. That is, CACHE tells Oracle to keep the blocks from the full table scan of a table in the SGA's data block buffer cache area, instead of quickly removing them from the SGA. Caching is particularly useful for small, frequently-used tables. The CACHE hint is useful if a non-cached table will be frequently scanned by separate parts of a query. An example of this hint is shown in the following listing. In the example, the blocks read from the full table scan of the COMPETITOR table (see the FULL hint later in this section) will be marked as "most recently used," so they will stay in the data block buffer cache longer than if the CACHE hint was not used.

```
select /*+ FULL(competitor) CACHE(competitor) */   *
  from COMPETITOR
 where Company_ID > 5;
```

CHOOSE

The CHOOSE hint tells the optimizer to choose between cost-based and rule-based optimization for the query. If the tables used by the query have been analyzed, the optimizer will use cost-based optimization. If no statistics are available, rule-based optimization will be used. As discussed in Chapter 7, applications that use a mix of the two should generally use cost-based optimization for the majority of the transactions, while using the RULE hint to specify rule-based optimization for specific queries. If you have set up the cost-based optimizer properly, the CHOOSE hint is unnecessary. The CHOOSE hint is available as of Oracle7.2.

CLUSTER

The CLUSTER hint tells the optimizer to use a TABLE ACCESS CLUSTER operation. The syntax for the CLUSTER hint is

```
/*+ CLUSTER(table) */
```

See the "TABLE ACCESS CLUSTER" operation description earlier in this chapter for information on cluster accesses.

FIRST_ROWS

The FIRST_ROWS hint is the logical opposite of the ALL_ROWS hint: it tells the operator to optimize the query with the goal of the shortest response time for the return of the first row from the query. FIRST_ROWS is ignored if set-based operations are used. If indexes or a NESTED LOOPS join is available, the optimizer will usually choose to use them. An example of this hint is shown in the following listing.

```
select /*+ FIRST_ROWS */
       COMPANY.Name
  from COMPANY, SALES
 where COMPANY.Company_ID = SALES.Company_ID
   and SALES.Period_ID =3
   and SALES.Sales_Total>1000;
```

NOTE
If you specify FIRST_ROWS, you must have previously analyzed the tables used by the query. If you have not done so, the optimizer estimates missing statistics and uses them while choosing an execution path.

FULL

The FULL hint tells the optimizer to perform a TABLE ACCESS FULL operation on the specified table. You may wish to use this hint if you know that the index normally used by the query would be a poor choice given the data distribution.

For example, consider the query shown in the following listing. Under normal data distribution, an AND-EQUAL of the City and State indexes would be appropriate for good performance.

```
select Name, City, State
  from COMPANY
 where City = 'Roanoke'
   and State = 'VA';
```

What if 90 percent of the records in the table have a City value of 'Roanoke' and a State value of 'VA'? If you use the indexes to access the 'Roanoke' records, you will have to read almost all of the index blocks and table blocks to satisfy the query. In that case, it would require fewer logical reads to simply scan the COMPANY table (via a TABLE ACCESS FULL operation). You can force a TABLE ACCESS FULL to occur by disabling the indexes or by using the FULL hint, as shown in the following listing.

```
select /*+ FULL(COMPANY) */
        Name, City, State
  from COMPANY
 where City = 'Roanoke'
   and State = 'VA';
```

HASH

The HASH hint tells the optimizer to use a TABLE ACCESS HASH operation. The syntax for the HASH hint is

```
/*+ HASH(table) */
```

See the "TABLE ACCESS HASH" operation description earlier in this chapter for information on hash cluster accesses.

HASH_AJ

The HASH_AJ hint specifies the type of join to use during an antijoin in Oracle7.3. See Chapter 13 for a description of antijoins.

Index

The INDEX hint can be used in three different ways:

1. If a single index is listed, that index will be used.

2. If multiple indexes are listed, the optimizer will choose which indexes to use.

3. If a table is listed, but no indexes are listed, the optimizer will choose an index or indexes to use for that table.

Given the query in the following listing, the optimizer may choose to use the index on City, the index on State, or both, as appropriate.

```
select /*+ INDEX(COMPANY) */
       Name, City, State
  from COMPANY
 where City = 'Roanoke'
   and State = 'VA';
```

INDEX_ASC

The INDEX_ASC hint is the same as the INDEX hint.

INDEX_DESC

The INDEX_DESC hint tells the optimizer to scan an index in descending order of the indexed values. INDEX_DESC is most commonly used with subqueries; see Chapter 11 for an example of this usage.

MERGE_AJ

The MERGE_AJ hint specifies the type of join to use during an antijoin in
Oracle7.3. See Chapter 13 for a description of antijoins.

NO_MERGE

The NO_MERGE hint, available as of Oracle7.3, tells the optimizer to not merge a
view's SQL syntax with the syntax of a query that uses the view. See Chapter 11 for
tuning examples involving views.

NOCACHE

The NOCACHE hint specifies that blocks retrieved by a full table scan are not to be
cached within the SGA's data block buffer cache. The blocks will be marked as
"least recently used," and will be the first ones removed from the SGA when
additional space is needed in the cache. In the following example, the blocks from
the COMPETITOR table will be marked as "least recently used" within the cache
(this is the default behavior for noncached tables).

```
select /*+ FULL(competitor) NOCACHE(competitor) */    *
  from COMPETITOR
 where Company_ID > 5;
```

NOPARALLEL

The NOPARALLEL hint allows you to disable parallelism for a query, even if the
tables used by the query have been defined to have a default degree of parallelism.
See Chapter 12 for information on selecting the degree of parallelism for a query,
and for managing the Parallel Query Option.

ORDERED

The ORDERED hint, when used with NESTED LOOPS joins, influences the order in
which tables are joined—that is, the structure of the loops used by the join. If you
use this hint, you need to be certain that the relative distribution of values within
the joined tables will not change dramatically over time; otherwise, the specified
join order may cause performance problems in the future. The join order for
NESTED LOOPS joins is discussed in Chapter 11.

PARALLEL

The PARALLEL hint allows you to specify a degree of parallelism for a table in a query. The degree of parallelism specified by the PARALLEL hint will override any degree of parallelism already defined at the table level. See Chapter 12 for information on selecting and setting the degree of parallelism for a query, and for managing the Parallel Query Option.

ROWID

The ROWID hint tells the optimizer to use a TABLE ACCESS BY ROWID operation. The syntax for the ROWID hint is

```
/*+ ROWID(table) */
```

See the "TABLE ACCESS BY ROWID" operation description earlier in this chapter.

RULE

The RULE hint tells the optimizer to use rule-based optimization for the query. All other hints within the query will be ignored. The syntax is shown in the following listing.

```
select /*+ RULE */
       COMPANY.Name
  from COMPANY, SALES
 where COMPANY.Company_ID = SALES.Company_ID
   and SALES.Period_ID =3
   and SALES.Sales_Total>1000;
```

STAR

The STAR hint, available as of Oracle7.3, tells the optimizer to use a composite key/star query execution path when resolving a join. Star query execution paths are typically used by data warehousing applications that feature a master table with many small detail tables. See the "Use Composite Keys/Star Queries" section of Chapter 11 for a detailed discussion of the use of star query execution paths.

USE_CONCAT

The USE_CONCAT hint forces conditions that are combined via OR clauses in the WHERE clause to be treated as a compound query using the UNION ALL operation. USE_CONCAT is available as of Oracle7.2.

USE_HASH

The USE_HASH hint, available as of Oracle7.3, tells the optimizer to perform a hash join. See Chapter 13 for a full description of hash joins.

USE_MERGE

The USE_MERGE hint is the logical opposite of the USE_NL hint. USE_MERGE tells the optimizer to use a merge join between specific tables—and thus is a more detailed hint than ALL_ROWS.

For the query in the following listing, the COMPANY table and the SALES table will be joined via a MERGE JOIN operation. USE_MERGE is useful when you are joining three or more tables and need to specify a MERGE JOIN operation for specific sets of tables within the query.

```
select /*+ USE_MERGE(COMPANY, SALES) */
       COMPANY.Name
  from COMPANY, SALES
 where COMPANY.Company_ID = SALES.Company_ID
   and SALES.Period_ID =3
   and SALES.Sales_Total>1000;
```

USE_NL

The USE_NL hint tells the optimizer to perform a NESTED LOOPS join, using the specified table as the driving table in the join. USE_NL is more specific than the FIRST_ROWS hint, since FIRST_ROWS may lead to a NESTED LOOPS join being used, but USE_NL lets you influence the join order of the tables within the NESTED LOOPS join.

For example, for the query in the following listing, the COMPANY table will be used as the driving table in a NESTED LOOPS operation.

```
select /*+ USE_NL(COMPANY) */
       COMPANY.Name
  from COMPANY, SALES
 where COMPANY.Company_ID = SALES.Company_ID
   and SALES.Period_ID =3
   and SALES.Sales_Total>1000;
```

CHAPTER 11

The Top Ten SQL Tuning Tips

Most of the time, the execution path selected by the Oracle optimizer is the best possible path to use when resolving a query. In about 5 to 10 percent of the cases, however, a better execution path is available. When your tables are small, the performance impact of using a nonoptimal execution path may be minimal. As your tables grow in size, the performance impact of nonoptimized queries can grow exponentially.

As the performance of a single query rapidly worsens, it consumes resources that should be available to the rest of the application—and soon, the entire system's performance deteriorates. To avoid this scenario, you need to actively manage the performance of the queries within your application. In this chapter you will see the ten tuning tips that are most frequently used when improving the performance of SQL in Oracle7. Improving the poorly optimized queries will have a significant impact on the overall performance of your application.

The Objective of the SQL Tuning Tips

The goal of SQL tuning is to improve the performance of queries through manual intervention. The performance of a query is altered by changing its *execution path*—the set of operations that the database uses to access and manipulate the desired data. The execution path may be altered to use specific operations when processing the query. For a detailed description of operations and hints, see Chapter 10. You should be familiar with the available operations and hints to make the best use of this chapter.

The Ten Tips

The top ten SQL tuning tips are:

1. Avoid Unplanned Full Table Scans.

2. Use Only Selective Indexes.

3. Manage Multi-Table Joins (NESTED LOOPS and MERGE JOINs).

4. Manage SQL Statements Containing Views.

5. Tune Subqueries.

6. Use Composite Keys/Star Queries.

7. Properly Index CONNECT BY Operations.

8. Limit Remote Table Accesses.

9. Manage Very Large Table Accesses.

10. Revisit the Tuning Process.

In the following sections, you will see examples of queries that require manual tuning intervention, along with the execution paths before and after tuning. Both the theoretical basis for the tip and detailed implementation information are provided. The examples use the sample tables from Chapter 10.

1. Avoid Unplanned Full Table Scans

Full table scans sequentially read all data from a table—whether it is relevant to the query or not. There are two strong reasons for avoiding unnecessary full table scans:

- *Full table scans are not selective.* While nonselective searches may be appropriate for large batch jobs that operate on many records, they are usually inappropriate for online applications.

- *Data read via full table scans is removed from the SGA buffers quickly.* If the table being scanned is not a "cached" table (see Chapter 13), the data read via a full table scan is placed at the end of the Least Recently Used block list. As a result, the data blocks read from the full table scan are the first to be removed from the SGA. For a multiuser system, full table scans prevent users from sharing the tables' data in the SGA; the same blocks have to be read multiple times via physical reads of the datafiles.

When a Full Table Scan Is Used

Under rule-based optimization, a full table scan will be used on a table if any of the following conditions are met in a SQL statement:

- No indexes exist on the table.

- No limiting conditions are placed on the rows returned (that is, the query requests all rows). For example, if the query does not have a **where** clause, all rows will be returned.

- No limiting conditions placed on the rows correspond to the leading column of any index on the table. For example, if a three-column concatenated index is created on the City-State-Zip columns, then a query that had a limiting condition on only the State column would not be able to use that index, since State is not the leading column of that index.

- Limiting conditions placed on the rows correspond to the leading column of an index, but the conditions are used inside expressions. For example, if an index exists on the City column, then a limiting condition of

```
where City = 'TOKYO'
```

could use the index. However, if the limiting condition was instead

```
where UPPER(City) = 'TOKYO'
```

then the index on the City column would not be used because the City column is inside the UPPER function. If you had concatenated the City column with a text string, the index would not be used. For example, if the limiting condition was

```
where City||'X' like 'TOKYO%'
```

then the index on the City column would not be used.

■ Limiting conditions placed on the rows correspond to the leading column of an index, but the conditions are either NULL checks or inequalities. For example, if an index exists on the City column, none of the following will be able to use the index:

```
where City is null
where City is not null
where City != 'TOKYO'
```

If cost-based optimization is used, Oracle will use full table scans for all of the cases shown for rule-based optimization. Additionally, the cost-based optimizer may decide to use full table scans if the table has not been analyzed, if the table is small, if the indexed columns are not selective, or if the optimization goal is set to ALL_ROWS (see Chapter 10 for a description of ALL_ROWS).

To avoid unplanned full table scans, make sure the query can use an index.

How to Make Sure a Query Can Use an Index

To make sure a query can use an index, you should first index all of your primary key and foreign key columns. These are the columns most likely to be used during joins and limiting conditions, so indexing them immediately resolves several of the potential full table scan causes listed in the previous section. By default, Oracle will create a unique index for each primary key constraint; foreign keys are not automatically indexed.

The order of the columns within your concatenated indexes is critical. There are two issues that you must balance relative to the order of columns within indexes. First, the column most frequently used in limited conditions should be the leading column. As shown in the previous section, a query using only the second column of a three-column index will not be able to use the index. Second, the most selective column—the column with the most distinct values—should be the leading column. The selectivity of the leading column is critical if you are using the cost-based optimizer, since the optimizer will judge the index's selectivity based on the leading column's selectivity. Ideally, the column most used in limiting conditions is also the most selective column in the index. If that is not the case, you may need to create multiple indexes on the columns (see Tip #2, "Use Only Selective Indexes," for tips on index creation).

Within the query, you need to verify that the indexed columns are not being used within expressions such as concatenate (||), UPPER, and SUBSTR. Also, you need to verify that the limiting conditions for the query are equalities, and are not NULL checks or inequalities.

Issues Encountered When Creating Indexes

When creating indexes, always create them in a separate tablespace from the table they index; if the tablespaces are stored in datafiles that are on separate devices, you can reduce I/O contention that may occur during queries and transactions. The indexes should always be created under the same owner account as the table, and should use a consistent naming convention. The name for an index should include the name of the table it indexes, and indicate whether it is a unique or nonunique index.

The storage space used by indexes should be properly sized. See Chapter 5 for information on the implications of sizing and extents for indexes.

2. Use Only Selective Indexes

The *selectivity* of an index is the ratio of the number of distinct values in the indexed column(s) to the number of records in the table. If a table has 1000 records, and an indexed column on that table has 950 distinct values, then the selectivity of that index is 950/1000, or 0.95. The best possible selectivity is 1.00. Unique indexes on non-nullable columns always have a selectivity of 1.00.

The selectivity of an index is a measure of the index's usefulness in reducing the I/O required by queries against the index's table. For example, if an index on a 1000 record table had only five distinct values, then the index's poor selectivity (5/1000 = 0.005) would make it a poor choice when applying limiting conditions on rows. If there are only five distinct values among the 1000 records in the example table, the index would return an average of 200 records for each distinct value. In that case, it may be more efficient to perform a full table scan instead of multiple index scans and table accesses.

If you are using cost-based optimization, the optimizer should not use poorly selective indexes. If you are using rule-based optimization, the optimizer will not consider the selectivity of an index when determining the execution path (unless the index is created as a unique index), and you will have to manually tune your queries to avoid using nonselective indexes.

Measuring Index Selectivity

Index selectivity can be measured via manual and automated methods. To manually measure selectivity, query the base table for the number of distinct values for the given index. For example, if you are creating a two-column concatenated index on the City and State columns of the COMPANY table, the query shown in the following listing would return the number of distinct combinations of City and State values in COMPANY:

```
select COUNT(distinct City||'%'||State)
  from COMPANY;
```

Once you know the number of distinct values from the preceding query, you can compare it to the total number of rows in the table, as provided by the following query.

```
select COUNT(*)
  from COMPANY;
```

The ratio of the number of distinct values to the total number of rows is the selectivity of the columns. The advantage of the manual method is its ability to estimate the selectivity of an index before the index is created.

To automate the selectivity measurement process for existing indexes, you can use the **analyze** command. If you analyze a table, all of the table's indexes will automatically be analyzed as well. To determine the selectivity of an index, analyze the table, as shown in the following listing. In the example, the **compute statistics** option of the **analyze** command is used to generate the most accurate statistics possible.

```
analyze table COMPANY compute statistics;
```

NOTE
You can analyze tables when using both the rule-based and cost-based optimizers. The optimizer will only use the statistics if cost-based optimization is used.

Once the table and its indexes have been analyzed, you can determine the selectivity of the index. The number of distinct values in the index is shown in USER_INDEXES. The query in the following listing will display the number of distinct keys in the COMPANY$CITY index.

```
select Distinct_Keys
  from USER_INDEXES
```

```
where Table_Name = 'COMPANY'
   and Index_Name = 'COMPANY$CITY';
```

The total number of rows in the table is in USER_TABLES:

```
select Num_Rows
  from USER_TABLES
 where Table_Name = 'COMPANY';
```

The Distinct_Keys value, divided by the Num_Rows value, is the index's selectivity.

In Oracle7.2 and above, you can query USER_TAB_COLUMNS to see the selectivity of each column individually (after the table has been analyzed). As with the manual method shown previously, these statistics allow you to calculate the selectivity of a column before an index is created on the column.

```
select Column_Name, Num_Distinct
  from USER_TAB_COLUMNS
 where Table_Name = 'COMPANY';
```

The Num_Distinct column in USER_TAB_COLUMNS displays the number of distinct values in that column for all rows in the table. Divide Num_Distinct by the total number of rows for the table (the Num_Rows column in USER_TABLES) to determine a column's selectivity. Null values will count as separate distinct values.

Querying USER_TAB_COLUMNS will help you measure the selectivity of individual columns, but it will not allow you to accurately measure the selectivity of concatenated sets of columns. To measure the selectivity of a set of columns, you need to either use the manual method or create an index on the set of columns and re-analyze the table.

Choosing a Leading Column for a Concatenated Index

As described in the section on avoiding unplanned full table scans, concatenated indexes present a challenge to the DBA: the leading column should be the most selective column, and it should also be the column most often used by limiting conditions in queries. Most of the time, a single column will meet both of the conditions. If a single column meets both conditions, that column should be the leading column. The second-most-used and second-most-selective column should be the second column in the index.

If a nonselective column is the most frequently used column in limiting conditions, you may need to evaluate your application design. Users' queries should return the minimum number of records they need—forcing them to use a nonselective execution path in their queries will have a damaging effect upon their queries' performance.

If a highly selective column is not frequently used in the limiting conditions of queries, then why has an index been created on the column? If the column is a foreign key column, then it should be indexed; otherwise the requirement for the index should be reevaluated. It is appropriate to create lightly-used indexes to resolve performance problems with specific queries, but their impact on the performance and management of the rest of the application must be considered.

Choosing Between Concatenated Indexes and Multiple Single-Column Indexes

What is more selective in the COMPANY table—an index on City, or a concatenated index on City and State? If there are 200 unique City values in a 1000 record COMPANY table, the selectivity of City is 0.2. How many distinct combinations of City and State are there? Most likely, there are around 200—the number of distinct values will increase slightly (for example, to distinguish Portland, ME, from Portland, OR), but usually not enough to significantly alter the selectivity of the index. The largest single factor in determining the selectivity of a concatenated index is the selectivity of its leading column.

Because the selectivity of a concatenated index's leading column plays such a large role in determining the index's overall selectivity, there is usually little additional cost to index selectivity when more columns are added to the index. The overall size and complexity of the index should be considered when evaluating its column composition, but its selectivity should remain fairly constant as columns are added.

Choosing between a single concatenated index—City and State together—versus multiple single-column indexes—a City index and a State index—requires you to evaluate the ways in which the columns are used as limiting conditions. If both columns are used as limiting conditions, and if the second column is used by itself in many queries, the second column should be separately indexed. Your options are shown in Table 11-1.

As shown in Table 11-1, one index will be created on either the City column or the concatenation of the City and State columns. As previously described, the selectivity of these two indexes is likely to be very similar; if that is the case, then

Scenario	Index #1	Index #2
1	City, State	(none)
2	City, State	State
3	City	State

TABLE 11-1. *Concatenated versus Single-Column Index Options*

use the concatenated index. Scenario #3 in Table 11-1 is therefore disregarded. The only remaining question is whether an index should be created on the State column—and that determination is based on the State column's selectivity and the degree to which it is used as a limiting condition column.

Using a single concatenated index in place of multiple single-column indexes also limits the amount of input to AND-EQUAL operations during query processing, and may significantly improve performance of that operation. The AND-EQUAL operation merges lists of data returned from multiple index scans. AND-EQUAL scans the entire index range of all involved indexes for a given value, and then performs the merge. For example, if there are 100,000 records in the COMPANY table, and 10,000 of the records had a City value of 'Portland', then the index range scan of the City index for the 'Portland' value would require 10,000 reads. If 5000 of the records had a State value of 'OR,' then the index range scan of the State index for the 'OR' value would require 5000 reads. The AND-EQUAL operation involving the City and State indexes thus requires 15,000 index reads (10,000+5000) to resolve a query with limiting conditions specifying City = 'Portland' and State = 'OR'. If City and State had been concatenated into a single index, the AND-EQUAL operation may require far fewer logical reads. Since there are 10,000 COMPANY records with a City value of 'Portland,' you would need no more than 10,000 logical reads if City and State were concatenated into a single index—a reduction of at least 33 percent. Since only one index would be used, no AND-EQUAL operation would be necessary, and the RowIDs from the index would be passed on to the next operation in the execution path.

3. Manage Multi-Table Joins (NESTED LOOPS and MERGE JOINs)

Two join operations are available in Oracle: NESTED LOOPS and MERGE JOIN (a third option, hash joins, was added in Oracle7.3 and is explained in Chapter 13). As described in Chapter 10, MERGE JOIN is a set operation; it does not return records to the next operation until all of the rows have been processed. NESTED LOOPS is a row operation, returning the first records to the next operation quickly. In the following section, you will see how to use the size of the tables and nature of the query to determine which operation is most appropriate for your query.

Within each of the join options, there are a number of steps you must take to get the best performance from the join. If you do not properly tune a NESTED LOOPS or MERGE JOIN operation, then the performance of the join, if acceptable at first, may grow exponentially as the tables grow. In the following sections you will see how to tune each of these operations, and how to choose which to use.

Tuning your joins can have a significant impact on the performance of your queries, and there are many options available. Since it is an important area of focus, and so many choices are available, the following sections form the largest single tip in this chapter. Examples of each major option are provided.

Steps Involved in MERGE JOINs

A MERGE JOIN operation joins the results of two data scans. The MERGE JOIN operation usually comprises three steps:

1. TABLE ACCESS FULL of each table in the join

2. SORT JOIN to sort the results of the data access operations (such as TABLE ACCESS FULL)

3. MERGE JOIN to merge the results of the SORT JOIN operation

The use of MERGE JOINs indicates that indexes are either unavailable or disabled by the query's syntax. Figure 11-1 shows the execution path for a two-table MERGE JOIN between COMPANY and SALES.

As a set operation that performs full table scans of its tables, MERGE JOIN is usually not appropriate for use in multiuser online applications for the following reasons:

■ It may be slow to return the first row from the query. Since MERGE JOIN is a set operation, not a row operation (see Chapter 10), it does not return rows to the user until all of the rows are processed.

■ Its result set will not stay in the SGA very long. Since the blocks used to satisfy the table reads were read via full table scans, they will be the first blocks removed from the SGA when more space is needed in the SGA's data block buffer cache.

■ Temporary segments may need to be allocated to resolve the query, potentially resulting in temporary segment lock contention among users.

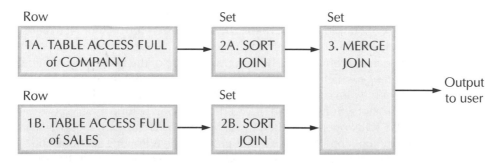

FIGURE 11-1. *MERGE JOIN example execution path*

There are, however, situations in which MERGE JOIN is the most efficient way to perform a join. In batch operations or large reports, MERGE JOIN may result in the best possible throughput for your query. In the following parts of this section, you will see the tuning implications for the MERGE JOIN operation and comparisons to the NESTED LOOPS join operation. Later sections of this chapter, including the tips on managing very large tables and remote queries, feature the MERGE JOIN operation.

Tuning Implications for MERGE JOINs

MERGE JOIN will be effective wherever a full table scan will be effective. That is, in situations in which a full table scan is preferable to an index range scan/table access by RowID combination, a MERGE JOIN operation will be preferable to a NESTED LOOPS join operation.

A full table scan is preferable under two conditions: when the table involved is very small or extremely large. If the table is very small, it may be quicker to perform a full table scan than to perform an index scan followed by a partial table scan. For example, if the table is completely stored in the number of blocks scanned during one read of the database, the entire table can be read in a single physical database read. If the entire table can be read during a single physical read from the database, a full table scan will be more efficient than an index range scan and table access by RowID combination (which would require multiple physical reads).

If a table is extremely large, it may be more efficient to perform a full table scan than to perform an index scan followed by a partial table scan, for three reasons. First, depending on the degree to which the data is physically stored in an ordered format, and the number of records selected, you may read fewer blocks to satisfy a full table scan than for a comparable index scan and table access by RowID. Second, the blocks read into the SGA's data block buffer cache by a full table scan are not held long in the SGA, so they will not hinder data sharing among users; blocks read via index scans are held long in the SGA, so a scan of a large index can prevent data sharing among users. Lastly, full table scans can take advantage of Oracle's Parallel Query Option. The choice of data access methods for extremely large tables is discussed in detail in the "Manage Very Large Table Accesses" section of this chapter. Implementation of the Parallel Query Option is described in Chapter 12.

During the SORT JOIN operation, Oracle sorts as much of the data as possible inside a memory area called the *sort area*. The maximum size of the sort area is defined by the SORT_AREA_SIZE parameter in the instance's init.ora file; it is allocated in 8K increments. If the sort area is not large enough to hold all the sorted data, Oracle will allocate a temporary segment for the duration of the query. The cost of the allocation and release of the temporary segment is roughly equivalent to the cost of about ten **insert/update/delete** statements. The allocation and release of temporary segments require locks to be allocated. When multiple users concurrently attempt to sort large result sets, they may experience contention during the temporary segment lock allocation process.

Data from the temporary segment is loaded into the sort area to be sorted. Every set of "load and sort" steps is called a *run*. If the result set is large relative to the sort area size, the data could be loaded and unloaded multiple times to and from the disk, generating excessive I/O.

NOTE
In Oracle7.2 and above, writes to temporary segments bypass the SGA via a technique called *Direct Sort Writes.* Direct Sort Writes in Oracle7.2 improve the performance of writes to temporary segments by at least 40 percent over earlier versions of the kernel. See Chapter 13 for parameters that you can use to tune Direct Sort Writes.

The third step of MERGE JOIN, the comparison and merge portion, is very efficient. The performance costs involved in MERGE JOINs are almost entirely found within the first two steps: the full table scans and the sorting operations. Tuning MERGE JOIN operations should therefore focus on improving the performance of the first two steps. The performance of full table scans can be improved through I/O tuning and improved use of Oracle's multiblock read capabilities (see Chapter 5), or by using the Parallel Query option (see Chapter 12). You can improve sort performance by setting a high value for SORT_AREA_SIZE, by upgrading to Oracle7.2 or 7.3, by dedicating a tablespace to temporary segment activity, or by some combination of these three.

How to Designate a Temporary-Only Tablespace

In Oracle7.3, you can specify a tablespace as "temporary." If you do so, the tablespace *cannot* be used to hold any permanent segments, only for temporary segments created during queries. The first sort to use the temporary tablespace allocates a temporary segment within the temporary tablespace; when the query completes, the space used by the temporary segment is *not* dropped. Instead, the space used by the temporary segment is available for use by other queries; this allows the sorting operation to avoid the costs of allocating and releasing space for temporary segments. This will reduce the temporary segment lock allocation contention and will save the cost of the ten **insert/update/delete** statements involved in temporary segment allocation.

To dedicate a tablespace as temporary in Oracle7.3, specify **temporary** in the **create tablespace** or **alter tablespace** command. The example shown in the following listing changes an existing tablespace named TEMP_1 to a **temporary** tablespace.

```
alter tablespace TEMP_1 temporary;
```

To change the TEMP_1 tablespace out of **temporary** state, and allow
permanent objects to be stored in it, use the **permanent** keyword in the **alter
tablespace** command, as shown in the following listing.

```
alter tablespace TEMP_1 permanent;
```

Steps Involved in NESTED LOOPS

A NESTED LOOPS operation joins two data sources. NESTED LOOPS is the most
common way that Oracle performs joins—it usually indicates that an index is
available for use during the join. As a row operation, NESTED LOOPS returns each
row to the next operation as it is processed rather than waiting for the entire set to
be processed. Because it is an index-based row operation, NESTED LOOPS is a
very effective join operation for multiuser online applications.

When performing a NESTED LOOPS join, the optimizer first selects a *driving
table* for the join. A full table scan may be performed on the driving table. For each
row in the driving table, an indexed access to the *driven table* is performed to see if
a match exists between the tables. If a matching value exists, that record is returned
to the user via the NESTED LOOPS operation.

For example, consider the SALES and COMPANY tables used throughout
Chapter 10. In the following query, COMPANY and SALES are joined by the
Company_ID column. In the example, Company_ID is the primary key of the
COMPANY table, and is the first column of a multicolumn primary key in SALES.

```
select COMPANY.Name
   from COMPANY, SALES
 where COMPANY.Company_ID = SALES.Company_ID
   and Period_ID = 2;
```

When executing this query, the optimizer will be able to use an index based on
the join criteria in the **where** clause. The execution path for the preceding query is
shown in the following listing.

```
NESTED LOOPS
   TABLE ACCESS FULL SALES
   TABLE ACCESS BY ROWID COMPANY
     INDEX UNIQUE SCAN COMPANY_PK
```

The execution path shows that SALES will be the driving table for the query.
The first step performed by the query will be the full table scan of SALES. For each
record in SALES, the COMPANY_PK index will be probed to see if a matching
Company_ID value exists for the SALES.Company_ID value in the current row. If a
match exists, a table access by RowID is performed to get the COMPANY.Name
column requested by the query.

The steps of the preceding example's NESTED LOOPS operation are:

1. Full table scan of the driving table.

2. Index range scan of the driven table.

3. If a match is found, a table access by RowID of the driven table.

These steps are illustrated in Figure 11-2. As an index-based row application, NESTED LOOPS will be effective for joins performed in multiuser online application environments. For single-user batch processing, particularly if you are dealing with very large tables, you may need to force MERGE JOINs to occur to improve your throughput.

Figure 11-2 shows the execution path.

NOTE
Since NESTED LOOPS joins, during their execution, reuse the index blocks they have already read into the SGA's data block buffer cache, they generate an artificially high hit ratio for the instance. See Chapter 8 for information on interpreting hit ratio statistics.

Implications of the Driving Table in a NESTED LOOPS Join
The key to the performance of a NESTED LOOPS join is the order in which the tables are joined. The selection of the driving table, the first table in the join, is critical. The amount of repetition in the nested loop is the product of the previous result set and the current accessed table.

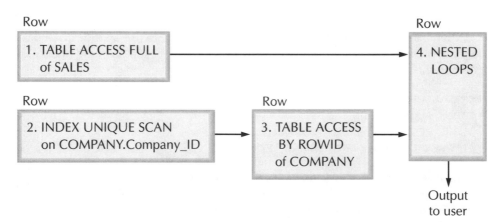

FIGURE 11-2. *NESTED LOOPS example execution path*

If more tables are used in the join, the selection of the driving table becomes even more critical, since the driving set of records is used for each successive join. As a result, the time needed to perform a join can grow exponentially as tables are added to the join unless the *driving set*—the join between the driving table and the first driven table—starts with very selective criteria.

In the previous example, SALES was used as the driving table. There are several important points to note about the selection of the driving table:

- Although all of the SALES table's primary key columns were specified in the query, the SALES_PK index was not used. The SALES_PK index was not used because there was not a limiting condition on the leading column (the Company_ID column) of the SALES_PK index. The only condition on SALES.Company_ID is a join condition.

- The optimizer could have selected either table as the driving table. If COMPANY was the driving table, it would have had a full table scan performed on it.

- In rule-based optimization, if there is an equal chance of using an index regardless of the choice of the driving table, the driving table will be the one that is listed *last* in the **from** clause.

- In cost-based optimization, the optimizer will consider the size of the tables and the selectivity of the indexes while selecting a driving table.

When selecting a driving table, the optimizer ranks all the tables in the **from** clause based on the limiting conditions and the join conditions. The optimizer ranks each table as a potential driving table. For each table, it evaluates the possible access paths that could be used during the query (unique index scans, nonunique index range scans, or table scans). The optimizer will choose an execution path that lets it best exploit the available indexes, considering the join conditions and the query's limiting conditions. The cost-based optimizer will consider the size of the tables and the selectivity of the indexes in evaluating possible driving tables. If the rule-based optimizer is used, and two or more tables have similar access paths available, then the optimizer will use the table mentioned last in the query's **from** clause as the driving table for the query.

How to Influence the Join Path
To modify the join path of a NESTED LOOPS join, you can either use hints (cost-based optimization only) or manually modify the **from** clause and **where** conditions in the query. Embedding hints is described in Chapter 10. Hints related to the join path of NESTED LOOPS joins include

ORDERED	Join the tables based on their order in the **from** clause.
INDEX	List specific indexes to use.
FULL	List a specific table for a full table scan—this table may serve as a driving table for the query.
USE_NL	List tables to join via NESTED LOOPS joins.

You can modify the **where** clause of a query to nullify the use of indexes on specific columns. By nullifying indexes, you can influence which tables will be more likely to have full table scans during the query—and thus more likely to be driving tables for the query.

As described in the first tip in this chapter, the optimizer will use an index if the indexed columns are used in a limiting condition. If an indexed column is used within a function, such as UPPER, then an index on that column would not be used by the optimizer. When you want to force the optimizer to *ignore* an index, use the following conventions:

1. For numeric or date columns, add zero to the value. For example, replace

   ```
   where Company_ID = 12345
   ```

   with

   ```
   where Company_ID+0 = 12345
   ```

   Adding 0 to the Company_ID value does not change the value, but it does prevent the optimizer from using the index on the Company_ID column during the query.

2. For character columns, concatenate an empty string (' ') to the value. For example, replace

   ```
   where City = 'ROANOKE'
   ```

   with

   ```
   where City||'' = 'ROANOKE'
   ```

Adding the empty string to the City value does not change the value, but it does prevent the optimizer from using the index on the City column during the query.

NOTE
You need to establish and follow a consistent syntax for nullifying indexes in commonly-used queries. Whenever you see a query that has been modified using this syntax, you will know that the query was modified for performance improvements, and the goal was to nullify the index rather than to indicate a significant business rule.

In the following sections you will see detailed examples on topics related to the selection of the driving table:

- what happens when you start from nonselective criteria
- tuning multi-table joins
- what happens when you add more tables to the join

Following those sections, you will see tips for reducing the number of tables used in joins.

What Happens When You Start from Nonselective Criteria

NESTED LOOPS is a directional operation; if you join two tables via a NESTED LOOPS operation, you will get different performance depending on which of the tables is the driving table. Consider SALES and COMPANY again. What if COMPANY has 5 records, and SALES has 100,000 records? If SALES is used as the driving table, the execution path will require a full table scan of SALES, plus repeated accesses to the same rows in COMPANY. If COMPANY were used as the driving table, the full table scan of COMPANY would read only 5 rows, and would be followed by indexed accesses to the larger SALES table. Changing the choice of the driving table can dramatically alter the number of rows read by the query—and can in turn dramatically alter the performance of the query. As more and more tables are added to the query, the size of the driving set passed to each successive join has a great impact on the performance of the query, as you will see in the following sections.

What Happens When You Add More Tables to the Join

The results from the first NESTED LOOPS operation—the join between the driving table and the first driven table—are called the *driving set*. If there are four tables involved in a NESTED LOOPS join, the steps taken by the optimizer are

1. Select a driving table.

2. Perform a NESTED LOOPS join between the driving table and a second table.

3. Perform a NESTED LOOPS join between the driving set returned from Step #2 and the third table.

4. Perform a NESTED LOOPS join between the driving set returned from Step #3 and the fourth table.

If you select the wrong driving table, the first NESTED LOOPS join will perform poorly, as described in the previous section. However, selecting the proper driving table does not guarantee good performance if you have three or more tables in your join. If you have more than two tables in a NESTED LOOPS join, you need to consider the size of the driving set of records involved in each successive join. If the driving set is not selective, the performance of each successive join will grow worse; as more tables are added, the time needed to complete the query will grow exponentially!

If there is a limiting condition in the **where** clause that is based on one of the columns used to join tables, consider which table the condition is applied to. For example, if there are four tables (named A, B, C, and D) in the query, all of which are the same size, and the **from** and **where** clauses are of the form

```
    from D, C, B, A
 where A.join_column = B.join_column
   and B.join_column = C.join_column
   and C.join_column = D.join_column
   and A.join_column = 12345
   and D.Name = 'MAGELLAN'
```

then a NESTED LOOPS join can be used if A, B, C, and D have indexes on their join columns. Table A will be joined to table B; the driving set from that join will be joined to table C; the driving set from that join will be joined to table D, and the limiting condition on D.Name will be applied.

If D.Name is selective, the performance of the query could be improved by joining D as part of the first NESTED LOOPS join in the execution path. The reason for the improvement is that fewer records will be returned by the first NESTED LOOPS join, so a smaller driving set will be used for each successive join. Just as large driving sets cause significant performance problems, changing to small driving sets can yield significant performance gains. In this example, the **where** clause could be rewritten, changing the limiting condition on A to be a limiting condition on D instead:

```
    from D, C, B, A
 where A.join_column = B.join_column
   and B.join_column = C.join_column
   and C.join_column = D.join_column
   and D.join_column = 12345
   and D.Name = 'MAGELLAN'
```

Given the revised **where** clause, the optimizer will now first join D to C, then the driving set from that join to C, then the driving set from that join to B, and finally the driving set from that join to A.

What is the significance of this change? Assume that each of the tables A, B, C, and D had exactly 100 records, and that there was only one record in D with a Name value of 'MAGELLAN'. The number of buffer gets (logical reads) needed to resolve the original query is shown in Table 11-2. An index access generates an average of two accesses inside the index "branches", plus one access to the index "leaf" blocks for each row and one RowID access to the table for each row. Thus, to access 100 rows by an index search, you need two buffer gets for the index branches, plus 100 index reads and 100 table reads, for a total of 202 reads. For the join from A to B, you need 100 buffer gets for each of the 202 buffer gets required by the read of table A.

As shown in Table 11-2, each successive join suffers if the driving set from the preceding join is large. Table 11-3 shows the number of buffer gets needed to resolve the modified query (in which the limiting condition on the join column was moved to table D, which had an additional limiting condition).

As shown in Table 11-3, the change to the order of the joins made a significant difference to the number of buffer gets the database needed to perform in order to resolve the query. In the original query, the limiting conditions on table D did not affect the size of the driving sets, because table D was the last table joined in the query. In the modified query, table D is part of the first NESTED LOOPS join—and as a result, the query requires one one-hundredth of the buffer gets in order to complete. The modified query will run significantly faster than the original query.

Operation	Original Query	Buffer Gets	Cumulative Buffer Gets
First Table Accessed	A	2+2*100	202
First Joined Table	B	100*202	20,402
Second Joined Table	C	100*100*202	2,040,402
Third Joined Table	D	100*100*100*202	204,040,402

TABLE 11-2. *Cumulative Buffer Gets for Original NESTED LOOP Join*

Operation	Table Accessed	Buffer Gets	Cumulative Buffer Gets
First Table Accessed	D	2+2*100	202 (1 row returned)
First Joined Table	C	1*202	404
Second Joined Table	B	100*1*202	20,604
Third Joined Table	A	100*100*1*202	2,040,604

TABLE 11-3. *Cumulative Buffer Gets for Modified NESTED LOOP Join*

How to Change the Database Design to Reduce the Number of Joins

You can reduce the number of joins performed during queries by denormalizing the data within your application. In a normalized database, the attributes of a table relate directly to the full primary key of the table. In a denormalized table, attributes may relate directly to only part of the primary key for the table.

For example, the COMPANY table used in the examples throughout Chapters 10 and 11 has a column named Active_Flag. You may have a lookup table of valid Active_Flag values, featuring the Flag_Code value and a description, as shown in the following listing.

```
select * from ACTIVE_FLAG_CODES;

ACTIVE_FLAG  DESCRIPTION
-----------  ----------------------
A            Active
I            Inactive
P            Pending Classification
U            Unknown
```

If you query the COMPANY table based on the Active_Flag code descriptions, you will need to join COMPANY to the ACTIVE_FLAG_CODES table as shown in the preceding listing unless you specify the code value in your query. The following listing shows a sample query that joins COMPANY to ACTIVE_FLAG_CODES.

```
select Company.Name
  from COMPANY, ACTIVE_FLAG_CODES
 where COMPANY.Active_Flag = ACTIVE_FLAG_CODES.Active_Flag
   and ACTIVE_FLAG_CODES.Description = 'Active';
```

To eliminate the join from the query, you must either change the query to use the code value (where COMPANY.Active_Flag = 'A'), or you must add

the ACTIVE_FLAG_CODES.Description column to the COMPANY table. If
the Description column is added to COMPANY, you can eliminate the
ACTIVE_FLAG_CODES table from your join, as shown in the following listing.

```
select Company.Name
  from COMPANY
 where Active_Flag_Description = 'Active';
```

Although this example only deals with two tables, the impact of denormalization
and reducing the number of tables involved in joins can be great when many tables
are involved in the initial join. Note that there are potential costs—this method
requires more storage space in the COMPANY table, and could cause problems if
the Description values for the Active_Flag codes change.

A second method of denormalization involves creating columns that store
values for specific ranges. For example, if your data is based on dates, there may be
logical divisions of date values. In the SALE table, the primary key is Company_ID
and Period_ID. For each record, a Sales_Total value is stored. In order to select the
data from four periods, you need to query four records.

If your periods are predetermined, and the number of periods you need is
unchanging, you may be able to denormalize the SALE table to contain additional
columns. The new columns could store the Sales_Total values for specific periods.
Instead of selecting four rows for a company:

```
select Period_ID, Sales_Total
  from SALE
 where Company_ID = 8791
   and Period_ID between 1 and 4;


PERIOD_ID    SALES_TOTAL
---------    -----------
        1           1000
        2           2300
        3           1890
        4           2410
```

you could instead select one row from a modified SALE table:

```
select Period_1_Sales, Period_2_Sales, Period_3_Sales,
       Period_4_sales
  from SALE
 where Company_ID = 8791;


Period_1_Sales Period_2_Sales Period_3_Sales Period_4_Sales
-------------- -------------- -------------- --------------
          1000           2300           1890           2410
```

By storing fewer records in the table, you reduce the size of the driving set of records used in joins with the table. However, you need to consider the likelihood that the data, or the divisions of the data (called the *partitions*), may change. If the data or the partitions change frequently, storing values according to their ranges may not be appropriate for your application.

A third denormalization method involves keeping the most current detail record in the same table as the master record. In many applications, the master table (for example, an EMPLOYEE table) stores data that is constant over time, and the detail table (for example, SALARY_HISTORY) stores data that changes over time. In many master-detail relationships, the most important detail record is the most recent one. In that case, the current active detail record could be stored in the master table to reduce the number of subqueries involved in the query. Based on the application, the DBA could decide to have the data stored redundantly in both the master table and the detail table. See the tips regarding subqueries later in this chapter for further information on master-detail queries.

Managing Joins

In the preceding sections, you've seen descriptions of NESTED LOOPS and MERGE JOINS operations, and the impact and tuning methods for each. The optimal type of join for your application depends on a number of criteria (such as the type of application and the database design). If you use a NESTED LOOPS join, you need to make sure that the proper driving table—and the proper driving set—is used by the query. If you choose the proper execution paths for your queries, they will be better able to withstand the impacts of changes within the database as tables grow over time. A third join option, hash joins, is described in Chapter 13.

4. Manage SQL Statements Containing Views

If a query contains a view, then the optimizer has two ways of resolving the query: first resolve the view and then resolve the query, or integrate the view text into the query. If the view is resolved first, the *entire* result set of the view is first determined, and the rest of the query conditions are then applied as a filter.

Depending on the relative sizes of the tables involved, resolving the view first can cause performance degradation for your queries; if the view is integrated into the query, the query's conditions can be applied within the view, and a smaller result set can be used. In some situations, however, you may improve your query's performance by separating grouping operations via views. Both of these situations will be described in the following sections. When you use views in your joins, you need to actively manage how the views are resolved.

If a view contains a set operation—such as GROUP BY, SUM, COUNT, or DISTINCT—then the view cannot be integrated into the query. For example, the following listing creates a view called COMPANY_COUNT that counts the records in the COMPANY table, by State.

```
create view COMPANY_COUNT as
select State, COUNT(*) Company_Count
   from COMPANY
 group by State;
```

If the COMPANY_COUNT view is joined to another table in a query, the COMPANY_COUNT view will be resolved first, its full result set will be determined, and the results will be used as input to the rest of the query. Because it contains a GROUP BY clause, the view's SQL syntax cannot be integrated into a larger query.

The SQL syntax of views that do not use grouping functions can be integrated into the larger query. For example, the PERIOD3_NAMES view shown in the following listing contains a join operation, with no grouping or set operations.

```
create view PERIOD3_NAMES as
select COMPANY.Name
   from COMPANY, SALES
 where COMPANY.Company_ID = SALES.Company_ID
   and SALES.Period_ID =3;
```

If the PERIOD3_NAMES view is joined to another table, the SQL syntax of PERIOD3_NAMES can be integrated with the SQL syntax of the rest of the query.

NOTE
Since Oracle7.1, and further improved in Oracle7.3, using UNION in a view does not prevent the view's SQL syntax from being integrated with the query's syntax. If there is a UNION, the optimizer can still integrate the query with the view by integrating each part of the UNIONed SQL separately.

Improving Integration of Views into Queries

If a view returns a large result set, or if the view's result set is to be filtered by additional limiting conditions in a query, the query would likely benefit from having the view's SQL integrated into the query. The optimizer will automatically perform the integration if it can.

To avoid having views that cannot be integrated into queries, do not use grouping functions in the views—defer the grouping operations to the query that joins with the view. Such a deferral is not always a feasible solution, but needs to be investigated on a view-by-view and query-by-query basis.

For example, suppose you had a view called SALES_TOTAL_VW that summed the Sales_Total column of SALES, by Company_ID. The view's SQL, shown in the following listing, groups by Company_ID.

```
create view SALES_TOTAL_VW as
select Company_ID, SUM(Sales_Total) Sum_Sales_Total
  from SALES
 group by Company_ID;
```

The SALES_TOTAL_VW view could be joined to the COMPANY table to get the company's name (Company.Name) and the company's cumulative sales total (SALES_TOTAL_VW.Sum_Sales_Total), as shown in the following listing.

```
select COMPANY.Name, Sum_Sales_Total
  from COMPANY, SALES_TOTAL_VW
 where COMPANY.Company_ID = SALES_TOTAL_VW.Company_ID;
```

The grouping is performed within the view. The explain plan for the query, in the following listing, shows that the view's output is used as the driving set of records for a NESTED LOOPS join.

```
NESTED LOOPS
   VIEW  SALES_TOTAL_VW
     SORT GROUP BY
        TABLE ACCESS FULL SALES
   TABLE ACCESS BY ROWID COMPANY
     INDEX UNIQUE SCAN COMPANY_PK
```

You can improve the level of integration in the example query. In SALES_TOTAL_VW, records are grouped by Company_ID. In the query, one record is returned for each Company_ID (since SALES_TOTAL_VW and COMPANY are joined on Company_ID). Therefore, the view and the query display records at the same level—the Company_ID level.

You can therefore perform the grouping operation at the query level instead of at the view level. Join SALES to COMPANY using the Company_ID column, and perform the grouping at the Company_ID level. In the example in the following listing, the GROUP BY clause groups by COMPANY.Name, which is an attribute of Company_ID.

```
select COMPANY.Name, SUM(Sales_Total)
  from COMPANY, SALES
 where COMPANY.Company_ID = SALES.Company_ID
 group by COMPANY.Name;
```

The SQL in the preceding listing will generate the following execution path:

```
SORT GROUP BY
   NESTED LOOPS
      TABLE ACCESS FULL SALES
      TABLE ACCESS BY ROWID COMPANY
         INDEX UNIQUE SCAN COMPANY_PK
```

The grouping operation is now performed *after* the NESTED LOOPS join.

Forcing Views to Remain Separate

Sometimes, you may wish for the view's SQL to not be integrated with the rest of the query. For example, if you are performing a GROUP BY operation on a NESTED LOOPS join of two tables, the grouping operation is not completed until the two tables have been fully joined. The examples in this section will use the same objects as the previous section, with the opposite outcome—a view that is deliberately resolved separately instead of being integrated into a larger query.

In the following example, COMPANY and SALES are joined, and the Sales_Total column from the SALES table is summed by company Name.

```
select COMPANY.Name, SUM(Sales_Total)
  from COMPANY, SALES
 where COMPANY.Company_ID = SALES.Company_ID
 group by COMPANY.Name;
```

Given the SQL in the preceding listing, and the table and operations descriptions from Chapter 10, the execution path would be

```
SORT GROUP BY
   NESTED LOOPS
      TABLE ACCESS FULL SALES
      TABLE ACCESS BY ROWID COMPANY
         INDEX UNIQUE SCAN COMPANY_PK
```

As the explain plan listing shows, SORT GROUP BY is the last operation performed—it follows the NESTED LOOPS join operation. But what if the columns being grouped are all from just one of those tables? You could perform the grouping function on the table prior to performing the join. If SALES is much larger than COMPANY, performing the SORT GROUP BY *after* the join requires the query to perform extra work. To reduce the resource requirements, you can rewrite the query to use a view that contains a GROUP BY clause. The following listing shows a sales summary view that contains the SALES grouping information from the prior query.

```
create view SALES_TOTAL_VW as
select Company_ID, SUM(Sales_Total) Sum_Sales_Total
  from SALES
 group by Company_ID;
```

The SALES_TOTAL_VW view can now be joined to the COMPANY table to get the original query's result set (the Company.Name and the Sales_Total).

```
select COMPANY.Name, Sum_Sales_Total
  from COMPANY, SALES_TOTAL_VW
 where COMPANY.Company_ID = SALES_TOTAL_VW.Company_ID;
```

In the modified version, the query does not contain the GROUP BY clause—the grouping operation is inside the SALES_TOTAL_VW view and cannot be integrated with the rest of the query. The explain plan for this version of the query is shown in the following listing.

```
NESTED LOOPS
   VIEW  SALES_TOTAL_VW
     SORT GROUP BY
       TABLE ACCESS FULL SALES
   TABLE ACCESS BY ROWID COMPANY
     INDEX UNIQUE SCAN COMPANY_PK
```

In the explain plan shown in the preceding listing, the SORT GROUP BY operation is performed only on the SALES table and the view's result set is determined; the result of that operation is then joined to the COMPANY table via a NESTED LOOPS join. If the SALES table is significantly larger than the COMPANY table, performing the SORT GROUP BY before the join may result in great performance gains.

As of Oracle7.2, you can embed view queries directly within the **from** clauses of queries, and therefore do not have to create the views (such as SALES_TOTAL_VW earlier) separately. In the following listing, the SALES_TOTAL_VW syntax is embedded in the query's **from** clause, and the view is joined to the COMPANY table.

```
select Name, Sum_Sales_Total
  from COMPANY,
       (select Company_ID Sales_Co_ID,
               SUM(Sales_Total) Sum_Sales_Total
         from SALES
        group by Company_ID)
 where COMPANY.Company_ID = Sales_Co_ID;
```

The explain plan for the query in the preceding listing is functionally identical to the explain plan for the query that used SALES_TOTAL_VW. The view is resolved before the join is performed. As shown in the following listing, the only difference is the name of the view.

```
NESTED LOOPS
   VIEW  from$_subquery$_  2
      SORT GROUP BY
         TABLE ACCESS FULL SALES
   TABLE ACCESS BY ROWID COMPANY
      INDEX UNIQUE SCAN COMPANY_PK
```

> **NOTE**
> If you have a view that does not contain a grouping operation, and you do not want the view's SQL to be integrated into the rest of the query, Oracle7.3 has a hint named NO_MERGE that can help. The NO_MERGE hint prevents the view's query syntax from being merged into the rest of the query.

5. Tune Subqueries

When using subqueries, you may encounter several unique problems. Potential problems with queries involving subqueries include the following:

- Subqueries may be resolved before the rest of the query is resolved (similar to views that perform grouping functions—see the previous section on views).

- Subqueries may require specific hints that are not directly related to the query that calls the subquery.

- Subqueries that could be performed as a single query may instead be written as several distinct subqueries.

- Subqueries may not perform existence checks in the most efficient manner, either by using a NOT IN clause or by failing to use an EXISTS clause.

In the following sections, you will see each of these problems addressed, and solutions provided.

When Subqueries Are Resolved

If a query contains a subquery, the optimizer has two ways of resolving the query: first resolve the subquery and then resolve the query (the "view" method), or integrate the subquery into the query (the "join" method). If the subquery is resolved first, the *entire* result set of the subquery is first calculated, and the rest of the query conditions are applied as a filter. If the subquery is integrated into the query, the subquery's conditions and tables can be joined to the rest of the query. If you are not using the subqueries to perform existence checks, the "join" method will usually perform better than the "view" method.

If a subquery contains a set operation—such as GROUP BY, SUM, or DISTINCT—then the subquery cannot be integrated into the rest of the query. As described in the "Manage SQL Statements Containing Views" section of this chapter, a nonintegrated subquery restricts the options available to the optimizer. Since the subquery cannot be integrated into the query that calls it, the subquery will be resolved before the rest of the query is resolved.

The query in the following listing contains a subquery with a DISTINCT clause. Because the subquery contains a DISTINCT clause, the subquery is treated as a view and is resolved separately from the rest of the query. The query returns the Names of companies that had a Sales_Total > 10000 in Period 4.

```
select COMPANY.Name
  from COMPANY
 where COMPANY.Company_ID in
       (select distinct SALES.Company_ID
          from SALES
         where Period_ID = 4
           and Sales_Total > 10000);
```

Although the query in the preceding listing does not contain a view, it is called a "view"-type subquery because it contains a grouping function (DISTINCT). The execution path for the preceding query is shown in the following listing.

```
NESTED LOOPS
  VIEW
    SORT UNIQUE
     TABLE ACCESS FULL SALES
   TABLE ACCESS BY ROWID COMPANY
    INDEX UNIQUE SCAN COMPANY_PK
```

As shown in the execution path, the "view" representing the subquery serves as the driving table for a NESTED LOOPS join. However, the subquery can be rewritten to act as a join. In the example, the DISTINCT clause in the subquery is unnecessary, since the subquery is merely generating a list of valid values for COMPANY.Company_ID. Instead of using a subquery, the query could be rewritten as a join of the COMPANY and SALES tables. The revised version of the query is shown in the following listing.

```
select COMPANY.Name
  from COMPANY, SALES
 where COMPANY.Company_ID = SALES.Company_ID
   and SALES.Period_ID = 4
   and Sales_Total > 10000;
```

Since the query has been rewritten as a join, the optimizer can now evaluate potential driving tables for the query. The revised execution path is shown in the following listing. Although the SALES table is still chosen as the driving table (for this particular query), the VIEW operation is no longer used. The optimizer can choose how to drive the query instead of being forced to use the subquery "view" to drive the query.

```
NESTED LOOPS
   TABLE ACCESS FULL SALES
   TABLE ACCESS BY ROWID COMPANY
      INDEX UNIQUE SCAN COMPANY_PK
```

Hints for Subqueries That Return the Maximum Value

In some applications, both historical and current data are stored. For example, you may store all current employee demographic information in a single table, with an employee's salary history data in a separate table. To determine the current salary of an employee, you need to select the record with the maximum effective date for that employee from the historical table. To do so, you need to use a subquery—and there is a very useful hint that applies to this sort of query.

Consider an EMPLOYEE table that has two columns—Employee_ID and Name. Employee_ID is the single-column primary key of the EMPLOYEE table. A second table, EMPLOYEE_HISTORY, comprises three columns: Employee_ID, Salary, and Effective_Date. To select the current salary for an employee, you would execute the query shown in the following listing.

```
select *
  from EMPLOYEE, EMPLOYEE_HISTORY EH
 where EMPLOYEE.Employee_ID = EH.Employee_ID
   and EMPLOYEE.Name = 'George Washington'
   and EH.Effective_Date =
       (select MAX(Effective_Date)
          from EMPLOYEE_HISTORY E2
         where E2.Employee_ID = EH.Employee_ID);
```

The execution path for the preceding query is shown in the following listing. It shows that the indexes on the Employee_ID columns in both the EMPLOYEE and EMPLOYEE_HISTORY tables are used.

```
FILTER
  NESTED LOOPS
    TABLE ACCESS FULL EMPLOYEE_HISTORY
    TABLE ACCESS BY ROWID EMPLOYEE
      INDEX UNIQUE SCAN EMPLOYEE$EMPLOYEE_ID
  SORT AGGREGATE
    TABLE ACCESS BY ROWID EMPLOYEE_HISTORY
      INDEX RANGE SCAN EMPLOYEE_HISTORY$EMPLOYEE_ID
```

Since a MAX function is used on the Effective_Date column, the index on that column could be used during the execution of the subquery. You can specify that index to be used via an INDEX_DESC hint—that will force the index to be read from its maximum to its minimum value, instead of in the usual ascending direction. As a result, the MAX(Effective_Date) will be returned to the calling portion of the query more quickly. In the following listing, the query has been rewritten to use the INDEX_DESC hint. The INDEX_DESC hint tells the optimizer to use the index on the EMPLOYEE_HISTORY.Effective_Date column. Only a single row will be returned because of the RowNum criteria in the **where** clause—and that single row will be the one with the highest value in the EMPLOYEE_HISTORY$EFF_DT index.

```
select /*+ INDEX_DESC(eh employee_history$eff_dt)*/
       *
  from EMPLOYEE, EMPLOYEE_HISTORY EH
 where EMPLOYEE.Employee_ID = EH.Employee_ID
   and EMPLOYEE.Name = 'George Washington'
   and EH.Effective_Date < SysDate
   and RowNum = 1;
```

The execution path of the revised query is shown in the following listing. The index on the Effective_Date column is now used, and the sorting operations have disappeared from the explain plan.

```
COUNT STOPKEY
  NESTED LOOPS
    TABLE ACCESS BY ROWID EMPLOYEE_HISTORY
      INDEX RANGE SCAN EMPLOYEE_HISTORY$EFF_DT
    TABLE ACCESS BY ROWID EMPLOYEE
      INDEX UNIQUE SCAN EMPLOYEE$EMPLOYEE_ID
```

Rewriting the query to use the Effective_Date index may improve the performance of the overall query, since the Effective_Date column may be more selective than the Employee_ID column in EMPLOYEE_HISTORY.

How to Combine Subqueries

A single query may contain multiple subqueries. The more subqueries you use, the more difficult it is to integrate or rewrite them into larger joins. Since having multiple subqueries makes integration difficult, you should try to combine multiple subqueries where possible.

You can even combine subqueries that at first seem unrelated. For example, consider the EMPLOYEE table again. In addition to the two columns it already contains—Employee_ID and Name—add three new columns: Active_Code (indicating if the employee is an active or retired employee), Hourly_Code (indicating full-time or part-time workers), and Start_Date. For each code, a separate code table will be created, as shown in the following listing.

```
create table ACTIVE_CODE
(Active_Code NUMBER,
 Description VARCHAR2(20));

create table HOURLY_CODE
(Hourly_Code NUMBER,
 Description VARCHAR2(20));
```

Applications that query the EMPLOYEE table are more likely to reference the code descriptions than the code values. A typical update of the EMPLOYEE table (updating a person's status when he or she starts) is shown in the following listing.

```
update EMPLOYEE
   set Active_Code = 1
 where Active_Code in
       (select Active_Code from ACTIVE_CODE
          where Description = 'HIRED')
   and Hourly_Code in
       (select Hourly_Code from HOURLY_CODE
          where Description = 'FULLTIME')
   and Start_Date <= SysDate;
```

The **update** command in the preceding listing will set the Active_Code value to '1' for any full-time employee who has been hired before the current date.

For each record of the EMPLOYEE table, the subqueries will be performed. To avoid having multiple subqueries performed per record, you can combine these two unrelated subqueries into a single subquery, as shown in the following listing. The ANY operator is used to evaluate which rows are returned from the combined subquery.

```
update EMPLOYEE
   set Active_Code = 1
 where (Active_Code, Hourly_Code) = ANY
       (select Active_Code, Hourly_Code
          from ACTIVE_CODE, HOURLY_CODE
         where ACTIVE_CODE.Description = 'HIRED'
           and HOURLY_CODE.Description = 'FULLTIME')
   and Start_Date <= SysDate;
```

The combined subquery is a Cartesian product of the two codes tables—but since they are small codes tables and each returns only one row, this should not place an undue burden on your performance. Any performance costs from combining the queries in this manner may be offset by the performance improvements gained by reducing the number of subqueries performed per row.

How to Perform Existence Checks

Often, subqueries do not return rows, but instead perform a data validation purpose. For example, you may check that a table with a primary key does not have any "children" records in a foreign key table for specific values of the primary key column. Such logical checks—that records in related tables either exist or do not exist—are called *existence checks*. You can use the EXISTS and NOT EXISTS operators to improve the performance of existence checks.

Using EXISTS   Whenever a join does not return any columns from one of the tables, or if you only care that a row exists, the join can use the EXISTS clause. Using the EXISTS clause may eliminate unnecessary table accesses.

The two queries in the following listing are functionally equivalent; they return a row from the COMPANY table if it has a matching record that meets the limiting conditions placed on the SALES table.

```
select COMPANY.Name
  from COMPANY, SALES
 where COMPANY.Company_ID = SALES.Company_ID
   and SALES.Period_ID = 4
   and Sales_Total > 10000;

select COMPANY.Name
  from COMPANY
 where COMPANY.Company_ID in
       (select SALES.Company_ID
          from SALES
         where SALES.Period_ID = 4
           and Sales_Total > 10000);
```

Both of the queries in the preceding listing could be rewritten using the EXISTS operator, as shown in the following listing.

```
select COMPANY.Name
  from COMPANY
 where EXISTS
   (select 1 from SALES
     where COMPANY.Company_ID = SALES.Company_ID
       and SALES.Period_ID = 4
       and Sales_Total > 10000);
```

The value of the EXISTS operator is that it only needs to check for a single row returned by the subquery. An **in** clause selects all rows from the subquery. The NOT EXISTS operator can also help you realize great performance gains for subqueries, for the types of existence checks described in the next section.

Using NOT EXISTS   In the examples used throughout this chapter, the SALES table's Company_ID column refers back to the Company_ID column of the COMPANY table. To select the Company_IDs from COMPANY that do *not* have records in the SALES table, the query shown in the following listing uses a NOT IN clause:

```
select Company_ID
  from COMPANY
 where Company_ID NOT IN
       (select Company_ID from SALES);
```

The main query in the preceding listing uses a NOT IN clause—so there is no limiting condition in the main query (see the section on avoiding full table scans in this chapter for a discussion of limiting conditions). Since there is no limiting condition on the query, Oracle will perform a full table scan of the COMPANY table. For each record in COMPANY, the subquery will be executed. Since the subquery has no **where** clause, it has no limiting condition. Thus, this query will perform a full table scan of SALES for every record in the full table scan of COMPANY. You need to rewrite the query to eliminate the full table scans.

To improve the performance of the query, you need to take a different approach. The query does not return any columns from the SALES table; you are only using SALES as a logical check for the COMPANY records—an existence check. Since you are checking to see which records do *not* meet a given criteria, a NOT EXISTS clause should be used. The following listing shows the syntax for the preceding query after it has been rewritten to use the NOT EXISTS clause.

```
select Company_ID
  from COMPANY
 where NOT EXISTS
         (select 1 from SALES
            where SALES.Company_ID = COMPANY.Company_ID);
```

When the query in the preceding listing is executed, the main query will perform a full table scan of the COMPANY table, since there are no limiting conditions on the query. For each record in COMPANY, the NOT EXISTS clause will be evaluated.

When the NOT EXISTS clause is evaluated, the value of COMPANY.Company_ID from the main query is compared to values of the Company_ID column in the SALES table. If there is a match—the Company_ID exists in both COMPANY and SALES—then a '1' is returned by the subquery. The logic of the NOT EXISTS clause tells Oracle to not return the row from the main query if the subquery returns a '1'. The only records that will be returned from COMPANY are those that return no rows from the subquery.

The performance improvements for this type of existence check can be enormous. When using NOT IN, the query performs nested full table scans. When using NOT EXISTS, the query can use an index within the subquery. Since

```
where SALES.Company_ID = COMPANY.Company_ID
```

can be used as a limiting condition in the subquery, the index on the SALES.Company_ID column can be used in resolving the query. For each record in the COMPANY table, an index probe of the SALES_PK index (which has Company_ID as its leading column) will be performed. Instead of iteratively performing full table scans, you can use an index scan. Because a single character is selected (the '1' in the subquery) instead of a column, there is no need for the database to do a subsequent table access by RowID after searching the SALES_PK index.

6. Use Composite Keys/Star Queries

Queries using tables created with a data warehousing style of application design can realize significant performance improvements by using "star" query execution paths. These performance benefits are also available to some queries based on traditional relational table layouts. In this section you will see a simple data warehouse design, the traditional execution path for a typical query, and the paradigm shift that occurs when tuning a "star" query.

How to Create a Star Schema

A "star" query selects data from a *star schema*. Star schemas are common to data warehouse table designs. Each type of data that is used in grouping columns (such as Product, if you sum data by Product, or Period, if you sum data by Period) is represented by a separate table. For example, the PRODUCT table, shown in the following listing, has a Product_ID and Product_Name column. A primary key is created on the Product_ID column (and a unique index is implicitly created on the Product_ID column).

```
create table PRODUCT
  (Product_ID    NUMBER,
   Product_Name VARCHAR2(20),
   constraint    PRODUCT_PK primary key (Product_ID));
```

Within the context of data warehousing design, PRODUCT is called a *dimension*, and the PRODUCT table is called a *dimension table*. In the following listing, two additional dimension tables are created: one for periods, and one for customers.

```
create table PERIOD
  (Period_ID    NUMBER,
   Period_Name VARCHAR2(20),
   constraint    PERIOD_PK primary key (Period_ID));

create table CUSTOMER
(Customer_ID    NUMBER,
 Customer_Name VARCHAR2(20),
 constraint     CUSTOMER_PK primary key (Customer_ID));
```

Three dimension tables—PRODUCT, PERIOD, and CUSTOMER—have been created. Each of the dimension tables has an ID column and a Name column, and each has a unique index on its ID column.

To store data about the dimensions, create a *fact* table. A fact table has a primary key that is created by combining the primary keys of its related dimension tables. For each record in the fact table, record the attributes being measured. For example, you could choose to track orders, by product, period, and customer. In the following listing, an ORDERS table is created to track sales orders totals by the three dimensions that have been created. The primary key of the ORDERS table is a three-column concatenation of Product_ID, Period_ID, and Customer_ID. For each record, the Order_Amount attribute records the total sales for the product, period, and customer.

```
create table ORDERS
  (Product_ID   NUMBER,
   Period_ID    NUMBER,
   Customer_ID  NUMBER,
   Order_Amount NUMBER,
   constraint   ORDERS_PK primary key
                   (Product_ID, Period_ID, Customer_ID),
   constraint   ORDERS_PRODUCT_FK foreign key (Product_ID)
                   references PRODUCT(Product_ID),
   constraint   ORDERS_PERIOD_FK foreign key (Period_ID)
                   references PERIOD(Period_ID),
   constraint   ORDERS_CUSTOMER_FK foreign key (Customer_ID)
                   references CUSTOMER(Customer_ID));
```

As shown in the preceding listing, the ORDERS table has a primary key on Product_ID, Period_ID, and Customer_ID, and therefore has a unique index implicitly created on those columns. ORDERS also has foreign keys back to each of the dimension tables it references. The graphical representation of the relationships between the ORDERS table and its dimension tables is shown in Figure 11-3. The "star" nature of the graphical layout of the schema gives it its name.

Querying the Star Schema

When a star schema is queried, dimension tables are usually involved in the query. Since the dimension tables contain the Name or Description columns commonly used by queries, dimension tables will always be used by star queries unless the queries specifically refer to the ID values. A star query therefore typically has two parts to its **where** clause: a set of joins between the fact table and the dimension tables, and a set of criteria for the Name columns of the dimension tables.

The following listing shows a star query using the ORDERS table and its PRODUCT, PERIOD, and CUSTOMER dimension tables.

```
select PRODUCT.Product_Name,
       PERIOD.Period_Name,
       CUSTOMER.Customer_Name,
       ORDERS.Order_Amount
  from ORDERS, PERIOD, CUSTOMER, PRODUCT
 where PRODUCT.Product_Name = 'WIDGET'
   and PERIOD.Period_Name = 'Last 3 Months'
   and CUSTOMER.Customer_Name = 'MAGELLAN'
   and ORDERS.Period_ID = PERIOD.Period_ID
   and ORDERS.Customer_ID = CUSTOMER.Customer_ID
   and ORDERS.Product_ID = PRODUCT.Product_ID;
```

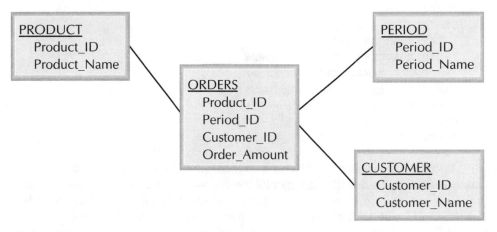

FIGURE 11-3. *Star Schema featuring the ORDERS table*

The **where** clause of the preceding query contains a section that specifies the criteria for the dimension tables:

```
where   PRODUCT.Product_Name = 'WIDGET'
   and PERIOD.Period_Name = 'Last 3 Months'
   and CUSTOMER.Customer_Name = 'MAGELLAN'
```

and a section that joins the fact table to the dimension tables:

```
   and ORDERS.Period_ID = PERIOD.Period_ID
   and ORDERS.Customer_ID = CUSTOMER.Customer_ID
   and ORDERS.Product_ID = PRODUCT.Product_ID;
```

The select list of the query retrieves the Order_Amount from the ORDERS table for the product, period, and customer specified.

The Traditional Execution Path

Given the example star schema, and the example star query, the execution path shown in the following listing will be used to resolve the query. The execution path uses a series of NESTED LOOPS joins. First, the PRODUCT table is used as the driving table for the query. Each row of PRODUCT is joined to ORDERS via the index on ORDERS' primary key (since Product_ID is the first column of the ORDERS_PK index). The output of that join is then joined to CUSTOMER, and then to PERIOD.

```
NESTED LOOPS
  NESTED LOOPS
    NESTED LOOPS
      TABLE ACCESS FULL PRODUCT
      TABLE ACCESS BY ROWID ORDERS
        INDEX RANGE SCAN ORDERS_PK
    TABLE ACCESS BY ROWID CUSTOMER
      INDEX UNIQUE SCAN CUSTOMER_PK
  TABLE ACCESS BY ROWID PERIOD
    INDEX UNIQUE SCAN PERIOD_PK
```

If ORDERS is very large relative to its dimension tables—and in a data warehousing application, this is typically the case—then the execution path shown in the preceding listing may perform poorly. Despite its usage of all of the available indexes, and a small driving table, the first join—between PRODUCT and ORDERS—may doom the performance of the query. If a large number of records are returned from that join, that large driving set of records will be used during the subsequent joins. If ORDERS is very large relative to its dimension tables, you should consider using a star query or *composite key* execution path instead.

How to Create a Star Query Execution Path

The first step toward using a star query is to properly index the dimension tables. Since star queries will typically refer to the Name columns of the dimension tables in their **where** clauses, you need to create indexes on those columns. The commands in the following listing create indexes on the Name columns of the PRODUCT, PERIOD, and CUSTOMER dimension tables.

```
create index PRODUCT$PRODUCT_NAME
    on PRODUCT(Product_Name);

create index PERIOD$PERIOD_NAME
    on PERIOD(Period_Name);

create index CUSTOMER$CUSTOMER_NAME
    on CUSTOMER(Customer_Name);
```

With these three indexes available, the optimizer will now be able to create a different execution path. It will create Cartesian joins of the three dimension tables, using the Name columns to eliminate records as it does. The three dimension tables, when joined together in this manner, will form a virtual table that Oracle will hold in memory during the query. The virtual table will contain all of the columns from all of the dimension tables involved. Its primary key will be the composite of the primary keys of all of the dimension tables involved—which is the same primary key as the fact (ORDERS) table!

The composite table of the three dimension tables will have a primary key of (Product_ID, Period_ID, and Customer_ID). It will contain three attribute columns (Product_Name, Period_Name, and Customer_Name). The **where** clause conditions of the star query will eliminate rows from the dimension tables, so the Cartesian join of the three dimension tables may contain very few records. Figure 11-4 shows the composite key table for this example, with sample data for the row returned. The Name columns show values specified by the **where** clause, and sample ID values associated with those Name values. The three ID columns, taken together, form the primary key for the composite key table. For this example, each of the dimension tables has a limiting condition on its Name column, so only one row is returned from each table and the composite of the three tables has only one row.

Once the virtual table has been created in memory, it is joined to the ORDERS table. The execution path is shown in the following listing.

```
NESTED LOOPS
  NESTED LOOPS
    NESTED LOOPS
      TABLE ACCESS BY ROWID PRODUCT
        INDEX RANGE SCAN PRODUCT$PRODUCT_NAME
      TABLE ACCESS BY ROWID CUSTOMER
        INDEX RANGE SCAN CUSTOMER$CUSTOMER_NAME
    TABLE ACCESS BY ROWID PERIOD
      INDEX RANGE SCAN PERIOD$PERIOD_NAME
  TABLE ACCESS BY ROWID ORDERS
    INDEX UNIQUE SCAN ORDERS_PK
```

Product_ID	Period_ID	Customer_ID	Product_Name	Period_Name	Customer_Name
17	3	427	WIDGET	Last 3 Months	MAGELLAN

Primary Key

FIGURE 11-4. *Composite key table used for star query*

The accesses to the ORDERS table and the ORDERS_PK index shown in bold in the preceding listing can result in significant performance impact for star queries. In the traditional execution path, a range scan was performed on ORDERS_PK, since only the first column of that index was used while joining ORDERS to PRODUCT; in the star query execution path, all three columns of the ORDERS_PK index are used via a unique index scan. The placement of the access to the ORDERS table, as the last join performed, eliminates the potential of a large driving set of records being used during each join. ORDERS is joined last, in the most efficient manner possible. If ORDERS is large compared to the composite of its dimension tables, the performance of the star query can improve by orders of magnitude when using the revised execution path.

Management Issues for Star Queries

The cost-based optimizer explicitly identifies star schemas as of Oracle7.2. The optimizer may evaluate a traditional application design—such as a master table with many detail tables—as a star schema. If the optimizer evaluates the table layout as a star schema, it may use a star schema execution path for the query. You need to be aware of the circumstances in which a star schema is being used; otherwise, your performance may suffer. If a master table is not significantly larger than its detail tables, or if the limiting conditions on the detail tables return many rows, you may obtain better performance from a traditional execution path.

To see if the optimizer is using star query execution paths on your queries, check the execution paths for the queries via the **explain plan** command. The telltale sign of a star query execution path is the use of indexes that are not part of the join criteria. In the preceding example, the indexes on the Name columns of the dimension tables were used; the indexes on the ID columns of the dimension tables (the join columns for the query) were not used.

In versions of Oracle prior to Oracle7.3, a star query execution path will only be used if five or fewer tables are used in the star query. In Oracle7.3, there is no limit to the number of tables used in the star query. In Oracle7.3, you can force a query to use a star query execution path via the new STAR hint. In versions prior to Oracle7.3, you can force a query to use a star query execution path by giving the optimizer hints about which indexes to use—but if the right indexes are in place, the optimizer may choose a star query execution path without being given a hint. Depending on the sizes of the tables involved and the query's limiting conditions, the star query execution path may significantly improve your query's performance.

7. Properly Index CONNECT BY Operations

The CONNECT BY operation is used to query data that is related in a hierarchical fashion. For example, an organization chart for a corporation has a hierarchy of levels; you can use CONNECT BY to traverse the hierarchy in a single query. Since CONNECT BY is an iterative join, you must properly index the table used by the query; otherwise, the query will perform nested full table scans on the same table. In the examples below, you will see the proper indexing strategy, as applied to a common CONNECT BY query.

A hierarchical query has three clauses:

- **start with** identifies the root of the hierarchy, that is, the point from which the query will begin to traverse up or down the hierarchy.

- **connect by** identifies the manner in which the hierarchy is to be traversed (from the root downward, or upward from a lower level). The direction in which the hierarchy is traversed is determined by the placement of the **prior** keyword within the **connect by** clause.

- **where** filters rows before they are returned to the user.

The **start with** and **connect by** clauses should be the focus of your tuning efforts when tuning queries that use the CONNECT BY operation.

Throughout the listings in this section, you will see the Explain Plan query from Chapter 10 used as the example query. The query syntax is

```
select
  LPAD(' ',2*Level)||Operation||' '||Options
        ||' '||Object_Name  Q_Plan
  from PLAN_TABLE
 where Statement_ID = 'TEST'
connect by prior ID = Parent_ID and Statement_ID = 'TEST'
 start with ID=1;
```

PLAN_TABLE is used to store the output of the **explain plan** command. The query shown in the preceding listing queries PLAN_TABLE and returns a listing of the operations involved in resolving the query. The operations in the resulting listing are shown in hierarchical order by the use of the **connect by** clause. The

LPAD function is used to indent the "child" operations of "parent" operations. For information on the creation and use of PLAN_TABLE, see Chapter 10.

By default, PLAN_TABLE does not have any indexes created on it. What is the execution path of the preceding query? You can use the **explain plan** command on the preceding query, as shown in the following listing.

```
explain plan
set Statement_ID = 'TEST' for
select
  LPAD(' ',2*Level)||Operation||' '||Options
       ||' '||Object_Name  Q_Plan
  from PLAN_TABLE
 where Statement_ID = 'TEST'
connect by prior ID = Parent_ID and Statement_ID = 'TEST'
 start with ID=1;
```

The execution path for the Explain Plan query is shown in the following listing.

```
FILTER
  CONNECT BY
    TABLE ACCESS FULL PLAN_TABLE
    TABLE ACCESS BY ROWID PLAN_TABLE
    TABLE ACCESS FULL PLAN_TABLE
```

As shown in the plan, the PLAN_TABLE is read via a full table scan (to get the starting point for the query). For each record read, Oracle performs a table access by RowID. For each table access by RowID, Oracle then performs another full table scan of PLAN_TABLE. The FILTER operation applies the

```
where Statement_ID = 'TEST'
```

condition after the CONNECT BY operation has completed.

You can avoid performing nested full table scans of the same table during CONNECT BY queries. First, the columns used in the **start with** clause should be indexed, thereby preventing the optimizer from performing a full table scan to find the root for the query. For the Explain Plan query, the **start with** clause is

```
start with ID=1;
```

so the ID column should be indexed, as shown in the following listing.

```
create index PLAN_TABLE$ID on PLAN_TABLE(ID);
```

The PLAN_TABLE$ID index created in the preceding listing will be used during the evaluation of the START WITH clause. The new execution path for the query is shown in the following listing.

```
FILTER
  CONNECT BY
    INDEX RANGE SCAN PLAN_TABLE$ID
    TABLE ACCESS BY ROWID PLAN_TABLE
    TABLE ACCESS FULL PLAN_TABLE
```

As shown in bold in the preceding listing, the first full table scan of PLAN_TABLE has been replaced with an index scan using the index on the ID column of PLAN_TABLE.

Two additional indexes are needed for the **connect by** queries: one for each set of columns in the **connect by** clause. In the case of the Explain Plan query, the **connect by** clause is

```
connect by prior ID = Parent_ID and Statement_ID = 'TEST'
```

The ID column has already been indexed, so the next step is to create an index on the Parent_ID column. The index on Parent_ID is created via the command shown in the following listing.

```
create index PLAN_TABLE$PARENT_ID on PLAN_TABLE(Parent_ID);
```

The PLAN_TABLE$PARENT_ID index created in the preceding listing will be used during the evaluation of the **connect by** clause. The new execution path for the query is shown in the following listing.

```
FILTER
  CONNECT BY
    INDEX RANGE SCAN PLAN_TABLE$ID
    TABLE ACCESS BY ROWID PLAN_TABLE
    TABLE ACCESS BY ROWID PLAN_TABLE
      INDEX RANGE SCAN PLAN_TABLE$PARENT_ID
```

As shown by the bold lines in the preceding listing, the full table scan of PLAN_TABLE has been replaced by an index scan using the PLAN_TABLE$PARENT_ID index, followed by table access by RowID.

The outermost FILTER operation cannot be avoided, since there is a **where** clause in the query. However, since the Statement_ID column is also used in the

connect by clause, an index on Statement_ID could also be used during the resolution of the query. The index on Statement_ID is created by the command in the following listing.

```
create index PLAN_TABLE$STATEMENT_ID
    on PLAN_TABLE(Statement_ID);
```

The PLAN_TABLE$STATEMENT_ID index created in the preceding listing will be used during the evaluation of the **connect by** clause, but not when applying the limiting condition in the **where** clause. The new execution path for the query is shown in the following listing.

```
FILTER
  CONNECT BY
    INDEX RANGE SCAN PLAN_TABLE$ID
    TABLE ACCESS BY ROWID PLAN_TABLE
    TABLE ACCESS BY ROWID PLAN_TABLE
       AND-EQUAL
          INDEX RANGE SCAN PLAN_TABLE$PARENT_ID
          INDEX RANGE SCAN PLAN_TABLE$STATEMENT_ID
```

As shown in the preceding listing, the index scan of the Parent_ID index has been replaced by an AND-EQUAL of the separate Parent_ID and Statement_ID indexes. The usefulness of the additional Statement_ID index is therefore dependent on its selectivity; if Statement_ID is more selective than the Parent_ID index, then indexing Statement_ID may improve your query performance. If Statement_ID is not selective, do not index it.

To improve your indexing scheme further, you can create two indexes on the columns used in the **connect by** clause. Consider the ID and Parent_ID columns used in the examples in this section. You can create an index on (ID, Parent_ID), and a second index on (Parent_ID, ID), alternating the leading column of the index. The optimizer would then be able to use an index in resolving the query regardless of the direction in which you traverse the hierarchy. That is, the index on (ID, Parent_ID) will be useful when going down the hierarchy (finding all the children of a given parent record). The index on (Parent_ID, ID) will be useful when going up the hierarchy (finding the parentage of a given child record). All of the examples in this section focus on traveling down the hierarchy from a parent record.

If both the (ID, Parent_ID) and (Parent_ID, ID) indexes are created, the execution path would be the similar to the execution path shown earlier in this section when the PLAN_TABLE.ID and PLAN_TABLE.Parent_ID columns were indexed separately. The following listing shows the commands needed to index the ID and Parent_ID columns together, along with the subsequent execution path. In this listing, the old indexes are dropped prior to the creation of the new indexes.

```
drop index PLAN_TABLE$ID;

drop index PLAN_TABLE$PARENT_ID;

drop index PLAN_TABLE$STATEMENT_ID;

create index PLAN_TABLE$ID$PARENT
    on PLAN_TABLE(ID, Parent_ID);

create index PLAN_TABLE$PARENT$ID
    on PLAN_TABLE(Parent_ID, ID);
```

The new execution path for the Explain Plan query is shown in the following listing.

```
FILTER
  CONNECT BY
    INDEX RANGE SCAN PLAN_TABLE$ID$PARENT
    TABLE ACCESS BY ROWID PLAN_TABLE
    TABLE ACCESS BY ROWID PLAN_TABLE
      INDEX RANGE SCAN PLAN_TABLE$PARENT$ID
```

The examples in this section show the significant impact of incremental changes in the indexing strategy for CONNECT BY queries. At the start, the query used nested full table scans. By properly indexing the columns used in the **start with** and **connect by** clauses, you can eliminate full table scans from your CONNECT BY queries.

8. Limit Remote Table Accesses

Whenever a SQL statement uses a database link or a synonym for a remote object, a portion of the SQL statement is extracted to be executed on the remote node. A query involving a remote table can have significant impact on your tuning efforts: instead of just tuning the main query, you now need to also tune the SQL on the remote node and the method by which the remote tables are accessed. NESTED LOOPS joins are a common cause of problems during remote table accesses, as you will see in the examples in this section.

The total cost of a query that uses remote objects is the sum of the costs of the local and remote portions of the query and of the cost of the manner in which the portions are executed. You need to tune first the local, then the remote, portion of the query. The SQL that is sent to be executed on the remote node is stored in the "Other" column of PLAN_TABLE during **explain plan** commands (see Chapter 10 for a description of PLAN_TABLE).

Once the two separate portions of the query have been tuned, you need to consider the method by which they are joined. In the following example, the COMPANY and SALES tables are joined (see Chapter 10 for a full description of these example tables).

```
select COMPANY.Name
  from COMPANY, SALES@REMOTE1
 where COMPANY.Company_ID = SALES.Company_ID
   and SALES.Period_ID =3
   and SALES.Sales_Total>1000;
```

The execution path for the NESTED LOOPS join query in the preceding example is shown in the following listing.

```
NESTED LOOPS
  REMOTE (TABLE ACCESS FULL SALES@REMOTE1)
  TABLE ACCESS BY ROWID COMPANY
    INDEX UNIQUE SCAN COMPANY_PK
```

The plan shows that the SALES table in a remote database (defined by the database link named "REMOTE1") is used as the driving table for the query (during NESTED LOOPS joins, one table is always used to drive the query). For each Company_ID value in the SALES table, the Company_PK index on COMPANY.Company_ID will be checked to see if a matching value exists. If a match exists, that record is returned to the user via the NESTED LOOPS operation. The query to be executed remotely is stored in the Other column of PLAN_TABLE (see the REMOTE operation description in Chapter 10).

What if SALES is located in a remote database? If SALES, as the driving table, were in a remote database, no tuning problem would be anticipated. What if COMPANY is located in a remote database? If COMPANY, as the driven table, is in a remote database, then the query's performance could be dramatically affected.

Since a NESTED LOOPS operation is performed, with SALES as the driving table, the query for COMPANY values from the remote database will be executed repeatedly—once for each record in SALES. The repeated accesses to the remote database could severely impact the performance of the query. Even if the query for the COMPANY data from the remote database is efficient, the cost of performing that query thousands of times will negatively affect the performance of the overall query.

To resolve the potential performance problem, you must manage how remote table accesses are executed during NESTED LOOPS joins. Either use the remote table as the driving table, or use MERGE JOINs instead of NESTED LOOPS joins. The section on managing multi-table joins earlier in this chapter described how to influence the choice of a driving table for a query. To force the use of a MERGE JOIN, embed the USE_MERGE hint within the query, as shown in the following listing.

```
select /*+ USE_MERGE(COMPANY,SALES) */
       COMPANY.Name
  from COMPANY@REMOTE1, SALES
 where COMPANY.Company_ID = SALES.Company_ID
   and SALES.Period_ID =3
   and SALES.Sales_Total>1000;
```

The execution path for the MERGE JOIN query in the preceding example is shown in the following listing.

```
MERGE JOIN
   SORT JOIN
     TABLE ACCESS FULL SALES
   SORT JOIN
     REMOTE (TABLE ACCESS FULL COMPANY@REMOTE1)
```

As shown in the preceding listing, the MERGE JOIN method prevents the iterative remote accesses that the NESTED LOOPS method causes; however, the cost of performing a full table scan on both tables may be great. The query to be executed in the remote database is stored in the PLAN_TABLE.Other column for the PLAN_TABLE record whose Operation value is equal to 'REMOTE'.

If you have multiple remote table accesses in the same query, and no remote table can be easily chosen as the driving table, you have two options:

- Use a view on one of the remote databases, to force the execution to be driven from there. See the Tip #4, on managing SQL statements containing views, earlier in this chapter.

- Force every join to execute as a MERGE JOIN via USE_MERGE hints.

Using remote tables in queries forces you to choose between MERGE JOINs and NESTED LOOPS joins that may have a nonoptimal driving table. If the tables are large, MERGE JOINs may not be an acceptable choice. The more remote table accesses you perform, the more tuning issues you will encounter with them—and as described here, there is no guarantee that you will be able to develop a successful solution. Often, your remote table accesses will prevent the database from using its best NESTED LOOPS combination. Once you prevent the database from using the best driving table in a NESTED LOOPS join, the second-best option available to you may not be acceptable.

For frequently-accessed remote tables, consider using Oracle's replication options. These include read-only snapshots and multisite ownership of data. See Chapter 13 for information on the management of the replication options.

9. Manage Very Large Table Accesses

As a table grows to be significantly larger than the size of the SGA's data block buffer cache, you need to approach tuning queries against that table from a different perspective. Whereas multiple users can benefit from sharing data from small tables in the SGA, that benefit disappears when very large tables are accessed. In the following sections you will see how to address the tuning of queries against very large tables, using the following methods:

- Managing data proximity
- Avoiding unhelpful index scans
- Creating fully indexed tables
- Creating hash clusters
- Creating partitioned tables
- Implementing parallel options

The tips within this section differ from those earlier in this chapter, since an application with a very large table is fundamentally different from the transaction-processing environment typical of relational database applications. The tips provided in this section apply only if the table being queried is significantly larger than the size of the SGA's data block buffer cache.

The Problem

When a table and its indexes are small, there can be a high degree of data sharing within the SGA. Multiple users performing table reads or index range scans can use the same blocks over and over. As a result of the reuse of blocks within the SGA, the *hit ratio*—a measure of the reuse of blocks within the SGA—increases.

As a table grows, the table's indexes grow too. As the table and its indexes grow larger than the available space in the SGA, it becomes less likely that the next row needed by a range scan will be found within the SGA. The reusability of data within the SGA's data block buffer cache will diminish. The hit ratio for the database will decrease. Eventually, each logical read will require a separate physical read.

The SGA is designed to maximize the reuse (among multiple users) of the blocks read from the datafiles. To do this, the SGA maintains a list of the blocks that have been read; if the blocks were read via index accesses or via table access by RowID, those blocks are kept in the SGA the longest. If a block is read into the SGA via a full table scan, that block is the first to be removed from the SGA when more space is needed in the data block buffer cache.

For applications with small tables, the data block buffer cache management in the SGA maximizes the reuse of blocks and increases the hit ratio. What happens, though, if an index range scan is performed on a very large table? The index's blocks will be kept for a long time in the SGA, even though it is likely that no other users will be able to use the values in the index's blocks. Since the index is large, many of its blocks may be read, consuming a substantial portion of the available space in the SGA's data block buffer cache. A greater amount of space will be consumed by the table blocks accessed by RowID, and those blocks will be even less likely to be reused. The hit ratio will begin to drop—ironically, because index scans are being performed. The tuning methods used for very large tables therefore focus on special indexing techniques and on alternatives to indexes.

Manage Data Proximity

If you intend to continue using indexes during accesses of very large tables, you must be concerned about *data proximity*—the physical relationship between logically related records. To maximize data proximity, insert records into the table sequentially, ordered by columns commonly used in range scans of the table. For example, the primary key of the large COMPANY table is Company_ID. Accesses that use Company_ID as a limiting condition will be able to use the unique index on the primary key. If range scans are commonly performed on the COMPANY.Name column, the data should be stored in order of Name.

If the data is stored in an ordered format, then during range searches, such as

```
where Name like 'AA%'
```

you will more likely be able to reuse the table and index blocks read into the SGA, because all of the Name values beginning with 'AA' would be stored together. Fewer index and table blocks will be read into the SGA's data block buffer cache, minimizing the impact of the index range scan on the SGA. Storing data in an ordered fashion helps range scans regardless of the size of the table, but it is particularly critical for large tables due to the negative implications of large range scans.

Avoid Unhelpful Index Scans

If you are going to use index scans against a large table, you cannot assume that the index scan will perform better than a full table scan. Unique scans or range scans of indexes that are not followed by table accesses perform well, but a range scan of an index followed by a table access by RowID may perform poorly. As the table grows to be significantly larger than the data block buffer cache, the break-even point between index scans and full table scans decreases—eventually, if you read more than 1 percent of the rows in a 10,000,000 row table, you are better off performing a full table scan rather than an index range scan and table access by RowID combination.

For example, the COMPANY table has a primary key of Company_ID. If COMPANY has 10,000,000 rows, the Company_ID values range sequentially from 1 to 10,000,000. In a multiuser environment, should the following query use an index to retrieve the first 1,000,000 records from COMPANY?

```
select *
  from COMPANY
 where Company_ID between 1 and 1000000;
```

The query in the preceding listing selects 10 percent of the COMPANY table. The rule-based optimizer's execution path for the query is shown in the following listing.

```
TABLE ACCESS BY ROWID COMPANY
   INDEX RANGE SCAN COMPANY_PK
```

Because the **select** clause selects all columns, Oracle has to access the table after performing the index range scan. If each index block contains entries for 100 records, you will need to scan 10,000 index blocks (1,000,000 rows selected/100 rows per index block). If each table block contains 10 records, you will need to access 100,000 table blocks (1,000,000 rows selected/10 records per table block) during the table access by RowID—and that's the best-case scenario. This scenario assumes that the data is stored in ordered fashion, so that no data is stored in the table blocks read except for the data required to resolve the query.

If the data is not stored in an ordered fashion, you may need to access 1,000,000 table blocks (1 block read per row for 1,000,000 rows selected)—for a total of 1,010,000 block accesses. Depending on data proximity, the total number of blocks read will therefore range between 110,000 and 1,010,000. Because these blocks are read via index range scans, they will be kept in the SGA for as long as possible. For a 2K block size, that means that this query would try to use and retain at least 220MB (2K per block * 110,000 blocks) of its blocks in the data block buffer cache. Unless you have an extremely large SGA, this query's block reads would effectively remove all other data from the data block buffer cache.

Conversely, how many blocks will be read during a full table scan? If there are 10 records per block, a full table scan will read 1,000,000 blocks. Not only is that fewer than the worst-case index range scan/table access by RowID combination, but also *the blocks read by the full table scan are not marked for long-term storage in the SGA.* The blocks read by the full table scan into the data block buffer cache are removed from the SGA as quickly as possible—thus reducing the query's impact on other users in the database. The only blocks held in the SGA because of the full table scan are those blocks read in via the last read; the number of blocks read is determined by the setting of the DB_FILE_MULTIBLOCK_READ_COUNT INIT.ORA parameter. Table 11-4 summarizes the block usage and data block buffer cache usage for the COMPANY "10 percent query" example.

What if only 1 percent (100,000 rows) of the records had been read? The full table scan would still require 1,000,000 block reads. The index range scan would scan 1,000 blocks. If each table block contained 10 records, you would need between 10,000 and 100,000 table block reads, depending on data proximity. The total for the index range scan/table access by RowID combination is therefore between 11,000 and 101,000 blocks—between 22MB and 202MB of space used in the data block buffer cache (if each block is 2K in size). Table 11-5 summarizes the block usage and data block buffer cache usage for the COMPANY "1 percent query" example.

When comparing the two methods' results in Tables 11-4 and 11-5, you must consider the rightmost column: the number of blocks that will be held long-term in the SGA by the data read by the query. If the query is run in batch mode, with no other users in the database, it may be acceptable to completely remove all other data from the SGA. If there are multiple users of the database, the performance cost of keeping the data in the SGA can be significant. The performance cost of the changes to the SGA could be so great for the other users of the database (due to the size of the table and indexes) that you may be better off using the full table scan method even when querying just 1 percent of the table.

Method	Best-Case Blocks Read	Worst-Case Blocks Read	Marked as Least-Recently-Used?	Blocks Held in SGA
Index Range Scan	10,000	10,000	Y	10,000
Table Access by RowID	100,000	1,000,000	Y	<=1,000,000
	=========	=========		==========
	110,000	1,010,000		<=1,010,000
Full Table Scan	1,000,000	1,000,000	N	(multiblock read count)

TABLE 11-4. *Block Reads and Memory Usage for Large Table Access Methods for 10 Percent Scan of a Very Large Table*

Method	Best-Case Blocks Read	Worst-Case Blocks Read	Marked as Least-Recently-Used?	Blocks Held in SGA
Index Range Scan	1,000	1,000	Y	1,000
Table Access by RowID	10,000	100,000	Y	<=100,000
	========	========		==========
	11,000	101,000		<=101,000
Full Table Scan	1,000,000	1,000,000	N	(multiblock read count)

TABLE 11-5. *Block Reads and Memory Usage for Large Table Access Methods for 1 Percent Scan of a Very Large Table*

In addition to the cache management issues, the full table scan method also benefits by Oracle's multiblock read mechanism. As described in Chapter 5, multiblock reads allow for quick data access during full table scans. The one-consistent-get-per-block feature used during full table scans also helps improve the performance of full table scans.

As noted earlier, favoring full table scans is not a typical tuning method. However, if a table is so large that its index-based accesses will override the SGA, you should consider using a full table scan for queries of very large tables in multiuser environments.

Create Fully Indexed Tables

To improve the use of indexes during large table accesses, you need to eliminate two operations: range scans and subsequent table accesses. The cost of index-only accesses to the SGA can still be high—as illustrated in Table 11-5, an index-only access of 1 percent of a very large table could still require 1000 index blocks to be read into the SGA (at a 2K block size, that equates to 2MB worth of index blocks). To achieve these index-related goals, you can fully index the table.

Fully indexing a table is useful if the table's data is fairly static. Create a concatenated index that contains all of the columns commonly selected during queries. During a query, all of the data requested by the query can be provided via index accesses, and no table accesses will be necessary.

If you have an associative table, which is used to maintain many-to-many relationships between major tables, the associative table's primary key is usually the composite of the primary keys of the tables it relates. For example, if there is a many-to-many relationship between COMPANY and PRODUCT, an associative table for those two tables (named COMPANY_PRODUCT) will have the primary key (Company_ID, Product_ID). If associative tables exist, create two concatenated indexes, one with each table's primary key as the leading set of columns. In the case of the COMPANY_PRODUCT, you should create one index with Company_ID as the leading column (Company_ID, Product_ID) and a second index with Product_ID as a leading column (Product_ID, Company_ID), to enable the optimizer to use either table as the driving table in the join.

Create Hash Clusters

In a *hash cluster*, the order in which records are inserted into a table does not matter; the physical location of a record is determined by its values in key columns. A *hashing function* is applied to the key values for the row, and Oracle uses the result to determine in which block to store the record. The rows within the hash cluster are quickly spread across all of the allocated blocks.

The use of a hash cluster eliminates the need for an index during a simple primary key value lookup. Hash clusters are useful under certain conditions, as follows.

If Equivalence Queries Are Used

An equivalence query contains a **where** clause that sets the primary key equal to a specific value, as shown in the following listing.

```
where Company_ID = 1234
```

When the query is resolved, the optimizer will apply the hashing function to the value specified in the **where** clause (in this case, 1234). The hashing function will provide the physical location of the row that matches the value in the **where** clause. The row can then quickly be located and returned to the user.

If There Is No Way to Enforce Row Proximity

If the rows are stored in sorted order, an index on the column will perform almost as well as a hash cluster for equivalence queries, and will use less storage space. If there are multiple successive equivalence queries of a range of values, and the rows are not in sorted order, then the index blocks read into the SGA's data block buffer cache will be less likely to be reused. If data proximity is poor, there is little chance of index block reusability. If you cannot reuse the index blocks read into the SGA, a hash cluster may be appropriate.

If Space Allocation Is Not a Problem

A hash cluster will typically require about 50 percent more space than a comparably indexed table.

To create a hash cluster, you must first create a cluster, as shown in the following listing. The **size** parameter specifies the amount of space allocated to each row in the table. To avoid *collisions*—multiple hashed rows stored in the same block—you should multiply the calculated **size** parameter for the cluster by a factor of 1.5. The **hashkeys** parameter specifies the expected number of rows within the hashed table. See the *Oracle7 Server Concepts Manual* for information on the **hashkeys** and **size** parameters.

```
create cluster COMPANY_CLUSTER (Company_ID NUMBER(12))
storage (initial 50M next 50M)
  hash is Company_ID
  size 60 hashkeys 10000000;
```

The **storage** parameters for the hashed table are specified at the cluster level, as shown in the preceding listing.

Once the cluster has been created, create the table within the cluster, as shown in the following listing.

```
create table COMPANY
(Company_ID   NUMBER(12),
 Name         VARCHAR2(20),
 Address      VARCHAR2(20))
cluster COMPANY_CLUSTER (Company_ID);
```

The table will be created using the storage parameters for the cluster, and the Company_ID column will be used as the hashed column for the COMPANY table.

As of Oracle7.2, you can specify a hashing formula for the cluster. Specifying your own hashing formula is particularly useful for applications that use system-generated sequence numbers for their tables' primary keys. The hash formula in that case would be the sequence column itself. Specifying a hash formula on a sequence column may eliminate many of the space and collision concerns associated with hash clusters. The more records that have the same hash value, the less efficient the hash cluster is. If the number of such "collisions" is unpredictable, use a fully indexed table instead.

Create Partitioned Tables

If a large table has several logical partitions—groups of records that share a common value for a key column—you may be able to break it into a several smaller tables. The smaller tables could be queried together via a **union all** involving separate queries against each of the smaller tables. Partitioning data based on its column values is called *horizontal partitioning*.

For example, consider the SALES table, which has three columns: Company_ID, Period_ID, and Sales_Total. There is a logical division of records among Period_ID values. If users frequently request data for just one Period_ID value, it may be appropriate to create multiple SALES tables, one for each Period_ID or set of Period_ID values.

If there are only four valid Period_ID values (for example, one for each quarter of the year), you may choose to create four smaller tables from the SALES table. Creating smaller tables simplifies the administration of the SALES data, since you can now truncate or replace one quarter's worth of the SALES data without directly affecting the rest of the data. You could also dynamically modify the **union** view to include or exclude particular quarters' tables.

When creating the quarters' tables, you need to create a CHECK constraint on the column used as the basis for partitioning. The **create table** command for Period 1's data is shown in the following listing.

```
create table SALES_PERIOD_1
(Company_ID, Period_ID, Sales_Total) as
select Company_ID, Period_ID, Sales_Total
  from SALES
 where Period_ID = 1;

alter table SALES_PERIOD_1
  add constraint CHECK_SALES_PERIOD_1
check (Period_ID = 1);

alter table SALES_PERIOD_1
  add constraint SALES_PERIOD_1_PK
primary key (Company_ID, Period_ID);

create index SALES_PERIOD_1$PERIOD_ID
    on SALES_PERIOD_1(Period_ID);
```

As shown in the preceding listing, there are several steps involved in properly creating the SALES_PERIOD_1 table. First, the table is created. Next, a CHECK constraint is created on the column used for partitioning. Indexes are then created for the primary key and the partition column for the SALES_PERIOD_1 table.

It is important that you create the CHECK constraint on the newly created table. If you create four SALES_PERIOD tables, and then create a view that performs a union across the four tables, then queries against the view can be optimized via a technique called *partition elimination* (available as of Oracle7.3). In partition elimination, the optimizer uses the CHECK constraints on the SALES_PERIOD tables to determine which tables could not have records that meet the query's **where** criteria. For example, the following listing shows the **create view** command for a view named SALES_ALL that performs a **union** across four SALES_PERIOD tables.

```
create view SALES_ALL as
select * from SALES_PERIOD_1
 union
select * from SALES_PERIOD_2
 union
select * from SALES_PERIOD_3
 union
select * from SALES_PERIOD_4;
```

If you query SALES_ALL using a Period_ID value as a limiting condition, most of the tables will not be involved in returning rows to the query. The query in the following listing selects only rows that have a Period_ID value of '1'.

```
select * from SALES_ALL
 where Period_ID = 1
   and Company_ID > 10000;
```

The query in the preceding listing will only return records from the SALES_PERIOD_1 table; there is no reason for the query to read from any other SALES_PERIOD table. As of Oracle7.3, the optimizer can use the CHECK clauses to determine which tables should not be used during the query resolution. Partitioned tables whose CHECK conditions prevent them from being used to return records to the query will not be scanned.

If your queries are based on strict partitions of data (whether they are related to exact values or exact ranges of values), partition elimination can significantly reduce the number of data blocks that must be read to resolve a query. If you cannot establish the partition boundaries, or if queries frequently cross many partitions, you may not see performance benefits from this design. The greatest performance benefits from a partitioned table design come from the partition elimination features of Oracle7.3.

Other very important management benefits of a partitioned design include:

- In the event of disaster, recovery could be much faster than if the table were not partitioned.

- It is easier to back up the table's partitions than to back up the entire table.

- You can improve I/O balancing by placing different portions of the table on different disk drives.

■ Oracle is planning to fully support horizontal partitioning of data in its future releases, so it will be easier to manage the data partitioning process.

Implement the Parallel Options

As noted earlier in this section, there are a number of conditions under which full table scans are preferable to index range scans. If you are using full table scans, you can use the Parallel Query Option available in Oracle7. Oracle7 cannot parallelize index scans. For full information on the administration and implementation of the available parallel options, see Chapter 12.

10. Revisit the Tuning Process

As stated earlier in this book, change is constant. Tables get larger, data may be moved, and new options may be available within the database. A well-tuned NESTED LOOPS join may work fine now, but if one of the tables is moved to a remote server, you may need to force the use of a MERGE JOIN instead. As your tables grow in size, the rate at which they grow may not be uniform; as a result, you may need to reevaluate the order of tables within a NESTED LOOPS join.

To make matters worse, the data is changing within the tables—and the statistics that the cost-based optimizer used to determine its optimal execution path during the creation of the query may change over time. As the statistics change, the query's execution path may change. Suddenly, a query that was once acceptable without manual tuning intervention may require tuning.

The changes to the tables' volume and data contents are largely in the hands of application users, so it is difficult to predict when the optimizer's chosen path will change. To manage the tuning changes as your application grows, schedule a routine audit of your application's queries. Determine which queries have nonoptimal execution paths. When queries use these paths, check the appropriate section of this chapter for information on how to manually intervene in the selection of the queries' execution paths. After correcting the query's tuning problem, schedule a time to check the query again—for unless its tables are static, the query's performance is constantly subject to change.

Tuning is not a simple process, but if you use the proper approach, it can quickly yield great benefits. The first chapter in this section, Chapter 7, provided five steps to follow during the tuning process, in the following order.

1. Ensure a consistent production environment.

2. Categorize the application's transactions and queries.

3. Focus on offensive SQL.

4. Tune specific long-running processes and batch jobs.

5. Tune the access to individual tables.

Given that five-step method for approaching tuning, you can use the information in this chapter and Chapter 10 to address points 3, 4, and 5. If your production environment is consistent, you should be able to identify the few SQL statements that cause most of the burden on your system. By focusing on those statements and the applications that call them, you can acquire great performance benefits.

Because of changes within the systems, though, you will need to revisit the tuning process every time you make a change to an application's database structures. For example, adding an index may help one query, but may change the execution path of an unrelated query. If a query has been tuned, be sure to use hints or comments to record the proper execution path for your query. If you properly comment your work, future tuning efforts will be less likely to undo the performance benefits you gained.

Within this chapter, the first focus was on the proper use of indexes and joins. If you use indexes and manage your joins correctly, you will resolve most of the tuning problems you are likely to encounter. As your system grows and moves over time, you can refer to the sections on managing large tables and remote tables for tuning advice specific to them. To avoid tuning queries while in crisis mode, schedule regular audits; if a major change is about to occur in the system, proactively evaluate its impact on your prior tuning efforts. Once the system has been reevaluated and provides a consistent production environment, you can again focus on tuning the most offensive SQL.

PART 4

Advanced
Tuning Options

CHAPTER 12

Parallel Options

Oracle7.1 introduced the ability to split a single database task, such as a **select** statement, into multiple units of work to be executed concurrently by multiple Oracle processes. This option, known as the Parallel Query Option (PQO), allows the database activity for a single query to be transparently processed by multiple coordinated processes. If adequate CPU and I/O capacity is available, the same task that previously was executed by a single process can complete much faster. Any application that requires large queries, frequent data loading, frequent indexing, or data aggregations (such as most data warehouse and decision support systems) can benefit from PQO.

In this chapter, you will see how to implement, monitor, and tune the usage of the PQO. Following the examples for the PQO, you will see how to implement the other parallel options available (Parallel Create Table, Parallel Create Index, Parallel Load, Parallel Recovery, and Oracle Parallel Server). Since many of the concepts are shared among the options, the implementation of parallelism in

Oracle will be discussed within the context of the PQO, but applies to the other parallel options as well, unless otherwise indicated.

The Impact of the Parallel Options

The parallel options invoke multiple processes to utilize spare system resources to reduce the time required to complete tasks. The parallel options do not reduce the amount of resources required by the processing; rather, they spread the processing burden across multiple CPUs. In order to get the most benefit from the parallel options, you should have underutilized CPUs and I/O on your disks. Since the goal of parallelism is to get more CPUs and disks involved concurrently in processing a database command, a server that is already out of CPU and I/O resources will not benefit from the parallel options.

Prior to the PQO, the execution of a single database task (such as a single SQL statement, database recovery, or data load) was completely *serialized*—only one process was involved in carrying out the task. Even if multiple processors were available, a single SQL statement could not make use of spare CPU and I/O capacity. With the parallel options, data-intensive SQL statements, database recovery, and data loads are handled by multiple processes. Figure 12-1 shows the difference between the serialized model and the parallel model. In the parallel model, multiple *query server processes* are created by the database. A *query coordinator* process distributes the load among the query server processes and coordinates the return of the output to the user. The arrows shown in Figure 12-1 show the direction of data flow.

If you have spare CPU and I/O resources available on your system, the parallel options can have significant impact on the performance of your database commands. In the following sections you will see how to set up and manage a database that uses the PQO.

What Are the Options?

In Oracle7.1 and above, parallelism can be used for the following database activities:

- **select** (for sorts and full table scans, including subqueries within **update** and **delete** statements)
- **create table as select** (as of Oracle7.1, for the query portion; as of Oracle7.2, the **insert** portion of **create table** can also be parallelized)
- **create index**
- SQL*Loader Direct Path
- **recover**

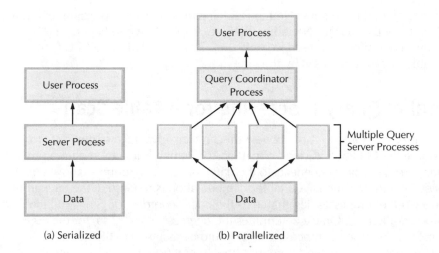

FIGURE 12-1. *Serialized versus parallelized query model*

NOTE
Index scans *cannot* be parallelized.

Since all of the options use the same type of architecture (query coordinators and multiple query server processes), the architecture for the PQO will be fully described; the architecture sections will not be repeated for each option.

How Parallel Query Works

In the following sections, you will see how PQO operates within your database. The impact of the change to the query architecture is shown by comparing a parallelized query with a conventional (serialized) query.

Conventional Query Processing

When a user process connects to a database, a background *shadow server process* is started to access the database on behalf of the user process. As shown in Figure 12-2, a query executed by the user is carried out by the shadow server process. There is only one shadow server process available per user process, so that process performs all of the work involved in resolving the query (in this example, a full table scan of the COMPANY table). In the example shown in Figure 12-2, one shadow server process is used, so only one CPU is used; if more CPUs are available, they are not used by the query.

Parallel Query Processing for a Table Scan

If you are using Oracle7.1 or above, you can take advantage of the PQO to distribute the CPU and I/O load of database commands among multiple processes. When the user process connects to the database, a background shadow server process is started. When a full table scan operation is requested, the background shadow server process is designated as the *query coordinator*. Since full table scans can be parallelized, Oracle determines the *degree of parallelism* for the query—the number of query server processes that should be assigned to the query.

The query coordinator determines how to partition the work among the assigned query server processes. The partitioning of work is based on ranges of contiguous blocks of data in the table. The query coordinator dynamically allocates table-scanning responsibilities to the query server processes. The query server processes go to work concurrently (on the same CPU or multiple CPUs, depending on your hardware configuration), scanning different parts of the table. Figure 12-3 shows the interaction of the user process, the query coordinator, and four query server processes that scan the COMPANY table.

The query server processes return their results to the query coordinator, which in turn assembles them and returns them to the user. As the query server processes complete the work assigned to them, more work is assigned to them dynamically by the query coordinator until the full table scan is complete. The management of the query server process loads is transparent to the user. Selecting the number of query server processes to use is described in the "How Oracle Determines the

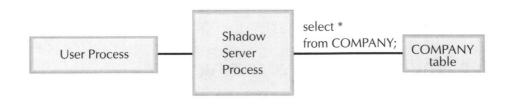

FIGURE 12-2. *Conventional scan*

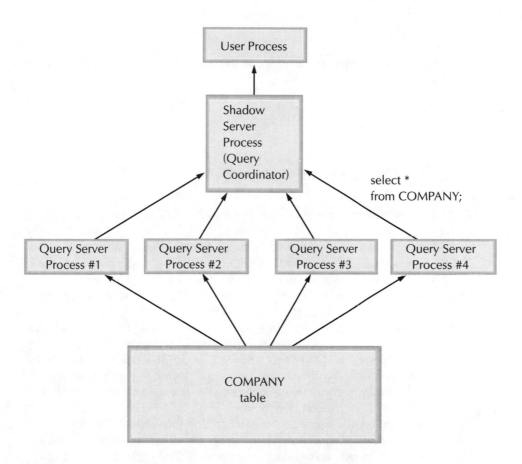

FIGURE 12-3. *Parallel scan with four query server processes*

Degree of Parallelism" and "The Art of Selecting a Degree of Parallelism" sections later in this chapter.

Parallel Query Processing for a Table Scan with One Sort

In addition to parallelizing full table scans, Oracle can also parallelize sorting operations. In the previous examples (Figure 12-2 and Figure 12-3), the example query was

```
select *
  from COMPANY;
```

A sorting operation will now be added to the example. The new query is shown in the following listing.

```
select *
  from COMPANY
 order by Name;
```

The explain plan for the new query is shown in the following listing.

```
SORT ORDER BY
  TABLE ACCESS FULL COMPANY
```

Since there is no **where** clause in the query, a full table scan (the TABLE ACCESS FULL operation) is performed. The SORT ORDER BY operation sorts the COMPANY records by the Name column values. See Chapter 10 for information regarding the generation and interpretation of explain plans; the script for creating the COMPANY table is provided later in this chapter.

When the query is executed, the background shadow server process acts as the query coordinator. Oracle checks the execution path for the query and determines that two separate operations (TABLE ACCESS FULL and SORT ORDER BY) used by the query can be parallelized. Oracle determines the degree of parallelism and assigns twice that many query server processes to the query—one set for the full table scan, and one set for the sort operation.

The query coordinator determines how to partition the work among the available query server processes. As with the previous table scan example, the partitioning is based on ranges of contiguous blocks of data in the table. The query coordinator dynamically allocates scanning responsibilities to the set of query server processes dedicated to the full table scan operation. Those query server processes work concurrently to access the COMPANY table's data, scanning different parts of the table.

The second set of query server processes performs the sorting operations. The query server processes performing the sorting operations receive results *directly* from the query server processes that perform the scanning operations. The query coordinator determines how to partition the sorting workload, based on contiguous values of the sort key (in this case, COMPANY.Name). The partitioning of the sorting workload is static, based on estimates of the data ranges. For example, the query coordinator may assign to the first sorting query server process all Name values starting with "A" through "F", while the second sorting query server process is assigned all Name values starting with "G" through "L". Based on the partitioning of the sort key values, the query server processes that perform the table scan check the sort keys of the rows being scanned and return the rows to the corresponding sorting query server processes. You cannot specify the ranges that the sorting operations use. Figure 12-4 illustrates the relationship between the query coordinator, the sorting query server processes, and the table scanning query server processes.

The sorted results from the sorting query server processes are returned to the query coordinator. The query coordinator assembles the results and returns them to the user process. As the scanning query server processes complete the work assigned to them, more work is assigned to them dynamically by the query coordinator until the full scan is complete. The assignment of work to the sorting query server processes is not dynamic; it is determined at the start of the query. As with the previous examples, the management of the query server loads is transparent to the user. Selecting the number of query server processes to use is described in the "How Oracle Determines the Degree of Parallelism" and "The Art of Selecting a Degree of Parallelism" sections of this chapter.

How to Manage and Tune the Parallel Query Option

If you do not properly manage the use of the PQO and the situations for which it is used, you may not derive much benefit from its use. In the following sections, you will see how to monitor the query server processes, how to tell if parallel query is being used, and how to select the proper degree of parallelism for your queries. You will also see how to use the **explain plan** command to see the impact of parallelism on the execution path of your queries.

Make sure that each user of the PQO can use the processes created by the query server processes. For the query server processes to be created, the user who executes the query must be able to create the processes. Most operating systems limit the maximum number of processes that can be created by a single account; you will need to factor in this limit when sizing the query server pool. Also, each user within Oracle has a profile that limits the user's resources. If you have previously limited the number of sessions allowed per user, you will need to alter the user profile to allow users to create the query server sessions they need for the PQO. The example shown in the following listing sets the default maximum number of sessions per user to **unlimited**, which is the default value, via the **alter profile** command.

```
alter profile default limit sessions_per_user unlimited;
```

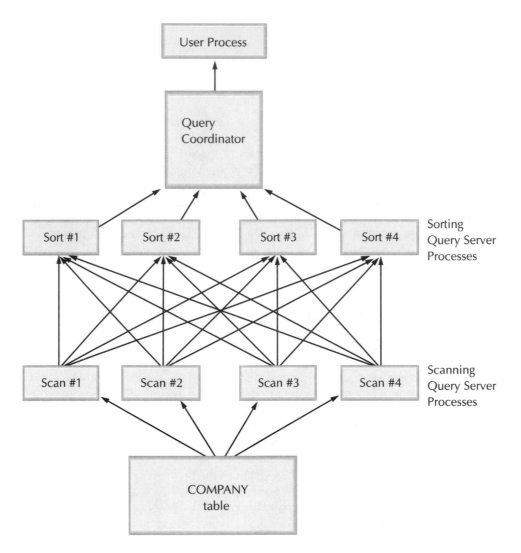

FIGURE 12-4. *Parallel scan and sort with degree of parallelism of four (eight query server processes)*

How Query Server Processes Are Assigned

The number of query server processes assigned to a query is based on the *degree of parallelism* for the query. As shown in Figures 12-3 and 12-4, the degree of parallelism determines the number of scanning and sorting processes used by the query. The degree of parallelism can be specified at the query level (via the PARALLEL hint), at the table level, or at the instance level. In Oracle7.3, the degree of parallelism can only be set at the query or table level. Setting the degree of parallelism at the table level overrides the instance setting; setting it at the query level overrides the table setting. Once the degree of parallelism for a query has been determined, query server processes can be assigned.

As shown in Figure 12-4, query server processes are assigned to parallelize both table scan and sorting operations. For a parallelized query, the degree of parallelism determines the maximum number of query server processes assigned to either a table scan or sorting operation. Therefore, the maximum number of query server processes for a query is two times the degree of parallelism. In the example shown in Figure 12-4, the degree of parallelism is four, and a total of eight query server processes are used. After a query completes, the query server processes are returned to the *query server pool*—the common set of query server processes available in an instance.

How to Manage the Query Server Pool

A query, if run at different times, could get processed by a different number of query server processes, depending on the resources available in the query server pool. Oracle maintains the query server pool based on the settings of several init.ora parameters. The parameters are

- *PARALLEL_MIN_SERVERS.* This parameter sets the number of query server processes started when the instance starts. These query server processes are available to the query pool, eliminating the performance penalties of frequent query server process startups and shutdowns. PARALLEL_MIN_SERVERS sets the minimum size of the query server pool at any time.

- *PARALLEL_MAX_SERVERS.* As needed, Oracle adds query server processes to the query server pool. Oracle stops adding new query server processes when the PARALLEL_MAX_SERVERS setting is reached. This parameter sets the maximum size of the query server pool.

- *PARALLEL_SERVER_IDLE_TIME.* When a query server process is no longer in use, it goes into an idle state and is available for subsequent operations. If a query server process is idle for longer than the PARALLEL_SERVER_IDLE_TIME setting (expressed in minutes), the query server process will be terminated (provided the size of the query server pool remains at least PARALLEL_MIN_SERVERS).

PARALLEL_MIN_SERVERS, PARALLEL_MAX_SERVERS, and PARALLEL_SERVER_IDLE_TIME determine how many query server processes are in the query server pool at any time. The number of available query server processes will be bounded at the low end by PARALLEL_MIN_SERVERS, and at the high end by PARALLEL_MAX_SERVERS. PARALLEL_SERVER_IDLE_TIME helps minimize the number of unused query server processes in the query server pool. You can monitor the changes in the size of the query server pool via the techniques described in the "How to Monitor the Parallel Query Option" section later in this chapter.

Init.ora Parameters Affecting the Degree of Parallelism

For databases using Oracle7.1 and Oracle7.2, you can enable PQO for all tables and queries in an instance. The following init.ora parameters determine the way Oracle parallelizes queries.

- *PARALLEL_DEFAULT_SCANSIZE.* This parameter, which is obsolete in Oracle7.3, is used to estimate the degree of parallelism. In Oracle7.1 and Oracle7.2, the query coordinator divides the number of blocks in the table by the PARALLEL_DEFAULT_SCANSIZE setting to estimate the degree of parallelism; this value is compared with the PARALLEL_DEFAULT_MAX_SCANS setting, and the smaller of the two is used as the degree of parallelism.

- *PARALLEL_DEFAULT_MAX_SCANS.* This parameter, which is obsolete in Oracle7.3, is used to estimate the degree of parallelism. In Oracle7.1 and Oracle7.2, the PARALLEL_DEFAULT_MAX_SCANS setting is the maximum degree of parallelism for any parallel operation.

- *PARALLEL_MIN_PERCENT.* Available as of Oracle7.3, this parameter allows you to prevent queries from running if the requested degree of parallelism is not available. If the requested number of query server processes is not available, and the PARALLEL_MIN_PERCENT parameter is set, Oracle calculates the minimum allowable number of server processes. For example, if eight query server processes are requested, and PARALLEL_MIN_PERCENT is set to 50, then at least four query server processes must be available for the query. *If the number of query server processes available is less than the calculated minimum, the query terminates with an error.* If the calculated minimum number of query server processes is available, the query will run with the available query server processes, reducing the effective parallelism of the query.

If the number of available query server processes is less than the number requested and the PARALLEL_MIN_PERCENT parameter is *not* set, only the available number of query server processes is used by the operation, reducing the effective parallelism of the statement. If the number of available query server processes is not sufficient to parallelize the query, Oracle processes the query sequentially. If you have set a value for PARALLEL_MIN_PERCENT, you can prevent queries from running unless they can be properly parallelized using the available resources. You may choose to use this option if you have a limited time window in which to run the query and would rather have the query fail than overrun the available time window.

If you are using Oracle Parallel Server, your queries can be parallelized across multiple instances on different nodes. The PARALLEL_DEFAULT_MAX_INSTANCES parameter defines the maximum number of instances involved in processing a parallelized query. The query can be parallelized across multiple instances, in addition to being parallelized within a single instance. You can involve multiple CPUs and multiple SGAs in the processing of a single query.

Defining the Degree of Parallelism at the Table Level

You can enable parallelism at three levels: the instance level (for Oracle7.1 and Oracle7.2), the table level, and the query level. To enable parallel query for any allowable statement (see the previous "What Are the Options?" section) that uses a specific table or cluster, specify the degree of parallelism via the **create table**, **alter table**, **create cluster**, or **alter cluster** command. Degree of parallelism settings at the table level override any instance settings.

To set the degree of parallelism at the table level, use the **parallel** clause of the **alter table** and **create table** commands. In the following example, the COMPANY table is defined to have a degree of parallelism of four.

```
alter table COMPANY
parallel(degree 4);
```

Queries that use the COMPANY table will now use a degree of parallelism of four. If you are using the Oracle Parallel Server, you can split the processing of a query across multiple instances. You can use the **instances** portion of the **parallel** clause to define the number of instances to involve in processing the query, as shown in the following listing. Up to four processes per instance will service the parallelzed operation, for an effective 20-way parallelism.

```
alter table COMPANY
parallel(degree 4 instances 5);
```

You may wish to define a table as always being processed serially—with no parallelization of its queries. You can indicate a serially processed table via the **noparallel** clause of the **alter table** and **create table** commands, as shown in the following listing.

```
alter table COMPANY noparallel;
```

You may want to specify a table as **noparallel** if it is not large enough to benefit greatly from parallelization. If this is the case, parallelizing queries against the table wastes the resources available in the query server pool. Since the query server pool is limited in size for the instance, you need to make sure that the available resources are properly used by the tables in the database.

If you do not set a **degree** parameter for a table, the table's **degree** setting is determined by the size of the table and the PARALLEL_DEFAULT_SCANSIZE instance parameter (for Oracle7.1 and Oracle7.2). As of Oracle7.3, the PARALLEL_DEFAULT_SCANSIZE instance parameter is obsolete, and you must specify the degree of parallelism at the table level or the query level to parallelize a query.

Using Query Hints to Force Parallelism

Two hints—PARALLEL and NOPARALLEL—directly control the degree of parallelism used for a query. Specifying a degree of parallelism at the query level will override any table-level or instance-level settings for the degree of parallelism.

The PARALLEL hint has three parameters: the table name, the degree of parallelism, and the instance setting (analogous to the table name, the **degree** setting, and the **instances** setting in the **alter table** examples in the preceding section). Within the hint, there are no keywords, so you need to be careful with the hint syntax. As described in the "Using Hints" section of Chapter 10, hints are embedded within SQL statements. The query in the following listing contains a hint that tells the optimizer to perform a full table scan on COMPANY (the FULL hint) with a degree of parallelism of five.

```
select /*+ FULL(company) PARALLEL(company,5) */  *
  from COMPANY;
```

When using the PARALLEL hint, you should always specify a degree of parallelism within the hint. Otherwise, Oracle will use the default degree of parallelism for the instance.

If you are using the Oracle Parallel Server, you can use hints to specify the number of instances that should be involved in resolving a query. Within the PARALLEL hint, include a value for the instances setting. In the following example, the query of the COMPANY table will have a degree of parallelism of five, with four instances involved in resolving the query for an effective 20-way parallelism.

```
select /*+ FULL(company) PARALLEL(company,5,4) */  *
  from COMPANY;
```

If you want to disable parallelism for a query, you can use the NOPARALLEL hint to override the table's default degree of parallelism. In the following example, the COMPANY table will be scanned serially because of the use of the NOPARALLEL hint.

```
select /*+ NOPARALLEL(company) */  *
  from COMPANY;
```

For information regarding the tuning implications of the degree of parallelism, see the "Tuning Parallelized Operations" section later in this chapter.

How to Monitor the Parallel Query Option

The query server pool can be monitored at both the operating-system and database levels. Operating system-level monitoring records the current state of the query server pool, while database-level monitoring displays information regarding both the current state of the query server pool and changes to its size and usage.

At the Operating-System Level

Each query coordinator and query server process currently in the query server pool has an associated process at the operating-system level. The process-naming conventions vary by operating system; in some versions of Unix, the instance name is included in the process name, along with a sequential number for each query server process. As shown in the following listing, the Unix *ps -ef* command lists the processes; the *grep* command searches for the string "ora_p0". In the listing, the query server process names all begin with the string "ora_p0", for the "dev" instance.

```
> ps -ef | grep ora_p0
oracle  1903    1  0 22:54:05 ?        1:56 ora_p000_dev
oracle  1907    1  0 22:54:07 ?        1:55 ora_p001_dev
```

The preceding listing shows two query server processes in the query server pool of the "dev" instance. The query server processes are sequentially numbered, starting with 0000. If the query server pool grows too large, the greater number of operating system processes may increase the likelihood of memory "paging," damaging the system throughput performance.

You should monitor the operating system's I/O statistics to make sure the I/O load is well balanced and spread across multiple drives. Overall I/O activity may increase when using the PQO; if you do not have spare I/O capacity, or if your parallel query server processes cause an I/O bottleneck, your performance may suffer. Use an operating system monitoring tool to check that the I/O activity is properly distributed.

Within Oracle

You can use several internal dynamic performance views to monitor the database's use of parallel query features. All of the views that report parallel query statistics begin with the prefix V$PQ_. The views are

V$PQ_SYSSTAT	System-level statistics for parallel queries
V$PQ_SESSTAT	Session-level statistics for parallel queries
V$PQ_SLAVE	Statistics for each active parallel query server in the instance
V$PQ_TQSTAT	New in Oracle7.3; lists statistics for all parallel queries and parallel query operations for the session

NOTE
The V$PQ_ objects are actually synonyms pointing to SYS-owned views whose names use the format V_$PQ_. All of the queries in the examples in this book use the synonyms.

As shown in the following example, you can use V$PQ_SYSSTAT to monitor the effectiveness of your query server pool settings. In the listing, the Statistic and Value columns of V$PQ_SYSSTAT are queried.

```
select Statistic, Value
  from V$PQ_SYSSTAT;

STATISTIC                         VALUE
------------------------------- ----------
Servers Busy                         16
Servers Idle                          0
Servers Highwater                    17
Server Sessions                      18
Servers Started                     226
Servers Shutdown                    209
Servers Cleaned Up                    1
Queries Initiated                    51
DFO Trees                            51
```

```
Local Msgs Sent                    40909
Distr Msgs Sent                        0
Local Msgs Recv'd                  40726
Distr Msgs Recv'd                      0
```

In order to correctly interpret the V$PQ_SYSSTAT results, you need to know the settings for your PARALLEL_MAX_SERVERS and PARALLEL_MIN_SERVERS parameters in the instance. As shown in the following listing, you can select the values for all of your parallel query parameters from V$PARAMETER. In versions prior to Oracle7.3, V$PARAMETER will also display the value for PARALLEL_DEFAULT_MAX_SCANS and PARALLEL_DEFAULT_SCANSIZE and Parallel_MIN_PERCENT will not be displayed.

```
select Name, Value
  from V$PARAMETER
 where Name like 'parallel%';
```

```
NAME                                          VALUE
---------------------------------------    ----------

parallel_min_percent                          90
parallel_default_max_instances                 1
parallel_min_servers                          16
parallel_max_servers                          32
parallel_server_idle_time                     30
```

If the "Servers Busy" value from V$PQ_SYSSTAT is consistently less than the "parallel_min_servers" value from V$PARAMETER, your PARALLEL_MIN_SERVERS parameter is set too high—the servers are not all being used. You could reduce the PARALLEL_MIN_SERVERS setting to release the system resources used by the idle query server processes. The "Servers Busy" value from V$PQ_SYSSTAT shows the number of query server processes that are currently in use.

If the "Servers Busy" value from V$PQ_SYSSTAT is greater than the "parallel_min_servers" value from V$PARAMETER, and the "Servers Started" value from V$PQ_SYSSTAT grows over time, you need to increase the PARALLEL_MIN_SERVERS setting. Since more than the minimum number of query server processes is in use, Oracle is forced to start new query server processes to the query pool on demand. The "Servers Started" value in V$PS_SYSSTAT is cumulative, recording the number of query server processes started since the instance was started.

If the "Servers Busy" value from V$PQ_SYSSTAT is close to the "parallel_max_servers" value from V$PARAMETER, you may need to increase the PARALLEL_MAX_SERVERS setting. If increasing the maximum size of the query pool impacts the available system resources, you may need to add more system resources (CPU, memory, and I/O), or limit the parallelization of queries.

V$PQ_SESSTAT shows the overall statistics for parallel queries for a session. V$PQ_SLAVE shows the statistics (such as its idle time and CPU time) for each active parallel query server for the instance. A fourth view, V$PQ_TQSTAT, shows the number of rows and bytes processed at each stage of the query and can help identify any imbalances in the parallelization of queries. The statistics in V$PQ_TQSTAT are compiled after the completion of each query and are valid only for the duration of the session.

Understanding Explain Plan Outputs

You can use the **explain plan** command to see the impact of parallelism on the execution path of your queries. As described in Chapter 10, the **explain plan** command determines the execution path for a query and inserts records that describe the execution path into a table called PLAN_TABLE. See Chapter 10 for a description of PLAN_TABLE and instructions for interpreting the execution path.

For the examples in this chapter, the COMPANY and SALES tables from Chapter 10 will be used. The **create table** commands for COMPANY and SALES are shown in the following listing.

```
create table COMPANY
(Company_ID          NUMBER,
Name                VARCHAR2(10),
Address             VARCHAR2(10),
City                VARCHAR2(10),
State               VARCHAR2(10),
Zip                 VARCHAR2(10),
Parent_Company_ID   NUMBER,
Active_Flag         CHAR,
constraint COMPANY_PK primary key (Company_ID),
constraint COMPANY$PARENT_ID foreign key
     (Parent_Company_ID) references COMPANY(Company_ID));

create index COMPANY$CITY on COMPANY(City);
create index COMPANY$STATE on COMPANY(State);
create index COMPANY$PARENT on COMPANY(Parent_Company_ID);

create table SALES
(Company_ID  NUMBER,
Period_ID    NUMBER,
Sales_Total  NUMBER,
```

```
constraint SALES_PK primary key (Company_ID, Period_ID),
constraint SALES$COMPANY_FK foreign key (Company_ID)
        references COMPANY(Company_ID));
```

As shown in the table creation scripts, the SALES table has a foreign key that references the Company_ID column of the COMPANY table. The primary key of SALES is the combination of the Company_ID and Period_ID columns.

A default degree of parallelism of four can be set for each table for these examples, as shown in the following listing.

```
alter table SALES
parallel(degree 4);

alter table COMPANY
parallel(degree 4);
```

For the examples in this section, NESTED LOOPS and MERGE JOIN operations will be used. The NESTED LOOPS example will show the operations before and after parallelization, and the MERGE JOIN example will show the parallel-related PLAN_TABLE columns.

NOTE
The examples in the following sections were all generated using Oracle7.3.2.

The query in the following listing joins COMPANY to SALES via an indexed NESTED LOOPS join (see Chapter 10 for descriptions of the different types of joins).

```
select COMPANY.Name, SALES.Sales_Total
  from COMPANY, SALES
 where COMPANY.Company_ID = SALES.Company_ID
   and SALES.Period_ID = 3;
```

When the query shown in the preceding listing is executed, the optimizer will use a NESTED LOOPS join to join COMPANY to SALES. The execution path is shown in the following listing.

```
NESTED LOOPS
    TABLE ACCESS FULL SALES
    TABLE ACCESS BY ROWID COMPANY
      INDEX UNIQUE SCAN COMPANY_PK
```

As shown in the execution path, SALES is the driving table for the NESTED LOOPS join. For each record in SALES, the COMPANY_PK index is checked for a matching Company_ID value. If a match exists, the COMPANY table is accessed via a TABLE ACCESS BY ROWID operation to find the COMPANY.Name value requested by the query.

NOTE

Depending on the version of Oracle you are using and the size of the tables, the optimizer may choose to use a hash join for this query instead. The explain plan for the hash join version of the execution path is shown in the following listing.

```
HASH JOIN
    TABLE ACCESS FULL SALES
    TABLE ACCESS FULL COMPANY
```

Hash joins are only available as of Oracle7.3. For the remainder of this chapter, the focus will be on NESTED LOOPS and MERGE JOIN operations for joins, which are available in all versions of Oracle7. The concepts of parallelization are the same regardless of the join operation used; but if you are using hash joins, your explain plans will differ from those shown in this chapter's examples.

Since the query contains a parallelizable operation (the TABLE ACCESS FULL of SALES), PQO can be used during the query execution. As noted earlier, index scans cannot be parallelized. As shown in the execution path, COMPANY is accessed via an index scan followed by a TABLE ACCESS BY ROWID; neither of these operations can be parallelized. Therefore, if you set a degree of parallelism for the COMPANY table, it will have no impact on the query's execution.

If you set a degree of parallelism on the SALES table (or use a query hint), the TABLE ACCESS FULL operation on the SALES table can be parallelized. In the previous listing, a degree of parallelism of four was set for the SALES table.

```
alter table SALES
parallel(degree 4);
```

Although the SALES table's scan can be parallelized, the operations involved in the query, and their order, has not changed. The explain plan appears to be the same as if no parallelization was in effect.

```
NESTED LOOPS
    TABLE ACCESS FULL SALES
```

```
TABLE ACCESS BY ROWID COMPANY
   INDEX UNIQUE SCAN COMPANY_PK
```

> **NOTE**
> See previous note regarding hash join execution paths.

The explain plan operations for the query have not changed. However, the TABLE ACCESS FULL operation can be parallelized. The information about the parallelization of the query is found in the Object_Node, Other_Tag, and Other columns in PLAN_TABLE.

> **NOTE**
> The PLAN_TABLE.Other_Tag column, along with the Bytes, Cardinality, and Cost columns, is only available as of Oracle7.3. If you upgrade to Oracle7.3 from a prior version, you will need to reexecute the utlxplan.sql script to see all of the new PLAN_TABLE columns.

The Object_Node column provides information on the query server processes involved. The Other_Tag column describes the function of the Other column's entries. The Other column contains a derived SQL statement—either for a remote query (see Chapter 11) or for Parallel Query operations, as you will see in the following MERGE JOIN example. The possible values for Other_Tag and their associated Other values are shown in Table 12-1. In the MERGE JOIN example, you will see sample values from the Object_Node, Other_Tag, and Other columns of PLAN_TABLE for parallel operations.

When a full table scan is parallelized, the scan of the table is partitioned to multiple query server processes based on ranges of RowID values; the ranges are based on contiguous blocks of data in the table. You can use the Other_Tag column to verify the parallelism within different operations of the query, and can see the parallelized query in the Other column. For example, the following query forces a MERGE JOIN to occur between the COMPANY and SALES tables; since a MERGE JOIN involves full table scans and sorts, multiple operations can be parallelized. You can use the Other_Tag column to show the relationships between the parallel operations.

```
select
 /*+ FULL(company) FULL(sales) USE_MERGE(company sales)*/
       COMPANY.Name, Sales.Sales_Total
   from COMPANY, SALES
```

```
where COMPANY.Company_ID = SALES.Company_ID
  and SALES.Period_ID = 3;
```

The explain plan for the MERGE JOIN query is shown in the following listing.

```
MERGE JOIN
  SORT JOIN
    TABLE ACCESS FULL COMPANY
  SORT JOIN
    TABLE ACCESS FULL SALES
```

As shown in the plan, Oracle will perform a full table scan (TABLE ACCESS FULL) on each table, sort the results (using the SORT JOIN operations), and merge the result sets. The following query of PLAN_TABLE shows the Other_Tag for each operation. The query shown in the following listing is the same as the query used

Value	Description
PARALLEL_COMBINED_WITH_CHILD	The parent of this operation performs the parent and child operations together; Other is null.
PARALLEL_COMBINED_WITH_PARENT	The child of this operation performs the parent and child operations together; Other is null.
PARALLEL_FROM_SERIAL	The SQL operation consumes data from a serial operation and outputs it in parallel: Other is null.
PARALLEL_TO_PARALLEL	The SQL in the Other column is executed in parallel, and results are returned to a second set of query server processes.
PARALLEL_TO_SERIAL	The SQL in the Other column is executed in parallel, and the results are returned to a serial process (usually the query coordinator).
SERIAL	The SQL statement is executed serially (the default); the Other column will be null.
SERIAL_FROM_REMOTE	The SQL in the Other column will be executed at a remote site.
SERIAI_TO_PARALLEL	The SQL in the Other column is partitioned to multiple query server processes.

TABLE 12-1. *Possible Values for PLAN_TABLE.Other_Tag for PQO*

throughout Chapter 10 to generate the explain plan listings, with the addition of the Other_Tag column (shown in bold).

NOTE
Since the query references the Other_Tag column, it will not work *unless* you are using the Oracle7.3 version of PLAN_TABLE.

```
select
  LPAD(' ',2*Level)||Operation||' '||Options
              ||' '||Object_Name   Q_Plan, Other_Tag
from PLAN_TABLE
where Statement_ID = 'TEST'
connect by prior ID = Parent_ID and Statement_ID = 'TEST'
start with ID=1;
```

The result of the preceding query for the MERGE JOIN example is shown in the following listing.

```
Q_PLAN                          OTHER_TAG
------------------------------  --------------------------
MERGE JOIN                      PARALLEL_TO_SERIAL
  SORT JOIN                     PARALLEL_COMBINED_WITH_PARENT
    TABLE ACCESS FULL COMPANY   PARALLEL_TO_PARALLEL
  SORT JOIN                     PARALLEL_COMBINED_WITH_PARENT
    TABLE ACCESS FULL SALES     PARALLEL_TO_PARALLEL
```

From the preceding listing, you can see (by their Other_Tag values of PARALLEL_TO_PARALLEL) that each of the TABLE ACCESS FULL operations is parallelized, and provides data to a parallel sorting operation. Each of the TABLE ACCESS FULL operations' records in PLAN_TABLE will have the parallel query text in their Other column values. The Other column values for the TABLE ACCESS FULL operations will show that the table will be scanned based on ranges of RowID values. The SORT JOIN operations, which are PARALLEL_COMBINED_WITH_PARENT (their "parent" operation is the MERGE JOIN) will have null values for their Other column values. The MERGE JOIN operation, which is PARALLEL_TO_SERIAL (the merge is performed in parallel; output is provided to the serial query coordinator process), will have an Other column value that shows how the merge occurs. The processing path is a more complex version of the path shown in Figure 12-4, with two sets of sorting and scanning processes and two table scans involved.

If you had not defined a degree of parallelism for one of the tables, then its Other_Tag value would be PARALLEL_FROM_SERIAL. As described in Table

12-1, PARALLEL_FROM_SERIAL means that the operation (the table scan) is performed serially, and the output (to the sorting operations) is handled by parallel query processes.

The Object_Node column values display information about the query server processes involved in performing an operation. The following listing shows the Object_Node and Other columns for the TABLE ACCESS FULL of COMPANY operation performed for the preceding MERGE JOIN query.

```
set long 1000
select Object_Node, Other
  from PLAN_TABLE
 where Operation||' '||Options = 'TABLE ACCESS FULL'
   and Object_Name = 'COMPANY';


OBJECT_NODE OTHER
----------- ------------------------------------------------
:Q15000     SELECT /*+ ROWID(A1) */ A1."COMPANY_ID" C0,
                   A1."NAME" C1
              FROM "COMPANY" A1
             WHERE ROWID BETWEEN :1 AND :2
```

As shown in the preceding listing, the Object_Node column references a parallel query server process (Q15000 is an internal identifier Oracle assigned to the process for this example). The Other column shows that the COMPANY table is queried for ranges of RowID values. Each of the query server processes performing the full table scan performs the query shown in the preceding listing, for a different range of RowIDs. The SORT JOIN and MERGE JOIN operations sort and merge (in parallel) the results of the table scans.

When using the **explain plan** command for a parallelized query, you cannot rely on querying just the operations-related columns to see the parallelized operations within the explain plan. At a minimum, you should query the Other_Tag column to see which operations are performed in parallel. If an operation is not performed in parallel and you think it should be, you may need to add hints to the query, set a degree of parallelism for the tables, or check the size of the query server pool to make sure query server processes are available for use by the query.

Using set autotrace on

If you are using Oracle7.3, you can have the explain plan automatically generated for every transaction you execute within SQL*Plus. The **set autotrace on** command will cause each query, after being executed, to display both its execution path and high-level trace information about the processing involved in resolving the query.

In order to use the **set autotrace on** command, you must have first created the PLAN_TABLE table within your account. When using the **set autotrace on** command, you do not set a Statement_ID, and you do not have to manage the records within the PLAN_TABLE. To disable the autotrace feature, use the **set autotrace off** command.

If you use the **set autotrace on** command, you will not see the explain plan for your queries until *after* they complete. The **explain plan** command shows the execution paths without running the queries first. Therefore, if the performance of a query is unknown, use the **explain plan** command before running it. If you are fairly certain that the performance of a query is acceptable, use **set autotrace on** to verify its execution path.

The following listing shows the impact of the **set autotrace on** command. When the MERGE JOIN query is executed, the data is returned from the query, followed by the explain plan. The explain plan is in two parts; the first part shows the operations involved, and the second part shows the parallel-related actions. In the following listing, the first part of the autotrace output is shown.

```
set autotrace on

rem
rem for Oracle7.3, disable hash joins
rem to force merge joins to occur.
rem
alter session set hash_join_enabled/FALSE;
rem
select
 /*+ FULL(company) FULL(sales) USE_MERGE(company sales)*/
      COMPANY.Name, Sales.Sales_Total
 from COMPANY, SALES
where COMPANY.Company_ID = SALES.Company_ID
  and SALES.Period_ID = 3;

<records returned here>

Execution Plan
----------------------------------------------------------
   0      SELECT STATEMENT Optimizer=CHOOSE (Cost=10 Card=1 Bytes=59)
   1    0   MERGE JOIN* (Cost=10 Card=1 Bytes=59)                    :Q17002
   2    1     SORT* (JOIN)                                           :Q17002
   3    2       TABLE ACCESS* (FULL) OF 'COMPANY' (Cost=1 Card=1 Bytes :Q17000
         =20)
   4    1     SORT* (JOIN)                                           :Q17002
```

```
5    4        TABLE ACCESS* (FULL) OF 'SALES' (Cost=1 Card=1 Bytes=3 :Q17001
     9)
```

The autotrace output may be difficult to read because some of the data values wrap. In the preceding listing, line 3 (the full table scan of COMPANY) ends with "Bytes=20)", but the "=20" portion is on the line below it. For line 5, the Bytes value is 39, although the 9 is on the line below it.

NOTE
The Cost statistics and other values shown in this example will differ in your environment, based on the data in your tables.

The autotrace output shows the ID column of each row, along with the operations and the objects on which they act. The information at the far right (":Q17002" and so on) identifies the parallel query servers used during the query.

The second portion of the autotrace output uses the step ID values to describe the parallelism of the execution path's operations. The second portion of the autotrace output for the MERGE JOIN example is shown in the following listing.

```
1 PARALLEL_TO_SERIAL            SELECT /*+ ORDERED NO_EXPAND USE_MERGE(A2) *
                                / A1.C1,A2.C1,A2.C2 FROM :Q17000 A1,:Q17001
                                A2 WHERE A1.C0=A2.C0

2 PARALLEL_COMBINED_WITH_PARENT

3 PARALLEL_TO_PARALLEL          SELECT /*+ ROWID(A1) */ A1."COMPANY_ID" C0,A
                                1."NAME" C1 FROM "COMPANY" A1 WHERE ROWID BE
                                TWEEN :1 AND :2

4 PARALLEL_COMBINED_WITH_PARENT

5 PARALLEL_TO_PARALLEL          SELECT /*+ ROWID(A1) */ A1."COMPANY_ID" C0,A
                                1."SALES_TOTAL" C1,A1."PERIOD_ID" C2 FROM "S
                                ALES" A1 WHERE ROWID BETWEEN :1 AND :2 AND A
                                1."PERIOD_ID"=3
```

From the earlier discussions in this section, you should know how to read this output—the first column is the step's ID value, which allows you to find the operation it refers to (from the first portion of the autotrace output). The second value is the Other_Tag value for the step (see Table 12-1 for a description of possible values). The third column is the Other value for the step, showing the parallelized SQL.

Since the output of the **set autotrace on** command can be difficult to read, you may find it easier to use the **explain plan** command instead. The **set autotrace on** command is most useful when you are evaluating the execution paths of a large number of SQL statements and want to verify their parallelization. Since **set autotrace on** does not display the execution path until after the query completes, it is most useful for small queries.

Tuning Parallelized Operations

To effectively use the PQO, you must have adequate CPU and I/O resources available. If all of the query server processes access the same disk, I/O may become a bottleneck. If CPU availability is already a bottleneck, using the PQO will likely worsen the situation. Although using the PQO will not dramatically increase the total CPU required by the query, it will force the system to manage the CPU requests of a greater number of processes than a serialized query would use.

For table scan operations against large tables, you should spread the I/O across multiple disks. You can "stripe" the table via a number of methods: via operating system striping (see Chapter 4), by creating partitioned tables (see Chapter 11), or by creating the tablespace's datafiles (and the table's extents) on multiple disks. In general, operating system-level striping is easiest to set up and provides adequate performance gains for query operations, although it may make data manipulation operations slower (see Chapter 4).

The query coordinator distributes work to the query server processes based on contiguous blocks of the data. If the table is heavily fragmented, the query coordinator will estimate how the work can best be distributed among the available query server processes.

If multiple query server processes are used to sort data, each query server process will require a memory area for sorting. The size of the memory area used by each query server process is specified by the SORT_AREA_SIZE parameter in the instance's init.ora file. If you have four query server processes that perform sorts for your query, and SORT_AREA_SIZE is set to 4M, your query may require 16M of memory for sorting! Therefore, you need to balance the degree of parallelism of your queries and the available sorting area within memory.

By default, Sort Direct Writes are automatically enabled for Oracle7.2 and above. Sort Direct Writes (described in Chapter 13) bypass the SGA during writes to temporary segments. For best performance, Oracle recommends the following settings in your init.ora file:

```
SORT_DIRECT_WRITES = true
SORT_WRITE_BUFFERS = 4
SORT_WRITE_BUFFER_SIZE = 65536
```

Each query server process that performs a sort may create a temporary segment, so you may wish to stripe the temporary tablespace across multiple disks to minimize I/O contention during sort operations. You will very likely require more temporary segment space to support a parallelized query than a serialized query. As of Oracle7.3, you can designate dedicated temporary tablespaces to further improve sort performance; see "Dedicated Temporary Tablespaces" in Chapter 13.

How Oracle Determines the Degree of Parallelism

To determine the degree of parallelism, Oracle checks the instance settings, the table definitions, and the query hints, in the following order:

1. If the query has a PARALLEL or NOPARALLEL hint for a table, the query coordinator uses that value for the degree of parallelism for the table.

2. If no hints are used, the query coordinator checks the table definitions for each table to see if a default DEGREE setting has been defined for the table.

3. If no query hints are used and there is no default DEGREE setting for the table, and you are using Oracle7.1 or Oracle7.2, then the init.ora parameters PARALLEL_DEFAULT_SCANSIZE and PARALLEL_DEFAULT_MAX_SCANS are used to estimate the degree of parallelism. If you are using Oracle7.3, there is no instance-level degree of parallelism parameter. In Oracle7.3, Oracle checks to see how many CPUs are available on the system and how many disk drives are used by the table. The smaller of these two values is the default degree of parallelism for the query. The default degree of parallelism is only used when you give the PARALLEL hint with no degree of parallelism and the table does not have a default degree of parallelism.

4. If there are multiple tables involved in a query, the query coordinator determines the degree of parallelism for each table and uses the highest value as the degree of parallelism for the query.

5. If not enough query server processes are available, the query server may choose to run the query with the available servers, or, if PARALLEL_MIN_PERCENT is set, the query coordinator may return an error to the user. See the "Init.ora Parameters Affecting the Degree of Parallelism" section earlier in this chapter for details on PARALLEL_MIN_PERCENT.

NOTE
Since Oracle cannot parallelize index scans, you may have to use the FULL hint to force the query to use a full table scan (and therefore be parallelizable). See the "Using Hints" section of Chapter 10.

Since the degree of parallelism can be set in different ways, is highly tunable, and has a great influence on the way the query is processed, you should carefully select a degree of parallelism for your most resource-intensive queries.

The Art of Selecting a Degree of Parallelism

To select a degree of parallelism for a query, you first must know the characteristics of the query. Queries can be categorized as CPU-intensive, I/O-intensive, or both.

If the main objective is to parallelize a single, CPU-intensive query, use a degree of parallelism no greater than twice the number of CPUs. CPU- and memory-intensive operations (such as sorts) are limited by the number of CPUs and the amount of memory in the system. If many such queries need to be parallelized at the same time, you may need to reduce the degree of parallelism per query, increase the number of CPUs, or both.

For example, if the COMPANY table comprises two extents, each in a separate datafile, and the two datafiles are on separate devices, queries against COMPANY can be parallelized without causing an I/O bottleneck. If you have three CPUs on the server, set the degree of parallelism to six. If the query processing causes a CPU or memory bottleneck, lower the degree of parallelism to five and continue to monitor the system.

If the main objective is to parallelize a single, I/O-intensive query, first spread the data across multiple drives. If a disk drive is busy with one I/O request, adding more query server processes to query the disk will create an I/O bottleneck. Use a degree of parallelism equal to twice the number of participating drives. If many such queries need to be parallelized at the same time, you may need to reduce the degree of parallelism per query, increase the number of independent disks participating in the I/O operation, or both.

For example, if the SALES table comprises two extents, each in a separate datafile, and the two datafiles are on separate devices, queries against SALES can be parallelized without causing an I/O bottleneck. Because SALES is spread across two drives, set the degree of parallelism to four. If the query processing causes an I/O bottleneck on one of the disk drives, lower the degree of parallelism to three and continue to monitor the system.

If a query is both CPU- and I/O-intensive, begin the tuning process by spreading the data across multiple drives, and treat it as an I/O-intensive query. Start with a degree of parallelism equal to twice the number of participating drives. If more CPU resources are available when the query is now run, increase the degree of parallelism—while monitoring to make sure an I/O bottleneck is not created.

If multiple queries are being tuned, use table definitions to set a low average degree of parallelism, and increase the degree of parallelism for specific tables and queries.

NOTE
When creating a table or index via the PQO, multiple query server processes start creating subsets of the table or index. Each query server process allocates an extent equal in size to the **initial** setting for the table, and each query server process allocates multiple extents, as defined by the table's **minextents** setting. You should keep the degree of parallelism to less than or equal to the number of datafiles in the tablespace where the object is being stored, so no two processes are trying to write to the same datafile.

The degree of parallelism tells the query coordinator how may query server processes to start up; since the query coordinator is itself a process, the total number of processes involved is one greater than the degree of parallelism. If you set the degree of parallelism to one, the query coordinator does not start any query server processes for the query.

Disadvantages of Enabling Parallel Query at the Instance Level

You can set default parameters affecting query parallelization in Oracle7.1 and Oracle7.2. In Oracle7.3, the only way to force query parallelization is by defining the degree of parallelism at the table level or via query hints. Since you can set a default level of query parallelization in Oracle7.1 and Oracle7.2, you may be tempted to use the PARALLEL_DEFAULT_SCANSIZE and PARALLEL_DEFAULT_MAX_SCANS parameters to enable parallelization for all queries within an instance. However, there are significant potential problems with enabling PQO for all queries within an instance.

If you enable PQO for all queries within an instance, you must have infinite resources available on your system. If all queries can be parallelized, you will eventually run out of system resources to handle the query server processes. Since your query server processes will, unchecked, consume all of your system resources, you will need to set a maximum number of query server processes (limiting the size of the query server pool). If all queries can be parallelized, the available query server processes could be completely occupied by short queries, with none left over to handle large queries. To disable parallelization for the small queries, you would need to manually alter the table definitions (to set **noparallel** for each small table) or alter each query of a small table (using the NOPARALLEL hint). Even though this option is available in Oracle7.1 and Oracle7.2, it is far simpler to manage PQO if you target specific tables and queries for parallelization.

Additional Parallel Options

The concepts described in the PQO examples—the degree of parallelism and the query server pool—are common to all of the parallel options. In the following sections, you will see the usage of Parallel Create Table, Parallel Create Index, Parallel Data Loading, Parallel Recovery, and the Oracle Parallel Server.

Parallel create table

As of Oracle7.1, the query portion of a **create table as select** command can be parallelized (via hints, or via a table-level setting for the degree of parallelism). As of Oracle7.2, the **insert** portion of the **create table as select** operation can also be parallelized. Clustered tables cannot be created and populated in parallel.

As shown in the following example, as of Oracle7.2 you can specify a degree of parallelism for the table population and for the query that populates the table. In the example, both the table population and the query are assigned a degree of parallelism of four.

```
create table COMPANY2
parallel(degree 4)
as select /*+ PARALLEL(company,4) */
          *
  from COMPANY;
```

The **create table** command, when used in serial (nonparallel) mode, uses the **storage** clause supplied with the command (or the tablespace's default) and allocates space for the table based on the **minextents** and **initial** values for the table.

In PARALLEL mode, *each* of the query server processes responsible for creating the table allocates and populates **minextents** of size **initial**! For example, if **initial** is 10M and **minextents** is 2, a serial creation would start by creating two 10M extents. If you create the table in PARALLEL mode, with a degree of parallelism of four, then each of the four query server processes will allocate two 10M extents—a total of 80M! When the query coordinator combines all of the extents thus created and populated, it may reclaim some of the space. You need to balance the performance gains of parallelization with the additional space costs.

NOTE
If you are creating tables in PARALLEL mode, make sure adequate space is available to handle the allocation of multiple extents of size **initial**.

As of Oracle7.2, you can use the **unrecoverable** clause with the **create table as select** command. The **unrecoverable** clause prevents the writing of entries to the online redo log files for the **create table as select** command. As a result, you will not be able to recover the table by applying archived redo log files during a media recovery—but you will be able to recreate the table by reissuing the **create table as select** command. The **unrecoverable** clause can improve the performance of the **create table as select** command by 30 to 50 percent.

If you do not use **unrecoverable**, you may not be getting the full impact of parallelizing the **create table as select** command. The reason for the decreased impact of the parallelization is that writes to the online redo logs are always serialized. Even if multiple processes are writing transaction entries, the process of writing entries to the online redo logs cannot occur in parallel. If your degree of parallelism is greater than four, you will receive measurably less impact from parallelism of the **create table as select** command if you do not use the **unrecoverable** clause.

Parallel create index

As of Oracle7.1, you can create an index in PARALLEL mode—multiple query server processes will work together to create the various parts of the index in parallel. One set of query server processes will scan the table to get the column values and the RowIDs of the rows. A second set of query server processes sorts the rows based on column values (just like a sort operation in queries) and creates sorted entries. The sorted entries are combined by the query coordinator, which builds the completed index. The storage and performance implications of the Parallel Create Index option mirror those of the Parallel Create Table As Select option.

In the following example, the **create index** command uses a degree of parallelism of six to partition the sorting work across multiple processes.

```
create index COMPANY$CITY_STATE
    on COMPANY(City, State)
parallel(degree 6);
```

NOTE
You cannot create an index in parallel when adding or enabling a UNIQUE or PRIMARY KEY constraint (which automatically create indexes). You must first manually create the index using the **parallel** option and then add or enable the constraint (and Oracle will then automatically use the existing index).

The **create index** command, when used in serial (nonparallel) mode, uses the **storage** clause supplied with the command (or the tablespace's default) and allocates space for the index based on the **minextents** and **initial** values for the table.

In PARALLEL mode, *each* of the query server processes responsible for creating the index allocates and populates **minextents** of size **initial**. For example, if **initial** is 10M and **minextents** is 2, a serial creation would start by creating two 10M extents. If you create the index in PARALLEL mode, with a degree of parallelism of six, then each of the six query server processes will allocate two 10M extents—a total of 120M! When the query coordinator combines all of the extents thus created and populated, it may reclaim some of the space. You need to balance the performance gains of parallelization with the additional space costs.

> **NOTE**
> If you are creating indexes in PARALLEL mode, make sure adequate space is available to handle the allocation of multiple extents of size **initial**.

As of Oracle7.2, you can also use the **unrecoverable** clause with the **create index** command. The **unrecoverable** clause prevents the writing of entries to the online redo log files for the **create index** command. As a result, you will not be able to recover the index by applying archived redo log files during a media recovery—but you will be able to recreate the index by reissuing the **create index** command. The **unrecoverable** clause can improve the performance of the **create index** command by 30 to 50 percent.

If you do not use **unrecoverable**, you may not be getting the full impact of parallelizing the **create index** command. The reason for the decreased impact of the parallelization is that writes to the online redo logs are always serialized. Even if multiple processes are writing transaction entries, the process of writing entries to the online redo logs cannot occur in parallel. If your degree of parallelism is greater than four, you will receive measurably less impact from parallelism of the **create index** command if you do not use the **unrecoverable** clause.

Parallel Data Loading

The SQL*Loader Direct Path loading option provides significant performance improvements over the SQL*Loader Conventional Path loader in loading data into Oracle tables by bypassing SQL processing, buffer cache management, and unnecessary reads for the data blocks. As of Oracle7.1, the Parallel Data Loading option of SQL*Loader allows multiple loading processes to work on loading the same table, utilizing spare resources on the system, and thereby reducing the overall elapsed times for loading. Given enough CPU and I/O resources, this can significantly reduce overall loading times.

To use Parallel Data Loading, start multiple SQL*Loader sessions using the **parallel** keyword (otherwise, SQL*Loader puts an exclusive lock on the table). Each session is an independent session requiring its own control file. The following listing shows three separate Direct Path loads, all using the PARALLEL=TRUE parameter on the command line. Each SQL*Loader process loads data from a separate input file, which you must create prior to beginning the data load processes.

```
SQLLOAD USERID=ME/PASS CONTROL=PART1.CTL DIRECT=TRUE PARALLEL=TRUE
SQLLOAD USERID=ME/PASS CONTROL=PART2.CTL DIRECT=TRUE PARALLEL=TRUE
SQLLOAD USERID=ME/PASS CONTROL=PART3.CTL DIRECT=TRUE PARALLEL=TRUE
```

Each session creates its own log, bad, and discard files (part1.log, part2.log, part3.log, part1.bad, part2.bad, and so on), by default. Since you have multiple sessions loading data into the same table, only the **append** option is allowed for Parallel Data Loading. The SQL*Loader **replace**, **truncate**, and **insert** options are not allowed for Parallel Data Loading. If you need to delete the table's data before starting the load, you must manually delete the data (via **delete** or **truncate** command). You cannot use SQL*Loader to delete the records automatically if you are using Parallel Data Loading.

NOTE
If you use Parallel Data Loading, indexes are *not* maintained by the SQL*Loader session. Before starting the loading process, you must drop all indexes on the table and disable all of its PRIMARY KEY and UNIQUE constraints. After the loads complete, you can recreate the table's indexes.

In serial Direct Path loading (PARALLEL=FALSE), SQL*Loader loads data into extents in the table. If the load process fails before the load completes, some data could be committed to the table prior to the process failure. In Parallel Data Loading, each load process creates temporary segments for loading the data. The temporary segments are later merged with the table. If a Parallel Data Load process fails before the load completes, the temporary segments will not have been merged with the table. If the temporary segments have not been merged with the table being loaded, no data from the load will have been committed to the table.

You can use the SQL*Loader FILE parameter to direct each data loading session to a different datafile. By directing each loading session to its own datafile, you can balance the I/O load of the loading processes. Data loading is very I/O intensive and must be distributed across multiple disks for parallel loading to achieve significant performance improvements over serial loading.

After a Parallel Data Load, each session may attempt to reenable the table's constraints. As long as at least one load session is still underway, attempting to reenable the constraints will fail. The final loading session to complete should attempt to reenable the constraints, and should succeed. You should check the status of your constraints after the load completes. If the table being loaded has PRIMARY KEY and UNIQUE constraints, you can create the associated indexes in parallel prior to enabling the constraints (see the "Parallel **create index**" section earlier in this chapter).

Parallel Recovery

As of Oracle7.1, you can use the Parallel Recovery option to use multiple recovery processes. A single SQLDBA or Server Manager session can read the archived redo log files during a media recovery, and can pass the recovery information to multiple recovery processes, which apply the changes to the datafiles concurrently. The recovery processes are automatically started and managed by Oracle. If you have a very long recovery process, and your datafiles are distributed among many disks, using Parallel Recovery may improve your recovery performance.

To use Parallel Recovery, set a value for the RECOVERY_PARALLELISM parameter in your instance's init.ora file. RECOVERY_PARALLELISM specifies the number of concurrent processes that will participate in Parallel Recovery during instance or media recovery. A value of 0 indicates that recovery is performed serially by a single process.

For media recovery, the RECOVERY_PARALLELISM setting is the default degree of parallelism unless overridden by the **parallel** clause of the **recover** command. The RECOVERY_PARALLELISM setting cannot be greater than the PARALLEL_MAX_SERVERS setting.

If you have an I/O-intensive recovery process (which is typical), and you cannot spread the I/O across many disks, then you may not see any performance benefit from Parallel Recovery. In fact, the increased I/O bottleneck may degrade your performance. You should therefore be sure that your disk environment is highly distributed before implementing Parallel Recovery.

Oracle Parallel Server

Oracle Parallel Server (OPS) consists of multiple Oracle instances, running on different nodes of a system. Each of the nodes has its own memory, but the instances share a common physical database. The typical Oracle Parallel Server implementation is found on a server cluster or a Massively Parallel Processor (MPP) system, in which multiple nodes share a single set of disks.

Each instance has its own SGA, its own background processes, and its own redo logs. All instances share the same control files and the same datafiles. The Oracle Parallel Server architecture coordinates shared resources across instances via a Parallel Cache Manager (PCM) lock area and an operating system-specific Distributed Lock Manager (DLM). The PCM and DLM manage the sharing of data among the instances.

Users log into specific Oracle Parallel Server instances. If a node on the cluster goes down, the users can log into a separate instance and access the database, thus providing high availability for the database. Queries can be parallelized not only within an instance (the Parallel Query Option), but also across different instances of an Oracle Parallel Server installation. To parallelize a query across different instances, use the **instances** setting within the **parallel** clause of the **create table** and **alter table** commands, or specify the number of instances via a hint. See "Defining the Degree of Parallelism at the Table Level" and "Using Query Hints to Force Parallelism" earlier in this chapter. For installation and management instructions for the Oracle Parallel Server, see the Oracle manuals that are specific to your operating system.

Choosing Among the Parallel Options

Oracle Parallel Server was available before the Parallel Query Option, which did not appear until Oracle7.1. In an Oracle Parallel Server implementation, you can have multiple instances accessing your database. As a result, you can separate users into separate instances, and can have more memory available for data sharing. Oracle Parallel Server offers good scalability of performance for transaction-intensive systems with many users, especially if the users can be easily separated by instance based on which tables they will access. If users in different instances access the same table, the lock management efforts of the Oracle Parallel Server increase, quickly degrading your performance.

If your servers have multiple CPUs, you can use the Parallel Query Option to take advantage of idle CPU time during query processing. The Parallel Query Option is most useful when you can distribute the data across as many disks as possible, to avoid an I/O bottleneck on a disk. Many server environments are turning to Symmetric MultiProcessing (SMP) machines, and the Parallel Query Option can take great advantage of the additional CPU power. For example, a data warehousing application on an SMP server would likely see significant performance benefits by using the Parallel Query Option—provided the data was properly distributed and the query server pool was properly managed.

If your system is both CPU- and I/O-bound, you will need to add more resources in order to take advantage of the parallel options. The Parallel Query Option does not consume less CPU, less I/O, or less memory than your queries are already using. The Parallel Query Option shortens elapsed times by spreading the command's load across all available resources—potentially causing I/O bottlenecks (if the data is not distributed across many disks), and potentially improving your performance. As the number of CPUs and the amount of memory within SMP servers grows, it is likely that the performance objectives of an Oracle Parallel Server implementation can be met via the use of the Parallel Query Option. You would not have the high availability (in the case of server failure), but you should be able to get high performance from your system.

Tuning queries that use the Parallel Query Option requires careful preparation: you must first establish and manage the query server pool, and you must use the proper hints and operations to take advantage of parallelizable operations. See Chapters 10 and 11 for information on the use of hints and the tuning of SQL statements—particularly the sections on tuning queries involving large tables. To gain additional performance improvements for your index creation and sorting operations in Oracle7.3, see the "Fast Index Recreate" and "Dedicated Temporary Tablespaces" sections of Chapter 13.

CHAPTER 13

When All Else Fails: New and Improved Tuning Options

The previous chapters in this book have provided tuning and administrative tips that are specific to particular areas of the database, such as the datafiles, the tables, and the optimizer. The tips in Section III focused on many areas of the optimizer; many of the examples referred to tuning tips that became available after Oracle7.0.

In this chapter, you will see the major administrative and tuning options that are available with Oracle7.1, 7.2, and 7.3. For some of the options, there are extensive examples elsewhere in the book. Since Chapter 12 is dedicated to the implementation of the parallel options that were released with Oracle7.1, that subject will not be covered in this chapter.

The topics you will see covered here, organized by category, are shown in Table 13-1. An "Optimizer" change is one that affects only the Oracle optimizer; no objects have to be altered to implement the change. "Performance-Related" changes require modifications to database objects in order to achieve better performance for previously existing operations. "Object Administration" changes affect the creation and maintenance of database objects. "Database Administration" changes simplify or enhance the administration of a database. "New DBA Utilities" describes two new database administration utilities available with Oracle7.3: TRACE and DB_VERIFY.

Optimizer Changes

As of Oracle7.3, the optimizer has been updated by adding three major areas of new functionality: the implementation of data histograms, the ability to use hash joins, and the ability to use star query execution paths. In the following sections, you will see descriptions of each of these new options.

Histograms

Like many of the changes in Oracle7.3, histograms are partially implemented by default. However, you must tune them in order to derive the greatest impact from their usage. Histograms enable you to tune queries against tables whose data values are not uniformly distributed.

For example, consider a table that has one row for every person in the world. The table could have two columns—one for the country name and one for each person's name—as shown in the following listing.

```
create table   POPULATION
(Country        VARCHAR2(200),
Name            VARCHAR2(200));
```

Assume that there are 250 countries in the world, and 6 billion people. On average, there are 24 million people per country (6 billion divided by 250 countries). To speed queries that use Country as a limiting condition, an index is placed on the Country column:

```
create index POPULATION$COUNTRY
on POPULATION(Country);
```

Type of Change	Option
Optimizer	Histograms
	Hash joins
	Star queries
Performance-Related	Unrecoverable actions
	Direct path export
	Dedicated temporary tablespaces
	Sort direct writes
Object Administration	Maxextents unlimited
	Deallocation of unused space from tables and indexes
	Fast index recreate
	Bitmap indexes
	User-specified hash clusters
	Partitioned views
	Stored triggers
Database Administration	Resizeable datafiles
	Dynamically changeable init.ora parameters
	Tablespace coalesce
	Read-only tablespaces
	Shrinking rollback segments
	Standby databases
	Media recovery status
	Replication (including snapshots and advanced replication)
	Multi-threaded server
	Delayed-logging block cleanout
	Scalable buffer cache
New DBA Utilities	TRACE
	DB_VERIFY

TABLE 13-1.   *New Administrative and Tuning Options, by Category*

You can determine the selectivity of the index. The number of distinct values of the Country column is 250, and the number of records in POPULATION is 6 billion, so the selectivity will be 0.0000000416 (250 distinct values/6 billion records). For every one distinct value in the index, there are 24 million rows in the table. The selectivity of the index is so poor that it will likely never be used; however, the index could be useful for queries involving countries with small populations.

Until Oracle7.3, the optimizer did not know how many rows were associated with each distinct value in the Country column. The optimizer had to start by assuming that there were the same number of rows associated with each Country, and then make educated guesses about the distribution of Country values. Unfortunately, data is not uniformly distributed, just as people are not uniformly distributed among countries. There are many more people in some countries than there are in others. Similarly, the data in your tables is not likely to be uniformly distributed. As a result, the optimizer may not make the proper choice of indexes during queries.

The COMPANY table used throughout this book, for instance, has a number of demographic columns. As shown in the following listing, there are indexes on its State and City columns, among others.

```
create table COMPANY
(Company_ID          NUMBER,
Name                 VARCHAR2(10),
Address              VARCHAR2(10),
City                 VARCHAR2(10),
State                VARCHAR2(10),
Zip                  VARCHAR2(10),
Parent_Company_ID    NUMBER,
Active_Flag          CHAR,
constraint COMPANY_PK primary key (Company_ID),
constraint COMPANY$PARENT_ID foreign key
    (Parent_Company_ID) references COMPANY(Company_ID));

create index COMPANY$CITY on COMPANY(City);
create index COMPANY$STATE on COMPANY(State);
create index COMPANY$PARENT on COMPANY(Parent_Company_ID);
```

The values in the State column are very likely no more evenly distributed than the values in the theoretical POPULATION table. Thus, the index on the State column will be more useful for some State values than for other State values. For example, if half of the rows in COMPANY come from the same State, it would most likely be faster to perform a full table scan than an index range scan followed by a table access for queries of that State value. For the other State values, the State index may enhance query performance.

What is needed, therefore, is a data-aware optimizer that can understand the distribution of values within a column. Oracle7.3 uses *histograms*—maps of the distribution of data values in the column—to determine when to use an index. By having the information about the data distribution, the cost-based optimizer can make better judgments about the execution path to use.

Oracle uses *height-balanced histograms*; a number of *buckets* are established, and the same number of data values are placed in each bucket. To accommodate the same number of values, the width of each bucket will usually be different (if all of the buckets are the same width, then either the data is evenly distributed or you do not have enough buckets).

For example, the SALES table used throughout this book has three columns: Company_ID, Period_ID, and Sales_Total. The primary key of the SALES table is the concatenation of the Company_ID column and the Period_Id column. You—and the optimizer—may assume that there will be the same number of rows in SALES for each distinct Company_ID value. However, there is no guarantee that the data is evenly distributed. For this example, assume that there are 200 records in the SALES table and the Company_ID values are distributed unevenly (some Company_ID values have records for periods that others do not). There are 150 distinct Company_ID values, distributed among the 200 rows as follows:

40 of the Company_ID values are between 0 and 10.

20 of the Company_ID values are between 11 and 20.

10 of the Company_ID values are between 21 and 30.

10 of the Company_ID values are between 31 and 50.

40 of the Company_ID values are between 51 and 100.

20 of the Company_ID values are between 101 and 200.

20 of the Company_ID values are between 201 and 1000.

40 of the Company_ID values are between 1001 and 2000.

Figure 13-1 shows a height-balanced histogram with 5 buckets for the Company_ID value distribution.

As shown in Figure 13-1, there are five separate buckets, each containing 40 values (one-fifth of the values in the table). The first bucket contains the Company_ID values from 0 to 10; the second, the values from 11 through 50; the third, those from 51 through 100; the fourth, those from 101 to 1000; and the fifth, those from 1001 to 2000. As shown in Figure 13-1, each bucket has the same "height," thus making it a height-balanced histogram. The width of each bucket is

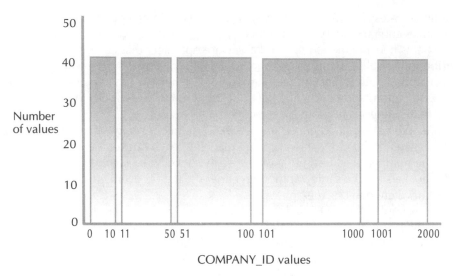

FIGURE 13-1. *Height-balanced histogram for the SALES table*

determined by the difference between its starting point and its endpoint (such as 10, 50, 100, 1000, and 2000 in the example).

The optimizer can use histograms to determine if an index should be used during a query. Consider the following query:

```
select * from SALES
where  Company_ID < 50;
```

Should the index on the Company_ID column be used during the query? If the table has not been analyzed using histograms, Oracle would estimate that the Company_ID column's selectivity is 150 distinct values divided by 200 rows, or 0.75. The query would be likely to use the index. However, the histogram shows that 40 percent of the table (two of the five buckets) would be returned by the query. Thus, the query may perform better if a full table scan were performed instead of an index range scan and table access of 40 percent of the table. The optimizer will make the choice; by using histograms, you give it the data it needs to make the choice.

Histograms will be useful whenever there is an uneven distribution of data values within a column. They are useful whenever an index may be used; see the "Avoid Unplanned Full Table Scans" section of Chapter 11 for a description of the limiting conditions that allow indexes to be used. As shown in the preceding example, histograms are most useful when the limiting conditions are ranges of values. If the limiting condition equates the column to a unique value, a histogram will still be used but will be less likely to alter the execution path.

Management Issues for Histograms

There are three critical management issues for histograms: the sample size, the frequency with which you analyze your tables, and the number of buckets used.

In Oracle7.3, the **analyze** command has been modified to include several new options. The new syntax for the **analyze** command contains a new set of clauses, as shown in the following listing.

```
ANALYZE
{INDEX    [user.]index] |
 TABLE    [user.]table] |
 CLUSTER [user.]cluster] }
  {COMPUTE STATISTICS  [FOR for_clause] |
   ESTIMATE STATISTICS [FOR for_clause]
      SAMPLE integer {ROWS | PERCENT } |
   DELETE STATISTICS |
   VALIDATE STRUCTURE [CASCADE] |
   LIST CHAINED ROWS [INTO [user.]table] }
```

The format of *for_clause* is

```
{FOR TABLE |
 FOR ALL [INDEXED] COLUMNS [SIZE integer] |
 FOR COLUMNS [SIZE integer] column [SIZE integer]... |
 FOR ALL INDEXES}
```

The use of the **for** clause is shown in the following example. The **for table** clause tells Oracle to calculate statistics for the table; if no other clauses are specified, **for table** tells Oracle not to calculate statistics for the table's indexes (which would have been calculated by default). The **for all indexed columns** clause tells Oracle only to perform column-level analysis on the indexed columns; histograms will not be generated for non-indexed columns, to improve the performance of the analysis process. The **size 250** clause tells Oracle to use histograms with 250 buckets each for each of the columns.

```
analyze table SALES compute statistics
    for table for all indexed columns size 250;
```

The sample size used in this example is the entire table—the **compute statistics** clause is used instead of **estimate statistics**. If at all possible, use **compute statistics**. The **compute statistics** option will require longer to run than **estimate**

statistics, and may need large temporary segments (usually not exceeding four times the size of the table), but the statistics will be accurate. If you use **estimate statistics**, you are assuming that analyzing part of the table will generate the same histogram endpoints as analyzing the entire table.

The frequency with which the **analyze** command is run is important. You must run it not only when new data is added to the table, but also when there are significant updates to indexed columns in the table. Once you start using histograms for a table, you have to keep the histograms current; otherwise, the optimizer will be using outdated data distribution information. Changes to the data are less important than changes to the data distribution; if the data changes but the data distribution remains unchanged, the old histogram values will still be valid.

Lastly, the number of buckets used must be large enough to show the distribution of the data. By default, the optimizer uses 75 buckets for each column. The first time you **analyze** a table, it is difficult to guess correctly at the number of buckets to use for a column. Once the column has been **analyze**d, you can use the DBA_HISTOGRAMS (or USER_HISTOGRAMS) data dictionary view to see the distribution of the values. The USER_HISTOGRAMS view contains information about each column's histogram, including the Table_Name, Column_Name, Endpoint_Number, and Endpoint_Value. The number of entries in USER_HISTOGRAMS for the table is the lesser of the number of buckets and the number of distinct values in the column. The values in USER_HISTOGRAMS are used by the optimizer to determine the distribution of the column values within the table.

In general, it is difficult to have too many buckets. The more buckets you have, the more accurately the optimizer will be able to estimate the distribution of data values in the table. In the example given previously in this section, the addition of more buckets may allow the optimizer to better estimate the distribution of the Company_ID values between 0 and 10. In the example, each endpoint value is distinct. If each endpoint value is distinct, you may benefit from increasing the number of buckets when you re-**analyze** the table. When one endpoint value appears multiple times, that means that multiple buckets have the same endpoint—indicating that the data distribution is skewed around that value. If the data is not distributed evenly, a repeated endpoint value indicates that you have enough buckets to detect at least one area of skewed data distribution in the table.

Oracle does not display the Endpoint_Value of each bucket in DBA_HISTOGRAMS. If the same Endpoint_Value is used for multiple buckets, the Endpoint_Value is only stored once. To see if an Endpoint_Value is repeated, you need to perform two queries.

First, the number of buckets is stored in USER_TAB_COLUMNS; the query in the following listing returns the number of buckets used for the SALES.Company_ID column.

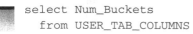

```
select Num_Buckets
  from USER_TAB_COLUMNS
```

```
where Table_Name = 'SALES'
  and Column_Name = 'COMPANY_ID';
```

The number of distinct values for the Endpoint_Value column for the analyzed column is equal to the number of records in USER_HISTOGRAMS for that column. The query in the following listing returns the number of distinct endpoints for the buckets generated during the analysis of the SALES.Company_ID column.

```
select COUNT(*)
  from USER_HISTOGRAMS
 where Table_Name = 'SALES'
   and Column_Name = 'COMPANY_ID';
```

If the result of the USER_HISTOGRAMS query is equal to the result of the USER_TAB_COLUMNS query, each Endpoint_Value is distinct. If each Endpoint_Value is distinct, you may be able to provide a better picture of the data distribution to the optimizer by increasing the number of buckets during the next analysis of the column. The goal is to use just enough buckets so that the data distribution is accurately represented and the optimizer can use data that is as accurate as possible while selecting an execution path.

Hash Joins

Oracle7.3 may dynamically choose to perform *hash joins* instead of NESTED LOOPS or MERGE JOINs. The following query shows a join between the COMPANY table and the SALES table. COMPANY and SALES both have the Company_ID column as the leading column of an index.

```
select COMPANY.Name
  from COMPANY, SALES
 where COMPANY.Company_ID = SALES.Company_ID
   and Period_ID = 2;
```

A traditional NESTED LOOPS explain plan for the indexed join between COMPANY and SALES is shown in the following listing.

```
NESTED LOOPS
   TABLE ACCESS FULL SALES
   TABLE ACCESS BY ROWID COMPANY
     INDEX UNIQUE SCAN COMPANY_PK
```

As shown in the execution path, SALES is the driving table for the NESTED LOOPS join. For each record in SALES, the COMPANY_PK index is checked for a matching Company_ID value. If a match exists, the COMPANY table is accessed via a TABLE ACCESS BY ROWID operation to find the COMPANY.Name value requested by the query.

As of Oracle7.3, the optimizer may choose to ignore the index and use a hash join for this query instead. The explain plan for the hash join version of the execution path is shown in the following listing.

```
HASH JOIN
  TABLE ACCESS FULL SALES
  TABLE ACCESS FULL COMPANY
```

In a hash join, both of the tables are fully scanned. However, the way that the tables are manipulated during the query execution makes the join very efficient.

NOTE
Hash joins have nothing to do with hash clusters. Hash clusters are a way of storing data. Hash joins refer to the way in which a join is performed by Oracle.

During a hash join, two tables are joined based on a set of join conditions—columns whose values they have in common, as defined in the **where** clause of the query. In the preceding example, the join condition is

```
where COMPANY.Company_ID = SALES.Company_ID
```

During a hash join, one of the tables involved in the join (in this case, SALES) is read by Oracle, and a bitmap of unique keys from the joined columns from the table is built in memory. As the rows are read, they are separated into groups or partitions based on a hashing function that maps the join keys to a partition. *Partition-level hashing* is used to split both tables into matching sets based on the join criteria. Partition-level hashing allows you to manage hash joins of large tables without excessive I/O penalties. In addition to partitioning the table, the optimizer builds a hash table (in memory) for all the partitions of the table that fit into memory; this is a second hashing function performed on the join keys, to be used when performing the join. The bitmap of values created is then used as a filter when the rows of the second table (COMPANY) are read and processed.

If a row is successfully filtered through the bitmap (that is, it is present in the bitmap), the hashing algorithm is used for data lookup and the subsequent join. The hash join detects the joins as quickly as possible via in-memory processing of the join columns; the returned values from that processing tell Oracle which rows should be joined.

If both of the tables are large, a portion of the processing may involve writing the partitions to disk—incurring disk I/O costs in the process. The hash tables and bitmaps always remain in memory. When doing hash joins of large tables, the challenge is to minimize disk I/Os while joining the tables without index lookups and sorts (the traditional join methods, used in NESTED LOOPS and MERGE JOIN methods). When large tables are joined via hash joins, they are first partitioned in memory; the partitions of the tables are processed separately, and the results are merged. During its hash join process, Oracle always performs two levels of hashing to perform the join. Two-level hashing avoids potential problems with large I/Os for joins of large tables.

Several init.ora parameters affect the usage and performance of hash joins. They are:

HASH_JOIN_ENABLED	If TRUE (the default), the cost-based optimizer will use hash joins whenever the cost of hash joins is cheaper than NESTED LOOPS or MERGE JOINs. To disable hash joins, set this value to FALSE.
HASH_AREA_SIZE	Sets the maximum amount of memory that will be used for hash joins. The default is twice the SORT_AREA_SIZE setting.
HASH_MULTIBLOCK_IO_COUNT	Sets the number of blocks to be read/written at a time while doing disk I/O for hash joins. The default value is the setting for DB_FILE_MULTIBLOCK_READ_COUNT.

If HASH_JOIN_ENABLED is set to TRUE (its default value), queries that had been executed as NESTED LOOPS or MERGE JOINS prior to Oracle7.3 may suddenly start using hash joins when executed within Oracle7.3. If you have specifically tuned a query to use another join method, you may need to force that method to be used via hints (see Chapter 10).

The unit of I/O for hash joins is determined by the following equation:

Hash join I/O size = Database block size * HASH_MULTIBLOCK_IO_COUNT

The hash join I/O size should not exceed 64KB. Thus, for a database block size of 8K, the HASH_MULTIBLOCK_IO_COUNT value should not exceed 8.

Management Issues for Hash Joins

Hash joins are an alternative to MERGE JOINs and NESTED LOOPS joins. MERGE JOIN operations tend to be I/O-bound (especially if temporary segments are used during sorting operations); if I/O is spread across disks (see Chapter 4), the MERGE JOIN performance will perform well if both tables are large or both are small. See Chapter 11 for detailed tuning advice for MERGE JOINs. If you are able to use the Parallel Query option, you can improve the performance of MERGE JOINs, since the full table scans typically found in MERGE JOIN operations can be parallelized (see Chapter 12).

Most joins on large tables are I/O-bound; hash joins tend to consume more CPU than other join methods. A full table scan will not benefit from having the table's data striped across multiple disks unless the query is parallelized or the distribution of I/O minimizes the table scan's impact on other I/O operations on the system.

Hash joins can take advantage of the Parallel Query option. However, there will be a limit to the extent to which a hash join query can improve with parallelism. Parallelism does not reduce the amount of CPU and memory needed by an operation; instead, it creates multiple processes and distributes the CPU and memory costs of the query across the processes concurrently. Since the hash join operation is already demanding a great deal of CPU and memory resources, there may not be enough resources available to fully exploit parallelism. If you plan to use hash joins extensively, you must have adequate memory and CPU resources available. If inadequate memory is available, the partitioning process used by the hash join may require a great deal of I/O to temporary segments.

The init.ora settings for the hash join parameters can be overridden at the session level via the **alter session** command, as shown in the following listing. The settings for the HASH_AREA_SIZE and HASH_MULTIBLOCK_IO_COUNT parameters can be set at the session level.

```
alter session set hash_multiblock_io_count=8;
```

In general, the larger the hash area size is, the better the performance of the hash join will be. The default value for the hash area size is twice the sort area size; if your sort area size is large enough, your hash area size should be acceptable. The minimum memory used is at least six times the product of the database block size and the HASH_MULTIBLOCK_IO_COUNT parameter setting. For example, if the database block size is 8KB, and the HASH_MULTIBLOCK_IO_COUNT is set to 8, then the minimum memory used by a hash join is 384KB (6*8KB*8).

The HASH_MULTIBLOCK_IO_COUNT parameter has a large impact on performance. In systems where the amount of data in the smaller table of the join is orders of magnitude larger than the size of the available memory, set this value to 1. If you set it too large, you will have few partitions with a large amount of data in each, resulting in a negative impact on query performance. If you are using the Multi-Threaded Server, the setting for this parameter is ignored and a value of 1 is used instead.

To force the use of a hash join, you can use the USE_HASH hint in your queries (see the "Using Hints" section of Chapter 10). The HASH_AJ hint in a query enables the use of the hashing method for an anti-join (such as a query containing a **not in** clause with a subquery).

> **NOTE**
> Since hash joins are enabled by default, be sure to check your explain plans after upgrading to Oracle7.3 to check which join method is used in your queries.

Star Queries

Star query execution paths are fully described, with examples, in the "Use Composite Keys/Star Queries" topic in Chapter 11. Star query execution paths improve the performance of data-warehousing style queries by joining the small dimension tables together in a Cartesian join, and joining the result set to the fact table.

Star query execution paths are available in all versions of Oracle7.0; you can force them to occur via hints (see Chapter 10). As of Oracle7.2, the optimizer dynamically identifies star queries, and may use a star query execution path to resolve a star query. In Oracle7.2, the optimizer can only use a star query execution path if five or fewer tables are involved; in Oracle7.3, the limitation on the number of tables involved is removed and a new STAR hint is provided.

The optimizer may choose to use a star query execution path if your query references a single large table that is joined to multiple smaller tables in the query. See Chapter 11 for a detailed example of a star query, star query execution paths, and methods for detecting when star query execution paths are being used. If the size of the fact table is much greater than that of the dimension tables used, and selective limiting conditions are specified for the dimension tables, the star query execution path may require over 1000 times fewer block reads than the traditional execution path.

Performance-Related Changes

A number of the non-optimizer changes made in Oracle exist solely to improve the performance of specific operations. These changes, as described in the following sections, include the unrecoverable actions, direct path exports, dedicated temporary tablespaces, and sort direct writes. In the following sections you will see examples illustrating how to implement each of these new options.

unrecoverable Actions

As of Oracle7.2, you can execute the **create table as select** and **create index** commands without generating entries in the online redo logs. Being able to execute these commands without generating online redo log entries significantly improves the performance of these operations—by up to 50 percent. The potential cost, as you will see in the following examples, is the potential loss of data if the use of the **unrecoverable** clause is not managed properly.

When you create a new table via a **create table as select** command, there is no "old" information to rollback; the table did not exist before. Similarly, when you create a new index, there is no "old" information to rollback. In each case, the data in the new object is created from data in another object. If you need to reconstruct the index, you could recreate it based on the table, with no data lost.

When the **unrecoverable** clause is added to the **create table as select** command, the table creation and population operations do not generate rollback segment or online redo log entries. The I/O costs of writing rollback segment and online redo log entries are eliminated. The performance benefit must be measured against the potential cost. In the event of media failure, you will not be able to recover the table by applying the archived redo log files; there will be no entries in those files for the table creation and population.

The **unrecoverable** clause is extremely useful when creating large aggregate tables such as those commonly found in data warehousing applications. In such environments, the base data is always available; if you had to recreate the table from the base data, you could. Since you can recreate the data from the base data, you do not need to be able to recreate it from the archived redo log files during recovery.

NOTE
If you use the **unrecoverable** clause for your tables or indexes, you must document that usage so that the person performing the database recovery will know that manual intervention will be necessary to recreate certain objects.

The **unrecoverable** clause is also useful when creating large temporary tables during batch or report processing. Such tables are temporary in nature, yet their creation may be enough to overwhelm the amount of archived redo log space available to your database! By creating the tables as **unrecoverable**, their creation will have no impact on the archived redo log file space usage.

The following example shows the SALES_BY_COMPANY table being created from the SALES table. SALES has three columns: Company_ID, Period_ID, and Sales_Total. The SALES_BY_COMPANY table is an aggregate table that stores the sum of the Sales_Total column, by Company_ID.

```
create table SALES_BY_COMPANY
unrecoverable
as select Company_ID, SUM(Sales_Total) Sum_Sales_Total
  from SALES
group by Company_ID;
```

The SALES_BY_COMPANY table can be created using the **unrecoverable** clause because it is a temporary table whose data is based on another table (SALES). The command in the preceding listing should be 40 to 50 percent faster than a comparable **create table as select** command that does not use the **unrecoverable** clause. The amount of performance benefit depends on the existing I/O distribution within your database and operating system (see Chapter 4).

When creating indexes, the **unrecoverable** clause is the last clause in the **create index** command, as shown in the following example. As with the **create table as select** command, the performance benefits can be significant, depending on your I/O layout.

```
create index SALES_BY_CO$CO_ID
on SALES_BY_COMPANY(Company_ID)
unrecoverable;
```

You can specify **recoverable** (the default option) explicitly for an object if your database is running in ARCHIVELOG mode.

Using the **unrecoverable** clause may help you get more performance from your usage of the Parallel Query option. If you have parallelized the query used as part of a **create table as select** command, or you have parallelized the **create index** command, then writing transaction entries to the online redo log files may create an I/O bottleneck, since the online redo log file entries will be serialized. In general, failing to use the **unrecoverable** clause will reduce the effective parallelism of your operations if your degree of parallelism is 4 or greater. See Chapter 12 for information on implementing and managing the parallel options.

When you are recovering a database that has a combination of recoverable and unrecoverable objects, the unrecoverable objects will be marked as logically corrupt by the recovery operation. Following a recovery, you will have to drop and recreate the unrecoverable objects before they can be accessed. Because the objects are marked as logically corrupt, you should not use the **unrecoverable** clause if your database is the master database in a standby database configuration.

Direct Path Export

Direct path export improves the performance of your exports by bypassing the SQL command processing layer used by conventional exports. To use direct path exports, you have to have the COMPATIBLE parameter in your database's init.ora file set to 7.1.5 or higher.

Direct path export does not work in the interactive mode of the Export utility; you must specify it either on the command line or in an Export parameter file. The parameter that causes a direct path export to be used is DIRECT, as shown in the following example.

```
exp system/manager DIRECT=Y
```

NOTE
The export dump file generated via a direct path export cannot be imported into a pre-Oracle7.3 database.

For direct path export to work, the NLS_LANG environment variable in your operating system session must be equivalent to the character set defined in the database. If the character sets are different, the export will terminate with an error. The BUFFER parameter of the Export utility has no effect when a direct path export is performed.

NOTE
The default value for DIRECT is N, so conventional exports will be performed by default.

Dedicated Temporary Tablespaces

As described in Chapter 11, you can specify a tablespace as "temporary" as of Oracle7.3. If you do so, the tablespace *cannot* be used to hold any permanent segments, only for temporary segments created during queries. The first sort to use the temporary tablespace allocates a temporary segment within the temporary tablespace; when the query completes, the space used by the temporary segment is *not* dropped. Instead, the space used by the temporary segment is available for use by other queries; this allows the sorting operation to avoid the costs of allocating and releasing space for temporary segments. This will reduce the temporary segment lock allocation contention and will save the costs involved in temporary segment allocation (equivalent to approximately ten **insert/update/delete** statements).

To designate a tablespace as temporary in Oracle7.3, specify **temporary** in the **create tablespace** or **alter tablespace** command. The example shown in the following listing changes an existing tablespace named TEMP to a **temporary** tablespace.

```
alter tablespace TEMP temporary;
```

If there are any permanent segments (tables or indexes, for example) stored in TEMP, the command shown in the preceding listing will fail.

You can query DBA_TABLESPACES to see if a tablespace has been created as a dedicated temporary tablespace. The DBA_TABLESPACES.Contents column will have a value of 'TEMPORARY' for dedicated temporary tablespaces, and 'PERMANENT' for tablespaces that can store both temporary sort segments and permanent objects.

You can query V$SORT_SEGMENTS for statistics about the usage of the sort segments in your database. There is one record in V$SORT_SEGMENTS for each dedicated temporary tablespace, storing data such as the current number of users (Current_Users), the maximum number of blocks used (Max_Used_Blocks), and the maximum sort size (Max_Sort_Size). The statistics in V$SORT_SEGMENT will help you verify your estimates regarding the amount of sort activity requiring temporary segments in your database.

To change the TEMP tablespace out of **temporary** state, and allow permanent objects to be stored in it, use the **permanent** keyword in the **alter tablespace** command, as shown in the following listing.

```
alter tablespace TEMP permanent;
```

You will now be able to store both temporary and permanent objects in the TEMP tablespace. However, the temporary segments will be dropped after each use, and the cost of the temporary segment allocation will be paid by each user who performs a sort requiring a temporary segment. In DBA_TABLESPACES, the Content column for the TEMP tablespace's row will now have a value of 'PERMANENT', and there will be no row for TEMP in V$SORT_SEGMENTS.

Sort Direct Writes

In Oracle7.2 and above, *sort direct writes* bypass the SGA when writing data to temporary segments. Sort direct writes greatly improve the performance of transactions that use temporary segments. Sort direct writes are enabled by default in some versions, but you should specify the sort size parameters in your init.ora file.

The three init.ora parameters affecting sort direct writes are:

SORT_DIRECT_WRITES	Set to TRUE (the default in some versions) to enable sort direct writes, or to FALSE to disable sort direct writes.
SORT_WRITE_BUFFER_SIZE	The size of each sort buffer to be allocated in memory during sorts. Sort buffers are allocated when SORT_DIRECT_WRITES is set to TRUE.
SORT_WRITE_BUFFERS	The number of sort buffers to allocate, ranging from 2 to 8.

Oracle recommends the following settings for optimal performance:

```
SORT_DIRECT_WRITES = TRUE
SORT_WRITE_BUFFERS = 4
SORT_WRITE_BUFFER_SIZE = 65536
```

The performance improvement from using sort direct writes is dramatic. For example, if an index creation takes 10 minutes in an Oracle7.1 instance (unparallelized), then upgrading the instance to Oracle7.2 and using the default sort direct write parameters should lower the index creation time by almost 50 percent, to about 5 minutes. Tuning the sort direct write process with the parameters shown above should reduce the sorting time even further.

There is no penalty for using sort direct writes, and you do not have to use a dedicated temporary tablespace to use them. Sort direct writes are available as of Oracle7.2.

Object Administration Changes

As of Oracle7.2 and 7.3, the ability to manage the space within your database greatly improves. In Oracle7.2, you can specify the hashing function to use in hash clusters. In Oracle7.3, you can reclaim space from tables and indexes, set an unlimited value for maxextents, quickly recreate indexes, use bitmap indexes, and manage partitioned views. In the following sections, you will see examples of the usage of each of these new options.

maxextents unlimited

As of Oracle7.3, the number of extents an object can obtain is greatly increased. You can use the **maxextents unlimited** clause of the **storage** clause to increase the maximum number of extents to 2,147,483,645 (prior to Oracle7.3, the maximum number of extents was dependent on the database block size). You can use **maxextents unlimited** for all tables, indexes, and clusters.

To specify **maxextents unlimited** for an object, you must set the COMPATIBLE parameter in the init.ora file to 7.3.0.0 or greater. In the following example, the SALES table is created with **maxextents unlimited**; you could also use the **alter table** command to modify the **storage** clause for SALES after it has been created.

```
create table SALES
(Company_ID  NUMBER,
Period_ID   NUMBER,
Sales_Total NUMBER,
```

```
constraint SALES_PK primary key (Company_ID, Period_ID),
constraint SALES$COMPANY_FK foreign key (Company_ID)
        references COMPANY(Company_ID))
tablespace DATA_1
storage (initial 100M next 100M pctincrease 0
        minextents 1
        maxextents unlimited);
```

You can query DBA_SEGMENTS to see the maximum number of extents allowed for a segment. If you have specified **maxextents unlimited** for a segment, the DBA_SEGMENTS.MaxExtents column will have a value of 2147483645 for the segment.

NOTE
Do not specify **maxextents unlimited** for temporary segments or rollback segments; otherwise, they could grow uncontrollably due to runaway transactions or queries.

Deallocation of Unused Space from Tables and Indexes

As of Oracle7.3, unused space in a segment can be released. Only the space above the highwatermark of the table can be released (see Chapters 2 and 5 for a discussion of highwatermark-related tuning issues).

The ability to release unused space is most useful for objects whose size has been greatly overestimated (resulting in a large amount of unused space in the initial extent) or whose **pctincrease** value is high (resulting in large amounts of unused space in each new extent created). To release unused space from a segment, use the **alter table**, **alter index**, or **alter cluster** command. To see the impact of the space release, you need to use the new DBMS_SPACE package.

To deallocate space from a table, you need to specify how much unused space is to be kept past the current highwatermark for the table. The format of the command for tables is shown via the following example, in which the COMPETITOR table is modified to retain only 100KB of unused space.

```
alter table COMPETITOR deallocate unused keep 100K;
```

The **alter table** command in the preceding listing tells Oracle to find the highwatermark of the COMPETITOR table—the highest point in the segment to which data has been written. Beyond that point, Oracle should leave 100KB in the table; the rest should be deallocated and returned to the tablespace. If you had not specified the **keep** clause, the **minextents** and **initial** sizes would have been preserved. If **keep** is used, you can reduce the size of the initial extent(s).

Before deallocating space, you should determine how much space is available in the table. You can use the DBMS_SPACE package to see the space allocation in the table, as shown in the following listing. The first three parameters passed to the DBMS_SPACE.UNUSED_SPACE procedure shown below are the schema that owns the object, the name of the object, and the object type (table, index, or cluster). Seven variables are defined to hold the output of the DBMS_SPACE.UNUSED_SPACE procedure.

```
declare
        OP1 number;
        OP2 number;
        OP3 number;
        OP4 number;
        OP5 number;
        OP6 number;
        OP7 number;
begin
dbms_space.unused_space('APPOWNER','COMPETITOR','TABLE',
                        OP1,OP2,OP3,OP4,OP5,OP6,OP7);
    dbms_output.put_line('OBJECT_NAME       = COMPETITOR');
    dbms_output.put_line('--------------------------');
    dbms_output.put_line('TOTAL_BLOCKS      = '||OP1);
    dbms_output.put_line('TOTAL_BYTES       = '||OP2);
    dbms_output.put_line('UNUSED_BLOCKS     = '||OP3);
    dbms_output.put_line('UNUSED_BYTES      = '||OP4);
    dbms_output.put_line('LAST_USED_EXTENT_FILE_ID  = '||OP5);
    dbms_output.put_line('LAST_USED_EXTENT_BLOCK_ID = '||OP6);
    dbms_output.put_line('LAST_USED_BLOCK   = '||OP7);
end;
/
```

The output of the preceding script for the COMPETITOR table is shown in the following listing.

```
OBJECT_NAME       = COMPETITOR
--------------------------
TOTAL_BLOCKS      = 300
TOTAL_BYTES       = 2457600
UNUSED_BLOCKS     = 100
UNUSED_BYTES      = 819200
LAST_USED_EXTENT_FILE_ID  = 6
LAST_USED_EXTENT_BLOCK_ID = 2292
LAST_USED_BLOCK = 5
```

The output shown in the preceding listing shows that the COMPETITOR table currently has 300 database blocks allocated. The database block size is 8KB, so the total bytes allocated is 300*8KB, or 2400KB, as shown in the TOTAL_BYTES line in the output. Of the 300 blocks allocated to COMPETITOR, 100 blocks are free (the UNUSED_BLOCKS line). Since the database block size is 8K, there are 800KB unused blocks in the table. The rest of the information shows the location information for the last used block and extent.

Since one-third of the table is empty, you can reclaim space from the table. The **alter table** command shown in the following listing will reclaim all but 100KB of the 800KB of unused space in the COMPETITOR table.

```
alter table COMPETITOR deallocate unused keep 100K;
```

You can verify the results of the **alter table** command by executing the DBMS_SPACE.UNUSED_SPACE procedure again for the COMPETITOR table.

```
declare
        OP1 number;
        OP2 number;
        OP3 number;
        OP4 number;
        OP5 number;
        OP6 number;
        OP7 number;
begin
dbms_space.unused_space('APPOWNER','COMPETITOR','TABLE',
                        OP1,OP2,OP3,OP4,OP5,OP6,OP7);
    dbms_output.put_line('OBJECT_NAME          = COMPETITOR');
    dbms_output.put_line('---------------------------');
    dbms_output.put_line('TOTAL_BLOCKS         = '||OP1);
    dbms_output.put_line('TOTAL_BYTES          = '||OP2);
    dbms_output.put_line('UNUSED_BLOCKS        = '||OP3);
    dbms_output.put_line('UNUSED_BYTES         = '||OP4);
    dbms_output.put_line('LAST_USED_EXTENT_FILE_ID  = '||OP5);
    dbms_output.put_line('LAST_USED_EXTENT_BLOCK_ID = '||OP6);
    dbms_output.put_line('LAST_USED_BLOCK      = '||OP7);
end;
/
```

The new output for the DBMS_SPACE.UNUSED_SPACE procedure is shown in the following listing.

```
OBJECT_NAME      = COMPETITOR
--------------------------
TOTAL_BLOCKS     = 213
TOTAL_BYTES      = 1744896
UNUSED_BLOCKS    = 13
UNUSED_BYTES     = 106496
LAST_USED_EXTENT_FILE_ID  = 6
LAST_USED_EXTENT_BLOCK_ID = 2292
LAST_USED_BLOCK = 5
```

The last three parameters did not change—the deallocation of space does not affect the currently used blocks. The UNUSED_BLOCKS value shows that over 100KB of space was kept as unused space. When you specified 100KB of space to keep, Oracle rounded that value up to the nearest whole increment of database blocks. Since the database block size in the example is 8KB, there is no way to have exactly 100KB free without splitting a database block in half. Oracle rounded the number of unused blocks to keep up from 12.5 to 13 (see the UNUSED_BLOCKS line). The total number of blocks now allocated by the table is 200 (the number of used blocks, as before) plus 13 unused blocks (because you kept 100KB of unused space allocated to the table). The total number of kept blocks is shown in the TOTAL_BLOCKS line of the output.

Fast Index Recreate

Prior to Oracle7.3, the only way to rebuild an index is to drop and recreate the index. Since dropping and recreating the index requires locking the table, you may not be able to rebuild the index for an application that has a high availability requirement.

As of Oracle7.3, the *fast index recreate* feature allows you to recreate an index without having to drop the existing index. The currently available index is used as the data source for the index, instead of using the table as the data source. During the index recreation, you can change its **storage** parameters and **tablespace** assignment. You can take advantage of the **parallel** and **unrecoverable** options during the index recreation. See Chapter 12 for information on the parallel options, and the "**unrecoverable** Actions" section of this chapter for information on the **unrecoverable** clause.

In the following example, the COMPANY_PK index is rebuilt (via the **rebuild** clause). Its storage parameters are changed to use an initial extent size of 100MB and a next extent size of 50MB, in the INDX_2 tablespace.

```
alter index COMPANY_PK rebuild
storage (initial 100M next 50M pctincrease 0)
tablespace INDX_2;
```

NOTE
When the COMPANY_PK index is rebuilt, there must be enough space for both the old index and the new index to exist simultaneously. After the new index has been created, the old index will be dropped and its space will be freed.

When you create an index that is based on previously indexed columns, Oracle may be able to use the existing indexes as data sources for the new index. For example, if you create a two-column index on (Company_ID, Period), and later decide to create an index on just the Company_ID column, Oracle will use the existing index as the data source for the new index. As a result, the performance of your **create index** commands will improve—if you create the indexes in an order that can take advantage of this feature.

Bitmap Indexes

In Chapter 11, one of the first SQL tuning tips involved using only selective indexes during your queries. To help tune queries that use nonselective columns in their limiting conditions, Oracle has made bitmap indexes available as of Oracle7.3. Bitmap indexes should only be used if the data is infrequently updated, as they add to the cost of all data manipulation transactions against the tables they index.

Bitmap indexes are appropriate when multiple nonselective columns are used as limiting conditions in a single query. For example, if an EMPLOYEE table has a column for Sex (with two possible values, 'M' or 'F'), and another for Active_Flag (with two possible values, 'Y' or 'N'), then you would not normally create an index on either the Sex or Active_Flag column. If queries frequently reference both Sex and Active_Flag in their **where** clauses, those columns may be good candidates for bitmap indexes.

Internally, a bitmap index maps the distinct values for the columns to each record. For example, for the Active_Flag column, there are two possible values, so there are two separate bitmap entries. If the first five rows in the table have an Active_Flag value of 'Y', and the next five have an Active_Flag value of 'N', then the Active_Flag bitmap entries would resemble those shown in the following listing.

```
Active_Flag bitmaps:
   Y: < 1 1 1 1 1 0 0 0 0 0 >
   N: < 0 0 0 0 0 1 1 1 1 1 >
```

In the preceding listing, each number represents a row in the EMPLOYEE table. Since there are ten rows considered, there are ten bitmap values shown. Reading the bitmap for Active_Flag, the first five records have a value of 'Y' (the '1' values), and the next five do not (the '0' values). You could have more than two possible values for the column, in which case there would be a separate bitmap entry for each possible value.

If the even-numbered records have a Sex value of 'M', the bitmap entries for the Sex column would resemble those shown in the following listing.

```
Sex bitmaps:
   M: < 0 1 0 1 0 1 0 1 0 1 >
   F: < 1 0 1 0 1 0 1 0 1 0 >
```

The value of bitmap indexes is that for queries involving multiple columns, the rows to be returned can be derived very quickly. Consider the query in the following listing, which selects from EMPLOYEE based on both Sex and Active_Flag.

```
select *
  from EMPLOYEE
 where Active_Flag = 'Y'
   and Sex = 'F';
```

If bitmap indexes are available for the Sex and Active_Flag columns, the optimizer can choose to use the bitmap indexes in resolving the query. The bitmaps for the limiting conditions are shown in the following listing.

```
Active_Flag = Y: < 1 1 1 1 1 0 0 0 0 0 >
        Sex = F: < 1 0 1 0 1 0 1 0 1 0 >
```

The optimizer can quickly compare the two bitmaps and see that rows 1, 3, and 5 meet the criteria for the query (since all three have '1' values for both criteria). Those rows will be returned when the query is resolved. The more columns used as limiting conditions, the more valuable bitmap indexes will be.

To create a bitmap index, use a modified version of the **create index** command, as shown in the following listing. You should indicate its status as a bitmap index within the index name so that it will be easy to detect during tuning operations.

```
create bitmap index EMPLOYEE$BITMAP_SEX
    on EMPLOYEE(Sex);
```

To enable bitmap indexes in Oracle7.3.2, you should add the following lines to your database's init.ora file:

```
event = "10111 trace name context forever"
event = "10112 trace name context forever"
event = "10114 trace name context forever"
```

If you choose to use bitmap indexes, you will need to weigh the performance benefit during queries against the performance cost during data manipulation commands. The more bitmap indexes there are on a table, the greater the cost will be during each transaction.

User-Specified Hash Clusters

In a *hash cluster*, the physical location of a record is determined by its values in key columns. A *hashing function* is applied to the key values for the row, and Oracle uses the result to determine in which block to store the record. The rows within the hash cluster are quickly spread across all of the allocated blocks. The use of hash clusters for large tables is described in the "Manage Very Large Table Accesses" section of Chapter 11.

Hash clusters are useful if equivalence queries are used; if your queries use ranges of values as limiting conditions, you should use an index instead of a hash cluster.

As of Oracle7.2, you can specify a hashing formula for the cluster. Specifying your own hashing formula is useful for applications that use system-generated sequence numbers for their tables' primary keys. In that case, the hash formula would be the sequence column itself.

An example of a user-specified hash cluster is shown in the following listing. The **size** parameter specifies the amount of space allocated to each row in the table. To avoid *collisions*—multiple hashed rows stored in the same block—you should multiply the calculated **size** parameter for the cluster by a factor of 1.5. The **hashkeys** parameter specifies the expected number of rows within the hashed table. The **hash is** clause specifies that the Company_ID column is to be used as the hash function for the cluster.

```
create cluster COMPANY_CLUSTER (Company_ID NUMBER(12))
storage (initial 50M next 50M)
   hash is Company_ID
   size 60 hashkeys 10000000;
```

The **storage** parameters and the hashing function for the hashed table are specified at the cluster level, as shown in the preceding listing.

Once the cluster has been created, create the table within the cluster, as shown in the following listing.

```
create table COMPANY
(Company_ID   NUMBER(12),
 Name         VARCHAR2(20),
 Address      VARCHAR2(20))
cluster COMPANY_CLUSTER (Company_ID);
```

The table will be created using the storage parameters for the cluster, and the Company_ID column will be used as the hashed column for the COMPANY table.

Partitioned Views

Partitioned views allow you to spread the data from a single table across multiple tables. The tables can be queried in a single query by using the **union** operator. Partitioned views can be used to improve the performance of queries against very large tables, as described in the "Manage Very Large Table Accesses" section of Chapter 11. However, they also improve the ease of administration of large tables, as you will see in the following examples.

For example, the SALES table has three columns: Company_ID, Period_ID, and Sales_Total. If there is a limited and constant set of valid Period_ID values, you may be able to partition the SALES data across multiple tables. Each of the tables will store the SALES record for a separate Period_ID value.

If there are three valid Period_ID values (1, 2, and 3), there will be three separate tables, each with a check constraint that specifies the limiting condition that defines its part of the partition. As shown in the following listing, the first table, SALES_1, is created and populated with data from the original SALES table.

```
create table SALES_1
(Company_ID, Period_ID, Sales_Total) as
select Company_ID, Period_ID, Sales_Total
  from SALES
 where Period_ID = 1;

alter table SALES_1
  add constraint CHECK_SALES_1
check (Period_ID = 1);

alter table SALES_1
  add constraint SALES_1_PK
primary key (Company_ID, Period_ID);

create index SALES_1$PERIOD_ID
    on SALES_1(Period_ID);
```

After the SALES_1 table has been created, the check constraint is added to the table (an important step from a performance standpoint in Oracle7.3). The primary key columns of the table are indexed, and the Period_ID column is indexed by itself.

The second SALES partition table, SALES_2, and the third, SALES_3, are created in similar fashion. Each of the partitioned tables contains data from only one period, and each has a check constraint that defines the limiting condition used to populate the table. The creation script for SALES_2 is shown in the following listing; the only difference from the SALES_1 creation script is the limiting condition used.

```
create table SALES_2
(Company_ID, Period_ID, Sales_Total) as
select Company_ID, Period_ID, Sales_Total
  from SALES
 where Period_ID = 2;

alter table SALES_2
  add constraint CHECK_SALES_2
check (Period_ID = 2);

alter table SALES_2
  add constraint SALES_2_PK
primary key (Company_ID, Period_ID);

create index SALES_2$PERIOD_ID
    on SALES_2(Period_ID);
```

SALES_3 is created in a similar fashion, containing all the records for which Period_ID=3.

You can use the **union** operator to create a view that shows the data from all three tables in a single query. The SALES_VIEW view shown in the following listing will query SALES_1, SALES_2, and SALES_3. Each of the tables has a primary key on the combination of Company_ID and Period_ID, and each table has a check constraint on Period_ID. There will be no duplicate records within any of the SALES tables, and there will be no records that are stored in more than one of the SALES tables. Therefore, you can use the **union all** version of the **union** operator, improving the performance of the operation.

```
create or replace view SALES_VIEW as
select * from SALES_1
union all
select * from SALES_2
```

```
union all
select * from SALES_3;
```

If you are using Oracle7.3, partitioned views such as SALES_VIEW can improve the performance of your queries via a technique called *partition elimination*. The query in the following listing selects records from only one of the three SALES tables, via the SALES_VIEW view:

```
select * from SALES_VIEW
 where Period_ID = 2
   and Company_ID between 1000 and 2000;
```

Since the query only retrieves records for which the Period_ID value equals 2, only the SALES_2 table is needed to satisfy the query. Prior to Oracle7.3, all three of the SALES tables will be queried whenever SALES_VIEW is queried. Oracle7.3 uses the check constraints defined on the partition tables to determine which tables might participate in the query. Thus, in an Oracle7.3 database, only SALES_2 will be queried; the accesses of SALES_1 and SALES_3 will be eliminated from the query execution path.

To enable partition elimination, you must set the PARTITION_VIEW_ENABLED parameter in your database's init.ora file to TRUE (the default is FALSE). You must create check constraints on the tables to define the partitions. You can see the modification to the query execution path by generating the explain plan for the query (see Chapter 10).

Using a partitioned view enables you to perform maintenance on one of the partition tables without affecting the rest of the view's tables. For example, suppose you need to **truncate** SALES_3 and reload it with updated data. During the process of rebuilding SALES_3, you can use a modified version of SALES_VIEW that does not reference SALES_3. When SALES_3 is once again available, you can revert to the original SALES_VIEW. In the following example, SALES_3 is removed from the partitioned view, maintenance is performed, and then SALES_3 is added back to the partitioned view.

```
REM  SALES_VIEW without SALES_3:
REM
create or replace view SALES_VIEW as
select * from SALES_1
union all
select * from SALES_2;
REM
REM
REM  Perform maintenance, such as Truncate/build of SALES_3
REM
```

```
REM  Then add SALES_3 back into SALES_VIEW:
REM
create or replace view SALES_VIEW as
select * from SALES_1
union all
select * from SALES_2
union all
select * from SALES_3;
```

During the maintenance period, no user can access SALES_3's data; however, they can access the data from SALES_1 and SALES_2. By comparison, if all of the SALES data is stored in a single table, you could not have easily provided partial data availability during the maintenance period, nor could you have used **truncate** without deleting all periods' records from the table. Using partition tables enables you to use DDL commands such as **truncate** during your maintenance operations without impacting the rest of the tables in the partitioned view.

Stored Triggers

As of Oracle7.3, Oracle treats triggers as a new form of executable object with bind variables; the compiled form of the trigger is stored in the database, loaded into memory, and executed directly, eliminating the need for run-time recompilation of the trigger. Prior to Oracle7.3, triggers were implemented as anonymous PL/SQL blocks that were compiled and stored in the shared SQL area of the database. If the PL/SQL block was not used recently enough, it may have been removed from the shared SQL area, forcing it to be recompiled the next time it was used.

When you create a new trigger in Oracle7.3, it is automatically compiled. To manually compile triggers that were created prior to Oracle7.3, use the **alter trigger** command, as shown in the following example.

```
alter trigger APPOWNER.MY_TRIGGER compile;
```

When a trigger is created, the items listed in Table 13-2 are stored in the data dictionary. For each item type, the data dictionary table that holds the associated records is listed. Note that although triggers are now stored objects similar to procedures, the source code for procedures is stored in SOURCE$, while the source code for triggers is still stored in TRIGGER$. Since more data is stored for each trigger than was stored prior to Oracle7.3, you should expect that the space requirements within the SYSTEM tablespace will increase for trigger-intensive applications.

Dictionary Table	Item Type
TRIGGER$	Source code for the trigger
IDL$ tables	P-code and debug code for the trigger
DEPENDENCY$	Dependencies for trigger objects
OBJ$	The status of the trigger object
ERROR$	Errors generated during compilation
DBA_OBJECT_SIZE	The sizes of various pieces of the stored trigger

TABLE 13-2. *Records Created When a Trigger is Created*

When you migrate from a pre-Oracle7.3 database to an Oracle7.3 database, you can run the appropriate catalog script (see the README.DOC file for your database) to mark all triggers as having an 'INVALID' state. An "invalid" trigger will be recompiled the next time it is executed. You can also manually recompile all of your triggers (to avoid run-time recompilation) via **alter trigger** commands as shown in the previous example.

Database Administration Changes

In the following sections, you'll see descriptions of changes that are intended to make the administration of an Oracle database easier or more flexible. The changes include resizeable datafiles, coalescing of free space in tablespaces, shrinking of rollback segments, and enhancements to advanced replication.

Resizeable Datafiles

As of Oracle7.2, the size of existing datafiles can be extended, and the extensions can take place automatically as more space is needed. Also as of Oracle7.2, space can be reclaimed from existing datafiles. The following examples show how to execute the commands needed to modify the size of your datafiles.

NOTE
Depending on your operating system's implementation of raw devices and logical volume management, you may not be able to use the file resizing commands in this section if you use raw devices.

When creating datafiles, you can specify parameters that will allow Oracle to automatically extend your datafiles. The datafiles could then be automatically extended whenever their current allocated length is exceeded. You can specify three sizing parameters for each datafile:

AUTOEXTEND	A flag, set to ON or OFF to indicate if the file should be allowed to automatically extend. If set to OFF, the other sizing parameters will be set to zero.
NEXT *size*	The size, in bytes, of the area of disk space to allocate to the datafile when more space is required. You can qualify the size value with 'K' and 'M' for KB and MB, respectively.
MAXSIZE *size*	The maximum size, in bytes, to which the datafile should be allowed to extend. You can qualify the size value with 'K' and 'M' for KB and MB, respectively.

If no **maxsize** value is specified, the maximum size of the datafile will be limited only by the available space on the file's disk.

The **autoextend**, **next**, and **maxsize** parameters can be specified for a datafile via the **create database**, **create tablespace**, and **alter tablespace** commands. In the following example, the **create tablespace** command is used to create a datafile that will automatically extend as needed.

```
create tablespace DATA
datafile '/db05/oracle/DEV/data01.dbf' size 200M
autoextend ON
next 10M
maxsize 250M;
```

The tablespace created in the preceding example will have a single datafile with an initial size of 200MB. When that datafile fills, and the objects within it require additional space, the datafile will extend itself by 10MB. The extension process will continue as needed until the file has reached 250MB in size, at which point the file will have reached its maximum size.

To verify the **autoextend** settings for the datafile, query SYS.FILEXT$. The FILEXT$ table will contain one record for each datafile that can autoextend. If you have multiple files that can autoextend, you can refer to the File_ID# value from DBA_DATA_FILES to identify the files shown in SYS.FILEXT$.

```
select * from SYS.FILEXT$;

FILE#        MAXEXTEND        INC
----------  ----------  ----------
         7       32000        1280
```

The **inc** and **maxextend** parameters are expressed in terms of database blocks. In this case the database block size is 8KB. Therefore, **maxextend** is 32000 blocks * 8KB per block = 250MB. The **next** parameter in the preceding example was specified to be 10MB. The **inc** parameter was set to 1280 blocks (10MB extent/8KB per block). If the **next** parameter is not specified, it is set to 1 block. If **maxextend** is not specified, it is set to 4,194,302 blocks.

You cannot modify an existing datafile in a tablespace via the **alter tablespace** command. You can add a new datafile, via the **alter tablespace** command, to enable **autoextend** capabilities for the tablespace. The command in the following listing adds a new datafile to the DATA tablespace, specifying **autoextend on** and **maxsize unlimited**.

```
alter tablespace DATA
add datafile '/db05/oracle/DEV/data02.dbf'
size 50M
autoextend on
maxsize unlimited;
```

Another way of making the same change is shown in the following example. The **alter database** command can be used to modify the storage values for datafiles, as shown here.

```
alter database
datafile '/db05/oracle/DEV/data01.dbf'
autoextend on
maxsize unlimited;
```

If you use the **autoextend** feature of datafiles, you need to be sure that your file systems have enough space to support an extended datafile. In previous versions of Oracle, datafiles could not extend; as a result, you may have become accustomed to an unchanging size of a datafile. If you use datafiles whose size can change, you need to document this change for your database and operating system administration personnel.

As of Oracle7.2, you can reclaim space from existing datafiles via the **alter database** command. As shown in the following listing, you can specify the size to which the file should be shrunk.

```
alter database datafile '/db05/oracle/DEV/data01.dbf'
resize 50M;
```

The shrinking of the datafile will succeed if the datafile is empty beyond the point specified in the **alter database** command. In the preceding example, a new size of 50MB was specified; if space is used within the datafile beyond the first 50MB, an error will be returned. As shown in the following listing, the error will show the amount of space that is used within the datafile beyond the specified **resize** value.

```
alter database datafile '/db05/oracle/DEV/data01.dbf'
resize 50M;
*
ERROR at line 1:
ORA-03297: file contains 912 blocks of data beyond
requested RESIZE value
```

Dynamically Changeable init.ora Parameters

As of Oracle7.3, a number of the parameters set via init.ora can be changed while the database is running. These dynamic initialization parameters are available at the system and session levels.

If a parameter is modified at the session level, the change is in effect for the duration of that session. Parameters that can be modified at the session level are shown in Table 13-3. Note that a number of the dynamic initialization parameters shown in Table 13-3 are listed as "undocumented"; the ability to change them is not documented, but they are changeable as of Oracle7.3.2.

If a parameter is modified at the system level, the change is in effect even after the database is shutdown and restarted. To see the current value of your init.ora parameters, you can no longer rely on reading the init.ora file; you should select all of the parameter names and values from V$PARAMETER instead. Parameters that can be modified at the system level are shown in Table 13-4. All of the dynamic initialization parameters shown in Table 13-4 are "undocumented"; the ability to change them is not documented, but they are changeable as of Oracle7.3.2.

You can use the **alter session** and **alter system** commands to set the parameter values, as shown in the following listing.

```
alter session set PARTITION_VIEW_ENABLED=TRUE;
alter system set TIMED_STATISTICS=TRUE;
```

Parameter	Description	Default Value
Documented:		
HASH_AREA_SIZE	Size of in-memory hash work area	2*SORT_AREA_SIZE
HASH_JOIN_ENABLED	Enable/disable hash joins	TRUE
HASH_MULTIBLOCK_IO_COUNT	Number of blocks hash join will read at once	1
Undocumented:		
DB_FILE_MULTIBLOCK_READ_COUNT	Number of database blocks read during each I/O	O/S-dependent
MAX_DUMP_FILE_SIZE	Maximum size (in blocks) of trace dump files	500 blocks
OPTIMIZER_PERCENT_PARALLEL	Optimizer percent parallel	0
PARALLEL_MIN_PERCENT	Minimum percent of threads required for parallel query	0
PARTITION_VIEW_ENABLED	Enable/disable partitioned views	FALSE
TEXT_ENABLE	Enable text searching	FALSE
TIMED_STATISTICS	Maintain internal timing statistics	FALSE

TABLE 13-3. *Session-Level Dynamic Initialization Parameters*

Parameter	Description	Default Value
DB_FILE_MULTIBLOCK_READ_COUNT	Number of database blocks read during each I/O	O/S-dependent
HASH_MULTIBLOCK_IO_COUNT	Number of blocks hash join will read at once	1
LOG_CHECKPOINT_INTERVAL	Number of redo blocks—checkpoint threshold	O/S-dependent
LOG_CHECKPOINT_TIMEOUT	Maximum interval between checkpoints, in seconds	0
LOG_SMALL_ENTRY_MAX_SIZE	Maximum size of a redo entry that does not require redo latch	O/S-dependent
TEXT_ENABLE	Enable text searching	FALSE
TIMED_STATISTICS	Maintain internal timing statistics	FALSE
USER_DUMP_DEST	User process dump directory	O/S-dependent

TABLE 13-4.   *System-Level Dynamic Initialization Parameters (all are undocumented)*

Tablespace Coalesce

As described in Chapter 5, the extents of a segment are marked as free extents when the segment is dropped. If the extents are next to each other, they can be combined, or *coalesced,* into a single free extent. The coalesced extent will be larger than either of the two separate free extents, and thus will be more likely to be reused. See Chapter 5 for details on extent sizing to maximize reuse of free extents.

As of Oracle7, the SMON background process periodically coalesces neighboring free extents into larger free extents. However, there is a potential problem with the SMON-based free space coalesce implementation.

The SMON background process only coalesces free extents in tablespaces whose default **pctincrease** storage parameter is non-zero. Since temporary and rollback segment tablespaces typically use a **pctincrease** of 0, the free space in their tablespaces will not be coalesced. If you have set the default **pctincrease** to 0 for a data tablespace, you may be experiencing free space fragmentation in the tablespaces. You may think that SMON is coalescing the tablespace's free space, but in fact it will skip the tablespace.

There are several solutions available to resolve the free space coalescing problem. First, you can size your extents properly, as described in Chapter 5. If this is done, the reuse of free extents will be maximized and the impact of noncoalesced free extents will be minimized. Second, you can set the default **pctincrease** value for your data and index tablespaces to a non-zero value. You could, for example, set the default **pctincrease** for each tablespace to a value of 1, and then override the default setting when creating objects within the tablespace. Third, as of Oracle7.3, you can manually coalesce the free space in a tablespace.

The **alter tablespace** command shown in the following example coalesces the free space in the DATA_1 tablespace. Other users of the DATA_1 tablespace will not be affected by the free space coalesce.

```
alter tablespace DATA_1 coalesce;
```

To determine if a tablespace needs to be coalesced, you can use a new data dictionary view, DBA_FREE_SPACE_COALESCED. The columns of DBA_FREE_SPACE_COALESCED are shown in Table 13-5. Ideally, the Percent_Blocks_Coalesced column of DBA_FREE_SPACE_COALESCED should be 100 percent. You can display the free space coalescence percentage for tablespace via the query in the following listing.

```
select Tablespace_Name,
       Percent_Blocks_Coalesced
  from DBA_FREE_SPACE_COALESCED
 order by Percent_Blocks_Coalesced;
```

The tablespace with the lowest percentage of free extents coalesced will be displayed first. Use the **alter tablespace** command shown earlier to coalesce the free extents. If a tablespace frequently has uncoalesced free extents, you should

Column	Description
Tablespace_Name	Name of the tablespace
Total_Extents	Number of free extents in the tablespace
Extents_Coalesced	Number of coalesced free extents in the tablespace
Percent_Extents_Coalesced	Percentage of coalesced free extents in the tablespace
Total_Bytes	Number of free bytes in the tablespace
Bytes_Coalesced	Number of coalesced free bytes in the tablespace
Total_Blocks	Number of free database blocks in the tablespace
Blocks_Coalesced	Number of coalesced database blocks in the tablespace
Percent_Blocks_Coalesced	Percentage of coalesced free blocks in the tablespace

TABLE 13-5. *Columns of DBA_FREE_SPACE_COALESCED*

check the default **pctincrease** value for the tablespace and the extent sizes for the segments stored in the tablespace (see Chapter 5).

Read-Only Tablespaces

As of Oracle7.1, you can define a tablespace as being *read-only*. A read-only tablespace can be created to avoid backup and recovery of static data stored in the tablespace. Static data can include reference data, historical data, or read-only lookup data. Read-only tablespaces, once configured, can be stored on low-cost media such as CD-ROMs or WORM (write once, read many) drives.

NOTE
Before making a tablespace read-only, you should back up the tablespace. Also, make sure that the COMPATIBLE parameter in the database's init.ora file is set to 7.1.0 or higher.

To make a tablespace read-only, it must be online and have no active transactions against it. The tablespace cannot contain any rollback segments. Use

394 Advanced Oracle Tuning and Administration

the **alter tablespace** command to convert the tablespace to read-only status, as shown in the following listing.

```
alter tablespace REFERENCE_DATA read only;
```

After the tablespace has been converted to read-only status, you can move it to a WORM drive or CD-ROM drive. You cannot move the tablespace to such a drive until it has been converted to read-only status.

To convert a read-only tablespace back to normal status, use the **alter tablespace** command shown in the following listing.

```
alter tablespace REFERENCE_DATA read write;
```

NOTE
Tablespaces containing SYSTEM-owned objects, temporary segments, or rollback segments should **never** be made read-only.

Shrinking Rollback Segments

As of Oracle7.2, you can force rollback segments to shrink. You can use the **shrink** clause of the **alter rollback segment** command to shrink rollback segments to any size you want. If you do not specify a size the rollback segment should shrink to, it will shrink to its **optimal** size. You cannot shrink a rollback segment to fewer than two extents.

In the following listing, the R1 rollback segment is altered twice. The first command shrinks R1 to 15MB. The second command shrinks the R1 rollback segment to its **optimal** size. The **shrink** option of the **alter rollback segment** command is only available in Oracle7.2 and above.

```
alter rollback segment R1 shrink to 15M;
alter rollback segment R1 shrink;
```

See the "Shrink Rollback Segments that have Extended Past optimal" section of Chapter 6 for information on shrinking rollback segments in databases prior to Oracle7.2.

Standby Databases

A *standby database* is a copy of the primary (production) database that is constantly in recovery mode. As archived redo log files are generated by the primary database, they are moved to the server on which the standby database resides, and are applied to the standby database. When a disaster occurs, the standby database can be quickly activated; the amount of data lost will be limited to the redo log files that were not applied because of the disaster.

Standby databases are available with all versions of Oracle7, but they are much simpler to create and administer in Oracle7.3 because of a new command set. To create a standby database, you need to create a replica of your production environment on a separate server. The two servers should use the same version of the database software (including patches), and the two databases should have the same name. The version of the operating system (including patches) should be the same on both servers.

Within the database, the COMPATIBLE parameter in the databases' init.ora files must have the same value. For ease of use, the datafiles, directories, log files, and control files should be the same for both the primary and standby databases.

The Oracle7.3 SQL commands for creating and activating a standby database are:

```
alter database create standby controlfile as filename;
alter database mount standby database [parallel];
alter database recover standby database;
alter database activate standby database;
recover standby database;
```

When a standby database is activated following a disaster, it is available for use as the primary database for the application. When the original primary database server is once again available, you can enable the original primary database as the new standby database if you wish. See the Oracle7.3 **alter database** and **recover** command descriptions for a full discussion of standby database management.

Media Recovery Status

As of Oracle7.3, you can use two new V$ dynamic views to monitor the progress of media recovery on a file-by-file basis.

V$RECOVERY_FILE_STATUS contains one row for each datafile within the scope of the **recover** command. For the **recover datafile** command, all datafiles listed in the command will be displayed in this view. For the **recover database** command, all online datafiles are shown via this view.

V$RECOVERY_STATUS contains information about the overall recovery session, including the details on the logs applied, error information, and overall status. If the recovery process is complete, this view will contain no rows.

The information for V$RECOVERY_FILE_STATUS and V$RECOVERY_STATUS is stored in the private database memory area for the user session and is destroyed when the recovery session is complete.

Replication

Replication permits you to have copies of data stored in multiple databases, allowing remote databases to query and possibly update the replicated data locally. The local access to the data eliminates the need to access data remotely each time the data is accessed by an online transaction processing application. The cost of the data movement is assumed by batch processes coordinated by the database. Oracle7 offers a number of administration options for replication administration. In the following sections, you will see descriptions of Oracle's replication offerings and the changes available with each successive version of Oracle7, as well as management advice for determining which replication option best suits your needs.

General Replication Issues

The techniques used to keep the replicated data in sync with the master copy of the data have a direct impact on the cost, performance, and effectiveness of replication. For small, infrequently replicated tables, a complete refresh (or full refresh) technique is simple and effective. In a full refresh, the replicated data is dropped or truncated, and the full set of master data is copied to the target database. Application reference tables (see Chapter 2) are good candidates for full refresh replication because they are typically small and nonvolatile.

For medium-to-large volume tables with low volatility (such as business reference tables), a fast refresh (or net change) technique is useful. In net change replication, only the changed data is transmitted and applied to the replicated data. Net change replication is preferred if the network and processing resources are limited. In general, the weakest link in data distribution is the network; access to the network can be expensive, and the network traffic is generally outside the direct control of the DBA.

Changes to the master data can be identified, transmitted, and applied either *columnwise* (applying changes to specific columns) or *rowwise* (replacing the entire row). With columnwise replication, the volume of data exchanged between the source and the target is kept to a minimum at the expense of more complexity of identification and application of changes. On the other hand, rowwise replication simplifies the replication process at the cost of the full row being transmitted and applied for any changes to the row.

During a net change replication, a unique key must be used for quick access to the changed row. If a primary key can be identified for the subset of the master data being replicated, the primary key can be used at the target for applying changes. Alternately, if a distinct RowID is available at the source for the replicated data, the RowID can be stored with the data at the target and used for unique identification of the row for applying changes.

In addition to planning the replication, you need to consider whether the data will be updateable at the target site. If the copy of the data is modified, do those changes need to be replicated back to the master data? As of Oracle7.1.6, you can use the database to automate the management of advanced replication, in which multiple sites can update the data. If the target data is read-only, the management of the replication process can be simplified.

Read-only replication makes use of commands and utilities that have long been available in Oracle. Copying data from one database to another can be accomplished via the Export and Import utilities, the SQL*Plus **create table as select** command, the SQL*Plus **copy** command, and the SQL*Loader used in combination with loadable data files. If you use the **create table as select** method, see the section on **unrecoverable** actions earlier in this chapter. As of Oracle7, snapshots are available to facilitate read-only replication.

To choose the proper replication option, you need to consider the volatility of the data, whether the target data can be updated, and the timing of the replication actions. If the data in the target database and the master database must always be the same, you will need to use synchronous replication. If the data in the target and master databases can be different until the next refresh action occurs, you can use one of the many asynchronous replication mechanisms available in Oracle7.

Asynchronous and Synchronous Replication

In *synchronous replication*, the master data and the target data are continuously in sync. Synchronous replication is implemented by creating triggers on the master tables. When a transaction occurs against a master table, the triggers on that table are executed; the triggers execute the same transaction against the target tables. If the transaction against the target tables fails, the transaction against the master table fails.

Synchronous replication uses Oracle7's *two-phase commit* capability. Two-phase commit allows transactions to occur across multiple databases. The entire transaction involving the master tables and the target tables is either committed or entirely rolled back. When you use synchronous replication, you are therefore depending on the availability and performance of the network and the server hardware for the triggered transaction. If the server that is used by the target database is not available, you will not be able to commit transactions against the master tables. You can also create triggers that allow changes at either the master or target database to be propagated to the other database, but setting up such a system is difficult because of the possibility of creating triggers that call each other recursively. Because it relies on the availability of remote systems, synchronous replication is usually only used if the master and target data must be identical at all times. If the master and target data do not have to be continuously in sync, you should use an asynchronous replication method instead.

In *asynchronous* replication, you refresh the target tables with data from the master tables at predetermined intervals. Between the refreshes, the data in master and target systems are out of sync. When a transaction occurs in the master table, it is not dependent on the availability of the network or the performance of a remote server. Instead, the transaction may be recorded locally, for use during the next refresh of the target system. The only time you need to worry about the network performance is during the refresh processes. Most applications can use asynchronous replication as a means of moving their data between databases; only the most critical and time-sensitive information requires synchronous replication. For example, most data warehousing applications do not record transactional data, but rather load data via batch processes. Since the data is not transactional, there is no need to use synchronous replication; instead, an asynchronous replication method is typically used in data warehousing implementations.

Oracle7 offers many options for asynchronous replication, including snapshots and advanced replication. In the following sections, you will see the administrative issues associated with each option.

Snapshots

A *snapshot* is an asynchronous local copy of data from a master database. The snapshot's data is based on the query used by the snapshot; the snapshot query can be based on queries involving multiple tables. A snapshot is periodically refreshed, either automatically or manually, to reflect the current state of the data it replicates. Snapshots require the Oracle7 procedural option and distributed option at both the master and target databases.

The **create snapshot** command is executed from the target database. As shown in the following listing, the **create snapshot** command specifies the snapshot query, the snapshot refresh timing, and storage parameters (for the table that will hold the query results in the target database). Before the snapshot can be created, you must first create a database link from the target database to the master database. The database link will be used each time the snapshot is populated with data from the master database.

```
create snapshot COMPANY
tablespace SNAP_1
storage (initial 100K next 100K pctincrease 0)
refresh complete
start with SysDate
next SysDate+7
as select * from COMPANY@link_to_master;
```

The COMPANY snapshot is a *simple snapshot* because its query does not perform any grouping functions, and selects from only one table. There is a one-to-one relationship between records in the snapshot and records in the master COMPANY table. If the snapshot's query contained a join or a grouping operation (such as MAX or DISTINCT), the snapshot would be a *complex snapshot*. In a complex snapshot, a single row in the snapshot may be derived from multiple rows in the master table, or from the join of multiple tables.

When the COMPANY snapshot is created, Oracle will create the following objects in the target database:

1. A view named MVIEW$_COMPANY will be created to record the query text of the snapshot. The view will be used each time the snapshot is refreshed. Since COMPANY is a simple snapshot, the RowID pseudo-column from the master COMPANY table will be selected via MVIEW$_COMPANY along with the other columns. The pseudo-column for the RowID is named M_ROW$$.

2. A table named SNAP$_COMPANY will be created, populated via an **insert as select** command using MVIEW$_COMPANY. The table will be created using the storage parameters specified in the **create snapshot** command.

3. Because COMPANY is a simple snapshot, an index will be created on the RowID column (named M_ROW$$ in SNAP$_COMPANY). In Oracle7.0, you cannot specify the storage parameters for this index; as of Oracle7.1, you can use the **using index** clause of the **create snapshot** command to specify the index location and storage parameters. By default, the index will be placed in your default tablespace, using that tablespace's default storage parameters. In Oracle7.0, the name of the index is system-assigned. As of Oracle7.1, the index name contains the name of the snapshot; for this example, the index name will be I_SNAP$_COMPANY.

4. A view named COMPANY is created, selecting all but the M_ROW$$ column from SNAP$_COMPANY. Ordinarily, such a view would be updateable, since it is based on only one table. However, unless you have created the snapshot as an updateable snapshot, Oracle7 creates the COMPANY view using the undocumented (until Oracle7.2) **with read only** clause of the **create view** command. As a result, you will not be able to update records via the COMPANY view of the SNAP$_COMPANY table.

When a user in the target database executes the following query:

```
select *
  from COMPANY
 where State = 'DE';
```

the user is selecting records from the COMPANY view of the local SNAP$_COMPANY table. Therefore, once the snapshot has been created, you should index SNAP$_COMPANY appropriately, based on the columns used in limiting conditions against the snapshot (see Chapter 11). Do not create constraints on the SNAP$_COMPANY table, and avoid creating unique indexes on it as well.

The **refresh**, **start with**, and **next** clauses of the **create snapshot** command tell Oracle how and when to refresh the snapshot. For Oracle to refresh the snapshots automatically, you need to set the appropriate init.ora parameter to a non-zero value ('1' is adequate unless you will be frequently refreshing multiple snapshots simultaneously). In Oracle7.0, the parameter name is SNAPSHOT_REFRESH_PROCESSES. In Oracle7.1 and above, the parameter name is JOB_QUEUE_PROCESSES. The **start with** clause tells Oracle when to first populate the snapshot table, with the next refresh scheduled based on the date calculation specified in the **next** clause. You can also manually refresh the snapshot via the REFRESH procedure of the DBMS_SNAPSHOT package.

The **refresh** clause is used to specify whether a *full refresh* or a *complete refresh* should be performed when refreshing the snapshot. A complete refresh **truncate**s the SNAP$_COMPANY table and issues an **insert as select** command using the MVIEW$_COMPANY view. Complete refreshes can generate very large transactions, and can take very long since all of the SNAP$_COMPANY table's indexes are left in place during the refresh.

In a fast refresh, only the changes to the master table are applied to the snapshot table. Fast refreshes are only available for simple snapshots. To execute a fast refresh, you must have first created a *snapshot log* on the master table (via the **create snapshot log** command). A snapshot log is a combination of a trigger and an audit table. Each time the master table is modified, the trigger inserts the RowID of the changed row into the audit table. When the snapshot that uses the master table is refreshed, the RowIDs from the snapshot log are used to determine which changes need to be applied to the snapshot. Therefore, there is a linkage between the RowIDs in the master table and the M_ROW$$ values in the snapshot's SNAP$_COMPANY table. If something causes the RowIDs in the master table to change (such as an Export/Import of the master table's data), you will need to perform a complete refresh of the snapshot.

The trigger created for the snapshot log is named TLOG$_*master_table_name* (for example, TLOG$_COMPANY). The snapshot log's audit table is named MLOG$_*master_table_name* (for example, MLOG$_COMPANY). The records in MLOG$_COMPANY can be used for the refreshes of multiple simple snapshots against the master COMPANY table; the records will be deleted from

MLOG$_COMPANY when all of the simple snapshots that use COMPANY have been refreshed.

Since only the modified records are sent from the master table to the target snapshots in fast refreshes, fast refreshes greatly reduce the amount of rollback segment space and time required for refreshes. Fast refreshes will complete faster than complete refreshes if less than 30 percent of the master table has been modified. If more than 30 percent of the master table has been modified, complete refreshes will complete faster than fast refreshes (but at a higher cost in terms of rollback segment space and network traffic).

Snapshot Refresh Groups

Snapshots do not have foreign key relationships to other snapshots. Therefore, if you have multiple snapshots in a target database, there is no referential integrity among the snapshots. This can cause data-related problems, since the snapshots may be refreshed at different times and therefore may contain data that would violate referential integrity in the master tables. To avoid potential referential integrity problems among snapshots, you have several options.

First, you could perform the refresh operations at a time when no users are using the master database (such as when it is operating in RESTRICTED mode). The snapshots' data, although refreshed at different times, would be refreshed at the same point in the transactional history of the replicated tables.

Second, you could lock the master tables during the refresh process. Locking the tables would help prevent modifications to the master tables while allowing queries against the tables, guaranteeing that the refreshes occur at the same point in the transactional history of the replicated tables.

As of Oracle7.1, a third option, snapshot refresh groups, is available. You can establish a group of snapshots that should be refreshed via a consistent transaction; regardless of the transaction activity occurring in the master database, the snapshots will all be refreshed as of the same point in the transactional history of the master database. Snapshot refresh groups are created via the MAKE procedure of the DBMS_REFRESH package.

In general, you should use one of the first two methods to maintain referential integrity while refreshing snapshots. Snapshot refresh groups place a heavy burden on your target database. Even if there are no transactions occurring in the master database, refreshing snapshots via a snapshot refresh group will more than double the amount of rollback segment space and time required to perform the refreshes.

Advanced Replication

Oracle's *Advanced Replication Option* is an asynchronous replication method (with a limited synchronous option in Oracle7.3) that allows changes made from multiple copies of a table to be propagated to all other copies of the table. The term "Advanced Replication Option" is new for Oracle7.2 and Oracle7.3; when first introduced with Oracle7.1.6, it was called *Symmetric Replication.* All references to "advanced replication" within this section refer to the components of the Advanced Replication Option, which include multi-master replication and updateable snapshots.

In advanced (multi-master) replication, each copy of the table can update the data. You cannot use advanced replication to replicate part of table; the entire table must be replicated. The replication of data among the multiple "master" copies of the data is performed via a transaction-oriented mechanism. In this mechanism, all row-level changes are captured within the database where the changes occur; the changes are later propagated to other copies of the data in a transaction-consistent fashion. The changes are applied to the remote copies of the tables directly, using remote procedure calls. The site where the data modification occurred drives the scheduling of the data replication. Note that this is a "push" mechanism for moving data from the master table, whereas snapshots are a "pull" mechanism executed from the target database.

In advanced replication, the objects to be replicated are registered in *replication schemas* and are replicated to other sites. Oracle maintains a global catalog of all replicated objects. The database procedures that support replication are generated automatically for the replicated objects. An AFTER ROW trigger is created for each table (for COMPANY, the trigger will be named COMPANY$RT). The COMPANY$RT trigger captures changes and stores them in deferred queues for later propagation.

The queued code generated via the COMPANY$RT trigger is a set of calls to remote procedures in a package generated and stored at all master sites for every table being replicated. This package, COMPANY$RP, contains code to handle incoming changes from other sites. The periodic updates are applied using Oracle's internal job queue, which forwards the transactions from the deferred queues to all other participating sites.

If the same row is updated at two locations simultaneously, a potential conflict can occur during data propagation. The procedures that perform the data propagation call code from COMPANY$RR to detect and resolve conflicts. Some of the standard choices available for conflict resolution include timestamps (earliest or latest record is kept), site priority (records from one database are given precedence over those from other databases), and adding values (values from conflicting records are added to create a new value). Custom conflict resolution routines are also supported. Advanced replication is based on primary keys—updates are applied to the receiving sites based on the primary key values of the rows.

When setting up an advanced replication environment, there are a number of critical administration tasks. First, the names of the replicated tables must be identical at all sites. Second, you must create database links between all participating databases. If you have three databases participating in your advanced replication environment, you will need two database links from each database to each of the others, for a total of six database links.

Each site participating in the advanced replication will have the following objects (assuming the COMPANY table is being replicated). Oracle automatically creates the triggers and packages used for advanced replication.

- The full COMPANY table.

- COMPANY_PK, the primary key constraint and associated index for the COMPANY table. You must define a primary key for the replicated table.

- An AFTER ROW trigger on COMPANY, named COMPANY$RT. The trigger captures changes made to the COMPANY table. It generates calls to procedures from the COMPANY$RP package, and the calls are queued to be propagated to other participating databases.

- A package named COMPANY$RP, containing the code to handle incoming data manipulation commands for the COMPANY table. Changes are applied on a row-by-row basis.

- A package named COMPANY$RR used to support conflict resolution for updates from multiple participating databases.

- A package named REP$WHAT_AM_I that contains standard code to detect within other procedures and triggers whether the code being executed is part of a snapshot refresh, a master-to-master data propagation, or a simple application update. The distinction among execution types is necessary to avoid recursive execution of changes among the master sites.

Advanced replication allows multiple databases to share ownership of the same data. Advanced replication is appropriate for transaction-intensive systems in which the response time for references to application reference tables and business reference tables can have a significant impact on the performance of the application. For example, if you had two separate divisions of a company recording a high number of customer orders, and the two divisions are connected via a wide area network (WAN), you could start by replicating the reference tables to each site via snapshots. The order information, however, may be entered or queried by either division. To avoid requiring one of the divisions to record all of their orders in a remote database (and avoid the network access performance costs associated with the remote access), you could create multiple copies of the orders table via advanced replication. Orders recorded in one database could be scheduled for replication to a second database, so that each database's orders records would be kept almost in sync.

Object Groups

Prior to Oracle7.3, replication was implemented using a replicated schema concept. For example, if the tables belonging to the HOBBES user are to be replicated, the tables must all be registered with a replicated schema named HOBBES. At all replicated sites, the schema name for the tables has to be HOBBES, and all sites have to have the same group of tables replicated. Thus, if the COMPANY table has to be replicated to one site, and the SALES table to a different site, then COMPANY and SALES should be kept under different schemas!

Oracle7.3 eliminates this limitation by introducing the concept of an *object group*. Object groups are named groups of objects that span schemas. Objects must be part of an object group to be replicated; objects cannot belong to more than one object group. As of Oracle7.3, it is no longer necessary to spread tables across multiple schemas in anticipation of having to replicate the tables selectively.

Updateable Snapshots

As of Oracle7.1.6, you can create updateable snapshots. Updateable snapshots use a combination of the "pull" mechanism used by snapshots and the "push" mechanism involved in advanced replication to propagate changes. Conflict detection and resolution are available only in the database that has the master table.

In an updateable snapshot environment, the master database is set up to capture changes to the master table (via snapshot logs) and to receive incoming changes from the snapshots. To receive changes from the snapshots, the master table must have the advanced replication objects used to accept transactions and detect conflicts. If, in addition to being a master site for updateable snapshots, the master also participates in advanced replication with other databases, the master database will have additional components of an advanced replication master site as well as the snapshot master site objects. The master database will have the snapshot log objects (TLOG$_COMPANY trigger and MLOG$_COMPANY table), and all of the advanced replication procedures and triggers.

The snapshot site will contain all the components of a read-only snapshot (see the "Snapshots" section previously in this chapter) to receive changes from the master. In addition, the snapshot's database also has an AFTER ROW trigger (like a master database in an advanced replication environment) to capture and queue changes to the snapshot into the local deferred queue. The snapshot database also has an updateable snapshot log, supported by another trigger, to capture the RowIDs of records changed in the local database. All changes to the snapshot are logged into the updateable snapshot log and put into the deferred queue.

The propagation and refreshes of the snapshot are controlled by the snapshot site. Periodically, the changes in the snapshot's deferred queue are pushed to the master where conflicts are resolved and changes applied to the master. All changes from the master are then pulled by the snapshot site and combined with the information registered in the updateable snapshot log locally. The combined changes are applied to the local snapshot to provide a guaranteed, point-in-time copy of the master at the local site. Changes to the snapshot are based on RowIDs in the master and snapshot tables. Changes from the snapshot are applied to the master using primary keys, just like standard advanced replication.

Updateable snapshots must be simple snapshots on a single table, with all the columns being replicated. The benefit of updateable snapshots over advanced replication is that you can limit the rows that are replicated from the master to the snapshot.

Row-Level and Procedural Replication

In *row-level replication*, any changes applied at the originating site are captured as individual row changes to the table and propagated to other sites. The advanced replication and snapshot techniques described in the previous sections use row-level replication. In addition to row-level replication, Oracle7 also supports procedural-level replication.

In *procedure-level replication*, procedure calls, not rows, are registered for replication across multiple sites. The procedures are copied to every participating site. Any call to the procedure is queued and later sent to the other sites as an identical call with the same parameters and reexecuted at other locations. If a SQL statement updates 1000 rows, row-level replication treats changes to each of the rows as a separate call by the trigger mechanism and applies the changes to other sites as individual row changes. On the other hand, if the procedure that issued the update statement is replicated, it is executed at other sites as *one* call, updating all 1000 rows in one procedure call. Procedure-level replication is very efficient for batch-oriented replication. On the other hand, all conflict detection and resolution must be custom-coded within the procedures. Procedural replication is suited for bulk operations that are run in a serial manner and it must generally not be combined with row-level replication. Row-level replication should be used for replication of data generated via user transactions.

Additional Changes in Oracle7.3

In addition to the object group improvements already described, a number of utilities and general improvements can also be used in Oracle7.3. In the following sections, you will see descriptions of each new replication-related feature not previously described in this chapter.

Comparing Replicated Tables

When operating in a replicated environment, it is a good idea to periodically check whether the various copies of replicated tables are identical. Data of replicated tables could diverge instead of converging to identical values because of either operational errors or unresolved conflicts. Oracle7.3 introduces a new package, DBMS_RECTIFIER_DIFF, to compare replicated tables.

The DBMS_RECTIFIER_DIFF package contains two procedures for use during table comparisons:

- DIFFERENCES to detect the differences between two copies of a replicated table.

- RECTIFY to rectify the two tables using the information generated by the DIFFERENCES procedure.

The DIFFERENCES procedure in DBMS_RECTIFIER_DIFF can be used to compare two copies of a replicated table to determine the differences between the copies. The output of the comparison is stored in two user-defined tables, the first containing the rows that are missing (missing rows data) and the second identifying the site information for the missing rows (missing rows location). The missing rows location data shows which site has the row and which one is missing it.

The RECTIFY procedure uses the output from the DIFFERENCES procedure to apply the missing rows to the proper table and synchronize the two tables.

The table comparison utility can be used to compare either replicated masters at two locations, or a master and a snapshot. The table rectification process need not be applied to the snapshot site, since the snapshot can be refreshed from its master.

Advanced replication environments are usually *quiesced* prior to administrative changes being made. When the system is quiesced, all data is synchronized with the master sites. Once all outstanding transactions in the replication queues are processed, all replication activity stops until the system is manually reactivated.

Although it is not necessary to quiesce the replicated schema during comparison or rectification, active replicated transactions during the process can cause indeterminate results in the table comparison process. Also, the RECTIFY procedure temporarily disables replication at the target site while it performs the necessary updates to avoid unintended propagation of those changes.

When comparing the replicated tables, start by selecting a master reference site for comparisons. Once the master site has been selected, go through the DIFFERENCES/RECTIFY steps with each of its replicas, one pair at a time, to check all of them.

Choice of Synchronous and Asynchronous Advanced Replication Capabilities

Prior to Oracle7.3, the only advanced replication option available was asynchronous—the changes to masters are accumulated in the deferred queues first and then propagated to other sites asynchronously in separate transactions. In Oracle7.3, replicated transactions can now be optionally propagated synchronously between master sites or from a snapshot site to the master. The transaction-oriented master-to-master mechanism can now also be specified to work synchronously so that the transactions are not deferred but applied to the other site in the same **update** transaction.

It is possible to set up a mixed environment where some sites propagate changes synchronously and others propagate them asynchronously. Snapshot sites must get changes from the master asynchronously (the point-in-time snapshot process is by definition asynchronous).

Conflicts do not occur during synchronous propagation since the updates will give error messages and fail if a conflict occurs. Therefore, the application must be designed to avoid conflicts. Mixed configurations of synchronous and asynchronous propagations can cause transactional inconsistencies and must be designed carefully. If the communications links are weak or slow, synchronous propagation significantly affects performance (see the "Asynchronous and Synchronous Replication" section earlier in this chapter). The main advantage from mixing the two replication methods is that the propagation can be designed to be synchronous for critical sites where current data is needed, while other sites could continue to operate asynchronously.

Conflict Notification

Oracle7.3 introduces a concept of *conflict notification routine*. A conflict notification routine does not resolve conflicts, it only detects them and provides a notification. The conflict information can be logged into the database or sent outside the database as electronic mail or other notification. Conflict notification eliminates the need for the DBA to constantly have to check for errors in the replicated environment.

Offline Instantiation

Instantiation is the process of copying the contents of a master to another location, such as while adding new master sites to a replicated environment. During the instantiation process, the entire replicated schema or group must be quiesced! For remote sites (especially over WANs), the instantiation process could take a long time if the tables are large. Even if the underlying table is exported, transferred, and imported at the target site, all sites must wait until the import (or initial refresh) is completed at the remote site. The duration of the instantiation process may be unacceptable for the application using the data. If a table already exists at the target site, Oracle can be instructed to use the table when the site is added as a master site in an advanced replication environment.

In Oracle7.3, a capability has been provided to minimize the wait for instantiation when using the Export/Import utilities. The environment must be quiesced while the master is exported and then the replication transactions can resume on all previous sites with minimal quiescing time. The Export dump file is transferred to the new location, data is imported, and then the new site can participate in the replication activity.

Connection Qualifier

Connection qualifiers allow you to open multiple connections to the same database from within one process. The propagation mechanism in replication is inherently single-threaded between two sites—all changes accumulated at a master site A are pushed to site B serially. Replication now supports connection qualifiers such that multiple database links can be used between sites A and B to propagate changes. The use of multiple connections increases the throughput for large volume replication, if appropriate network and CPU resources are available.

Replication Challenges

Regardless of the replication method used, there are a number of challenges common to replicated environments. The challenges include:

- *Replicating date/time columns* If your replication environment spans time zones, the servers involved may not agree what time it is! If you use a timestamp-based method of conflict resolution, the time differences may cause problems regarding which record should "win" the conflict. You may need to set each server to the same time zone to avoid timestamp-related problems. Choose a common time zone such as GMT (in the date/time columns) to avoid date/time problems.

- *Global sequence numbers* Instead of setting up a global sequence server, partition ranges of values to the servers or use a location identifier as part of the primary keys to avoid conflicting sequence-generated values. If you use ranges of values distributed to the servers, you need to anticipate growth in the number of servers and in the size of the data. A location identifier added to the primary keys could also be used when limiting the rows distributed to a snapshot from a master table.

- *Referential integrity constraints*   Unique indexes and referential integrity constraints between tables can cause unforeseen errors in a replicated environment (see the previous section on snapshot refresh groups). The more tightly enforced referential integrity is in a database, the more challenging it will be to correctly replicate it.

- *Structural changes*   A database that undergoes many structural changes to its tables is not a good candidate for replication. During the replication of DDL changes, the replication environment must be quiesced. Bundle structural changes into sets that can be performed together, with minimal downtime for the system.

- *LONG and LONG RAW*   Columns with LONG and LONG RAW datatypes cannot be replicated.

Multi-Threaded Server

The multi-threaded server (MTS), introduced with Oracle7, allows many client processes to share a small number of server processes. As a result, you can minimize the server's memory and processing resources needed as the number of database connections increases. Without MTS, each client process requires a dedicated server process that remains associated with the user process for the duration of the session. If the session is idle, and MTS is not used, the memory resources dedicated to the session are wasted.

NOTE
MTS requires SQL*Net V2. To use shared servers, a user process must connect via SQL*Net, even if the user is on the same server as the database.

In MTS, many client processes connect to a shared dispatcher process. The dispatcher routes client requests to the next available shared server process. MTS consists of a SQL*Net network listener process that connects client processes to one or more dispatchers and one or more shared server processes.

You configure MTS via a set of init.ora parameters:

- MTS_DISPATCHERS and MTS_MAX_DISPATCHERS define the type of dispatcher connection used, the initial number of dispatchers, and the maximum number of dispatchers. If MTS decides more than the initial number of dispatchers is required, it will add more dispatchers but will not exceed the MTS_MAX_DISPATCHERS setting.

- MTS_SERVERS and MTS_MAX_SERVERS define the initial and maximum number of server processes used. If MTS decides more than the initial number of server processes is required, it will add more server processes but will not exceed the MTS_MAX_SERVERS setting.

- MTS_SERVICE defines the instance being accessed via the MTS.

- MTS_LISTENER_ADDRESS defines the connection information used by SQL*Net V2 for the instance. The listener address syntax is dependent on the network protocol used.

To see if MTS is in use, look for Oracle background processes whose names start with "ora_s0" for the server processes and "ora_d0" for the dispatcher processes.

NOTE
If you use MTS, you will need to greatly increase the amount of space in the shared SQL area. In general, the shared SQL area for an MTS-enabled database should be one-half of the total SGA size.

Delayed-Logging Block Cleanout

When a transaction occurs within a block of records, Oracle writes the "before" image of the block to a rollback segment and the actual changes to the data block. When a **commit** is issued, the rollback entries are not cleaned out. Instead, the transaction is marked as committed, and the rollback segment entry is marked as inactive. The next time a user tries to access that data block, Oracle finds an entry in the rollback segment and tries to generate a read-consistent view.

When inactive data is accessed in the rollback segment, the database assumes that the transaction has been committed and goes back to the data block for the data. In the meantime, the database will also clean out the block from the rollback segment. The process of cleaning the blocks from the rollback segment is known as *block cleanout*. When a block is cleaned out, cleanout redo records are generated and the block is "dirtied."

As of Oracle7.3, when a transaction is committed, all blocks changed by the transaction are cleaned out immediately using a *fast version cleanout*. The fast version cleanout does not generate redo logs and does not reread the block. For Oracle Parallel Server, fast version cleanout does not cause data or index block pings during current reads since the blocks are not dirtied.

A new initialization parameter, DELAYED_LOGGING_BLOCK_CLEANOUTS, is available as of Oracle7.3; its value is TRUE by default. Also introduced in Oracle7.3 is a no-I/O delayed block cleanout, to be done by DBWR when writing dirty (but not yet cleaned-out) blocks to disk. Delayed-logging block cleanout improves system performance, especially when running Oracle Parallel Server.

Scalable Buffer Cache

As of Oracle7.3, you can use a *scalable buffer cache* feature to provide scalable Least Recently Used (LRU) latches in support of large SMP (Symmetric Multi-Processor) machines. LRU latches are required under the following conditions:

- The DBWR background process holds the LRU latch while it is scanning the LRU list for potential candidate blocks to write to disk.

- The DBWR background process holds the LRU latch while returning clean buffers for reuse.

- User processes scan the LRU list for usable buffers.

If the system is under heavy load and many transactions are waiting for LRU latches, a negative impact on performance is observed. In SMP installations, there is typically a large number of users performing transactions. The scalability of the buffer cache could enable you to reduce LRU latch contention in systems with many online users.

A new init.ora parameter, DB_BLOCK_LRU_LATCHES, configures the buffer cache by specifying an advisory upper bound for the desired number of sets of latches. The default value is one-half the number of CPUs on the server. The maximum value is twice the number of CPUs on the server. If the current workload is causing latch waits (as detected by monitoring programs or via the utlbstat.sql/utlestat.sql scripts), you could benefit by increasing the DB_BLOCK_LRU_LATCHES parameter.

New Database Administration Utilities

Two new database administration utilities are available with Oracle7.3. In the following sections, you will see brief descriptions of each: TRACE for performance data collection and DB_VERIFY to validate datafiles.

TRACE

Oracle Trace (TRACE) is a flexible, powerful tool for performance data collection for the Oracle database and SQL*Net. Server-side support is provided in Oracle7.3.

In TRACE, event-based collectors gather statistics on the resources used by specific events in an application. Events can be of two types: duration events (such as transactions), and point-specific events, such as database connections. Events are classified into predefined categories (including monitoring, performance, capacity planning, and debugging) or user-defined categories. Data items are collected for each event occurrence.

To use TRACE, you need to set ORACLE_TRACE_ENABLE to TRUE in your database's init.ora file. Other init.ora parameters used by TRACE include:

- ORACLE_TRACE_COLLECTION_NAME—the collection name.

- ORACLE_TRACE_COLLECTION_PATH—the pathname for the directory used by TRACE for collection definitions and log files.

- ORACLE_TRACE_COLLECTION_SIZE—the maximum size, in bytes, of the collection data files. Once the maximum size is reached, the collection is aborted.

A GUI tool for TRACE is available as part of the Enterprise Manager tool.

DB_VERIFY

DB_VERIFY is an external utility (like Export/Import or SQL*Loader) that performs physical datafile structure integrity checks. DB_VERIFY can be used against offline or online, complete or partial datafiles. You can use DB_VERIFY as part of your backup process and to validate the datafiles restored during a recovery process. You can also use DB_VERIFY as a diagnostic tool to troubleshoot data corruption problems.

The name and location of the DB_VERIFY utility depends on the operating system. On Unix systems, the name is **dbv**. To get help on this utility, type the command shown in the following listing.

```
dbv help=y
```

Sample output from the preceding command is shown in the following listing.

```
DBVERIFY: Release 7.3.2.1.0 - Production

Copyright (c) Oracle Corporation 1979, 1994.  All rights reserved.

Keyword    Description         (Default)
-----------------------------------------------
FILE       File to Verify      (NONE)
START      Start Block         (First Block of File)
END        End Block           (Last Block of File)
```

```
BLOCKSIZE Logical Block Size (2048)
LOGFILE   Output Log         (NONE)
FEEDBACK  Display Progress   (0)
```

The FILE parameter is used to specify the name of the file to be verified. The default starting point for the verification is the first Oracle block in the file; you can set a different starting point via the START parameter. By default, the entire file will be verified; you can set a different ending point via the END parameter.

If the database block size is not 2KB, you must specify the block size (in bytes) via the BLOCKSIZE parameter. The output of the verification process is displayed to the terminal screen, or, if LOGFILE is specified, to an output file. If the FEEDBACK parameter is set to 0, no progress information is displayed. If FEEDBACK is non-zero, Oracle displays (on the terminal only) a period ('.') for every *n* pages verified.

The following example shows a verification of the datafile users01.dbf using a parameter file verify.par to provide the parameter settings. The contents of verify.par are shown in the following listing.

```
file=users01.dbf
blocksize=8192
logfile=indy
feedback=1000
```

The output is written to a file named indy.txt. The contents of indy.txt are shown in the following listing.

```
DBVERIFY: Release 7.3.2.1.0 - Production

Copyright (c) Oracle Corporation 1979, 1994.  All rights reserved.

DBVERIFY - Verification starting : FILE = users01.dbf

DBVERIFY - Verification complete

Total Pages Examined          : 5120
Total Pages Processed (Data)  : 4362
Total Pages Failing   (Data)  : 0
Total Pages Processed (Index) : 256
Total Pages Failing   (Index) : 0
Total Pages Empty             : 482
Total Pages Marked Corrupt    : 0
Total Pages Influx            : 0
```

The verification output shows that there are no corrupt or failing sections of the datafile.

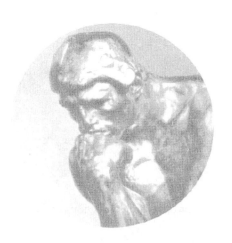

PART 5

The Oracle DBA Certification Exam

CHAPTER 14

Oracle7 DBA Certification Exam Candidate Bulletin of Information

The Chauncey Group International Ltd. (Chauncey) and Educational Testing Service would like to acknowledge the professional contributions of the International Oracle Users Group–Americas and the Oracle Corporation during the research and development phase of this program.

417

We would also like to express our gratitude to the following individuals for their time and professional commitment in order to provide their Database Administrator (DBA) colleagues with a meaningful program that will recognize highly skilled individuals in the DBA profession.

Michael Abbey, Database Consultant, MASC
Michael Ault, Senior Database Administrator, Marion Merrell Dow
Paul Collins, Database Administrator, Datastorm, Inc.
Daniel Dechichio, Database Administrator, First National Bank of Boston
Mark W. Farnham, President, Rightsizing, Inc.
Angela Foster, Database Administrator, Eastman Kodak
Michael Gangler, Database Administrator, MIACO, Inc.
Mark Gokman, Lead Database Administrator, New York Power Authority
John Hunt, Astra Merck
James Hussy
David Kreines, Database Consultant, The Ultimate Software Consultants
Brian Laskey, Database Administrator, Parke-Davis Pharmaceutical
Kevin Loney, Database Administrator, Astra Merck
Scott Nelson, Database Administrator Consultant, Results Through Technology, Inc.
Rich Niemic, The Ultimate Software Consultants
Tim Olesen, University of California, Davis
Scott A. Shelton, Database Administrator, American Bankers Association
Nadji Sid, Database Administrator/Trainer, Oracle Corporation
William Smith, Database Administrator, Oracle Corporation

Contacting the Oracle7 Database Administrator Examination Program Staff

If you have questions or comments about The Oracle7 Database Administrator Examination, the CBT Center facilities and/or supervision, test content, or any other matter related to the testing program, you should complete the exit evaluation questionnaire on the computer at the test center or write to **The Chauncey Group International** at the following address:

Oracle7 DBA Examination
The Chauncey Group International
PO Box 6541
Princeton, NJ 08541

Program staff may be reached at 1-800-258-4914 or by fax at 1-609-951-6767. Our e-mail address is **dbatest@cgi.com**. **All correspondence must include your name and address**. If the questions or comments concern a test already taken, the correspondence should include the name of the test, the date of the test, the location of the CBT Center, and your Social Security number. Chauncey will investigate each complaint and reply to comments within a reasonable period of time. Inquiries about scores and procedures for reexamination should also be directed to the address above.

The Oracle7 Database Administrator Examination

The Oracle7 Database Administrator (DBA) Examination measures an individual's mastery of the knowledge, skills, and abilities necessary to perform proficiently the job of Oracle7 DBA. The examination was developed in cooperation with the International Oracle Users Group–Americas and the Oracle Corporation and is based on a significant body of research to define the characteristics of the job of an Oracle DBA. A committee of expert DBAs, specifically chosen for their high level of knowledge and experience, was assembled to develop the actual examination questions and to validate the examination content. This examination is available to all Oracle DBAs.

A Word about The Chauncey Group International

The Chauncey Group International Ltd. (Chauncey) is a wholly-owned subsidiary of Educational Testing Service (ETS). Chauncey is a global company established to assist individuals and organizations with career advancement and certification of skills and achievement.

Through innovative programs, strategic alliances, and aggressive deployment of technical solutions, we will offer consulting, assessment, diagnostic information and training, recordkeeping, and database services for the convenience of the customers.

In serving our clients, we draw upon our dedicated staff, our vast experience and demonstrated expertise in psychometrics and research, our unique relationship with ETS, our expertise in computer-based testing, and our relationship with Sylvan [Sylvan Prometric Centers, administrators of the Oracle7 DBA Certification Exam].

The Certified Oracle DBA designation will document the attainment of this level of competence. It will be useful to candidates in assessing their qualifications and abilities, and to employers in making hiring decisions and evaluating the applicable technical skills of existing staff for diverse purposes.

Oracle DBA Job Analysis

The first step in the development of the Oracle DBA Examination was to conduct a job analysis to define the tasks and knowledge that are important for the professional position of Oracle DBA. The study took a multimethod approach to identify a content domain related to the performance requirements of an Oracle DBA. The study included meetings with Oracle DBA experts, telephone interviews with DBA professionals, and the posting of a final survey of the Oracle job-task domain to the general population of Oracle DBAs. The results from the job analysis were used to determine test specifications for the examination.

About the Examination

The Oracle7 DBA Examination consists of 60 computer-delivered, multiple-choice or free-response questions in a variety of formats. Candidates are asked to choose the best answer for each question. Each question is scored separately and only correct responses will contribute to a candidate's final score. Although no candidate is expected to obtain a perfect score, candidates are expected to have a high degree of familiarity with Oracle7. Oracle7 DBA Examination candidates will be given 1 hour and 45 minutes to complete the examination and a brief biographical questionnaire. An additional 15 minutes is allotted for a pretest tutorial and exit evaluation. Fifteen minutes will be added to appointments in certain countries that have been identified as non-English speaking countries.

Test Development

The Oracle7 DBA Examination was developed with the assistance of several committees of Oracle DBAs who were specifically chosen for their knowledge of the Oracle7 DBA position. Also participating were hundreds of DBA volunteers, who helped define the test content, the relative emphases, and the professional knowledge to be covered by the examination.

The Oracle7 DBA Examination offers multiple-choice questions in which a candidate selects one of several displayed choices. It also features scenario questions in which a candidate is provided with a variety of online exhibits as part of the testing process. There are also questions in which a candidate is asked to identify incorrect information in a command or process. All of the questions are designed to measure knowledge of Oracle7, breadth of preparation, and both analytical and problem-solving skills.

Test Dates

The Oracle7 DBA Examination is available year-round at participating Sylvan Prometric Centers. When registering, ask the Sylvan Prometric operator to advise you of the closest test center and the center's available hours.

Fees

The examination fee is $195. This fee applies to first-time test takers and to retesters.

NOTE
International test fees may vary. Candidates will be provided with the appropriate fee during registration.

Test Preparation

The examination consists of computer-delivered multiple-choice and exhibit-based scenario questions. With either question type, sound preparation in Oracle7 is the key to successful performance on the examination. Such preparation includes effective long-term study and use of Oracle that allows the development of knowledge, skills, and abilities related to the test content. An understanding of the examination—the test content, the types of questions, and the responses called for—is also important. Sound preparation in Oracle7 and an understanding of the examination will enhance your confidence in your ability to demonstrate your knowledge and skills.

To be well prepared for the Oracle DBA Examination, you should know the following:

- Testing requirements—read the Registration Bulletin for registration procedures.

- Subject matter to be tested—use this descriptive material to provide a study framework of material to review, and familiarize yourself with the question types and their explanations.

- Test format—know how much time is allotted for the test. Be familiar with the total number of questions and the types of questions included in the test.

Test-Taking Strategies

The following strategies may be of help to you when taking this test:

- UNDERSTAND the tutorial. The tutorial is provided to help you navigate throughout the test. The tutorial will explain to you how to access the many exhibit documents you will need to answer the test questions.

- READ the directions and all of the test questions carefully, including all the response options.

- PACE your activities. Know the total number of test questions and the amount of time allotted for the test. Allow time to read each question, to respond, and to review your answers. Work rapidly without being careless. Answer all questions that seem easy before you spend time on those that seem difficult. You earn as much credit for correctly answering easy questions as you do for correctly answering hard ones. You can put a mark next to questions you wish to come back to. At the end of the test, you will be presented with a screen that summarizes how many questions you have answered, as well as how many and which questions need to be answered. By utilizing the test review screen you can return to any question.

- GUESS. If you are uncertain about the correct answer, eliminate as many of the response options as possible and then guess. Your test score is based on the number of questions that you answer correctly. Incorrect answers will not be counted against you. Therefore, if you are uncertain about the answer to a question, you should guess at the answer rather than not respond at all. You risk nothing by guessing. If you do not respond, you lose the chance to raise your score by making an educated guess.

- REVIEW your responses. If you finish the examination before time is called, review the questions, particularly those about which you may have been uncertain.

Test Content

There are seven major content areas covered in the examination. The major emphasis is placed on the comprehension and application of concepts, principles, and practices rather than on the recall of isolated facts. There are, however, some questions based on knowledge of specific terms, tools, and techniques.

The content areas and a representative description of topics covered in each category are provided below.

I. Oracle Architecture and Options (11-13%)

- Demonstrate an understanding of memory structures and processes that make up an Oracle instance.
- Demonstrate an understanding of the logical and physical structures associated with an Oracle database.
- Demonstrate an understanding of PL/SQL constructs (triggers, functions, packages, procedures) and their processing.
- Demonstrate an understanding of distributed architecture and client server.
- Demonstrate an understanding of locking mechanisms.

II. Security (13-15%)

- Create, alter, and drop database users.
- Monitor and audit database access.
- Develop and implement a strategy for managing security (roles, privileges, authentication).
- Demonstrate an understanding of the implications of distributed processing on the security model.

III. Data Administration (11-13%)

- Manage integrity constraints.
- Implement the physical database from the logical design.
- Evaluate the implications of using stored procedures and constraints to implement business rules.

IV. Backup and Recovery (16-18%)

- Understand backup options.
- Develop backup and recovery strategies.
- Manage the implementation of backup procedures.
- Recover a database.

V. Software Maintenance and Operation (13-15%)

- Configure and manage SQL*Net.
- Install and upgrade Oracle and supporting products.
- Configure the Oracle instance using the initialization parameters.
- Distinguish among startup and shutdown options.
- Create a database.
- Demonstrate an understanding of the capabilities of underlying operating systems as they relate to the Oracle database.

VI. Resource Management (13-15%)

- Create and manage indexes.
- Evaluate the use of clusters and hash clusters.
- Allocate and manage physical storage structures (e.g., data files, redo logs, control files).
- Allocate and manage logical storage structures (e.g., tablespaces, schemas, extents).
- Control system resource usage by defining proper profiles.
- Perform capacity planning.

VII. Tuning and Troubleshooting (13-15%)

- Diagnose and resolve locking conflicts.
- Use data dictionary tables and views.
- Monitor the instance.
- Collect and analyze relevant database performance information.

- Identify and implement appropriate solutions for database performance problems.
- Use vendor support services when necessary.
- Solve SQL*Net problems.

Registration–Scheduling Your Computer-Based Assessment (U.S. and Canada)

1. Contact the Sylvan Prometric main registration number at 1-800-967-1100.

2. The CBT Center staff will ask you to supply your name and telephone number. You will be asked to give your preference for date and time of testing at a CBT Center. They can also advise you as to the center nearest to you.

3. If your first-choice date or time is unavailable, you will be offered an alternative as close to your first choice as possible.

4. Make note of when and where you have been scheduled for the examination. No confirmation of your appointment will be sent to you. Be sure to ask for directions to the CBT Center if you need them.

5. There are no specified testing dates. Testing will be available at any time throughout the year.

6. Plan for your testing session to last two hours.

7. You may use MasterCard, Visa, or American Express to pay the test fee. Information on method of payment is to be supplied to the CBT Center staff when you register for your appointment. You may also register in person at the CBT Center of your choice. The examination fee may be paid by credit card only. Your credit card statement will serve as a receipt.

Note: Americans with Disabilities Act

Candidates seeking special testing arrangements under the Americans with Disabilities Act of 1990 must call the Oracle7 DBA Examination program staff at Chauncey **prior to registering** for the exam. Formal written requests and documentation may be required. Documentation should be in the form of a letter on official letterhead of a licensed or certified professional qualified to evaluate the disability. A description of the special accommodation(s) requested should be included. Chauncey staff will assist in the registration process. There is no extra charge to the candidate for making these special arrangements.

Changing or Canceling Your Oracle7 DBA Appointment

If you need to reschedule or cancel your appointment, you must do so by noon of the second business day before the appointment. Call the Sylvan toll-free number 1-800-967-1100. **If you fail to arrive for your appointment without giving at least two business days' notice, you will forfeit ALL of your test fee.**

A candidate who needs to reschedule an examination appointment because of a medical emergency may mail a written request and official documentation to the Oracle7 DBA Certification Administrator. Requests must be made within the two-week period following the scheduled exam date.

Refunds

No cash refunds will be granted.

Inclement Weather

If a test administration is canceled due to weather conditions, the CBT centers will, whenever possible, announce the cancellation on local radio stations. If cancellation is necessary, you will be rescheduled without penalty for another appointment.

Retake Policy

Candidates must wait 30 days after their **first** test date to retest. Candidates must wait **270 days between subsequent attempts**. Candidates will be permitted to take the examination a total of four (4) times only. Chauncey encourages candidates who do not pass to use the time before they retest to review the content areas in which they received low diagnostic ratings.

Attempt	Waiting Period
#2	30 days from attempt 1
#3	270 days from attempt 2
#4	270 days from attempt 3

Identification Requirements

You should always use the same form of your name. Do not change the spelling and do not change the order of your names.

Use the same name when you register for your CBT appointment and if you need to contact Chauncey for assistance.

When you arrive at the test center, you will be required to present two forms of identification. **You will not be admitted to the examination without the proper identification**. Both pieces of identification must be signed and one must bear a recent photograph of you.

Examples of acceptable forms of *primary identification* (must include your signature and photograph) are

- current driver's license
- employee identification card
- state identification card
- current (valid) passport

Examples of acceptable forms of *secondary identification* (must include your signature) are:

- valid credit cards
- bank automated teller
- machine cards
- check cashing cards

On the Day of the Examination

The following activities will occur when you arrive at the CBT Center for your Oracle DBA Examination appointment:

1. Plan to arrive at the CBT Center at least 30 minutes (domestic) or 15 minutes (international) before your scheduled testing appointment. If you arrive 30 minutes after your scheduled appointment, you may be required to forfeit your appointment. If you forfeit your appointment, you will be required to register again and pay an additional test fee.

2. Waiting areas at the CBT Centers are small. Friends or relatives who accompany you to the test center will not be permitted to wait in the test center or contact you while you are taking the examination.

3. You must present your photo-bearing identification that includes your signature and your second form of identification that includes your signature.

4. You will be asked to sign in at the center. Your signature will be compared to those on your identification documents.

5. You will be required to leave your personal belongings outside the testing room. Secure storage will be provided. However, keep the two forms of identification with you at all times. If you leave the testing room for any reason, you will be required to show the test administrator your identification to be readmitted to the room. Storage space is small, so candidates should plan appropriately. CBT Centers assume no responsibility for candidates' personal belongings.

6. The test center administrator will give you a short orientation and will then escort you to a computer terminal. You must remain in your seat during the examination, except when authorized to leave by a test center staff member.

7. Raise your hand to notify the test center administrator if you

- believe you have a problem with your computer,

- need to take a break,

- need assistance for any reason.

8. You will have up to 1 hour and 45 minutes to complete the Oracle7 DBA examination and demographic questions. An additional 15 minutes will be provided for a short tutorial at the beginning of the examination and an exit evaluation questionnaire. An additional 15 minutes will be added to appointments in certain countries that have been identified as non-English speaking countries. There will be no scheduled breaks.

9. The clock will continue to run and will not be turned off for unplanned, unscheduled breaks.

10. If there is a power outage, the test will resume at the point where it left off.

11. After your examination is finished, you will see an unofficial examination performance report. You will be asked to complete a brief computer-delivered questionnaire about your testing experience.

12. When you have finished with the questionnaire the test administrator will dismiss you.

Please Note: On rare occasions, technical problems due to power outages, transmission problems, etc., may require rescheduling of a candidate's examination.

Test Center Regulations

To ensure that all candidates' results are earned under comparable conditions and represent fair and accurate measurement, it is necessary to maintain a standardized testing environment. The following regulations are strictly enforced:

- No papers, books, food, or purses are allowed in the testing room.
- No eating, drinking, or use of tobacco are allowed in the testing room.

Additional Security Measures

Security of the test and the testing environment is important for maintaining the validity of the Oracle7 DBA Examination program. Candidates will be observed at all times while taking the examination. This observation will include direct observation by test center staff as well as video and audio monitoring of the examination session.

Grounds for Dismissal

The test scores of a candidate who engages in misconduct will be canceled. A candidate who does not heed an administrator's warning to discontinue behavior which is possibly misconduct behavior may be dismissed from the test center. Chauncey, in its sole discretion, may choose to cancel the test scores of candidates if it has substantial evidence that misconduct has occurred. All of the following behaviors are considered to be misconduct:

- Giving or receiving assistance of any kind
- Using any unauthorized aids
- Attempting to take the examination for someone else, or having the examination taken for you
- Failing to follow test regulations or the instructions of the test administrator
- Creating a disturbance of any kind
- Removing or attempting to remove test questions and/or responses (in any format) or notes about the examination from the testing room
- Tampering with the operation of the computer or attempting to use it for any function other than taking the examination

Name Registry

Prior to the start of each test session, you will be asked whether or not you would like your name and address released in our certification registry. Only individuals who indicate "yes" to this question and successfully pass the examination will be entered into the registry database.

Chauncey program staff will maintain and regularly update the registry. Access to the registry will be limited to corporations and employers seeking DBA job candidates and to industry groups interested in the advancement of Oracle DBA skills, use, and education.

Reporting Test Results and Passing Scores

Candidates will be notified of their pass/fail status at the test center immediately after testing. Official confirmation of these results will be mailed from Chauncey approximately ten working days after the administration for domestic candidates and within a four- to six-week period for international candidates.

Candidates who pass the examination will receive a "pass" indication along with their certification. Passing candidates **will not** receive their individual scores.

Domestic candidates who do not pass the examination will be mailed their final score and diagnostic information based on the content categories while international candidates will receive this information at the test center immediately after testing.

Candidates will be able to determine their areas of relative strength and weakness based on the content categories and design their study accordingly prior to retaking the test.

Final Scores

Final scores on the examination will be determined by converting the number of questions answered correctly to a scale that ranges from 300 to 1000. The minimum passing score that corresponds to the level of achievement judged to represent minimum competency is 740. Test forms are equated, which will make it possible to compare candidates' final scores across different forms of the Oracle7 DBA Examination. The equating process makes appropriate adjustments so that equivalent final scores on forms with different difficulty levels are made comparable. This means that candidates will not be penalized or advantaged if the test form they take is harder or easier than a form given to other candidates.

Score Reliability

Reliability refers to the precision with which something is measured. If you were to measure the length of a room with a yardstick and repeat the measurement the next day with the same yardstick, you might expect the two measurements to be very close. Two close measurements would mean the yardstick has high reliability. If you could know the "true length" of the room, you might also expect the two measurements to be extremely close to the room's true length (within a very small margin of error).

The reliability of test score functions is based on the same principle: reliability is the degree to which test scores reflect the "true abilities" of the candidates. Although the true abilities, or true scores, of individual candidates can never be known, the average errors of measurement can be calculated, statistically, based on the distribution of the observed test scores.

For an individual, some slight variation in two or more test scores can be due to a number of factors. Individuals may perform differently on two or more occasions based on how well they feel, how motivated they are, how familiar they are with the particular test questions administered, or how lucky they are at guessing. There could also be environmental conditions that impact an individual's performance.

Another type of reliability for the Oracle7 DBA Examination is the reliability of the pass/fail decisions. Although the classification of a candidate as passing or failing is done with extremely high consistency, it is impossible to perfectly classify candidates, given the measurement error that comes into play. So, a very small percentage of "true passers" will fail the test and "true failers" will pass the test. Therefore, even if you fail the test the first time, you have a chance of passing a retest.

Determination of Passing Scores

To ensure a consistent standard of competence of Certified Oracle7 DBAs, the Examination will use a criterion-referenced passing standard. This ensures that passing or failing will depend solely on a candidate's level of performance in relation to the established point that represents competence. There is no fixed percentage of candidates who pass or fail the test. To set the passing standard, a panel of qualified judges convened following the beta test. The Angoff method was employed and a systematic cut-score study was conducted.

The Angoff method is based on the idea that qualified candidates should pass, unqualified candidates should fail, and borderline candidates should score right at the pass/fail cutpoint. This distinction between qualified and unqualified candidates was provided by the panel of judges. For each test form, the judges considered each question and estimated the probability that a borderline candidate would answer that particular question correctly. The average probabilities across all items are summed to determine the expected number of total correct answers for the borderline candidate. This expected number of total correct answers is the choice for the passing score.

FAQs

Q. HELP! I need to speak to someone about the exam. Whom do I call?
A. **Program Assistance**—for questions regarding test background or development, scoring, examination regulations, results, certifications, or name and/or address updates, call 1-800-258-4914.

Registration Assistance—to register for testing, to change or cancel an appointment, or for test center locations, call 1-800-967-1100.

Q. I called the test center in my local phone book and they were unable to register me. What should I do?
A. When registering, call the MAIN registration number, not your local center. The toll-free number is 1-800-967-1100.

Q. I am an ADA candidate. Whom do I call to make special arrangements for testing?
A. Call Oracle7 DBA program staff at 1-609-951-6149.

Q. When is the test available and where?
A. The test is delivered at Sylvan Prometric test centers. It is available anytime throughout the year during regular center hours. Some centers have Saturday testing available. When you call 1-800-967-1100 to register, the operator will tell you the closest available center that can meet your needs.

Q. When will I get my results?
A. Pass/Fail results will be presented at the center. Official results will be mailed in approximately ten business days.

List of Computer-Based Testing Centers

Below is a list of test centers where the Oracle7 DBA Examination will be available. New sites may be available that are not listed here. Ask the CBT Registration Staff for the testing center closest to you. **When registering, please call the CBT registration hot line at 1-800-967-1100.**

ALASKA
Anchorage

ALABAMA
Birmingham
Decatur
Mobile
Montgomery

ARKANSAS
Ft. Smith
Little Rock

AMERICAN SAMOA
Pago Pago

ARIZONA
Chandler
Phoenix
Tucson

CALIFORNIA
Anaheim Hills
Brea
Burlingame
Diamond Bar
Fair Oaks
Fresno
Garden Grove
Irvine
La Jolla
Oakland
Rancho Cucamonga
Redlands
Riverside
San Francisco
San Jose
Santa Monica
Santa Rosa
Torrance
Walnut Creek
Westlake

CANADA
Calgary
Cambridge
Delta, BC
Edmonton
Etobicoke
Kelowna, BC
Montreal
Ottawa
Whitby
Winnipeg, Manitoba

COLORADO
Boulder
Colorado Springs
Littleton
Pueblo

CONNECTICUT
Glastonbury
Hamden

DELAWARE
Dover

**DISTRICT OF
COLUMBIA**
Washington

FLORIDA
Davie
Gainesville
Jacksonville
Miami Lakes
Ormond Beach
Sarasota
Tallahassee
Temple Terrace
Wellington
Winter Park

GEORGIA
Augusta
Columbus
Jonesboro
Macon
Savannah
Smyrna

GUAM
Agana

HAWAII
Kailua
Wailuku

IDAHO
Boise

ILLINOIS
Bloomington
Carbondale
Carpentersville
Chicago
Homewood
Northbrook
Peoria
Springfield
Westchester

INDIANA
Evansville
Ft. Wayne
Indianapolis
Lafayette
Merrillville
Mishawaka

IOWA
Bettendorf
Cedar Rapids
Des Moines

KANSAS
Topeka
Wichita

KENTUCKY
Lexington
Louisville

LOUISIANA
Baton Rouge
Bossier City
New Orleans

MAINE
Portland

MARYLAND
Bethesda
Columbia
Frederick
Pikesville

MASSACHUSETTS
Boston
Springfield
Woburn
Worcester

MICHIGAN
Ann Arbor
Grand Rapids
Lansing
Livonia
Troy
Utica

MISSISSIPPI
Jackson

MINNESOTA
Bloomington
Duluth
Maplewood

MISSOURI
Ballwin
Creve Coeur
Gladstone
Springfield

MONTANA
Billings
Helena

NEBRASKA
Lincoln
Omaha

NEVADA
Las Vegas
Reno

NEW HAMPSHIRE
Concord

NEW JERSEY
East Brunswick
Hamilton
Toms River
Verona

NEW MEXICO
Albuquerque

NEW YORK
Albany
Fayetteville
Forest Hills-Queens
Garden City
Manhattan
Rochester
Staten Island
Tonawanda
Vestal
Wappingers Falls

NORTH CAROLINA
Asheville
Charlotte
Greensboro
Greenville
Raleigh

NORTH DAKOTA
Bismarck

N. MARIANAS
Saipan

OHIO
Akron
Cincinnati (2)
Columbus
Dayton
Mentor
Niles
Reynoldsburg
Solon
Strongsville
Toledo

OKLAHOMA
Oklahoma City
Tulsa

OREGON
Eugene
Portland

PENNSYLVANIA
Allentown
Erie
Harrisburg
North Wales
Philadelphia
Pittsburgh (2)
Scranton

PUERTO RICO
Hato Rey

RHODE ISLAND
Cranston

SOUTH CAROLINA
Charleston
Greenville
Irmo

SOUTH DAKOTA
Sioux Falls

TENNESSEE
Chattanooga
Knoxville
Madison
Memphis

TEXAS
Amarillo
Arlington

Austin
Beaumont
Corpus Christi
El Paso
Ft. Worth
Houston (2)
Longview
Lubbock
Mesquite
Midland
San Antonio
Waco

UTAH
Provo
Salt Lake City

VERMONT
Williston

VIRGINIA
Arlington
Newport News

Richmond
Roanoke

VIRGIN ISLANDS
St. Croix
St. Thomas

WASHINGTON
Everett
Lynwood
Puyallup
Spokane

WEST VIRGINIA
South Charleston
Morgantown

WISCONSIN
Brookfield
Madison

WYOMING
Casper

Registration–International

The registration process varies by country. To register for the Oracle7 DBA Examination, you will need to contact either the Sylvan Prometric Regional Service Center or your local test center. Again, who you contact depends on the country in which you are testing. The following table will assist you.

Step 1 Locate in Column 1 the country where you plan to take the exam.

Step 2 Go to the corresponding number in Column 2 for the country you have chosen and locate the telephone number for the Regional Service Center that serves that country. NOTE: This number and location is for registration purposes only. You will be able to test in the country you chose in Column 1. The regional service center will assist you by either registering you or providing you with information on where to register.

Column 1	Column 2
Country	**Service Center/Phone**
Argentina	Sylvan Minneapolis/Latin America 1-612-820-5200
Australia	Sylvan Sydney/from Australia toll-free 1-800-806-944
Austria	Sylvan Düsseldorf/from Austria toll-free 0660-8582
Bahrain	Sylvan London/44-181-607-9090
Belgium	Sylvan Düsseldorf/from Belgium toll-free 0800-1-7414
Bermuda	Sylvan Minneapolis/Latin America 1-612-820-5200
Botswana	Sylvan London/44-181-607-9090
Brazil	Sylvan Minneapolis/Latin America 1-612-820-5200
Chile	Sylvan Minneapolis/Latin America 1-612-820-5200
China	Sylvan Sydney/from China toll-free 10800-3538
Columbia	Sylvan Minneapolis/Latin America 1-612-820-5200
Croatia	Sylvan Düsseldorf/492159-9233-50
Curacao	Sylvan Minneapolis/Latin America 1-612-820-5200
Czech Republic	Sylvan Düsseldorf/492159-9233-50
Denmark	Sylvan London/44-181-607-9090
Ecuador	Sylvan Minneapolis/Latin America 1-612-820-5200
Egypt	Sylvan London/44-181-607-9090
Fiji	Sylvan Sydney/61-2-414-3666
Finland	Sylvan London/44-181-607-9090
France & DOM-TOM (French Islands, Martinique and Guadeloupe)	Sylvan Paris/33-1-4289-3122
Germany	Sylvan Düsseldorf/from Germany toll-free 0130-83-97-08
Greece	Sylvan London/44-181-607-9090
Hong Kong	Sylvan Sydney/from Hong Kong toll-free 800-8444
Hungary	Sylvan Düsseldorf/492159-9233-50
India	Sylvan Sydney/61-2-414-3666
Indonesia	Sylvan Sydney/from Indonesia toll-free 011-800-612-401
Ireland	Sylvan London/from Ireland toll-free 1-800-626-104
Israel	Sylvan London/44-181-607-9090

Column 1	Column 2
Country	**Service Center/Phone**
Italy	Sylvan Düsseldorf/from Italy toll-free 1-6787-8441
Ivory Coast	Sylvan Paris/33-1-4289-3122
Jamaica	Sylvan Minneapolis/Latin America 1-612-820-5200
Japan	Sylvan Tokyo/0120-387737
Kenya	Sylvan London/44-181-607-9090
Kuwait	Sylvan London/44-181-607-9090
Latvia	Sylvan Düsseldorf/492159-9233-50
Luxembourg	Sylvan Düsseldorf/492159-9233-50
Malaysia	Sylvan Sydney/from Malaysia toll-free 800-0508
Mexico	Sylvan Minneapolis/Latin America 1-612-820-5200
Morocco	Sylvan Paris/33-1-4289-3122
Netherlands	Sylvan Düsseldorf/from the Netherlands toll-free 06-022-7584
Netherlands Antilles	Sylvan Minneapolis/Latin America 1-612-820-5200
New Zealand	Sylvan Sydney/from New Zealand toll-free 080-044-1689
Norway	Sylvan London/44-181-607-9090
Oman	Sylvan London/44-181-607-9090
Pakistan	Sylvan Sydney/61-2-414-3666
Peru	Sylvan Minneapolis/Latin America 1-612-820-5200
Philippines	Sylvan Sydney/from the Philippines toll-free 102-718-0061-02161
Poland	Sylvan Düsseldorf/492159-9233-50
Portugal	Sylvan Paris/33-1-4289-3122
Romania	Sylvan Düsseldorf/492159-9233-50
Russia	Sylvan Düsseldorf/492159-9233-50
Saudi Arabia	Sylvan London/44-181-607-9090
Singapore	Sylvan Sydney/from Singapore toll-free 800-6161-132
Slovakia	Sylvan Düsseldorf/492159-9233-50
Slovenia	Sylvan Düsseldorf/492159-9233-50
South Africa	Sylvan London/44-181-607-9090
South Korea	Sylvan Sydney/from South Korea toll-free 007-8611-3095

Column 1	Column 2
Country	**Service Center/Phone**
Spain	Sylvan Paris/33-1-4289-3122
Sweden	Sylvan London/44-181-607-9090
Switzerland	Sylvan Düsseldorf/from Switzerland toll-free 155-6966
Taiwan	Sylvan Sydney/from Taiwan toll-free 008-061-1141
Thailand	Sylvan Sydney/from Thailand toll-free 011-800-611-2401
Trinidad	Sylvan Minneapolis/Latin America 1-612-820-5200
Turkey	Sylvan London/44-181-607-9090
Ukraine	Sylvan Düsseldorf/492159-9233-50
United Arab Emirates	Sylvan London/44-181-607-9090
United Kingdom	Sylvan London/from the UK toll-free 08-00-592-873
Uruguay	Sylvan Minneapolis/Latin America 1-612-820-5200
Venezuela	Sylvan Minneapolis/Latin America 1-612-820-5200
Zimbabwe	Sylvan London/44-181-607-9090

Step 3   Call the Regional Service Center and inform the customer service representative that you are interested in taking the Oracle7 Database Administrator Examination. You should be prepared to give the following information.

- Name
- Sylvan Prometric Identification Number—a Sylvan Prometric ID Number will be assigned if the candidate has not tested with Sylvan previously
- Phone Number (Home and Work)
- Mailing Address
- Billing Address (if needed)
- Exam Number: 9P0-001
- Exam Name: Oracle7 Database Administrator Examination
- Method of Payment
  1. cash or personal checks (certain locations only)
  2. credit cards

Walk-in Registration—Candidates may register/pay at their local test center; however, they may not be able to test for 48 hours.

Candidates must pay for the exam prior to testing. Scheduling may be arranged up to six weeks in advance. (In certain countries in Asia payment is made at the test site on the day of testing.)

Oracle Education

To help you prepare for certification, Oracle education is available. For more information on Oracle courses, call a center convenient to you.

Argentina	Buenos Aires	541-313-0102
Australia	North Sydney	61-2-9900-1685
Austria	Vienna	43-1-33-777-400
Bahrain	Manama	973-533912
Belgium	Brussels	32-2-7191294
Brazil	São Paulo	55-11-548-9111
Caribbean	*see Puerto Rico*	
Centro America	*see Costa Rica*	
Chile	Santiago	562-203-5353
China	Beijing	861-0857-1506
Colombia	Bogota	571-621-2066
Costa Rica	San José	506-296-1530
Croatia	Zagreb	385-1-530-926
	Osijek	385-54-101-042
	Rijeka	385-51-217-477
	Split	385-21-44-729
Czech Republic	Praha	422-24408-150
Denmark	Ballerup	45-44-80-80-80
Ecuador	Quito	593-222-0809
Egypt	Cairo	202-574-8952
Finland	Espoo	358-0-804-661
France	Paris	33-1-47-62-20-81
	Aix-en-Provence	
	Bordeaux	
	Lyons	

	Nantes	
	Strasbourg	
	Toulouse	
	Brest	33-98-44-01-66
	Clermont-Ferrand	33-72-26-24-74
	Nice	33-93-65-22-29
Germany	Munich	49-89-9-93-11-3
	Berlin	
	Düsseldorf	
	Frankfurt	
	Hamburg	
	Stuttgart	
	Dresden	49-35-1-498-1260
Greece	Athens	301-88-31-511
Hong Kong	Kowloon	85-2-2856-2626
Hungary	Budapest	36-1-214-0050
		36-1-251-5949
Iceland	Reykjavik	354-561-8131
India	New Delhi	9111-372-0570
Indonesia	Jakarta	6221-572-4221
Italy	Milano	39-2-24959-230
	Florence	39-55-475603
	Rome	39-6-50261-401
	Ivrea (Turin)	39-125-529359
	Naples	39-81-8533684
	Venice	39-41-5310863
Kazakhstan	Alma-Aty	7-3272-32-22-73
Korea	Seoul	822-369-9680
Kuwait	Kuwait City	965-242-9734
Malaysia	Kuala Lumpur	603 241 7531
Mexico	Col. Granada	525-728-6463
Netherlands	De Meern	31-30-669-4211
New Zealand	Auckland	649-309-1946

Norway	Oslo	47-67-52-6700
	Bergen	
	Trondheim	
Oman	Muscat	968-702907
Peru	Lima	511-221-1566
Philippines	Metro	632-812-3551
Poland	Warsaw	48-22-622-5830
Portugal	Lisbon	351-1-410-2837
	Oporto	351-2-600-1938
Puerto Rico	San Juan	1-809-793-3377
Romania	Bucharest	40-1-250-3235
Russia	Moscow	7-095-258-4180
Saudi Arabia	Riyadh	966-1-481-1551
	Al-Khobar	966-3-857-8577
	Jeddah	966-2-661-2000
Singapore	Singapore	65-434-7828
Slovakia		42-7-322-239
Slovenia	Ljubljana	386-61-1687004
	Slovenj Gradec	
South Africa	Midrand	27-11-313-5136
	Cape Town	
	Durban	
Spain	Barcelona	34-3-419-50-50
	Bilbao	34-4-476-39-39
	Madrid	34-1631-20-00
Sweden	Goteborg	46-31-703-24-00
	Stockholm	46-8-705-38-80
		46-8-703-24-00
		46-8-629-8000
Switzerland	Dietikon	41-1-745-8787
	Bern	
	Lausanne	41-21-320-3821
	Basel	
	Zurich	

Taiwan	Taipei	886-2-719-3966
Thailand	Bangkok	662-632-9400
Turkey	Ankara	90-312-446-7575
	Istanbul	90-212-285-2950
Vietnam	Hanoi	84 426 9970
UAE	Dubai	971-4-313-828
	Abu Dhabi	
United Kingdom	Bracknell	44-1344-860-230
	Dublin	44-1344-860-230
	Edinburgh	44-131-228-4583
	Glasgow	44-1344-860-230
	London	44-1344-860-230
	Manchester	44-1344-860-230
	Richmond	44-1344-860-230
Venezuela	Caracas	582-993-2170

CHAPTER 15

Oracle7 DBA Practice Questions

T he Oracle7 DBA Certification Exam was developed by the International Oracle Users Group—Americas, Oracle Corporation, and the Education Testing Service. The goal of the exam, according to the exam bulletin, is to measure "the DBA candidate's mastery of the knowledge, skills, and abilities necessary to perform proficiently the job of the Oracle DBA."

How do you know if you have mastered the necessary skills? Better yet, how can you tell which areas you need to study prior to taking the exam? In this chapter, you'll find questions designed to determine which areas of DBA skills you need to enhance.

The question categories provided here are based on the description of the exam provided in the exam bulletin (see Chapter 14). The exam bulletin provides the percentage of questions in each category, and the questions in this chapter mimic those percentages. For example, the exam bulletin states that questions about backup/recovery account for 16 to 18 percent of the exam questions—so of the 100 questions in this chapter, 18 are related to backup/recovery.

The questions provided here have been developed to provide test candidates with an opportunity to identify areas for further study. The questions provided here do not concentrate solely on syntax, but rather reflect real-life issues and problems faced by Oracle DBAs. **As these questions are not directly from the exam, and are administered in a different fashion, successful completion of these questions does not guarantee success on the Certification exam. These questions should be used solely to identify areas in which you need further study in order to perform well as a DBA and, by extension, on the Certification exam. These questions are not designed to replace the Certification exam or undermine its integrity in any way. All DBAs are encouraged to seek certification.**

For information on the Oracle DBA Certification Exam fees and schedules, see Chapter 14.

Question Format

For almost all of the questions, the answer will be a single letter, representing a choice from a list of multiple answers to a question. Questions may be TRUE/FALSE, YES/NO, sentence completions, or word problems. The question categories have been mixed throughout the exam.

The candidate bulletin of information for the Oracle7 DBA Certification Exam shown in Chapter 14 is reprinted by permission of The Chauncey Group International, Ltd., the copyright owner. Permission to reprint the Oracle7 DBA Certification Exam candidate bulletin of information does not constitute review or endorsement by The Chauncey Group International, Ltd., of this publication as a whole or of any testing information it may contain.

The Chauncey Group International, Ltd., did not participate in the development or review of the practice questions shown in this chapter. Any resemblance to questions on the Oracle7 DBA Certification Exam is coincidental.

Recording Your Answers

For each question, mark your answer in the box provided. For all but one question, the answer will be a single letter. At the end of this chapter, you will find an answer sheet with places for all 100 answers. After you have completed the questions, mark your answers on the answer sheet. As an additional exercise, you may wish to record your level of confidence in each of your answers.

What to Do If You're Stumped

Don't guess. An unanswered question counts as a wrong answer in this format, but sheer guesswork undermines the value of answering these questions. Guessing right on these questions may increase your "grade," but *the "grade" is unimportant—the important goal is to identify things you do not know.* Guessing right on these questions will not guarantee that you can guess right on any subsequent questions or when you encounter the problem during your work as a DBA. After you've completed the answer sheet, turn to Chapter 16 and read through the questions and their explanations.

What's a Passing Grade?

There is no passing grade. If you've completed the questions and learned what you need to study, consider this exercise a success. Don't expect to be perfect—the questions require in-depth knowledge on a diverse set of topics.

Time Limits

Limit yourself to two-and-a-half hours to complete the questions. That gives you an average of a minute and a half to answer each question.

The Questions

1. By default, what is the frequency of commits during an Import?

    A. After each table.
    B. After each 100 records.

C. After the import completes.

D. After each user is imported.

2. Lines A through E of the following script form a single SQL command. In the script, which line contains an error?

A. create rollback segment ROLLBACK2

B. storage (initial 1M

C. next 1M

D. pctincrease 10

E. optimal 50M);

F. There are no errors in the command.

3. What is the default password for the SQL*Net V2 Listener?

A. LISTENER

B. TNSNAMES

C. ORACLE

D. LSNRCTL

4. A user logs into SQL*Plus and gets the following message:

"Warning: Product user profile information not loaded! Error in disabling roles in product user profile."
What is the proper way to eliminate this message?

A. Run the pupbld.sql file.

B. Execute the command **alter database enable product privileges**.

C. Execute the command **alter session enable product privileges**.

D. Shut down and restart the instance in SHARE mode.

5. Which of the following correctly describes the actions Oracle performs during a Complete Refresh of a simple snapshot?

    A. **Truncate**s the local snapshot table, leaving all indexes on the table; then performs an **insert ... as select** ... from the master view into the local snapshot table.

    B. **Delete**s all records from the local snapshot table, disables all of the indexes on the table; then performs a full **insert ... as select** ... from the master view into the local snapshot table; then reenables all indexes.

    C. **Truncate**s the local snapshot table, leaving all indexes on the table; then performs an **insert ... as select** ... from the master table's snapshot log into the local snapshot table.

    D. **Delete**s all records from the local snapshot table, disables all indexes on the table; then performs an **insert ... as select** ... from the master table's snapshot log into the local snapshot table.

6. A Production instance, running in ARCHIVELOG mode, has the following backup schedule: nightly exports, nightly online backups, and offline backups each Saturday night.

On Wednesday afternoon, the Production host machine suffers a media failure to a single disk. The disk that fails contains only datafiles, and the tablespaces associated with those datafiles do not contain SYSTEM objects, rollback segments, or temporary segments. What recovery path will recover the database with the least data lost?

    A. Apply the Tuesday night's export.

    B. Apply the Tuesday night's export to the database, and then recover using the archived redo log files.

    C. Restore the damaged files, plus the control files, from Tuesday night's online backup, and apply the archived redo log files.

    D. Restore only the damaged files from the Tuesday night online backup, and apply the archived redo log files.

7. A user creates a table without specifying storage parameters or a tablespace for the table. What will Oracle use for the storage and tablespace parameters for the table?

   A. The user's default storage parameters, in the SYSTEM tablespace.

   B. The user's default storage parameters, in the user's default tablespace.

   C. The tablespace's default storage parameters, in the SYSTEM tablespace.

   D. The tablespace's default storage parameters, in the user's default tablespace.

8. The following command is executed from within SQLDBA, after connecting as INTERNAL:

```
drop tablespace DATA_03 including contents;
```

At what point will the datafiles associated with the DATA_03 tablespace be deleted by Oracle?

   A. Never; you have to delete them manually after dropping the tablespace.

   B. As soon as the **drop tablespace** command is parsed.

   C. As soon as the **drop tablespace** command has completed.

   D. As soon as all of the tablespace's contents have been deleted.

9. During a long-running SELECT, a user receives a message that the query cannot be completed because the database is unable to allocate an extent. What is the most likely cause?

   A. The rollback segment used by the query exceeded the space available in the rollback segment's tablespace.

   B. The temporary segment used by the query exceeded the space available in the temporary tablespace.

   C. The user's default tablespace ran out of space.

   D. Another user has locked the table being queried, and a lock extent cannot be acquired.

10. What will be the result of the following query:

```
select
 count(distinct(substr(ROWID,1,8))||substr(ROWID,15,4))
  from EMP;
```

    A. The number of rows in the EMP table.

    B. The number of blocks used by the EMP table.

    C. The number of extents in the EMP table.

    D. The number of blocks allocated to the EMP table.

11. To improve database administration activity performance, you can create multiple SMON processes for a single instance.

    A. TRUE

    B. FALSE

12. If a database has been running in ARCHIVELOG mode, can you apply archived redo log files to datafiles that were backed up via an offline ("cold") backup?

    A. YES

    B. NO

13. The following listing comes from which file?

```
tcpdb.us.oracle.com =
  (DESCRIPTION =
    (ADDRESS_LIST =
        (ADDRESS =
          (COMMUNITY = tcp.us.oracle.com)
          (PROTOCOL = TCP)
          (Host = tcp_server.us.oracle.com)
          (Port = 1521)
```

```
       )
     )
     (CONNECT_DATA = (SID = oracle7)
     )
   )
```

    A. init.ora

    B. tnsnames.ora

    C. config.ora

    D. listener.ora

14. The following command is executed to grant the CLERK role to the user named LYNN:

```
grant CLERK to LYNN;
```

What must be done to have the CLERK role automatically enabled for LYNN during LYNN's next login?

    A. Nothing; the CLERK role will automatically become a default role for LYNN.

    B. Execute the command **alter user LYNN add default role LYNN**.

    C. Execute the command **alter role CLERK default.**

    D. Execute the command **grant CLERK to LYNN with admin option**.

15. Which of the following data dictionary views displays the setting of the OPTIMAL parameter for a rollback segment?

    A. DBA_ROLLBACK_SEGS

    B. V$ROLLSTAT

    C. V$SETTINGS

    D. DBA_SEGMENTS

16. Which of the following constraints, when applied to a table, will automatically create an index?

    A. FOREIGN KEY

B. CHECK

C. UNIQUE

D. NOT NULL

17. TRUE or FALSE: You can recompile the body of a package without recompiling the package specification.

A. TRUE

B. FALSE

18. What is the impact of specifying IGNORE=Y during an Import?

A. It causes Import to ignore the default Import parameters, using your account's default parameters instead.

B. It causes rows to be imported into existing tables.

C. It deletes data currently in the tables before inserting the records from the Export dump file.

D. It causes Import to ignore data integrity constraints during the Import.

19. What will be the result of the following command, when issued by the SYSTEM user? Assume that the SCOTT and TONY users exist, and that SCOTT owns a table named DEPT.

```
create synonym TONY.DEPT for SCOTT.DEPT;
```

A. A synonym named TONY.DEPT, pointing to SCOTT.DEPT, will be created in the SYSTEM schema.

B. A synonym named DEPT, pointing to SCOTT.DEPT, will be created in the TONY schema.

C. A synonym named DEPT, pointing to SCOTT.DEPT, will be created in the TONY schema, and TONY will be granted SELECT access to the SCOTT.DEPT table.

D. An error will be returned.

20. A user has been granted three roles, named CONNECT, SELECT_USER, and CLERK. All three roles are enabled by default. After login, which of the following commands will allow the user to enable only the CONNECT and SELECT_USER roles, while disabling the CLERK role?

    A. alter session disable role CLERK;

    B. alter session set role all except CLERK;

    C. set role none;

    D. execute DBMS_ROLES.DISABLE('clerk');

21. TRUE or FALSE: When tuning a transaction-intensive system, it is important to separate the rollback segments and online redo log files onto different I/O devices.

    A. TRUE

    B. FALSE

22. If an AFTER ROW trigger fails, does the transaction that caused the trigger to execute also fail?

    A. YES

    B. NO

23. Can a trigger contain a COMMIT?

    A. YES

    B. NO

24. What will be the result of the following command, when issued by the SYSTEM user? Assume that the TONY user exists, and that the service name and remote account information are accurate.

```
create database link TONY.REMOTE_LINK
connect to REMOTE_ACCT identified by REMOTE_PASS
 using 'HQ';
```

A. A database link named TONY.REMOTE_LINK, pointing to a remote database, will be created in the SYSTEM schema.

B. A database link named REMOTE_LINK, pointing to a remote database, will be created in the TONY schema.

C. A database link named REMOTE_LINK, pointing to a remote database, will be created in the TONY schema, and the remote account will be granted CONNECT privileges.

D. An error will be returned.

25. RELOAD is an option for which of the following utilities?

A. SQLLOAD

B. LSNRCTL

C. IMPORT

D. SQLDBA

26. Which of the following privileges cannot be granted to a role?

A. CREATE SESSION

B. UNLIMITED TABLESPACE

C. INSERT ANY TABLE

D. ANALYZE ANY

27. In which V$ table can you find the maximum number of users that were concurrently logged into an instance since it was started?

A. V$LICENSE

B. V$SESSIONS

C. V$SYSSTAT

D. V$PROCESS

28. Which of the background processes periodically coalesces free space in tablespaces?

    A. SMON

    B. PMON

    C. IMON

    D. FMON

29. During a recovery using online backups and archived redo log files, you discover that one of the archived redo log files is missing. Which of the options below best describes your recovery options?

    A. Skip the missing log file and apply the rest of the archived redo log files, and then open the database without the data in the missing log file.

    B. Stop the recovery at the last available log file prior to the missing archived redo log file.

    C. Skip the missing log file, apply the rest of the archived redo log files, and recover the missing log file's data from the rollback segments.

    D. Skip the missing log file, apply the rest of the archived redo log files, and use the **alter database resetlogs** command when opening the database.

30. When a rollback segment entry expands from one extent to another,

    A. an ORA-1555 ("snapshot too old") error is returned.

    B. the data in its first extent is marked as "inactive."

    C. the expansion is called a "wrap."

    D. it always acquires additional space in the tablespace.

31. Which of the following can you NOT change after a database has been created?

    A. The shared pool size.

    B. The default number of listeners.

    C. The number of control files.

    D. The database block size.

32. A user creates a PRIMARY KEY constraint while creating the COMPANY table with the following command.

```
create Table COMPANY
 (Company_ID NUMBER,
  Name        VARCHAR2 (20),
  constraint COMPANY_PK primary key (COMPANY_ID))
tablespace DATA
storage (initial 50M next 50M pctincrease 0);
```

What will Oracle use for the storage and tablespace parameters for the associated unique index?

    A. The default storage and tablespace parameters designated in the user's profile.

    B. The storage and tablespace parameters used by the COMPANY table.

    C. The default tablespace for the user, and the default storage parameters for that tablespace.

    D. The default tablespace for the user, and the storage parameters used by the COMPANY table.

33. What will be the outcome of the following command?

```
alter database backup controlfile to TRACE;
```

    A. The **create controlfile** command for the instance will be written to a trace file in the trace file destination directory.

    B. An existing controlfile will be backed up to the trace file destination directory.

    C. An existing controlfile will be copied to a file named *trace*.

    D. The **create controlfile** command for the instance will be written to a file named *trace*.

34. The CLERK role has been granted SELECT access to the TONY.EMP table. The following commands are executed by the SYSTEM user.

```
create user MARY identified by LAMB;
grant CONNECT, CREATE VIEW to MARY;
grant CLERK to Mary;
```

Which of the following actions, when run under the MARY account, will fail?

    A. select * from TONY.EMP;

    B. create synonym EMP for TONY.EMP;

    C. create view EMP as select * from TONY.EMP;

    D. describe TONY.EMP

35. Lines A through D of the following script form a single command. Which of the lines in the following command will cause an error?

    A. create user OPS$MARY

    B. identified externally

    C. quota 10M on SYSTEM

    D. default role CONNECT;

36. What data dictionary view displays the status of an INDEX ('DIRECT LOAD' or 'VALID') following a SQL*Loader Direct Path load?

    A. V$LOADER

    B. DBA_INDEXES

    C. DBA_SEGMENTS

    D. V$LOADSTAT

37. In your database's init.ora file, OPTIMIZER_MODE is set to CHOOSE. Which of the following is true about queries in your database?

A. Oracle will dynamically decide whether rule-based or cost-based optimization will resolve each query the fastest, and will choose an execution path accordingly.

B. During each query, you will be prompted to choose either rule-based or cost-based optimization.

C. Each query will use the choice-based optimizer.

D. If statistics are available for the tables in the queries, the cost-based optimizer will be used; otherwise, the rule-based optimizer will be used.

38. In the following listing, the archive log list command is executed within SQLDBA, and the results are shown.

```
SQLDBA> archive log list
Database log mode             NOARCHIVELOG
Automatic archival            ENABLED
Archive destination           /db01/oracle/arch/arch
Oldest online log sequence    966
Current log sequence          968
```

Is the database currently writing archive log files to the archive log destination directory?

A. YES

B. NO

39. Which of the following would cause a SHUTDOWN IMMEDIATE to fail?

A. A transaction that has just started.

B. A user process that is not disconnected.

C. A transaction that is in the process of rolling back.

D. A deadlock between two processes.

40. The EMPLOYEE table has a single-column, nonunique index on its City column, and a second single-column nonunique index on its State column. Given the following query, which of the listed operations will be used during the query's execution, assuming rule-based optimization?

```
select count(*)
  from EMPLOYEE
 where City = 'Baltimore'
   and State = 'MD';
```

    A. NESTED LOOPS

    B. AND-EQUAL

    C. CONCATENATION

    D. TABLE ACCESS FULL

41. During a conventional path SQL*Loader load, some of the input records fail the WHEN clause. Which file will record the records that fail the WHEN clause criteria?

    A. The Discard file.

    B. The Bad file.

    C. The Log file.

    D. No file, since they failed the WHEN clause.

42. In the following listing, the archive log list command is executed within SQLDBA, and the results are shown.

```
SQLDBA> archive log list
Database log mode              NOARCHIVELOG
Automatic archival             ENABLED
Archive destination            /db01/oracle/arch/arch
Oldest online log sequence     966
Current log sequence           968
```

How many online redo log files are there for this instance?

    A. 968

B. 3

C. 2

D. 966

43. Can you create a PUBLIC snapshot log?

A. YES

B. NO

44. Which of the following roles is not created automatically during a database creation?

A. CONNECT

B. MONITORER

C. IMP_FULL_DATABASE

D. RESOURCE

45. TRUE or FALSE: The WITH ADMIN OPTION clause of the grant command allows users to create views based on the objects being granted to the users.

A. TRUE

B. FALSE

46. A large table has all of its records deleted, and the deletion is committed. To verify that there are no records in the table, you perform the following query:

```
select COUNT(*) from EMP;
```

Several minutes later, the query returns a value of 0 for the number of records in the table. What is the most likely reason that the query took so long?

A. The table was fragmented into multiple extents.

B. The table had more than five indexes on it.

C. The table had not been analyzed since its records had been deleted.

D. The table's highwatermark had not been reset.

47. The number of query server processes associated with a single operation

A. is known as the "degree of parallelism."

B. can only be specified at the query level.

C. is limited by the database block size.

D. is limited at the user level.

48. What will be the outcome of the following command?

```
archive log all;
```

A. When issued during a recovery, this command forces all archive log files to be applied to the damaged datafiles without further prompting.

B. All full unarchived online redo log files will be manually archived.

C. The log of all database connections will be archived in SYS.AUD$.

D. The ARCH background process will be enabled for all instances.

49. A tablespace named DATA contains three datafiles, each of which is 100MB in length. A user who has a quota of 200MB on the DATA tablespace attempts the following command:

```
create table TABLE_X
(column1   VARCHAR2(10))
tablespace DATA
storage (initial 75M next 75M pctincrease 0 minextents 2);
```

What will be the result of the create table command shown?

A. The command will fail.

B. TABLE_X will be created in the DATA tablespace; its first extent will be in the first datafile, and its second extent will be in the second datafile.

C. TABLE_X will be created in the DATA tablespace; its first extent will be in the first datafile, and its second extent will be split across the first and second datafile.

D. TABLE_X will be created in the DATA tablespace; only one extent will be created.

50. What will be the output of the following command?

```
lsnrctl status netstat
```

A. The status of SQL*Net V2 on the host named NETSTAT will be reported.

B. The status of SQL*Net V2 on the current host will be reported, along with network traffic statistics.

C. The status of SQL*Net V2 for the instance identified by the NETSTAT service name in the tnsnames.ora file will be reported.

D. The status of SQL*Net V2 on the current host will be written to a file named NETSTAT.

51. What is the name of the default user profile?

A. DEFAULT

B. USER

C. CONNECT

D. PROFILE

52. Following an aborted SQL*Loader Direct Path load, the COMPANY table's unique index on the Mail_ID column, named COMPANYUMAIL_ID, is left in 'DIRECT LOAD' state. Which of the following procedures will restore the index to a valid state in the shortest time possible?

A. alter index COMPANYUMAIL_ID valid;

B. validate index COMPANYUMAIL_ID;

    C. alter table COMPANY enable index COMPANYUMAIL_ID;

    D. Drop and re-create the index.

53. An automated shutdown/startup process fails due to a media failure. In which file will you be able to view the errors that the database encountered?

    A. The alert log.

    B. The online redo log.

    C. The control file.

    D. The archived redo log.

54. An empty tablespace named DATA contains one datafile, 300MB in length. A user who has a 50MB table named TABLE_Y (in a different tablespace) and a quota of 200MB on the DATA tablespace attempts the following command:

```
create table TABLE_X
as select * from TABLE_Y
tablespace DATA
storage (initial 40M next 40M pctincrease 0);
```

What will be the result of the create table command shown, assuming that the database has adequate space to handle the transaction?

    A. The command will fail because of a syntax error.

    B. TABLE_X will be created in the DATA tablespace, with no rows.

    C. TABLE_X will be created in the DATA tablespace and populated with rows from the TABLE_Y table.

    D. TABLE_X will be created in the same tablespace as TABLE_Y.

55. What will be the outcome of the following command?

```
audit INSERT, UPDATE, DELETE on DEFAULT;
```

A. **insert**, **update**, and **deletes** against the table named DEFAULT will be recorded.

B. **insert, update**, and **deletes** by users with DEFAULT profiles will be recorded.

C. **insert, update**, and **deletes** will be recorded for all tables in the database.

D. **insert**, **update**, and **deletes** will be set as the DEFAULT auditing option for all tables.

56. TRUE or FALSE: There is no limit to the length of the time period between the running of utlbstat.sql and utlestat.sql, provided the database is not shut down at any point during that period—the results will always be valid.

A. TRUE

B. FALSE

57. Can a CHECK constraint on the COMPANY table reference any table other than COMPANY?

A. YES

B. NO

58. Queries against a non-updateable snapshot retrieve data

A. from a local read-only view of a local table.

B. from a local read-only view of a remote table.

C. directly from a local table.

D. directly from a remote table.

59. In your development environment, the backup schedule is:

■ **Sunday nights: Full export**

■ **Monday & Tuesday: Incremental export**

■ **Wednesday: Cumulative export**

- **Thursday, Friday, Saturday: Incremental export**

On Friday afternoon, you need to recover the database to the latest point possible from your exports. What files will you need?

    A. Thursday night's Incremental export and Sunday night's Full export.

    B. Thursday night's Incremental export, Sunday night's Full export, and Wednesday night's Cumulative export.

    C. Sunday night's Full export, and the Incremental exports from Monday, Tuesday, and Thursday.

    D. Thursday night's Incremental export and Wednesday night's Cumulative export.

60. Place the database creation steps listed below in their proper chronological order.

    1. create database...

    2. create tablespace ROLL_SEGS...

    3. create rollback segment R_1 tablespace ROLL_SEGS;

    4. create rollback segment R1 tablespace SYSTEM;

    5. alter rollback segment R1 online;

61. Which data dictionary view records the creation date of tables?

    A. DBA_OBJECTS

    B. DBA_TABLES

    C. DBA_SEGMENTS

    D. DBA_TAB_COLUMNS

62. Which of the following is correct?

    A. You can perform Complete refreshes only on complex snapshots.

    B. You can perform Fast refreshes only on complex snapshots.

C. You can perform Fast refreshes on either complex or simple snapshots.

D. You can perform Complete refreshes on simple snapshots.

63. In a client-server environment using SQL*Net V2 (prior to 2.3, and not using Oracle*Names), which machines must have SQL*Net V2 configuration files on them?

A. The server, but not the client.

B. Both the client and the server.

C. The client, but not the server.

D. Neither the client nor the server.

64. TRUE or FALSE: An Incremental export backs up only the records that have changed since the last export; records that have not changed are not backed up.

A. TRUE

B. FALSE

65. The space allocation within a tablespace is shown in the following listing.

```
select Segment_Name, Block_ID, Blocks
  from DBA_EXTENTS
 where Tablespace_Name = 'DATA'
 union
select 'free space', Block_ID, blocks
  from DBA_FREE_SPACE
 where Tablespace_Name = 'DATA'
 order by 2,3;
```

Segment_Name	Block_ID	Blocks
TABLE_A	2	20
TABLE_A	22	20
TABLE_B	42	50
free space	92	10
free space	102	45
TABLE_A	147	20

As shown in the preceding listing, TABLE_A's first extent starts at block #2 and is twenty blocks in length. Can TABLE_B extend to a second extent if its NEXT value is equal to its INITIAL value, and it has a PCTINCREASE value of 50?

A. YES

B. NO

66. TRUE or FALSE: You can use the SQL*Net V2 tnsnames.ora file to facilitate SQL*Net V1 connections by setting service names equal to SQL*Net V1 connect strings.

A. TRUE

B. FALSE

67. What will be the outcome of the following command?

```
analyze table COMPANY compute statistics;
```

A. By default, roughly 10 percent of the COMPANY table will be scanned and its statistics will be estimated.

B. The COMPANY table and all of its indexes will be fully scanned and their statistics will be collected.

C. The COMPANY table will be scanned and its statistics will be collected, but its indexes will not be analyzed.

D. Each row of the COMPANY table will be matched against the index column values in its associated indexes.

68. An SCN is a

A. Source Code Number.

B. System Control Number.

C. System Change Number.

D. Session Commit Node.

69. What is the outcome of the following command?

```
audit session;
```

   A. All successful connections to the database will be recorded.

   B. All unsuccessful connections to the database will be recorded.

   C. All successful and unsuccessful connections to the database will be recorded.

   D. The command will return an error.

70. TRUE or FALSE: There is a 1-to-1 relationship between V$ROLLNAME and V$ROLLSTAT.

   A. TRUE

   B. FALSE

71. In a distributed transaction environment, the Commit Point Site for a transaction is designated by

   A. setting COMMIT_POINT = TRUE in the init.ora file of the Commit Point Site, and COMMIT_POINT = FALSE for the other sites.

   B. using a COMMIT_POINT hint in the transaction.

   C. having the highest value for COMMIT_POINT_STRENGTH among the init.ora files of participating sites.

   D. using a NOT_IN_DOUBT hint in the transaction.

72. An application will be using stored procedures and packages extensively. Which of the following system tables will most likely require a large amount of space?

   A. TS$

   B. SOURCE$

   C. CODE$

   D. PROC$

73. What will be the outcome of attempting to use the REMOTE_CONNECT database link, whose create database link command is shown below?

```
create database link REMOTE_CONNECT
using 'dev';
```

    A. Attempts to use this database link will fail, since no username/password is identified.

    B. Using this database link will succeed if current username/password combination in the current database is a valid username/password combination in the 'dev' instance.

    C. Attempts to use this database link will succeed if REMOTE_OS_AUTHENT is set to 'TRUE' in the 'dev' instance's init.ora file.

    D. When used, the REMOTE_CONNECT database link will log into the 'dev' instance using the default username and password for that instance.

74. What will be the outcome of the following command?

```
truncate table COMPANY;
```

    A. The records in COMPANY will be deleted, its non-**initial** extents will be marked as free space, and its associated indexes will also be reduced to a single extent.

    B. The records in COMPANY will be deleted, it will keep all of its allocated space, and its associated indexes will keep all of their allocated space.

    C. The records in COMPANY will be deleted, it will keep all of its allocated space, and its indexes will be dropped.

    D. The status of COMPANY table will change to 'TRUNCATED', as shown in the Status column of the DBA_TABLES view.

75. During an attempted login, you receive the message "archiver is stuck, connect INTERNAL only until freed". To properly resolve the problem that caused this message, you should

    A. execute the command **alter database archive log free**.

    B. free up space in the archive log destination directory.

C. require all users to use the **connect internal** command for all application database connections.

D. execute the command **alter database archivelog**.

76. In a tablespace that has default storage parameters of INITIAL 30K, NEXT 30K, PCTINCREASE 0, a user specifies INITIAL 12K, NEXT 12K, PCTINCREASE 0 in a create table command. If the database block size is 2K, how large is the first extent of the table?

A. 12K

B. 15K

C. 20K

D. 30K

77. Which of the following is NOT an option for ORASRV?

A. dbaoff

B. debugoff

C. logoff

D. waitoff

78. The COMPANY table in a remote database contains only CHAR, VARCHAR2, and NUMBER columns. Can you create a view of COMPANY in a different database, using a database link?

A. YES

B. NO

79. Which of the following is NOT a lockmode option for the lock table command?

A. share update

B. share row exclusive

C. row share

D. update

80. If you are using multiple online redo log threads, then you are

A. logged in multiple times to the same instance.

B. using the Parallel Query option.

C. using the Parallel Server option.

D. using an instance that has specified MULTIPLE_REDO_THREADS = TRUE in its init.ora file.

81. When you create a new tablespace, do the control files increase in size?

A. YES

B. NO

82. During an insert into a table in an Oracle7.2 database, an "unable to allocate extent of size 100 in tablespace DATA" error is returned. The table has no indexes or constraints, and has reached 121 extents (the maximum allowed for the database's block size of 2K). Which of the following is the best way to resolve this problem and complete the data insertion process?

A. Alter the **next** parameter for the table.

B. Alter the **pctincrease** parameter for the table.

C. Increase the DB_BLOCK_SIZE parameter in the init.ora file.

D. Drop and re-create the table with higher **initial** and **next** storage parameters.

83. Which init.ora parameter enables the writing of records to the audit trail?

A. SECURE=TRUE

B. AUDIT_TRAIL=TRUE

C. AUDIT_LOG=TRUE

D. None of the above. You need to execute the **alter database audit log** command from within SQLDBA.

84. The following commands are issued by the MARY user, and all succeed. Company_ID is the primary key of the COMPANY table.

```
commit;
update COMPANY set Active_Flag = 'Y'
 where Company_ID = 12345;
savepoint A1;

insert into COMPANY (Company_ID, Active_Flag)
   values (12346,'N');
savepoint A2;

rollback to savepoint A1;
commit;
```

What will be the result when a different user now executes the query

```
select Active_Flag from MARY.COMPANY
 where Company_ID = 12346;
```

    A. 'N'

    B. 'Y'

    C. Null.

    D. 'no rows selected.'

85. If a CKPT process is not used, which other background process performs the CKPT process's function?

    A. LGWR

    B. DBWR

    C. SMON

    D. PMON

86. During an attempted normal shutdown of an instance, a memory error prevents the database from shutting down. What should be done to resolve the situation?

    A. Use the **shutdown immediate** command.

    B. Nothing has to be done; since the instance never shutdown all the way, it is still available to the application users.

    C. Use the **shutdown abort** command.

    D. Use the **startup** command.

87. Which of the following queries will tell you how much space is allocated to the COMPANY table in the DATA tablespace?

    A. Select count(distinct(substr(ROWID,1,8)||substr(ROWID,15,4))) from COMPANY;

    B. Select SUM(Blocks) from DBA_FREE_SPACE where Table_Name = 'COMPANY';

    C. Select SUM(blocks) from DBA_EXTENTS where Segment_Name = 'COMPANY' and Segment_Type = 'TABLE';

    D. Select MAX(Blocks) from DBA_SEGMENTS where Table_Name = 'DATA';

88. How often are a table's statistics re-collected?

    A. Every time the table is accessed.

    B. Every time the table is manually analyzed.

    C. Every time the database is restarted.

    D. Every time records in the table are inserted, updated, or deleted.

89. Can a role be granted to another role?

    A. YES

    B. NO

90. Given the create table command below:

```
create table COMPANY_ADDRESS
(Company_ID    NUMBER
    constraint fk_company_address
      references COMPANY.Company_ID,
Address_Code   CHAR(1),
constraint pk_company_address
     primary key (Company_Id, Address_Code));
```

Which of the following is true?

A. You cannot insert records into COMPANY_ADDRESS unless a matching Company_ID already exists in COMPANY.

B. You cannot insert records into COMPANY unless a matching Company_ID already exists in COMPANY_ADDRESS.

C. The Address_Code column is nullable.

D. You cannot delete records from COMPANY_ADDRESS if a matching Company_ID still exists in COMPANY.

91. TRUE or FALSE: To simplify your backup/recovery procedures, it is a good idea to leave tablespaces in BEGIN BACKUP state at all times.

A. TRUE

B. FALSE

92. A third-party package requires the Oracle Version 6 data dictionary views. To install these views, you should do which of the following?

A. Do a Full Import from an Export of an Oracle Version 6 database.

B. Do a User Import of the SYSTEM user from an Export of an Oracle Version 6 database.

C. Run ddviews6.sql.

D. Run catalog6.sql.

93. What will be the outcome of the following command?

```
audit profile;
```

   A. Any user statistics that exceed their prescribed profile values will be recorded in the audit log.

   B. All **create profile, alter profile,** and **drop profile** commands will be recorded in the audit log.

   C. All queries against the USER_PROFILES table will be audited.

   D. The command will fail.

94. Querying DBA_IND_COLUMNS for the MARY.EMPLOYEE table shows the following:

```
select Column_Name, Column_Position from DBA_IND_COLUMNS
 where Owner = 'MARY' and Table_Name = 'EMPLOYEE';
```

Column Name	Column Position
City	1
State	2
Zip	3

Will the following query use an index, given rule-based optimization?

```
select distinct City from EMPLOYEE
 where State = 'DE';
```

   A. YES

   B. NO

95. Which of the following is NOT an Oracle background process?

   A. Dispatcher (Dnnn)

   B. Server (Snnn)

   C. Recoverer (RECO)

   D. Monitorer (Mnnn)

96. Which of the following is NOT true about conditions that must be met prior to starting a database recovery from a media failure?

    A. All datafiles must be either available or marked as 'OFFLINE'.

    B. You must be connected as INTERNAL.

    C. You must be connected via a multi-threaded server process.

    D. You must have all control files available.

97. The number of rollback segments in a database should most directly correspond to

    A. the number of concurrent users.

    B. the number of concurrent transactions.

    C. the size of the largest transaction.

    D. the size of the largest stored procedure.

98. Which program is used to verify SQL*Net V2 connectivity from a Windows client?

    A. TNSNAMES

    B. LISTENER

    C. ORASRV

    D. TNSPING

99. What will be the outcome of the following command?

```
revoke CONNECT from MARY;
```

    A. MARY's current sessions will be disconnected.

    B. MARY's account will be dropped.

    C. MARY will no longer be able to use the CONNECT privilege.

    D. MARY will no longer be able to enable the CONNECT role.

☐ 100. Querying DBA_IND_COLUMNS for the MARY.EMPLOYEE table shows the following:

```
select Column_Name, Column_Position from DBA_IND_COLUMNS
 where Owner = 'MARY' and Table_Name = 'EMPLOYEE';
```

```
Column Name      Column Position
City                    1
State                   2
Zip                     3
```

Will the following query use an index, given rule-based optimization?

```
select distinct City from EMPLOYEE
 where City not in ('New York', 'Boston', 'Dallas');
```

A. YES

B. NO

Answer Form for the Practice Questions

Fill in your answers in the blanks provided in Figure 15-1, on the space following the number of each question. The answer form is designed to make it easier to analyze your answers by category in Chapter 16 (hence its somewhat unusual design). There are forty unnumbered blank areas in the answer form; do not place marks in the unnumbered areas, as they were inserted to vary the frequency of the question categories.

When the answer form is complete, turn to Chapter 16 to analyze your study needs in the different question categories.

1. __	2. __	3. __	4. __		5. __
6. __	7. __	8. __		9. __	10. __	11. __
12. __		13. __	14. __	15. __	16. __	17. __
18. __	19. __		20. __	21. __	22. __	23. __
	24. __	25. __	26. __	27. __		28. __
29. __	30. __	31. __			32. __
33. __	34. __		35. __	36. __		37. __
38. __		39. __		40. __	41. __
42. __	43. __	44. __	45. __	46. __		47. __
48. __	49. __	50. __	51. __		52. __
53. __	54. __		55. __	56. __	57. __	58. __
59. __		60. _____		61. __	62. __	63. __
64. __	65. __	66. __			67. __
68. __			69. __	70. __		71. __
	72. __		73. __		74. __
75. __	76. __	77. __	78. __	79. __		80. __
81. __	82. __	83. __		84. __		85. __
86. __	87. __	88. __	89. __		90. __
91. __		92. __	93. __	94. __		95. __
96. __	97. __	98. __	99. __	100. __	

FIGURE 15-1. *Answer Form for the Practice Questions*

CHAPTER 16

Analysis of the Practice Questions

The practice questions provided in Chapter 15 were designed to help you gauge your knowledge of Oracle database administration theory and practice. In this chapter, you'll see how to interpret your answers to these questions in a manner that will let you quickly determine which categories you should study or practice to become a more fully-rounded DBA. You'll also find specific reference materials for each category to assist in your study.

Following the answer sheet and the references, you'll find each of the practice questions repeated, with its category, answer, and explanation provided.

Answer Key to the Practice Questions

In the process of going through the practice questions, you may have sensed that you performed better in some categories than others. After completing the following answer key, you'll see how well you answered the questions from each category. In order to start the analysis process, check that you have completed the process of putting your answers in the Answer Sheet provided in Figure 15-1.

The correct answers for the questions are shown in Figure 16-1. The labels across the top of the columns in Figure 16-1 identify the question categories as they are specified in Chapter 14. The interpretation of the results and the explanations of the answers follow Figure 16-1.

General Analysis of the Practice Questions

To analyze your performance by question category, correct your answer sheet as it appears in Figure 15-1, given the answers from Figure 16-1. Each column of answers corresponds to a different category of questions. For example, the first column of questions (1, 6, 12, ... 96) covers the "Backup and Recovery" category.

Backup & Recovery	Resource Management	Maintenance & Operations	Security	Tuning and Trouble-shooting	Data Administration	Architecture & Options
1. A	2. D	3. A	4. A		5. A	
6. D	7. D	8. A		9. B	10. B	11. B
12. A		13. B	14. A	15. B	16. C	17. A
18. B	19. B		20. B	21. A	22. A	23. B
	24. A	25. B	26. B	27. A		28. A
29. B	30. C	31. D			32. C	
33. A	34. C		35. D	36. B		37. D
38. B		39. D		40. B	41. A	
42. B	43. B	44. B	45. B	46. D		47. A
48. B	49. B	50. C	51. A		52. D	
53. A	54. A		55. D	56. B	57. B	58. A
59. B		60. 14523		61. A	62. D	63. B
64. B	65. A	66. A			67. B	
68. C			69. C	70. A		71. C
	72. B		73. B		74. A	
75. B	76. C	77. D	78. A	79. D		80. C
81. B	82. D	83. B		84. D		85. A
86. C	87. C	88. B	89. A		90. A	
91. B		92. D	93. B	94. B		95. D
96. C	97. B	98. D	99. D	100. B		

FIGURE 16-1. *Correct answers for the practice questions*

Category	Number of Correct Answers	Number of Questions
Backup and Recovery	_____	18
Resource Management	_____	15
Maintenance and Operations	_____	15
Security	_____	14
Tuning and Troubleshooting	_____	14
Data Administration	_____	12
Architecture and Options	_____	12

TABLE 16-1. *Category analysis with number of correct answers from Figure 16-1*

For each category, count the number of correct answers on your answer sheet. Enter the number of correct answers for each category in the space provided in Table 16-1.

Your results by category, as shown in Table 16-1, should point out areas in which you could benefit by further study and practice. As shown in Table 16-1, all areas of a DBA's role are measured by the practice questions. If you had problems with specific categories, check the reference sections provided below for further information. You may wish to first check the questions that you missed, as some questions could have been assigned to multiple categories. For example, a question about a Unique constraint could be categorized as a Data Administration question (considering the constraint) or a Resource Management question (considering the constraint's associated index). Look for patterns among the questions you missed to further specify the areas in need of study.

References

In each of the following sections, you'll find references to specific works that were consulted during the development of the practice questions.

NOTE
You must not only read the sections listed, but also practice the commands and utilities described. Relying on a knowledge of syntax alone will not help you to resolve scenario-type problems or error-condition problems.

General Reference

Every Oracle7 DBA should have practical working knowledge of the material in the following books provided by Oracle:

- *Oracle7 Application Developer's Guide*
- *Oracle7 Server Administrator's Guide*
- *Oracle7 Server Concepts Manual*
- *Oracle7 Server Utilities User's Guide*
- *SQL Language Reference Guide*
- *SQL*Net Administrator's Guide*

You should also know the architecture and concepts for all of the major Oracle features and configurations, as described in the books listed above.

In addition, a number of books (such as this one) are available to supplement your Oracle database administration knowledge. During the development of the practice questions, the books most frequently used were:

- *Oracle DBA Handbook* by Kevin Loney (Osborne McGraw-Hill, 1994)
- *Oracle Backup and Recovery Handbook* by Rama Velpuri (Osborne McGraw-Hill, 1995)

The tuning and resource management sections of this book were also used in the development of the practice questions.

You need to have a good working knowledge of the data dictionary views and tables in order to answer a number of the practice questions. For information on the data dictionary views and tables, see the *Oracle7 Server Administrator's Guide* and the data dictionary chapter of *Oracle: The Complete Reference, Third Edition* by George Koch and Kevin Loney (Osborne McGraw-Hill, 1995).

In the following sections, you'll see specific references for the practice question categories. The categories are listed in the order of their weighting in the Certification exam.

NOTE
If you are only familiar with Oracle Version 6, you will need to study the use and administration of Oracle7 in order to do well on the practice questions. Each category contains questions that are unique to Oracle7.

Backup and Recovery

The Backup and Recovery practice questions cover architecture concepts, Import/Export, offline backups, online backups, recovery scenarios, control files, redo log files, and trace/log files. The Backup and Recovery practice question numbers are 1, 6, 12, 18, 29, 33, 38, 42, 48, 53, 59, 64, 68, 75, 81, 86, 91, and 96.

For Further Reading
The Backup and Recovery category requires knowledge of almost all of the files used by the database. For general architecture knowledge, see the books listed previously in the "General Reference" section.

For information on Import and Export, including sample scenarios, see the *Oracle7 Server Utilities User's Guide*. For information on designing backups for your environment, see the backup procedures chapters in the *Oracle7 Server Administrator's Guide* and the *Oracle DBA Handbook*. Also, read through the **alter database** command syntax.

For examples of backup and recovery scenarios, see the *Oracle7 Server Administrator's Guide* (the chapter on recovery is particularly useful) and the *Oracle Backup and Recovery Handbook*. You should also read through the **recover** command syntax.

Once you have studied the available options, test them out by creating a small database. After the database has been backed up, test your ability to recover from the loss of a datafile or from a missing archived redo log file. Practice both logical and file system-based recovery methods.

Resource Management

The Resource Management questions cover rollback segments, space allocation and usage, database links, synonyms, views, indexes, and tables. Other Resource Management questions could have included clusters and sequences. The Resource Management question numbers are 2, 7, 19, 24, 30, 34, 43, 49, 54, 65, 72, 76, 82, 87, and 97.

For Further Reading

You cannot excel in the Resource Management category questions without a thorough working knowledge of the way Oracle7 manages space inside the database; how it calculates extent sizes; how rollback segments and temporary segments work; and how to manage objects that have grown. In addition to the resource management sections of this book, the *Oracle7 Server Concepts Manual* and the *Oracle7 Server Administrator's Guide* provide information on all of the Resource Management topics. You should also read through the **create, alter,** and **drop** commands for each of the object types, and practice using those commands.

The Resource Management category contains some of the most difficult questions in the set of practice questions. Significant hands-on experience, including subsequent queries of the data dictionary views, is critical to being successful in this category.

Maintenance and Operations

The Maintenance and Operations questions cover SQL*Net (V1 and V2), monitoring, shutdown/startup, database creation, the **analyze** command, init.ora parameters, and the data dictionary views. The Maintenance and Operations question numbers are 3, 8, 13, 25, 31, 39, 44, 50, 60, 66, 77, 83, 88, 92, and 98.

For Further Reading

Like Resource Management, the Maintenance and Operations category requires significant hands-on experience. Among the reference books, the *SQL*Net Administrator's Guide* provides the architectural concepts for SQL*Net, and the *Oracle7 Server Administrator's Guide* describes the init.ora parameters. The usage of the data dictionary views is covered in the *Oracle DBA Handbook* and the "Hitchhiker's Guide to the Data Dictionary" chapter of *Oracle: The Complete Reference, Third Edition.*

Once you are familiar with the architecture and concepts involved in maintenance and operations, it is imperative that you use and practice them. Since the Maintenance and Operations category deals with the day-to-day management of your databases, the more experience you have, the better.

Security

The Security category's questions cover roles, profiles, database links, product user profiles, and the **audit, grant, revoke,** and **create user** commands. All other user account manipulation commands (such as **drop user** and **alter user**) would be valid Security questions as well. The Security category's question numbers are 4, 14, 20, 26, 35, 45, 51, 55, 69, 73, 78, 89, 93, and 99.

For Further Reading
Security questions are fairly straightforward: either you can access the data or you can't. Start by reading the *Oracle7 Server Administrator's Guide* for an overview of the security architecture, and then read the **audit, noaudit, grant, revoke, create user, alter user,** and **drop user** command syntax in the *SQL Language Reference Guide*—the syntax sections contain useful information about topics such as statement groups.

The product user profile information is described in the *SQL*Plus User's Guide*. Not as much practice is required to master this category as to master Resource Management.

Tuning and Troubleshooting

Tuning and Troubleshooting questions could cover just about any topic. In the practice questions, the Tuning and Troubleshooting category covers locking, index usage, the V$ dynamic performance tables, I/O distribution, savepoints, and data dictionary views. The Tuning and Troubleshooting question numbers are 9, 15, 21, 27, 36, 40, 46, 56, 61, 70, 79, 84, 94, and 100.

> **NOTE**
> Be sure to review and try out the documentation for the Monitoring features of SQLDBA and Server Manager.

For Further Reading
Since Tuning and Troubleshooting could involve resolving any given performance problem, the best approach to studying this category is to develop a grounding in the areas that are most critical to performance: index usage, execution paths, locking, and resource utilization. Become familiar with the V$ dynamic performance tables and the data dictionary views.

Locking is well described in the *Oracle7 Server Concepts Manual*, and is also covered in the *Oracle7 Application Developer's Guide*. The Oracle optimizer is also described in the *Oracle7 Server Concepts Manual*; the available operations and most important SQL tuning tips are provided in Chapters 10 and 11 of this book. There are a number of publications available from Oracle that provide operating-specific tuning advice. The V$ dynamic performance tables are described in the tuning portion of the *Oracle7 Server Administrator's Guide*. *Tuning Oracle* by Michael J. Corey, Michael Abbey, and Daniel J. Dechichio, Jr. (Osborne McGraw-Hill, 1995) provides an overview of many areas of Oracle database tuning.

Data Administration

The Data Administration questions cover a wide array of categories. The Certification bulletin refers to questions that focus on constraints and stored procedures, but the practice questions expand this category to also cover snapshots, RowIDs, SQL*Loader, and the **analyze** and **truncate** commands. The Data Administration question numbers are 5, 10, 16, 22, 32, 41, 52, 57, 62, 67, 74, and 90.

For Further Reading

The Data Administration category requires a thorough understanding of the uses and implications of constraints. For background information on constraints, read the "Data Integrity" chapter of the *Oracle7 Server Concepts Manual*. You should also understand the **constraint** clause, as described in the *SQL Language Reference Guide*. The different levels of normalization in a relational database are not covered in the practice questions, but you should be familiar with them; see *Oracle: The Complete Reference, Third Edition*, for a description of data normalization.

You will find SQL*Loader concepts and examples shown in the *Oracle7 Server Utilities User's Guide*. Snapshots are described the *Oracle7 Server Concepts Manual* and the *Oracle7 Server Administrator's Guide*.

Architecture and Options

The Architecture and Options questions cover background processes, triggers, packages, Parallel Query option, Parallel Server option, the System Global Area (SGA), and distributed transactions. The architecture of any part of an Oracle installation could be used as the basis for a question in this category. The Architecture and Options question numbers are 11, 17, 23, 28, 37, 47, 58, 63, 71, 80, 85, and 95.

For Further Reading

Most Architecture and Options questions do not require hands-on experience; rather, they require you to understand the concepts and terminology used within the Oracle7 database—a particularly important area of study for DBAs who previously used other relational databases. You should have a good general understanding of the different options available within Oracle7, and the way in which those options are implemented. For example, you should be familiar with the workings of the different Parallel options and their impact on your database environment (see Chapter 12). The books listed in the "General Reference" section are important resources when studying this material.

To excel in this category, you should understand the uses of the background processes, memory objects, and other core database components. The *Oracle7 Server Concepts Manual* provides an overview of the architectural options; the *Oracle Backup and Recovery Handbook* describes the internals with an implementation focus. In addition to these books, you should be sure to read the readme.doc files that are shipped with each new release of the Oracle7 software. The readme.doc files often offer detailed examples of the implementation or modification of architectural features within the database.

Although the Architecture and Options category is the most lightly weighted category in the Certification exam, it is nonetheless important, as questions in the other categories may concern the architecture of features instead of the features' implementations.

Question Analysis

In the following section, you'll see each question as it appears in Chapter 15, along with the question's category, answer, and an explanation of the answer. Rather than indicate reference materials within the answers, the reference materials are cited in the "References" section earlier in this chapter. When a question could have been assigned to multiple categories, a single category was chosen.

1. By default, what is the frequency of commits during an Import?

    A. After each table.

    B. After each 100 records.

    C. After the import completes.

    D. After each user is imported.

Category   Backup and Recovery

Answer   A. After each table.

Explanation   By default, the Import COMMIT flag is set to 'N', and records are committed after each table is imported. You can override this action by setting COMMIT=Y and setting a value for the BUFFER variable—a commit will then be issued after the number of bytes specified by the BUFFER setting. For example, specifying COMMIT=Y and BUFFER=100000 will issue a commit after every 100000 bytes—potentially reducing the amount of rollback segment space needed during the Import.

2. Lines A through E of the following script form a single SQL command. In the script, which line contains an error?

    A. create rollback segment ROLLBACK2

    B. storage (initial 1M

    C. next 1M

    D. pctincrease 10

    E. optimal 50M);

    F. There are no errors in the command.

Category   Resource Management

Answer   D. PCTINCREASE 10

Explanation   Rollback segments must have a PCTINCREASE of 0. Therefore, line D has an error. With a PCTINCREASE of 0, and with **initial** set to the same value as **next**, each extent of the rollback segment will be the same size.

3. What is the default password for the SQL*Net V2 Listener?

    A. LISTENER

    B. TNSNAMES

    C. ORACLE

    D. LSNRCTL

Category   Maintenance and Operations

Answer   A. LISTENER

Explanation   The LISTENER password is used to access commands within LSNRCTL, the SQL*Net V2 listener control utility. From the command line of your operating system, entering

```
lsnrctl
```

should give you the "LSNRCTL>" prompt. At the "LSNRCTL" prompt, you can then enter

LSNRCTL> SET PASSWORD LISTENER

(where LISTENER is the Listener password—it's the default) to gain access to SQL*Net commands. You can change the password by setting the PASSWORDS_LISTENER parameter in the server's listener.ora file.

4. A user logs into SQL*Plus and gets this message: "Warning: Product user profile information not loaded! Error in disabling roles in product user profile." What is the proper way to eliminate this message?

    A. Run the pupbld.sql file.

    B. Execute the command **alter database enable product privileges**.

    C. Execute the command **alter session enable product privileges**.

    D. Shut down and restart the instance in SHARE mode.

Category   Security

Answer   A. Run the pupbld.sql file.

Explanation   This message occurs when the PRODUCT_USER_PROFILE table has not been created. To create it, log in as SYSTEM and run the pupbld.sql file found in the /SQLPLUS/ADMIN subdirectory under the Oracle home directory. You can use PRODUCT_USER_PROFILE to prevent a user from executing commands (such as **set role, insert,** or **connect**) from within SQL*Plus.

5. Which of the following correctly describes the actions Oracle performs during a Complete Refresh of a simple snapshot?

    A. **Truncate**s the local snapshot table, leaving all indexes on the table; then performs an **insert ... as select** ... from the master view into the local snapshot table.

    B. **Delete**s all records from the local snapshot table, disables all of the indexes on the table; then performs a full **insert ... as select** ... from the master view into the local snapshot table; then reenables all indexes.

    C. **Truncate**s the local snapshot table, leaving all indexes on the table; then performs an **insert ... as select** ... from the master table's snapshot log into the local snapshot table.

    D. Deletes all records from the local snapshot table, disables all indexes on the table; then performs an **insert ... as select** ... from the master table's snapshot log into the local snapshot table.

Category   Data Administration

Answer   A. **Truncate**s the local snapshot table, leaving all indexes on the table; then performs an **insert ... as select** ... from the master view into the local snapshot table.

Explanation   The entries in a snapshot log are only used during Fast Refreshes, so C and D are not applicable. To speed up the record deletion process and minimize the amount of rollback space needed, Oracle performs a **truncate** on the local base table prior to completely repopulating it by querying the master snapshot view. All of the indexes are left on throughout the entire process.

6. A Production instance, running in ARCHIVELOG mode, has the following backup schedule: nightly exports, nightly online backups, and offline backups each Saturday night. On Wednesday afternoon, the Production host machine suffers a media failure to a single disk. The disk that fails contains only datafiles, and the tablespaces associated with those datafiles do not contain SYSTEM objects, rollback segments, or temporary segments. What recovery path will recover the database with the least data lost?

    A. Apply the Tuesday night's export.

    B. Apply the Tuesday night's export to the database, and then recover using the archived redo log files.

    C. Restore the damaged files, plus the control files, from Tuesday night's online backup, and apply the archived redo log files.

    D. Restore only the damaged files from the Tuesday night online backup, and apply the archived redo log files.

Category   Backup and Recovery

Answer   D. Restore only the damaged files from the Tuesday night online backup, and apply the archived redo log files.

Explanation   Since the problem was a media failure, the most appropriate method for recovery is via either the online or offline backups. The exports, although they might be useful, cannot be rolled forward to recover transactions that occurred after the exports completed. Answer A therefore results in a loss of all data in the lost files that was entered on Wednesday. Answer B is not correct because you apply archived redo log files to restored datafiles, not imported data.

Since the Production instance is run in ARCHIVELOG mode, you should be able to fully recover all transactions in the database via the archived redo log files. To apply the archived redo log files, you first need to restore the damaged files from a previous night's backup. To minimize recovery time, use the backups from the most recent night—in this case, Tuesday night's backups. Do not bring back the control files from the backup tape—this fact makes Answer C inappropriate. Then apply the archived redo log files to the database, and the restored files will be brought current with the rest of the database's files. The best answer is D.

7. A user creates a table without specifying storage parameters or a tablespace for the table. What will Oracle use for the storage and tablespace parameters for the table?

    A. The user's default storage parameters, in the SYSTEM tablespace.

    B. The user's default storage parameters, in the user's default tablespace.

    C. The tablespace's default storage parameters, in the SYSTEM tablespace.

    D. The tablespace's default storage parameters, in the user's default tablespace.

Category   Resource Management

Answer   D. The tablespace's default storage parameters, in the user's default tablespace.

Explanation   The table will be created in the user's default tablespace, using the default storage parameters for that tablespace. The user's default tablespace is defined via the **default tablespace** clause of the **create user** and **alter user** commands. The default storage parameters for a tablespace are specified via the **default storage** clause of the **create tablespace** and **alter tablespace** commands.

8. The following command is executed from within SQLDBA, after connecting as INTERNAL:

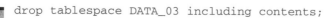

```
drop tablespace DATA_03 including contents;
```

At what point will the datafiles associated with the DATA_03 tablespace be deleted by Oracle?

    A. Never; you have to delete them manually after dropping the tablespace.

    B. As soon as the **drop tablespace** command is parsed.

    C. As soon as the **drop tablespace** command has completed.

    D. As soon as all of the tablespace's contents have been deleted.

Category   Maintenance and Operations

Answer   A. Never; you have to delete them manually after dropping the tablespace.

Explanation   Oracle does not automatically drop the datafiles associated with tablespaces. File deletion is a manual step, performed via operating system commands.

9. During a long-running SELECT, a user receives a message that the query cannot be completed because the database is unable to allocate an extent. What is the most likely cause?

    A. The rollback segment used by the query exceeded the space available in the rollback segments tablespace.

    B. The temporary segment used by the query exceeded the space available in the temporary tablespace.

    C. The user's default tablespace ran out of space.

    D. Another user has locked the table being queried, and a lock extent cannot be acquired.

Category   Tuning and Troubleshooting

Answer   B. The temporary segment used by the query exceeded the space available in the temporary tablespace.

Explanation   Large queries that require space for sorting often use temporary tables. Temporary tables are created in the user's default temporary tablespace (set via the **temporary tablespace** clause of the **create user** and **alter user** commands). The long-running query's sort area in the temporary tablespace cannot extend, resulting in the error. To resolve the error, change how the user acquires space in the temporary tablespace (by altering that tablespace's default storage characteristics), or add space to the temporary tablespace, or use a different tablespace for temporary segments.

10. What will be the result of the following query?

```
select
 count(distinct(substr(ROWID,1,8))||substr(ROWID,15,4))
 from EMP;
```

    A. The number of rows in the EMP table.

    B. The number of blocks used by the EMP table.

    C. The number of extents in the EMP table.

    D. The number of blocks allocated to the EMP table.

Category   Data Administration

Answer   B. The number of blocks used by the EMP table.

Explanation   Columns 1 through 8 of the RowID are the block identifier. Columns 15 through 18 are the file identifier. The concatenation of the block identifier and the file identifier uniquely identifies each block in the table, so the query shown in this question counts the number of blocks used by the rows in the table. The result of this query may be different than the result of the **analyze** command (as shown in DBA_TABLES), because the **analyze** command counts all the blocks up to the highwatermark of the table.

11. To improve database administration activity performance, you can create multiple SMON processes for a single instance.

    A. TRUE

    B. FALSE

Category   Architecture and Options

Answer   B. FALSE

Explanation   You cannot create multiple SMON processes for an instance. You can, however, create multiple DBWR processes for a single instance to improve database I/O performance.

12. If a database has been running in ARCHIVELOG mode, can you apply archived redo log files to datafiles that were backed up via an offline ("cold") backup?

A. YES

B. NO

Category   Backup and Recovery

Answer   A. YES

Explanation   Archived redo log files can be applied to datafiles that were backed up via either online or offline backups. To use them with offline backups, you should have the database in ARCHIVELOG mode prior to the backup. If a database is running in ARCHIVELOG mode, then its online redo log files are being archived prior to being overwritten. The archived redo log files can be applied to the database during a recovery operation. You can apply the archived redo log files to datafiles recovered from backups, as long as the database had been in ARCHIVELOG mode prior to the backup. If the database was running in ARCHIVELOG mode prior to the backup, then it does not matter whether the backup was done via an online backup or an offline backup.

13. Which file does the following listing come from?

```
tcpdb.us.oracle.com =
  (DESCRIPTION =
    (ADDRESS_LIST =
      (ADDRESS =
        (COMMUNITY = tcp.us.oracle.com)
        (PROTOCOL = TCP)
        (Host = tcp_server.us.oracle.com)
        (Port = 1521)
      )
    )
    (CONNECT_DATA = (SID = oracle7)
    )
  )
```

     A. init.ora

     B. tnsnames.ora

     C. config.ora

     D. listener.ora

Category   Maintenance and Operations

Answer   B. tnsnames.ora

Explanation   The tnsnames.ora file is used to define service names. In this case, the service name is 'tcpdb.us.oracle.com'. The service name description tells SQL*Net V2 which host to connect to, the protocol and port to use, and the instance to connect to. This example came from the sample tnsnames.ora file provided with SQL*Net V2.

14. The following command is executed to grant the CLERK role to the user named LYNN:

```
grant CLERK to LYNN;
```

What must be done to have the CLERK role automatically enabled for LYNN during LYNN's next login?

     A. Nothing; the CLERK role will automatically become a default role for LYNN.

     B. Execute the command **alter user LYNN add default role LYNN**.

     C. Execute the command **alter role CLERK default.**

     D. Execute the command **grant CLERK to LYNN with admin option**.

Category   Security

Answer   A. Nothing. The CLERK role will automatically become a default role for LYNN.

Explanation   Once a role is granted to a user, it is enabled as a default role for that user on the user's next login.

15. Which of the following data dictionary views displays the setting of the OPTIMAL parameter for a rollback segment?

    A. DBA_ROLLBACK_SEGS

    B. V$ROLLSTAT

    C. V$SETTINGS

    D. DBA_SEGMENTS

Category   Tuning and Troubleshooting

Answer   B. V$ROLLSTAT

Explanation   **Optimal** is the only parameter of a rollback segment that is not shown in either DBA_ROLLBACK_SEGS or DBA_SEGMENTS. This is one of the five most difficult practice questions.

16. Which of the following constraints, when applied to a table, will automatically create an index?

    A. FOREIGN KEY

    B. CHECK

    C. UNIQUE

    D. NOT NULL

Category   Data Administration

Answer   C. UNIQUE

Explanation   Unique indexes are automatically created whenever UNIQUE or PRIMARY KEY constraints are added to a table. Use the **using index** clause of the **alter table** or **create table** command to force the UNIQUE or PRIMARY KEY indexes to use nondefault storage values.

17. TRUE or FALSE: You can recompile the body of a package without recompiling the package specification.

    A. TRUE

    B. FALSE

Category   Architecture and Options

Answer   A. TRUE

Explanation   Use the **alter package ... compile body** command to compile the body of a package without compiling the package specification.

18. What is the impact of specifying IGNORE=Y during an Import?

    A. It causes Import to ignore the default Import parameters, using your account's fault parameters instead.

    B. It causes rows to be imported into existing tables.

    C. It deletes data currently in the tables before inserting the records from the Export dump file.

    D. It causes Import to ignore data integrity constraints during the Import.

Category   Backup and Recovery

Answer   B. It causes rows to be imported into existing tables.

Explanation   "IGNORE", within Import, tells the Oracle to ignore object creation errors during Import. If a table already exists prior to starting an Import, attempting to Import that table with IGNORE=N will cause an error. To load records into an existing table, you must specify IGNORE=Y to force Import to ignore that error.

19. What will be the result of the following command, when issued by the SYSTEM user? Assume that the SCOTT and TONY users exist, and that SCOTT owns a table named DEPT.

```
create synonym TONY.DEPT for SCOTT.DEPT;
```

    A. A synonym named TONY.DEPT, pointing to SCOTT.DEPT, will be created in the SYSTEM schema.

    B. A synonym named DEPT, pointing to SCOTT.DEPT, will be created in the TONY schema.

    C. A synonym named DEPT, pointing to SCOTT.DEPT, will be created in the TONY schema, and TONY will be granted SELECT access to the SCOTT.DEPT table.

    D. An error will be returned.

Category   Resource Management

Answer   B. A synonym named DEPT, pointing to SCOTT.DEPT, will be created in the TONY schema.

Explanation   The synonym will be created in the TONY schema. No privileges will be granted as a result of the synonym creation.

20. A user has been granted three roles, named CONNECT, SELECT_USER, and CLERK. All three roles are enabled by default. After login, which of the following commands will allow the user to enable only the CONNECT and SELECT_USER roles, while disabling the CLERK role?

    A. alter session disable role CLERK;

    B. alter session set role all except CLERK;

    C. set role none;

    D. execute DBMS_ROLES.DISABLE('clerk');

Category   Security

Answer   B. alter session set role all except CLERK;

Explanation   Only two of the answers—B and C—are valid commands in Oracle. You can use the **set role** clause of the **alter session** command to enable all roles, specifically listed roles, or all except specifically listed roles, as shown in answer B, the correct solution to the question.

21. TRUE or FALSE: When tuning a transaction-intensive system, it is important to separate the rollback segments and online redo log files onto different I/O devices.

    A. TRUE

    B. FALSE

Category   Tuning and Troubleshooting

Answer   A. TRUE

Explanation   During a transaction, data is being written concurrently to both the rollback segments and the online redo log files. To avoid I/O contention in transaction-intensive systems, rollback segments and online redo log files should be placed on separate I/O devices.

22. If an AFTER ROW trigger fails, does the transaction that caused the trigger to execute also fail?

    A. YES

    B. NO

Category   Data Administration

Answer   A. YES

Explanation   The transactions within triggers must succeed; otherwise, the transaction that caused the trigger to be executed must be rolled back.

23. Can a trigger contain a COMMIT?

    A. YES

    B. NO

Category   Architecture and Options

Answer   B. NO

Explanation   Triggers cannot contain COMMITs; the success or failure of transactions within the trigger must be tied to the success or failure of the transaction that executed the trigger.

24. What will be the result of the following command, when issued by the SYSTEM user? Assume that the TONY user exists, and that the service name and remote account information are accurate.

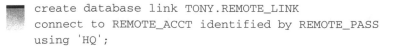

```
create database link TONY.REMOTE_LINK
connect to REMOTE_ACCT identified by REMOTE_PASS
using 'HQ';
```

A. A database link named TONY.REMOTE_LINK, pointing to a remote database, will be created in the SYSTEM schema.

B. A database link named REMOTE_LINK, pointing to a remote database, will be created in the TONY schema.

C. A database link named REMOTE_LINK, pointing to a remote database, will be created in the TONY schema, and the remote account will be granted CONNECT privileges.

D. An error will be returned.

Category   Resource Management

Answer   A. A database link named TONY.REMOTE_LINK, pointing to a remote database, will be created in the SYSTEM schema.

Explanation   Database links cannot be created in other users' accounts—the only options are to create **public** database links or links that exist solely in the creator's account. Oracle will create a database link named TONY.REMOTE_LINK (database link names can contain periods) in the schema of the user issuing the command—in this case, SYSTEM.

25. RELOAD is an option for which of the following utilities?

A. SQLLOAD

B. LSNRCTL

C. IMPORT

D. SQLDBA

Category   Maintenance and Operations

Answer   B. LSNRCTL

Explanation   RELOAD, when executed within LSNRCTL, forces the SQL*Net V2 Listener process to reread the listener.ora file and reset itself based on the parameters in that file.

26. Which of the following privileges cannot be granted to a role?

A. CREATE SESSION

B. UNLIMITED TABLESPACE

C. INSERT ANY TABLE

D. ANALYZE ANY

Category Security

Answer B. UNLIMITED TABLESPACE

Explanation UNLIMITED TABLESPACE must be granted on a user-by-user basis. Many system privileges can be granted to roles, but space-related privileges (such as space quotas and the UNLIMITED TABLESPACE system privilege) cannot be granted via roles.

27. In which V$ table can you find the maximum number of users that were concurrently logged into an instance since it was started?

A. V$LICENSE

B. V$SESSIONS

C. V$SYSSTAT

D. V$PROCESS

Category Tuning and Troubleshooting

Answer A. V$LICENSE

Explanation To see the high-water mark for concurrent sessions since the instance was started, execute the following query:

```
select Sessions_Highwater from V$LICENSE;
```

28. Which of the background processes periodically coalesces free space in tablespaces?

A. SMON

B. PMON

C. IMON

D. FMON

Category   Architecture and Options

Answer   A. SMON

Explanation   SMON will coalesce neighboring free extents into a single free extent, provided the default **pctincrease** for the tablespace is non-zero.

29. During a recovery using online backups and archived redo log files, you discover that one of the archived redo log files is missing. Which of the options below best describes your recovery options?

    A. Skip the missing log file and apply the rest of the archived redo log files; then open the database without the data in the missing log file.

    B. Stop the recovery at the last available log file prior to the missing archived redo log file.

    C. Skip the missing log file, apply the rest of the archived redo log files, and recover the missing log file's data from the rollback segments.

    D. Skip the missing log file, apply the rest of the archived redo log files, and use the **alter database resetlogs** command when opening the database.

Category   Backup and Recovery

Answer   B. Stop the recovery at the last available log file prior to the missing archived redo log file.

Explanation   You cannot skip the missing log file; you have to stop at that point and open the database. Since all of the other answers involve skipping the missing redo log file, B is the only valid answer.

30. When a rollback segment entry expands from one extent to another,

    A. an ORA-1555 ("snapshot too old") error is returned.

    B. the data in its first extent is marked as "inactive".

    C. the expansion is called a "wrap".

    D. it always acquires additional space in the tablespace.

Category   Resource Management

Answer   C. the expansion is called a "wrap".

Explanation   Data in a rollback segment entry is always considered "active" while the transaction is active, so B is incorrect. If there is enough free space already within the rollback segment, the rollback segment will not extend, so D is incorrect. An ORA-1555 error (answer A) occurs when a transaction relies on data that has since been marked as "inactive"; that error is not related to the scenario described.

Wraps indicate that the extents within a rollback segment are not large enough to handle a transaction without involving other extents. The number of wraps that has occurred within each rollback segment since the instance was started is reported in V$ROLLSTAT; the utlbstat and utlestat scripts will report on the number of wraps that occur in a given time period.

31. Which of the following can you NOT change after a database has been created?

    A. The shared pool size.

    B. The default number of listeners.

    C. The number of control files.

    D. The database block size.

Category   Maintenance and Operations

Answer   D. The database block size.

Explanation   All of the answers except for the database block size can be changed via the database's init.ora file. Adding an additional controlfile involves changing the init.ora file (the CONTROL_FILES parameter) and, while the database is down, copying an existing controlfile to the new location. Changing the database block size requires completely re-creating the database.

32. A user creates a PRIMARY KEY constraint while creating the COMPANY table with the following command.

```
create Table COMPANY
 (Company_ID NUMBER,
  Name        VARCHAR2 (20),
  constraint COMPANY_PK primary key (COMPANY_ID))
```

```
tablespace DATA
storage (initial 50M next 50M pctincrease 0);
```

What will Oracle use for the storage and tablespace parameters for the associated unique index?

    A. The default storage and tablespace parameters designated in the user's profile.

    B. The storage and tablespace parameters used by the COMPANY table.

    C. The default tablespace for the user, and the default storage parameters for that tablespace.

    D. The default tablespace for the user, and the storage parameters used by the COMPANY table.

Category   Data Administration

Answer   C. The default tablespace for the user, and the default storage parameters for that tablespace.

Explanation   The index will be created in the user's default tablespace. The table will be created in the DATA tablespace, but the index will not inherit that tablespace designation. To specify a tablespace during index creations within **create table** commands, use the **using index** clause. Since no storage parameters are specified, the index will use the default storage parameters for the tablespace in which it is created. The default tablespace for a user is set via the **default tablespace** clause of the **create user** and **alter user** commands. The default storage parameters for a tablespace are set via the **default storage** clause of the **create tablespace** and **alter tablespace** commands.

33. What will be the outcome of the following command?

```
alter database backup controlfile to TRACE;
```

    A. The **create controlfile** command for the instance will be written to a trace file in the trace file destination directory.

    B. An existing controlfile will be backed up to the trace file destination directory.

    C. An existing controlfile will be copied to a file named *trace*.

    D. The **create controlfile** command for the instance will be written to a file named *trace*.

Category   Backup and Recovery

Answer   A. The **create controlfile** command for the instance will be written to a trace file in the trace file destination directory.

Explanation   The full syntax for your current **create controlfile** command will be written to a trace file. This command is useful when you have lost your controlfiles or when you need to modify a system parameter such as MAXDATAFILES—or just to have current documentation of the database's physical configuration.

34. The CLERK role has been granted SELECT access to the TONY.EMP table. The following commands are executed by the SYSTEM user:

```
create user MARY identified by LAMB;
grant CONNECT, CREATE VIEW to Mary;
grant CLERK to Mary;
```

Which of the following actions, when run under the MARY account, will fail?

A. select * from TONY.EMP;

B. create synonym EMP for TONY.EMP;

C. create view EMP as select * from TONY.EMP;

D. describe TONY.EMP

Category   Resource Management

Answer   C. **create view EMP as select * from TONY.EMP;**

Explanation   You cannot create a view, procedure, function, or package based on privileges obtained via a role. In order to create a view based on another user's table, you would first need to have been explicitly granted privileges on the table, as shown in the following listing:

```
grant SELECT on TONY.EMP to MARY;
```

The CONNECT role granted to the Mary account includes the CREATE SYNONYM and CREATE VIEW system privileges.

35. Lines A through D of the following script form a single command. Which of the lines will cause an error?

    A. create user OPS$MARY

    B. identified externally

    C. quota 10M on SYSTEM

    D. default role CONNECT;

Category   Security

Answer   D. **default role CONNECT;**

Explanation   You can't grant roles to a user via the **create user** command. Line C, which grants a space quota to the OPS$MARY user for the SYSTEM tablespace, will succeed; however, users generally should not be granted space quotas on the SYSTEM tablespace. To alter a user's default roles, use the **alter user** command.

36. What data dictionary view displays the status of an INDEX ('DIRECT LOAD' or 'VALID') following a SQL*Loader Direct Path load?

    A. V$LOADER

    B. DBA_INDEXES

    C. DBA_SEGMENTS

    D. V$LOADSTAT

Category   Tuning and Troubleshooting

Answer   B. DBA_INDEXES

Explanation   The Status column of DBA_INDEXES displays this information:

```
select Index_Name, Status from DBA_INDEXES
 where Table_Name = 'EMP';
```

37. In your database's init.ora file, OPTIMIZER_MODE is set to CHOOSE. Which of the following is true about queries in your database?

A. Oracle will dynamically decide whether rule-based or cost-based optimization will resolve each query the fastest, and will choose an execution path accordingly.

B. During each query, you will be prompted to choose either rule-based or cost-based optimization.

C. Each query will use the choice-based optimizer.

D. If statistics are available for the tables in the queries, the cost-based optimizer will be used; otherwise, the rule-based optimizer will be used.

Category   Architecture and Options

Answer   D. If statistics are available for the tables in the queries, the cost-based optimizer will be used; otherwise, the rule-based optimizer will be used.

Explanation   If any of the tables in the query has been analyzed, and the optimizer mode is CHOOSE, then Oracle will use the cost-based optimizer. If none of the tables have been analyzed, and the optimizer mode is CHOOSE, then Oracle will use the rule-based optimizer. The execution path choices can be influenced via hints. See Chapters 7 and 10.

38. In the following listing, the archive log list command is executed within SQLDBA, and the results are shown.

```
SQLDBA> archive log list
Database log mode             NOARCHIVELOG
Automatic archival            ENABLED
Archive destination           /db01/oracle/arch/arch
Oldest online log sequence    966
Current log sequence          968
```

Is the database currently writing archive log files to the archive log destination directory?

A. YES

B. NO

Category   Backup and Recovery

Answer   B. NO

Explanation   Since the database is in NOARCHIVELOG mode, it is not writing archived redo log files to the archive log destination directory. "Automatic archival" is marked as "ENABLED" because the database's init.ora file has LOG_ARCHIVE_START set to 'TRUE', but the database is not in ARCHIVELOG mode.

39. Which of the following would cause a shutdown immediate to fail?

   A. A transaction that has just started.

   B. A user process that is not disconnected.

   C. A transaction that is in the process of rolling back.

   D. A deadlock between two processes.

Category   Maintenance and Operations

Answer   D. A deadlock between two processes.

Explanation   The **shutdown immediate** command will wait for all ongoing processes to rollback, and will disconnect users who are still logged in. The database will not shutdown if the **shutdown immediate** encounters a deadlock between two processes. In a deadlock situation, the shutdown will hang and you will have to **shutdown abort** the instance.

40. The EMPLOYEE table has a single-column, nonunique index on its City column, and a second single-column nonunique index on its State column. Given the following query, which of the listed operations will be used during the query's execution, assuming rule-based optimization?

```
select count(*)
  from EMPLOYEE
  where City = 'Baltimore'
  and State = 'MD';
```

A. NESTED LOOPS

B. AND-EQUAL

C. CONCATENATION

D. TABLE ACCESS FULL

Category   Tuning and Troubleshooting

Answer   B. AND-EQUAL

Explanation   Since two indexes are available, Oracle will perform range scans on both indexes and will merge the result sets of the index scans. The merging of the result sets from index scans is called an AND-EQUAL operation. This is one of the five most difficult practice questions. See Chapter 10.

41. During a conventional path SQL*Loader load, some of the input records fail the WHEN clause. Which file will record the records that fail the WHEN clause criteria?

A. The Discard file.

B. The Bad file.

C. The Log file.

D. No file, since they failed the WHEN clause.

Category   Data Administration

Answer   A. The Discard file.

Explanation   Records that fail the WHEN clause get written to the Discard file.

42. In the following listing, the archive log list command is executed within SQLDBA, and the results are shown.

```
SQLDBA> archive log list
Database log mode              NOARCHIVELOG
Automatic archival             ENABLED
Archive destination            /db01/oracle/arch/arch
Oldest online log sequence     966
Current log sequence           968
```

How many online redo log files are there for this instance?

    A. 968

    B. 3

    C. 2

    D. 966

Category   Backup and Recovery

Answer   B. 3

Explanation   There are three online redo log files; their sequence numbers are 966, 967, and 968. The current online redo log has a sequence number of 968.

43. Can you create a PUBLIC snapshot log?

    A. YES

    B. NO

Category   Resource Management

Answer   B. NO

Explanation   Snapshot logs are created under the schema that owns the base table for a simple snapshot. The **create snapshot log** command creates an audit table to record rows that have been modified and a trigger to populate the audit table—and neither a table nor a trigger can be declared as a public object. The snapshot log cannot be declared PUBLIC in the same way that a synonym or database link can be.

44. Which of the following roles is not created automatically during a database creation?

    A. CONNECT

    B. MONITORER

    C. IMP_FULL_DATABASE

    D. RESOURCE

Category   Maintenance and Operations

Answer   B. MONITORER

Explanation   The MONITORER role is created via the utlmontr.sql script in the /RDBMS/ADMIN subdirectory under the Oracle home directory; it is not part of the standard database creation.

45. TRUE or FALSE: The WITH ADMIN OPTION clause of the GRANT command allows users to create views based on the objects being granted to the users.

   A. TRUE

   B. FALSE

Category   Security

Answer   B. FALSE

Explanation   The **with admin option** clause of the **grant** command is used when a role is granted to a user; it grants the user the ability to alter or drop the role. The **with grant option** clause of the **grant** command allows users to create (and pass along privileges to) views based on the objects being granted to the users.

46. A large table has all of its records deleted, and the deletion is committed. To verify that there are no records in the table, you perform the following query:

```
select COUNT(*) from EMP;
```

Several minutes later, the query returns a value of 0 for the number of records in the table. What is the most likely reason why the query took so long?

   A. The table was fragmented into multiple extents.

   B. The table had more than five indexes on it.

   C. The table had not been analyzed since its records had been deleted.

   D. The table's highwatermark had not been reset.

Category Tuning and Troubleshooting

Answer D. The table's highwatermark had not been reset.

Explanation A table's highwatermark is reset when it is **truncate**d or dropped and re-created. The highwatermark indicates the highest block that contained records. The COUNT(*) query forces Oracle to read every block up to the highwatermark—even if there are no records in the table. This is one of the five most difficult practice questions. See Chapter 2.

47. The number of query server processes associated with a single operation

    A. is known as the "degree of parallelism."

    B. can only be specified at the query level.

    C. is limited by the database block size.

    D. is limited at the user level.

Category Architecture and Options

Answer A. is known as the "degree of parallelism."

Explanation The degree of parallelism is set via the **degree** parameter, at either the instance, table, or query level. See Chapter 12 and the *Oracle Release 7.1 Server Administrator's Addendum.*

48. What will be the outcome of the following command?

```
archive log all;
```

    A. When issued during a recovery, this command forces all archive log files to be applied to the damaged datafiles without further prompting.

    B. All full unarchived online redo log files will be manually archived.

    C. The log of all database connections will be archived in SYS.AUD$.

    D. The ARCH background process will be enabled for all instances.

Category Backup and Recovery

Answer   B. All full unarchived online redo log files will be manually archived.

Explanation   The **archive log all** command is often used during online backups to force all online redo log entries to be written to the archived redo log files. This command is frequently used during online backup procedures, to make sure all online redo log entries have been archived prior to the start of the backup.

49. A tablespace named DATA contains three datafiles, each of which is 100MB in length. A user who has a quota of 200MB on the DATA tablespace attempts the following command:

```
create table TABLE_X
(column1 VARCHAR2(10))
tablespace DATA
storage (initial 75M next 75M pctincrease 0 minextents 2);
```

What will be the result of the create table command shown?

A. The command will fail.

B. TABLE_X will be created in the DATA tablespace; its first extent will be in the first datafile, and its second extent will be in the second datafile.

C. TABLE_X will be created in the DATA tablespace; its first extent will be in the first datafile, and its second extent will be split across the first and second datafile.

D. TABLE_X will be created in the DATA tablespace; only one extent will be created.

Category   Resource Management

Answer   B. TABLE_X will be created in the DATA tablespace; its first extent will be in the first datafile, and its second extent will be in the second datafile.

Explanation   An extent cannot span datafiles, so C is incorrect. **minextents** is set to 2, so D is incorrect. The extents (75 MB each) fit within the datafiles (100 MB each), so the extents will be created and the command will succeed.

50. What will be the output of the following command?

```
lsnrctl status netstat
```

    A. The status of SQL*Net V2 on the host named NETSTAT will be reported.

    B. The status of SQL*Net V2 on the current host will be reported, along with network traffic statistics.

    C. The status of SQL*Net V2 for the instance identified by the NETSTAT service name in the tnsnames.ora file will be reported.

    D. The status of SQL*Net V2 on the current host will be written to a file named NETSTAT.

Category   Maintenance and Operations

Answer   C. The status of SQL*Net V2 for the instance identified by the NETSTAT service name in the tnsnames.ora file will be reported.

Explanation   The **lsnrctl status** command checks the status of SQL*Net V2; when followed by a service name (in this example, "netstat"), it will check the status of SQL*Net V2 on the host used by the service name's instance. Service names are defined via the tnsnames.ora file.

51. What is the name of the default user profile?

    A. DEFAULT

    B. USER

    C. CONNECT

    D. PROFILE

Category   Security

Answer   A. DEFAULT

Explanation   You can change the default profile values via the **alter profile default** command.

52. Following an aborted SQL*Loader Direct Path load, the COMPANY table's unique index on the Mail_ID column, named COMPANYUMAIL_ID, is left in 'DIRECT LOAD' state. Which of the following procedures will restore the index to a valid state in the shortest time possible?

A. alter index COMPANYUMAIL_ID valid;

B. validate index COMPANYUMAIL_ID;

C. alter table COMPANY enable index COMPANYUMAIL_ID;

D. Drop and re-create the index.

Category   Data Administration

Answer   D. Drop and re-create the index.

Explanation   When an index is left in 'DIRECT LOAD' state, you must drop and re-create the index for it to have a status of 'VALID'.

53. An automated shutdown/startup process fails due to a media failure. In which file will you be able to view the errors that the database encountered?

A. The alert log.

B. The online redo log.

C. The control file.

D. The archived redo log.

Category   Backup and Recovery

Answer   A. The alert log.

Explanation   All database shutdowns and startups write entries to the alert log. The alert log also contains data about errors it encounters, log switches, and many DBA activities.

54. An empty tablespace named DATA contains one datafile, 300MB in length. A user who has a 50MB table named TABLE_Y (in a different tablespace) and a quota of 200MB on the DATA tablespace attempts the following command:

```
create table TABLE_X
as select * from TABLE_Y
tablespace DATA
storage (initial 40M next 40M pctincrease 0);
```

What will be the result of the create table command shown, assuming that the database has adequate space to handle the transaction?

A. The command will fail because of a syntax error.

B. TABLE_X will be created in the DATA tablespace, with no rows.

C. TABLE_X will be created in the DATA tablespace and populated with rows from the TABLE_Y table.

D. TABLE_X will be created in the same tablespace as TABLE_Y.

Category   Resource Management

Answer   A. The command will fail because of a syntax error.

Explanation   The **as select** clause should follow the **tablespace** and **storage** designations. The command should read:

```
create table TABLE_X
tablespace DATA
storage (initial 40M next 40M pctincrease 0)
as select * from TABLE_Y;
```

55. What will be the outcome of the following command?

```
audit INSERT, UPDATE, DELETE on DEFAULT;
```

A. insert, **update**, and **deletes** against the table named DEFAULT will be recorded.

B. insert, **update**, and **deletes** by users with DEFAULT profiles will be recorded.

C. **insert**, **update**, and **deletes** will be recorded for all tables in the database.

D. **insert**, **update**, and **deletes** will be set as the DEFAULT auditing option for all tables.

Category   Security

Answer   D. **insert**, **update**, and **deletes** will be set as the DEFAULT auditing option for all tables.

Explanation   The "on DEFAULT" clause changes the default auditing options; the next time an **audit** command is executed, it will use the default auditing options.

56. TRUE or FALSE: There is no limit to the length of the time period between the running of utlbstat.sql and utlestat.sql, provided the database is not shutdown at any point during that period—the results will always be valid.

A. TRUE

B. FALSE

Category   Tuning and Troubleshooting

Answer   B. FALSE

Explanation   There *is* a limit to the time period between utlbstat.sql and utlestat.sql. The internal statistics are stored in a 32-bit unsigned counter. If the counter exceeds this range (0 to 2,147,483,647), the counter will wrap and start from zero again. When selecting from V$SYSSTAT using SQL*Plus, the numbers are returned as signed 32-bit counters, so high values (over one-half of the 32-bit value above) will appear as negative numbers, yielding erroneous results.

57. Can a CHECK constraint on the COMPANY table reference any table other than COMPANY?

A. YES

B. NO

Category   Data Administration

Answer   B. NO

Explanation   A CHECK constraint can only reference the table it is constraining—in this case, COMPANY.

58. Queries against a non-updateable snapshot retrieve data

   A. from a local read-only view of a local table.

   B. from a local read-only view of a remote table.

   C. directly from a local table.

   D. directly from a remote table.

Category   Architecture and Options

Answer   A. from a local read-only view of a local table.

Explanation   The local table is populated via snapshot refreshes. The local view that accesses the local table is non-updateable.

59. In your development environment, the backup schedule is:

   ■ **Sunday nights: Full export**

   ■ **Monday & Tuesday: Incremental export**

   ■ **Wednesday: Cumulative export**

   ■ **Thursday, Friday, Saturday: Incremental export**

On Friday afternoon, you need to recover the database to the latest point possible from your exports. What files will you need?

   A. Thursday night's Incremental export and Sunday night's Full export.

   B. Thursday night's Incremental export, Sunday night's Full export, and Wednesday night's Cumulative export.

   C. Sunday night's Full export, and the Incremental exports from Monday, Tuesday, and Thursday.

   D. Thursday night's Incremental export and Wednesday night's Cumulative export.

Category Backup and Recovery

Answer B. Thursday night's Incremental export, Sunday night's Full export, and Wednesday night's Cumulative export.

Explanation You'll need the most recent Full export, the most recent Cumulative export (if performed after the most recent Full export), and every Incremental export since either the most recent Cumulative or the most recent Full, whichever comes later.

60. Place the database creation steps listed below in their proper chronological order:

1. **create database**...
2. **create tablespace ROLL_SEGS**...
3. **create rollback segment R_1 tablespace ROLL_SEGS;**
4. **create rollback segment R1 tablespace SYSTEM;**
5. **alter rollback segment R1 online;**

Category Maintenance and Operations

Answer 1, 4, 5, 2, 3

Explanation The second rollback segment (R1) must be created in the SYSTEM tablespace and brought online before the ROLL_SEGS tablespace can be created. You cannot create and use the ROLL_SEGS tablespace until the second rollback segment is brought online in the SYSTEM tablespace.

61. Which data dictionary view records the creation date of tables?

A. DBA_OBJECTS

B. DBA_TABLES

C. DBA_SEGMENTS

D. DBA_TAB_COLUMNS

Category Tuning and Troubleshooting

Answer   A. DBA_OBJECTS

Explanation   Query the Created column from DBA_OBJECTS:

```
select Created from DBA_OBJECTS
 where Object_Name = '&table_name';
```

62. Which of the following is correct?

A. You can perform Complete refreshes only on complex snapshots.

B. You can perform Fast refreshes only on complex snapshots.

C. You can perform Fast refreshes on either complex or simple snapshots.

D. You can perform Complete refreshes on simple snapshots.

Category   Data Administration

Answer   D. You can perform Complete refreshes on simple snapshots.

Explanation   You can perform Complete refreshes on either simple or complex snapshots. You can only perform Fast refreshes on simple snapshots.

63. In a client-server environment using SQL*Net V2 (prior to 2.3, and not using Oracle*Names), which machines must have SQL*Net V2 configuration files on them?

A. The server, but not the client.

B. Both the client and the server.

C. The client, but not the server.

D. Neither the client nor the server.

Category   Architecture and Options

Answer   B. Both the client and the server.

Explanation   The client must have the tnsnames.ora file to find the remote service, and the server must have a Listener process running (as defined by its listener.ora file).

64. TRUE or FALSE: An Incremental export backs up only the records that have changed since the last export; records that have not changed are not backed up.

  A. TRUE

  B. FALSE

Category   Backup and Recovery

Answer   B. FALSE

Explanation   An Incremental export backs up any table that contains a changed record—and it backs up every record in those tables.

65. The space allocation within a tablespace is shown in the following listing.

```
select Segment_Name, Block_ID, Blocks
 from DBA_EXTENTS
 where Tablespace_Name = 'DATA'
 union
select 'free space', Block_ID, blocks
 from DBA_FREE_SPACE
 where Tablespace_Name = 'DATA'
 order by 2,3;
```

Segment_Name	Block_ID	Blocks
TABLE_A	2	20
TABLE_A	22	20
TABLE_B	42	50
free space	92	10
free space	102	45
TABLE_A	147	20

As shown in the preceding listing, TABLE_A's first extent starts at block #2 and is 20 blocks in length. Can TABLE_B extend to a second extent if its NEXT value is equal to its INITIAL value, and it has a PCTINCREASE value of 50?

  A. YES

  B. NO

Category   Resource Management

Answer   A. YES

Explanation   If TABLE_B's **next** value is the same as its **initial** value (50 blocks), Oracle can combine the two contiguous free extents to handle the free space requirements. The **pctincrease** value does not impact the space requirements of the *second* extent for a table, only for the third extent and beyond. TABLE_B's space requirements, by extent, are 50 blocks (**initial**) for the first, 50 blocks (**next**) for the second, 75 blocks (**next***(1+(**pctincrease**/100))) for the third. This is one of the five most difficult practice questions.

66. TRUE or FALSE: You can use the SQL*Net V2 tnsnames.ora file to facilitate SQL*Net V1 connections by setting service names equal to SQL*Net V1 connect strings.

   A. TRUE

   B. FALSE

Category   Maintenance and Operations

Answer   A. TRUE

Explanation   The entry in the tnsnames.ora file would be of the form

```
dev_v1 = t:server1:dev
```

where "t" tells SQL*Net V1 to use the TCP/IP protocol, and "server1" is the host machine on which the "dev" instance resides.

67. What will be the outcome of the following command?

```
analyze table COMPANY compute statistics;
```

   A. By default, roughly 10 percent of the COMPANY table will be scanned and its statistics will be estimated.

   B. The COMPANY table and all of its indexes will be fully scanned and their statistics will be collected.

   C. The COMPANY table will be scanned and its statistics will be collected, but its indexes will not be analyzed.

D. Each row of the COMPANY table will be matched against the index column values in its associated indexes.

Category   Data Administration

Answer   B. The COMPANY table and all of its indexes will be fully scanned and their statistics will be collected.

Explanation   Since the **compute** option is used, the entire table will be scanned. When you collect statistics for a table, Oracle automatically also collects statistics for its associated indexes. Answer D would be correct if you had used the **validate structure** option of the **analyze** command.

68. An SCN is a

A. Source Code Number.

B. System Control Number.

C. System Change Number.

D. Session Commit Node.

Category   Backup and Recovery

Answer   C. System Change Number.

Explanation   The System Change Number is used to maintain a chronological order for the changes within a database.

69. What is the outcome of the following command?

```
audit session;
```

A. All successful connections to the database will be recorded.

B. All unsuccessful connections to the database will be recorded.

C. All successful and unsuccessful connections to the database will be recorded.

D. The command will return an error.

Category   Security

Answer   C. All successful and unsuccessful connections to the database will be recorded.

Explanation   Since no **whenever [not] successful** clause is specified in the example, both successful and unsuccessful connection attempts will be audited.

70. TRUE or FALSE: There is a 1-to-1 relationship between V$ROLLNAME and V$ROLLSTAT.

    A. TRUE

    B. FALSE

Category   Tuning and Troubleshooting

Answer   A. TRUE

Explanation   There is one record per rollback segment in both V$ROLLNAME and V$ROLLSTAT.

71. In a distributed transaction environment, the Commit Point Site for a transaction is designated by

    A. setting COMMIT_POINT = TRUE in the init.ora file of the Commit Point Site, and COMMIT_POINT = FALSE for the other sites.

    B. using a COMMIT_POINT hint in the transaction.

    C. having the highest value for COMMIT_POINT_STRENGTH among the init.ora files of participating sites.

    D. using a NOT_IN_DOUBT hint in the transaction.

Category   Architecture and Options

Answer   C. having the highest value for COMMIT_POINT_STRENGTH among the init.ora files of participating sites.

Explanation   The COMMIT_POINT_STRENGTHs of the participating databases are checked during each distributed transaction. The value of the COMMIT_POINT_STRENGTH parameter cannot exceed 255.

72. An application will be using stored procedures and packages extensively. Which of the following system tables will most likely require a large amount of space?

A. TS$

B. SOURCE$

C. CODE$

D. PROC$

Category   Resource Management

Answer   B. SOURCE$

Explanation   The source code for procedures and packages is stored in the SOURCE$ data dictionary table in the SYSTEM tablespace. In applications that use stored procedures and packages extensively, SOURCE$ may expand rapidly.

73. What will be the outcome of attempting to use the REMOTE_CONNECT database link, whose create database link command is shown below?

```
create database link REMOTE_CONNECT
 using 'dev';
```

A. Attempts to use this database link will fail, since no username/password is identified.

B. Using this database link will succeed if current username/password combination in the current database is a valid username/password combination in the 'dev' instance.

C. Attempts to use this database link will succeed if REMOTE_OS_AUTHENT is set to 'TRUE' in the 'dev' instance's init.ora file.

D. When used, the REMOTE_CONNECT database link will log into the 'dev' instance using the default username and password for that instance.

Category   Security

Answer   B. Using this database link will succeed if current username/password combination in the current database is a valid username/password combination in the 'dev' instance.

Explanation   Since no username/password combination is specified for the database link, it will use the current user's username and password when attempting to log into the 'dev' instance.

74. What will be the outcome of the following command?

```
truncate table COMPANY;
```

    A. The records in COMPANY will be deleted, its non-**initial** extents will be marked as free space, and its associated indexes will also be reduced to a single extent.

    B. The records in COMPANY will be deleted, it will keep all of its allocated space, and its associated indexes will keep all of their allocated space.

    C. The records in COMPANY will be deleted, it will keep all of its allocated space, and its indexes will be dropped.

    D. The status of COMPANY table will change to 'TRUNCATED', as shown in the Status column of the DBA_TABLES view.

Category   Data Administration

Answer   A. The records in COMPANY will be deleted, its non-**initial** extents will be marked as free space, and its associated indexes will also be reduced to a single extent.

Explanation   By default, **truncate** will drop all non-**initial** extents for objects. You can also specify **reuse storage** to force it to keep its allocated space. When you **truncate** a table, its indexes will be **truncate**d too.

75. During an attempted login, you receive the message "archiver is stuck, connect INTERNAL only until freed". To properly resolve the problem that caused this message, you should

    A. Execute the command **alter database archive log free**.

    B. Free up space in the archive log destination directory.

    C. Require all users to use the **connect internal** command for all application database connections.

    D. Execute the command **alter database archivelog**.

Category   Backup and Recovery

Answer   B. Free up space in the archive log destination directory.

Explanation   The problem is that the archive log destination directory is filled, and the ARCH background process cannot write any more archived redo log files to that directory. Once space is available in the archive log destination directory, the database can once again be used for transactions. This error also points out that the archive log destination directory is not properly sized for the transaction volume of your database.

76. In a tablespace that has default storage parameters of INITIAL 30K, NEXT 30K, PCTINCREASE 0, a user specifies INITIAL 12K, NEXT 12K, PCTINCREASE 0 in a create table command. If the database block size is 2K, how large is the first extent of the table?

    A. 12K

    B. 15K

    C. 20K

    D. 30K

Category   Resource Management

Answer   C. 20K

Explanation   In order to avoid tablespace free space fragmentation, Oracle rounds up storage specifications so that space is allocated in groups of five blocks. Since the database block size is 2K, the smallest extent you can create is 10K (five 2K blocks). The **create table** storage specification exceeds 10K (five blocks), so ten blocks, 2K each in size, will be allocated, yielding an **initial** extent size of 20K (ten 2K blocks). In Oracle Version 6, the initial extent size would have been 12K; the rounding action was added in Oracle7.

    Despite the fact that it has given you a different quantity of space than you requested, Oracle will still save your **initial** and **next** values and will use them when calculating the size of subsequent extents—and it will round the sizes of those extents, too.

If you use a different block size, Oracle will round the block allocations differently; and if the tablespace is already in use, Oracle may round the block allocations based on the size of the available free extents in the tablespace. This is one of the five most difficult practice questions.

77. Which of the following is NOT an option for ORASRV?

   A. dbaoff

   B. debugoff

   C. logoff

   D. waitoff

Category   Maintenance and Operations

Answer   D. waitoff

Explanation   ORASRV is the executable for SQL*Net V1. "dbaoff" prevents remote users from using **connect internal** to connect to the local database. "debugoff" turns off debugging, and "logoff" turns off the writing of SQL*Net V1 log file entries. "waitoff" is not a valid option.

78. The COMPANY table in a remote database contains only CHAR, VARCHAR2, and NUMBER columns. Can you create a view of COMPANY in a different database, using a database link?

   A. YES

   B. NO

Category   Security

Answer   A. YES

Explanation   For example,

```
create view TEST as select * from COMPANY@some_db_link;
```

You cannot select LONG values across a database link.

79. Which of the following is NOT a lockmode option for the lock table command?

    A. share update

    B. share row exclusive

    C. row share

    D. update

Category   Tuning and Troubleshooting

Answer   D. **update**

Explanation   The others are all valid options, as are **share**, **row share**, and **exclusive**.

80. If you are using multiple online redo log threads, then you are

    A. logged in multiple times to the same instance.

    B. using the Parallel Query option.

    C. using the Parallel Server option.

    D. using an instance that has specified MULTIPLE_REDO_THREADS = TRUE in its init.ora file.

Category   Architecture and Options

Answer   C. using the Parallel Server option.

Explanation   When you use the Parallel Server option, multiple instances reference the same datafiles. Redo log threads help distinguish among the entries from various instances.

81. When you create a new tablespace, do the control files increase in size?

    A. YES

    B. NO

Category   Backup and Recovery

Answer   B. NO

Explanation   The size of the controlfile is set via the parameters specified in the **create database** and **create controlfile** commands.

82. During an insert into a table in an Oracle7.2 database, an "unable to allocate extent of size 100 in tablespace DATA" error is returned. The table has no indexes or constraints, and has reached 121 extents (the maximum allowed for the database's block size of 2K). Which of the following is the best way to resolve this problem and complete the data insertion process?

  A. Alter the **next** parameter for the table.

  B. Alter the **pctincrease** parameter for the table.

  C. Increase the DB_BLOCK_SIZE parameter in the init.ora file.

  D. Drop and re-create the table with higher **initial** and **next** storage parameters.

Category   Resource Management

Answer   D. Drop and re-create the table with higher **initial** and **next** storage parameters.

Explanation   Since the table has already reached the maximum number of extents allowable for the database block size, it cannot extend. The only option is to drop and re-create the table using a better set of storage parameters. The Export and Import utilities are often used for this purpose (and help preserve the data in the table). Export and Import can compress the current data extents into a single large **initial** extent; changes to the **next** parameter must be performed manually.

83. Which init.ora parameter enables the writing of records to the audit trail?

  A. SECURE=TRUE

  B. AUDIT_TRAIL=TRUE

  C. AUDIT_LOG=TRUE

  D. None of the above. You need to execute the **alter database audit log command** from within SQLDBA.

Category   Security

Answer   B. AUDIT_TRAIL=TRUE

Explanation   Once the AUDIT_TRAIL parameter is set in init.ora and the database goes through a shutdown/startup cycle, AUDIT commands will cause records to be written to the audit log.

84. The following commands are issued by the MARY user, and all succeed. Company_ID is the primary key of the COMPANY table.

```
commit;
update COMPANY set Active_Flag = 'Y'
 where Company_ID = 12345;
savepoint A1;

insert into COMPANY (Company_ID, Active_Flag)
 values (12346,'N');
savepoint A2;

rollback to savepoint A1;
commit;
```

What will be the result when a different user now executes the following query?

```
select Active_Flag from MARY.COMPANY
 where Company_ID = 12346;
```

    A. 'N'

    B. 'Y'

    C. Null.

    D. 'no rows selected.'

Category   Tuning and Troubleshooting

Answer   D. 'no rows selected.'

Explanation   D. Since the transaction was rolled back to Savepoint A1, the transaction that inserted the record for Company_ID 12346 was rolled back and was not committed to the database.

85. If a CKPT process is not used, which other background process performs the CKPT process's function?

    A. LGWR

    B. DBWR

    C. SMON

    D. PMON

Category   Architecture and Options

Answer   A. LGWR

Explanation   CKPT performs the checkpointing operations; if it is not present, LGWR assumes these responsibilities.

86. During an attempted normal shutdown of an instance, a memory error prevents the database from shutting down. What should be done to resolve the situation?

    A. Use the **shutdown immediate** command.

    B. Nothing has to be done; since the instance never shutdown all the way, it is still available to the application users.

    C. Use the **shutdown abort** command.

    D. Use the **startup** command.

Category   Backup and Recovery

Answer   C. Use the **shutdown abort** command.

Explanation   Since the database did not shutdown cleanly, if you attempt to log into the database you will get the message "shutdown in progress." You will get the same message if you attempt to **startup** the database. The only solution is to use the **shutdown abort** command to shutdown the instance.

87. Which of the following queries will tell you how much space is allocated to the COMPANY table in the DATA tablespace?

A. Select count(distinct(substr(ROWID,1,8)||substr(ROWID,15,4)))
from COMPANY;

B. Select SUM(Blocks) from DBA_FREE_SPACE
where Table_Name = 'COMPANY';

C. Select SUM(Blocks) from DBA_EXTENTS where Segment_Name =
'COMPANY' and Segment_Type = 'TABLE';

D. Select MAX(Blocks) from DBA_SEGMENTS
where Table_Name = 'DATA';

Category   Resource Management

Answer   C. select SUM(Blocks) from DBA_EXTENTS where Segment_Name =
'COMPANY' and Segment_Type = 'TABLE';

Explanation   The query in answer C sums the blocks allocated to all the extents
of the COMPANY table. DBA_SEGMENTS could also have been queried for the
same information:

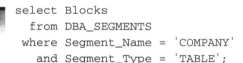

```
select Blocks
  from DBA_SEGMENTS
 where Segment_Name = 'COMPANY'
   and Segment_Type = 'TABLE';
```

88. How often are a table's statistics re-collected?

A. Every time the table is accessed.

B. Every time the table is manually analyzed.

C. Every time the database is restarted.

D. Every time records in the table are inserted, updated, or deleted.

Category   Maintenance and Operations

Answer   B. Every time the table is manually analyzed.

Explanation   Statistics are updated manually, via the **analyze** command.

89. Can a role be granted to another role?

    A. YES

    B. NO

Category   Security

Answer   A. YES

Explanation   A role can be granted to either a user or a role.

90. Given the create table command below:

```
create table COMPANY_ADDRESS
(Company_ID    NUMBER
   constraint fk_company_address
     references COMPANY.Company_ID,
Address_Code    CHAR(1),
constraint pk_company_address
    primary key (Company_Id, Address_Code));
```

Which of the following is true:

    A. You cannot insert records into COMPANY_ADDRESS unless a matching Company_ID already exists in COMPANY.

    B. You cannot insert records into COMPANY unless a matching Company_ID already exists in COMPANY_ADDRESS.

    C. The Address_Code column is nullable.

    D. You cannot delete records from COMPANY_ADDRESS if a matching Company_ID still exists in COMPANY.

Category   Data Administration

Answer   A. You cannot insert records into COMPANY_ADDRESS unless a matching Company_ID already exists in COMPANY.

Explanation   Since COMPANY_ADDRESS has a foreign key back to COMPANY, Company_ID values must be present in the COMPANY before they can be used in COMPANY_ADDRESS. Since Address_Code is part of the primary key, it will set to NOT NULL. The delete restriction in D is backwards—you cannot delete from COMPANY if matching Company_IDs exist in COMPANY_ADDRESS.

91. TRUE or FALSE: To simplify your backup/recovery procedures, it is a good idea to leave tablespaces in BEGIN BACKUP state at all times.

A. TRUE

B. FALSE

Category   Backup and Recovery

Answer   B. FALSE

Explanation   Tablespaces in BEGIN BACKUP state write much more data than normal to the online redo log files. Also, if a tablespace is in BEGIN BACKUP state during a media failure, you will have to recover that tablespace from a prior backup.

92. A third-party package requires the Oracle Version 6 data dictionary views. To install these views, which of the following should you do?

A. Do a Full Import from an Export of an Oracle Version 6 database.

B. Do a User Import of the SYSTEM user from an Export of an Oracle Version 6 database.

C. Run ddviews6.sql.

D. Run catalog6.sql.

Category   Maintenance and Operations

Answer   D. Run catalog6.sql.

Explanation   While connected as INTERNAL within SQLDBA or Server Manager, run the catalog6.sql file in the /RDBMS/ADMIN directory under the Oracle home directory.

93. What will be the outcome of the following command?

```
audit profile;
```

    A. Any user statistics that exceed their prescribed profile values will be recorded in the audit log.

    B. All **create profile, alter profile,** and **drop profile** commands will be recorded in the audit log.

    C. All queries against the USER_PROFILES table will be audited.

    D. The command will fail.

Category   Security

Answer   B. All **create profile, alter profile,** and **drop profile** commands will be recorded in the audit log.

Explanation   "PROFILE" is a statement option for auditing. Others include "INDEX" (for **create, drop,** and **alter index**), TABLE, and TABLESPACE.

94. Querying DBA_IND_COLUMNS for the MARY.EMPLOYEE table shows the following:

```
select Column_Name, Column_Position from DBA_IND_COLUMNS
 where Owner = 'MARY' and Table_Name = 'EMPLOYEE';

Column_Name      Column_Position
City                         1
State                        2
Zip                          3
```

Will the following query use an index, given rule-based optimization?

```
select distinct City from EMPLOYEE
 where State = 'DE';
```

    A. YES

    B. NO

Category   Tuning and Troubleshooting

Answer   B. NO

Explanation   There is only one index on the MARY.COMPANY table (since there is only one column that has a Column_Position of '1'). The index has three columns. The columns in the index are, in order, City, State, and Zip, as shown by the Column_Position values. Since the index is a concatenated index, it will be used if its leading column—City—is used in the **where** clause. City is not in the **where** clause, so the index is not used.

95. Which of the following is NOT an Oracle background process?

    A. Dispatcher (Dnnn)

    B. Server (Snnn)

    C. Recoverer (RECO)

    D. Monitorer (Mnnn)

Category   Architecture and Options

Answer   D. Monitorer (Mnnn)

Explanation   The rest are all Oracle7 background processes. MONITORER is a role that is created via the **utlmontr** script in the /RDBMS/ADMIN subdirectory under the Oracle home directory.

96. Which of the following is NOT true about conditions that must be met prior to starting a database recovery from a media failure?

    A. All datafiles must be either available or marked as 'OFFLINE'.

    B. You must be connected as INTERNAL.

    C. You must be connected via a multi-threaded server process.

    D. You must have all controlfiles available.

Category   Backup and Recovery

Answer   C. You must be connected via a multi-threaded server process.

Explanation   During a recovery, you must be connected via a dedicated server process.

97. The number of rollback segments in a database should most directly correspond to

    A. the number of concurrent users.

    B. the number of concurrent transactions.

    C. the size of the largest transaction.

    D. the size of the largest stored procedure.

Category   Resource Management

Answer   B. the number of concurrent transactions.

Explanation   Ideally, each transaction has a rollback segment to itself; when this level of isolation is not possible, each transaction should have an extent within a rollback segment to itself. The number of rollback segments only corresponds to the number of concurrent users if all of the users are actively performing transactions or using inactive data from prior transactions. V$ROLLSTAT shows the current number of transactions. By monitoring V$ROLLSTAT over time, you can verify the number of rollback segments you need.

98. Which program is used to verify SQL*Net V2 connectivity from a Windows client?

    A. TNSNAMES

    B. LISTENER

    C. ORASRV

    D. TNSPING

Category   Maintenance and Operations

Answer   D. TNSPING

Explanation   TNSPING will prompt you for a service name from the client's tnsnames.ora file; it will verify that you can reach the instance.

99. What will be the outcome of the following command?

```
revoke CONNECT from MARY;
```

A. MARY's current sessions will be disconnected.

B. MARY's account will be dropped.

C. MARY will no longer be able to use the CONNECT privilege.

D. MARY will no longer be able to enable the CONNECT role.

Category Security

Answer D. MARY will no longer be able to enable the CONNECT role.

Explanation CONNECT is a role in Oracle7, comprising several system privileges (such as CREATE SESSION). MARY would still be able to log in provided she has been granted CREATE SESSION either directly or via another role.

100. Querying DBA_IND_COLUMNS for the MARY.EMPLOYEE table shows the following:

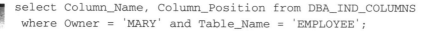

```
select Column_Name, Column_Position from DBA_IND_COLUMNS
 where Owner = 'MARY' and Table_Name = 'EMPLOYEE';
```

```
Column_Name  Column_Position
City                       1
State                      2
Zip                        3
```

Will the following query use an index, given rule-based optimization?

```
select distinct City from EMPLOYEE
 where City not in ('New York', 'Boston', 'Dallas');
```

A. YES

B. NO

Category Tuning and Troubleshooting

Answer B. NO

Explanation City is the leading column of a three-column index, but the index can't be used because the NOT operator is used. Indexes are useful when equating

a column's value to a given value, not when excluding values via NOT IN or !=
clauses. See the comments on limiting conditions in Chapter 11.

CHAPTER 17

The Oracle7 Database Administrator Practice Test

The Oracle7 Database Administrator (DBA) Examination measures an individual's mastery of the knowledge, skills, and abilities necessary to perform proficiently the job of Oracle7 DBA. The examination was developed in cooperation with the Oracle Users Group-Americas and the Oracle Corporation and is based on a significant body of research to define the characteristics of the job of Oracle DBA. A committee of expert DBA's, specifically chosen for their high level of knowledge and experience, was assembled to develop the actual examination questions and to validate the examination content.

The Certified Oracle DBA designation will document the attainment of this level of competence. It will be useful to candidates in assessing their qualifications and abilities, and to employers in making their hiring decisions and evaluating the applicable technical skills of existing staff for diverse purposes.

The Oracle7 DBA Practice Test has been developed to help familiarize prospective candidates for certification with the structure and the content focus of the test itself. By reading the commentary, taking the practice test, scoring your own responses, and reviewing the rationale for each correct answer, you will have taken an important step in approaching your test date with confidence. The practice test consists of 36 questions (the actual test has 60 questions) including both multiple-choice and exhibit-based scenario questions. The practice test was designed to produce a sample of item types across the content areas, closely proportionate to the actual test (see the section later in this chapter called "Test Content").

Trainers and educators can use this practice test as a supplement to their training and education efforts. By reviewing the detailed test content, becoming familiar with the type of questions asked, and using the test to preassess knowledge, individual plans can be prepared for certification candidates.

The Chauncey Group is a wholly-owned subsidiary of Educational Testing Service. THE CHAUNCEY GROUP, THE CHAUNCEY GROUP INTERNATIONAL, and its design logo are trademarks of the Chauncey Group International Ltd.

Oracle™ is a trademark of the Oracle Corporation.

How to Use the Practice Test Material

To get the most from the practice test material, follow these simple steps:

1. Review the portions of the material that describe test content and test-taking strategies.

2. Follow the instructions on using the self-scoring answer sheet.

3. Read the test-taking strategies and the advice about guessing at answers.

4. Time the test, allowing one hour for completion.

5. Take the test under conditions that are similar to those in an actual test administration. Select a well-lighted and properly ventilated room. The room should be quiet and one in which you are unlikely to be interrupted. Do not use any aids such as textbooks, notes, etc.

Once you begin the test, you may skip questions and go back to them if you like. If you do skip questions, be sure to mark the corresponding space on the answer sheet. Always be sure the number of the question you are answering is the same as the number on the answer sheet where you darken your response.

1. At the end of the test, go back and reconsider each skipped test question.

2. After you have answered all the questions on the answer sheet, check your work to be sure that you have darkened the appropriate number of choices for each question and filled in the blanks for open ended response questions.

3. Follow the instructions for marking the answer sheet.

4. Evaluate your performance by comparing your results to the score interpretation guide which is on the Answer Sheet later in this chapter.

5. Review the questions you have answered incorrectly and read the rationale for those questions. Review the reasons given in the rationale for why each of the other choices is incorrect.

After you have completed the review and considered your scores, decide if you need additional training or more test review. To help you determine areas for further study the relevant content area(s) is listed within the rationale explanations for each question.

Marking the Answer Sheet

Use the answer sheet included in this chapter to record your answers to the questions. After you have completed the practice test, check your work to insure that you have responded to all the questions. Compare your responses to the correct answers provided within the answer rationale, clearly marking only incorrect responses. After you complete marking the answer sheet, count the total number of correct responses and place this value in the space provided on the answer sheet. Check your final result against the Score Interpretation guide on the practice test answer sheet to determine your readiness to take the certification examination.

Test Taking Strategies

Read the directions and all the test questions carefully, including all the response options. Work as rapidly as you can without being careless. Do not waste time on questions you find extremely difficult or unfamiliar; no question carries greater weight than any other.

It is not good to follow any test taking strategy that is based on the assumption that any particular pattern of answer choices will or will not appear in a test. In general, test makers strive for patterns of answer choices that are similar to those that would typically occur by chance. Also, the order and distribution of answer choices vary from test-to-test, so a test-taking strategy based on the distribution of choices in one version of a test may not be useful for another version.

Your score on the Oracle7 DBA Certification test is based on the number of questions you answer correctly—that is, the number for which you choose the best answer from among the choices given. There is no penalty for an incorrect answer. So, if you are uncertain about the answer to a question, you should guess rather than not respond at all. You risk nothing by guessing, but if you do not respond you lose the chance to raise your score by making a lucky guess.

Test Content

There are seven major content areas covered in the examination. The major emphasis is placed on the comprehension and application of concepts, principles, and practices rather than on the recall of isolated facts. There are, however, some questions based on knowledge of specific terms, tools, and techniques.

The content areas and a representative description of topics covered in each category is provided below:

I. Oracle Architecture and Options (11-13%)

A. Demonstrate an understanding of memory structures and processes that make up an Oracle instance

B. Demonstrate an understanding of the logical and physical structures associated with an Oracle database

C. Demonstrate an understanding of PL/SQL constructs (triggers, functions, packages, procedures) and their processing

D. Demonstrate an understanding of distributed architecture and client server

E. Demonstrate an understanding of locking mechanisms

II. Security (13-15%)

A. Create, alter, and drop database users

B. Monitor and audit database access

C. Develop and implement a strategy for managing security (roles, privileges, authentication)

D. Demonstrate an understanding of the implications of distributed processing on the security model

III. Data Administration (11-13%)

A. Manage integrity constraints

B. Implement the physical database from the logical design

C. Evaluate the implications of using stored procedures and constraints to implement business rules

IV. Backup and Recovery (16-18%)

A. Understand backup options

B. Develop backup and recovery strategies

C. Manage the implementation of backup procedures

D. Recover a database

V. Software Maintenance and Operation (13-15%)

A. Configure and manage SQL*Net

B. Install and upgrade Oracle and supporting products

C. Configure the Oracle instance using the initialization parameters

D. Distinguish among startup and shutdown options

E. Create a database

F. Demonstrate an understanding of the capabilities of underlying operating systems as they relate to the Oracle database

VI. Resource Management (13-15%)

A. Create and manage indexes

B. Evaluate the use of clusters and hash clusters

C. Allocate and manage physical storage structures (e.g., datafiles, redo logs, control files)

D. Allocate and manage logical storage structures (e.g., tablespaces, schemas, extents)

E. Control system resource usage by defining proper profiles

F. Perform capacity planning

VII. Tuning and Troubleshooting (13-15%)

A. Diagnose and resolve locking conflicts

B. Use data dictionary tables and views

C. Monitor the instance

D. Collect and analyze relevant database performance information

E. Identify and implement appropriate solutions for database performance problems

F. Use vendor support services when necessary

G. Solve SQL*Net problems

Overview and Directions

The purpose of the Oracle7 Database Administrator Examination is to measure an individual's mastery of the knowledge, skills, and abilities of an individual who works with Oracle7 as Database Administrators.

The Oracle7 Database Administrator Practice Examination consists of 36 questions. The test contains a variety of question types. You should be able to complete this test in one hour.

Most of the questions or statements are followed by four possible answers, from which you must select the best or most appropriate answer. Some of the questions ask you to enter an answer (fill in the blank) or to indicate an appropriate sequence. Specific instructions will indicate this type of question. Read each question carefully to make sure you understand what you are asked to do before you answer. Try to answer every question; there is no penalty for guessing. The exhibits needed for questions 33-36 follow the questions.

1. The Program Global Area (PGA) for a dedicated server connection resides in the

A. SGA

B. sort area

C. user process

D. shared SQL area

2. Which combination is NOT a valid backup combination?

A. Off-line "cold" backups and archiving redo logs

B. Online "hot" backups and archiving redo logs

C. Export and archiving redo log files

D. Export and off-line "cold" backups

3. User kelly has been given access to an Oracle7 database. The following commands have been issued by the DBA, and kelly is unaware that they have been executed.

```
create role DET.UPDATE1                          identified by BLACKHAWKS;
grant select, insert, update, delete on DET.CUSTOMER
to DET.UPDATE1;
grant DET.UPDATE1 to KELLY;
alter user KELLY default role CONNECT;
```

Which of the following is true?

A. User kelly will be able to connect to the database using SQL*Plus and issue commands against the DET.CUSTOMER table.

B. User kelly needs to be granted one more privilege before his privileges on DET.CUSTOMER can take effect.

C. After connecting to the database, user kelly cannot issue any SQL commands against DET.CUSTOMER until given the password BLACKHAWKS.

D. Synonyms need to be created for user kelly on the DET.CUSTOMER table before kelly can access the table.

4. To help correct a severe swapping problem at the Operating System (OS) level, which action is most appropriate?

A. Increasing DB_BLOCK_BUFFERS

B. Decreasing DB_BLOCK_BUFFERS

C. Increasing SORT_AREA_SIZE

D. Decreasing OPEN_CURSORS

5. A bulk data load from a 250,000-record file will be inserted into a single table. Each record in the file will become a row in the table. The table has 3 foreign key constraints that reference 3 other tables (lookup codes). A Before-Insert trigger for each row inserts conditionally into another table. Which of the following processes is fastest and logically correct?

A. Drop all constraints on the load table and its trigger, run SQL*LOADER on the table, and reapply the foreign key constraints.

B. Leave the constraints on and drop the trigger, run SQL*LOADER, and re-create the trigger.

C. Leave the trigger on the table, drop all constraints on the table, run SQL*LOADER on the table, and reapply the constraints.

D. Leave both the triggers and constraints on the table and run SQL*LOADER on the table.

6. Online operating systems (OS) backups of the files making up a tablespace are valid if

A. the tablespace is in backup mode

B. the tablespace is off-line

C. no users are executing transactions

D. a redo log switch does not occur during the backup

7. Which line in the SQL statement below contains an error?

A. `grant select,update,insert,`
       `delete`

B. `on TABLE_DEPT`

C. `to USER_KELLY`

D. `with admin option;`

8. When running Oracle7, which privilege is required for use of the TRUNCATE command on a table in another user's schema?

A. DELETE_ANY_TABLE

B. TRUNCATE_ANY_TABLE

C. ALTER_ANY_TABLE

D. DROP_ANY_TABLE

9. An exclusive table lock prevents all of the following transactions on a locked table EXCEPT

A. performing any DML

B. selecting data

C. deleting rows

D. adding rows

10. A site has no archive logging and performs no exports, but performs weekly operating system backups with the database shutdown. Choose from the list below all of the possible recovery options. Select all that apply.

    A. [ ] Recover a dropped table and its data easily.

    B. [ ] Recover a table with great difficulty.

    C. [ ] Recover a lost datafile with no loss of data.

    D. [ ] Restore the database to the date and time of the last backup.

    E. [ ] Restore the database to a specific point in time since the last backup.

11. The following command has been issued:

```
create index XFK1PAYROLL on PAYROLL (Last_Name);
```

Which of the following about the command is true?

    A. It will fail because no tablespace was specified.

    B. It will be created in the user's default tablespace.

    C. It will be created in the tablespace defined by the application manager when the application was defined.

    D. It will be created in the SYSTEM tablespace because no tablespace was specified.

12. In an Oracle database that uses the rule-based optimizer, which condition in a WHERE clause will provide the fastest path to a single row?

    A. Entire non-UNIQUE concatenated index=constant

    B. ROWID=constant

    C. UNIQUE indexed column=constant

    D. Full table scan

13. The purpose of the SMON process is to act as

    A. a table size monitor to automatically notify users when they approach size constraints, reclaiming leaf nodes from dropped index values

    B. a database space monitor to automatically notify the DBA when a tablespace needs extension, automatically coalescing "swiss cheese" type fragmentation

C. a system monitor performing instance recovery on startup and cleaning up temporary segments during operation, automatically coalescing "honeycomb" type fragmentation

D. the sequence monitor, automatically generating and caching sequence values as they are used

14. An Oracle Forms user receives the error message:

```
Error on Pre-Insert trigger. . . duplicate records are not allowed.
```

The DBA should do which of the following?

A. Tell the user to **commit** the transaction.

B. Tell the user the values entered are invalid and to correct the values entered.

C. Tell the user to exit, to re-connect, and to try the insert again.

D. Do a **shutdown abort** and restart the instance before using this form.

15. In order for user Pat to create a table in the USERS tablespace in a default installation of Oracle7, which of the following commands must be issued by a DBA?

A. grant connect to PAT

B. alter user PAT quota 500K on USERS

C. grant resource on USERS to PAT

D. alter user PAT default tablespace USERS

16. While importing a full export after a fresh install, the DBA receives the following error message:

```
Unable to allocate extent of size nnn in tablespace SYSTEM
```

Which of the following actions is most likely to solve the problem?

A. Reinstall Oracle

B. Call Oracle Support immediately

C. Shut down the database with **shutdown abort**

D. Ensure that the importing user is not assigned to SYSTEM for temporary or default tablespaces

17. What is the first action a DBA should take when the reference to a stored procedure from an application receives the response that the procedure is no longer valid?

   A. Re-grant privileges on the underlying objects.

   B. Compile the procedure.

   C. Drop and re-create the procedure.

   D. Query USER_OBJECTS and inspect the value in the Status column.

18. When running Oracle version 7.2, which of the following will have precedence in determining the degree of parallelism for a database table?

   A. The value of the PARALLEL_DEFAULT_MAXSCAN initialization parameter

   B. The value of the PARALLEL clause in the **create table** command

   C. The parallel hint in a SQL query

   D. The number of system CPUs and disks that the driving table is spread across

19. When performing an online "hot" backup of a database in archive log mode, the DBA should backup all of the following Oracle files EXCEPT

   A. control files

   B. online redo log files

   C. archived redo log files

   D. system tablespace file(s)

20. User Fran owns table EMP. User Pat has created a stored procedure called PROC_1 which updates table EMP. Which of the following must occur in order for user Kelly to sucessfully run PROC_1?

   A. Fran must grant UPDATE on EMP to Pat.

   B. Pat must grant UPDATE on EMP to Kelly.

   C. Fran must grant UPDATE on EMP to Kelly.

   D. Pat must grant UPDATE on EMP to Fran.

21. After a new database has been created, all of the following initialization parameters can change EXCEPT

   A. DB_FILES

   B. DB_DOMAIN

    C. DB_BLOCK_SIZE

    D. LOG_ARCHIVE_FORMAT

22. To be most efficient, physical resources for an Oracle database should be allocated in which way?

    A. Indexes should be deployed on as few physical disks as possible.

    B. Data and indexes should always be placed in the same tablespace so they will be on the same physical disk.

    C. Data and indexes should be placed on different physical disks when possible.

    D. Datafiles corresponding to the system tablespace should be deployed on as many physical disks as possible.

23. The following is the physical setup of an Oracle7 database.

```
DISK      CONTENTS
----      --------
  1       SYSTEM tablespace
          online redo log files

  2       USER tablespace

  3       ROLLBACK tablespace
          archived redo logs

  4       INDEX tablespace

  5       Application software
```

Which action is most likely to improve the performance of this database?

    A. Placing the online redo log files on disk 3

    B. Placing the USER tablespace on disk 4

    C. Placing the archived redo logs on disk 5

    D. Placing ROLLBACK tablespace on disk 1

24. Which of the following is required in order to perform a "hot" backup of an Oracle database?

A. The database must be running in ARCHIVELOG mode.

B. The database must have enough redo log files online; otherwise the ARCHMON process will be stopped.

C. All tablespaces must be placed in BEGIN BACKUP mode prior to performing the backup.

D. The archiving process must be stopped.

25. An index corresponds to a table from which many records are being deleted. To reclaim or reuse space used by the deleted index rows, which action would be best?

A. Alter the index to decrease **pctused** to 20.

B. Alter the index to increase **pctused** to 80.

C. Alter the index to increase **next**.

D. Drop and re-create the index.

26. Assume that the instance has a 4KB blocksize. Which of the following is a proper storage clause?

A. ```
STORAGE (INITIAL_EXTENT 50K
NEXT_EXTENT 50K MINEXTENTS 1 MAXEXTENTS 249
PCTINCREASE 0)
```

**B.** ```
STORAGE (INITIAL=EXTENT 50K NEXT=EXTENT 50K
MIN_EXTENTS 1
MAX_EXTENTS 249 PCTINCREASE 0)
```

C. ```
STORAGE(INITIAL_EXTENT 50K NEXT_EXTENT 50K
MINEXTENTS 1
MAXEXTENTS 249) PCTINCREASE 0
```

**D.** ```
STORAGE (INITIAL 50K NEXT 50K MINEXTENTS 1
MAXEXTENTS 249
PCTINCREASE 0)
```

27. Given the following tablespaces: SYSTEM, TEMP, TABLE_DATA1, and SORTS, a DBA executes the following 3 commands.

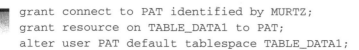

```
grant connect to PAT identified by MURTZ;
grant resource on TABLE_DATA1 to PAT;
alter user PAT default tablespace TABLE_DATA1;
```

Where do temporary sorts take place when pat runs a SQL statement?

   A. Temporary tablespace TEMP

   B. System tablespace SYSTEM

   C. Data tablespace TABLE_DATA1

   D. Sort tablespace SORTS

28. In what sequence must the four steps below be carried out to start up a database? Beginning with 1, enter the appropriate sequence number in each box.

   1. [ ] alter database open

   2. [ ] connect internal

   3. [ ] alter database mount

   4. [ ] startup nomount

29. Which strategy would be most appropriate for a heavy TPS server?

   A. Yearly backup of exports, archive logs, all Oracle datafiles, and INIT.ORA

   B. Daily exports, weekly backups, database running in ARCHIVELOG mode

   C. Complete exports yearly, cumulative exports biyearly, incremental exports monthly

   D. Image backup of all Oracle-related files (including databasefiles) on a daily basis while database is in normal operation

30. When tables that participate in a parent-child foreign key relationship are dropped, which of the following is true?

   A. The parent table must be dropped first, regardless of the delete rule that has been specified.

   B. The parent table must be dropped first if the delete rule is restrict.

   C. The child table must be dropped first if the delete rule is restrict.

   D. The order of dropping the tables does not matter if the delete rule is restrict.

31. Which of the following is NOT a part of the CREATE INDEX statement?

A. pctfree

B. pctused

C. initrans

D. freelist

32. The system tablespace is contained in one datafile. The datafile becomes corrupt. The database is in ARCHIVELOG mode. A valid online backup of the system tablespace was completed last night. Which is the most appropriate action to recover to the time of the corruption?

A. Restore datafile from backup and apply all archived logs

B. Apply ARCHIVELOG

C. Restore entire database from backup

D. Perform point-in-time recovery

The next four questions are based on an actual database system. To answer these questions you will need to look up information about the system in the "Practice Database Description" section, which follows this test.

33. How many bytes of the SGA are allocated to database buffer? Indicate your answer in either bytes or Kbytes and indicate which you are using.

34. In the sample database, tablespace USERS consists of how many datafiles?

35. When starting the sample database, the following errors are displayed:

```
LCC-00209: missing value for keyword at end of string
    [log_archive_start]

ORA-01078: failure in processing system parameters
```

Which of the following initialization parameters needs to be corrected?

A. LOG_ARCHIVE_START

B. LOG_ARCHIVE_ERROR

C. LOG_ARCHIVE_LCC

D. LOG_ARCHIVE_DEST

36. For which of the following tables has the ANALYZE command been run in the sample database?

A. PROSPECTS

B. CODES

C. MENU_ITEMS

D. ORDERS

End of Test.

Practice Database Description

The following pages contain information about an actual database which will be useful to you when answering items 33-36 in the practice examination.
    The following information is available:

1. SGA Information

2. Initialization Parameters (init.ora)

3. Tablespace Information

4. Rollback Segment Information

5. User Information

6. List of Roles

7. Granted Roles

8. Tablespace Quotas

9. Table Information

Section 1-SGA Summary

```
Total System Global Area      4386244 bytes
             Fixed Size         48452 bytes
          Variable Size       3920000 bytes
       Database Buffers       1024000 bytes
           Redo Buffers          8192 bytes
```

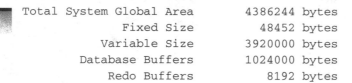

NOTE
This database is currently running Oracle7 version 7.1 in NOARCHIVELOG mode.

Section 2-Initialization Parameters (init.ora)

```
archive_log_dest             =
archive_log_format           = NONE
archive_log_start            = FALSE
audit_file_dest              = ?/rdbms/audit
background_dump_dest         = /disk2/home/oracle/admin/orac/
control_files                = /disk1/ctrl01.ctl,/disk2/ctrl02.ctl
core_dump_dest               = /disk2/home/oracle/admin/orac/
db_block_buffers             = 250
db_block_size                = 4096
db_file_multiblock_read_count = 16
db_file_simultaneous_writes  = 4
db_files                     = 12
db log_archive_start         = FALSE
log_buffer                   = 8192
_name                        = prac
dblink_encrypt_login         = FALSE
dml_locks                    = 100
enqueue_resources            = 155
license_max_sessions         = 100
license_max_users            = 100
license_sessions_warning     = 90
log_archive_buffer_size      = 16
log_archive_buffers          = 4
log_archive_dest             = ''
log_archive_format           = %t_%s.dbf
```

```
log_checkpoint_interval          = 1000
log_checkpoint_timeout           = 0
log_files                        = 255
max_rollback_segments            = 30
open_cursors                     = 500
open_links                       = 4
optimizer_mode                   = CHOOSE
os_authent_prefix                = " "
processes                        = 1
rollback_segments                = (RBS1,RBS2,RBS3,RBS4)
single_process                   = FALSE
sort_area_size                   = 65536
sort_mts_buffer_for_fetch_size   = 0
sql_trace                        = FALSE
timed_statistics                 = TRUE
transactions                     = 66
transactions_per_rollback_segment = 16
user_dump_dest                   = /disk2/home/oracle/admin/orac/
```

Section 3-Tablespace Information

FILE NUM	FILE NAME	TABLESPACE	BYTES	BLOCKS	STATUS
1	/disk1/system01.dbf	SYSTEM	26214400	12800	AVAILABLE
2	/disk1/rbsa01.dbf	RBS1	25600000	12500	AVAILABLE
3	/disk1/rbsa02.dbf	RBS1	4194304	2048	AVAILABLE
4	/disk1/temp01.dbf	TEMP	4194304	2048	AVAILABLE
5	/disk2/users01.dbf	USERS	104857600	51200	AVAILABLE
6	/disk2/users02.dbf	USERS	104857600	51200	AVAILABLE
7	/disk2/data01.dbf	DATA1	5242880	2560	AVAILABLE
8	/disk2/data02.dbf	DATA2	1048576	512	AVAILABLE
9	/disk2/indx01.dbf	INDEX	2097152	1024	AVAILABLE

Section 4-Rollback Segment Information

SEGMENT NAME	TABLESPACE NAME	CUR EXTS	INITIAL EXTENT	NEXT EXTENT	MIN EXTENT	MAX EXTENT	CURRENT SIZE	STATUS
SYSTEM	SYSTEM	2	51200	51200	2	121	102400	ONLINE

R01	RBS1	32	131072	131072	2	121	4194304	ONLINE
R02	RBS1	121	131072	131072	2	121	15859712	ONLINE
R03	RBS1	2	131072	131072	2	121	262144	OFFLINE
R04	RBS1	2	131072	131072	2	121	262144	ONLINE

Section 5-User Information

USERNAME	DEFAULT TABLESPACE	TEMPORARY TABLESPACE	PROFILE
ASHBURN	USERS	TEMP	DEFAULT
BERMAN	USERS	TEMP	DEFAULT
BROWN	USERS	TEMP	DEFAULT
DALEY	USERS	TEMP	DEFAULT
DEVLIN	USERS	TEMP	DEFAULT
GIBSON	USERS	TEMP	DEFAULT
MARSHALL	USERS	TEMP	DEFAULT
NICHOLS	USERS	TEMP	DEFAULT
PRACTICE	USERS	TEMP	DEFAULT
SCHMIDT	USERS	DATA1	DEFAULT
SCOTT	USERS	TEMP	DEFAULT
SMITH	USERS	TEMP	DEFAULT
SYS	SYSTEM	TEMP	DEFAULT
SYSTEM	TOOLS	TEMP	DEFAULT

Section 6-List of Roles

ROLE	PASSWORD
CONNECT	NO
RESOURCE	NO
DBA	NO
ORAFORMS$DBG	NO
ORAFORMS$OSC	NO
ORAFORMS$BGM	NO
EXP_FULL_DATABASE	NO
IMP_FULL_DATABASE	NO
PRAC_INPUT	NO
PRAC_USER	NO
PRAC_MGR	YES
USERS	NO

Section 7-Granted Roles

GRANTEE	GRANTED_ROLE	ADM	DEF
BROWN	PRAC_INPUT	NO	YES
BROWN	PRAC_USER	NO	YES
GIBSON	PRAC_USER	NO	YES
PRACTICE	PRAC_INPUT	NO	YES
SCOTT	CONNECT	NO	YES
SCOTT	PRAC_USER	NO	YES
SCOTT	RESOURCE	NO	YES
SMITH	PRAC_INPUT	NO	YES
SMITH	PRAC_USER	NO	YES
SYS	CONNECT	YES	YES
SYS	DBA	YES	YES
SYS	EXP_FULL_DATABASE	YES	YES
SYS	IMP_FULL_DATABASE	YES	YES
SYS	RESOURCE	YES	YES
SYSTEM	CONNECT	NO	YES
SYSTEM	DBA	YES	YES
SY	PRAC_INPUT	YES	YES
SYSTEM	PRAC_MGR	YES	YES
SYSTEM	PRAC_USER	YES	YES
SYSTEM	ORAFORMS$BGM	YES	YES
SYSTEM	ORAFORMS$DBG	YES	YES
SYSTEM	ORAFORMS$OSC	YES	YES
SYSTEM	USERS	YES	YES

Section 8-Tablespace Quotas

TABLESPACE	USER NAME	BYTES USED	MAX BYTES	BLOCKS USED	MAX BLOCKS
DATA1	BROWN	102400	102400	50	50
DATA1	PRACTICE	724992	1.0E+07	354	5120
DATA2	ASHBURN	12288	102400	6	50
DATA2	PRACTICE	10240	1.0E+07	5	5120
DATA1	SCHMIDT	0	102400	0	50
INDEX	SCOTT	362496	1.0E+07	177	5120
INDEX	SCHMIDT	10240	1.0E+07	5	5120
TOOLS	DEVLIN	4096	102400	2	50

TOOLS	SCHMIDT	40960	102400	20	50
TOOLS	SYSTEM	40960	1024000	20	500
USERS	BERMAN	0	0	0	0
USERS	BROWN	20480	102400	10	50
USERS	DALEY	69632	102400	34	50
USERS	GIBSON	102400	102400	50	50
USERS	SCHMIDT	0	1.0E+07	0	5120

Section 9-Table Information

OWNER	TABLE NAME	TABLE SPACE	PCT FREE	PCT USED	INITIAL EXTENT	NEXT EXTENT	MAX EXT	CUR EXT	PCT INC	NUM ROWS
SCHMIDT	AV_ITEMS	DATA1	10	40	10240	10240	121	1	50	
SCHMIDT	CUSTOMERS	DATA1	10	40	4096	1024	121	121	0	
SCHMIDT	DEPTS	DATA1	10	40	10240	10240	121	1	50	
SCHMIDT	EMPS	DATA1	10	40	10240	10240	121	1	50	
SCHMIDT	EVENTS	DATA1	10	40	10240	10240	121	1	50	
SCHMIDT	MENU_ITEMS	DATA1	10	40	10240	10240	121	1	50	
SCHMIDT	ORDERS	DATA1	10	40	10240	12288	121	3	50	204
SCHMIDT	ORDER_DETAILS	DATA11	0	40	10240	10240	121	1	50	
SCHMIDT	PERSONS	DATA1	0	40	10240	10240	121	1	50	
SCHMIDT	PROSPECTS	DATA1	10	40	10240	10240	121	1	50	
SCHMIDT	RESERVATIONS	DATA1	10	40	10240	10240	121	1	50	
SCHMIDT	ROOMS	DATA1	10	40	10240	10240	121	1	50	
SCHMIDT	MASTER_CODES	USERS	10	40	10240	10240	121	1	50	
SCOTT	BONUS	USERS	10	40	10240	10240	121	1	50	
SCOTT	CUSTOMER	USERS	10	40	10240	10240	121	1	50	
SCOTT	DEPT	USERS	10	40	10240	10240	121	1	50	
SCOTT	EMP	USERS	10	40	10240	10240	121	1	50	
SCOTT	ITEM	USERS	10	40	10240	10240	121	1	50	
SCOTT	ORD	USERS	10	40	10240	10240	121	1	50	
SCOTT	PRICE	USERS	10	40	10240	10240	121	1	50	
SCOTT	PRODUCT	USERS	10	40	10240	10240	121	1	50	
SCOTT	SALGRADE	USERS	10	40	10240	10240	121	1	50	
SCOTT	SEQ	USERS	10	40	10240	10240	99	1	50	

Answer Sheet/Score Interpretation Guide
Oracle7 DBA Practice Examination

Please shade-in / fill-in the correct answer.

Item # Answer(s)

	A	B	C	D	E
1.	O	O	O	O	
2.	O	O	O	O	
3.	O	O	O	O	
4.	O	O	O	O	
5.	O	O	O	O	
6.	O	O	O	O	
7.	O	O	O	O	
8.	O	O	O	O	
9.	O	O	O	O	
10.	O	O	O	O	O
11.	O	O	O	O	
12.	O	O	O	O	
13.	O	O	O	O	
14.	O	O	O	O	
15.	O	O	O	O	
16.	O	O	O	O	
17.	O	O	O	O	
18.	O	O	O	O	

Item # Answer(s)

	A	B	C	D
19.	O	O	O	O
20.	O	O	O	O
21.	O	O	O	O
22.	O	O	O	O
23.	O	O	O	O
24.	O	O	O	O
25.	O	O	O	O
26.	O	O	O	O
27.	O	O	O	O
28.	___	___	___	___
29.	O	O	O	O
30.	O	O	O	O
31.	O	O	O	O
32.	O	O	O	O
33.	_____
34.	_____
35.	O	O	O	O
36.	O	O	O	O

Number Correct _____ Out of 36

Score Interpretation for the Oracle DBA Sample Exercise

Functions Performed Correctly	Interpretations
33-36	Excellent work. You performed all of the functions efficiently and as directed.
29-32	Good work. You performed most of the functions efficiently and as directed.
21-28	Marginal. You made some mistakes and should review how you performed the functions tested.
20 or less	Deficient. You need to practice more and consult your training materials regarding the functions that were tested.

Rationale for Correct Answers

The following section provides a brief rationale for each of the correct answers in the practice examination. These explanations are not intended to be comprehensive; for further information please reference the Oracle7 Server Administrator's Guide, the Oracle7 Server Concepts Manual, or any of the excellent Oracle7 DBA-related books on the market today.

1. The correct answer is C—user process. The PGA is allocated by Oracle when a user process connects to an Oracle database and a session is created. The Sort Area and Shared SQL Area are both components of the SGA, which is shared by all processes.

Test Content Area: I A

2. The correct answer is C—Export and archiving redo log files. In order to use archive log files to restore a database, it is necessary to have a full system backup as a starting point. The arched redo log files are then applied to the "base" restore to bring the database "up to date"; this could be accomplished with either option A or C. Option D describes a method which provides individual table recovery (the Export) as well as full database recovery via the "cold" backup.

Test Content Area: IV B

3. The correct answer is C—After connecting to the database, user kelly cannot issue any SQL commands against the DET.CUSTOMER until he is given the password BLACKHAWKS. Although the role contains a full set of privileges on the customer table, it was created with a password which is required to utilize it. Option A is not correct since the password is not available. No additional privileges are required (option B), and a synonym is never required to access a table as described in option D.

Test Content Area: II C

4. The correct answer is B—Decreasing DB_BLOCK_BUFFERS. Swapping is caused by system demand for more physical memory than is available, and since each DB_BLOCK_BUFFERS will use the same amount of memory as a single database block, reducing this value will reduce overall memory demand. Increasing this parameter as suggested by option A would increase paging, as would increasing SORT_AREA_SIZE as in option C. Decreasing OPEN_CURSORS (option D) would have negligible effect.

Test Content Area: V C& V F

5. The correct answer is C—Leave the trigger on the table, drop all constraints on the table, run SQL*LOADER on the table, and reapply the constraints. Using this option, the subsidiary table would be populated by the trigger as the table is loaded, and constraints would be applied after the load. Both A and B would prevent any inserts into the other table since the trigger would be dropped, so these would be logically incorrect. Option D would not be as efficient, since the constraints would still be in place.

Test Content Area: III C

6. The correct answer is A—the tablespace is in backup mode. The online (or "hot") backup requires the database to be placed in backup mode, which writes all transactions to log files while the database files are being backed up. There is no need for the tablespace to be offline (B), and users can be executing transactions (C). If transactions are taking place, it is likely that a redo log switch will occur (D), and this is normal.

Test Content Area: IV A

7. The correct answer is D—**with admin option**;. This is not a valid option for the **grant** statement shown.

Test Content Area: II C

8. The correct answer is A—DELETE_ANY_TABLE. Since **truncate** is essentially a **drop table** command without a provision for rollback, the same privilege is required. A table owner may always **drop** a table in that owner's schema, but to **drop** a table in another schema, the DELETE_ANY_TABLE system privilege is required.

Test Content Area: II C

9. The correct answer is B—selecting data. An exclusive lock prevents any change to data in the table, including deleting and inserting rows, as well as other DML, but allows other users to select a consistent view of the data.

Test Content Area: VII A

10. The correct answers are B and D—Recover a table with great difficulty and Restore the database to the date and time of the last backup. A table can be recovered by restoring the database backup to another machine, and then exporting or copying the table, but this is time- and resource-consuming, so the first statement does not apply. The purpose of a "cold" backup is to allow recovery of the database as of the time of the backup. Since the backup is taken at a particular point in time, any data added or modified could not be recovered, and without log files it is not possible to restore to a particular point in time.

Test Content Area: IV A & IV D

11. The correct answer is B—It will be created in the user's default tablespace. In the absence of a **tablespace** parameter, all Oracle objects are created in the default tablespace specified for the user. Objects will be created in SYSTEM only when no other default tablespace is defined.

Test Content Area: VI A & D

12. The correct answer is B—ROWID=constant. This is the basic method used by Oracle to access data, and provides a direct path to the data. Access by index requires an access to the index, which in turn contains the ROWID, so A and C are not correct. A full table scan is the slowest route to a single row, since it requires a read of every row in the table.

Test Content Area: I B & VII D

13. The correct answer is C—Act as a system monitor performing instance recovery on startup and cleaning up temporary segments during operation, automatically coalescing "honeycomb" type fragmentation. Options A and B describe features which might be desirable but do not exist in Oracle, while option D describes the function of the sequence generator, which is provided by the server process.

Test Content Area: I A

14. The correct answer is B—Tell the user the values entered are invalid, correct the values entered. It is clear from the description that the Pre-Insert trigger is implemented to prevent the insertion of duplicate records, and no action will allow the user to override this constraint.

Test Content Area: III C & VII E

15. The correct answer is B—alter user PAT quota 500K on USERS. This command permits Pat to utilize space in the USERS tablespace to create an object - up to 500K in this case. **grant connect** only allows a user to log into the database, while **grant resource** is an obsolete command formerly used in Oracle version 6 to allow the authorize the creation of objects. **alter user** PAT **default tablespace** USERS defines USERS as the default choice of tablespace when no tablespace name is explicitly mentioned in the CREATE TABLE command, but without quota on that tablespace, an object still cannot be created.

Test Content Area: II A

16. The correct answer is D—Ensure that the importing user is not assigned to SYSTEM for temporary or default tablespaces. If the DBA does not assign a default tablespace to a user, when an object is created it will be created in the SYSTEM tablespace, which may not be large enough to hold it. Likewise, in the absence of an assigned temporary tablespace, temporary tables (required for index creation) will also be created in the SYSTEM tablespace. Reinstalling Oracle will not change this condition, nor will a shutdown of the database. A call to Oracle Support will probably yield the correct solution to the problem, but is not a very efficient approach.

Test Content Area: V B & VI D

17. The correct answer is B—Compile the procedure. Oracle stores procedures in a compiled form, and if the procedure is no longer valid, it means it requires compilation. Regranting privileges will have no effect on this condition, and the Status column of USER_OBJECTS will simply confirm the fact that the procedure is invalid. Dropping and recreating the procedure will work, since that includes compilation, but is certainly not the first action to take.

Test Content Area: I C

18. The correct answer is C—The parallel hint in a SQL query. Any hint provided will override any other database parameter relating to parallelism, and so it always has precedence. Note that in Oracle version 7.3 the PARALLEL_DEFAULT_MAXSCAN parameter no longer exists.

Test Content Area: I D

19. The correct answer is B—online redo log files. All of the other files listed are required to restore the database, but the online log files contain current transactions not subject to backup. It is imperative to backup at least one control file, as well as all database files (especially those associated with the systerm tablespace). Archived redo log files will also be required to bring the database "up to date" as of the time of the backup.

Test Content Area: IV D

20. The correct answer is A—Fran must grant UPDATE on EMP to Pat. When a procedural object is executed, it relies on the table privileges of its owner, not those of the user who is executing it. A user executing a procedure does not need to have been granted access to the table that the procedure accesses. Therefore, before Kelly can execute the procedure, the table owner (Fran) must grant privileges to the procedure owner (Pat).

Test Content Area: II C & III C

21. The correct answer is C—DB_BLOCK_SIZE. Once a database is created, the only way to change the blocksize is to re-create the database "from scratch". DB_FILES may be raised (up to the limit set by MAXDATAFILES in the control file) and the new value will be effective at the next startup of the database. The DB_DOMAIN parameter indicates a logical location of the database within a network, and may be changed as the network changes.

Test Content Area: V C & V E

22. The correct answer is C—Data and indexes should be placed on different physical disks when possible. This is because typical Oracle access to an indexed table requires one or more read of the index file to determine the location of the data block containing the row to be accessed, followed by a read of the appropriate data file block (if it is not cached in memory). If both of these files are on the same disk, the disk head must move from one physical area to another, and this is a relatively slow operation. If the files are on different disks, this "head contention" will be reduced or eliminated. Further efficiencies may be gained by spreading both index and data tablespaces over multiple disks (if available), so option A is not correct. B is incorrect for the reason just explained (head contention), and while the situation described in option D may yield some small performance gain, I/O on the system tablespace is not normally a problem.

Test Content Area: VI C & VII E

23. The correct answer is C—Placing the archived redo logs on disk 5. As shown, the archived redo log files are on the same disk as the ROLLBACK tablespace, and since any update transaction will write to the rollback segments as well as online log files (which will be archived to this disk), there will be a very heavy I/O load on disk 3 each time a log file fills and needs to be archived. The Application software disk (disk 5) will typically be lightly used, since applications are loaded once at the beginning of execution, and then remain in memory. Option A is not correct, since placing the online redo log files on the same disk as the archived log files will increase the I/O load on that disk. Option B is not correct, since data and index files should be on different disks (see rational for item 22 above). Likewise, option D would not be correct for the same reason option A is not correct.

Test Content Area: VI C & VII E

24. The correct answer is A—The database must be running in ARCHIVELOG mode. During online or "hot" backups, data which would normally be written to the database files is temporarily stored in the online log files. As these files fill, they must be automatically archived and then reused so the database can continue to run, hence the requirement that the database be running in ARCHIVELOG mode. B is not correct, since only the normal number of online log files are required, and these are archived and reused as required. C is not correct since tablespaces can be backed up one at a time, and there is no requirement that all tablespaces be placed in backup mode prior to the backup. D is also not correct, since the archiving process (ARCH) must be running in order for the database to run in ARCHIVELOG mode.

Test Content Area: IV A & VI C

25. The correct answer is D—Drop and re-create the index. This is the only way to reclaim space from a fragmented index. Changes to the storage parameters (**pctused** and **next**) may have an effect on future index space utilization and fragmentation, but cannot help reclaim space in the index structure.

Test Content Area: I B & VI A

26. The correct answer is D—

```
STORAGE    (INITIAL 50K NEXT 50K
           MINEXTENTS 1 MAXEXTENTS 249
           PCTINCREASE 0)
```

This is really a question of proper syntax for a **storage** clause—the parameters "INITIAL_EXTENT" and "NEXT_EXTENT" in options A and C are incorrect, as are the parameters "INITIAL=EXTENT" and "NEXT=EXTENT" in option B. In addition, the left parenthesis is improperly placed in option C.

Test Content Area: VI D

27. The correct answer is B—System tablespace SYSTEM. Temporary tables are always created in the SYSTEM tablespace unless a specific temporary tablespace is assigned using the statement "**alter user** *username* **temporary tablespace** *tempspace*".

Test Content Area: II A & VI D

28. The correct answer to this item is:

[4] alter database open
[1] connect internal
[3] alter database mount
[2] startup nomount

The DBA must first login to the database (using INTERNAL, since the database is not yet up and running). Although it is possible to simply issue a **startup** command at this point, the actual sequence of commands executed is then **startup nomount**, then **alter database mount**, and finally **alter database** OPEN.

Test Content Area: V E

29. The correct answer is B—Daily exports, weekly backups, database running in ARCHIVELOG mode. The weekly backup would allow archived log files to be applied in case of failure, but even without such a backup, the daily export would allow the system to be restored to the time of the last export. Option A would only allow the system to be restored to a single point each year, and option C would get the system no closer than the last monthly export. Option D would not work at all, since backups taken with the database up are invalid unless a "hot" backup is taken with the database in "backup" mode.

Test Content Area: IV B

30. The correct answer is C—The child table must be dropped first if the delete rule is restrict. The purpose of a parent-child foreign key relationship is to ensure that no "child" record can exist without a "parent" record. Therefore, regardless of the delete rule, the "child" rows must be deleted prior to deleting the "parent" row.

Test Content Area: III A

31. The correct answer is B—PCTUSED. While **pctused** may be specified for tables, it is not a valid storage option for an index. All of the other choices are valid index storage options.

Test Content Area: VI A

32. The correct answer is A—Restore datafile from backup and apply all archived logs. This is the standard method for restoring a corrupted data file. Restoring the file from the backup ensures a valid data file, and then applying all arched logs brings the tablespace back up-to-date by re-applying all transactions that had been made. Option B is not correct, because you cannot apply archived log files without first restoring a valid datafile. Option C is not correct, since there is no need to restore the entire database when only a single tablespace is damaged. In addition, option C does not mention applying archived log files, which would be required to bring the database back up-to-date. Point-in-time recovery is a method of restoring the database to a particular time prior to the failure (typically an incomplete recovery) and would not be appropriate here.

Test Content Area: I B & IV D

33. The correct answer is 1024000 bytes, or 1000K. Since the database block size is 4096 (or 4K) and there are 250 database buffers (DB_BLOCK_BUFFERS=250), it is a simple calculation:

4096 * 250 = 1024000

to determine the size of the database buffers.

Test Content Area: I A

34. The correct answer is 2. Section 3 of the Database Information shows the operating system files associated with each tablespace, and it can be seen that USERS consists of two files.

Test Content Area: VI C

35. The correct answer is D—LOG_ARCHIVE_DEST. An examination of the LOG_ARCHIVE_DEST parameter in the init.ora file (Database Information Section 2) shows that there is not a complete entry for this parameter.

Test Content Area: V C

36. The correct answer is D—ORDERS. An examination of Section 11 of the Database Information shows that only ORDERS has a n entry in the column "NUM ROWS", indicating that the **analyze** command has been run for that table. If **analyze** has not been run, this column will contain NULLs.

Test Content Area: VII B

Index

A

Ad hoc application SQL monitoring, 138
Ad hoc database monitoring, 138, 152
Administration of a growing database, 17-131
Administration space (application), estimating, 56
Advanced replication, 401-403, 407
Alert logs, 122-123

allocate extent clause (alter table command), 63
ALL_ROWS hint, 251-252
alter database resize, 388-389
alter index rebuild, 30, 378-379
alter profile unlimited, 327
alter rollback segment command, 103, 106
alter rollback segment shrink, 130, 394
alter session command, 389
alter session set optimizer_goal, 143
alter system command, 389
alter table command, 24
       allocate extent clause, 63

cache clause, 36
deallocate unused keep clause,
375, 377
nocache clause, 36
parallel clause, 331
alter tablespace command
coalesce clause, 111, 392
default storage clause, 100
permanent clause, 273
read only clause, 394
read write clause, 394
temporary clause, 101, 272-273
alter trigger command, 385
alter user temporary tablespace, 99
analyze command
compute statistics method, 85,
92, 128, 145-146, 266, 363
estimate statistics method,
145-146, 364
for all indexed columns clause,
363
for table clause, 363
table list chained rows clause, 95
AND-EQUAL operation, 203-205,
252, 269
Answer form for Practice Questions,
478-479
Answer key to Practice Questions,
482-483
Answer sheet for Practice Test, 567
Answers to Practice Questions,
analysis of, 481-543
Application administration space,
estimating, 56
Application deployment, 4-5
Application deployment spiral cycle,
11
Application development cycle, 4-10
another redeployment, 8-9
application deployment, 4-5
application redeployment, 7-8

hardware upgrades and tuning,
5-6
major redeployment, 9-10
Application redeployment, 7-10
Application reference tables, 23-24
growth profiles, 22-24
tuning, 22-24
Application SQL monitoring, ad hoc,
138
Applications
categorizing transactions and
queries, 139-140
custom vs. packaged, 139-140
tuning, 191
APP_REF tablespace
free extents in, 109
free space fragmentation in, 110
honeycomb fragmentation in,
112
segments in, 110
Architecture references, 489-490
Archiving old trace files and logs,
120-122
Array controller, RAID configuration
with, 67
Asynchronous advanced replication,
407
Asynchronous I/O, 189
Asyncronous replication, 397-398,
407
autoextend parameter, 387-388

B

Background timeouts statistic, 166
BACKGROUND_DUMP_DEST, 120,
122
Backup and recovery references, 486
Backups, and raw devices, 76

Batch applications, 34
    data access, 37-39
    and hit ratio, 46
Batch jobs, tuning, 141-142
Batch operations, vs. OLTP, 140
Bibliographical references, 484-490
Bitmap indexes, 379-381
Block cleanout, 410
Block reads for large table access
    methods, 311-312
Blocks (database), 94-97. *See also*
    Extents
Buckets (histogram), 361
Buffer aging (batch applications), 38
Buffer cache, scalable, 411
Buffer contention types,
    V$WAITSTAT, 168
Buffer waits statistic, 167
Business reference tables, 21-22
    growth profiles, 20-22
    tuning issues, 21-22
Business transaction tables
    growth profiles, 25-27
    tuning, 25-27

C

cache clause (create/alter table
    command), 36
CACHE hint, 252
Cache issues of parity-based RAID
    systems, 71
Cache table, marking, 36
Cached table, 24
Candidate Bulletin (Oracle7 DBA
    Exam), 417-442
Categorizing application transactions
    and queries, 139-140
Certification Exam. *See* Oracle7 DBA
    Certification Exam
Chained rows in batch applications, 39

Changing requirements, 11
Chauncey Group International,
    417-420, 546
CHOOSE hint, 253
Client-centric monitoring, 151
CLUSTER hint, 253
Cluster key, 97, 160-161
Clusters, 97-98
coalesce clause (alter tablespace
    command), 111, 392
Coalesced tablespaces, 391-393
Collisions, avoiding, 314, 381
Columnwise replication, 396
Combining subqueries, 291-292
COMPANY table, 200, 202
COMPANY table Parallel Query
    Option, 325-348
Comparing replicated tables, 406-408
COMPATIBLE parameter, 395
COMPETITOR table, 200, 202
Complete refresh, 400
Composite key table for star query,
    299
Composite keys, 298-299
compute statistics method, 85, 92,
    128, 145-146, 266, 363
Concatenated index
    choosing a leading column,
        267-268
    vs. single-column index, 268-269
CONCATENATION operation,
    204-207
Concurrent processing. *See* Parallel
    options
Conflict notification, 407
Conflict notification routine, 407
connect by clause, 301, 303-304
CONNECT BY operations, 206,
    208-209, 301-305
Connection qualifiers, 408
Consistent changes statistics, 43, 159

Consistent gets statistics, 152-153, 156-157

Consistent production environment, ensuring, 136-139

Cost associated with queries, 249

Cost-based optimizers, 143-146

COUNT operation, 209-211

COUNT STOPKEY operation, 211-212

CPU requirements, 48-49

CPU tuning issues, 46-47, 190-191

create controlfile command, generating, 123

create index command, 24, 99, 102, 371

create rollback segment command, 103

create snapshot command, 398-400

create table command, 23
    as select clause, 102, 397
    cache clause, 36
    parallel clause, 331
    for partitioned tables, 315
    unrecoverable clause, 99, 370-371

create tablespace command
    default storage clause, 100
    temporary clause, 101, 272-273

create user temporary tablespace, 99

Crisis level
    explained, 4
    is cyclic, 8
    lowering, 11-13

Cumulative buffer gets (NESTED LOOP join), 279-280

Custom applications, vs. packaged applications, 139-140

Cycle of application development, 4-10

D

Data access
    batch applications, 37-39
    OLTP applications, 34-36

Data administration references, 489

Data block buffer cache, 35, 136

Data block gets (batch applications), 38-39

Data blocks consistent reads statistics, 43

Data dictionary cache load statistic, 164

Data location, managing, 137-138

Data partitions, 282

Data proximity, 138, 309

Data striping, 62-64, 69, 77

Data warehousing
    RAID systems, 72
    table querying, 294-300

Database access operations. *See* Operations (database access)

Database administration, Oracle7 changes, 386-411

Database Administration Toolset, 173

Database administration utilities, new Oracle7.3, 411-413

Database blocks, 94-97. *See also* Extents

Database growth
    and disk capacity requirements, 58
    planning for, 19-31
    supporting, 76-77

Database growth profiles, 20-31

Database management statistics, 166-169

Database monitoring. *See* Monitoring (database)

Database service outage causes, 150

Database shutdown/startup kit,
    119-131
        implementing, 131
        items in, 120-130
Database size, 4
        growth over time, 8
        planning for growth, 11
Database space
        estimating requirements, 52-54
        managing, 79-116
Datafiles
        managing extent usage, 137-138
        ownership of objects in, 128
        resizable, 386-389
Date/time columns, replication
    challenges, 408
db block changes statistic, 158
db block gets statistic, 157
DBA (database administrator), 4
DBA_FREE_SPACE, 108
DBA_FREE_SPACE_COALESCED,
    392-393
DB_BLOCK_BUFFERS, 136, 178-179
DB_BLOCK_LRU_LATCHES, 411
DB_BLOCK_SIZE, 37, 178
DB_FILE_MULTIBLOCK_READ_COUN
    T, 38, 87-88, 180-181
DBMS_SHARED_POOL, 124
DBMS_SPACE, 93-94
dbv utility, 412
DB_VERIFY utility, 412-413
DBWR processes, multiple, 189
DB_WRITERS, 180
dd command, 76
Deallocation of unused table/index
    space, 375-378
Dedicated temporary tablespaces,
    372-373
default storage clause (alter/create
    tablespace command), 84, 100
Degree of parallelism, 328
        art of selecting, 347-348

defining at table level, 331-332
        determining, 346-347
Delayed-logging block cleanout,
    410-411
delete command, 92
Deleting old trace files and logs,
    120-122
Denormalization methods, 281-282
Development team
        hardware questions for, 14
        integrating with operating
            system management, 14-15
Dictionary tables, and hit ratio, 41-42
Dimension (data warehousing), 295
Dimension table (data warehousing),
    295
Direct path export, 371-372
Direct Path problem (SQL*Loader),
    28-29
Direct Sort Writes, 272
Disk access performance, tuning, 51-77
Disk capacity requirements
        and database growth, 58
        estimating, 52-57
DISTINCT clause, 288
Distributed I/O, 188-190
DLM (Distributed Lock Manager), 354
Driving set, 275, 277
Driving/driven table, 273
Dynamic initialization parameters
        session-level, 390
        system-level, 391
Dynamically changeable init.ora
    parameters, 389-391

E

Educational courses, 439-442
Emergency storage space, estimating,
    57

Enterprise Manager architecture, 172
Enterprise Manager Console, 173
Enterprise Manager (EM), 171-174
Enterprise Manager Performance
    Pack, 173-174
Environment tuning, 177-191
Equivalence queries, 313
estimate keyword, 129
estimate statistics option (analyze
    command), 145-146, 364
Exam. *See* Oracle7 DBA Certification
    Exam
Execution path illustrations, 248. *See
    also* Explain plans
        AND-EQUAL, 205
        CONCATENATION, 207
        CONNECT BY, 209
        conventions used, 202-203
        COUNT, 210
        COUNT STOPKEY, 212
        FILTER, 214
        FOR UPDATE, 215
        HASH JOIN, 216
        INDEX RANGE SCAN, 218
        INDEX UNIQUE SCAN, 219
        INTERSECTION, 221
        MERGE JOIN, 224, 270
        MINUS, 225
        NESTED LOOPS, 227, 274
        OUTER JOIN, 229
        PROJECTION, 230
        REMOTE, 232
        SEQUENCE, 233
        SORT AGGREGATE, 234
        SORT GROUP BY, 235
        SORT JOIN, 236
        SORT ORDER BY, 237
        SORT UNIQUE, 239
        TABLE ACCESS BY ROWID, 240
        TABLE ACCESS CLUSTER, 241
        TABLE ACCESS FULL, 242
        TABLE ACCESS HASH, 243
        UNION, 245
        VIEW, 246
Existence checks, performing, 292-294
EXISTS clause, 292-293
Expectations from users, 12
explain plan command, 193-259
        interpreting the output, 246-249
        operations, 199-250
Explain plans, 141, 193-259. *See also*
    Execution path illustrations
        generating, 194-199
        Oracle7.3, 198-199
        parallelism and, 336-345
        PLAN_TABLE, 194-197
        and set autotrace on, 343-344
Extents
        benefits of multiple, 90-91
        explained, 80-81
        and full table scans, 89
        how Oracle allocates, 81-86
        location of, 90
        managing, 81-91, 137-138
        sizing, 62-63, 86-91
External space used by Oracle,
    estimating, 54-56
Extremely large tables, tuning access
    to, 142
Extremely volatile tables, tuning
    access to, 142

F

Fact table (data warehousing), 295
Fast index rebuild method, 98
Fast index recreate, 378-379
Fast version cleanout, 410
File separation (for I/O bottlenecks),
    61-62

File systems, vs. raw devices, 73-76
FILTER operation, 212-214
FIRST_ROWS hint, 253-254
Focus on offensive SQL, 140-141
FOR UPDATE operation, 213-215
Free extents
    in APP_REF tablespace, 109
    explained, 107
Free list, 92
Free space
    database block, 95
    fragmentation in APP_REF
      tablespace, 110
    managing, 107-113
freelist groups storage parameter, 115
freelist storage parameter, 115
Frequently-used tables, tuning access
    to, 142
from clause, 278, 286
FULL hint, 254
Full refresh, 400
Full table scans
    avoiding unplanned, 263-265
    and extent size, 89
    optimization techniques, 37-39
    when to use, 263-264
Fully indexed tables, creating, 312-313
Future, preparing for, 15-16

G

Gets per block (batch applications),
    38-39
Global sequence numbers, replication
    challenges, 408
grep command (Unix), 333
group by clause, 97
Growing database
    administration of, 17-131
    tuning, 133-317

Growth profiles, 20-31
    for application reference tables,
      22-24
    for business reference tables,
      20-22
    for business transaction tables,
      25-27
    explained, 20
    for temporary/interface tables,
      27-29
    using in planning, 30-31

H

Hardware issues, managing, 14-15
Hardware tuning, 5-6, 51-77
    RAID technologies, 64-73
    traditional approaches, 60-64
Hardware upgrades, 5-6
Hash clusters, 98, 313
    creating, 313-314
    user-specified, 381-382
HASH hint, 254-255
hash is clause, 381
HASH JOIN operation, 215-216
Hash joins, 338, 365-369
    explained, 365
    managing, 367-369
Hash key, 98
HASH_AJ hint, 255
HASH_AREA_SIZE, 367
Hashing, partition-level, 366
Hashing function, 313
HASH_JOIN_ENABLED, 367
hashkeys parameter, 381
HASH_MULTIBLOCK_IO_COUNT,
    367-368
Header area, database block, 95
Height-balanced histograms, 361-362
Hiccup syndrome, 60, 73

Hierarchical query, clauses, 301
High expectations from users, 12
Highwatermarks (HWMs), 27-29,
   92-94
Hints
      explained, 250
      for NESTED LOOPS join path,
         275-276
      for subqueries returning
         maximum value, 289-290
      using, 250-259
      using to force parallelism,
         332-333
Histogram buckets, 361
Histogram management, 363-365
Histograms, 358, 360-365
Hit, 46
Hit ratio
      application target, 47-48
      calculating, 39-41
      explained, 33, 137
      factors impacting, 41-46
      large increases in, 308
Honeycomb fragmentation in
   APP_REF tablespace, 112
Horizontal partitioning, 315
Hot spot, 35
Hybrid database monitoring, 151,
   171-174

I

Ignoring an index, 276
inc parameter, 388
INDEX hint, 255
INDEX RANGE SCAN operation, 43,
   217-218
Index scans, avoiding unhelpful,
   309-312
Index selectivity, 265-267

Index space
      deallocation of unused, 375-378
      estimating requirements, 53
Index stagnation, 25, 98
INDEX UNIQUE SCAN operation,
   218-219
INDEX_ASC hint, 255
INDEX_DESC hint, 255
Indexes
      bitmap, 379-381
      concatenated, 267-268
      concatenated vs. single-column,
         268-269
      creating, 265
      deallocation of unused space,
         375-378
      estimating space requirements,
         53
      explained, 35
      fast index rebuild method, 98
      and hit ratio, 43-44
      ignoring, 276
      making sure queries can use,
         264-265
      managing, 98-99
      root and leaf nodes, 43-44
      selective, 265-269
      very large, 308
initial storage parameter, 82, 85,
   100-101, 113
init.ora parameters
      dynamically changeable,
         389-391
      key, 178-182
initrans storage parameter, 116
Inodes, 74
Instance-level Parallel Query Option,
   348
Instantiation, 407-408
International exam registration,
   435-439
INTERSECTION operation, 219-222

I/O
  distributed, 188-190
  Optimal Flexible Architecture
    (OFA), 187-188
I/O bottlenecks
  data striping, 62-64, 69, 77
  identifying, 57-60
  RAID technologies, 64-73
  separation of files, 61-62
  traditional approaches, 60-64
I/O management, 137-138
I/O tuning, 186-190

J

Joins. *See also* MERGE JOIN; NESTED
  LOOPS
    managing, 269-282
    reducing the number of, 280-282

L

Large table access, managing, 308-317
Lazy write technique, 60, 73
Leading column (concatenated index),
  267-268
Leaf nodes (index), 43-44
Least Recently Used (LRU) list, 35
Library Cache, 137
list chained rows clause (analyze table
  command), 95
List I/O, 189
Listener log file (SQL*Net V2), 121
Log files, managing, 121-122
Log switch, 54
LOG_BUFFER, 179-180

Logical read statistics
  for indexed table accesses, 44
  viewing, 40-41
Long-running processes, tuning,
  141-142

M

Maintenance and operations
  references, 487
Managing, 1-16
  data location, 137-138
  data proximity, 309
  database space, 79-116
  development and operating
    system, 14-15
  extents, 81-91
  free space, 107-113
  hardware issues, 14-15
  hash joins, 367-369
  histograms, 363-365
  indexes, 98-99
  I/O, 137-138
  joins, 282
  memory requirements, 136-137
  memory tradeoffs, 186
  multitable joins, 269-282
  for performance, 135-146
  and preparing for the future, 15-16
  raw devices, 75-76
  resource requirements, 13-14
  rollback segments, 102-107
  SQL statements containing
    views, 282-287
  star queries, 300
  tables, 91-98
  temporary segments, 99-102
  very large table access, 308-317
Massively Parallel Processor (MPP), 353

maxextents storage parameter, 84, 114, 388

maxextents unlimited clause, 91, 374-375

maxsize parameter, 387

maxsize unlimited clause, 388

maxtrans storage parameter, 116

Media recovery status, 395

Memory
  contention for overall memory, 183-184
  for large table access methods, 311-312
  managing, 136-137
  managing tradeoffs, 186
  paging, 184
  requirements, 48-49
  setting up semaphores, 185-186
  setting up shared, 184-185
  swapping, 184
  tuning, 33-49, 182-186
  usage statistics, 163-166

MERGE JOIN, 222-224, 250, 269-282, 307, 340-345
  example execution path, 270
  steps involved in, 270-271
  tuning implications for, 271-272

MERGE_AJ hint, 256

Migrated rows in batch applications, 39

minextents storage parameter, 84

MINUS operation, 223-225

Mirrored RAID systems, 66, 70, 72-73, 77

Mirroring, explained, 66

Miss, explained, 46

Monitoring (database), 149-174
  ad hoc, 152
  for a consistent production environment, 138
  developing a plan, 174
  hybrid, 171-174

types of, 150-152

V$ and X$ views, 151

MPP (Massively Parallel Processor), 353

Multiblock reads (batch applications), 37-38

Multi-threaded server (MTS), 409-410

N

Negative hit ratio, 42

NESTED LOOPS, 225-228, 250, 269, 273-282, 297-298, 337-338
  adding more tables, 277-280
  cumulative buffer gets, 279-280
  driving table, 274-275
  example execution path, 274
  influencing the join path, 275-277
  starting from nonselective criteria, 277
  steps involved in, 273-274

New tuning options (Oracle7 on), 357-413

next storage parameter, 53, 82-83, 100-101, 114, 387-388

nocache clause (create/alter table command), 36

NOCACHE hint, 256

NO_MERGE hint, 256

NOPARALLEL hint, 256, 332-333

NOT EXISTS clause, 293-294

NOT IN clause, 293-294

O

Object administration changes (Oracle7), 374-386

Object allocation statistic, 164
Object groups, 404
Object ownership in tablespaces,
    querying, 126-128
OFA (Optimal Flexible Architecture),
    187-188
Offensive SQL, focusing on, 140-141
Offline instantiation, 407-408
OLTP (on-line transaction processing),
    140
OLTP (on-line transaction processing)
    applications, 34
        vs. batch operations, 140
        creating rollback segments,
            104-105
        data access, 34-36
        and hit ratio, 45
        RowID value, 87
Operating system management,
    integrating, 14-15
Operations (database access),
    199-250. *See also* MERGE JOIN;
    NESTED LOOPS
        AND-EQUAL, 203-205
        CONCATENATION, 204-207
        CONNECT BY, 206, 208-209
        COUNT, 209-211
        COUNT STOPKEY, 211-212
        FILTER, 213-214
        FOR UPDATE, 213-215
        HASH JOIN, 215-216
        INDEX RANGE SCAN, 217-218
        INDEX UNIQUE SCAN, 218-219
        INTERSECTION, 219-222
        listed, 201
        MINUS, 223-225
        order of, 199
        OUTER JOIN, 228-229
        PROJECTION, 229-230
        REMOTE, 231-232
        row vs. set, 200

        SEQUENCE, 233
        SORT AGGREGATE, 234
        SORT GROUP BY, 234-235
        SORT JOIN, 235-236
        SORT ORDER BY, 237
        SORT UNIQUE, 238
        TABLE ACCESS BY ROWID,
          238-240
        TABLE ACCESS CLUSTER,
          240-241
        TABLE ACCESS FULL, 241-242
        TABLE ACCESS HASH, 242-243
        UNION, 243-245
        VIEW, 244-246
OPS (Oracle Parallel Server), 353-354
Optimal Flexible Architecture (OFA),
    187-188
Optimal size (rollback segment),
    shrinking to, 129-130
optimal storage parameter, 103,
    105-106, 116
Optimizer changes (Oracle7.3),
    358-369
OPTIMIZER_MODE, 142
OPTIMIZER_MODE set to CHOOSE,
    143-144
Optimizers
    choosing, 144
    cost-based, 143-144
    goals of, 146
    hybrid, 143-144
    ruler-based, 143
    using, 142-146
Options references, 489-490
Oracle educational courses, 439-442
Oracle Parallel Server (OPS), 353-354
Oracle7 changes
    database administration, 386-411
    object administration, 374-386
    performance-related, 369-374

Oracle7 DBA Certification Exam,
   415-575. *See also* Practice
   Questions; Practice Test
      arrangement for disabilities,
         425-426
      Candidate Bulletin, 417-442
      changing/canceling, 426
      computer-based testing centers
         list, 432-435
      contacting exam program staff,
         419
      determination of passing scores,
         431-432
      FAQs, 432
      fees, 421
      final scores, 430
      grounds for dismissal, 429
      identification requirements, 427
      inclement weather, 426
      international registration,
         435-439
      job analysis, 420
      name registry, 430
      on the day, 427-428
      preparation courses, 439
      refunds, 426
      registration, 425
      retake policy, 426
      score reliability, 431
      security measures, 429
      test center regulations, 429
      test content, 423-425
      test dates, 421
      test development, 421
      test preparation, 421-422
      test results and passing scores, 430
      test-taking strategies, 422
Oracle7 DBA Practice Test. *See*
   Practice Test
Oracle7.0 and on
      changes, 405-413
      explain plans, 198-199
      new database administration
         utilities, 411-413
      new tuning options, 357-413
      optimizer changes, 358-369
      PLAN_TABLE Cost column, 249
orasrv log file (SQL*Net V1), 121
Order of operations, interpreting, 199
ORDERED hint, 256
OUTER JOIN operation, 228-229
Overall memory, contention for,
   183-184
Owner-to-datafile location map,
   creating, 128
Owner-to-object location map,
   creating, 126-128

P

Packaged applications, vs. custom
   applications, 139-140
Packages, pinning, 124-126
Paging memory, 184
Parallel Cache Manager (PCM), 354
Parallel Create Index option, 350-351
Parallel Create Table option, 349-350
Parallel Data Loading option, 351-353
PARALLEL hint, 257, 332-333
Parallel options, 321-355
      choosing among, 354-355
      impact of, 322
      list of, 322
Parallel Query Option. *See* PQO
   (Parallel Query Option)
Parallel query views, 334-336
Parallel Recovery option, 353
Parallel table scan, 325
PARALLEL_DEFAULT_MAX_INSTANCES,
   331
PARALLEL_DEFAULT_MAX_SCANS,
   330

PARALLEL_DEFAULT_SCANSIZE, 330
Parallelism
    and explain plan, 336-345
    using query hints to force,
      332-333
Parallelized operations, tuning,
    345-346
Parallelized vs. serialized processing,
    322-323
PARALLEL_MAX_SERVERS, 329-330
PARALLEL_MIN_PERCENT, 330-331
PARALLEL_MIN_SERVERS, 329-330
PARALLEL_SERVER_IDLE_TIME,
    329-330
Parity-based RAID systems, 66, 70-73,
    77
Parsing, 169
Partition elimination, 315-316, 384
Partitioned tables
    benefits of, 316-317
    creating, 314-316
Partitioned views, 382-385
Partition-level hashing, 366
Partitions (data), 282
PCM (Parallel Cache Manager), 354
pctfree storage parameter, 52, 95, 99,
    115
pctincrease storage parameter, 53,
    82-83, 100-101, 111-114
pctused storage parameter, 95, 115
Performance, managing for, 135-146
Performance Pack (EM), 173-174
Performance statistics. *See* Statistics
    views
Performance-related changes in
    Oracle7, 369-374
permanent keyword, 273, 373
Personnel availability, 12
Physical reads statistics, 40-41,
    157-158
Physical writes statistics, 158
Pinning packages, 124-126

Planning
    for database growth, 11, 19-31
    for spiral cycle of application
      development, 10-15
    using growth profiles in, 30-31
PLAN_TABLE, 194
    column descriptions, 196-197
    column structures, 195
    Cost column, 249
    Other_tag column, 339-341
PQO (Parallel Query Option), 27,
    317, 321-348
    for all queries within an
      instance, 348
    how it works, 323-327
    managing and tuning, 327
    monitoring, 333-336
    for a table scan, 324-325
    for a table scan with one sort,
      325-328
Practice Questions, 445-479
    analysis of, 490-543
    answer form for, 478-479
    answer key, 482-483
    format of, 446
    general analysis of, 482, 484
    the questions, 447-479
    references used, 484-490
    time limit, 447
Practice Test, 545-575
    answer sheet, 567
    content summary, 549-551
    database used in, 561-566
    how to use, 547-548
    overview and directions, 551-561
    rationale, 568-575
    score interpretation, 568
    strategies, 548
Preparing for the future, 15-16
Procedure-level replication, 405
Process tuning, applying query tuning
    to, 250

Processing, serialized vs. parallelized, 322-323
Production environment, consistency in, 136-139
Production monitoring, 138
PROJECTION operation, 229-230
ps -ef command (Unix), 333

Q

Query coordinator processes, 322
Query processing
    conventional, 323-324
    parallel, 321-355
    statistics, 156-162
Query server pool, managing, 329-330
Query server process assignments, 328-329
Query server processes, 322
Questions. See Practice Questions; Practice Test
Quiesced replication environments, 406

R

RAID configuration
    with array controller, 67
    choosing, 72-73
RAID levels, 65, 68
RAID system types, 66
RAID technologies, 64-73
    advantages of, 64
    with array controller, 67
    choosing a configuration, 72-73
    how RAID works, 65-69
    mirrored systems, 66, 70, 72-73, 77

parity-based systems, 66, 70-73, 77
    RAID levels, 65, 68
Random hot-spot pattern, 35
Raw devices
    explained, 73
    vs. file systems, 73-76
    managing, 75-76
Read I/O, 57. See also I/O bottlenecks
read only clause (alter tablespace command), 394
Read statistics, viewing, 40-41
read write clause (alter tablespace command), 394
Read-only tablespaces, 393-394
rebuild option (alter index command), 30, 378-379
Recompute statistics, 128-129
recover datafile command, 395
Recursive query, 41, 163
Recursive SQL statements, 41, 163
Redo log space requests statistic, 162-163
Redundancy/emergency storage space, estimating, 57
References (bibliographical), 484-490
Referential integrity constraints, 409
REMOTE operation, 231-232
Remote table access, tuning, 142, 305-308
Renaming the alert log, 122-123
Replicated tables, comparing, 406-408
Replication
    advanced, 401-403, 407
    asyncronous and syncronous, 397-398
    challenges, 408-409
    explained, 396
    general issues of, 396-397
    row-level and procedural, 405
    symmetric, 402
Replication schemas, 402

Requirements change, 11
Resizable datafiles, 386-389
resize parameter, 389
Resource management references, 486-487
Resource requirements, managing, 13-14
Response time
    explained, 4
    is cyclic, 8
Rollback activity, 43
Rollback segment header activity, 43
Rollback segments
    explained, 102
    and hit ratio, 43
    managing, 102-107
    minimizing need for large, 107
    shrinking, 129-130, 394
ROLLBACK_SEGMENTS, 182
Root node (index), 43-44
Row cache, 137
Row operations, 200
Row proximity
    explained, 96
    no way to enforce, 313
ROWID hint, 257
Rowwise replication, 396, 405
RULE hint, 257
Ruler-based optimizer, 143
Runs (sorting steps), 272

S

SALES table, 200, 202
Scalable buffer cache, 411
SCN (System Change Number), 38-39
Security references, 487-488
Segments. *See also* Rollback segments
    in APP_REF tablespace, 110

estimating space requirements, 53
    explained, 80-81
    temporary, 42, 99-102
select count command, 29-30
Selective indexes, 265-269
Selectivity of an index, 265
Semaphores, setting up, 185-186
Sequence numbers, replication
    challenges, 408
SEQUENCE operation, 233
Serialized vs. parallelized processing, 322-323
Server Manager 2.3, 172
Server-centric monitoring, 151
Service outage causes, 150
Session connect time statistic, 170-171
Session logical reads statistic, 165
Session-level dynamic initialization
    parameters, 390
set autotrace on command, 198, 342-345
Set operations, 200
set transaction use rollback segment
    command, 102
SGA memory areas
    managing, 136
    tuning, 33-49
    and very large tables, 308-317
Shadow server process, 323
Shared memory, setting up, 184-185
Shared Pool, 137
Shared SQL area, 35, 49, 137
SHARED_POOL_SIZE, 137, 179
shrink option (alter rollback segment
    command), 129-130, 394
Shrinking rollback segments, 129-130, 394
Shutdown/startup kit, 119-131
    implementing, 131
    items in, 120-130
Simple snapshot, 399

size storage parameter, 115
Sizing extents, 62-63, 86-91
Sizing raw devices, 76
SMP (Symmetric Multi-Processing),
    190
Snapshot log, 400
Snapshot refresh groups, 401
Snapshots, 398, 400-401
        simple, 399
        updateable, 404-405
SORT AGGREGATE operation, 234
Sort area, 42
Sort Direct Writes, 345, 373-374
SORT GROUP BY operation, 234-235
SORT JOIN operation, 235-236
SORT ORDER BY operation, 237
Sort steps (runs), 272
SORT UNIQUE operation, 238
SORT_AREA_RETAINED_SIZE, 181
SORT_AREA_SIZE, 42, 181, 345
SORT_DIRECT_WRITES, 181-182,
    373-374
Sorts (memory and disk) statistic,
    161-162
SORT_WRITE_BUFFERS, 373-374
SORT_WRITE_BUFFER_SIZE, 373-374
Space allocation of raw devices, 76
Space (database)
        estimating requirements, 52-54
        managing, 79-116
Space (external) used by Oracle,
    estimating, 54-56
Space (segment), estimating
    requirements, 53
Space (table/index)
        deallocation of unused, 375-378
        estimating requirements, 53
Spanned rows, 39
Spiral cycle of application
    deployment, 11
Spiral cycle of application
    development, 4-15

SQL, offensive, 140-141
SQL statement tuning, 193-259
SQL statements containing views,
    managing, 282-287
SQL*Loader Direct Path problem,
    28-29
SQL*Net roundtrips statistics, 167-169
SQL*Net V1 orasrv log file, 121
SQL*Net V2 Listener log file, 121
Standby databases, 394-395
STAR hint, 257
Star queries, 369
        composite key table, 299
        creating an execution path,
            298-300
        management issues, 300
        using, 294-300
Star schemas, 295-297
start with clause, 301-302
Statistics views (V$SESSTAT and
    V$SYSSTAT), 152-171
        database management, 166-169
        gathering, 154-156
        interpreting, 156-171
        memory and CPU usage,
            163-166
        naming, 154
        performance of, 153-154
        precision of, 153
        query processing, 156-162
        transaction management,
            162-163
        user, 169-171
        value ranges, 152-153
storage clause, 81-86
storage parameter reference, 113-116
Stored triggers, 385-386
Striping (data)
        hardware-based, 69
        for I/O bottlenecks, 62-64, 69, 77
        methods of, 345

Structure changes, replication
    challenges, 409
Subqueries
    combining, 291-292
    resolving, 287-289
    returning maximum value,
        289-290
    tuning, 287-294
Swap space, 183
Swapped in process, 183
Swapped out process, 183
Swapping memory, 184
Symmetric Multi-Processing (SMP),
    190
Symmetric replication, 402
Synchronous advanced replication,
    407
Synchronous replication, 397
System Change Number (SCN), 38-39
SYSTEM tablespace requirements,
    estimating, 53-54
System-level dynamic initialization
    parameters, 391

T

Table access
    limiting remote, 305-308
    managing for very large tables,
        308-317
TABLE ACCESS BY ROWID operation,
    238-240
TABLE ACCESS CLUSTER operation,
    240-241
TABLE ACCESS FULL operation,
    241-242, 338-342
TABLE ACCESS HASH operation,
    242-243
Table fetch statistic, 160

Table joins. *See also* MERGE JOIN;
    NESTED LOOPS
    managing, 269-282
    reducing the number of, 280-282
table scan PQO, 324-328
Table scans
    conventional, 324
    and hit ratio, 44-45
    parallel, 325
Table scans statistic, 159-160
Table striping methods, 345
Tables. *See also* Tablespaces
    deallocation of unused space,
        375-378
    managing, 91-98
    types of, 80
Tables used in examples, 200, 202
tablespace coalesce, 391-393
tablespace storage parameter, 114
Tablespaces
    estimating space requirements,
        53
    ownership of objects in, 126-128
    read-only, 393-394
    temporary, 53, 99, 372-373
    temporary/interface tables, 27-29
    temporary-only, 272-273
Target hit ratio, application, 47-48
TEMP tablespace, 100
temporary keyword, 101, 272-273,
    372-373
Temporary segments
    and hit ratio, 42
    managing, 99-102
temporary tablespace clause
    (alter/create user command), 99
Temporary tablespace requirements,
    estimating, 53
Temporary tablespaces, dedicated,
    372-373
Temporary/interface tables
    explained, 27

growth profiles, 27-29
tuning, 27-29
Temporary-only tablespaces,
designating, 272-273
Test. *See* Oracle7 DBA Certification
Exam; Practice Questions; Practice
Test
Testing centers (Oracle7 DBA Exam),
432-435
TOOLS tablespace, 54
Top ten tuning tips, 261-318
Trace files
creating, 123
deleting or archiving, 120-122
TRACE utility, 411-412
Transaction management statistics,
162-163
Transaction processing, on-line, 140
Trend monitoring, 138
Triggers
records created, 386
stored, 385-386
Troubleshooting references, 488
truncate command, 28-29, 84, 86,
384-385
Truncated tables, 28
Tuning
access to individual tables, 142
application reference tables,
22-24
applications, 191
business reference tables, 21-22
business transaction tables,
25-27
CPU, 190-191
disk access performance, 51-77
effectively, 11
environment, 177-191
five-step process, 136, 317-318
a growing database, 133-317
hardware, 5-6, 51-77

implications for MERGE JOIN,
271-272
I/O, 186-190
long-running processes and
batch jobs, 141-142
memory, 182-186
memory and CPU, 33-49
parallelized operations, 345-346
query to process, 250
references, 488
shared SQL area, 49
SQL statement, 193-259
subqueries, 287-294
temporary/interface tables, 27-29
top ten tips, 261-318
Tuning hardware
RAID technologies, 64-73
traditional approaches, 60-64
Tuning options
advanced, 319-413
new to Oracle7, 357-413
Tuning process, five-step, 136,
317-318
Tuning tips, top ten, 261-318
Two-phase commit, 397

U

union all, 314, 383
union operator, 382-383, 243-244
union view, 315
unrecoverable actions, 370-371
unrecoverable clause (create
index/table command), 99, 370-371
update command, 291
Updateable snapshots, 404-405
Upgrades, hardware, 5-6
USE_CONCAT hint, 258
USE_HASH hint, 258
USE_MERGE hint, 258, 307

USE_NL hint, 258-259
User calls statistic, 170
User expectations, 12
User statistics, 169-171
USER_DUMP_DEST, 123
User-specified hash clusters, 381-382
USER_TAB_COLUMNS, 267
using index clause, 98
utlbstat.sql, 154-155
utlestat.sql, 154-155

V$FILESTAT, 59, 74
V$LOG_HISTORY, 54-55
V$PQ_SYSSTAT, 334-335
V$RECOVERY_FILE_STATUS, 395
V$RECOVERY_STATUS, 395
V$SESS_IO, 47
V$SESSTAT, 152-171
V$SYSSTAT, 40, 152-171
V$WAITSTAT, 168

V

Very large table access, managing, 308-317
VIEW operation, 244-246
Views. *See also* Statistics views
    forcing to remain separate, 285-287
    integration into queries, 283-285
    managing SQL statements containing, 282-287
    monitoring, 151
    partitioned, 382-385
V$DATAFILE, 74

W

Where clause, 278-279, 290, 296-297, 313
Write cache, 71
Write I/O. *See also* I/O bottlenecks
Write requests statistic, 158

X

X$ views, monitoring, 151

About the CD-ROM

The CD-ROM that comes with this book contains SQLab and Scripts required to create demo tables.

SQLab is an Oracle application tuning tool. SQLab is built by Eyal Aronoff and is used by all the authors of this book on a regular basis to identify SQL statements that require tuning and to facilitate the tuning process. With SQLab you will be able to practice the tuning tips that are described in the book. You will be able to identify the most "offensive" SQL statements, collect them, explain them, incorporate hints, and execute them to show the performance improvements that could be achieved. The version that is attached to the book is a demo version. This version is good for 60 days, can only connect to one Oracle instance and enables you to collect only 10 SQL statements at a time. If you find that this product is useful, you can contact Quest Software at the phone number below or at **http://www.quests.com**.

Creating Demo Tables used in
Advanced Oracle Tuning and Administration

The ./scripts directory contains all of the scripts shown in *Advanced Oracle Tuning and Administration*. The commands from the chapters are stored by chapter (chapt03.sql, chapt04.sql, etc.). Within each chapter's script, the remarks describe the use of each command. Refer to the book for detailed descriptions of the uses of the commands.

The script named "common.sql" will create tables, constraints and indexes used throughout the book. The scripts are stored as ASCII text files, so they can be opened and edited with any text editor.

SQLab Installation

System requirements:

1. 8MB on Hard Disk and 486 CPU is recommended.

2. For the Installation of SQLab tables, at least 1MB of free space is needed in any tablespace other than SYSTEM.

3. It is recommended to have SORT_AREA_SIZE between 500KB and 2MB depending on the size of your SHARED_POOL.

The CD contains:
> READ.ME
> READ1.ME (This File)
> INSTALL.EXE
> GETTING.DOC
> GENSQLAB.001
> SQLAB.INI
> GENSQLAB.002
> GENSQLAB.003
> LOGO1.BMP
> LOGO.BMP
> SCRIPTS <DIR> (Directory of Scripts)

To install:
> Run: **D:\Install**

For tech support please contact:
> Quest Software
> 1-800-306-9329
> or
> (714) 720-1434

WARNING: BEFORE OPENING THE DISC PACKAGE, CAREFULLY READ THE TERMS AND CONDITIONS OF THE FOLLOWING COPYRIGHT STATEMENT AND LIMITED CD-ROM WARRANTY.

Copyright Statement

This software is protected by both United States copyright law and international copyright treaty provision. Except as noted in the contents of the CD-ROM, you must treat this software just like a book. However, you may copy it into a computer to be used and you may make archival copies of the software for the sole purpose of backing up the software and protecting your investment from loss. By saying, "just like a book," The McGraw-Hill Companies, Inc. ("Osborne/McGraw-Hill") means, for example, that this software may be used by any number of people and may be freely moved from one computer location to another, so long as there is no possibility of its being used at one location or on one computer while it is being used at another. Just as a book cannot be read by two different people in two different places at the same time, neither can the software be used by two different people in two different places at the same time.

Limited Warranty

Osborne/McGraw-Hill warrants the physical compact disc enclosed herein to be free of defects in materials and workmanship for a period of sixty days from the purchase date. If the CD included in your book has defects in materials or workmanship, please call McGraw-Hill at 1-800-217-0059, 9am to 5pm, Monday through Friday, Eastern Standard Time, and McGraw-Hill will replace the defective disc. For all technical support issues, please contact Quest Software at 1-800-306-9329 or (714) 720-1434.

The entire and exclusive liability and remedy for breach of this Limited Warranty shall be limited to replacement of the defective disc, and shall not include or extend to any claim for or right to cover any other damages, including but not limited to, loss of profit, data, or use of the software, or special incidental, or consequential damages or other similar claims, even if Osborne/McGraw-Hill has been specifically advised of the possibility of such damages. In no event will Osborne/McGraw-Hill's liability for any damages to you or any other person ever exceed the lower of the suggested list price or actual price paid for the license to use the software, regardless of any form of the claim.

OSBORNE/McGRAW-HILL SPECIFICALLY DISCLAIMS ALL OTHER WARRANTIES, EXPRESS OR IMPLIED, INCLUDING BUT NOT LIMITED TO, ANY IMPLIED WARRANTY OF MERCHANTABILITY OR FITNESS FOR A PARTICULAR PURPOSE. Specifically, Osborne/McGraw-Hill make no representation or warranty that the software is fit for any particular purpose, and any implied warranty of merchantability is limited to the sixty-day duration of the Limited Warranty covering the physical disc only (and not the software), and is otherwise expressly and specifically disclaimed.

This limited warranty gives you specific legal rights; you may have others which may vary from state to state. Some states do not allow the exclusion of incidental or consequential damages, or the limitation on how long an implied warranty lasts, so some of the above may not apply to you.

This agreement constitutes the entire agreement between the parties relating to use of the Product. The terms of any purchase order shall have no effect on the terms of this Agreement. Failure of Osborne/McGraw-Hill to insist at any time on strict compliance with this Agreement shall not constitute a waiver of any rights under this Agreement. This Agreement shall be construed and governed in accordance with the laws of New York. If any provision of this Agreement is held to be contrary to law, that provision will be enforced to the maximum extent permissible, and the remaining provisions will remain in force and effect.

PLEASE SEE REVERSE SIDE FOR INSTALLATION INSTRUCTIONS AND DISC CONTENTS.